The Living Planet

The State of the World's Wildlife

Since 1970, there has been an overall decline in wildlife populations in the order of 52%. Freshwater species populations have declined by 76%, species populations in Central and South America have declined by 83% and in the Indo-Pacific by 67%. These are often not complete extinctions, but large declines in the numbers of animals in each species, as well as habitat loss. This presents us with a tremendous opportunity, before it is too late to rescue many species. This book documents the present state of wildlife on a global scale, using a taxonomic approach, and serving as a one stop place for people involved in conservation to be able to find out what is in decline, and the success stories that have occurred to bring back species from the brink of extinction – primarily due to conservation management techniques – as models for what we might achieve in the future.

NORMAN MACLEAN is Emeritus Professor of Biology at the University of Southampton and a lifelong wildlife enthusiast. He has visited and studied wildlife in more than 50 countries around the world and has given numerous radio and TV interviews on the subject. He is the editor of *Silent Summer* (Cambridge, 2010), co-editor of *Austral Ark* (with Adam Stowe and Greg Holwell, Cambridge, 2015) and author of *A Less Green and Pleasant Land* (Cambridge, 2015).

The Living Planet

The State of the World's Wildlife

Edited by

NORMAN MACLEAN
University of Southampton

CAMBRIDGE
UNIVERSITY PRESS

CAMBRIDGE
UNIVERSITY PRESS

Shaftesbury Road, Cambridge CB2 8EA, United Kingdom

One Liberty Plaza, 20th Floor, New York, NY 10006, USA

477 Williamstown Road, Port Melbourne, VIC 3207, Australia

314–321, 3rd Floor, Plot 3, Splendor Forum, Jasola District Centre, New Delhi – 110025, India

103 Penang Road, #05–06/07, Visioncrest Commercial, Singapore 238467

Cambridge University Press is part of Cambridge University Press & Assessment,
a department of the University of Cambridge.

We share the University's mission to contribute to society through the pursuit of
education, learning and research at the highest international levels of excellence.

www.cambridge.org
Information on this title: www.cambridge.org/9781108499828

DOI: 10.1017/9781108758826

First published 2023

A catalogue record for this publication is available from the British Library.

Library of Congress Cataloging-in-Publication Data
Names: Maclean, Norman, 1932– author.
Title: The living planet : the state of the world's wildlife / edited by Norman Maclean,
    University of Southampton.
Description: First edition. | Cambridge, United Kingdom ; New York, NY, USA : Cambridge University
    Press, [2023] | Includes bibliographical references and index.
Identifiers: LCCN 2022044113 (print) | LCCN 2022044114 (ebook) | ISBN 9781108499828 (Hardback) |
    ISBN 9781108731652 (Paperback) | ISBN 9781108758826 (epub)
Subjects: LCSH: Wildlife conservation. | Wildlife reintroduction.
Classification: LCC QL82 .M325 2023 (print) | LCC QL82 (ebook) | DDC 333.95/4–dc23/eng/20221027
LC record available at https://lccn.loc.gov/2022044113
LC ebook record available at https://lccn.loc.gov/2022044114

ISBN 978-1-108-49982-8 Hardback
ISBN 978-1-108-73165-2 Paperback

Contents

Contributors

OCTAVIO ABURTO-
OROPREZA
Scripps Institution of Oceanography,
UC San Diego, San Diego, CA,
USA

JESSICA L. ALLEN
Eastern Washington University
IUCN SSC Lichen Specialist Group

TRISTRAM ALLINSON
Senior Conservation Scientist, Birdlife
International, Cambridge, UK

ARIADNE ANGULO
IUCN SSC Amphibian Specialist Group,
Toronto, Canada

PHILLIP J. BISHOP[†]
Department of Zoology, University
of Otago, Dunedin, New Zealand
and
IUCN SSC Amphibian Specialist Group,
Toronto, Canada

PHILIPPE BOUCHET
Muséum National d'Histoire Naturelle,
Paris, France

BRIAN W. BOWEN
Hawai'i Institute of Marine Biology,
University of Hawai'i, Kāne'ohe, HI,
USA

PHILIP BOWLES
Coordinator, IUCN SSC Snake and Lizard
Red List Authority, Cambridge, UK

ROBERT H. COWIE
Pacific Biosciences Research Center,
University of Hawai'i,
Honolulu, HI, USA

BENOÎT FONTAINE
Muséum National d'Histoire Naturelle,
Paris, France

LAUREN GARDINER
Cambridge University Herbarium,
Department of Plant Sciences, University
of Cambridge, Cambridge, UK

MARY GIBBY
Royal Botanic Garden Edinburgh,
Edinburgh, UK

GONZALO GIRIBET
Museum of Comparative Zoology and
Department of Organismic and
Evolutionary Biology, Harvard University,
Cambridge, MA, USA

MOLLY GRACE
Department of Biology, University of
Oxford, Oxford, UK and IUCN Red List
Committee Green Status of Species
Working Group

RICHARD A. GRIFFITHS
Durrell Institute of Conservation and
Ecology, School of Anthropology and
Conservation, University of Kent,
Canterbury, UK

MATT W. HAYWARD
School of Environment and Life Sciences,
University of Newcastle, Australia

MARK A. HIXON
School of Life Sciences, University of
Hawai'i, Honolulu, HI, USA

THOMAS A. JEFFERSON
Clymene Enterprises and VIVA Vaquita,
Lakeside, CA, USA

SIMON LEATHER[†]
Harper Adams University, Newport,
Australia

ROBERT A. LEIDY
Department of Environmental Science,
Policy and Management, University of
California, Berkeley, CA, USA

NORMAN MACLEAN
University of Southampton, UK

PATRICIA MILOSLAVICH
Scientific Committee on Oceanic
Research (SCOR), University of
Delaware, College of Earth, Ocean and
Environment, Newark, DE, USA
and
Universidad Simón Bolívar, Departamento
de Estudios Ambientales, Caracas, Venezuela

PETER B. MOYLE
Department of Wildlife, Fish, and
Conservation Biology, Center for
Watershed Sciences, University of
California, Davis, CA, USA

GREGORY M. MUELLER
Negaunee Institute for Plant
Conservation Science and Action,
Chicago Botanic Garden,
Chicago, IL, USA
and
IUCN SSC Fungal Conservation
Committee

ALEXIS M. MYCHAJLIW
Departments of Biology and
Environmental Studies, Middlebury
College, VT, USA
and
Department of Rancho La Brea, Natural
History Museum of Los Angeles County,
CA, USA

DAVID OBURA
CORDIO East Africa, Mombasa, Kenya

SARA OLDFIELD
IUCN SSC Global Tree Specialist Group,
Cambridge, UK

ALEX DAVID ROGERS
REV Ocean, Lysaker, Norway

MANU E. SAUNDERS
School of Environmental and Rural
Science, University of New England,
Armidale, Australia

JENNI A. STOCKAN
James Hutton Institute, Aberdeen, UK

SALLY WREN
IUCN SSC Amphibian Specialist Group,
Toronto, Canada
and
Department of Zoology, University of
Otago, Dunedin, New Zealand

DAVID YEATES
CSIRO Australian National Insect
Collection, Canberra, Australia

Preface

Like the wildlife which it discusses, this book has an evolutionary history. Back in 2010, a book which I had edited and partly written was published. It was entitled 'Silent Summer: The State of Wildlife in Britain and Ireland'. The book was multiauthored and chapters on all the major wildlife groups and the factors affecting them were written by acknowledged experts in these areas. It proved to be a publishing success and its structure a winning formula.

There followed in 2015 a book with a similar structure entitled 'Austral Ark: The State of Wildlife in Australia and New Zealand', to which I made an editorial contribution. I initially planned to compile similar books on the wildlife of all the major world continents, but this proved to be an impossible task. After taking stock I determined to try to compile a book which discussed the world's wildlife in toto, and this is the book that has now emerged. Its compilation has been a long haul but finally proved possible.

Writing such books poses a major problem for the contributing authors, namely that wildlife is not doing well, and so the books could easily become catalogues of woe. Aware of this dilemma, we have tried to provide an honest and informed account, but to partly balance the bad news with accounts of modern nature conservation and the many species which have prospered as a result of such activity. Thus, the cessation of whale hunting by most countries has led to a dramatic increase in the numbers of most whale species.

There is little doubt that *Homo sapiens*, supposedly wise, has not proved to be very smart in managing Planet Earth and its resources. So what with climate change, widespread pollution and agricultural intensification, the effects on wildlife communities have been fairly disastrous. I personally think that it is too late to completely reverse the damage, but even partial recovery will be a most happy prospect. Let's hope that we can make it happen.

It is perhaps appropriate for me to share with our readers where my passion for wildlife has come from. It began in my early boyhood. I was brought up in a very strictly religious family, which meant that I could not play sport at school or even read novels (until my English master mercifully explained to my father that without reading novels, his son could not hope to pass an exam in English; when my father gave in on this, I read classical novels as other boys read comics!). Nor did we have a radio at home and the cinema was prohibited. But my home in a village on the outskirts of Edinburgh was set amongst fields and farmland, and as a somewhat lonesome boy, I became fascinated by the local birds, insects and flowers. Thus was initiated what became a lifelong interest and passion, for which I remain ever grateful.

I should not conclude this preface without mentioning IUCN, the International Union for the Conservation of Nature. This is the body which gives a red listing to species threatened with extinction, and other listings to species less threatened. All the chapters in the book which are devoted to particular groups of animals and plants include an introductory section detailing the IUCN status of the relevant species. In addition, many of the authors are themselves affiliated to IUCN in some way, and the organisation has given me much help and advice personally. So, without IUCN this book would never have seen fulfilment.

Acknowledgements

First and foremost, I want to thank all the contributing authors to this book for giving their time, expertise and energy to writing their chapters. All the chapters have been independently vetted by authorities in the relevant fields, and this has led to many improvements. Although I am a retired academic with an Emeritus Chair in Genetics at the University of Southampton, England, and have always had a passionate interest in wildlife, I do not have the detailed knowledge which the authors provide, and can only stand back and admire their knowledge and achievement. I am also greatly indebted to Southampton University for providing constant encouragement and outstanding computing services, even when most of my work on this book has been carried out at home. Sir David Attenborough, who wrote a foreword for 'Silent Summer', also deserves praise for the way in which his television expertise has kept us all aware of what is currently happening to the world's wildlife.

Dr Gyulin Hwang, who used to be a member of my research team, has also made a great contribution to the preparation of many of the chapters.

The staff at Cambridge University Press, and especially Dominic Lewis and Aleksandra Serocka, have provided support and advice over an extended period of time, and I am most grateful to them. I am also very grateful to Jo Tyszka (freelance copyeditor for Cambridge University Press) for her careful and critical reading of the chapters. The book has been greatly improved thereby.

My wife Jean has also ensured a supportive home environment and has been very tolerant of the piles of books and paperwork which have stacked up in some of our rooms. Without her love and support I could not function.

ONE

Introduction and the Evolution of Life on Earth

NORMAN MACLEAN

Summary

This chapter serves as an introduction to the book. It discusses the origin of Planet Earth and its Moon, their dependence on the Sun for energy, and the evolution of life on Earth. The evolution of the first living cell seems to have been a single event and all life on Earth is directly derived from this individual primary organism. The first life forms were anaerobic bacteria, but these later gave rise to photosynthesising cyanobacteria, which produced oxygen. The presence of oxygen eventually led to the emergence of aerobic animals and plants. The chapter then details the emergence of the oceans and supercontinents Pangea and Gondwanaland, the eventual break-up of the supercontinents and the development of the varied ecosystems which characterise Planet Earth at the present time.

1.1 Introduction

We are currently in the middle of a so-called great extinction of the world's wildlife, one to add to many past extinctions. These include the extinction of the dinosaurs some 65 million years ago (sometimes called the K–T or K–Pg extinction), apparently caused by a huge meteorite striking Earth in the vicinity of the Gulf of Mexico and the Yucatan peninsula, the catastrophic Triassic–Jurassic extinction of 2000 million years ago (2000 Mya), resulting from a mix of climate change and volcanism, and causing the extinction of 75% of all the species living at that time, and the even more disastrous Permian–Triassic extinction with 96% of all marine species dying out, including the trilobites.

The present extinction, sometimes called the Holocene extinction event, began about 10,000 years ago and is ongoing, and is uniquely attributed to human activity. The agents by which humans have brought about this devastation are the use of fire and hunting by early hominids (think of the demise of the mammoths) followed by more recent habitat destruction and deforestation, together with overexploitation of other biological resources, agricultural intensification often preceded by slash and burn, overextraction of water and land drainage, pollution of land, water and air by oil, pesticides and herbicides (consider Rachel Carson and her predictions of DDT damage), spread of urban and industrial areas with construction of road and rail networks, and destruction of corridors between surviving islands of suitable wildlife habitat. Also the accidental or intentional release of many destructive exotic species such as mice, rats, cats, pigs, mongoose, cane toads, brown snakes and many others, such as possum in New Zealand and lion fish in the Caribbean. So this book sets out to detail which species have recently become extinct and which ones remain, and of these, which are prospering and which declining, together with some success stories of recent conservation efforts.

The present scenario is not without hope, in fact there are many recent success stories, such as the redesign of fishing methods (involving hooks that are only effectively exposed on reaching a certain depth) to avoid accidental death of albatrosses, the global moratorium on whaling and recovery of stocks of many whale species, and the successful exploitation of human habitats by species as diverse as polar and brown bears, nighthawks, peregrine falcons and the successful reintroduction programmes with condors, red kites, white-tailed sea eagles, wolves and others.

The section that follows will consider the history of Planet Earth, how early life evolved, and how the break-up of Pangea has led to the subdivision and distribution of species on the remaining continents.

1.2 The Origin of Planet Earth and its Moon

Recent evidence has led to a revision of our understanding of the relationship between Earth and Moon. Initially it was believed that a small planet called Theia grazed the Earth at a 45 degree angle and broke up after this impact, one of the resulting chunks being caught by the gravitational pull of Earth and forming the orbiting Moon. But in more recent years it has become apparent that Earth and Moon have identical chemical compositions. So the revised view is that the violent collision between Earth and Theia led to the formation of a single larger planet from which a chunk of the mantle layer became detached to form the Moon. The crash between the original Earth and Theia happened about 100 million years after the Earth originally formed, which was about 4.5 billion years ago. Rocks brought back to Earth from the Moon by Apollo missions 12, 15 and 17 reveal that the Moon has an identical oxygen isotope signature to Earth, having 99.9% of its oxygen atoms as ^{16}O, the remainder being a mix of ^{17}O and ^{18}O (the numbers indicate the sum of the protons and neutrons in the oxygen atom).

The age of the Earth is approximately one-third the age of the Universe, 4.5 billion years rather than the 13.8 billion years since the Big Bang. The Moon has, together with the Sun, led to the tidal flows and ebbs, the combined effect of their gravitational pull, when in line, providing the regular dramatic spring tides. The Moon also stabilises the axial tilt of the Earth and this results in climatic changes being reduced to moderate levels.

Evolution of the first life forms on Earth seems to have occurred soon after conditions became permissible by the availability of water and the stabilisation of temperatures, and

Figure 1.1 Image of Planet Earth from space.

this occurred probably about 4000 Mya, only 500 million years after Earth's formation. There is now agreement that the ocean was present very early, so the date for the origin of life lies somewhere between 4000 and 4400 Mya.

One of the necessary prerequisites for the development of life was the presence of water and recent thinking about the arrival of water on Earth has changed. A large proportion of the Earth's surface is water and so from space Earth looks to be a largely blue planet (see Figure 1.1). This water is 96% oceanic and 1.2% freshwater, with the remainder locked up in polar ice, glaciers and permafrost.

It used to be argued that most of the Earth's water arrived in comets, but it is now accepted that water was already integral to the interstellar dust grains which accreted to form our planet. Calculations about the possible adhesion of water to the dust grains in the harsh conditions of interstellar dust clouds support this new interpretation of events.

Initially much of the Earth was molten because of volcanism and frequent collisions with other bodies, but quite rapidly a cooler crust formed, interspersed by the oceans. The initial atmosphere contained almost no oxygen, but was made up of 60% hydrogen, 20% water vapour, 10% carbon dioxide and 6% hydrogen sulfide, with lesser amounts of nitrogen, methane, carbon monoxide and inert gases. The Earth's atmosphere also helped to shield the surface from too much solar radiation. Early oceans probably had temperatures of about 250 °C, at least for brief periods, with the dense atmosphere preventing complete vaporisation. Ocean cooling then followed. In years gone by it was assumed that life could not survive at temperatures much above 60 °C, since most proteins are denatured at higher temperatures, but more recently we have learned about the so-called extremophile microorganisms, including organisms called Archaea, which will thrive at temperatures above 120 °C. Such organisms can still be found in hot springs, such as those in Yellowstone Park in the United States, as well as occurring in the hydrothermal vents in the deep oceans. Enzymes from bacteria such as *Thermus aquaticus* (Taq polymerase) have revolutionised molecular biology and underlie the important polymerase chain reaction (PCR) now used to replicate DNA sequences worldwide. Other extremophile bacteria include species such as *Thermus brockianus, Halobacterium volcanii* and *Deinococcus radiodurans*.

Although cells similar to the Archaea certainly evolved early in the Earth's history, it is likely that originally living systems were acellular, employing membranous surfaces and enzymatic forms of RNA (ribonucleic acid) rather than DNA (deoxyribonucleic acid), together with amino acids, which are the building blocks of protein.

Soon after cellular life evolved, involving DNA as well as RNA as genetic material, it is likely that photosynthetic cells evolved. Notice that the earliest life grew independently of oxygen, and indeed oxygen would have been highly toxic to this early life, but then oxygen was released by photosynthetic bacteria (cyanobacteria) using solar energy with carbon dioxide and water.

One of the hardest steps to envisage in cellular evolution is to conceive how early cells became self-replicating, and the improbable nature of this evolutionary step is underscored by the fact that all modern life seems to have evolved from a single evolutionary event in the production of the first replicating cell (see the publication by Douglas L. Theobald (2010), 'A formal test of the theory of universal common ancestry').

So the earliest cellular life was not aerobic (oxygen requiring) but some 2.3 Bya, photosynthetic cells (cyanobacteria) evolved, which produced oxygen as a by-product, and this paved the way for the evolution of oxygen-dependent life, which accounts for most of the species that we know of as living organisms on Planet Earth.

Rocky formations known as stromatolites, which are layered biochemical accretionary structures, can still be found today in shallow seas such as exist in Shark Bay in Western Australia. These structures include microbial biofilms (mats) of bacteria, especially cyanobacteria, which are photosynthetic, and fossilised stromatolites dating to 3.5 Mya. Some geologists now think that the earliest stromatolites may have been inert, and that the release of oxygen by cyanobacteria did not occur until 2.3 Bya.

It thus appears that life evolved on Earth soon after the presence of water and moderate surface temperatures provided appropriate conditions. It has been estimated that more than 99% of the five billion or so species that have evolved on Earth are now extinct. Estimates about the number of present species on Earth range from 10 to 14 million, although some naturalists put the figure at more than 20 million. An entomologist called Terry Erwin has tried to tackle the question by addressing the question of how many species remain undescribed. The majority of these are small insects, especially ants, in rainforest canopy. What Erwin has done is to visit various rainforest areas, put down extensive plastic sheets under the trees and, on climbing up into the canopy, he has released a fog cloud of dense insecticidal vapour and allowed this to descend through the canopy. The casualties are collected from the plastic sheets and identification attempted. By estimating the number of species caught and the number of secured species which are currently not recorded in taxonomy, Erwin has estimated the number that represent new species. The estimates are highly variable but the total is usually over 30 million species. This number breaks down into 300,000 to 400,000 plant species, 1.4 million non–insect animals (85,000 molluscs, 1.1 million mites and spiders, 47,000 crustaceans, 31,000 fish, 7,000 amphibians, 10,000 reptiles, 10,000 birds and 5,500 mammals). The insects make up the rest, between 10 to 15 million of them, and fungi at 1.5 million. The total numbers of species of bacteria and Archaea is hard to know but will certainly be in millions. Some of these figures, such as the number of bird species, is certainly accurate, but others, such as the figures for the number of insect and bacterial species, are less certain.

1.3 What is a Species?

Having thought of these millions of different life forms on Earth which are separated by taxonomy (the science of classification) into different species, it is high time to try to define what exactly is meant by a species.

Biologists define a species as a group of freely interbreeding individuals which do not breed with other neighbouring individuals of different species; the individuals within a species are morphologically the same, except for the separate sexes. Sometimes even within a species there is some morphological variation, and this is referred to as poly-morphism. For example the little land snail *Cepaea nemoralis* appears with different amounts of banding, and some individuals have no banding. When the ratios between these variant individuals remain the same, it is referred to as a balanced polymorphism, sometimes explained by the success of the variant individuals in differing environmental situations.

Occasionally, neighbouring species will interbreed, and this is referred to as hybridisa-tion. This may occur if one individual cannot find a mate within the same species. Duck species quite often hybridise, especially if an individual duck of the American wigeon (*Anas americana*) flies the Atlantic Ocean and finds itself in a population of European wigeon (*Anas penelope*). Hybridisation between the two 'sister-species' will then readily occur. There are examples of so-called 'clines', where individuals show increasing vari-ation in one parameter so that the individuals at each end of the cline do not recognise one another as being con-specific. This can result in so-called 'ring speciation' as has occurred with the greenish warblers (*Phylloscopus trochiloides*) which forms a ring species around the Himalayas, and the subspecies at the ends of the ring, *P. trochiloides plumbeitarsus* and *P. trochiloides viridanus*, overlap but do not interbreed. The plane tree so widely planted in London is also a plant hybrid between the oriental plane (*Platanus orientalis*), and the American plane (*Platanus occidentalis*); it is now referred to as *Platanus hispanica*.

1.4 Latin Names and Genera

All species have a Latin binomial (ever since the scheme drawn up by the father of taxonomy, Linnaeus). The first name indicates the genus (which is a group of related species) and the second name the species. So we, *Homo sapiens*, belong to the genus *Homo*, which includes *erectus*, *neandertalensis* and many others, while *sapiens* denotes our species, the 'wise' hominid. There are further levels of hierarchy which need not concern us much. They are, going up from Genus, Family, Order, Class, Phylum and Kingdom. There are also some fine subdivisions such as subclasses and suborders. A group of organisms classified together is normally assumed to be monophyletic (having one common ancestor) but some groupings are seen as paraphyletic, that is 'not quite monophyletic'. Taxonomy must always beware of evolutionary convergence, where two organisms look alike but are not related. For example, in Madagascar there is an animal called a hedgehog tenrec. The animal closely resembles a European hedgehog, but is actually a tenrec. Selective evolution has led to convergence in appearance since both have adapted to similar ecological conditions. The birds called barbets in the New World of Latin America closely resemble the barbets of Asia, but the two groups of birds are not at all related. It is another example of convergent evolution.

A group of related organisms in one or more populations is referred to as a 'taxon' of which the plural word is 'taxa'. In taxonomy, the Archaea and true Bacteria are referred to as Prokaryotes (before nuclei) while all the higher groupings of organisms are referred to as Eukaryotes (with nuclei). There has been a vexed question over the years about how many kingdoms exist in life forms. There is little doubt that the mitochondria of eukaryotic cells are derived from bacteria and that chloroplasts and other plastids are derived from cyanobacteria, but the precise derivation of the original eukaryotic cell, with its bacterial and cyanobacterial inclusions, remains a little uncertain in terms of the derivation from Archaea and true Bacteria. It is worth emphasising that viruses are not in the lineage of organisms, they are in fact escaped parts of organisms and can only replicate by re-entering a living cell and using its cellular machinery to make more virus particles. Bacteria have their own viruses, called 'bacteriophage'. Just where the chromosome-possessing nucleus of the eukaryotic cell came from remains somewhat mysterious, but the eukaryotes with their elaborate membranes, mitochondria, nuclei and, if a plant, their chloroplasts, has proved to be a winning formula.

There used to be only five Kingdoms, the Prokaryotes (bacteria etc.), Protista (Protozoa etc.), Fungi, Plants and Animals. However it is now clear that neither of the first two Kingdoms is a single taxonomic grouping, the Archaea and Eubacteria being quite distinct and not closely related, while the Protista (the Protozoa) are now known to be a taxonomic rag-bag of unicellular forms of life.

Early in the history of life on Earth the original Kingdom diverged, leading to primitive Protozoa and primitive Fungi, Plants and Animals. There are still living fossils around which represent some of the early forms of life. These include the curious sago palms (*Cycads*), the horsetails (*Equisetum*), red seaweeds and the curious welwitschia plants of the Namibian desert. Potato blight (*Phytophthora infestans*) seems to be a very primitive Fungus and the two groups of slime moulds Plasmodium and Acrasiomycota are somewhere between Fungi and Protozoa.

1.5 Pangea and the Break-up of the Continents

It is time for us to return from our preoccupation with taxonomy to what happened to Planet Earth itself after the origin of life. The Earth's crust and oceans were themselves subject to major changes, and here we must now follow up on these.

The crust of the Earth was (and still is) highly dynamic, especially in the early life of the planet, and the tectonic plates that lay beneath it were frequently moving. Tectonic plates are large solid slabs which lie under the surface of the Earth's crust. The lithosphere, which is the rigid outermost shell of the planet, is divided into separate plates, of which there are seven or eight major plates and many minor ones. Where the plates meet, the boundaries are areas of earthquake and volcanic activity, together with mountain building and oceanic trench formation. Plate movement may be up to 10 cm annually. Along plate boundaries, plates may crunch together or slide under one another. The lithosphere is about 100 km thick and becomes thicker with time as the surface cools. Most of the world's active volcanoes lie along plate boundaries, as in the 'Ring of Fire' of the Pacific plate, Africa's Rift Valley and the San Andreas fault.

Two supercontinents were evident some 200 million years ago, a southerly one called Gondwana and a northerly one called Laurasia. The former included Antarctica, South America, Africa, Madagascar, India and Australasia, while the latter included North America, Europe and Asia. About 300 million years ago a larger supercontinental mass called Pangea (see Figure 1.2) existed, and its first break-up yielded the two separate masses which characterised the Triassic some 200 million years ago.

Many plants are believed to have a Gondwana distribution, as, for example, the Proteaceae family now found in southern South America, South Africa and Australasia. The eucryphia trees are today found in the southern areas of South America and Australia once joined in Gondwana. Similarly the existence of marsupial mammals in Australia and South America is also explained in this way, although in the latter they have now been largely superseded by the more successful Eutherian placental mammals that spread from North America.

The existence of Pangea is also strongly supported by fossil evidence, as, for example, fossil remains of *Cynognathus*, a 3 m long Triassic land reptile, in both South America and West Africa, fossil evidence of the Triassic land reptile *Lystrosaurus* in Africa, India and Antarctica, fossil remains of the freshwater reptile *Mesosaurus* in southern parts of South

Figure 1.2 Pangea chart.

America and South Africa, and fossil remains of the plant *Glossopteris* in Australia, South Africa, South America and parts of Antarctica. The supercontinent Pangea eventually broke up under the influence of the moving tectonic plates, to yield the continents as we know them today, separated as they are by the large tracts of ocean, Atlantic, Pacific, Indian and Southern, and many smaller seas. Some distribution anomalies remain which are hard to reconcile with Pangea and its break-up. One such is the existence of boa snakes in Madagascar, with their nearest relatives being in South America.

1.6 Early Evolution of Multicellular Life

We should now return to consider how the early eukaryotic cells evolved into the huge array of multicellular life which followed. One recent technique which has greatly helped in understanding early evolution and the relationships between the resulting organisms is the use of DNA sequencing. The DNA of both mitochondria and chloroplasts is itself quite simple, carrying only a few genes, and analysis of these sequences in different organisms allows one to trace early relationships. Some of the simpler conserved sequences in the nuclear DNA have also proved useful in this regard. The recent development of PCR, referred to earlier in the context of the DNA polymerase enzymes recovered from extremophile Archaea bacteria, has greatly assisted in this analysis.

There is an excellent reference book to consult on the diversity of life forms. It is *The Variety of Life* by Colin Tudge (2000). As mentioned before, the Protozoa, the single-celled organisms, have proved to be very diverse and are hard to classify accurately. The bacteria themselves have become diverse, developing cell walls, flagellae and spiral morphology, as in the Spirochaetes. Some also became obligate intracellular parasites like *Chlamydia*. Many higher vertebrates are entirely dependent on intestinal bacteria to help digest their food.

Amongst Protozoa, few have become more complex than the multiflagellated *Trichonympha*, which lives in the guts of termites and helps them to digest the wood on which they feed. Some of the algal Protozoa with chloroplasts have become partially multicellular for part of their life cycle, as displayed by *Pandorina* with 16 cells and *Volvox* with many hundreds.

Early multicellularity prepared the way for the great leap forward in Eukaryotic life, namely the development of different kinds of cells within the same organism. This development, first evident in the most primitive plants and animals, allowed the development of differentiated cell types to take on different roles within the same organism. In turn, this allowed the specialisation of sex cells in different sexes of the same species, a major advance in the Eukaryotes.

Soon after the development of multicellularity (which actually evolved independently in several groups of organisms), the Plants, Fungi and Animals diverged from one another, all retaining the mitochondria derived from intracellular bacteria, but only the plants retaining chloroplasts derived from cyanobacteria. This scenario of evolution has also been shown by looking at the nucleus, mitochondrial and chloroplast genomes, and comparing them with those of the presumed prokaryotic originals.

Photosynthetic algae and Protozoa preceded the evolution of proper plants, but by the Cambrian period some 500 million years ago fossil plant spores become evident. The earliest plants probably resembled liverworts (Hepatophyta) which formed small tetrads of spores. They grow in wet terrestrial environments and today many of these early primitive plants, including mosses, clubmosses, hornworts and *Selaginella* (examples of which are still alive today) are lumped together as Bryophytes. Other early plants included horsetails (*Equisetum*) and ferns (Pterophyla). Some 370 million years ago in the Devonian, the seed-bearing plants evolved. Early examples included cycads and ginkos, both still with us today, but the really major advances were the evolution of gymnosperms (conifers) and the dramatic and hugely varied angiosperms (flowering plants). Angiosperms first appeared some 130 million years ago in the early Cretaceous and in that period we can find examples of some of the earliest angiosperms, magnolias, water lilies and arums. By the late Devonian there were forests of tree-like plants with internal conducting vessels.

The appearance of all these large plants, which coincided with the earliest tetrapods, the amphibians, has been called the 'Devonian Explosion'.

Fungi are first found about 1500 Mya and 'higher fungi' about 600 Mya. They probably first colonised the land in the Cambrian, but only became common in the Devonian, some 400 Mya. Since fungi do not mineralise to form good fossils, early fungi are shrouded in mystery. The first fungi were probably aquatic, but became terrestrial when they exploited growth on dead or dying Devonian trees.

The earliest animal evolution seems to have been jump-started by increases in marine oxygen levels associated with the so-called 'snowball Earth' glaciations (see Lyons and Planavsky (2012) 'Extreme climate change linked to early animal evolution'). The first fossil evidence for early animals comes from the remains of burrows made by worm-like organisms in rocks found in China. Animals really diversified during the 'Cambrian Explosion', and one of the most famous assemblages are those found in the 'Burgess Shale' (see 'Wonderful Life' by S. J. Gould (2000)).

The oldest fossil of undoubted animal character is that of *Charnia masoni*, found in pre-Cambrian rocks in Charnwood Forest in Leicestershire, England. It was first discovered by Roger Mason when a schoolboy. Originally thought to be a plant, it is now recognised to be a sessile sea pen or crinoid (a sister group to the soft corals). But it was in the later Cambrian explosion that animal life really diversified. Sponges, Ctenophores and worms were amongst the simplest but starfish and Mollusca soon followed. They also conquered land as the early arthropod insects and the marine sea squirts, tunicates placed in the subphylum Urochordata, which have tadpole-like larvae with the beginnings of a noto-chord (early backbone). Other arthropods, besides insects, the Crustaceans, radiated hugely in the sea to give crabs, shrimps and lobsters, and the once-abundant trilobites. The latter flourished in the Cambrian but all became extinct in the great Permian extinction 250 million years ago. Their success can be measured in part by their speciation, which reached almost 4000 separate species. The trilobites included predators and species which fed on both marine plants and animals, and even plankton. They were heavily armoured with numerous walking legs, although these were not evident in the initial fossils found. Some were as large as 45 cm long and weighed up to 4.5 kilos. For details of these animals see the book 'Trilobite!: Eyewitness to Evolution' by Richard Fortey (2000). They had excellent eyesight with multifaceted eyes and lenses of calcite. Fossil trilobites are abundant, especially in Morocco, where there is a special museum dedicated to Trilobites.

'Onychophora' are often called velvet worms or *Peripatus*. These animals occur mainly on the forest floor of tropical rainforest in Africa, Australia and South America. They resemble intermediates between worms and insect larvae, walking by means of paired oncopods or stub feet. Their main importance in animal evolution is that they were amongst the earliest life forms to move from an aquatic environment to a terrestrial one. To this end they have lost gills and breathe air through a tracheal network for aerobic respiration. They seem to be distant relatives of Arthropods and Tardigrades (water bears). Velvet worms are mainly predatory on other small animals such as worms and woodlice, hunting at night and enmeshing their prey in a sticky slime secreted from special slime glands on either side of the mouth. They are faintly segmented and very prone to desiccation, and so live in moist environments. The main evolutionary significance of the Onychophora is that they left a purely aquatic environment dependent on gills for respiration, to move onto land and develop trachea for air breathing. So living examples are referred to as 'Living Fossils'. For more information on these animals see the relevant Wikipedia entry under Onychophora (https://en.wikipedia.org/wiki/Onychophora).

But we must return to the ascidian tadpole to trace the dramatic rise of the vertebrates, first as simple fishes like lampreys, hagfish and the sand-dwelling Amphioxus, but soon to conquer the land at the end of the Cambrian as the first amphibians. Reptiles were soon to follow, and although some species such as turtles remained sea-bound, most laid eggs on land. The embryos inside the egg remained in their own shelled watery environment. From the hugely successful reptilian dinosaurs came the first flying birds and others remain with us today as the crocodiles and alligators. The demise of the dinosaurs not only left space for the birds but also for the small mammal-like reptiles (Cynodonts) although we can trace mammalian evolution back to the Synapsids which occurred in the late Permian around 250 Mya. Mammal-like reptiles co-existed with dinosaurs for over 150 million years, but somehow survived the great dinosaurs extinction event at the end of the Cretaceous, some 65 Mya. This is emphasised in a recent publication by Grossnickle and Newham (2016).

Mammals have proved very successful, first as marsupials which colonised both Australia and South America before the break-up of Pangea, but were later out-competed by the placental mammals, the Eutherians which have no pouch and give birth to independent youngsters, albeit often requiring frequent sustenance from the female breast milk and, in the most highly developed, female care and attention for over a year. We must not leave the mammals without recording the astonishing rise of the primates, and eventually of the apes and hominids which evolved on the plains of Africa, from which they migrated to spread around the planet (see 'The Origin of Our Species' by Chris Stringer, 2011).

Some mammals returned to the sea, none more remarkable than the toothed and baleen whales, which diverged from the hoofed ungulates, and seals, sea lions and walruses, which evolved from land carnivores.

1.7 Habitats and Ecosystems

No introduction to a book on the world's wildlife would be complete without reference to the communities in which the wild species live. These are particular habitats, with distinctive climates and geographical features, and are often referred to as ecosystems. Although an ecosystem such as grassland or rainforest may occur in different parts of the Earth, the species which occupy the same ecosystem in different places are themselves quite different. Thus the species that characterise coral reefs in Indonesia are quite distinct from those found in the coral reefs of the Caribbean.

Let us now consider some of these ecosystems and the species which occupy them. There are too many ecosystems in the world to be able to discuss them all, and some, like chalk downlands in England, have a very restricted distribution. But the following are of more global occurrence:

- Tropical rainforest
- Grassland
- Desert
- Coral reef
- Mangrove swamp
- Salt marshes
- Rivers and river deltas
- Deciduous woodland
- Taiga
- Seagrass meadows
- Kelp forests
- Coniferous woodland
- High mountains
- Polar ice
- Islands
- Oceans

Ecosystems are in general balanced energy systems, so that plants produce starch by photosynthesis and nitrogen fixation, and the local animals support the plants by pollination, but also depend on the plants for food. In coral reefs the photosynthetic algae (zooxanthellae) in the corals provide much of the energy but, the corals predating microplanktonic organisms also provides more.

Tropical rainforest occurs in small patches in Australia, in Borneo, Indonesia and Africa, and very substantially in Amazonia. It is characterised by tall trees and high rainfall, and the topmost canopy layer is rich in insects and birds such as hornbills and barbets, which feed on the figs and other fruits. Many of the tallest trees have buttress root systems supporting the massive trunks. Selective logging of rainforest trees has proved to be much more ecologically friendly than clear-felling sections, as has occurred so widely in Indonesia, where much of the rainforest has given way to plantations of oil palms. There are also temperate rainforests, found in areas such as the Pacific Northwest, New Zealand, Tasmania and southeast Australia, and also boreal rainforests found in Canada, Alaska and Russia.

Grassland occurs in the wide open steppes of Asia, the African plains and the prairies of North America. Huge herds of wildebeest, zebra, buffalo and gazelle feed on the African grasses and migrate with the rains to find the new grass. Birds such as the very numerous red-billed quelea feed on the grass seeds and large numbers of vultures feed on carcasses of animals killed by the abundant lions and other predators. The soils of the Serengeti are volcanic and are ideal for the grass, but form a hard pan in which trees other than acacia struggle to survive. Bison which once migrated across the American prairie are now sadly diminished and no longer migrate. The Asian steppe in Hungary and stretching over to

Siberia, once had large herds of wild horses, but these are also much diminished, as are the once-abundant saiga antelopes.

Desert. There are many desert areas in, for example, central Australia, the Asian Gobi, American Nevada and Arizona, the African Namib, Sahara and Kalahari, and the almost rainless Atacama of northern Chile. Deserts are highly variable, some being stony or rocky, others primarily sand like the Namib and Sahara. The Arizona desert in the US has numerous cacti, including the huge Saquaro, and also the succulent Joshua trees. The Namib has quite a lot of underground water, which allows animals such as oryx, giraffe and even elephants to thrive there. The coastal areas are watered only by fog rolling in from the sea.

Coral reefs. These dramatic ecosystems are to be found in Indonesia, the Red Sea, the Indian Ocean and many Pacific islands, as well as the Great Barrier Reef of Australia and in the Caribbean, the world's second largest barrier system, the Mesoamerican Barrier Reef. They are characterised, of course, by numerous coral species, which thrive in the shallow water and contain photosynthetic algae to help provide energy. The abundant fish are often brightly coloured, and the reefs also provide food for visiting turtles, sharks, and even whale sharks. Coral can die due to bleaching in sunlight and warming of the coastal waters. The reefs are also characterised by abundant invertebrate species of worms, Molluscs, Crustaceans and Echinoderms, and host about a quarter of all marine fish species.

Mangrove swamps. The trees and chunks of mangrove colonies are not all closely related, although some, the red mangroves, belong to a distinct family, the Rhizophoraceae. Many mangroves have upright columns of aerial roots, called pneumatophores. Usually there is mud under the mangroves which provides a home to numerous fiddler crabs and mudskipper fishes. The mangroves help protect the shore from excessive wave erosion, and their roots provide a haven for innumerable young fish, even of ocean-going species. Some mammals like proboscis monkeys feed exclusively on the leaves of mangroves.

Salt marshes. There are important ecosystems situated at the interface of the land and the ocean. They are home to a range of salt-tolerant herbs, grasses and shrubs, which in turn provide habitat for both marine and terrestrial species.

Rivers and river deltas. The huge rivers of Nile, Yangtze and Amazon bring down large amounts of silt which help fertilise the fields adjoining the delta regions. Many large fish such as sturgeon migrate up these rivers, while areas like the Ganges delta, the Sunderbans, provide livelihoods for millions of Indian small farmers. The delta of the Danube is characterised by extensive reed beds and immense numbers of fish-eating birds such as pelicans, storks and cormorants live there. The fertile mud brought down by the Nile River has been cultivated for many centuries by Egyptian farmers.

Deciduous woodland. Such woodland is mainly a northern European phenomenon, and the beech and oak trees protect a rich understorey of flowering herbs before the leaves appear each spring. The leaves provide food for large numbers of insect caterpillars, which are in turn predated by incoming migratory birds such as warblers, redstarts and flycatchers. Many deer browse on the understorey herbs and shrubs, and indeed an overabundance of deer species in the UK is causing ecological problems in these deciduous forests. Wild boars are another characteristic mammal of these ecosystems.

Taiga. The taiga is the woodland heath which characterises northern Europe to America, and is sometimes called boreal rainforest. It provides breeding habitat for numerous species of ducks and wading birds. It is the world's largest terrestrial biome, extending over most of Canada and Alaska, as well as northern Scandinavia and Russia. It is often referred to as boreal or snow forest, since the abundant pines, spruces and larches are covered by snow in winter. Reindeer occur in large numbers, as do wolves and wolverine, and immense hordes of mosquitoes occur in summer. The rivers of the Taiga support large runs of many species of salmon, providing food for bears and eagles and indirectly for the adjacent forest. Although winters are long and very cold, there are 24 hours of sunlight in summer, allowing long feeding periods for the birds and mammals which breed in the Taiga.

Seagrass meadows. These are formed by marine angiosperms in shallow lagoonal, coastal or estuarine waters from the tropics to temperate waters. They are also characterised by a high diversity of animals and are important as feeding grounds for a wide range of animals, including marine turtles, manatees and dugongs, birds, fish and a range of invertebrates. They can also be important habitats in the lifecycle of coral reef fish.

Kelp forests. These are also important biogenic habitats formed by macroalgae that occur from Arctic and sub-Antarctic latitudes to temperate. The main structural species in these forests vary between oceans (e.g. *Laminaria* in the north Atlantic; *Ecklonia* in the Indian Ocean; *Macrocystis* in the Pacific and South Atlantic) but these habitats are all highly productive and are important to a range of fish and invertebrate species, including those with commercial value. Kelp are also important in the formation of organic detritus which supplies coastal food webs and is also transported into deeper waters.

Coniferous woodland. This ecosystem substantially overlaps with the former one, the Taiga, but stretches further south on the American west coast and also down into northern India and southwestern South America. It is temperate in climate, with high rainfall and the immense stands of redwood cypress, fir and pine trees are characteristic. These are also a rich understorey of shrubs in many places. Fur-bearing animals such as mink, fox, lynx and beaver are characteristic, as are numerous squirrels. The coniferous trees are often characterised by needle-like leaves which have a waxy coating and can curl up to avoid frost damage. The old Caledonian pine forest of Scotland was a British extension of this biome.

High mountains. The dramatic ranges of the American Sierras and Andes, the Asian Himalayas, and the European Alps and Pyrenees are all expressions of this biome. The mountain tops often have year-round snow cover, but enough melts in summer to provide numerous rivers and lakes. There is often moorland below the topmost peaks, and mountain birds such as bar-headed geese, dotterel, snow bunting and snow finch breed here during the brief summer. These is also a characteristic flora of alpine plants including many species of gentians, saxifrages, and dwarf bulbs such as crocus. As one goes north, these species are found at lower levels and indeed in Iceland and Spitzbergen they occur abundantly at sea level.

Polar ice. The North Pole has little permanent sea ice and indeed global warming has opened the Northwest Passage from east to west. Not so with Antarctica, where the permanent ice shelves are hundreds of metres thick and the annual sea ice extends to cover a vast area of the Southern Ocean. The low water temperatures mean high dissolved oxygen levels, supporting large shoals of fish and krill. The areas are beloved by feeding whales, some like bowheads, beluga and narwhals more or less permanently in the Arctic, others in the Antarctic, such as humpbacked whales and fin whales, visit in summer. There are huge numbers of nesting fish-eating birds including the southern penguin and the northerly auks, puffins, kittiwakes and shearwaters. Polar bears and Arctic foxes are present in the north, leopard seals in the south. The numerous Antarctic whaling stations at one time accounted for thousands of visiting blue, fin, right and humpback whales, and the northern Inuit people in the Arctic are still permitted to harvest bowhead, beluga and pilot whales. Visiting pods of killer whales also account for many penguins in the south and many seals and walruses in the north and now killer whales (orca) are present in the Southern Ocean more or less year round. Different groups of orca in different parts of the world do not mix and have different prey items and hunting strategies. They may well constitute different orca subspecies.

Islands. The archipelagos of Hawaii and Galapagos are of ongoing volcanic origin, while the large island of Madagascar is a remaining relic of Gondwanaland. Island species are amongst many recent extinctions, partly because they are often highly specialised, and introductions of non-native cats, rats, pigs and mongoose have often helped eradicate many native species. Islands provide rich areas for speciation, as evidenced by the tortoises and finches on the Galapagos, the Hawaiian honeycreeper birds, and the lemurs and vanga bird species of Madagascar. Intensive efforts are underway to clear rat populations from many islands. New Zealand has set a good example in clearing exotic species from some of its many islands prior to then introducing native bird species such as takahe and kokako in their place. Islands often have large visiting seabird populations of albatrosses and other petrels. The sensitivity of island populations is emphasised by the introduction of the brown tree snake (*Boiga irregularis*) to Guam, where it has essentially eliminated the entire populations of native small birds.

Oceans. Oceans are not so much ecosystems in themselves but include many other ecosystems. Some of these we have already considered under Deltas, Mangrove swamps, Islands, and Coral reefs. But some remain to be considered. In the middle of the Southern Atlantic is a quiet zone called the Sargassum Sea, characterised by the floating seaweed of the same name. It provides a haven for many fish species, especially when young, and is believed to be the breeding area of the European Eel. The deep ocean comprises the vast pelagic realm, the waters between the surface and the seafloor. This is probably the least explored ecosystem on Earth and is zoned by depth into the sunlit euphotic zone, the mesopelagic or twilight zone, where sunlight is detectable and the bathypelagic/abyssopelagic zone. The seafloor mainly comprises the vast abyssal plains surrounded by continental margins. There are also the mid-ocean ridges, vast ranges of underwater mountains or seamounts that run across the ocean floor around the Earth. Seamounts can also be formed by intraplate hotspots creating chains or clusters of seamounts. There are also ocean trenches, including the deepest place on Earth, the Challenger Deep, part of the Marianas Trench system, at around 11,000 m deep. Canyons incise the continental margins and can be productive ecosystems which attract marine predators. By far the most productive regions of the ocean are the upwelling zones along the western continental margins of Africa and South America which are extremely important in the production of seafood. The deep ocean has been found to be a more physically heterogeneous and biologically diverse range of ecosystems than previously recognised. There are also extreme environments such as the hydrothermal vents, which are places where hot fluids enriched in minerals escape from the seafloor. Some are known as black smokers because the fluid escape is highly focused, issuing from mineral chimneys and resembling smoke because of the precipitation of metallic sulfides on contact with the cold waters of the deep sea. They support huge numbers of sulfur-dependent bacteria, which in turn provide food for worms, shrimps and other crustaceans. Two aspects of these strange biomes deserve attention. One is that the water in their vicinity is often very hot, which demands heat tolerance of the extremophile bacteria living there, as well as of the motile shrimps and other animals which are exposed to the hot water. However, these organisms can only tolerate temperatures of 120 °C for microorganisms and around 60 °C for animals, so they live a perilous existence on the interface between the hot vent fluids and the cold waters of the deep sea. The other significant aspect of thermal vents is that life is in no way dependent on the Sun for energy, only on the reduced chemicals emitted by the vents. So life in these areas is cut off and independent of all other life on Earth, although it should be pointed out that the larvae of some of the animals, such as vent shrimp, are distributed in the pelagic zone and feed on phytoplankton. Since these vents only occur in certain regions, often hundreds of miles from other such vents, it is puzzling how organisms can move from one to another, especially when colonising new vents, although evidence suggests this is through larvae with long pelagic durations. Another ecosystem characterised by the use of chemical energy are hydrocarbon seeps, places where methane and other hydrocarbons leak from the seafloor. Some of the organisms that are found around these seeps are related to those found at vents. Another aspect of life in the oceans is the remarkable adaptation of many deep-water fish, squid and crustaceans which communicate by bioluminescence. These animals mostly occur in the twilight zone and bioluminescence has evolved to be used not just for communication but also camouflage, as a defence and also to lure or stun prey. Also, when animals such as whales die, their bodies sink to the ocean bottom, where they provide food for hagfish and other deep water forms of life.

In the last few years Conservation International has listed 25 areas in the world which are current biodiversity hotspots for conservation priority. They are listed here:

* Forests of Hawaii and other Pacific archipelagos
* Forests of New Caledonia
* Heathland of southwest Australia
* Rainforest of the Philippines
* Most of the forests of Indonesia
* Forests of southwest China
* Himalayan forests
* Rainforest of Sri Lanka

* Rainforest of Indian Western Ghats
* Many habitats in Madagascar
* Habitats of the Horn of Africa
* Multiple habitats in the African Southern Cape
* Guinean forests of West Africa
* Forest of Caucasus Mountains
* Brazil's Cerrado and Atlantic forest
* Forest and dryland of Mediterranean basin
* Tropical forest of Andean slopes
* Forests and drylands of Caribbean islands, especially Cuba and Hispaniola
* Tropical forests of southern Mexico and Central America
* Californian coastal and foothill sage

Just before completion of this book, an important volume appeared. It is David Attenborough's new book 'A Life on Our Planet: My Witness Statement and a Vision for the Future', published by Witness Books of Penguin Random House, UK. In this book Attenborough (2020) recounts his lifetime experience of the human impact on the planet and the resulting dramatic reductions in biodiversity. This is followed by an account of his vision that even at this late time, a supreme effort by human civilisation could yet reverse the dreadful declines.

I do not share David Attenborough's optimism in this latter section. However, I want to stress that his book casts this present volume about the state of the world's wildlife into sharp focus, since our book provides the detailed analysis of the state of the planet's biodiversity on which his analysis depends.

Acknowledgement

I wish to thank Professor Alex Rogers (an author of Chapter 12 of this book) who identified some errors and also suggested many improvements to this chapter.

References

Attenborough, D. (2020) *A Life on Our Planet: My Witness Statement and a Vision for the Future.* London: Witness Books/Penguin Random House.

Fortey, R. (2000) *Trilobite!: Eyewitness to Evolution.* New York: Vintage Books.

Gould, S.J. (2000) *Wonderful Life: The Burgess Shale and the History of Nature.* New York: Vintage Books.

Grossnickle D.M. and Newham E. (2016) Therian mammals experience an ecomorphological radiation during the Late Cretaceous and selective extinction at the K–Pg boundary. *Proc R Soc B* 283(1832): 20160256.

Lyons, T. and Planavsky, N. (2012) Extreme climate change linked to early animal evolution. *Science Daily* (Sept. 26, 2012).

Stringer, C. (2011) *The Origin of Our Species.* London: Penguin Books.

Theobald, D.L. (2010) A formal test of the theory of universal common ancestry. *Nature*, 465: 219–222.

Tudge, C. (2000) *The Variety of Life: A Survey and a Celebration of all the Creatures that Have Ever Lived.* Oxford: Oxford University Press.

TWO

Flowering Plants

SARA OLDFIELD AND LAUREN GARDINER

Summary

The importance of plant diversity to humankind is immense. Plants are primary producers defining and supporting ecosystems worldwide and providing a wide range of ecosystem goods and services. Vascular plants are species characterised by a well-developed system of specialised cells that transport water, minerals and photosynthetic products and provide structural support enabling plants to grow on land. Flowering plants, also known botanically as angiosperms, are by far the largest group of vascular plants. They are characterised by their distinctive reproductive structures, the flowers. Designed to be pollinated by wind, insects or other animals, all flowers have ovules, which become seeds after fertilisation, enclosed within an ovary. In contrast, the gymnosperms (see Box 2.1), which include conifers and cycads, have reproductive structures with naked seeds that are not enclosed. The other groups of vascular plants are ferns and fern allies which do not produce seeds.

Flowering plants are commonly divided into two broad groups, monocotyledons and dicotyledons, based on the presence of either one or two embryonic leaves (cotyledons) contained within each seed. Monocotyledons (usually shortened to 'monocots') include families of plants such as grasses, palms and orchids, and comprise about 20% of all flowering plants. Monocots can usually be recognised by having simple leaves with parallel veins, and flowers with parts in threes or multiples of threes. Dicots, although not considered to be a formal, scientifically valid grouping, make up the remainder of flowering plants, and include a huge range of diverse plant species, from the buttercups (Ranunculaceae) and magnolias (Magnoliaceae) to the daisies (Asteraceae).

Box 2.1

Gymnosperms

Conifers are one of the four distinct lineages of surviving gymnosperms, the other three being *Ginkgo* (with only one species, the commonly cultivated *Gingko biloba*), gnetophytes (112 spp.) and cycads (about 350 spp.). There are about 630 conifer species around the world. Conifers are native to all continents except Antarctica. Some species are very widespread, for example the pine, fir, larch and spruce of boreal forests, whereas others are narrow endemics, surviving in tiny patches of tropical forest. Conifers have a long history dating back to the time of the earliest trees which evolved as land plants, 300 million years ago.

There are eight families of conifers. The largest is the Pinaceae with 231 species, including pine, spruce, larch and fir trees, all found in the Northern Hemisphere. The Podocarpaceae family has 174 species mainly found in the tropics with some species in temperate mountainous regions of the Southern Hemisphere. The Cupressaceae has 135 species native to both temperate and tropical regions. The other five families are Araucariaceae, Cephalotaxaceae, Phyllocladaceae, Sciadopityaceae and Taxaceae.

Because of their great international interest as economically and culturally important trees, there have been major conservation efforts for conifers. All species have been assessed for the IUCN Red List of Threatened Species, with this task completed in 2013. Sadly over one-third of all conifer species are now threatened with extinction, as a result of logging pressures and forest clearance, including some species that have only been scientifically described in recent years. The wollemi pine (*Wollemia nobilis*) is an iconic survivor. Described as a new species in 1994, this tree of the Araucariaceae family is Critically Endangered in the wild. Surviving in a small area of deep gorges in New South Wales, miraculously it survived the intense bush fires of early 2020.

There are about 350 species of cycads in 10 genera and three families. 307 species have been assessed for the IUCN Red List. Of these, four are recorded as Extinct in the Wild, and a further 192 species fall within a threatened category. They are considered the most threatened group of plants with the main threats to cycads being habitat loss and overcollection.

2.1 Taxonomic Diversity

Current knowledge of the taxonomic diversity of flowering plants recognises that there are around 400,000 species in over 450 families. The largest plant families of dicots are Asteraceae (the daisy family), with over 32,000 species, and Fabaceae (the pea family), with nearly 21,000 species. In the monocots, the largest families are Orchidaceae, with some 30,000 species, and Poaceae (grasses) with over 11,000 species (Willis, 2017). Taxonomic knowledge of flowering plants remains incomplete, with estimates that there may be around 70,000 additional species still awaiting discovery and description, and around

Box 2.2

The Value of Herbaria for Plant Conservation

In order to most effectively and efficiently conserve plant species and the ecosystems in which they grow, we need to understand the species under threat, how they are related to each other, and how and why they are threatened. We need to know how species are geographically distributed, where they grow now and ideally where they used to grow in the past, to inform strategies to conserve as much as possible.

Herbaria are essential resources in the gathering of this essential data. Fundamentally made up of preserved collections of plant (and often mycological) specimens, usually collected from the wild, herbaria most commonly comprise systematically arranged collections of dried pressed specimens, but may include material stored in other ways (e.g. preserved in alcohol-based liquids, wood samples, bulky dried fruits and seeds, and silica-dried material stored specifically for DNA preservation). Each specimen represents a single, verifiable, citable point in time and space where a plant was growing, and is accompanied by collection information, usually in the form of one or more typed or handwritten labels. This information includes what the plant is, where it was collected, when, by whom, associated collections (such as DNA, photographs and flowers preserved in alcohol), and often additional information encompassing subjects such as vegetation types, associated species, local uses and threats. A large, historic herbarium can ultimately represent several hundred years of plant collecting and documentation, from around the world, but smaller collections often focus on specific regions of the world, particular plant groups, and even individual collectors.

With more than 3000 herbaria worldwide, holding an estimated 380 million specimens, these collections represent a powerful – and highly collaborative – research dataset, and tool, for plant conservation. Traditionally used and thought of as centres for the documentation of biodiversity, describing and cataloguing plant taxa, herbaria have long been used for the identification of plants collected in the wild by comparison with previously collected material, and the naming of new species. Floristic and monographic studies of plants are commonly based out of herbaria, utilising specimens from the network of collections around the world.

Herbaria remain major centres of species discovery, with many of the approximately 2000 new species described each year being identified in them, often from specimens collected some time ago. Increasingly, herbarium specimens are being used in a range of newer ways, such as studying morphological changes and geographical shifts in response to changing climates, documenting the extirpation of populations – and even extinction of species, vegetation mapping, molecular studies investigating genetic change over decades or even hundreds of years and the origin of domesticated varieties used by man, and even isotope analysis revealing changes in atmospheric gases and soils. With an estimated two in five plant species being thought to be threatened with extinction (work which was itself heavily dependent on herbarium collections from around the world, in the Sampled Red List Index of Plants project) (Nic Lughadha, 2020), and a third of all plants being barely known at all, herbaria are at the coalface of plant conservation research.

2000 new species are described each year (Willis, 2017). The mean time lag between the time a new flowering plant is first collected in its natural habitat and formal species description is over 30 years. About 50% of the plant species awaiting 'discovery' are thought to have already been collected and stored as herbarium specimens, but not yet studied more closely (Bebber et al., 2010, see also Box 2.2). There are many outstanding challenges in the understanding and quantification of plant diversity. These include collecting challenges in species-rich understudied regions of the world, particularly in the tropics, understanding diversity in large complicated genera and reconciliation of species accounts between different geographical regions (Hollingworth et al., 2017). Nevertheless, based on what is known, there is a wealth of data with which to assess, conserve and utilise sustainably the global diversity of flowering plants.

2.2 Life Form Diversity

Across the diversity of flowering plants, life forms include trees, shrubs, herbs, succulents, submerged aquatics, vines and epiphytes. Species evolution has resulted in adaptations which enable plants to thrive and compete in many different habitats (see Box 2.3), maximising the efficient use of essential resources including sunlight, water and minerals. Trees, with their rigid trunks enabling massive growth to great heights, first evolved over 300 million years ago with gymnosperms being the earliest trees. The characteristic of 'woodiness' has subsequently evolved independently in many plant families, with the arrival of flowering plants in the Cretaceous period, 130 million years ago (Kenrick and Crane, 1997; Fitzjohn et al., 2014). It is currently estimated that there are about 60,000 tree species (Beech et al., 2017), of which around 500 are gymnosperms and the rest are flowering plants. Monocots do not have the ability to increase their stem diameter by secondary growth and do not produce true wood. Some species, such as palm trees in the Arecaceae and *Dracaena* spp. (dragon trees) in the Asparagaceae family, do, however, attain a tree-like habit through various growth mechanisms and function ecologically as trees. Nearly half of all tree species (45%) are found in just 10 flowering plant families. The family with the most tree species is the Fabaceae, with 5405 tree species, followed by Rubiaceae (4827) and Myrtaceae (4330). The most diverse tree genera are *Syzygium* (1069 species), *Eugenia* (884 species) and *Eucalyptus* (747 species), all in the family Myrtaceae (Beech et al., 2017).

The plant trait of succulence, the ability to store water in one or more organs, has also evolved repeatedly among many flowering plant lineages (Grace, 2019). Overall 83 plant families include succulent species, about 12,500 species in total (Nyffeler and Eggli, 2010). Plant families with the largest number of succulent species, adapted to survive regular

---

Box 2.3
Examples of Major Ecosystems, Plant Life Forms
And Plant Diversity

Forests
Forest ecosystems, dominated and defined by tree species, cover approximately 31% of the world's land surface. They provide critical ecosystem services, including the direct provision of food, fodder and water. Forests play a major role in the Earth's biogeochemical processes, influencing hydrological, nutrient and carbon cycles, as well as global climate (Millenium Ecosystem Assessment (MA), 2005). In turn, forests provide habitat for a wide range of species supporting at least half of the Earth's terrestrial biodiversity (MA, 2005) including 80% of amphibians, 75% of birds and 68% of mammal species (Vié et al., 2009). In the Sampled Red List Index for Plants study (see main text) forest was the habitat with the greatest number of threatened plant species, comprising 79% of the species in the sample found to be threatened.

Grasslands
Grasslands form a major component of the world's dryland ecosystems (the others being deserts and woodlands) which cover approximately 40% of the world's land surface (excluding Greenland and Antarctica). Grasslands are found in every region of the world. Sub-Saharan Africa and Asia have the largest total area in grassland, 14.5 and 8.9 million km², respectively. Worldwide, grassland ecosystems provide livelihoods for nearly 800 million people. Grasslands are home to many wild relatives of important human food crops derived from the grasses (Poaceae) that dominate them – namely wheat, maize, rice, rye, millet and sorghum. They remain the primary source of genetic material for improving these crops. At least 30% of the world's cultivated plants originate in dryland ecosystems, including grasslands. Most drylands are poorly monitored in terms of biodiversity and it is difficult to disaggregate plant species that are restricted to grasslands from those found in desert habitats. In the Sampled Red List Index for Plants study grassland species formed 10% of the threatened species.

Deserts
Desert ecosystems cover over 19 million km², almost 15% of the world's land surface, and are defined by low and unpredictable rainfall. Many plant species have specialised adaptations to cope with arid conditions and succulents are a plant life form particularly associated with deserts. In the Sampled Red List Index for Plants study desert species formed a low proportion of threatened species within the sample.

---

drought and typically associated with desert habitats, include the Euphorbiaceae (with more than 2000 succulent species), Aizoaceae (1800), Cactaceae (1500) and Apocynaceae (1100) (Grace, 2019). The huge and highly diverse Orchidaceae family has about 4400 species that can be considered to be succulent. It is thought that evolutionary radiations among large lineages of succulent species in Africa and the Americas occurred nearly simultaneously during the Miocene (Arakaki et al., 2011). Globally, xeromorphic succulent species diversity is concentrated in five geographical regions. South Africa is by far the most diverse region per unit area with over 4600 taxa, from 350 genera and 58 families (Smith et al., 1997). Other succulent-rich arid and semi-arid floras with high levels of succulent endemism are found in Madagascar, East Africa and the Arabian Peninsula, Eastern Brazil, and Mexico and the US, which results in distinctive floristic affinities between these regions (van Wyk and Smith, 2001; Barthlott et al., 2015).

2.3 Biogeographic Regions

Flowering plant diversity, in terms of number of species, is not evenly distributed around the world. As with other living organisms, diversity is generally highest in regions between the Tropics and dramatically decreases towards the Poles. Regions with so-called Mediterranean climates (such as the Mediterranean Basin itself, the Cape Region of South Africa, California) are, however, also of great importance for plant diversity. Taking geographical area into account, the regions of the world which have the greatest vascular plant species richness (more than 3000 species per 10,000 km^2) have been determined to be: Central America extending into northwest South America, Southern Mexico, tropical eastern Andes and northwest Amazonia, eastern Brazil, northern Borneo and New Guinea, the Cape Region of South Africa, east Himalaya, western Sumatra, Malaysia and eastern Madagascar (Barthlott et al., 2007). All these geographical areas fall within the 36 parts of the world considered to be global biodiversity hotspots, based on the concept proposed by Myers et al. (2000). Plant species diversity was one of the primary factors used to define biodiversity hotspots using Myers' methodology. To qualify, an area must have high endemism, with at least 1500 endemic vascular plants, and to be under threat, with 30% or less of its original natural vegetation remaining. The 36 global biodiversity hotspots cover only 2.4% of terrestrial land worldwide, but support more than half of the world's endemic plant species. These hotspots are likely to contain most of the as yet undescribed plant species (Joppa et al., 2011).

Important areas for plant diversity in Mediterranean climatic zones include Central Chile, the Cape Floristic Province and Succulent Karoo of southern Africa, the California Floristic Province, the Mediterranean Basin and southwest Australia. The exceptional plant diversity and endemism of Mediterranean regions are explained by evolutionary processes induced by the characteristic climate of extended summer drought and cool wet winter, together with high topographic variation and low soil fertility (Huston, 1994). Other important centres of plant diversity located in temperate regions include New Zealand and the Caucasus mountains of southwest China.

Islands are frequently renowned for high levels of plant endemism compared with mainland regions. It has been estimated that there are around 50,000 insular endemic plant species. Factors accounting for the high degree of endemism include geographical isolation, both in terms of speciation in isolation and also the absence of competitors, predators and pests. Globally, islands cover about 5% of the land surface, but have over 25% of the world's vascular plant species (Caujapé-Castells et al., 2010). Of the global biodiversity hotspots, 14 are islands, archipelagos or have a significant proportion of land in the form of islands. Six other hotspots include offshore islands within their limits

(Bramwell, 2011). One such island, Madagascar, is renowned for its high level of plant diversity and endemism. In a flora of some 12,000 plant species, Madagascar has some 5800 tree and shrub species, of which over 5200 (90%) are endemic and, as noted above, Madagascar is also a centre of endemism for succulent plant species.

2.4 Rarity and Threats

The present-day distribution of a plant species may provide an indication of its ability to survive threatening factors. Many plant species are naturally rare and may be adapted to very particular habitats, and the majority of plant species are restricted in range (Joppa et al., 2013). Naturally rare plant species may not be of particular conservation concern so long as their habitat remains secure. However, naturally rare species may have more limited genetic variability in contrast to more widespread species, which generally have greater genetic variability and ecological plasticity and enables the latter to adapt or evolve in response to threats more readily than narrow endemics can. Intrinsic factors such as adaptation to a particular soil type, specific mutualistic relationships with other organisms (such as pollinators or dispersers) and genetic incompatibility (for instance having dioecious flowers), all influence the potential for long-term survival of a flowering plant species at a particular site.

As mentioned above, flowering plants first evolved in the Cretaceous period, 130 million years ago. Over time they have diversified, with the evolution of new species and decline of others as a result of competition and the impact of natural phenomena, providing strong selective pressures. Humans have had a profound impact over recent millennia. Initially this impact was small, but it is now clear that the impacts of human activities are greatly outweighing natural threats to plant species and their habitats (Brummitt and Bachman, 2010). Plant diversity is under threat worldwide, with many species facing genetic erosion or extinction. The main threats to biodiversity worldwide are habitat loss, overexploitation and the impacts of pollution, invasive species and climate change (MA, 2005). Plant species are experiencing all these threats to varying degrees and in different combinations around the world.

As noted by Rivers (2017), there is not yet a comprehensive analysis of which factors are most important in threatening plant species with extinction. Studies which have analysed information on threats specified in over 20,000 IUCN Red List assessments for plant species have, however, shown that agriculture is the most frequently identified human activity threatening plant species in the wild. The primary impact of agriculture is habitat loss and fragmentation, as natural vegetation, and its component plant species, is cleared to make way for crop production. Secondary factors include soil disturbance and modification, changes in water availability and the excessive use of synthetic agrochemicals, including pesticides, herbicides and fertilisers that frequently form part of modern agricultural land use.

2.5 Habitat Loss

Habitat loss is considered to be the single most important threat to plant diversity, particularly in the tropics (Corlett, 2016). Habitat loss includes the total removal of vegetation, as well as degradation and fragmentation of persisting habitat. Agricultural conversion of land from primary habitat occurs on many different scales: from small-scale slash and burn farming, to medium-scale conversion of habitat for cash crops (such as coffee and tea), to large-scale plantations of commercial crops (such as oil palm, rubber and soybean). Only regions unsuited to crop plants (including deserts, boreal forest and tundra), have remained largely unaffected by land conversion (MA, 2005).

Other causes of habitat loss include conversion of land for livestock production, conversion and degradation of forest caused by industrial logging, mining, dam infrastructure, and coastal, urban and industrial development. Fragmentation at the landscape level is a significant factor reducing plant diversity (Kettle and Koh, 2014). Fragmentation is caused both by natural causes such as storms and fires, but also more systematically via anthropogenic land use change. As larger areas of vegetation are divided and fragmented, remnant areas of habitat may only be able to support small species populations, which will be more vulnerable to stochastic effects, disease, and inbreeding and genetic bottlenecking. Edge-effects in fragmented habitats may impact species that are unable to withstand these conditions. Pollination and seed dispersal may also be reduced as the wider ecosystem and associated species are affected by increasing habitat fragmentation, and fragmentation is known to provide increased access for pests and invasive species, as well as easier access for poachers and the illegal collection of plants by humans.

2.6 Overexploitation

The second most common threat recorded for plants in IUCN Red List assessments is biological resource use leading to overexploitation. Many plant species are harvested from the wild for a wide variety of uses, including timber, food, medicine and ornamental use. Harvesting of timber from natural forests remains the major use of plant diversity in terms of scale, volume and value. Timber extraction from the wild (rather than from plantations) applies particularly to tropical hardwoods, of which approximately 300 million cubic metres of timber is harvested annually, equivalent to an estimated 100 million trees (Jenkins et al., 2018). Exploitation of timber trees through clear felling, where whole areas of forest are cut, or selective logging, where individual species are targeted, continues under various forms of forest management. Where particular species are sought after for the quality of their timber, logging can be a direct threat to that species' survival, especially when felling controls are ignored. Selective logging of prime timber species also has secondary impacts, increasing fragmentation and degradation of the habitat of other species and opening up the forest through road construction, leading, for example, to further clearance for settlement and agriculture. In tropical regions where tree diversity is greatest, 'intact forest landscapes' comprise only 20% of forest area. An intact forest landscape (IFL) is defined as 'a seamless mosaic of forest and naturally treeless ecosystems with no remotely detected signs of human activity and a minimum area of 500 km^2' (Potapov et al., 2017). Industrial timber extraction has been recorded as the primary cause of the reduction in IFL area globally between 2000 and 2013. During this time period, in Africa and Southeast Asia, selective logging was the dominant cause of IFL loss (77 and

75% of the total loss of IFL area, respectively), whereas clear felling was the main cause of IFL loss in the less diverse temperate and southern boreal regions of North America and Eurasia (Potapov et al., 2017).

In many cases, logging of tropical hardwoods is driven by international demand. For over 600 years, timbers such as *Swietenia* spp. (mahogany) have been traded around the world. In recent years there has been a dramatic increase in demand for hardwoods of 'precious timbers' from genera such as *Diospyros* spp. (commonly known as ebony) and *Dalbergia* spp. (commonly known as blackwood, rosewood and sometimes ebony), particularly for the Chinese market. The pressure on individual species is intense and illegal logging is rife. In Madagascar, for example, the trade in timber of these groups, which remains poorly regulated, is threatening the survival of species, many of which remain poorly known botanically with very limited data on their extant distribution and abundance. Illegal logging of Madagascar's precious timbers has been a major problem for at least 20 years and has increased over the past decade as a result of political turbulence. This has resulted in unprecedented levels of illegal timber harvesting in protected areas, particularly in the northeast of the island (Ratsimbazafy et al., 2016). Recently, 23 Madagascan species of *Dalbergia* have been assessed as threatened with extinction, together with 74 species of *Diospyros*. *Dalbergia* spp. are also heavily exploited in Southeast Asia and Latin America. At an IUCN meeting in Costa Rica in March 2019, 18 of the 19 *Dalbergia* species found in Central America were assessed as threatened with extinction. Six of these are particularly valued for their attractive timber, and have experienced dramatic declines in species' population sizes as a consequence in recent decades.

In addition to the overexploitation of timber trees, non-timber forest products (NTFP) are also extensively collected from the wild and may become overharvested. NTFP are biological resources other than timbers that are harvested directly from forests. They include fruit, nuts, spices, latexes, resins, gums, medicinal plants and dyes. Millions of people around the world depend on wild-collected plants for at least part of their livelihoods, using them for subsistence purposes, local trade or collection as the basis for international trade commodities. Information on the level of use and trade is scattered and generally sparse, and the impact of collecting on the abundance and regeneration of individual plant species remains generally not fully understood.

An estimated 30,000 plant species are used medicinally around the world (Jenkins et al., 2018) and relatively few of these are present in cultivation. It has been estimated that 70–90% of market demand for medicinal and aromatic plants is supplied by wild or 'natural' resources (Bhattacharya et al., 2008). As with other NTFP species, the impact of collection and trade on medicinal plants has been quantified for relatively few species. *Panax* spp. (ginseng) is an example of a heavily traded medicinal plant, harvested from the wild. There are 13 species of *Panax* with a natural distribution in North America and East Asia. Ginseng has been used in traditional medicine in China for thousands of years and by the early eighteenth century, intense wild harvesting had led to the near extinction of the Asian *Panax ginseng*. Today wild *P. ginseng* occurs in only a few localities in Russia and

China. Demand for ginseng roots in the eighteenth century led to a boom in wild-harvesting of American ginseng (*Panax quinquefolius*) causing the decline in wild populations in North America (Manzanilla et al., 2018). *Panax quinquefolius* grows in the eastern woodlands of Canada and the US and is still highly sought after for its medicinal value. Ginseng harvesters remove the fleshy taproot of this slow-growing perennial herbaceous plant, and in doing so kill the plant. Of the 19 states where the species grows, 15 do not allow the harvest of wild roots of *P. quinquefolius* and of those states, five have formally designated the species as either Endangered or threatened at state level due to population decline. The main destination for US exports of roots of *P. quinquefolius* is Hong Kong, with smaller amounts exported to Singapore, Taiwan and other East Asian countries (Ford, 2008).

African cherry (*Prunus africana*) is another important medicinal plant species. This tree species has a wide range of local uses in Africa and yields a valuable medicinal product used to manufacture treatments for benign prostatic hyperplasia. The manufactured drugs are sold globally and the international market is projected to continue to increase. The bark of *P. africana* is harvested in the largest quantity of any tree species worldwide and this has led to international concerns about the sustainability of its use. The retail value of *P. africana* products is estimated at over USD 200 million annually, and may be considerably higher. So far, commercial plantations of the species have only been developed on a very small scale.

Collection of species for ornamental use is another threatening factor for plants. For certain groups of species, including cacti and other succulents, orchids, many bulbs, bromeliads and palms, specialist collectors target desirable species in the wild specifically for their rarity. Wild collection affects a relatively small group of species, but can have extremely detrimental effects and lead to extinction for those plants.

It has been suggested that orchids may be particularly vulnerable to overexploitation because of natural factors such as the limited distribution of many species and low population density because of interacting factors such as recent speciation, specialised pollination mechanisms, habitat specificity and the restricted distribution of mycorrhizal symbionts (Hinsley et al., 2018). These factors combine with the desirability of orchids for humans, both for their attractive flowers and their medicinal properties, to exacerbate their risk of extinction as a result of wild collection. Orchids have been prized in China since ancient times and have exerted an increasing fascination in the Western horticultural world since the seventeenth century. Since that time, cultivation of exotic orchids has been highly prized in Europe, with ownership of rare species becoming extremely fashionable and lucrative in the latter part of the nineteenth century. Enormous quantities of wild-collected orchids were imported, especially to the UK, during Victorian times, with intense rivalry between collectors and commercial companies. Now the vast majority of orchids traded worldwide are artificially propagated hybrids, but demand for wild plants, particularly of rare species and those of medicinal value continues.

One orchid genus that has been severely impacted by overcollection is *Paphiopedilum*. Currently 85 species of this genus of Southeast Asian slipper orchids are included as

Threatened or Near Threatened on the IUCN Red List, nearly the entire genus. At the end of nineteenth century these were the most sought after of all orchids with European collectors, and commanded enormous prices when changing hands. They subsequently fell out of fashion but the discovery of a new species, *P. sukhakulii*, in Thailand in the 1960s followed by other species new to science and horticulture, revived interest in the genus and led to large quantities of wild plants appearing in trade. Similarly, new discoveries in southwest China in the 1980s triggered intense international demand, which continues today. A recent study has shown the importance of social media as a means of trading in rare orchid species, including those from the genus *Paphiopedilum* (Hinsley et al., 2016).

Cacti and other succulent plants are also popular with collectors who often favour wild-collected plants for their 'authenticity' and seek specimens of particularly rare species. The Global Assessment of Cacti, published by the IUCN SSC Cactus and Succulent Specialist Group, found that 31% of cactus species are threatened with extinction. The main threats to cacti are the illegal trade in live plants and seeds for the horticultural industry and private collections, as well as their unsustainable harvesting for medicinal use. These threats affect 47% of the threatened species (Goettsch et al., 2015.)

2.7 Climate Change

Temperature and rainfall are fundamental determinants of plant growth, and climatic factors directly influence the distribution of plant species. With the growing impact of climate change, plant ranges are known to be shifting altitudinally and latitudinally. Phenological changes, such as time of flowering and fruiting, are also being observed. In response to climate change, species can adapt, migrate, or face extinction. Widespread plant species with greater genetic variation are more likely to be able to adapt more effectively than naturally rare species that are more likely to have a more restricted gene pool. Restricted range plants, such as alpines, which are likely to be adapted to and isolated at higher elevations, may simply have nowhere to migrate to. Despite current constraints in the form of limited species distribution data and with anticipated future changes in rainfall and temperature, information on the predicted impact of climate change on rare plant species is going to be essential to consider long-term management options for the species and the ecosystems within which they are found. As yet, there is limited evidence for climate change directly being a factor in plant species extinctions, but it is highly likely to be more clearly revealed to be so in future (Willis, 2017). As noted by the World Wide Fund for Nature (WWF, 2018), the influence of climate change on populations of wild species is rapidly accelerating and may take a dominant role in shaping future biodiversity. It is also likely that losses of wild species that are already declining as a result of threats such as habitat loss and overexploitation, are being exacerbated by the ability of species to respond to changes in climate being compromised.

There have been various studies modelling the impact of anticipated changes in climate on plant distributions. Still et al. (2016) modelled the future distributions of 565 rare plant species in the US and predicted that 45% will be at the highest risk of extinction by the

2080s. Of the taxa studied, 16.8% are currently listed under US Federal legislation as Endangered or Threatened. The study indicated that these federally listed taxa are not more likely to be at risk from climate change than non-listed species. Similarly, a higher rarity status (as indicated by NatureServe Global Rank) does not indicate increased vulnerability to climate change. The authors summarised that the majority of the rare plants in the western US are predicted to be threatened by climate change, however, current rarity – as defined by threat status – is not necessarily correlated to climate change vulnerability.

The ability of plant species to tolerate both current and future climate change has been attributed to various different plant traits, including physical characteristics such as plant height, leaf size and rooting depth, physiological measures such as efficiency of water use, and traits associated with life history and life cycle events, such as flowering times and reproduction mechanisms (Willis, 2017). It has been suggested that the slow growth rate of trees may limit their adaptability to climate change. Succulent species, with their ability to store water might be expected to cope relatively well with increased drought in environments that become hotter and drier. Under altered drought regimes though, forced functional shifts may affect the ecological distinction between xeromorphic succulents and (non-succulent) xerophytes, resulting in reduced diversity among succulent plant communities, as has been observed in grasslands both in South Africa and North America (Forrestel et al., 2017).

2.8 Invasive Species

A major threat to wild plant species, associated with modern agriculture and the globalisation of goods and services, has been the spread of invasive species which outcompete native plants, particularly those which are naturally restricted in range. Climate change is exacerbating the threat to these species. In the US alone, over 3700 exotic plant species have been introduced either accidently or deliberately, with the largest concentrations of non-native species arising in and around large coastal cities (Kartesz, 1999). Particularly rapid establishment by weedy introduced species occurs in habitats which have already been degraded by other factors such as wild fires, overgrazing and logging. It is estimated that invasive species are a threatening factor for 42% of US Federally Listed Threatened and Endangered plant species and are the main threat for 18% of these (Pimentel et al., 2005).

Introduced pests and diseases are also becoming a major threat to native species around the world, as well as having huge economic consequences. A recent analysis of 1300 known invasive pests and pathogens estimated their potential cost to global agriculture at over US$540 billion per year unless their spread can be stopped. China and the US are reported to represent the richest potential sources for new invasions to other countries, because of the number of invasive species already present and their volume of trade (Willis, 2017). One invasive pest species in the US and Canada, the emerald ash borer *Agrilus planipennis*, has caused major problems at the landscape level over the past two decades. Six abundant North American species of *Fraxinus* (ash) trees have become

Critically Endangered as a result of predation by this beetle which was accidentally introduced through infested shipping pallets (Barstow et al., 2018).

2.9 Threat Assessments

Assessing the threat status of plant species began at a global level in the 1970s, but progress in assessing the status of all flowering plants remains relatively slow. In 1970–1971, Robert Melville at the Royal Botanic Gardens, Kew produced an account of threatened angiosperms, forming Volume 5 of the IUCN Red List series, adding to Volumes 1–4 all covering animal groups. Melville doubted that detailed Red List accounts, similar to those prepared for birds and mammals, would ever be possible, given the overall number of plant species, with so many rare or likely to be threatened, and the limited information for most plants in the wild (Scott *et al.*, 1987). In 1978, the IUCN Plant Red Data Book, also prepared at the Royal Botanic Gardens, Kew, was published and provided 250 examples of globally threatened plants (239 angiosperms; 6 gymnosperms and 5 pteridophytes). These species were chosen to be representative of the 20,000–25,000 vascular plant species considered likely to be threatened at the time based on the IUCN Red Data categories (Lucas and Synge, 1978). Twenty years later a list of over 33,000 globally threatened vascular plant species was published by IUCN (using the same threat categories of Endangered, Vulnerable, Rare or Indeterminate), with the authors stating that the number of threatened plant species recorded represented 'the tip of the iceberg' (Walter and Gillett, 1998).

In 1994, a revised system of IUCN Red List categories was introduced, designed to produce more objective and transparent conservation assessments for all species. This system had three threatened categories of Critically Endangered (CR), Endangered (EN) and Vulnerable (VU) together with five associated criteria to measure symptoms of extinction risk. The five different criteria related to biological processes underlying population decline and extinction. The IUCN Red List system for categorising extinction risk has subsequently been modified, but retains the same three categories of threat and the five criteria. In a species assessment, the species is evaluated against the criteria which relate to: (A) population reduction, (B) geographic range (C) small population size and decline (D) very small or restricted population and (E) quantitative analysis. Each criterion has quantitative thresholds and is qualified by several subcriteria. If species do not fall into an IUCN threatened category they may be considered Near Threatened (NT), if they nearly meet the criteria. If there is insufficient information to determine whether a species can be considered threatened or not, it can be categorised as Data Deficient (DD). In some cases, this may be due to taxonomic uncertainty and in others due to the lack of data on a species' distribution, ecology and threats. Species that do not meet the criteria for the threatened categories may be assessed as Least Concern (LC).

At present, more than half of all species assessed as threatened (i.e. as Vulnerable, Endangered or Critically Endangered) on the IUCN Red List are vascular plants (25,483 of 43,212, as of September 2022). This figure is not directly comparable with the 33,000 species included in the 1998 Red List of Threatened Plants because many species have not yet been reassessed using the system introduced in 1994, which requires more explicit supporting documentation. Furthermore, the current IUCN Red List system measures extinction risk and no longer specifically covers the concept of rarity. The 1998 IUCN Red List included 14,504 species listed as Rare (Walter and Gillett, 1998), whereas an equivalent category is no longer utilised.

The threat assessments currently on the IUCN Red List are not representative of all flowering plants. This is partly because there has been a tendency to assess species already known to be at risk and partly because assessments have been undertaken on an ad hoc basis by a wide range of different groups and experts. Furthermore, there has been an emphasis on assessment of woody plants because of strategic opportunities. Current information on woody plants on the IUCN Red List builds on a global survey carried out in 1995–1998 and reported by Oldfield et al. (1998).

As of late 2022, more than 63,000 vascular plant species have been assessed globally and added to the IUCN Red List. Given this relatively small number of global assessments for plants, it is difficult to estimate what proportion of the total number of plant species are at risk of extinction. In a systematic initiative to increase understanding of the global plant extinction risk, the IUCN Sampled Red List Index (sRLI) for Plants assessed the status of a random sample of plant species around the world (Brummitt et al., 2015). The random sample consisted of 7000 species selected from bryophytes, pteridophytes, gymnosperms, monocots and the family Fabaceae (chosen as a large family for which a comprehensive nomenclatural checklist was available and the family which is considered to best mirror overall patterns of global angiosperm diversity). The IUCN Red List categories and criteria were applied to all the species in the sample. Given that we lack verifiable and quantifiable data on population sizes or trends over time for most plant species around the world, most plant conservation assessments were (and still are) based strongly on Criterion B which focuses on species distribution, although all criteria were considered for each assessment. The best source of distribution data for plants comes from preserved specimens held in the world's herbaria (Box 2.2).

The results of the sRLI for plants indicated that 11% of legume species are likely to be threatened (i.e. assessed as Vulnerable, Endangered or Critically Endangered), 18% of monocots, 40% of gymnosperms and 16% of pteridophytes. The results indicated that 21% of all plants are likely to be at risk of extinction. The region of the world with the greatest threats affecting plant diversity, based on this study, was revealed to be the Neotropics, with 23% of assessed species being found to be threatened. Tropical Africa has 22% of assessed species threatened, tropical Asia has 21% of assessed species recorded as threatened and Australasia, with a very large number and high proportion of endemic species, has 18% of assessed species recorded as threatened. In this study, relatively low proportions of the flora were found to be threatened in temperate Eurasia (12%) and North America (10%) (Brummitt et al., 2015).

A specific global initiative which aimed to assess the conservation status of all 60,000 tree species worldwide by the end of 2020, as far as possible using the IUCN Red List categories and criteria made enormous progress in its targets. The Global Tree Assessment took two strategic approaches in tackling this major task. One approach was to undertake a rapid assessment of Least Concern tree species using Global Biodiversity Information Facility (GBIF) data as a basis for the assessment process. Initially over 10,000 tree species were identified in this process as being globally widespread and also not considered threatened in any global, regional or national conservation status appraisal. The second approach was to identify the countries with the greatest number of endemic species and work with national partners to assess the species fully. A total of 20,900 endemic tree species were found to be present in the ten countries with the highest recorded number of endemic trees. The Global Tree Assessment also paid particular attention to timber species that are traded internationally and to specific plant families that are relatively well known taxonomically and for which expertise is available.

Analysis for the Global Tree Assessment shows that 45% of all tree species have some form of conservation assessment. This includes all the trees found on the IUCN Red List of Threatened Species (www.iucnredlist.org; 13,964 assessments) together with single-country endemic tree species assessed nationally as threatened. Combined information in this analysis indicates that at least 19% of all tree species are likely to be threatened with extinction globally.

Many countries have national approaches to the conservation assessment of plants which align with the IUCN Red List system to varying degrees. Plants are currently by far the most common taxa represented in the National Red List database maintained by IUCN and the Zoological Society of London, with 98 countries having a national plant red list. Various different methodologies are used to categorise degree of threat at a national level, some of which are enshrined in national law. Whereas over 63,000 plant species have global IUCN Red List assessments, over 180,000 plant taxa have some form of global, national, regional or non-IUCN conservation assessments, as recorded in the ThreatSearch database maintained by Botanic Gardens Conservation International (BGCI). According to a recent analysis of the IUCN Red List, national red lists and other assessments, around 30,000 plant species (vascular plants and bryophytes) have been assessed at least once with a threatened category (Bachman et al., 2018).

Assessing the threat status of all plant species is an international priority in biodiversity conservation, as recognised, for example, in the Global Strategy for Plant Conservation (GSPC) of the Convention on Biological Diversity (CBD). One particularly urgent task is to assess the threat status of useful plant species which support human livelihoods. As yet it is not clear how many timbers, medicinal plants, ornamentals, wild-sourced food species and Crop Wild Relatives (CWR), for example, are threatened with extinction. Over 1000 tree species used for timber have been recorded as threatened (Oldfield et al., 1998) and assessments are being updated as part of the Global Tree Assessment. Detailed assessment of the conservation status of the 30,000 medicinal and aromatic plant species has not been undertaken, with a recent report noting that the conservation status of 93% of medicinal and aromatic plant species remains unknown (Jenkins et al., 2018). While the majority of commercial medicinal plant material comes from cultivated sources, no more than a few hundred of the estimated 2500 internationally traded medicinal plant species are thought to be commercially cultivated, so both international trade and unsustainable local use put wild medicinal plants under significant pressure. In India around 90% of the plants used by the country's medicinal plant industry are collected from the wild, and 315 of the 6560 known medicinal species are threatened with extinction (Sharrock et al., 2014).

Crop wild relatives (CWR) are wild plant taxa that have relatively close genetic relationships to crop plants, enabling their potential use in plant breeding to improve agricultural varieties. Almost all modern varieties of crop plants contain some genes derived from a CWR and they are now recognised as a critical resource for food security and economic stability, as well as contributing to environmental sustainability (Maxted and Kell, 2009). The diversity of crop wild relatives has decreased in some areas and appears to be particularly threatened in places where the climatic conditions are changing, but species migration is prevented by ecogeographical barriers (Food and Agriculture Organisation of the United Nations (FAO), 2019).

A recent prioritised inventory of CWR includes 3546 species (Vincent et al., 2013). As yet, the conservation status of relatively few of these species has been assessed. Globally, despite the immense importance of grasses as CWR relating to the major cereals, only 757 species of grasses have been assessed for the IUCN Red List (15 April 2019). A comprehensive assessment of the threatened status of European CWR has been undertaken, covering 572 species relating to 25 economically important crops (Kell et al., 2012). The study showed that at least 11.5% of the species are threatened, with 3.3% being Critically Endangered, 4.4% Endangered and 3.8% evaluated as Vulnerable. A further 29% were recorded as Data Deficient, which is somewhat disappointing, given the level of botanical knowledge there is about the flora of Europe compared with much of the rest of the world. Over half the species assessed were considered to be Least Concern globally, but of these around a third are considered to be threatened at national level (Kell et al., 2012).

Considering plant species of ornamental value, Red List assessments have been completed for the Cactaceae (Goettsch et al., 2015) but are far from complete for other families of succulent plants, for example only 1.6% of Aizoaceae and 18% of Asphodelaceae have been assessed (Grace, 2019). Full global assessments using IUCN Red List categories and criteria have been published for only 1377 orchid species (as of 15 April 2019). As noted by Hinsley et al. (2018), assessments for orchids are predominantly for species of China and Madagascar, and also for certain charismatic groups such as the genus *Paphiopedilum*. Some orchid assessments also result from the Sampled Red List Index. Hinsley et al. (2018) suggest that the lack of global conservation assessments for orchids reflects major gaps in taxonomic and ecological knowledge about orchids and other specific challenges of studying the species of this diverse family. As noted above, many orchid species have restricted distributions, they may also have short flowering seasons, and/or epiphytic growth habits that make them physically hard to access, and in conservation assessments there may be a need to consider horizontal and vertical distributions of epiphytic species. However, in addition to these intrinsic difficulties, factors such as lack of incentives and the sheer scale of the task may also be reasons for the low number of assessments. At a national level, however, there are many threat assessments for orchid species and so likely more data is available than initially may be apparent.

Bringing together data from the Sampled Red List Index project and BGCI's ThreatSearch database, further modelling of the likely extinction risks to plants has now estimated that as many as 39% of all plant species are threatened in the wild (Nic Lughadha, 2020).

2.10 Looking Ahead

Understanding the diversity of flowering plants, global patterns of distribution and the threats faced by flowering plants is vital to ensure effective biodiversity conservation. Targets for documentation, conservation and sustainable use of plant diversity were first agreed at a global level in 2002 under the auspices of the GSPC. The targets were updated in 2010 and linked to the Aichi Targets of the CBD which are also known as the United Nations (UN) Biodiversity Targets. In turn, the global biodiversity targets are linked with the Sustainable Development Goals, adopted through the UN in September 2015.

Reporting on the 2010 GSPC targets takes place in 2022. Progress has been mixed. The GSPC has galvanised action to develop a World Flora Online, which was called for in Target 1, and more than 40 organisations are working together in an international consortium to deliver the World Flora Online. GSPC Target 2 calls for 'An assessment of the conservation status of all known plant species, as far as possible, to guide conservation action'. As outlined in this chapter, progress towards this Target remains slow at a global level, with less than 10% of vascular plant species assessed and added to the global IUCN Red List. Progress on recording the *ex situ* conservation of threatened plant diversity has been relatively good, but progress on *in situ* plant conservation for species globally is more difficult to evaluate. At a global level, it is not yet possible to estimate the extent to which protected areas conserve plant diversity and/or threatened plant species.

It remains a global priority to complete the task of documenting flowering plant diversity worldwide, and new species continue to be discovered each year. The ecological, cultural and economic values of plants need to be emphasised and the increasing threats they face need to be better understood. With an estimated 39% of all plants likely to be facing extinction, many as a result of human activities, action is urgently required.

Acknowledgement

We gratefully acknowledge the help of Suzanne Sharrock in reviewing this chapter.

References

Arakaki, M., Christin, P.-A., Nyffeler, R., et al. (2011) Contemporaneous and recent radiations of the world's major succulent plant lineages. *Proc Natl Acad Sci USA* 108(20): 8379–8384.

Bachman, S., Nic Lughadha, E.M. and Rivers, M.C. (2018) Quantifying progress toward a conservation assessment for all plants. *Conserv Biol* 32(3): 516–524.

Barstow, M., Oldfield, S., Westwood, M., et al. (2018) *The Red List of Fraxinus*. Richmond, UK: Botanic Garden Conservation International.

Barthlott, W., Hostert, A., Kier, G., et al. (2007) Geographic patterns of vascular plant diversity at continental to global scales. *Erdkunde* 61: 305–315.

Barthlott, W., Burstedde, K., Geffert, J.L., et al. (2015) Biogeography and biodiversity of cacti. *Schumannia* 7: 255–284.

Bebber, D.P., Carine, M.A., Wood, J.R.I., et al. (2010) Herbaria are a major frontier for species discovery. *PNAS* 107(51): 22169–22171.

Beech, E., Rivers, M., Oldfield, S. and Smith, P. (2017) GlobalTreeSearch: The first complete global database of tree species and country distributions. *J Sustain For* 36(5): 454–489.

Bhattacharya, P., Bhattacharyya, R., Asokan, A. and Prasad, R. (2008) Towards certification of wild medicinal and aromatic plants in four Indian states. *Unasylva* 230(59): 35–44.

Bramwell, D. (2011) Introduction: islands and plants. In: Bramwell, D. and Caujapé Castells, J. (Eds.), *The Biology of Island Floras*. Cambridge, UK: Cambridge University Press.

Brummitt, N. and Bachman, S. (2010) *Plants under Pressure – A Global Assessment: The First Report of the IUCN Sampled Red List Index for Plants*. Kew, UK: Royal Botanic Gardens.

Brummitt, N.A., Bachman, S.P., Griffiths-Lee, J., et al. (2015) Green plants in the red: a baseline global assessment for the IUCN Sampled Red List Index for Plants. *PloS One* 10(8): p.e0135152.

Caujapé Castells, J., Tye, A., Crawford, D.J., et al. (2010) Conservation of oceanic island floras: present and future global challenges. *Perspect Plant Ecol Evol Syst* 12(2): 107-129.

Corlett, R.T. 2016. Plant diversity in a changing world: status, trends and conservation needs. *Plant Divers* 1:11-18.

Fitzjohn, R.G., Pennell, M.W., Zanne, A.E., et al. (2014) How much of the world is woody? *J Ecol* 102(5): 1266–1272.

Food and Agriculture Organisation of the United Nations (FAO); Bélanger, J. and Pilling, D. (Eds.) (2019) *The State of the World's Biodiversity for Food and Agriculture*, Rome: FAO Commission on Genetic Resources for Food and Agriculture Assessments.

Ford, P. (2008) The yin and the yang of ginseng – making a non-detriment finding for *Panax quinquefolius*: a case study with two perspectives (United States of America and Canada). NDF Workshop Case Studies 2 – Perennials. Case Study 6.

Forrestel, E.J., Donoghue, M.J., Edwards, E.J., et al. (2017) Different clades and traits yield similar grassland functional responses. *Proc Natl Acad Sci USA* 114: 705–710.

Goettsch, B., Hilton-Taylor, C., Cruz-Piñón, G., et al. (2015) High proportion of cactus species threatened with extinction. *Nat Plants* 1: 15142.

Grace O.M. (2019) Succulent plant diversity as natural capital. *Plants, People, Planet* 2019; 00:1–10.

Hinsley, A., Lee, T.E., Harrison, J.R., and Roberts, D.L. (2016) Estimating the extent and structure of trade in horticultural orchids via social media. *Conserv Biol* 30(5): 1038–1047.

Hinsley, A., De Boer, H.J., Fay, M.F., et al. (2018) A review of the trade in orchids and its implications for conservation. *Bot J Linn* 186: 435–455.

Hollingworth, P. Neaves, L.E. and Twyford, A.D. (2017) Using DNA sequence data to enhance understanding and conservation of plant diversity at the species level. In: Blackmore, S. and Oldfield, S. (Eds.), *Plant Conservation Science and Practice: The Role of Botanic Gardens*. Cambridge, UK: Cambridge University Press.

Huston, M.A. (1994) *Biological Diversity: The Coexistence of Species on Changing Landscapes*. Cambridge, UK; New York: Cambridge University Press.

Jenkins, M., Timoshyna, A. and Cornthwaite, M. (2018) *Wild at Home: Exploring the Global Harvest, Trade and Use of Wild Plant Ingredients*. Cambridge, UK: TRAFFIC International.

Joppa, L.N., Roberts, D.L., Myers, N. and Pimm, S.L. (2011) Biodiversity hotspots house most undiscovered plant species. *PNAS* 108(32): 13171–13176.

Joppa, L.N., Visconti, P., Jenkins, C.N. and Pimm, S.L. (2013) Achieving the Convention on Biological Diversity's Goals for Plant Conservation. *Science* 341: 1100.

Kartesz, J. (1999) Exotic vascular plant species: where do they occur? In: Ricketts TH, Dinertein E, Olson DM, et al. (Eds.), *Terrestrial Ecoregions of North America: A Conservation Assessment*. Washington, D.C.: Island Press.

Kell, S.P., Maxted, N. and Bilz, M. (2012) European crop wild relative threat assessment: knowledge gained and lessons learnt. In: Maxted, N., Dulloo, M.E., Ford-Lloyd, B.V., et al. (Eds.), *Agrobiodiversity Conservation: Securing the Diversity of*

Crop Wild Relatives and Landraces. Wallingford, UK: CAB International.

Kenrick, P. and Crane, P.R. (1997) The origin and early evolution of plants on land. *Nature* 389: 33–39.

Kettle, C.J. and Koh, L.P. (Eds.) (2014) *Global Forest Fragmentation*. Wallingford, UK: CAB International.

Lucas, G. and Synge, S. (1978) *The IUCN Plant Red Data Book*. Morges, Switzerland: IUCN.

Manzanilla V., Kool A., Nguyen Nhat L., et al. (2018) Phylogenomics and barcoding of *Panax*: toward the identification of ginseng species. *MC Evol Biol* 18(1): 44.

Maxted, N. and Kell, S.P. (2009) *Establishment of a Global Network for the In Situ Conservation of Crop Wild Relatives: Status and Needs*. FAO Consultancy Report. Rome: FAO.

Millennium Ecosystem Assessment (MA) (2005) *Ecosystems and Human Well-being: Current State and Trends*. Washington D.C.: Island Press.

Myers, N., Mittermeier, R.A., Mittermeier, C.G., Da Fonseca, G.A. and Kent, J. (2000) Biodiversity hotspots for conservation priorities. *Nature* 403 (6772): 853–858.

Nic Lughadha, E., Bachman, S.P., Leão, T.C.C., et al. (2020) Extinction risk and threats to plants and fungi. *Plants, People, Planet* 2: 389–408.

Nyffeler, R. and Eggli, U. (2010) An up-to-date familial and suprafamilial classification of succulent plants. *Bradleya* 28: 125–144.

Oldfield, S.F., Lusty, C. and MacKinven, A. (1998) *The World List of Threatened Trees*. Cambridge, UK: World Conservation Press.

Pimentel, D., Zuniga, R. and Morrison, D. (2005) Update on the environmental and economic costs associated with alien-invasive species in the United States. *Ecol Econ* 53(3): 273–288.

Potapov, P., Hansen, M.C., Laestadius, L., et al. (2017) The last frontiers of wilderness: tracking loss of intact forest landscapes from 2000 to 2013. *Sci Adv* 2017(3): e1600821.

Ratsimbazafy, C., Newton, D.J. and Stéphane, R. (2016) *Timber Island: Rosewood and Ebony Trade of Madagascar*. Cambridge, UK: TRAFFIC International.

Rivers, M. (2017) Conservation assessments and understanding the impacts of threats on plant biodiversity. In: Blackmore, S. and Oldfield, S. (Eds.). *Plant Conservation Science and Practice: The Role of Botanic Gardens*. Cambridge, UK: Cambridge University Press.

Scott, P., Burton, J.A. and Fitter, R. (1987) Red Data Books: the historical background. In: IUCN/ UNEP, Fitter R. and Fitter, M. (Eds.) *The Road to Extinction*. Gland, Switzerland; Cambridge, UK: IUCN.

Sharrock, S., Oldfield, S. and Wilson, O. 2014. *Plant Conservation Report 2014: A Review of Progress in Implementation of the Global Strategy for Plant Conservation 2011–2020*. Technical Series No. 81. Richmond, UK: Secretariat of the Convention on Biological Diversity, Montréal, Canada and Botanic Gardens Conservation International.

Smith, G., van Jaarsveld, E.J., Arnold, T.H., Steffens, F.E. (Eds.) (1997). *List of Southern African Succulent Plants*. Pretoria, South Africa: Umdaus Press.

Still, S.M., Havens, K. and Havens, P. (2016) *Assessing the Vulnerability to Climate Change for Rare Plants in the Western United States*. Report to USDI Bureau of Land Management. Washington, DC: Plant Conservation Program.

van Wyk, A. and Smith, G. (2001). *Regions of Floristic Endemism in Southern Africa*. Pretoria, South Africa: Umdaus.

Vié, J-C., Hilton-Taylor, C. and Stuart, S.N. (2009) *Wildlife in a Changing World: An Analysis of the 2008 IUCN Red List of Threatened Species*. Gland, Switzerland; Cambridge, UK: IUCN.

Vincent, H., Wiersema, J., Kell, S., et al. (2013) A prioritized crop wild relative inventory to help underpin global food security. *Biol Conserv* 167: 265–275.

Walter, K.S. and Gillett, H.J. (Eds.) (1998) *1997 IUCN Red List of Threatened Plants*. Gland, Switzerland; Cambridge, UK: IUCN.

Willis, K.J. (Ed.) (2017) *State of the World's Plants 2017*. Kew: Royal Botanic Gardens.

World Wide Fund for Nature (WWF) (2018) *Living Planet Report – 2018: Aiming Higher*. Grooten, M. and Almond, R.E.A. (Eds). Gland, Switzerland: WWF.

THREE

Bryophytes and Pteridophytes: Spore-Bearing Land Plants

MARY GIBBY

Summary

Spore-bearing land plants are much fewer in number than flowering plants, with around 20,000 bryophytes and 12,000 pteridophytes, but they have a much longer history, with the first recognisable land plant fossil dating from the Silurian. Bryophytes and pteridophytes are not a significant food source for man, nor do they provide essential commodities like timber or cloth, but they have a significant role in maintaining healthy ecosystems and storing carbon, and bryophytes deliver key ecological functions in arctic, boreal and peatland ecosystems. The major threats to bryophytes and pteridophytes are habitat loss and climate change, followed by overexploitation. Global conservation assessments are available for just 1.5 percent of bryophyte species and 5.7 percent of pteridophytes. However, progress towards an accessible worldwide flora is growing through international collaboration and coordination, and molecular studies are increasing understanding of relationships between species, genera and families.

Ferns and mosses remain very understudied, especially with regard to their many unique features, including photosynthetic mechanisms, desiccation tolerance, secondary metabolites, and resistance to diseases and pests.

IUCN Section: IUCN global conservation assessments have been made on 282 bryophytes and 678 pteridophytes, of which a high percentage – approximately half of those assessed, some 56% for bryophytes and 46% for pteridophytes, are classed as threatened (EX+CR+EN+VU) in the IUCN Red List (IUCNredlist.org).

3.1 Introduction

Spore-bearing land plants were recognised by Linnaeus as belonging to the cryptogamic plants, as their mechanism for reproduction was hidden (cryptic), unlike seed-bearing plants that have more obvious floral structures. The cryptogamic land plants comprise two groups, the smaller bryophytes – mosses, liverworts and hornworts that lack vascular tissue, and the usually larger pteridophytes – lycophytes, horsetails and ferns. Bryophytes and pteridophytes differ from seed plants in reproducing via single-celled spores, rather than multicellular seeds, the spores germinating to form a distinct gametophyte stage where fertilisation takes place, producing the sporophyte stage. Fertilisation is dependent on the availability of water to allow the motile male gametes to swim to the egg cell. Bryophytes lack vascular tissue, but have the ability to dry out or re-wet rapidly, depending on external conditions. As a result, they are sensitive to subtle changes in the environment, to humidity, water quality, atmospheric pollution and acidification. The development of internal vascular tissue enables pteridophytes to reach much greater sizes than bryophytes, with tree ferns achieving up to 20 metres in height. Although fewer in number than flowering plants, and less conspicuous, bryophytes and pteridophytes are widely distributed in a range of habitats, from forest and woodland, arable land and grasslands to bogs, moor and mountains, and can even thrive as desert plants when afforded shelter amongst rocks. Despite their small size, mosses are a dominant component of the vegetation in cool, northern, temperate regions, and here the bog moss, *Sphagnum*, is a major element of the vegetation and forms peatlands that sequester vast stores of carbon. These spore-bearing land plants are not a significant food source for man, nor do they provide essential commodities like timber or cloth, but they have a significant role in maintaining healthy ecosystems and storing carbon, yet remain very understudied, especially with regard to their many unique features, including photosynthetic mechanisms, desiccation tolerance, secondary metabolites, and resistance to diseases and pests.

3.2 Taxonomic Diversity

The Global Strategy for Plant Conservation (GSPC) (see Oldfield and Gardiner, Chapter 2, this volume) provides a framework for plant conservation, and among its goals is an accessible documentation of all plant species, with assessments of their status to guide conservation actions. Recent assessments of the numbers of species of bryophytes and pteridophytes suggest figures of some 18,000–23,000 bryophytes (Villarreal et al., 2010) and 11,000–13,500 pteridophytes (PPG 1, 2016), significantly lower than the number of flowering plant species, which is estimated at 370,000, where speciation events may be driven by adaptive radiation in pollinators and limited dispersal of seeds, in comparison with the more mobile wind-borne spores of bryophytes and pteridophytes (Givnish, 2010).

Both bryophytes and pteridophytes have a long evolutionary history, although there is poor representation of bryophytes in the fossil record. The earliest recognisable land plant fossil is *Cooksonia* from the Silurian, with a simple stem with stomata and terminal sporangia (Edwards et al., 1983). Recent studies suggest that the first land plants date back to the middle Cambrian–Early Ordovician, with the first vascular plants appearing in the Late Ordovician–Silurian period, and a burst of diversification in the Early Devonian (Morris et al., 2018). Throughout history there have been periods of rapid diversification in both bryophytes and pteridophytes, but also major extinctions (Kenrick and Crane, 1997; Laenen et al., 2014). Today we recognise just 15 horsetails, *Equisetum* species, yet these represent the extant relatives of an ancient plant group, the Sphenopsids, which first appeared in the Devonian, and formed a major element of the Carboniferous flora, together with some ferns and ancestors of modern lycophytes (Kenrick and Crane, 1997). The mid-Jurassic was a period of rapid diversification in liverworts, and the mid-Cretaceous for mosses (Laenen et al., 2014), but much of the present-day diversity found in bryophytes and ferns has evolved since the rise of the angiosperms (Schneider et al., 2004; Feldberg et al., 2014).

Bryophytes belong to three distinct lineages, the mosses with some 11,000–13,000 species, the liverworts with around 7000–9000 species and the hornworts with 200–250 species (Söderström et al., 2016). There are over 100 distinct families of mosses, 80 families of liverworts (Goffinet and Shaw, 2008) and 14 families of hornworts (Villarreal et al., 2010). Their diversity is emphasised by their classification into three separate phyla, the Bryophyta (mosses), Marchantiophyta (liverworts) and the Anthoceratophyta (hornworts), each equivalent to the vascular plant phylum, Tracheophyta. Classification of bryophytes has benefitted hugely in recent years from incorporation of molecular data in phylogenetic studies (e.g. Liu et al., 2019). Mosses are divided into five subphyla (Goffinet and Shaw, 2008), with two of these represented by just three species, the monotypic *Andreaeobryum macrosporum*, and two species of *Takakia*. The characteristic bog mosses typified by *Sphagnum* with 380 species represent the third group; the rock mosses, *Andreaea*, with 100 species, are the fourth, and all other *c.* 11,000–13,000 mosses are classified within the subphylum Bryophytina, encompassing 30 orders and over 100 families (Goffinet and Shaw, 2008; Liu et al., 2019). There are two major groups of liverworts, the complex thalloid group comprising some 340 species (Class Marchantiopsida), and a group (Class Jungermanniopsida) that includes over 7000 species of simple thalloids and leafy liverworts, with a third, much smaller group of just 17 species (Class Haplomitriopsida) (Villarreal et al., 2016).

Ferns, horsetails, quillworts, spike mosses and clubmosses have been grouped together in the past as pteridophytes because they share some significant features, including reproduction by spores, the presence of vascular tissue and a unique life cycle, with independent free-living sporophyte and gametophyte generations. Today we recognise two distinct classes; the lycophytes (Lycopodiopsida), with 1500 species in three families, clubmosses, quillworts and spike mosses, and the much bigger 'Fern' class (Polypodiopsida), with about 11,000 species in 48 families, and including the small family of 15 horsetail species, Equisetaceae (PPG 1, 2016). Fern families range in size from Dryopteridaceae (wood ferns, 2115 species), Pteridaceae (brake ferns, 2111 species), Polypodiaceae (polypodies, 1652 species) and Hymenophyllaceae (filmy ferns, 434 species), to Matoniaceae (four species with fan-shaped fronds confined to Malaysia and Indonesia) and Thyrsopteridaceae (a single species of tree fern endemic to Juan Fernandez Is, Chile) (PPG 1, 2016).

Taxonomic knowledge of bryophytes and pteridophytes remains incomplete, with significant gaps, particularly in tropical regions, where diversity is most rich. While pteridophytes have benefitted from being included with flowering plants in botanical surveys, checklists and floral accounts (e.g. Cámara-Leret et al., 2020), knowledge of bryophyte diversity remains understudied in comparison (e.g. van Rooy et al., 2019). However, for both bryophytes and pteridophytes, significant progress in documenting taxonomic diversity has been made, particularly over the last 20 years, and has benefitted from collaboration and coordination by botanists worldwide, wider accessibility of herbarium collections through databasing and digitisation, targeted collecting trips in under-explored regions, and advances in molecular methods that are clarifying relationships amongst species, genera and families, and uncovering many new cryptic species (e.g. Carter, 2012; Hollingsworth et al., 2016; Dauphin et al., 2017).

3.3 Life Form Diversity

Bryophytes are small, relatively inconspicuous plants with a clonal growth form, as cushions, short or tall turfs, mats, pendants, fans, dendroids (Figure 3.1) and streamers (Mägdefrau, 1982), and may be terrestrial, but also grow as epiphytes on trees on the surface of the trunk, on branches and on leaves, on dead wood, on rock and even as aquatics. The major part of their life cycle is dominated by the gametophyte generation, while the short-lived sporophyte is a usually a small, stalked spore-bearing capsule that remains attached to the gametophyte (see Box 3.1). In comparison with other land plants, bryophytes have a much simpler morphology, lacking vascular tissue, roots and stomata in gametophytes, although some families of mosses and hornworts have stomata on the sporangia; however, their function may be in drying and dehiscence of the sporangium, rather than gaseous exchange, as in vascular plants (Merced and Renzaglia, 2017). Bryophytes have the property of poikilohydry, the ability to take up water rapidly or dry out, depending on the local conditions. They absorb water and nutrients over their entire surface, and are therefore sensitive to water quality, atmospheric pollution and acidification, and have been shown to be valuable ecological indicators (Harmens et al., 2010).

Figure 3.1 Tree moss, *Climacium dendroides*, has a tree-like habit; it is frequent in damp places in Europe and North America. © D.G. Long.

Box 3.1
The Life Cycle of Spore–Bearing Plants: Alternation of Generations

Bryophytes and pteridophytes have two phases to their life cycle, a haploid gameto-phyte generation that has a single set of chromosomes, and a diploid sporophyte generation that produces the spores. In bryophytes the major part of the life cycle is dominated by the gametophyte generation that develops from a spore, initially forming a green protonema and then either a structure with stem and leaves, as in mosses and leafy liverworts, or a flattened thalloid structure, as seen in the thalloid liverworts and hornworts. A monoecious gametophyte produces both male and female sex organs – the antheridia and archegonia, and water is essential to allow the swimming sperm (antherozooid) to fertilise the egg cell in the archegonium. However, 70% of liverworts and 60% of mosses are dioecious (Patiño and Vanderpoorten, 2018), and for fertilisation to produce a sporophyte, the separate male and female gameto-phytes need to be in relatively close contact to enable the male gametes to swim to the archegonium. The sporophyte is a small, stalked, spore-bearing capsule that remains attached to the gametophyte. The wind-dispersed spores are the normal method of dispersal, but the clonal habit of the gametophyte also allows reproduction through fragmentation. Some bryophytes have very restricted dispersal, with some dioecious species never producing sporophytes (Goffinet and Shaw, 2008), but they can spread locally through clonal growth. For some species dispersal is also through specialised vegetative propagules, as found in *Tortula pagorum*, where populations are entirely female in Europe and entirely male in North America (Frahm, 2008). *Sphagnum subnitens* is another species that has dispersed solely by asexual propagules over 4000 km in North America (Patiño and Vanderpoorten, 2018).

The life cycle in lycophytes and ferns follows a similar pattern, except that both gametophyte and sporophyte stages are independent plants, and the sporophyte is the visibly dominant phase. The larger, more complex diploid sporophytes produce haploid single-celled spores within sporangia. The wind-borne spores develop into relatively simple, haploid gametophytes with reproductive cells, the female archego-nia and the male antheridia. The form of the gametophyte varies in the pterido-phytes, but they are usually inconspicuous, often ephemeral, and normally green, but occasionally lack chlorophyll and are subterranean, and are then dependent on a fungus to supply nutrients. The green thalloid gametophyte of ferns is referred to as a prothallus, although in some families the gametophyte may be more ribbon-like, or even filamentous. Like bryophytes, pteridophytes are dependent on water for repro-duction and the antherozooids use flagellae to swim in a thin film of water to fertilise the egg cell.

In the lycophytes the sporangia are derived laterally from the meristem, and are found on the upper side of the small, simple leaves. In contrast, the sporangia are derived terminally in horsetails and ferns; in horsetails the sporangia are within the terminal cone, whereas in the ferns they are usually found on the underside of the fern 'leaf' or frond, or on a modified section of frond.

Vegetative propagation in ferns and lycophytes is common, especially in those with creeping rhizomes that spread successfully through clonal growth; one clone of bracken, *Pteridium aquilinum*, was reported to cover 390 metres (Sheffield et al., 1989). Bulbils, small young sporophytes, may develop on a fern frond and root below the parent plant, and the gametophytes of filmy ferns, Hymenophyllaceae, and Vittariaceae, can disperse via gemmae (Farrar, 1974; Rumsey et al., 1999).

Figure 3.2 Great hairy screw-moss, *Syntrichia ruralis*, forms loose cushions on walls, rocks and sandy ground. © D.G. Long

Some bryophytes grow in large clonal mats, but others may exist as small clumps limited to very specific sites – the trunk of a tree, in a rock crevice, as epiphytes, or epiphyllic on a leaf. The trunks and branches of moist temperate and tropical montane forest can be festooned with mosses and liverworts (Fenton and Bergeron, 2008), providing shelter for a range of organisms. Liverwort diversity increases with increasing humidity, cloud cover and mist in Southern Hemisphere forests (Frahm and Ohlemüller, 2001). Bryophytes are great primary colonisers, as evidenced in the rapid establishment of mosses on the new island of Surtsey, following the volcanic eruption in Iceland in 1963–1967 (Ingimundardóttir et al., 2014).

Typical mosses are small, delicate plants with short stems and simple leaves. Some mosses are unbranched and grow upright as cushion plants, like the great hairy screw-moss, *Syntrichia ruralis* (Figure 3.2), whereas others are branched and have a creeping habit, like the feather-moss *Brachythecium rutabulum*. The hair-cap mosses, *Polytrichum* species, have stiffer stems, with leaves arranged spirally, and the cushions can reach half a metre in height. In contrast, the rock mosses, *Andreaea*, grow as small, dark brown or black tufts on

Figure 3.3 Two peat-forming bog mosses: (a) red bog moss, *Sphagnum capillifolium*, and (b) papillose bog moss, *S. papillosum*. © M. Gibby

rocks in mountainous regions. Bog moss or peat moss, *Sphagnum* (Figure 3.3), is one of the most remarkable of all plants, and by far the most economically important of all bryophytes. It is unique amongst bryophytes in its capacity to take up water very quickly and release it relatively slowly, thus acting as a sponge; once established in an area with a suitably high water table, *Sphagnum* will flourish and enhance the water-retaining property of the vegetation, giving rise to landscapes dominated by bogs and mires (see Box 3.2). This water-retaining ability emphasises the key role played by *Sphagnum* in uplands by controlling run-off after heavy rain, and thus helping to prevent flooding in valleys below.

Box 3.2
Northern Bryophyte-Rich Ecosystems

Bryophytes are involved in key ecological processes in arctic, boreal and peatland ecosystems that impact on carbon and nitrogen cycles (Lindo et al., 2013). They act as thermal insulators of the soil with their turf-like and mat-forming growth forms, they produce slow-decomposing litter and, through association with nitrogen-fixing cyanobacteria (*Nostoc* species), they are a primary source of nitrogen in these ecosystems (Lindo et al., 2013). They are able to capture carbon dioxide emissions from the soil and provide habitat for a wide range of microbiota and arthropods, and species of *Sphagnum* especially serve as keystone components of arctic ecosystems (Kauserud et al., 2008; Whiteley and Gonzalez, 2016).

Box 3.2.1 Northern Peatland Ecosystems
Peatlands are ecosystems where the processes of plant production exceed decomposition of the organic material, and this organic material accumulates as peat (Goffinet and Shaw, 2008). Peatlands cover 3% of the world's land area, but provide some 30% of the world's carbon stock, storing some 550 gigatonnes of carbon

globally – more than that stored in all the world's forests. Peatlands occur in tropical swamps in Southeast Asia, at high altitudes in the Andes and Himalaya, and cover the northern boreal regions of Europe and great swathes of permafrost areas Canada and Russia (Bain et al., 2011). They are critical for carbon sequestration and the IPCC Climate Change and Land, Special Report (IPCC, 2019) highlights the importance of peatlands, as these can continue to sequester carbon for centuries, in contrast to reforestation that is much less effective, as forest may not store carbon indefinitely if subject to harvesting.

Northern peatlands (Figure 3.4) are almost completely covered by a continuous mat of moss, and the peat itself is composed largely of fragments of bryophytes that decompose slowly. Slow decomposition and water-saturated anaerobic conditions, together with short seasons and a cool climate, allows the accumulation of vast stores of organic material (Goffinet and Shaw, 2008).

Species of *Sphagnum* dominate in the wet conditions present in poor, acidic fens and bogs, including species like the circumboreal *S. magellanicum* and *S. papillosum*, emphasising the huge economic importance of this group of bryophytes. *Sphagnum* is largely replaced in the more alkaline-rich fens and bogs by weft-forming brown mosses such as *Campylium stellatum* and *Hamatocaulis vernicosus*, together with calcium-tolerant species of *Sphagnum*, e.g. *S. contortum* or *S. warnstorfii* (Vitt et al., 1995). The wide distribution of species across these northern peatlands illustrates the close association of each with its particular niche; for example, *Sphagnum fuscum*, that is circumboreal in its distribution, flourishes on hummocks across the wide spectrum of bog vegetation, from acid bogs to rich fens (Goffinet and Shaw, 2008); acidic pools may be dominated by *S. cuspidatum* or *S. denticulatum*; *S. capillifolium* (Figure 3.3a), *S. papillosum* (Figure 3.3b) and *S. subnitens* are hummock-forming species; *Scorpidium*

Figure 3.4 Peatland landscape in the Flow Country, Sutherland, Scotland. © M. Gibby

scorpioides is a widespread calciphilous, brown, rich-fen moss that thrives in shallow water (Goffinet and Shaw, 2008).

With their extensive and relatively undisturbed ranges, peatlands host a number of highly specialised species, including caribou and wolverine in Northern Canada. For many birds they provide a breeding site, or are a vital stopover, supporting global flyways for birds that migrate north to the arctic to breed (Minayeva et al., 2016).

Box 3.2.2 The Arctic Tundra

The Arctic flora is rich in bryophytes, with an estimated 900 species of mosses and liverworts, compared with *c.* 2218 species of vascular plants, and 80% have a circumboreal distribution (CAFF, 2013). Mosses and liverworts dominate wetter areas, in ponds, lakes, bogs and mires, and among dwarf shrub heaths and rocks, but also contribute significantly to other tundra vegetation types (Longton 1992). Arctic Russia is the most species rich (720 species), followed by Greenland (670), Arctic Alaska (543) and the Canadian Arctic Archipelago (543); the flora of Svalbard has a greater number of bryophytes (373) than vascular plants (200) (CAFF, 2013). The open vegetation of the High Arctic zone growing on thin mineral soils underlain by permafrost is dominated by low-growing bryophytes and lichens (40–60%), with few vascular plants (5–25%), but the percentage of vascular plants increases in the Low Arctic, with more herbaceous and dwarf shrub vegetation (50–80%) on peat-rich soils (Walker et al., 2005). Low wetlands in the Canadian High Arctic are dominated by mosses with a turf life form, species of *Drepanocladus* and *Cinclidium*, replaced by *Polytrichum juniperum* and mats of *Racomitrium lanuginosum* in mesic communities, with grasses and dwarf shrubs (Longton 1992).

Arctic tundra provides habitat for some charismatic species including reindeer/caribou, musk ox, arctic fox and snowy owl, a breeding site for summer avian migrants and supports the unique cultures of indigenous peoples.

Box 3.2.3 Northern Boreal Forests

The northern boreal forests are found in high latitudes distributed between the Arctic tundra and the temperate forest from Canada and Alaska, across Scandinavia and Russia, to China and Mongolia. Boreal forests cover 17% of the Earth's land surface, but contain a third of all soil carbon and can act as a carbon sink (O'Neill, 2001). The ground-cover mosses of northern boreal forests are dominated by pleurocarpus feather mosses (e.g. *Hylocomium splendens*, *Pleurozium schreberi*) and bog mosses (*Sphagnum* species), and perform key ecological functions in these forests despite contributing a small proportion of the total living biomass of the ecosystem. Timber has been harvested from boreal forests for centuries, but even a century ago in Scandinavia is was recognised that the timber was not an inexhaustible resource and measures were introduced to encourage reforestation after felling; however, the forests of Sweden and Finland remain some of the most intensively managed, and support a less diverse flora than those of Russia (https://www.borealforest.org/world/rus_mgmt.htm).

Figure 3.5 Interrupted clubmoss, *Lycopodium (Spinulum) annotinum*, Lanarkshire, Scotland. © M. Gibby

The largest group of liverworts, the jungermannioid or leafy liverworts, have three rows of small, thin leaves, with the underside row usually smaller; they show great diversity in the colour, shape and structure of the leaves, and may grow as deep cushions, creeping or epiphytes. In contrast, marchantioid liverworts have a complex thalloid structure, as seen in the widespread Common liverwort, *Marchantia polymorpha*. Hornworts resemble thallose liverworts, but are distinguished by their 'horn', the long, narrow structure of the sporophyte.

The clubmosses, Lycopodiaceae, are the most diverse lineage of the lycophytes, with a variety of life forms, including upright, tufted fir clubmoss, *Huperzia selago*, stag's-horn clubmoss, *Lycopodium clavatum*, with erect, paired cones and creeping rhizomes, and interrupted clubmoss, *Lycopodium annotinum* (Figure 3.5); neotropical species of *Phlegmarius* grow as epiphytes in humid montane forests or as terrestrial herbs in alpine grassland. Quillworts, *Isoëtes* species, have linear leaves growing from a thickened stem base, and are mostly aquatic or grow in damp ground. Spike mosses, *Selaginella* species, have a creeping or erect habit, and are particularly diverse in humid tropical forest, like the iridescent *S. willdenowii*; other species have adapted to desert environments and the resurrection plant, *S. lepidophylla*, curls into a ball in response to drought and can tolerate complete desiccation.

The horsetails stand apart from the remainder of the ferns in their unique structure, with hollow, jointed, ribbed stems, whorls of branches, terminal cones and leaves reduced to small sheath teeth that clasp the stem. Some species are aquatic, others terrestrial,

Figure 3.6 Unfurling crozier of 'Ama'u, *Sadleria cyatheoides*, an endemic fern from Hawaii that colonises new lava flows. © M. Gibby

and may be evergreen or produce new shoots annually from the wiry underground rhizome. The Mexican giant horsetail, *Equisetum myriochaetum*, can reach seven metres in height.

Ferns are characterised by their young fronds uncurling from croziers, often clad in dense scales or hairs (Figure 3.6). The classic fern has a shuttlecock structure, with the fronds emerging from an upright rhizome, but there is much variation, and the rhizome may be ascending or creeping, either below ground or on the surface, as seen in many epilithic or epiphytic species. Many ferns are ground dwelling, but epiphytes flourish, particularly in moist tropical and subtropical forest, including the spectacular stag's horn ferns, *Platycerium* species, bird's nest fern, *Asplenium nidus*, and species of *Phlebodium* (Figure 3.7) and Davalliaceae, hare's foot ferns, with characteristic creeping rhizomes. Rock ferns emerge from cracks and fissures on cliffs and rock faces, or adapt to crevices in man-made walls, and these ferns are invariably restricted by rock type, being either calcicoles or calcifuges. Filmy ferns of the family Hymenophyllaceae have delicate fronds, usually just one cell thick, and lack stomata, and so are restricted to moist and shady habitats, often growing as epiphytes in close association with bryophytes. The close association between ferns and their ecological niche has been seen in forests in Brazil, where environmental gradients can be predicted by fern species composition (Zuquim et al., 2014).

Marattiaceae (111 species) is a largely tropical family, with a fossil record dating back to the Jurassic. They have large rhizomes with tall erect fronds, and individual fronds of the giant *Angiopteris evecta* reach nine metres in height.

Figure 3.7 A large population of the epiphyte, *Phlebodium areolatum*, after renewing its seasonal leaves in May, one month after the beginning of the rainy season in the cloud forest zone at 1800 m elevation in Veracruz, Mexico. © K. Mehltreter

Tree ferns of the families Cyatheaceae (643 species) and Dicksoniaceae (28 species) develop tall, often massive trunks that carry the fronds high in the canopy. Tree ferns are distributed widely in the tropics and subtropics and in wet temperate forests of Australia and New Zealand. The trunks can reach 12–15 m in height, but are not woody, consisting of a modified rhizome surrounded by frond bases, and with a mass of small roots that grow down from the actively developing crown. They function ecologically as trees, often supporting a diverse flora of epiphytes on the trunks (see Figure 3.8). Tree ferns form an understorey canopy within forests, but can also extend above the tree line as, for example, in New Guinea where *Cyathea muelleri*, *C. macgregorii* and *C. atrox* (now *Alsophila muelleri*, *A. macgregorii* and *Sphaeropteris atrox*) grow in subalpine grasslands. New Guinea is particularly rich in species, with 110 species of Cyatheaceae, including 92 endemics, and seven species of *Dicksonia*, all of which are endemic (Cámara-Leret et al., 2020).

Small trunks also develop in some other ferns, including species of Blechnaceae (Figure 3.8). The Tristan da Cunha endemic bog fern, *Blechnum (Lomariocycas) palmiforme* (Figure 3.8), produces stout trunks up to 1.6 m and 30 cm diameter and forms a major scrub vegetation zone on the lower slopes of Tristan and Gough Island (Tristan da Cunha Government and RSPB, 2012; https://www.tristandc.com/wildbotany.php).

The small water ferns *Azolla* and *Salvinia* are floating plants of freshwater lakes and rivers. *Azolla* has been grown in rice paddies in the Far East for thousands of years, as its leaves harbour *Anabaena azollae*, a cyanobacterium that sequesters atmospheric nitrogen, increasing rice production. However, both *Azolla* and *Salvinia* can become problematic

Figure 3.8 Bog fern, *Lomariocycas* (*Blechnum*) *palmiforme*, endemic to the Tristan da Cunha archipelago, supports an array of epiphytes on its trunk. © J. McIntosh

and congest waterways outwith their native distributions, as in the case of the Kariba weed, *Salvinia molesta*, a Brazilian species that invaded Lake Kariba, following impoundment on the Zambezi river in the 1950s (Lee, 2001).

Ferns and mosses exhibit many unique features. Bryophytes have a remarkable facility to photosynthesise at very low light levels, and can be found growing deep in caves, even where the only available light source is artificial (Glime, 2017); gametophytes of the filmy fern *Vandenboschia speciosa* grow at extremely low light levels in small caverns and crevices, together with two cave bryophytes, *Isopterygium elegans* and *Calypogeia arguta* where there is 1% or less of the ambient light, with photon flux density well below 1 μmol m^{-2} s^{-1} (Johnson et al., 2000).

Desiccation tolerance is a feature of many bryophytes, with the ability to rehydrate rapidly when water is available; a range of drought-tolerant species are native to desert environments, or grow in the open on exposed bare soil or rock surfaces, but even the aquatic moss *Fontinalis antipyretica* is tolerant of slow drying, enabling it to survive summer periods of Mediterranean droughts (Cruz de Carvalho et al., 2019). Bryophytes grow and function within the boundary layer of the atmosphere next to the ground or other substrate, and drought tolerance can be viewed rather as a means of evading drought. Extreme drought tolerance is seen in the spike moss, *Selaginella lepidophylla*, which curls up in response to drought. Understanding of the mechanisms of drought tolerance in this plant may be of value in crop improvement; high levels of metabolites trahalose, sorbitol and xylitol have been identified, although their role, if any, in drought tolerance is not yet known, but the maintenance of high levels of the respiratory enzymes in dried tissue matches with the rapid resumption of respiratory activity in this species, and a critical level of cell order is maintained in the dry state in *S. lepidophylla* (Pampurova and Van Dijck, 2014).

The importance of the rich array of secondary compounds in ferns has been long appreciated, but still remains an issue for conjecture (Cooper-Driver, 1985). It is also well known that mosses and ferns are free of certain fungal pathogen groups that cause diseases in flowering plants, but the mechanisms associated with this resistance remain unknown (Davey and Currah, 2006; Antonovics, 2020).

3.4 Distribution and Diversity

The ability to be spread widely through minute airborne spores has resulted in many cryptogamic plants, and particularly mosses, having cosmopolitan distributions. The small, tufted silver-thread moss, *Bryum argenteum*, flourishes in open or disturbed habitats from the tropics to Antarctica, and has been described as probably the most widespread plant on Earth. Its occurrence in Antarctica is not a recent introduction, but resulted from multiple colonisations over the last four million years (Pisa et al., 2014). Although restricted to sites that remain moist throughout the year, the brittle-bladder fern, *Cystopteris fragilis*, is common throughout temperate regions and tropical montane ecosystems (Mehltreter et al., 2010). Long-range spore dispersal has enabled the colonisation of remote oceanic islands. Although on a worldwide scale pteridophytes represent just 3.6% of the vascular plant flora, this rises to 13% in montane habitats and 15% on islands, and up to 70% on some remote oceanic islands (Kreft et al., 2010; Mehltreter et al., 2010). Cultures of detritus from Antarctic glacial debris from Signey Island, South Atlantic Islands, produced several mosses and liverworts that were typical of Antarctic floras, but also a fern, *Elaphoglossum hybridum*, showing that viable fern spores can be carried to hostile environments, though none has yet established so far south (Smith, 2014); the nearest populations of this species are on Gough Island, some 2000 miles to the north.

An association between species richness and latitude, with a marked increase in diversity from the poles to the Equator, has been documented for a range of organisms (Hillebrand, 2004) and within the tropics montane regions are generally richer in species diversity than lowland areas (Barthlott et al., 2007). Two-thirds of all bryophyte species are found in the tropics (Frahm, 2008), although moss diversity shows similar richness across three major latitudinal zones, while liverwort diversity is greatest in high latitudes in the Southern Hemisphere (Shaw et al., 2005). Diversity of pteridophytes is at its peak in the humid montane tropics (Kreft et al., 2010; Mehltreter et al., 2010). Regions with the lowest levels of plant diversity are found in deserts, or in the Arctic tundra, yet bryophytes make an important contribution to ecosystems in northern latitudes (CAFF, 2013) in the high Arctic, boreal forest, moorland and heath, and are the dominant vegetation in northern peatlands (see Box 3.2), and within Europe, species richness of ferns and bryophytes increases towards the north (Mateo et al., 2016).

Oceanic islands have been shown to exhibit lower levels of species diversity than continents, owing to their geographical isolation (MacArthur and Wilson, 1967), but recent analyses suggest that spore-dispersing plants do not all follow this pattern. While very small islands have an impoverished flora, larger oceanic and continental islands show similar or even enhanced levels of species richness, particularly in ferns and liverworts, perhaps relating to higher levels of dispersal and environmental conditions on islands, where humidity and mild temperatures may be optimal for establishment and colonisation (Patiño et al., 2015).

Geographical patterns of species richness in plants show significant differences between groups. For mosses, high species richness is found not only in tropical and subtropical regions, but also in temperate broad-leaved forests, boreal forests and tundra (Geffert et al., 2013), while New Zealand, New Caledonia, Japan and Costa Rica show the greatest species richness for liverworts (von Konrat et al., 2010), and the Indian subcontinent, Japan and the Neotropics for hornworts (Villarreal et al., 2010). Pteridophyte and seed plant species richness have been shown to be highly correlated, with the greatest species richness in mountainous tropical areas – the Andes, Mesoamerica, Himalaya and Southeast Asia, and particularly in New Guinea, Sumatra and Borneo (Kreft et al., 2010). Ferns and lycophytes may contribute up to 70% of species richness in local tropical floras (Kreft et al., 2010), with spore-dispersal enabling them to colonise a diversity of terrestrial and epiphytic habitats (see Figure 3.7) (Aros-Mualin et al., 2021). In the montane forests of Ecuador the epiphyte habitat is richer in ferns and liverworts than is the terrestrial habitat, whereas mosses are mostly terrestrial (Mandl et al., 2010).

3.5 Hotspots

To help prioritise areas for conservation effort, Myers et al. (2000) identified 25 biodiversity hotspots across the globe, featuring high concentrations of endemic species of vascular plants and vertebrates with significant threats to habitat. These hotspots fall mostly within tropical and subtropical regions, and areas with a Mediterranean climate. Using frequency of endemism in a region as a measure to define hotspots has to be modified for bryophytes, as endemism is much lower in bryophytes than is found in flowering plants, probably reflecting the advantage of wind-dispersed spores. Widely disjunct distributions are frequent (Patiño and Vanderpoorten 2018); 45% of Antarctic mosses have bipolar disjunctions (Biersma et al., 2017), and there is a significant North Atlantic disjunction, with 43% of North American mosses found in Europe and 70% of European mosses found in North America (Patiño and Vanderpoorten 2018). Islands are renowned for their high levels of endemism. Hawaii is a rich biodiversity hotspot for all groups of land plants, but with lower percentages of endemics for spore-bearing plants than seed plants – mosses with 31.1%, liverworts 58.6%, ferns

77% and flowering plants 90% (Wagner et al., 2005; Geiger et al., 2007; Patiño and Vanderpoorten 2018).

The Critical Ecosystem Partnership Fund (CEPF) has used the hotspot concept to identify 36 regions where funding is targeted, through supporting civil society to protect ecosystems in tropical and subtropical regions in South America, Africa, Madagascar, Indo-Burma, Wallacea and the East Melanesian Islands, the Mediterranean and the mountains of Central Asia (https://www.cepf.net). These areas are hotspots for flowering plants, but global patterns of biodiversity hotspots for bryophytes show some differences; whilst tropical areas are important, outwith the tropics, the Mediterranean region is not a hotspot for bryophytes, but temperate regions of Patagonia, northwestern North America and Tasmania have significant levels of bryophyte diversity (Patiño and Vanderpoorten, 2018). There are also differences in distribution patterns for mosses and liverworts when considered separately. Important areas for mosses, based on a level of 15% endemism, are identified as Hawaii, northwestern North America, the Andes, Reunion, New Guinea, New Caledonia and New Zealand; for liverworts these are Patagonia, St Helena, South Africa, Madagascar, Borneo, New Guinea, Vanuatu, New Caledonia and Tasmania (Goffinet and Shaw 2008). For ferns, Suissa et al. (2021) found that 58% of global species richness occurred in eight tropical and subtropical montane hotspots, coinciding with areas of high environmental heterogeneity, that together comprise just 7% of terrestrial land worldwide, in Mesoamerica, Greater Antilles, Guianas, tropical Andes and Colombian montane forest, Southeastern Brazil, Madagascar, East Asia and Malesia. Total numbers of endemic fern species were similar in montane and lowland habitats, unlike patterns for other plants, where higher levels of endemism are found at higher elevations (Suissa et al., 2021), perhaps reflecting the high dispersibility of fern spores, and the close association of ferns with edaphic features (Lehtonen et al., 2017).

However, conservation efforts towards protecting areas of high species richness may overlook important areas for rare species, where these areas do not overlap. For example, in mainland Europe the highest species richness for pteridophytes is in montane regions – the Pyrenees, Alps, Massif Central, Corsica and the Carpathian mountains – while endemics are most frequent in and around the Alps, northern Sardinia, mainland Italy and southern Spain (García Criado et al., 2017). For bryophytes in mainland Europe, highest species richness is again in the montane regions, but hyper-oceanic areas of northwest Spain, Brittany, Ireland, western Britain and Norway support rich communities of globally rare montane liverworts (Figures 3.9, 3.10, 3.11) (Hodgetts et al., 2019). Not only are these communities of oceanic-montane liverwort-rich heaths strict habitat specialists, with a preference for areas with late-laying snow, but they are also restricted by their poor dispersal ability, and are particularly vulnerable to anthropogenic environmental change (Flagmeier et al., 2020).

Figure 3.9 Leafy liverworts of oceanic heath: arch-leaved whipwort, *Bazzania pearsonii*, growing with purple spoonwort, *Pleurozia purpurea*. *Bazzania pearsonii* has a disjunct distribution, being recorded in northwest Canada, northwest Scotland and western Ireland, and the Himalaya in Nepal, Bhutan, Myanmar and China. *Pleurozia purpurea* is not restricted to oceanic heath, but also grows in mire and wet heath; it has a disjunct distribution in northwest Canada and northwest Europe. © D.G. Long

Figure 3.10 Leafy liverworts of oceanic heath: northern prongwort, *Herbertus borealis*, Beinn Eighe, Scotland – a Scottish endemic species. © D.G. Long

Figure 3.11 Habitat of northern prongwort, *Herbertus borealis*, on Beinn Eighe, Scotland, where it grows in dwarf heath shrub on north and northeast facing slopes, and where snow-beds provide protection in winter. © D.G. Long

3.6 Rarity and Threats

Bryophytes have particular vulnerabilities relating to dispersal ability, genetic potential, reproduction and establishment, habitat tolerances, competitive ability and survival rates, with small populations being especially susceptible to damage (Goffinet and Shaw 2008). Of the 98 liverworts that have been assessed worldwide, 62 fall within a threatened category, with 40% of these from Europe. Fifteen of these threatened liverworts are endemic to Macaronesia, where habitat loss and increasing tourism present the main threats, and predicted climate changes will almost certainly lead to the extinction of 6 of the 35 bryophytes endemic to Macaronesia (Patiño et al., 2016). Worldwide assessments have been prepared for 96 lycophytes, of which 41 are threatened, including 26 species of quillworts, *Isöetes*, where their aquatic habitat is vulnerable to forest clearance, agricultural expansion, mining and pollution, and 13 clubmosses, *Huperzia* species, of the high Andean páramo that are threatened by grazing. Of the 24 Red Listed species of filmy fern, Hymenophyllaceae, 12 fall in the threatened categories (CR+EN+VU), with 7 from forests of Ecuador where they are vulnerable to forest disturbance, and 5 island endemics threatened by invasive non-native plants.

3.7 Habitat Loss

Analysis of the threats to bryophytes and pteridophytes based on over 1000 assessments in the IUCN Red Data List identifies habitat loss, climate change and agriculture as the greatest threats, followed by the impacts of overexploitation, urbanisation, pollution and invasive species.

Forest ecosystems are rich in bryophytes and pteridophytes, where a combination of shade, humidity and niche heterogeneity allows these organisms to flourish. Damage to forest ecosystems will inevitably impact on communities of bryophytes and pteridophytes. The State of the World's Forests Report (FAO and UNEP, 2020) emphasises the importance of forests to global terrestrial diversity and highlights the alarming rates of deforestation, fragmentation and degradation, driven by agricultural expansion and timber extraction (and see Oldfield and Gardiner, Chapter 2, this volume). Uncut stands of tropical forest support rich communities of epiphytic bryophytes and pteridophytes, and selective logging or fragmentation of the forest can lead to reduction in heterogeneity in the forest understorey, and an altered microclimate, with changes to humidity, temperature and light levels, presenting a severe threat to these communities (Mehltreter et al., 2010). The rich bryophyte flora of the forests of Madagascar and Indian Ocean Islands and the East Afromontane region is threatened by recent increases in logging, with epiphyllous bryophytes being particularly vulnerable (van Rooy et al., 2019). Fragmentation of forest areas in the Atlantic forests of northeastern Brazil has resulted in a decrease in species richness; large fragments of forest appear to be important for maintaining high abundance and diversity of ferns, but smaller fragments often hold a different suite of species, emphasising the need to preserve the mosaic of habitats (da Silva et al., 2014). Changes in forest management can also alter the forest ecosystem. In southeastern Australia, where fire is part of the natural cycle, tree ferns *Dicksonia antarctica* and *Cyathea australis* in old-growth forests are able to resprout after fire, but become less abundant in logged forests (Bowd et al., 2018) and continue to decline over subsequent years.

Agricultural expansion has been the main driver of change in peatland ecosystems around the world, particularly in Europe, followed by commercial forestry in North America, Scandinavia, countries of the former Soviet Union and the United Kingdom (Crump, 2017). Conversion for agriculture and forestry has involved drainage that releases nutrients and often leads to soil degradation. The harvesting of peat for fuel was a significant activity before the introduction of coal in the nineteenth century, but large-scale commercial extraction of peat for use in horticulture has contributed particularly to the conversion of lowland peat bogs in Europe (e.g. Alexander et al., 2008). Road building, construction of dams and reservoirs, development of wind farms in Europe, and oil and gas extraction in North America and Russia are all impacting on peatlands, adding to their degradation and resulting in widespread damage (Minayeva et al., 2016). In Britain, peatlands have not been viewed as an ecosystem resource, with the result that some 80% have been damaged or altered by development (Bain et al., 2011). There has been a long tradition of peat turf extraction for use as low-grade fuel, mostly on a domestic scale, but since the early twentieth century there has been major extraction of peat on a commercial scale for use in horticulture as a soil conditioner. In addition, peat-rich moorlands have been subject to intensive sheep grazing, burned (muirburn) to support grouse production, and blanket bog has been drained for afforestation or agriculture.

Peatlands are now recognised as the world's largest terrestrial carbon store, with the potential to act as a carbon sink, and this is highlighted by the UN Environment Programme's Global Peatlands Initiative that was established in 2016 to work at global and national levels to improve conservation, restoration and the sustainable management of peatlands (www.globalpeatlands.org). Between 1992 and 2018 the EU Life Programme has funded 363 projects to restore peatlands across Europe, through damming drainage channels, deforestation of commercial plantations on peat and removing invasive non-native species; amongst a range of achievements, some 170,000 hectares of mires in the United Kingdom and 40% of peatlands in Belgium have been restored (https://cinea.ec .europa.eu/news/protecting-our-precious-peat-2021-05-12_en). However, the biological diversity within peatlands depends on the complex ecosystem structure and function that has developed over centuries, and successful restoration of damaged peat will be a complex process. With appropriate management of the hydrology and geomorphology, native vegetation can be re-established, although this is more successful on damaged fen peat than on acid peat; however, not all species colonise successfully and may require artificial introduction (Minayeva et al., 2016). Successful restoration of peatlands will be measured over decades and longer, rather than in years.

3.8 Climate Change

Climate change and habitat loss are the two greatest threats to biodiversity, and they are inextricably linked. Changing patterns of rainfall and temperature are already influencing species ranges, causing these to shift in altitude or in latitude. The ability to adapt to the changing climate depends on the ability of a species to migrate and adapt, and this depends on a range of factors, including the availability of suitable habitat and the ability to disperse, where spore-bearing plants may be at an advantage. Habitat specialists with restricted distribution will be particularly susceptible to environmental changes in annual rainfall patterns and temperature, especially when coupled with poor colonising ability, and this susceptibility will be increased with habitat fragmentation (Travis, 2003). For example, the communities of oceanic-montane liverwort-rich heath of northwestern Europe are dependent on a late snow cover in winter to give protection from freezing and are increasingly susceptible to warmer winter temperatures (Flagmeier et al., 2020). Recent lack of snow cover in winter in the Scottish highlands drastically reduced populations of the Alpine lady fern, *Athyrium distentifolium*, with many crowns killed off by frost and subsequent encroachment of the habitat by grasses (McHaffie, 2006). Experimental studies in Swedish alpine meadow and heath demonstrated that both bryophyte cover and bryophyte species richness decline over an 18-year period of warming, and there is an increase in deciduous shrubs and litter cover (Alatalo et al., 2020).

Climate change impacts not only on species but also on whole ecosystems. Climate effects are greatest in arctic and boreal ecosystems, where warming is occurring more rapidly than in other parts of the planet, resulting in greater ice-melt to the point of extending the navigation season in northern sea passages during the summer months. Increased temperatures in northern latitudes are already affecting tundra in the low Arctic, with increased encroachment of shrubs and trees into the open vegetation dominated by mosses and lichens (CAFF, 2021). Although tundra ecosystems were considered net sinks for carbon storage, the fear is that recent increases in air and soil temperatures may have already converted large areas of tundra to net sources of carbon dioxide (O'Neill, 2001), making stocks of carbon and nitrogen in large areas of the northern peatlands vulnerable to permafrost thaw (Hugelius et al., 2020). Climate warming in the Arctic, together with anthropogenic peatland fragmentation and subsequent drying of peatlands, will increase the loss of carbon to the atmosphere, and thus produce a positive-feedback effect, greatly exacerbating climate warming (Nelson et al., 2021). In boreal regions where the treeline migrates northwards or the growing season lengthens, it is probable that warmer temperatures in winter will be enhanced by reduced snow cover, with consequent reduction in solar reflection; however, warming may be reduced during the growing season by increased levels of transpiration (IPCC, 2019). In contrast, drought is more likely to reduce levels of nitrogen fixation in boreal forests by cyanobacteria associated with bryophytes rather than increased temperatures (Whiteley and Gonzalez, 2016).

Wildfires are common in northern boreal forests, with huge areas of forest and peatlands burning during the summer months. Climate change is increasing the risk of fire frequency and intensity in these regions (Heim et al., 2021). Fires in Siberia during the summer of 2020 were estimated to have released a record 244 megatonnes of carbon dioxide, damaging northern peatlands and making them more vulnerable to further burning (Witze, 2020). Fires in peatlands are particularly devastating, as peat can continue to smoulder for long periods, and subsequent loss of vegetation cover exposes the soil to greater fluctuations in temperature, with thaw of the underlying permafrost (Heim et al., 2021). Recovery of the ecosystem after fire is slow; in Siberian subarctic tundra, although soil temperature, permafrost thaw layer thickness, and total vegetation cover were shown to have recovered to pre-fire levels after 44 years, the composition of the vegetation was altered, with shrub encroachment being one of the significant effects of fire (Heim et al., 2021).

3.9 Overexploitation

Sphagnum is the most economically important of all bryophytes, with living plants harvested for their water-retaining properties. During World War I, collection of dried *Sphagnum* moss – mostly *Sphagnum cuspidatum* and *S. palustre* – for use as wound dressings for servicemen became a highly organised activity in Scotland, and was then extended all over Britain and, as demand increased, imported from Canada (Ayres, 2015). This ceased after the war, but harvesting and drying of *Sphagnum* has continued for the horticulture trade, where it is used as a medium for growing orchids, or as liners for hanging baskets. *Sphagnum* moss is included in the EU Habitats Directive (Annex V) to 'ensure that their exploitation and taking in the wild is compatible with maintaining them in a favourable conservation status'. In a recent report on *Sphagnum* harvesting in Wales, the practice was found to have decreased considerably in the last 15 years in response to concerns over peat harvesting, reduction in traditional markets for wreath-making, and competition from importation of dried moss from New Zealand, Chile and China. Recent harvesting recorded in Wales has been mainly from young conifer plantations, targeted on mat-forming 'feather-mosses', *Rhytidiadelphus*, *Pseudoscleropodium* and *Pleurozium* species, rather than *Sphagnum* species (Wong et al., 2016). Commercial moss harvesting from the forests of the Pacific Northwest and Appalachians for decorative use in the florist and horticulture trades is common practice in the USA (Muir et al., 2006). Continuous 'moss mats', comprising a mixture largely of epiphytic mosses and liverworts, are collected from the wild in the USA for local sale and export, with financial returns estimated at somewhere between 6 million and 165 million US$ per year, a wide estimation as quantities of the annual harvest are difficult to determine (Muir et al., 2006). Much of the harvesting is unregulated, even from National Forests, yet it has a substantial impact on the bryophyte diversity of the forests, altering epiphytic bryophyte communities (Peck and Frelich, 2008).

Resurrection plant, *Selaginella lepidophylla*, is on the list of high volume imports into Europe (UNEP-WCMC, 2019), being sold as a horticultural novelty, sometimes under the name 'Rose of Jericho'. The species is difficult to cultivate and presumably is all harvested from its native habitat in the Chihuahuan desert in Mexico and southern USA.

The Australian soft tree fern, *Dicksonia antarctica*, grows in cloud forest and wet sclerophyll forest from Queensland, New South Wales and Victoria to Tasmania, and its trunks are frequently covered in epiphytic ferns and bryophytes. Although the species is widespread, the ability of the trunk to regrow from the crown after being cut at the base resulted in thousands of plants being removed from the wild and transplanted to northern temperate gardens, a practice that began in the 1860s and 1870s during the Victorian fern craze and continues today. Plants with tall trunks are particularly prized and although readily raised from spores, plants are slow-growing, with trunks increasing just 5 cm per year, and so export of wild origin material has continued. In Tasmania, tree ferns are officially harvested as 'salvage' following forest management, but in practice often resulting in forest clearance, and this reached a peak from 2002–2007 with *c.* 50,000 individuals taken per annum, raising concerns of continuing forest destruction (Roth, 2002; Hawkins 2019), and loss of habitat of the rich bryophyte flora.

Many tree ferns are covered by the Convention on International Trade in Endangered Species (CITES) that was established in 1975; all species in Cyatheaceae and Dicksoniaceae were originally included, but the list was amended in 2006 and is now limited to all species of *Cyathea* (643, including *Alsophila*, *Nephelea*, *Sphaeropteris* and *Trichipteris*) and eight species of American *Dicksonia*, plus Golden Chicken fern *Cibotium barometz* (also known as the Lamb of Tartary from the appearance of the 'woolly' rhizome), from Southeast Asia, that has been collected widely for its use in traditional medicine. Tree ferns continue to be exported as live plants for the horticultural trade, or as stems to be used as a medium for cultivating orchids and other epiphytes, or hollowed out to make flowerpots. The EU Wildlife Trade 2017 report (UNEP-WCMC, 2019) highlighted a sharp increase of imports of silver fern, *Cyathea dealbata*, and a high volume of tree fern sago, *Spharopteris medullaris*.

3.10 Conservation Assessments

A major goal of the GSPC is to make assessments of the conservation status of all known species to guide conservation actions. Currently IUCN global conservation assessments have been made on 282 bryophytes and 678 pteridophytes, with 56% of bryophytes and 46% of pteridophytes classified as threatened (EX+CR+EN+VU). However these numbers of global assessments represent very small fractions of the estimated total numbers of species, just 1.5% for bryophyte species and 5.7% for pteridophytes. In comparison, assessments have been made of 14% of flowering plants. Mounce et al. (2018) have demonstrated that assessments derived from Regional Red Lists can significantly increase information on the conservation status of plants, with the number of assessments made for bryophytes rising 40-fold, and ninefold for pteridophytes. They also identify geographical bias in the data, with many fewer assessments from African countries, and a taxonomic bias, with a notable, if predictable, deficiency in bryophyte species. The global and regional lists have now been merged in a global database by Botanic Gardens Conservation International (BGCI) to ensure that the taxonomic coverage of assessments is more complete (https://tools.bgci.org/threat_search.php). Another approach to improving the representation of species on the IUCN Red List has been through the selection of a Sampled Red List Index (sRLI) of 1500 pteridophyte species, including gathering information from herbarium specimens, literature and websites for initial assessments (Brummitt et al., 2016); by modelling species distributions, they highlight priority areas for conservation of small-range species in the tropics and subtropics, where the habitat is threatened by conversion to agriculture. The need for more assessments of threatened species from Africa is highlighted by van Rooy et al. (2019); of the 50 species of bryophytes they have assessed, 19 are from the Madagascar and Indian Island hotspot, while the highest species number is from the large Lejeuneaceae liverwort family, which includes 95% of all epiphyllous bryophytes. Their loss from the East Afromontane and Madagascan global hotspots is a consequence of the usual suspects, forest destruction and fragmentation, agricultural expansion, urbanisation and competition from invasive non-native species.

IUCN Conservation assessments have been made for only two of the c. 250 species of hornworts, and both of these are listed as Endangered, *Anthoceros neesii*, a species from the arable fields of Central Europe, where it is dependent on traditional management practices, and *Dendrocerus japonicus*, an epiphyte of forest tree-trunks, with very scattered populations from Taiwan and Japan to Micronesia, and threatened by deforestation.

Of 41 IUCN Red List assessments of quillworts, *Isoëtes* species, 26 are threatened (CR +EN+VU) and all are endemics; their aquatic habitat makes them vulnerable to a range of threats, including pollution, eutrophication, invasive macrophytes, disturbance and development for infrastructure or tourism. Six threatened aquatic ferns, *Marsilea* and *Pilularia* species, occupy ephemeral pools, and are threatened by urban and agricultural development, changing hydrology and competition from invasive species.

Twenty species of tree fern are assessed as threatened, and are from Ecuador (7), Tanzania (2), India + Sri Lanka (1), Madagascar (1), New Guinea (4), New Caledonia (3), Solomon Islands (1) and St Helena (1), with the greatest threats being loss of habitat and, in New Caledonia, grazing by invasive deer. The seven endemic species from Ecuador range from coastal forest to high Andean forest, and all with habitats threatened by deforestation for agricultural expansion (Navarrete and Pitman 2003). Clearly there are huge gaps in knowledge for all plants groups (e.g. Bachman et al., 2018), but especially for bryophytes and ferns.

3.11 Outlook

Understanding of species diversity and distributions is essential for the development of effective conservation strategies. In comparison with flowering plants, taxonomic knowledge of bryophytes and pteridophytes remains incomplete, with significant gaps, particularly in tropical regions, where diversity is most rich, and while ferns and lycophytes have benefitted from inclusion in vascular plant floras, bryophytes have been overlooked. The GSPC, in 2002 and updated in 2010, set out clear targets for documentation, conservation and sustainable use of plant diversity, and though this focused first on vascular plants, the international bryological community embraced this approach to increase knowledge of bryophyte diversity, distributions and threats. The recent report on the 2010 GSPC Targets (see Oldfield and Gardiner, Chapter 2, this volume) highlights progress on Target 1, with the establishment of the World Flora Online that includes vascular plants and bryophytes. Target 2, to develop conservation assessments to guide conservation action, has been less successful, particularly for bryophytes, with only 1.5% of global assessments achieved. However, sharing information developed in Regional Red Lists (Mounce et al., 2018) and highlighting priority areas for conservation through the Sampled Red List Index approach (Brummitt et al., 2016) are helping in progress towards Target 2, but there remain huge gaps in knowledge especially for bryophytes and ferns. We should advertise these less charismatic species and develop societal initiatives, like Citizen Science, that target neglected organisms to ensure that the breadth of biodiversity is comprehensively sampled while this is still possible (Troudet et al., 2017).

The greatest threats to bryophytes and pteridophytes remain habitat loss and climate change. The richest areas of bryophyte and pteridophyte diversity are in forest ecosytems, in the tropics, subtropics and in moist temperate and montane forests; this further emphasises the importance of forests to global biological diversity (State of the World's Forests Report, FAO and UNEP, 2020). The greatest effects of climate change are seen in alpine regions and the bryophyte-dominated arctic and boreal ecosystems, altering ecosystem functioning, with consequent permafrost melting, scrub encroachment and drying out, making the systems vulnerable to fire. Concerted effort on climate change mitigation, and conservation and restoration of natural ecosystems remain paramount. It must be remembered that bryophytes and pteridophytes are not only victims but also participants in the cascade of processes that are leading to climate change, and continuing assessment of their contribution to ecosystem processes, especially in the arctic and alpine regions is crucial for understanding the forces leading to global change.

Acknowledgements

I thank Janis Antonovics and Sara Oldfield for helpful advice and comments on the manuscript.

References

Alatalo, J.M., Jägerbrand, A.K., Erfanian, M.B., et al. (2020) Bryophyte cover and richness decline after 18 years of experimental warming in alpine Sweden. *AoB Plants* 12(6): plaa061.

Alexander, P.D., Bragg, N.C., Meade, R., Padelopoulos, G. and Watts, O. (2008) Peat in horticulture and conservation: the UK response to a changing world. *Mires and Peat* 3: 08.

Antonovics, J. (2020) Pathogenic fungi in ferns and angiosperms: a comparative study. *Amer Fern J* 110: 79–94.

Aros-Mualin, D., Noben, S., Karger, D.N., et al. (2021) Functional diversity in ferns is driven by species richness rather than by environmental constraints. *Front Plant Sci* 11: 615723.

Ayres, P.G. (2015) Isaac Bayley Balfour, *Sphagnum* moss, and the Great War (1914–1918). *Arch Nat Hist* 42(1): 1–9.

Bachman, S., Nic Lughadha, E.M. and Rivers, M.C. (2018) Quantifying progress toward a conservation assessment for all plants. *Conserv Biol* 32(3): 516–524.

Bain, C.G., Bonn, A., Stoneman, R., et al. (2011) *IUCN UK Commission of Inquiry on Peatlands. IUCN UK Peatland Programme.* Edinburgh: IUCN.

Barthlott, W., Hostert, A., Kier, G., et al. (2007) Geographic patterns of vascular plant diversity at continental to global scales. *Erdkunde* 61(4): 305–315.

Biersma, E.M., Jackson, J.A., Hyvönen, J., et al. (2017) Global biogeographic patterns in bipolar moss species. *Royal Soc Open Sci* 4: 170147.

Bowd, E.J., Lindenmayer, D.B., Banks, S.C. and Blair, D.P. (2018) Logging and fire regimes alter plant communities. *Ecol Appl* 28(3): 826–841.

Brummitt, N. Aletrari, E., Syfert, M.M. and Mulligan, M. (2016) Where are threatened ferns found? Global conservation priorities for pteridophytes. *J Syst Evol* 54(6): 604–616.

CAFF (Conservation of Arctic Fauna and Flora) (2013) Chapter 9: Plants. In: *Arctic Biodiversity Assessment 2013.* Akureyri, Iceland: CAFF.

CAFF (Conservation of Arctic Fauna and Flora) (2021) *State of the Arctic Terrestrial Biodiversity: Key Findings and Advice for Monitoring.* Akureyri, Iceland: CAFF.

Cámara-Leret, R., Frodin, D.G., Adema, F., et al. (2020) New Guinea has the world's richest island flora. *Nature* 584: 579–583.

Carter, B. (2012) Species delimitation and cryptic diversity in the moss genus *Scleropodium* (Brachytheciaceae). *Mol Phylogenet Evol* 63(3): 891–903.

Cooper-Driver, G. (1985) Anti-predation strategies in pteridophytes: a biochemical approach. *Proc Roy Soc Edinburgh* 86B: 397–402.

Crump, J. (Ed.) (2017) *Smoke on Water: Countering Global Threats From Peatland Loss and Degradation. A UNEP Rapid Response Assessment.* Nairobi, Kenya and Arendal, Norway: United Nations Environment Programme and GRID-Arendal.

Cruz de Carvalho, R., Maurício A., Pereira, M.F., Marques da Silva, J. and Branquinho, C. (2019) All for one: the role of colony morphology in bryophyte desiccation tolerance. *Front Plant Sci* 10: 1360.

Da Silva, A.A., Pereira, A.F. de N. and Barros, I.C.L. (2014) Fragmentation and loss of habitat: consequences for the fern communities in Atlantic forest remnants in Alagoas, north-eastern Brazil. *Plant Ecol Divers* 7(4): 509–517.

Dauphin, B. Farrar, D.R., Maccagni, A. and Grant, J.R. (2017) A worldwide molecular phylogeny provides new insight on cryptic diversity within the moonworts (*Botrychium* s. s., Ophioglossaceae). *Syst Bot* 42(4): 620–639.

Davey, M.L. and Currah, R.S. (2006) Interactions between mosses (Bryophyta) and fungi. *Canada J Bot* 84: 1509–1519.

Edwards, D., Feehan, J. and Smith D.G. (1983) A late Wenlock flora from Co. Tipperary, Ireland. *Bot J Linn Soc* 86(1–2): 19–36.

FAO and UNEP. (2020) *The State of the World's Forests 2020: Forests, biodiversity and people.* Rome: FAO and UNEP.

Farrar, D.R. (1974) Gemmiferous fern gametophytes: Vittariaceae. *Am J Bot* 61: 146–155.

Feldberg, K, Schneider, H., Stadler, T., et al. (2014) Epiphytic leafy liverworts diversified in angiosperm-dominated forests. *Sci Rep* 4: 5974.

Fenton, N.J. and Bergeron, Y. (2008) Does time or habitat make old-growth forests species rich?

Bryophyte richness in boreal *Picea mariana* forests. *Biol Conserv* 141: 1389–1399.

Flagmeier, M., Squirrell, J., Woodhead, M., et al. (2020) Globally rare oceanic-montane liverworts with disjunct distributions: evidence for long-distance dispersal. *Biodivers Conserv* 29: 3245–3264.

Frahm, J.-P. (2008) Diversity, dispersal and biogeography of bryophytes (mosses). *Biodivers Conserv* 17: 277–284.

Frahm, J.-P. and Ohlemüller, R. (2001) Ecology of bryophytes along altitudinal and latitudinal gradients in New Zealand: Studies in austral temperate rain forest bryophytes 15. *Trop Bryol* 20: 117–137.

García Criado, M., Väre, H., Nieto, A., et al. (2017) *European Red List of Lycopods and Ferns*. Brussels, Belgium: IUCN.

Geffert, J.L., Frahm, J.P., Barthlott, W. and Mutke, J. (2013) Global moss diversity: spatial and taxonomic patterns of species richness. *J Bryol* 35: 1–11.

Geiger, J.M.O., Ranker, T.A., Ramp Neale, J.M. and Klimas, S.T. (2007) Molecular biogeography and origins of the Hawaiian fern flora. *Brittonia* 59: 142–158.

Givnish, T.J. (2010) Ecology of plant speciation. *Taxon* 59(5): 1326–1366.

Glime, J.M. (2017) Light: reflectance and fluorescence. In: Glime, J.M. (Ed.), *Bryophyte Ecology, Volume 1: Physiological Ecology*. Ebook available at http://digitalcommons.mtu.edu/bryophyte-ecology/ (accessed September 2022).

Goffinet, B. and Shaw, A.J. (Eds.) (2008) *Bryophyte Biology*, Second Edn. Cambridge, UK: Cambridge University Press.

Harmens, H., Norris, D.A., Steinnes, E., et al. (2010) Mosses as biomonitors of atmospheric heavy metal deposition: spatial patterns and temporal trends in Europe. *Environ Pollut* 158(10): 3144–3156.

Hawkins, J. (2019) Tasmanian tree ferns…an indicator of corruption? *Tasmanian Times*, 5 February. www.tasmaniantimes.com/2019/02/tasmanian-tree-ferns-an-indicator-of-corruption/ (accessed September 2022).

Heim, R.J., Bucharova, A., Brodt, L., et al. (2021) Post-fire vegetation succession in the Siberian subarctic tundra over 45 years. *Sci Total Environ* 760(2021): 143425.

Hillebrand, H. (2004) On the generality of the latitudinal diversity gradient. *Am Nat* 163(2): 192–211.

Hodgetts, N., Cálix, M., Engleeld, E., et al. (2019) *A Miniature World in Decline: European Red List of Mosses, Liverworts and Hornworts*. Brussels, Belgium: IUCN.

Hollingsworth P.M., Li D., VanderBank M. and Twyford A.D. (2016) Telling plant species apart with DNA: from barcodes to genomes. *Philos Trans R Soc B* 371: 20150338.

Hugelius, G., Loisel, J., Chadburn, S., et al. (2020) Large stocks of peatland carbon and nitrogen are vulnerable to permafrost thaw. *PNAS* 117(34): 20438–20446.

Ingimundardóttir, G.V., Weibull, H. and Cronberg, N. (2014) Bryophyte colonization history of the virgin volcanic island Surtsey, Iceland. *Biogeosciences* 11: 4415–4427.

IPCC. (2019) Summary for Policymakers. In: Shukla, P.R., Skea, J., Calvo Buendia, E., et al. (Eds.), *Climate Change and Land: An IPCC Special Report on Climate Change, Desertification, Land Degradation, Sustainable Land Management, Food Security, and Greenhouse Gas Fluxes in Terrestrial Ecosystems*. Geneva, Switzerland: IPCC.

Johnson, G.N., Rumsey, F.J., Headley, A.D. and Sheffield, E. (2000) Adaptations to extreme low light in the fern *Trichomanes speciosum*. *New Phytol* 148: 423–431.

Kauserud, H., Mathiesen, C. and Ohlson, M. (2008) High diversity of fungi associated with living parts of boreal forest bryophytes. *Botany* 86:1326–1333.

Kenrick, P. and Crane, P.R. (1997) *The Origin and Early Diversification of Land Plants: A Cladistics Study*. Washington, DC: Smithsonian Institution Press.

Kreft, H., Jetz, W., Mutke, J. and Barthlott, W. (2010) Contrasting environmental and regional effects on global pteridophyte and seed plant diversity. *Ecography* 33: 408e419.

Laenen, B., Shaw, B., Schneider, H., et al. (2014) Extant diversity of bryophytes emerged from successive post-Mesozoic diversification bursts. *Nat Commun* 5: 5134.

Lee, W.G. (2001) Negative effects of introduced plants, II.B. *Salvinia molesta* (Salviniaceae). In:

Encyclopedia of Biodiversity. Cambridge, MA: Academic Press.

Lehtonen, S., Silvestro, D., Karger, D.N., et al. (2017) Environmentally driven extinction and opportunistic origination explain fern diversification patterns. *Sci Rep* 7(1): 4831.

Lindo, Z., Nilsson, M.-C. and Gundale, M.J. (2013) Bryophyte-cyanobacteria associations as regulators of the northern latitude carbon balance in response to global change. *Glob Change Biol* 19: 2022–2035.

Liu, Y., Johnson, M.G., Cox, C. J., et al. (2019) Resolution of the ordinal phylogeny of mosses using targeted exons from organellar and nuclear genomes. *Nat Commun* 10(1): 1485.

Longton, R.E. (1992) Bryophyte vegetation in polar regions. In: Smith, A.J.E. (Ed.), *Bryophyte Ecology*. London, UK: Chapman & Hall.

MacArthur, R.H. and Wilson, E.O. 1967. *The Theory of Island Biogeography*. Princeton, NJ: Princeton University Press.

Mägdefrau, K. (1982) Life-forms of bryophytes. In: Smith, A.J.E. (Ed.), *Bryophyte Ecology*. London, UK: Chapman & Hall.

Mandl, N., Lehnert, M., Kessler, M. and Gradstein, S.R. (2010) A comparison of alpha and beta diversity patterns of ferns, bryophytes and macrolichens in tropical montane forests of southern Ecuador. *Biodivers Conserv* 19: 2359–2369.

Mateo, R.G., Broennimann, O., Normand, S., et al. (2016) The mossy north: an inverse latitudinal diversity gradient in European bryophytes. *Sci Rep* 6: 25546.

McHaffie, H. (2006) Alpine lady ferns: are they suffering with climate change? *Pteridologist* 4(5): 162–164.

Mehltreter, K., Walker, L. and Sharpe, J. (Eds). (2010) *Fern Ecology*. Cambridge, UK: Cambridge University Press.

Merced, A. and Renzaglia, K.S. (2017) Structure, function and evolution of stomata from a bryological perspective. *Bryophyt Divers Evol* 39: 7–20.

Minayeva, T., Bragg, O. and Sirin, A. (2016) Peatland biodiversity and its restoration. In: Bonn, A., Allott, T., Evans, M., Joosten, H. and Stoneman, R. (Eds.), *Peatland Restoration and Ecosystem*

Services: Science, Policy and Practice (Ecological Reviews). Cambridge, UK: Cambridge University Press.

Morris, J.L., Puttick, M.N., Clark J.W., et al. (2018) The timescale of early land plant evolution. *Proc Natl Acad Sci USA* 115(10): E2274–E2283.

Mounce, R., Rivers, M., Sharrock, S., Smith, P. and Brockington, S. (2018) Comparing and contrasting threat assessments of plant species at the global and sub-global level. *Biodivers Conserv* 27: 907–930.

Muir, P.S., Norman, K.N. and Sikes, K.G. (2006) Quantity and value of commercial moss harvest from forests of the Pacific Northwestern and Appalachian regions of the US. *The Bryologist* 109 (2): 197–214.

Myers, N., Mittermeier, R. A., Mittermeier, C. G., Da Fonseca, G. A. and Kent, J. (2000) Biodiversity hotspots for conservation priorities. *Nature* 403 (6772): 853–858.

Navarrete, H. and Pitman, N. (2003) Cyathea. In: *IUCN 2010 Red List of Threatened Species*. Gland, Switzerland: IUCN.

Nelson, K., Thompson, D., Hopkinson, C., Petrone, R. and Chasmer, L. (2021) Peatland-fire interactions: a review of wildland fire feedbacks and interactions in Canadian boreal peatlands. *Sci Total Environ* 769: 145212.

O'Neill, K.P. (2001) Role of bryophyte-dominated ecosystems in the global carbon budget. In: Shaw, A.J. and Goffinet, B. (Eds.), *Bryophyte Biology*. Cambridge, UK: Cambridge University Press.

Pampurova, S. and Van Dijck, P. (2014) The desiccation tolerant secrets of *Selaginella lepidophylla*: What we have learned so far? *Plant Physiol Biochem* 80: 285–290.

Patiño, J., Solymos, P., Carine, M. A., et al. (2015) Island floras are not necessarily more species poor than continental ones. *J Biogeogr* 42: 8–10.

Patiño, J., Mateo, R.G., Zanatta, F., et al. (2016) Climate threat on the Macaronesian endemic bryophyte flora. *Sci Rep* 6: 29156.

Patiño, J. and Vanderpoorten, A. (2018) Bryophyte biogeography, *Crit Rev Plant Sci* 37(2–3): 175–209.

Peck, J.L.E. and Frelich, L.E. 2008. Moss harvest truncates the successional development of epiphytic bryophytes in the Pacific northwest. *Ecol Appl* 18(1): 146–158.

Pisa, S., Biersma, E.M., Convey, P., et al. (2014) The cosmopolitan moss *Bryum argenteum* in Antarctica: recent colonisation or in situ survival? *Polar Biol* 37 (10): 1469–1477.

PPG 1 (2016) A community-derived classification for extant lycophytes and ferns. *J Syst Evol* 54(6): 563–603.

Roth, S. (2002) Just a frond memory? *The Guardian*, 6 March. www.theguardian.com/society/2002/mar/06/highereducation.biologicalscience (accessed September 2022).

Rumsey, F.J., Vogel, J.C., Russell, S.J., Barrett, J.A. and Gibby, M. (1999) Population structure and conservation biology of the endangered fern *Trichomanes speciosum* Willd. (Hymenophyllaceae) at its northern distributional limit. *Biol J Linn Soc* 66: 333–344.

Schneider, H., Schuettpelz, E., Pryer, K.M., et al. (2004) Ferns diversified in the shadow of angiosperms. *Nature* 428(6982): 553–557.

Shaw, A.J., Cox, C. and Goffinet, B. (2005) Global patterns of moss diversity: taxonomic and molecular inferences. *Taxon* 4(2): 337–352.

Sheffield, E., Wolf, P.G. and Haufler, C.H. (1989) How big is a bracken plant? *Weed Res* 29: 455–460.

Smith, R.L. (2014) A fern cultured from Antarctic glacier detritus. *Antarct Sci* 26(4): 341–344.

Söderström, L., Hagborg, A., von Konrat, M., et al. (2016) World checklist of hornworts and liverworts. *PhytoKeys* 59: 1–821.

Suissa, J.S., Sundue, M.A. and Testo, W.L. (2021) Mountains, climate and niche heterogeneity explain global patterns of fern diversity. *J Biogeogr* 48(6): 1296–1308.

Travis, J.M.J. (2003) Climate change and habitat destruction: a deadly anthropogenic cocktail. *Proc Royal Soc. B* 270(1514): 467–473.

Tristan da Cunha Government & RSPB. (2012) *Biodiversity Action Plan for the Tristan da Cunha Islands (2012–2016)*. Edinburgh of the Seven Seas, Tristan da Cunha, South Atlantic: Tristan Conservation Department.

Troudet, J., Grandcolas, P., Blin, A., Vignes-Lebbe, R. and Legendre, F. (2017) Taxonomic bias in biodiversity data and societal preferences. *Sci Rep* 7: 9132.

UNEP-WCMC. (2019) *EU Wildlife Trade 2017: Analysis of the European Union's Annual Reports to CITES 2017*. Cambridge, UK: European Commission.

van Rooy, J., Bergamini, A. and Bisang, I. (2019) Fifty shades of red: lost or threatened bryophytes in Africa, *Bothalia* 49(1): a2341.

Villarreal, J.C., Cargill, D.C., Hagborg, A. Söderström, L. and Renzaglia, K.S. (2010) A synthesis of hornwort diversity: patterns, causes and future work. *Phytotaxa* 9: 150–166.

Villarreal A.J.C., Crandall-Stotler, B.J., Hart, M.L., Long, D.G. and Forrest, L.L. (2016) Divergence times and the evolution of morphological complexity in an early land plant lineage (Marchantiopsida) with a slow molecular rate. *New Phytol* 209: 1734–1746.

Vitt, D.H., Li, Y. and Belland, R.J. (1995) Patterns of bryophyte diversity in peatlands of continental western Canada. *Bryologist* 98: 218–227.

von Konrat, M., Söderström, L., Renner, M.A.M., Hagborg, A. and Briscoe, L. (2010) Early Land Plants Today (ELPT): how many liverwort species are there? *Phytotaxa* 9: 22–40.

Wagner, W.L., Herbst, D.R. and Lorence, D.H. (2005) Flora of the Hawaiian Islands. https://naturalhistory2.si.edu/botany/hawaiianflora/ (accessed September 2022).

Walker, D.A., Raynolds, M.K., Daniëls, F.J., et al.; CAVM Team. (2005) The Circumpolar Arctic vegetation map. *J Veg Sci* 16: 267–282.

Whiteley, J.A. and Gonzalez, A. (2016) Biotic nitrogen fixation in the bryosphere is inhibited more by drought than warming. *Oecologia* 181: 1243–1258.

Witze, A. (2020) The Arctic is burning like never before – and that's bad news for climate change. *Nature*, 10 September. www.nature.com/articles/d41586-020-02568-y (accessed September 2022).

Wong J.L.G., Dickinson B.G. and Thorogood A. (2016) Assessing the scale of Sphagnum moss collection from Wales. *NRW Evidence Reports*. Report No 185. Bangor, Wales: Natural Resources Wales.

Zuquim, G., Tuomisto, H., Jones, M.M., et al. (2014) Predicting environmental gradients with fern species composition in Brazilian Amazonia. *J Veg Sci* 25(5): 1195–1207.

FOUR

Terrestrial Mammals

ALEXIS M. MYCHAJLIW

Summary

Mammals are among the most recognisable and most threatened organisms on Earth. There are more than 6000 living species, ranging from the big (rhinoceroses) to the small (rats), the wondrous to the weird (even venomous, too!) (Figure 4.1). While mammals face accelerating extinction risks as human populations grow and alter the landscapes and climates of the world, hope for survival remains through productive collaborations between scientists, governments and most importantly, local communities and stakeholders. Achieving conservation goals for terrestrial mammals means recognising that:

- Our present-day extinctions actually started thousands of years ago!
- Extinction filters and centres of risk have changed over time. Today, large-bodied mammals and those with small ranges face the greatest risk, and many of these species are found in the tropics, particularly Southeast Asia.
- The most urgent threats include habitat loss and degradation, direct exploitation for bushmeat and trade, human–wildlife conflict, invasive species and infectious diseases. All of these threats intersect with each other and play out in the theatre of global climate change.
- In the midst of a mass extinction, some mammals are recovering, and even thriving, and new species are still being described.
- The biggest obstacle – and opportunity – for mammal conservation is our own behaviour.

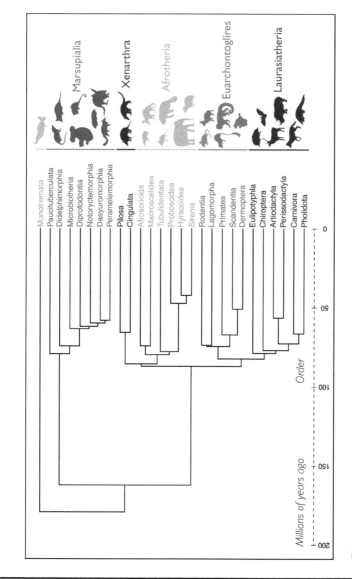

Figure 4.1 Evolutionary relationships of all living mammal groups by Order and Superorder, built using the VertLife mammal tree of 4098 species for which DNA sequences are available (Upham et al., 2019). One species was chosen to represent each extant order (27 total) from the maximum clade-credibility topology of the fossil node-dated phylogeny. Phylogeny provided by N. Upham and animal silhouettes courtesy of Phylopic users, including licenses from the public domain (Steven Traver, Daniel Stadtmauer, Gavin Prideaux, Xavier A. Jenkins, Yan Wong, Pearson Scott Foresman, 'An Ignorant Atheist', Jiro Wada, T. Michael Keesey, Jody Taylor, Margot Michaud) and CCA 3 Unported (Roberto Sibaja, Sarah Werning).

Box 4.1
IUCN Listed Terrestrial Mammals

The International Union for the Conservation of Nature (IUCN) considers species as threatened within the categories of Critically Endangered (CR), Endangered (EN) and Vulnerable (VU). Unfortunately, so many mammals fall within this elevated threat bracket that they are too numerous to list here. Of the nearly 5800 terrestrial mammals that have been evaluated, two are Extinct in the Wild (EW), 218 are CR, 515 EN,

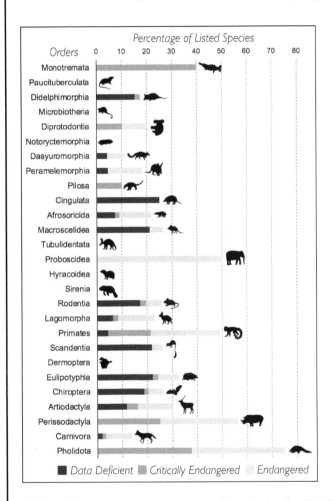

Figure 4.2 Percentage of mammal species, by order, listed as Data Deficient, Critically Endangered and Endangered by IUCN. Animal silhouettes courtesy of Phylopic users, including licenses from the public domain (Steven Traver, Daniel Stadtmauer, Gavin Prideaux, Xavier A. Jenkins, Yan Wong, Pearson Scott Foresman, 'An Ignorant Atheist', Jiro Wada, T. Michael Keesey, Jody Taylor, Margot Michaud) and CCA 3 Unported (Roberto Sibaja, Sarah Werning).

Figure 4.3 Mammal species of conservation concern, including the (A) eastern gorilla, *Gorilla beringei*, Critically Endangered (K. Solari), (B) social tuco-tuco, *Ctenomys sociabilis*, Critically Endangered (J. Hsu), (C) Jamaican flower bat, *Phyllonycteris aphylla*, Critically Endangered (A. Soto-Centeno), (D) giraffe, *Giraffa camelopardalis*, Vulnerable (K. Solari), (E) African bush elephant, *Loxodonta africana*, Vulnerable (K. Solari).

530 VU, 345 Near Threatened (NT) and 3230 Least Concern (LC) (Figure 4.2). About 15% of all listed species are considered Data Deficient (DD), and these obscure species disproportionately come from the most speciose clades, including rodents and eulipotyphlans (true 'insectivores'). IUCN recognises 81 species that have gone extinct since

1500 AD: numerous small mammals from island systems such as the Caribbean and the Galapagos, as well as more well-known species such as the thylacine or 'Tasmanian Tiger'. CR species include a large number of well-known primates including gorillas (Figure 4.3A), gibbons and orangutans, as well as lesser known but equally threatened species including a wide range of rodents (e.g. the social tuco-tuco (Figure 4.3B) and marsupials (e.g. the mountain pygmy possum). A complementary framework for assessing species is the Evolutionarily Distinct and Globally Endangered (EDGE) scheme, which prioritises species whose extinction would represent a disproportionate loss of evolutionary history. The top scoring EDGE mammals are two rare species of long-beaked echidnas.

4.1 Introduction

We live in the 'Age of Mammals', a nickname for the Cenozoic Era, reflecting the rise of furry, warm-blooded creatures from below the feet of dinosaurs. The evolution of mammals is also a story of extinction: mammals diversified after the Cretaceous–Paleogene mass extinction approximately 66 million years ago (Upham et al., 2019) (Figure 4.1). Closer in time, mammals themselves underwent massive extinctions starting in the Late Pleistocene (roughly the past 125,000 years) with the spread of humans worldwide, and such extinctions stretched through the Holocene (the past 10,000 years) as human populations grew and now continue into the present day.

Mammals are among the most recognisable organisms on the planet and receive a disproportionate share of research attention and conservation efforts among all vertebrates – perhaps because we ourselves are mammals! There are currently ~ 6400 mammal species currently recognised as alive today (Burgin et al., 2018). While many species that come to mind are threatened, large-bodied and actively monitored (e.g. tigers, elephants, pandas), the majority are actually small, cryptic and understudied in their basic natural history. Large herbivorous mammals exert important effects on vegetation structure, fire regimes and carbon sequestration, and in turn, carnivores regulate the effects of these herbivores from the top down. Small mammals also play key ecological roles by consuming insects, dispersing seeds and influencing disease dynamics; for example, the Virginia opossum eats thousands of ticks a season! Therefore, the loss of mammals – large and small – has cascading effects on the ecosystems around them. These services affect humans, too: for millennia, mammals have been a source of food, labour and raw materials, and they also have aesthetic and religious values to many cultures. Yet today, these different values and uses across different human populations worldwide has led to conflict and decline for many species. The story of mammal conservation today is one of humans interacting with their fellow mammals, and both the problems and the solutions are in our hands.

What makes a mammal a mammal? Despite their wide phenotypic and ecological diversity, mammals are distinguished by several uniting features. Visibly, mammals have hair and mammary glands that produce milk; internally, there are numerous other structures, such as the anatomy of their inner ears and jaw bones, and the lack of nuclei in their blood cells.

Mammal groups vary in their number of species, geographic distribution and evolutionary history, presenting conservation challenges and tradeoffs. In this chapter, we will consider the mammals typically featured for conservation, but also make a special effort to highlight the full diversity of mammals, including the cryptic, rare and quite frankly, weird species.

There are three major evolutionary groups of mammals living today (Figure 4.1):

Monotremes. While they lay eggs and lack nipples, it would be incorrect to describe them as 'primitive', as they have been evolving for millions of years to fulfill their own specialised lifestyles, including being some of the few venomous mammals on the planet. There are five known living species of Monotremes (Order Monotremata): four echidnas (Family Tachyglossidae) and one platypus (Family Ornithorhynchidae); these two families diverged nearly 50 million years ago from each other. Monotremes are found in Australasia, including Australia and New Guinea. The western long-beaked echidna and Attenborough's long-beaked echidna are the two highest ranked Evolutionarily Distinct and Globally Endangered (EDGE) species alive today.

Marsupials. The term marsupial derives from having a marsupium, or pouch, though many species don't have one. Marsupials are characterised by giving birth to relatively undeveloped young after a short gestation period. There are approximately 330 species spread across seven orders: Didelphimorphia, Paucituberculata, Microbiotheria, Dasyuromorphia, Peramelemorphia, Notoryctemorphia and Diprotodontia (Figure 4.1). These species range from the iconic kangaroos, wombats and koalas to the lesser known monito del monte, the only species in an entire order found in southern South America, and the recently extinct 'Tasmanian tiger' or thylacine. While their centre of diversity today is Australasia, the group originated in the Western Hemisphere and are found widely in South America. The only marsupial to live in North America is the Virginia opossum.

Placentals. The majority of extant mammals, >5000 species, are placental mammals, named for the distinctive features of their placenta, though there are also metabolic and morphological differences between placental and other mammals. After much debate between conflicting morphological and molecular datasets, the major groups (Superorders) of placental mammals have finally been resolved: Afrotheria (elephants, hyraxes and others), Xenarthra (sloths, armadillos, anteaters), Laurasiatheria (carnivores, ungulates, bats and others) and Euarchontoglires (rodents, primates and others) (Figure 4.1). Placental mammals are found across all continents except Antarctica. The most diverse groups include rodents, bats and eulipotyphlans (true 'insectivores').

4.2 A Long Legacy of Extinction and Survival

We are in the midst of an extinction event on par with the 'Big Five' mass extinctions of the distant past: a geologic event unfolding on ecological timescales, making it difficult to see how losses can be replaced in the near future ('extinction without replacement'). For example, recent bat extinctions in the Caribbean would require 8 million years to recover the evolutionary diversity that has been lost (Valente et al., 2017). Present-day mammal communities represent survivors that have already passed through several extinction filters, and the legacy of the past shapes our perception of present-day mammal diversity and extinction risk (Turvey and Fritz 2011). Data points of past abundance represent baselines that can help us trace the decline of species over time. For example, in North America, records of the number of pelts collected during the historical fur harvest industry change how we perceive the present-day population trends (and thus conservation needs) of fur-bearing mammals: population declines of several species are significantly greater when viewed from a baseline of 1850 AD, rather than 1970 AD (Collins et al., 2020). Understanding this longer history of extinction – encompassing the Late Pleistocene, Holocene and more recent historical record, with changing human pressures across all three intervals – is necessary to accurately contextualise present-day conservation priorities and reveal hidden opportunities. This view from the past also makes us appreciate that the mammals on the landscape today are in fact survivors, presenting a narrative of hope.

4.2.1 Living in the Shadow of Giants: Late Pleistocene Megafauna Extinctions

Fossil discoveries in the nineteenth century led Alfred Russel Wallace to observe that 'we live in a zoologically impoverished world, from which all the hugest and fiercest and strangest forms have recently disappeared'. The present-day landscape of mammal diversity and the ecosystems they inhabit were shaped by events of the Late Pleistocene, which included major climatic changes of glacial–interglacial cycles and, of paramount importance, the evolution of modern humans and their spread across the globe. Megafaunal mammals (those >45 kg or ~100 lbs) disproportionately went extinct at the end of the Late Pleistocene on continents from the tundra to the tropics, severely reducing the diversity of mammalian groups including sloths, proboscideans, cingulates (e.g. armadillos), ungulates and carnivores (Smith et al., 2018). Many now-threatened species began contracting their ranges during the Late Pleistocene, such as the giant panda, Malayan tapir and tiger in Southeast Asia (Louys, 2012). More than 100 genera of megafaunal mammals went extinct in total, with magnitudes of loss varying by continent, with some like South America losing >80% of genera (Smith et al., 2018). Debate still rages over the cause of these losses: was it natural climate change, the arrival of humans, or some synergy of the two? Understanding these ancient extinction forces can yield helpful clues for our present conservation dilemmas, and this is a very active area of research.

4.2.2 The Geography and Selectivity of Extinction

Today, more than 1000 species, or roughly a quarter, of all IUCN assessed mammals are threatened with extinction, with body size and geographic range size acting as the most important predictors of risk (Cardillo et al., 2005). A body size of 3 kg (~7 lbs) appears to be the threshold for which species begin to face multiple, compounding extinction threats. Species smaller than 3 kg are most at risk based on the human impacts they are exposed to in their geographic range (extrinsic risks), whereas those larger than 3 kg are additionally vulnerable to decline given their slow life history traits, including a low reproductive rate and long life span that make it difficult for populations to rebound (intrinsic risks). Given this dichotomy, in general, smaller mammals may benefit from a threatened areas or hotspot approach, whereas larger mammals can require approaches that are species-specific (Cardillo et al., 2005).

A small geographic range can predispose species to be vulnerable to catastrophic events, and in general, extinction risk is higher for species with ranges less than 1 million km^2 (Davidson et al., 2017). The CR social tuco-tuco (a rodent) has an area of occupancy of only 8 km^2, and the 2011 eruption of the Puyehue-Cordón Caulle volcano near Patagonia nearly halved its population density (Hsu et al., 2017) (Figure 4.3B). Species with the smallest ranges are disproportionately found on islands (e.g. Madagascar, Sri Lanka and Sulawesi) and tropical mountains (e.g. Andes, Cameroonian and Ethiopian Highlands) (Schipper et al., 2008). Some examples include the EN pygmy sloth, found only on the wildlife refuge Isla Escudo de Veraguas of Panama, the EN Nicobar island tree shrew (Order Scandentia) from the Great and Little Nicobar Islands, the EN Seram bandicoot, endemic to the island of Seram in Indonesia, and known only from seven specimens collected in 1920 at a single locality, and the CR Attenborough's long-beaked echidna, found on a single mountain (Berg Rara) in the Cyclops Mountains of New Guinea.

Extinction risk for mammals has changed over time both spatially and across the tree of life (Turvey and Fritz 2011). While in the Holocene, many extinctions were concentrated on islands, today, the largest concentrations of threatened mammals are found in South and Southeast Asia, the tropical Andes in South America, the Cameroonian Highlands and Albertine Rift in Africa, and the Western Ghats in India. These regions share the common feature of being at the intersection of intense anthropogenic pressures, rapidly growing human populations and high species richness, including those species with restricted ranges (Schipper et al., 2008; Davidson et al., 2017). Geographic patterns of risk can differ for different taxa. Large carnivores, such as lions and tigers, have experienced the greatest range contractions across Southeast Asia and Africa (Wolf and Ripple, 2017), whereas rodent 'threat spots' include the Philippines, New Guinea, Sulawesi, the Caribbean, Chinese temperate forests, the Brazilian Atlantic Forest, and drylands including Togo and the Mongolian–Manchurian steppes (Amori and Gippoliti, 2001).

4.3 Conserving Mammals in a Changing World

As we have seen, correlates of extinction risk and the location of geographic hotspots are not static but can change over time in response to different human and environmental conditions. Mammals in the Anthropocene face multiple global extinction threats that intersect with local ecological, cultural and socioeconomic conditions. Here we identify habitat loss, direct exploitation, human–wildlife conflict, invasive species and disease as the major Anthropocene threats facing mammals, all playing out in the overarching context of climate change.

4.3.1 Habitat Loss, Degradation and Fragmentation

By far the greatest immediate threat to mammalian biodiversity is the loss, degradation and fragmentation of habitat, often linked to agricultural and urban expansion. This affects

40% of IUCN assessed mammal species (Schipper et al., 2008). The ecological and behavioural needs of primates make them particularly vulnerable to habitat loss, which is the main driver of threat for species in primate hotspot countries including Brazil, Madagascar and Indonesia (Estrada et al., 2018). Under a worst-case scenario of agricultural expansion in the twenty-first century, primate ranges will severely contract by ~60–80% across these countries (Estrada et al., 2018). Illegal mining of precious metals and gems has affected many forests in Madagascar, the only place in the world where lemurs are found today (nearly 100 species of them!) (Estrada et al., 2018).

Mammals in Southeast Asia face devastating rates of habitat loss due to forest clearance for agriculture, international logging concessions, and oil palm and other agroforestry crops (e.g. rubber, biofuels, wood pulp) (Hughes, 2017). These causes of deforestation, combined with mining and dam construction, have destroyed more than 50% of the original forest cover in some places (e.g. the Philippines, parts of Indonesia), and up to 98% original forest loss is projected for some countries in the next decade (Hughes, 2017). It is estimated that more than 100,000 individual CR Bornean orangutans (half the population) were lost due to logging, deforestation or the construction of industrialised plantations from 1999–2015 (Voigt et al., 2018). Habitat loss in this region also affects smaller, lesser known species such as the EN flat-headed cat, which is rapidly losing its native Indonesian wetlands and lowland forest habitats to oil palm plantations and clearance of coastal mangroves (Wilting et al., 2010).

Many small mammals are also impacted by habitat loss, particularly those whose already small ranges unfortunately intersect with anthropogenic activities. Numerous shrews (Order Eulipotyphla) are threatened by habitat destruction, including the CR Nelson's small-eared shrew of Veracruz, Mexico and the CR Jenkin's shrew of India's Andaman Island. Their convergent cousins, the afrosoricid insectivores (Orders Afrosoricida and Macroscelidea) (Figure 4.1), are similarly threatened by habitat loss. The EN golden-rumped sengi relies on Kenyan forests with abundant leaf litter, such as the Arabuko-Sokoke Forest, which has been degraded by tree felling. Perhaps surprisingly, of the 21 known species of golden moles (Family Chrysochloridae), more than half are listed at an elevated threat level due to urbanisation, mining and agriculture, including the possibly extinct De Winton's golden mole of South Africa. Even bats, which are more vagile due to their flight capabilities, can vary in sensitivity based on roosting behaviours. Two CR bat species, the Jamaican flower bat (Figure 4.3C) and the Jamaican greater funnel-eared bat, are now each restricted to a single remaining cave roost, demanding urgent conservation attention to avoid the loss of their entire species.

4.3.2 Direct Exploitation

Humans exert direct pressure on mammal populations by removing wild individuals for food, trade, traditional medicine and sport, all within the context of a globalising economy and changing cultural norms. Such direct exploitation currently threatens more than 300 species of terrestrial mammals (Ripple et al., 2016). Those species threatened by overharvesting are typically large bodied and charismatic, such as elephants, primates and rhinoceroses, and their selective removal from an ecosystem can result in 'empty forest syndrome', creating landscapes devoid of large mammals. The drivers of direct exploitation are complex, and solutions require strengthening legal protections coupled with increased support of local communities in ways that do not recapitulate colonial power dynamics. Efforts to increase global awareness and change attitudes, such as World Pangolin Day, and emerging technologies in wildlife crime forensics are additional tools in the conservationist's toolbox.

Humans have been consuming mammals for millennia, with outcomes ranging from extinction to sustainable harvest. However, commercialisation, global supply chains and easier access to firearms have fundamentally altered these traditional practices; for example, drug cartels are now involved in poaching due to its profitability. Bushmeat hunting (in contrast with legal, regulated hunting) is a major conservation challenge because it is linked to economic inequality, food insecurity and cultural norms, and conservation responses must include alternative livelihoods and protein sources. Mammalian orders with the most species threatened by hunting include primates, bats, carnivores, even- and odd-toed ungulates, and rodents (Ripple et al., 2016). Civil wars and illegal mining in many primate-rich areas, such as the DRC, have led to elevated bushmeat exploitation affecting numerous species including CR Eastern lowland gorillas (Figure 4.3A). Popular as trophy hunting prizes, giraffes (Figure 4.3D) in Uganda have alarmingly declined by 90% over 30 years, and more than 39,000 giraffe derivatives were imported into the US from 2006–2015 (Brown et al., 2019). Small mammals are also exploited for both their meat and fur. The Russian desman, an aquatic mole (Family Talpidae), was overharvested for its water-resistant fur throughout the 1800s until the Soviet government enacted a hunting moratorium in 1957 (Rutovskaya et al., 2017), giving the species a chance to recover.

International trade is formally controlled by the Convention on International Trade in Endangered Species of Wild Fauna and Flora (CITES). More than 800 mammal species are currently regulated by CITES, but many species are traded illegally and smuggled across borders in response to global economic forces. For example, demand for ivory in Chinese markets drives poaching of African elephants (Figure 4.3E) (Hauenstein et al., 2019). Pangolins (Order Pholidota) are an unfortunate icon of the international illegal wildlife trade and, as the most trafficked mammal on the planet, have been described as literally being eaten to death. Pangolins are often called scaly anteaters due to their keratin scales and specialised diet of ants and termites, and are found across Africa and Asia. While they have been consumed on a local scale for decades, they are now highly sought after in the Chinese Traditional Medicine market and sold as delicacies in restaurants, resulting in African species being shipped for consumption and use in Asia. Recent estimates suggest that the equivalent of more than 895,000 pangolins were trafficked globally between 2000 and 2019 (Challender et al., 2020). All pangolin species were listed in the CITES Appendix I at CoP17 in 2016, establishing an international trade ban, though conservation solutions must target changing attitudes and norms in Asian markets to be successful.

Many mammals are traded as pets and for use in entertainment. Hundreds of thousands of primates are thought to be traded as pets each year, including the unfortunate viral video star, the CR Javan slow loris (Nijman et al., 2011). There are more tigers in captivity in the United States than in the wild, yet less than 5% of the estimated 10,000 tigers are held within accredited facilities, and many are severely inbred (Nyhus et al., 2010). White tigers are a particularly egregious case of genetic mismanagement, as the inbreeding required to produce a white coat is accompanied by birth defects including club feet and crossed eyes (Figure 4.4A). Raising awareness of the ethical issues surrounding captivity can lead to meaningful policy change through public pressure on governments, such as the continued amendments strengthening the Animal Welfare Act in the United States, though such protections still do not apply to less broadly charismatic species (e.g. rodents).

4.3.3 Human–Wildlife Conflict

As human populations grow, so does the potential for human–wildlife conflict through competition for the same resources, such as prey or habitat, or when wild mammals are perceived as a threat to the safety of humans or their property. Often, contentious wildlife management decisions are made in the shadow of political tensions and the power dynamics of human communities, such as the massive battles between ranchers and conservationists over grey wolves in Yellowstone National Park, United States. In North America and Europe, years of carnivore absence have led to a human population that lacks the social norms for responsibly behaving in places where carnivores are returning, leading to increased attacks reported in the media, which can reinforce negative attitudes (Penteriani et al., 2016). Because human–wildlife conflicts often centre on perceived, rather than real, threats and are enmeshed in complex sociopolitical landscapes, social science research is critical for conservation progress on this front.

Humans are considered 'super predators' – both consuming prey and killing off other predators to avoid competition. This manifests most clearly in the conflict associated with livestock predation by wild mammalian carnivores, which often results in retaliatory killings of the offending (or more often, suspected) individual. Carnivores are increasingly co-occurring with humans and livestock in shared spaces, particularly in the Global South where people rely directly on livestock and multiuse forests for their livelihoods. Government support for predator control and eradication has resulted in several historical carnivore extinctions and massive range extirpations, such as the range reduction of wolves in Asia, North America and Europe, lions and wild dogs in Africa, tigers in Asia and jaguars in the Americas (Wolf and Ripple, 2017). Historic carnivore extinctions associated with hunting bounties to 'protect' livestock include the thylacine, the Hokkaido wolf of Japan, the California grizzly bear and the Falkland Islands wolf. While common approaches to preventing livestock depredation include lethal control, other options can include translocation of problematic individuals, construction of barriers and the use of trained guard dogs. Governments and non-governmental organisations can also offer compensation to farmers who have lost individuals to predation events to ameliorate feelings of resentment and support livelihoods, despite economic losses.

Figure 4.4 Examples of mammal conservation scenarios featured in the text. (A) Kenny, a captive white tiger (*Panthera tigris*), was born with skull and jaw malformities due to inbreeding. While most tigers with this appearance would have been euthanised, Kenny was rescued by Turpentine Creek Wildlife Refuge (https://www.turpentinecreek.org/), (B) sacred sika deer (*Cervus nippon*), with antlers removed, peruse a store and are tolerated by the shop owner in Nara, Japan (A. Mychajliw), (C) a female Hispaniolan solenodon (*Solenodon paradoxus*) killed by a dog near Puerto Escondido, Dominican Republic – extended teats suggest that she was nursing (A. Mychajliw), (D) a pika (*Ochotona roylei*) in Spiti Valley, Himachal Pradesh, India, stuck between a rock and a hard place – rising temperatures and high elevation hypoxia (K. Solari), (E) despite their abundance in places such as Costa Rica, Xenarthrans such as the northern tamandua (*Tamandua mexicana*) remain understudied (K. Solari).

Carnivores are not the only species that may conflict with humans. Given their massive size, elephants often have major impacts on villages and agriculture, with records of crop raiding in Asia dating back centuries. In Africa, strategies to avoid conflict have taken advantage of elephants' natural fear of bees. Farmers who place beehives along their fences can simultaneously protect their crops and generate new sources of income, creating a conservation win-win scenario (Ngama et al., 2016).

While humans and wildlife conflict with certain cultural practices, others can promote conservation. Temples and shrines have served as important places for positive human–wildlife interactions for hundreds of years. The sacred herd of sika deer at the Kasuga-taisha Shrine in Nara, Japan (a UNESCO World Heritage Site) attracts thousands of visitors annually, generating income for local communities through tourism and the sale of special crackers (鹿煎餅, shika-senbei) for feeding the docile deer (Figure 4.4B). This particular deer herd has been protected for hundreds of years; killing of a deer was punishable by death up until the mid 1600s, and the deer remain protected under national treasure status, even as populations grow and spill outside of the shrine's perimeter onto city streets. Bucks' antlers are proactively removed each year to avoid injuries to humans, especially during mating season when males become aggressive. This relationship formed over hundreds of years provides insight into the strategies – both from the biological and social sciences – that do and don't work in facilitating co-existence.

4.3.4 Introduced and Invasive Species

Invasive species can impact mammals directly through predation, or indirectly, by competing with species for shared resources or altering ecosystem structures, leading to habitat degradation and loss. While mammals are highly threatened by the activities of introduced species, they themselves actually represent some of the most destructive invasive species globally: black and brown rats, feral cats and dogs, mongoose and domestic livestock, among others. These invasive mammals have insidiously significant and wide-ranging effects on island species. The numerous historical extinctions of Caribbean small mammals, including an entire endemic family of island shrews (Order Eulipotyphla), have been linked to the introduction of mongooses, cats and dogs associated with European colonial practices (Turvey et al., 2017a). Species such as the EN Hispaniolan hutia and the EN Hispaniolan solenodon (Figure 4.4C) remain severely threatened by predation, though recovery could be feasible where dog populations are controlled (Turvey et al., 2017a).

Australian mammals – both marsupial and placental – are particularly threatened by non-native predators. Similar to the Caribbean, feral cats have been proposed as the cause of more than 20 Australian endemic mammal extinctions historically, including the lesser bilby and the entire family of pig-footed bandicoots (Family Chaeropodidae) (Woinarski et al., 2015). This is why many conservationists suggest that if you have a pet cat, you should keep them inside to protect native species. Many of Australia's threatened mammals now occur only on small islands or fenced enclosures, and these predator-free environments represent important places for reintroductions. The EN numbat (Family

Myrmecobiidae), a termite specialist, nearly disappeared in the 1970s, but experimental fox control programmes showed significant numbat recovery potential. As a result, numbats are now successfully bred in captivity for reintroduction to predator-free reserves across southwestern Australia and translocated to two fenced mainland islands in eastern Australia.

New archaeological research continues to deepen our understanding of just how long humans have been moving species outside of their native ranges. In fact, the earliest documented translocation occurred 20,000 years ago (Hofman and Rick, 2018)! Such studies paint a complex picture of the underappreciated or unrecognised human components of mammal histories, including species we, perhaps ironically, now protect today. Dingoes were brought to Australia by people more than 3000 years ago and likely had significant ecological effects on native species, potentially precipitating the extirpation of Tasmanian devils from Australia. Similarly, Indigenous peoples likely introduced foxes to the previously canid-free California Channel Islands ~7000 years ago, eventually evolving into the 'endemic' and beloved island fox (Hofman and Rick, 2018). These examples reflect the truly coupled long-term history of humans and other mammals and are a window into what co-existence looks like over hundreds and even thousands of years.

4.3.5 Infectious Diseases and Spillovers

Our increasingly interconnected world is putting species together in new ways, in turn allowing them to share parasites, viruses, bacteria and other agents of disease across biogeographic boundaries. The Christmas Island rat, which went extinct around 1900, represents the earliest mammal extinction directly attributable to a human-mediated disease, as invasive ship rats were accompanied by pathogenic trypanosomes (Wyatt et al., 2008). More generally, the expansion of domestic mammals and bushmeat consumption, changing habitat conditions, due to deforestation, and shifting climates are all working to reshape the disease landscapes that species inhabit and lead to increasing disease spillovers of relevance to wildlife and human health.

The global popularity of domestic dogs is accompanied by an increase in the extent and transmission of canine distemper virus to wild canids, such as the EN Ethiopian wolf (Marino et al., 2017) and can impact numerous carnivore species aside from canids if not managed through vaccination. Plague, introduced to US shipping ports by invasive rodents in 1900, decimates immunologically naive black-tailed prairie dog populations, which are the main food item for EN black-footed ferrets. As a result, the ferrets are hit with a one-two punch of prey depletion and direct plague mortality (Salkeld, 2017). The oral vaccine for plague can be delivered to prairie dogs in the form of peanut-butter-flavoured baits, but such dissemination requires collaboration between US federal agencies and private landowners, which can be contentious. Yet, hope for combating such diseases comes from the case of rinderpest, which once spilled over from domestic livestock and caused massive mortality events in African ungulates, but is now considered to be globally eradicated (Morens et al., 2011).

Bats are often associated with zoonotic diseases in the minds of the public due to viral spillovers including Hendra, Nipah, Ebola, Marburg and now, COVID-19. These spill-over events occur as a result of habitat loss and degradation, which changes bat behavioural patterns and species interactions. Hunting of bats and other co-occurring mammals for bushmeat further increases the likelihood of transmission to humans (Schneeberger and Voigt, 2016). Humans have also facilitated the spread of diseases affecting bats, such as the deadly white-nose syndrome (WNS) in North America, a fungus that infects the skin and causes bats to wake up too frequently during hibernation (Schneeberger and Voigt, 2016). WNS has killed millions of bats since its introduction to a New York cave by tourists in 2006 and prompted the listing of several mouse-eared bat species under the US Endangered Species Act due to imminent threat of disease-related extinction. From this hard lesson, we have learned the vital importance of sterilising equipment and other precautions to avoid bringing pathogens from one location to another, whether in research or tourism.

Given their close relationship to us, non-human primates are particularly vulnerable to zoonotic diseases transmitted by humans. Ebola outbreaks killed over 90% of western gorillas (Figure 4.3A) and 80% of chimpanzees in the Lossi Sanctuary of Republic of Congo between 2002 and 2004 (Bermejo et al., 2006). In Kibale and Gombe Stream National Park of Tanzania – where Jane Goodall famously worked – human respiratory viruses are the leading cause of death for chimpanzees. In the new era of COVID-19, researchers must be extremely vigilant to avoid spillover of this highly infectious disease to the very non-human primate communities they are trying to protect.

4.4 Climate Change: Move, Adapt or Go Extinct

Anthropogenic climate change is transforming our planet and no mammal species is outside the reach of its impacts. Globally, hotspots of climate change risk for mammals include areas in Africa (northeastern South Africa, northeastern Tanzania, southwestern Kenya), the Yunnan region of China, the mountains of New Guinea and the western Amazon Basin in South America (Pacifici et al., 2017). In the past, species responded to natural climate change by either adapting to stay in place or moving to a new place to track their preferred ecological conditions; if neither of those options were feasible, the outcome was extinction. Today, these survival options are even more complicated: adaptation may be hindered by a population's low genetic diversity resulting from other threats (e.g. fragmentation and inbreeding) or may not be possible given how rapidly temperatures are rising relative to reproductive rates. Range shifts may not be possible because of anthropogenic barriers such as habitat conversion, roads and fences. As species continue to shift outside of protected areas and move across political boundaries, planning in the context of climate change requires conservation innovation and inter-national collaboration. In the Western Hemisphere, anywhere from ~9–39% of mammals at a given location may not be able to shift their ranges to match the velocity of suitable climate conditions changes (Schloss et al., 2012), and these impacts are worsened for dispersal-limited taxa, including primates, shrews and moles. Such species may benefit from a controversial but promising approach of assisted colonisation, in which managers translocate populations outside of their current range in anticipation of climate impacts.

Anthropogenic climate change is accompanied by an increased frequency of extreme weather events. In Mexico, threatened species including two subspecies of spider monkeys, two howler monkeys and the silky anteater are all vulnerable to population mortality events associated with hurricane exposure (Ameca et al., 2019). In the Pacific Islands, increasingly frequent tropical cyclones have devastated insular bat populations (80–90% of flying fox populations) through direct mortality and alteration of resources (Scanlon et al., 2018).

Small mammals with restricted ranges on islands, mountains or already arid areas are extremely sensitive to climate change. The Bramble Cay melomys, a rodent, is now considered the first mammal extinction caused directly by anthropogenic climate change (Waller et al., 2017). The species was formerly restricted to Bramble Cay (Maizab Kaur), an ~4 ha sand cay located in Australia's Torres Strait. This low elevation and small range made it vulnerable to sea-level rise and storm surges, which destroyed its habitat and also caused direct mortality (Waller et al., 2017). Pikas (Order Lagomorpha) (Figure 4.4D) are cold-temperature specialists distributed across mountain ranges in Asia and North America. The impact of climate change on pikas is twofold, placing pikas in a vice between two different selective pressures: at lower elevations, warming temperatures (hyperthermia) may be lethal, and at higher elevations, low oxygen levels (hypoxia) may be lethal. American pikas are already climbing higher in elevation in the US Great Basin at a rate of ~145 m per decade (Beever et al., 2011). Genetic research provides us with some hope, luckily – pikas may be able to flexibly alter how they express genes related to oxygen use, permitting them to occupy somewhat higher elevations (Solari et al., 2018).

Climate change is not purely its own force, but rather intersects with and amplifies all other ongoing threats to mammals in the specific local contexts where they live. Large mammals that migrate may need to alter their migration pathways in response to climate change. Caribou live at high latitudes in circumpolar regions of Europe, Siberia and North America, and play critical roles in the livelihoods of Indigenous peoples. The boreal caribou, a subspecies of caribou in Quebec, Canada, will have its migratory movements reduced due to climate change in a way that exacerbates existing fragmentation due to road construction. Positively, the removal of secondary roads inside protected areas could, however, offset these losses as a compensatory conservation action and benefit the subspecies (Bauduin et al., 2018). Climate change also influences the potential geographic ranges and activity periods of pathogens and their vectors. In Kazakhstan, the shocking death of >200,000 individual CR saiga (a type of antelope) over a three-week period in 2015 was due to an outbreak of haemorrhagic septicemia during a calving aggregation. This disease is caused by the bacterium *Pasteurella multocida*, which is normally endemic in saiga, but lethal levels were caused by abnormally high temperatures and humidity (Kock et al., 2018).

4.5 The Future of Mammals

If we do not act, the future of mammal communities will look very different from the recent past. Assuming all threatened mammals eventually go extinct, ~20–50% of all mammals will have been lost since 125,000 years ago, and the largest mammal on the planet in a few hundred years may very well be a domestic cow, representing the lowest average body mass for terrestrial mammals in 45 million years (Smith et al., 2018). But, with active management efforts that take into account the needs of both local communities and wild mammals, coupled with increasingly effective captive breeding strategies, there is hope for preserving many now-threatened species and even for discovering previously cryptic species with new genetic and monitoring tools.

4.5.1 There's More to Discover

Despite being among the most well studied of any taxa, many mammal species are insufficiently assessed by IUCN and therefore are 'Data Deficient', hindering our projections of conservation need (Figure 4.2). Spatial and taxonomic biases in international research agendas, often linked to funding priorities, means that many threatened species have not been assessed and may be lost before we can even appraise their status. Conversely, this also means that there may be species who are faring better than expected! While there is good research coverage of primate and carnivores – likely linked to their charismatic appearances and behaviours – small mammals such as shrews and rodents are poorly studied. For example, nearly 20% of the 2000 species of rodents, the 100 species of didelphimorphid marsupials and the 500 species of eulipotyphlans are Data Deficient (Figure 4.2). An entire Superorder, Xenarthra (Figure 4.4E), suffers from a lack of basic field-based natural history studies, and new genetic and morphological studies continue to expand the number of small-range endemic species.

4.5.2 Not Extinct Yet: Just in the Wild

IUCN currently lists two mammals as Extinct in the Wild (EW). While it is possible that these species will go extinct, they represent major opportunities for conservation innovation in developing tools for bringing species back from the brink. And it has been done before: through captive breeding of just 12 wild individuals, the Przewalski's horse, or takhi, moved from EW in the 1960s to being listed as EN today, with nearly 200 individuals spread across reintroduction sites in the Gobi steppe near the Mongolian–Chinese border.

The two currently EW species are both ungulates. The scimitar-horned oryx, an antelope adapted to arid areas that once ranged across North Africa, nearly disappeared by the 1990s. Today there are more than 15,000 individuals in captivity, many of which are thought to have resulted from a founder population of ~50 individuals from Chad (Woodfine and Gilbert, 2016). Studbook-managed breeding programmes and trial reintroductions into fenced areas in Morocco, Chad, Senegal and Tunisia are showing signs of success. The Père David's deer was formerly endemic to China and its survival shows just how much luck can be involved in dodging extinction. The species first became known to Western scientists in 1864, when the French missionary Père David encountered a small herd in the Nanyuan Royal Hunting Garden south of Beijing. Unfortunately, the remaining 20–30 individuals were eaten by soldiers during the 1900 Boxer Revolution – but (very!) luckily, several deer had been sent to Europe a few years prior, and the very last 18 deer in existence formed a breeding herd in England. Despite inbreeding, the population grew, and the first captive animals were sent to the Beijing Zoo in 1956, and there are now >2000 individuals in China across fenced areas of Beijing, Dafeng, Shishou and Yuanyang. This species was perhaps both imperilled but also saved by its cultural importance as a symbol of high status for people in China (Turvey et al., 2017b), with a history of management from the fifth century BCE that now stretches into the present day.

Even in cases where it seems like hope may be lost, new and improving assisted reproductive technologies may help species persist. The CR northern white rhino, a subspecies of white rhinoceros, is possibly extinct in the wild: the living population consists of two females, Najin and Fatu, at a private sanctuary in Kenya. While no living males persist, a sliver of hope of saving this subspecies can be found in technological advancements that transform northern white rhino cells into gametes that can be used in *in vitro* fertilisation with a southern white rhino surrogate (Tunstall et al., 2018).

4.5.3 Global Markets and Local Impacts

As we have seen, our increasingly connected world means that choices made at a supermarket or website on one side of the planet can affect mammal species on the other. This does not always have to be a negative transaction – rather, this should empower us to recognise the role we currently play in affecting local- and global-scale mammal conservation, and alter our behaviours if necessary by supporting conservation organisations, advocating for science-based government policies and most simply, modifying our day-to-day choices as consumers. While 40% of IUCN assessed species are impacted by habitat loss (Schipper et al., 2008), consumer decisions and technological advances in agriculture can blunt this trend through increasing crop yields, adjusting land zoning practices and implementing conservation-based agricultural trade (Tilman et al., 2017). Large carnivores are not only losing habitat directly to deforestation for livestock grazing, but they are also persecuted and, in some cases, actively culled, to protect livestock. Therefore, reducing meat consumption in the Global North represents a step that many individuals can take to benefit wild mammals and wild carnivores in particular. For example, Tilman et al. (2017) found that halving per capita meat consumption by 2060 would lead to significant conservation benefits for medium- and large-bodied mammals in the tropics, predominantly South America and Southeast Asia – the very places where mammals need conservation action the most.

4.5.4 Rewilding, Recovery and Resilience

Mammal conservation success happens when local communities are included in decision-making about the wildlife that they live alongside. This requires expanding the disciplines considered when implementing management strategies, and also changes what narratives we tell about mammal survival in a changing world. Indeed, carnivores are recovering in many places and there are many suitable reintroduction sites globally, from Mongolia, Canada and Thailand, to Namibia, Indonesia and Australia (Wolf and Ripple 2017). The return of carnivores in turn could help restore other components of ecosystems through their cascading ecological impacts across the food webs. Similarly, successful wildlife policies in Europe have led to 90% of the region having at least one native wild ungulate (Linnell et al., 2020), and the 'rewilding' of large herbivores is now seen as a major component of ecological restoration policy in Europe.

Ongoing human demographic trends means that more people now live in cities than anywhere else in the world, and such concentrated urbanisation may provide new conservation opportunities for mammals. Ageing human populations are resulting in countryside depopulation in places such as Europe and Japan, making space for the recovery of large mammals in unused agricultural lands (Tsunoda and Enari, 2020). Within urban areas, even the megacity of Los Angeles, California, supports a diverse carnivore guild that persists in the midst of millions of people. The iconic mountain lion named P-22 likely crossed two freeways to take up residence below the Hollywood sign in the city's famous Griffith Park, and despite likely predating a captive koala from the Los Angeles Zoo, P-22 remains beloved by many Angelinos, highlighting the central importance of human emotion and attitudes in conservation success.

While mammal diversity appears to be inexorably eroding, not all mammal stories are centred on loss. It is important to remember that of the nearly 6000 mammal species on Earth, more than half of the mammal species alive today are not considered to be threatened with extinction (3230 species are of Least Concern). And, since 1990, scientists have actually described more than 800 species of mammals, including large and charismatic species such as the olinguito, the Skywalker gibbon and the little black tapir (Burgin et al., 2018). Species once thought to be extirpated or extinct have reappeared following decades of absence, such as the short-tailed chinchilla in Bolivia, the silver-backed chevrotain in Vietnam and the Nelson's spiny pocket mouse in Mexico. Even the Machu Picchu arboreal tree rat virtually rose from the grave; known only from skulls in ancient Incan tombs for decades, it was unexpectedly photographed alive in 2014! From the humble beginnings of scurrying around dinosaurs' feet, mammals have come to dominate the planet's ecosystems, and their history of resilience prepares them (and by extension, us) for survival, even in the face of seemingly inescapable change.

Acknowledgements

I thank Sam Turvey for his constructive review of this chapter. Katie Solari, Angelo Soto-Centeno and Jeremy Hsu kindly provided permission to use their photos, and Nate Upham graciously shared his phylogeny. Kizmin Reeves (Tigers in America) and Ellie Armstrong generously shared photos and stories of captive white tigers. I drew heavily from species accounts found on the IUCN Red List website, and I thank the numerous authors working to assess and protect terrestrial mammals. I was supported as a postdoctoral research associate by the University of Oklahoma at the time of this writing. This chapter greatly benefitted from the diverse forms of knowledge shared with me over the years by colleagues and community members striving to protect some of the weirdest and most forgotten mammals on Earth. Long live the solenodons!

References

Ameca, E.I., Mace, G.M., Cowlishaw, G. and Pettorelli, N. (2019) Relative vulnerability to hurricane disturbance for endangered mammals in Mexico: a call for adaptation strategies under uncertainty. *Anim* 22(3): 262–273.

Amori, G. and Gippoliti, S. (2001) Identifying priority ecoregions for rodent conservation at the genus level. *Oryx* 35(2): 158–165.

Bauduin, S., McIntire, E., St-Laurent, M.H. and Cumming, S.G. (2018) Compensatory conservation measures for an endangered caribou population under climate change. *Sci Rep* 8(1): 1–10.

Beever, E.A., Ray, C., Wilkening, J.L., Brussard, P.F. and Mote, P.W. (2011) Contemporary climate change alters the pace and drivers of extinction. *Glob Change Biol* 17(6): 2054–2070.

Bermejo, M., Rodríguez-Teijeiro, J.D., Illera, G., et al. (2006) Ebola outbreak killed 5000 gorillas. *Science* 314(5805): 1564.

Brown, M.B., Bolger, D.T. and Fennessy, J. (2019) All the eggs in one basket: a countrywide assessment of current and historical giraffe population distribution in Uganda. *Glob Ecol Conserv* 19: e00612.

Burgin, C.J., Colella, J.P., Kahn, P.L. and Upham, N.S. (2018) How many mammal species are there? *J Mammal* 99: 1–14.

Cardillo, M., Mace, G.M., Jones, K.E., et al. (2005) Multiple causes of high extinction risk in large mammal species. *Science* 309(5738): 1239–1241.

Challender, D.W., Heinrich, S., Shepherd, C.R. and Katsis, L.K. (2020) International trade and trafficking in pangolins, 1900–2019. In: Challender, D., Nash, H. and Waterman, C. (Eds.), *Pangolins: Science, Society and Conservation*. Cambridge, MA: Academic Press.

Collins, A.C., Böhm, M. and Collen, B. (2020) Choice of baseline affects historical population trends in hunted mammals of North America. *Biol Conserv* 242: 108421.

Davidson, A.D., Shoemaker, K.T., Weinstein, B., et al. (2017) Geography of current and future global mammal extinction risk. *PloS One*, 12(11): e0186934.

Estrada, A., Garber, P.A., Mittermeier, R.A., et al. (2018) Primates in peril: the significance of Brazil, Madagascar, Indonesia and the Democratic Republic of the Congo for global primate conservation. *PeerJ* 6: e4869.

Hauenstein, S., Kshatriya, M., Blanc, J., Dormann, C.F. and Beale, C.M. (2019) African elephant poaching rates correlate with local poverty, national corruption and global ivory price. *Nat Commun* 10(1): 1–9.

Hofman, C.A. and Rick, T.C. (2018) Ancient biological invasions and island ecosystems: tracking translocations of wild plants and animals. *J Archaeol Res* 26(1): 65–115.

Hsu, J.L., Crawford, J.C., Tammone, M.N., et al. (2017) Genomic data reveal a loss of diversity in two species of tuco-tucos (genus *Ctenomys*) following a volcanic eruption. *Sci Rep*, 7(1): 1–14.

Hughes, A.C. (2017) Understanding the drivers of Southeast Asian biodiversity loss. *Ecosphere* 8(1): e01624.

Kock, R.A., Orynbayev, M., Robinson, S., et al. (2018) Saigas on the brink: Multidisciplinary analysis of the factors influencing mass mortality events. *Sci Adv* 4(1): eaao2314.

Linnell, J.D., Cretois, B., Nilsen, E.B., et al. (2020) The challenges and opportunities of coexisting with wild ungulates in the human-dominated landscapes of Europe's Anthropocene. *Biol Conserv* 244: 108500.

Louys, J. (2012) The future of mammals in Southeast Asia: conservation insights from the fossil record. In: Louys, J. (Ed.), *Paleontology in Ecology and Conservation*. Berlin and Heidelberg: Springer.

Marino, J., Sillero-Zubiri, C., Deressa, A., et al. (2017) Rabies and distemper outbreaks in smallest Ethiopian wolf population. *Emerg Infect Dis* 23(12): 2102.

Morens, D.M., Holmes, E.C., Davis, A.S. and Taubenberger, J.K. (2011) Global rinderpest eradication: lessons learned and why humans should celebrate too. *J Infect Dis* 204(4): 502–505.

Ngama, S., Korte, L., Bindelle, J., Vermeulen, C. and Poulsen, J.R. (2016) How bees deter elephants: beehive trials with forest elephants (*Loxodonta africana cyclotis*) in Gabon. *PLoS One* 11(5): e0155690.

Nijman, V., Nekaris, K.A.I., Donati, G., Bruford, M. and Fa, J. (2011) Primate conservation: measuring and mitigating trade in primates. *Endanger Species Res* 13(2): 159–161.

Nyhus, P.J., Tilson, R. and Hutchins, M. (2010) Thirteen thousand and counting: how growing captive tiger populations threaten wild tigers. In: Tilson, R. and Nyhus, P.J. (Eds.), *Tigers of the World*. Cambridge, MA: Academic Press.

Pacifici, M., Visconti, P., Butchart, S.H., et al. (2017) Species' traits influenced their response to recent climate change. *Nat Clim Change* 7(3): 205–208.

Penteriani, V., del Mar Delgado, M., Pinchera, F., et al. (2016) Human behaviour can trigger large carnivore attacks in developed countries. *Sci Rep* 6: 20552.

Ripple, W.J., Chapron, G., López-Bao, J.V., et al. (2016) Saving the world's terrestrial megafauna. *Bioscience* 66(10): 807–812.

Rutovskaya, M.V., Onufrenya, M.V. and Onufrenya, A.S. (2017) Russian desman (*Desmana moschata*: Talpidae) at the edge of disappearance. *Nat Conserv Res* 2(1): 100–112.

Salkeld, D.J. (2017) Vaccines for conservation: plague, prairie dogs and black-footed ferrets as a case study. *EcoHealth* 14(3): 432–437.

Scanlon, A.T., Petit, S., Tuiwawa, M. and Naikatini, A. (2018) Response of primary and secondary rainforest flowers and fruits to a cyclone, and implications for plant-servicing bats. *Glob Change Biol* 24(8): 3820–3836.

Schipper, J., Chanson, J. S., Chiozza, F., et al. (2008) The status of the world's land and marine mammals: diversity, threat, and knowledge. *Science* 322(5899): 225–230.

Schloss, C.A., Nuñez, T.A. and Lawler, J.J. (2012) Dispersal will limit ability of mammals to track climate change in the Western Hemisphere. *Proc Natl Acad Sci USA* 109(22): 8606–8611.

Schneeberger, K. and Voigt, C.C. (2016) Zoonotic viruses and conservation of bats. In Voigt, C.C. and Kingston, T. (Eds.), *Bats in the Anthropocene: Conservation of Bats in a Changing World*. New York: Springer Cham.

Smith, F.A., Smith, R.E.E., Lyons, S.K. and Payne, J.L. (2018) Body size downgrading of mammals over the late Quaternary. *Science* 360(6386): 310–313.

Solari, K.A., Ramakrishnan, U. and Hadly, E.A. (2018) Gene expression is implicated in the ability of pikas to occupy Himalayan elevational gradient. *Plos One* 13(12): e0207936.

Tilman, D., Clark, M., Williams, D.R., et al. (2017) Future threats to biodiversity and pathways to their prevention. *Nature* 546(7656): 73–81.

Tsunoda, H. and Enari, H. (2020) A strategy for wildlife management in depopulating rural areas of Japan. *Conserv Biol* 34(4): 819–828.

Tunstall, T., Kock, R., Vahala, J., et al. (2018) Evaluating recovery potential of the northern white rhinoceros from cryopreserved somatic cells. *Genome Res* 28(6): 780–788.

Turvey, S.T. and Fritz, S.A. (2011) The ghosts of mammals past: biological and geographical patterns of global mammalian extinction across the Holocene. *Phil Trans Royal Soc B* 366(1577): 2564–2576.

Turvey, S.T., Kennerley, R.J., Nuñez-Miño, J.M. and Young, R.P. (2017a) The last survivors: current status and conservation of the non-volant land mammals of the insular Caribbean. *J Mammal* 98 (4): 918–936.

Turvey, S.T., Barnes, I., Marr, M. and Brace, S. (2017b) Imperial trophy or island relict? A new extinction paradigm for Père David's deer: a Chinese conservation icon. *Royal Soc Open Sci* 4(10): 171096.

Upham, N.S., Esselstyn, J.A. and Jetz, W. (2019) Inferring the mammal tree: Species-level sets of phylogenies for questions in ecology, evolution, and conservation. *PLoS Biol* 17(12): e3000494.

Valente, L., Etienne, R.S. and Dávalos, L.M. (2017) Recent extinctions disturb path to equilibrium diversity in Caribbean bats. *Nat Ecol Evol* 1(2): 1–7.

Voigt, M., Wich, S.A., Ancrenaz, M., et al. (2018) Global demand for natural resources eliminated more than 100,000 Bornean orangutans. *Curr Biol* 28(5): 761–769.

Waller, N.L., Gynther, I.C., Freeman, A.B., Lavery, T.H. and Leung, L.K.P. (2017) The Bramble Cay melomys *Melomys rubicola* (Rodentia: Muridae): a first mammalian extinction caused by human-induced climate change? *Wildlife Res*, 44(1): 9–21.

Wilting, A., Cord, A., Hearn, A.J., et al. (2010) Modelling the species distribution of flat-headed cats (*Prionailurus planiceps*), an endangered South-East Asian small felid. *PloS One* 5(3): e9612.

Woinarski, J.C., Burbidge, A.A. and Harrison, P.L. (2015) Ongoing unraveling of a continental fauna: decline and extinction of Australian mammals since European settlement. *Proc Natl Acad Sci USA* 112(15): 4531–4540.

Wolf, C. and Ripple, W.J. (2017) Range contractions of the world's large carnivores. *Royal Soc Open Sci* 4(7): 170052.

Woodfine, T. and Gilbert, T. (2016) The fall and rise of the scimitar-horned oryx: a case study of ex-situ conservation and reintroduction in practice. In: Bro-Jorgensen, J. and Mallon, D.P. (Eds.), *Antelope Conservation: From Diagnosis to Action.* Hoboken, NJ: Wiley-Blackwell.

Wyatt, K.B., Campos, P.F., Gilbert, M.T.P., et al. (2008) Historical mammal extinction on Christmas Island (Indian Ocean) correlates with introduced infectious disease. *PloS One* 3(11): e3602.

FIVE

Marine Mammals: Exploited for Millennia, But Still Holding On

ALEXIS M. MYCHAJLIW AND THOMAS A. JEFFERSON

Summary

Marine mammals are a diverse collection of about 137 mammals that have returned, in varying degrees, to life in the water. This group includes cetaceans (whales, dolphins and porpoises), pinnipeds (seals and sea lions), sirenians (sea cows) and a few species of otters and bears.

- *Extinctions have occurred* within this group, and marine mammals are particularly vulnerable to human activities, due to their long life spans and limited reproductive potential.
- *Marine mammals are now recognised as important* in shaping their environment and in providing certain ecosystem services that benefit other species, including our own.
- *Threats to marine mammals are varied*, but the most serious ones include hunting, fisheries interactions, vessel collisions, pollution and various forms of behavioural disturbance, with captivity and live captures affecting only some species.
- *Anthropogenic climate change has become a serious concern* for marine mammal conservation. Deleterious effects on coastal species, especially those that live in high-latitude areas, have already become apparent.
- *The future for marine mammals is not looking particularly bright* at the moment. However, there is still time for us to change, and to take better care of these fascinating and ecologically important animals.

5.1 Introduction

What is a marine mammal? Despite what you might think, the answer is not so simple. Clearly, a marine mammal is one associated with the sea, but humans spend a lot of time at sea and we are never considered marine mammals. Some river dolphins never contact salt water, but they still are considered marine mammals (spoiler alert – it is due to their marine ancestry). So, how do we define this important and charismatic group of animals?

Marine mammals do not constitute a specific evolutionary group or clade, but rather are species hailing from several placental mammal groups that have evolved distinct adaptations for aquatic life (such as hair loss, blubber development, nostril migration, hindlimb reduction/loss and respiratory/circulatory adaptations for thermoregulation, diving and breath holding) (Berta et al., 2015). Of utmost importance is where they feed (Berta et al., 2015; Jefferson et al., 2015). Marine mammals get all or virtually all of their food from marine (or in a few cases, freshwater) habitats. While marine mammals exhibit the characteristics that define a mammal, including the presence of hair (Berta et al., 2015), these qualities can be obscured by morphological convergence with other marine organisms for life in the water, such as their streamlined body shape. Terrestrial mammals have evolved a diversity of routes towards marine life over geologic time, and some of these evolutionary 'experiments' went extinct long ago. For instance, 20 million years ago, bears in the extinct genus *Kolponomos* evolved specialised dentition to consume molluscs, acting ecologically like a sea otter, but morphologically like a saber-tooth cat! Nearly 8 million years ago, a marine giant ground sloth, *Thalassocnus*, swam along the Pacific coast of South America in search of seagrasses. We briefly describe the three main groups of extant marine mammals (cetaceans, sirenians and marine carnivores) in the paragraphs below.

5.1.1 Cetaceans

Cetaceans are the whales, dolphins and porpoises (Berta et al., 2015). Well over half of the extant marine mammal species (93 of 132) are cetaceans, and this group of marine mammals is most thoroughly adapted to life in seas and oceans (with ranges into the open ocean and deep-diving capabilities). The evolutionary history of cetaceans extends back more than 55 million years, so they are an ancient marine mammal lineage (Berta et al., 2015). All cetaceans live their entire lives and pursue all of their major life functions in water. They have broad paddle-like tail flukes for swimming, are largely free of fur and have lost their external hind limbs, meaning they cannot move efficiently on land. Their nostrils migrated to the tops of their heads and are now known as blowholes (baleen whales have two, but toothed whales only have one). Cetaceans are now known to be part of the order Cetartiodactyla (even-toed hoofed mammals such as deer, cattle, camels, llamas and pigs). Their closest living relatives are hippos, something not realised until quite recently, just 20–30 years ago (Berta et al., 2015).

5.1.2 Sirenians

Sirenians (dugongs, manatees and sea cows) are the only marine mammals that are primarily herbivores. There are only four living species. They are nearly as completely adapted to aquatic living as the cetaceans, having lost all traces of their hindlimbs and greatly reducing their body hair. All life functions occur in the water, but sirenians are all found in shallow nearshore waters, and are probably unable to survive long in deep ocean habitats. As Afrotherians, sirenians are most closely related to African mammals like elephants and hyraxes (Berta et al., 2015). Their evolutionary history dates back more than 50 million years, making them another very ancient lineage.

5.1.3 Pinnipeds

Pinnipeds – the 35 recent species of seals, sea lions and walruses – are a very specialised group of mammalian carnivores (order Carnivora) that are highly adapted to living in water, but still have links to land for some life functions (primarily moulting and reproduction, giving birth and mating on solid substrates). All pinnipeds have dense fur and both fore- and hindlimbs. They can all move on land, though some more efficiently than others. The skeletons of pinnipeds are much less modified than those of cetaceans or sirenians. Pinnipeds have a much shorter evolutionary history than the other two major marine mammal groups, only extending back approximately 27 million years (Berta et al., 2015). As we currently understand it, the two main types of pinnipeds (true or earless seals, and eared seals) have a monophyletic origin (i.e. all species share a common ancestor), dating back to a bear-like ancestor.

5.1.4 Other Carnivores

There are a few other species of mammals that are classified among terrestrial mammal groups but have nonetheless strongly adapted to lives at sea (Berta et al., 2015). These four 'oddball' marine mammals include the polar bear (*Ursus maritimus*), sea otter (*Enhydra lutris*), marine otter (*Lontra felina*) and the recently extinct sea mink. All have body forms that are not so different from their land-living relatives, with a coat of fur, well-developed hindlimbs and largely unmodified skulls. With the possible exception of the sea otter, they are all dependent on land to some extent. Their evolutionary history is quite recent, not extending back more than a couple of million years. The polar bear is closely related to the grizzly bear, and with a changing climate, these two species are increasingly coming into contact and creating hybrids known as 'pizzlies'. Sea and marine otters are most closely related to the river and freshwater otters and other species, such as weasels and minks.

5.1.5 Others

A few other mammals may rely on some marine resources seasonally (e.g. Arctic foxes, wolves, brown bears that eat salmon and forage on whale carcasses, etc.). A number of living species of bats feed in marine environments and could thus potentially be considered marine mammals. However, these species are not traditionally considered to be marine mammals and are thus outside the scope of this chapter.

5.2 Going, Going, Gone

Figure 5.1 summarises the current conservation status of marine mammals, as assessed by IUCN (see also Box 5.1). Below we detail the stories of some recently extinct species.

The sea mink (*Neovison macrodon*, Figure 5.2A) was a mustelid (weasel-like carnivore) closely related to the still-extant and widespread American mink (Prentiss, 1903). It was distinguished from other minks by its reddish coarse fur, supposedly fishy smell and large body size, and was found along the coastline and many small islands of the Gulf of Maine, North America. Sea mink bones are abundant in archaeological sites and have clear evidence of cutmarks, indicating millennial-scale relationships with Indigenous peoples. They declined

Box 5.1
IUCN Listed Marine Mammals

Out of roughly 137 marine mammals assessed by the International Union for the Conservation of Nature (the actual number varies, as taxonomic changes are made) (Figure 5.1), four marine mammals have been long been recognised as having gone extinct since 1500 AD: the sea mink (*Neovison macrodon*, a mustelid) (Figure 5.2A), Steller's sea cow (*Hydrodamalis gigas*, a sirenian) (Figure 5.2B), and two pinnipeds, the Caribbean monk seal (*Monachus tropicalis*) (Figure 5.2C) and the Japanese sea lion (*Zalophus japonicus*). The disappearance of most of these species has been linked to overharvest and exploitation for fur, blubber and meat. Unfortunately, a fifth species has likely joined this list in recent years: the baiji or Yangtze River dolphin (*Lipotes vexillifer*) (Figure 5.3A). Perhaps surprisingly, given the popularity of many marine mammals in the public eye, nearly 20% of species are considered Data Deficient and cannot be accurately categorised. As a group, most marine mammals (nearly 50%, 62 species) are Least Concern. There are currently four species listed as Critically Endangered – all cetaceans – including the North Atlantic right whale (*Eubalaena glacialis*), vaquita (*Phocoena sinus*), the Atlantic humpback dolphin (*Sousa teuszii*) and the Baiji (*Lipotes vexillifer*). Marine mammals from the order Carnivora have been hit the hardest: of the four species listed, one is Extinct (the sea mink), two are Endangered (sea otter, *Enhydra lutris*, marine otter, *Lontra felina*) and the

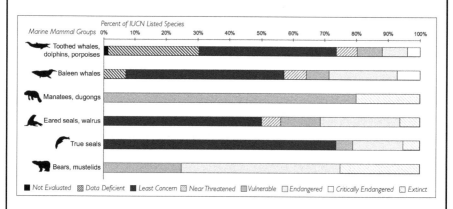

Figure 5.1 The conservation status of marine mammals, based on current IUCN species assessments. Animal silhouettes courtesy of PhyloPic with specific acknowledgement of PhyloPic users Craig Dylke, Steven Traver, 'An Ignorant Atheist', Margot Michaud and Tracy Heath.

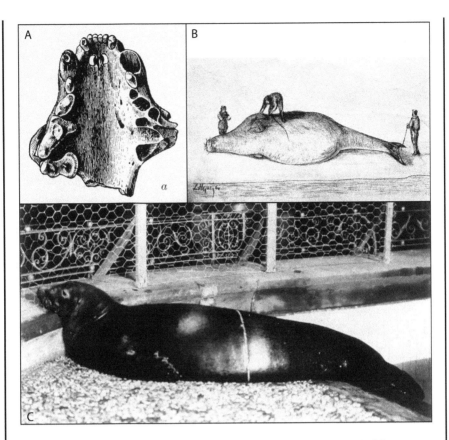

Figure 5.2 Marine mammals that went extinct in historical times: (A) skull of the type specimen of the sea mink (Prentiss, 1903), public domain, (B) reconstruction of men measuring a Steller's sea cow on Bering Island, from Stejneger, Steller's Journal of the Sea Voyage from Kamchatka to America, public domain, (C) a captive Caribbean monk seal held at the New York Aquarium, 1910, New York Zoological Society Bulletin, public domain.

remaining species, the polar bear, *Ursus maritimus*, is Vulnerable. Lamentably, some species that are listed as Critically Endangered may already be extinct, such as the case of the baiji. Those listed as Endangered will continue to decline unless action is taken, particularly in the face of rapid global climate change, underscoring the need for international cooperation and collaboration.

Figure 5.3 Historically decimated marine mammals: (A) QiQi, the last known member of a species now thought to be extinct, the baiji (W. Ding), (B) a humpback whale, a species that has recovered dramatically from past decimation (M. Cucuzza), (C) sea otters, once thought to be extinct, but now considered relatively safe (T. Jefferson), (D) an aggregation of harbour seals, a species that was depleted, but was never in danger of extinction (M. Cucuzza), (E) whale meat on sale at Tsukiji Fish Market in Tokyo, Japan, 2019 (A. Mychajliw).

rapidly following European and later American fur harvesting practices. By the time it was formally described as a species in 1903, the sea mink was likely already extinct. Unfortunately, despite this massive pelt harvest, no skins were ever deposited in scientific museum collections.

Steller's sea cow (*Hydrodamalis gigas*, Figure 5.2B) was a sirenian related to dugongs and manatees. It may have grown larger than 5 tons and measured up to 7.5 metres long, making it a prime target for human hunters, who exploited it for its blubber and meat. Up until its extinction it was restricted to the Commander Islands between Alaska and Russia, but fossils show it had a much wider range across the Late Pleistocene. It was a dietary specialist and relied almost exclusively on kelp for subsistence, which may have made it sensitive to environmental change. It was apparently found in large social groups and exhibited high levels of parental care. The sea cow had a particularly disturbing story, as it vanished just a few short years after its scientific discovery in 1741 by George W. Steller and his shipwrecked party. Today, we know more about this animal from its fossilised remains than from direct scientific observations, and sea cow bones have been sold as 'mermaid ivory' on the international market.

The Caribbean monk seal (*Neomonachus tropicalis*, Figure 5.2C) lived in the warm waters of the Caribbean Sea and Gulf of Mexico and was last sighted in 1952 near Jamaica. This species was mentioned in the log of Christopher Columbus: his men killed a group of them on their second voyage to the Caribbean, initiating a pattern of overharvest that would eventually lead to extinction, as officially declared in 2008 by the National Marine Fisheries Service. Their hauling out behaviour, in which they congregated in massive groups on coastlines, made them extremely vulnerable to exploitation. While several individuals had been captured and exhibited in North American zoos and aquaria, no successful breeding programme for conservation was initiated.

The baiji, or Yangtze River dolphin (*Lipotes vexillifer*, Figure 5.3A) is currently listed as Critically Endangered by IUCN, though unfortunately this species is almost certainly extinct. An intensive 6-week survey in 2006 across the species' entire historical range did not detect any evidence of survival, making the captive male Qi Qi (淇淇) the last (likely) recorded baiji upon his death in 2002. The baiji faced threats common to many freshwater cetaceans globally, including pollution, boat collisions and mortality due to fisheries bycatch. In particular, the use of rolling hooks, gillnets and electrofishing techniques decimated baiji populations through incidental mortality, rather than directed persecution of the species. Given the massive ecological degradation of the Yangtze today, hope for rediscovering straggling survivors is nearly non-existent. As the only species in the family Lipotidae, the extinction of this species represents the loss of 20 million years of evolutionary history (Turvey, 2008).

5.3 Shifting Baselines of Marine Mammal Conservation

In comparison with terrestrial mammals, which experienced massive size-biased extinctions in the Late Pleistocene (Chapter 4), marine mammals have persisted with a relatively low number of species extinctions. Humans have been using marine resources for thousands of years, and the industrialisation of fishing and whaling is relatively recent. Yet commercial activities have already left a significant mark on the abundance and geographic range of many species globally, and continued commercial harvest with increasingly sophisticated technology may lead to further species extinctions (McCauley et al., 2015). For example, pre-modern whaling harvests focused on species with coastal affinities that would have been easier to reach and collect, including humpback (*Megaptera novaeangliae*) (Figure 5.3B), grey (*Eschrichtius robustus*), bowhead (*Balaena mysticetus*) and right whales (*Eubalaena* spp.), but technological advances led to exploitation of more oceanic and fast-moving species.

Understanding how humans have shaped past marine mammal populations – and in turn how marine mammals have shaped human cultures – helps us reframe conservation goals and permits us to see marine mammals as part of coupled human–natural systems, emphasising that sustainable co-existence is possible. The syndrome of 'shifting baselines' is commonly discussed in fisheries management, wherein the limits of human memory lead us to forget the true natural range or abundance for a given species, because we only remember the reference point within our lifetime – the biggest fish on record today may have been one of the smaller ones in the past. Similarly, recognising these hidden marine mammal extirpations may help us better interpret the novelty of behaviour, range and/or ecology in recovering populations (Silliman et al., 2018). For example, today's sea otter (Figure 5.3C) populations are unexpectedly using inland estuaries and salt marshes as primary habitat, but data from pre-extirpation time periods suggests this was a normal dimension of their ecology in the past (Silliman et al., 2018).

Archaeological data can help us understand and contextualise historical trends, reveal unexpected opportunities and in many cases, sharpen trajectories of decline. New bio-molecular techniques are allowing us to identify marine mammal remains harvested hundreds to thousands of years ago. Ancient DNA extracted from whale bones found in archaeological sites revealed that Pacific grey whale populations were possibly three to five times larger in the past, speaking to the carrying capacity of the region for further whale recovery (Alter et al., 2012). While we know that grey whales were extirpated historically from the North Atlantic Ocean due to commercial whaling, specimens from Roman archaeological sites in the Strait of Gibraltar demonstrate that right and grey whales used the Mediterranean Sea as a calving area ~2000 years ago, and may have been a part of a 'forgotten whaling industry' of the Roman Empire (Rodrigues et al., 2018). This extends the historic range of right and grey whales geographically, accentuating just how substantially their ranges have contracted due to human activities today.

The exploitation of pinnipeds by Indigenous groups has a longer and more well-documented history, particularly because their aggregation and hauling out behaviour makes them easier to harvest on coastlines (Figure 5.3D). Different pinniped species have different histories and relationships with humans, and in turn different histories of genetic bottlenecks and extirpations (Stoffel et al., 2018). Northern elephant seals (*Mirounga angustirostris*) were heavily persecuted historically, but have since recovered; their presence in ~12,000 year old archaeological sites on the California Channel Islands suggests that perhaps human activities thousands of years ago precipitated the initial decline (Hofman et al., 2018). Conversely, South American fur seals (*Arctocephalus australis*) and sea lions (*Otaria flavescens*) have been exploited in South America for over 7000 years, yet did not show population declines until the advent of European/American harvest practices (Nye et al., 2018). As Indigenous peoples have interacted with marine mammals for millennia, these species have an enduring cultural importance that must be recognised and respected. Marine mammal conservation today can be enhanced by recognising these long ties and including Indigenous groups as valued partners in management.

5.4 The Ecological Importance of Protecting Marine Mammals

On land, large-bodied mammals exert important effects on the environments around them, acting as engineers to reshape landscapes and providing important ecological services. Marine megafaunal mammals are similarly vital components of ecosystems. However, the true extent of their ecological impacts may be difficult to discern from a present-day vantage point, given that today's whale populations represent anywhere from 30% to just 1% of their former abundance, and may even be considered 'functionally extinct' (Doughty et al., 2016). Further, the cryptic habits of many species mean that we are just beginning to study them as sufficiently sophisticated technologies become available.

While once being valued for only what raw materials they supplied after death, these species are now valued for ecosystem services they provision in life: they influence the dynamics of marine ecosystems by operating as consumers, by themselves being prey for other animals and through acting as vectors to move nutrients vertically and across latitudes (Roman and McCarthy, 2010), and when they die, they become detritus and nourish organisms at the ocean floor. Aside from these ecological roles, they provide aesthetic, cultural, religious and socioeconomic benefits to human communities globally.

Among marine mammals, perhaps the largest ecological effects are generated by great whales (baleen whales and sperm whales). Ocean waters are stratified by density and nutrient content; when whales dive to feed, their mechanical energy literally stirs these different layers together and supports productivity by bringing nutrients from feeding areas at deeper depths (below the thermocline) up closer to the surface (photic zone) (Roman and McCarthy, 2010). Whale faecal plumes can have an iron concentration at least 10 million times greater than ambient levels (Nicol et al., 2010). Because krill rely on nutrients such as iron to grow, and whales excrete nutrients in their faeces, the loss of whales may also cause krill population decreases due to lack of nutrient fertilisation, creating a negative feedback cycle in which fewer whales means less krill to feed whales as they recover. Thus, healthy whale populations may translate to healthy fisheries. In ecosystem models, decreases in whale abundance lead to decreases in fish stocks (Morissette et al., 2012), and empirically, blue whales (*Balaenoptera musculus*) in the Southern Ocean promote increased fishery yields through their faecal nutrients (Lavery et al., 2014). Whales are also living carbon banks, and when they die, they take this carbon (an estimated ~190,000 tons of carbon per year) down to the bottom of the ocean (Pershing et al., 2010). Therefore, as whale populations (hopefully) continue to recover, they may actually help us address global climate change.

Through food webs, the loss of marine mammals can have cascading ecological impacts and conservation dilemmas. Juvenile baleen whales are prey for other marine megafauna, such as killer whales (*Orcinus orca*) and great white sharks, and the loss of baleen whales likely had impacts on the animals that relied on them for prey. In the North Pacific Ocean, killer whales likely switched to feed on smaller marine mammals such as harbour seals (*Phoca vitulina*), sea otters and Steller sea lions (*Eumetopias jubatus*), in turn decreasing the abundance of these populations (Springer et al., 2008).

Sea otters (Figure 5.3C) are a classic example of a keystone species, whose removal leads to trophic cascades, as urchin populations increase and graze uncontrolled on kelp forests. Some have speculated that the role of sea otters in shaping kelp abundance was so important that the historic overharvest of sea otters may have indirectly contributed to the decline of the now-extinct Steller's sea cow (Estes et al., 2016). While the consumption of shellfish by sea otters has led to conflict with fishermen, ecological models show that sea otters actually increase the total ecosystem biomass where they live by nearly 40%, providing a diverse range of economically valuable services that exceed the monetary losses of invertebrate fisheries (Gregr et al., 2020).

Clearly, marine mammals play important ecological roles and their conservation yields numerous benefits to the environment and human societies. These ecological functions can be recognised in conservation planning and prioritisation by considering functional traits. The FUSE (functionally unique, specialised and endangered) metric combines functional uniqueness and specialisation with IUCN extinction status (Pimiento et al., 2020). The dugong (*Dugong dugon*) and sea otter have among the five highest FUSE scores of all marine megafauna (not just mammals). When considering all marine megafauna, marine mammals contain the largest global ecological trait space, despite being less speciose than bony fish, reflecting their incredible range of adaptations and use of near-shore resources (Pimiento et al., 2020). This highlights the relevance of marine mammal conservation to preserving the overall ecological and evolutionary diversity of our planet's oceans.

5.5 Governance of Marine Mammals

Most countries have legislation that protects, or at least attempts to regulate, potential negative impacts on marine mammals (Reeves 2017a). In the United States, marine mammals (and sea turtles) are known as 'protected species', due to the strong legislative protection they receive from the federal government. The Marine Mammal Protection Act of 1972, Endangered Species Act of 1973 and several other laws provide stringent protection for these animals, which are considered 'special' by most Americans. Similar laws exist in many other countries, such as Canada, the United Kingdom, Australia and New Zealand.

However, most marine mammal species freely move across boundaries between countries, thus requiring effective transnational conservation measures. There are real difficulties with international management of marine mammals, as goals and agendas often conflict, and jurisdictions are not always clear. Nonetheless, some international bodies have been established specifically to protect marine mammals, though some have done so more effectively than others. The International Whaling Commission (IWC, officially created in 1946) has a long and complicated history of trying to 'protect' large cetaceans and to a lesser extent, small cetaceans. It started out as a 'whaler's club' with its major goal being to maximise whale catches while still preventing the loss of its major source of income – large-scale commercial whaling operations. It has changed over the years, and now has a more conservation-focused orientation, though problems and conflicts still persist (Wright et al., 2016).

There are many other international bodies and treaties that regulate marine mammal impacts, such as the Convention on Trade in Endangered Species (CITES), International Union for the Conservation of Nature (IUCN), Convention on the Conservation of Migratory Species (CMS), North Atlantic Marine Mammal Commission (NAMMCO), Inter-American Tropical Tuna Commission (IATTC) and High North Alliance, to name just a few (Reeves, 2017a). Indigenous peoples often have their own regulatory bodies that set quotas for hunts, conduct monitoring and management, and collaborate in research.

Marine protected areas (MPAs) are another very important element of providing protection measures for marine mammal species (Hoyt, 2011). Some MPAs are very small, just a few tens of hectares, but others are extremely large, covering huge areas of the high seas. Sometimes they even match large sections of an entire ocean basin, such as the Indian Ocean Sanctuary, which prohibits commercial whaling in virtually the entire Indian Ocean.

5.6 Ongoing Threats to Survival

5.6.1 Hunting and Harvest

Without a doubt, in past centuries (i.e. before the mid-twentieth century), direct killing of marine mammals was the most serious threat these animals faced (Reeves, 2017b). Commercial whaling and sealing operations have been ongoing for many centuries, and in the 1800s and early 1900s, these activities brought many species of whales, seals and sea lions to drastically reduced population levels and even in some cases, near extinction. Other marine mammals in which hunting reduced populations to very low levels involved the sea otter, and several species of manatees. Fortunately, today hunting is generally much reduced, and usually regulated to be sustainable, but there are still concerns about its impact on some species of sirenians and cetaceans (Figure 5.3E). The impacts of overfishing on prey (see below), also lead to potential conflicts with humans over fisheries and the pressure to cull some marine mammal populations. This generally involves pinnipeds or some species of small cetaceans and can be exacerbated by tensions associated with species reintroductions and recoveries.

5.6.2 Fisheries Interactions

Fisheries can impact marine mammal populations primarily in one of two ways. First, fisheries can affect the environment and reduce potential prey resources for marine mammals (ecological or biological impacts). Second, marine mammals can get caught in fishing nets, lines and other gear, and then become injured, or worse yet, die (operational impacts). Both of these types of impacts are usually negative, though the major problem that many species of marine mammal populations have with fisheries is related to the second issue – entanglement or entrapment. This is a particularly severe problem for many species of small cetaceans – dolphins and porpoises, and also a few species of large whales. Indeed, it is believed that more marine mammals today die from gear entanglement or entrapment than from any other source. In some cases, like North Atlantic right whales (*Eubalaena glacialis*), Hector's dolphins (*Cephalorhynchus hectori*) and finless porpoises (*Neophocaena* spp.), it may be so serious as to endanger an entire population or subspecies with extinction (Brownell et al., 2019). And in the most serious case of all, the vaquita (*Phocoena sinus*) (Figure 5.4A), Mexico's endemic little porpoise, entanglement in nets is the sole reason for the entire species being driven to the very brink of extinction (Bessesen, 2018). The vaquita, as of 2022, may not last even another year (Figure 5.4B).

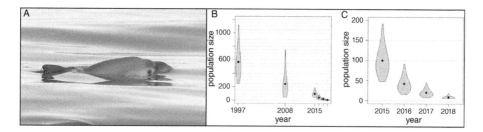

Figure 5.4 Without swift intervention, Mexico's endemic porpoise, the vaquita, may be the next marine mammal to go extinct. (A) A vaquita surfaces in the calm waters of the northern Gulf of California (T. Jefferson). (B) Decreasing trends of the vaquita population since 1997. (C) Close up of vaquita population trends, 2015–2018 (B and C from Jaramillo-Legorreta et al., 2019).

5.6.3 Vessel Collisions

Many types of boats and ships ply the world's seas, coastlines and rivers. While collisions with vessels undoubtedly occur for many marine mammal species, they generally do not occur frequently enough to be considered a highly significant form of morbidity and mortality on a population level (Schoeman et al., 2020). Examples of exceptions, where impacts are significant on a population level, are with some large rorqual whales (e.g. blue, fin and humpback whales) off Hawaii and California, North Atlantic right whales off the US and Canadian eastern seaboard (see Kraus and Rolland, 2007), finless porpoises in the Yangtze River of China and West Indian manatees (*Trichechus manatus*) in Florida. Large ocean-going cargo vessels and tankers, high-speed ferries and small outboard motor boats appear to be the worst offenders.

5.6.4 Behavioural Disturbance

Behavioural disturbance and stress, especially that caused by underwater noise, has become a very serious issue for many marine mammals in recent decades (Southall, 2017). Although disturbance by human activities can be problematic for any marine mammal species, this is most significant for cetaceans. All cetaceans use sound as a primary means of communication and navigation, and the odontocetes (toothed whales and dolphins) additionally use sound to sense their surroundings, navigate, find prey and avoid predators. They do this through echolocation or sonar, which is the active production of sound and reception of echoes that then provide information on the environment. This is something of a sixth sense for these animals. Human activities that create noise in the marine environment (such as naval sonars, shipping noise, marine construction activities, etc.) can cause disturbance, lessen communication ranges and even mask important echolocation or communication sounds. The issue of antisubmarine sonar used by the world's navies has also become a major conservation concern for deep-diving toothed cetaceans in the past 20 years or so (Popper and Hawkins, 2016).

5.6.5 Pollution and Environmental Toxins

Contamination and pollution can be loosely defined to include noise pollution (covered above) and marine debris, but generally when we talk about this issue in relation to marine mammals we are thinking of chemical contamination of the water, air, bottom sediments, and prey species that marine mammals feed on (Reijnders et al., 2017). There are many classes of chemicals that are harmful to marine mammals, some broad examples being oil/petrochemicals, DDTs and other pesticides, industrial chemicals like PCBs and butyltins, and various sorts of heavy/trace metals. The chemicals themselves may be toxic to the animals, or may give off substances that are, or they may simply work by reducing the immune responses of the animals that ingest them, and thereby increasing the likelihood of the subject dying from parasites, injuries or diseases that might not otherwise have been so detrimental.

5.6.6 Live Captures and Captivity

While some who have viewed dolphins and killer whales performing at Sea World, or other marine parks, may not consider captivity to be a threat to marine mammals, the truth is that in many cases it can be (Corkeron, 2017). Attempts at live capture may result in high levels of mortality and heavy disturbance/harassment of wild populations (especially so in the past). Additionally, not all marine mammal live capture operations have been tightly monitored or controlled, and when sometimes-greedy organisations remove marine mammals from their natural habitat and take them to oceanariums, research laboratories, military facilities or even personal 'zoos', the effect can be just the same as going out and killing the animals. Once removed from the wild population, these animals are effectively 'dead' in terms of contributing to natural stocks.

One case in which live captures can actually be a part of a valuable conservation strategy is that in which animals are removed from nature for protection and/or captive propagation, with the intention of conserving genetic diversity, breeding them in captivity and eventually restocking wild populations. This has been tried recently with several endangered dolphin and porpoise species, and while it has shown much promise for some pinniped and otter species, it has yet to be done successfully for any cetacean species.

5.7 The Synergistic Context of Global Climate Change

Due to human activities, global mean surface temperatures are now more than 1.0 °C above our pre-industrial reference point (Hoegh-Guldberg et al., 2019). Climate change can directly impact marine mammal species through changes in habitat and resource availability. But, perhaps, more insidiously, climate change also synergistically intersects with all other ongoing threats to marine mammal survival, exacerbating them and making their outcomes increasingly difficult to predict (Burek et al., 2008). While marine mammals have resiliently responded to natural climate change in the geologic past, today's anthropogenic climate change is unfolding so quickly and so widely that evolutionary responses are likely insufficient to cope. For example, Southern elephant seals (*Mirounga leonina*) responded to the climate-linked availability of new breeding habitat ~7000 years ago by expanding their populations, in turn forming a genetically diverse new breeding colony (de Bruyn et al., 2009). While this shows that marine mammals can respond to climate change, such responses are complicated by both the sheer speed of temperature rise today and the need to navigate new anthropogenic obstacles when shifting ranges, such as shipping routes. Given that warming impacts are intensified at circumpolar regions where many marine mammals occur, these species may act as sentinels of change for conservation biologists.

Increasing temperatures and severe weather events associated with climate change can chronically stress individuals, leading to hypothermia and drowning (Laidre et al., 2008). Range shifts of both marine mammals and their prey will require new approaches to conservation and increased intergovernmental cooperation as species move outside of existing protected areas. Such range shifts can also alter exposure to pollutants and toxins, which themselves may be altered in prevalence due to changes in hydrologic cycles. Perhaps most concerning, reduction in sea ice has opened circumpolar regions to increased human activities, including vessel traffic, mineral exploration and extraction, and fisheries (Burek et al., 2008).

Climate impacts will differentially affect marine mammal species based on their intrinsic characteristics (reproductive rate, behavioural plasticity, dietary generalism or specialisation) and exposure to extrinsic factors based on their geographic range. As a result, there will be climate winners and losers. The loss of Arctic sea ice represents a loss of habitat for some species and an expansion of habitat for others (Laidre et al., 2008; Moore and Reeves 2018). In Norway, two decades of biotelemetry data show that ringed seals (*Pusa hispida*) and belugas (*Delphinapterus leucas*) have divergent responses to the reduction of sea-ice cover and changes in tidal glacier fronts: ringed seals maintain their historical patterns and stay near tidal glaciers to consume Arctic prey, whereas belugas have more plastic behaviour and appear to be consuming newly available Atlantic fishes (Hamilton et al., 2019). Many seals rely on ice as a platform for nursing pups, and these species, as well as walruses, use ice as substrate on which to haul out and rest. Polar bear populations are already showing signs of stress, including emaciation and elevated cortisol levels when poor ice conditions prevent them from accessing marine protein (Bechshøft et al., 2013). Narwhals (*Monodon monoceros*) are perhaps the most sensitive of Arctic cetaceans, given their restricted distribution, reliance on pack-ice habitat, and extreme physiological adaptations, and bowhead whales similarly occupy waters covered by ice (Moore and Reeves, 2018). Conversely, ice reductions may present opportunities for species that seasonally use Arctic resources during times of open water, such as humpback and minke (*Balaenoptera acutorostrata*) whales, and indeed these species are increasingly common in areas north of the Bering Strait (Brower et al., 2018).

Reports of disease affecting marine species are increasing alongside warming temperatures (Burek et al., 2008). The loss of sea ice can change patterns of mobility and species interactions, leading to potential new venues of disease transmission. Species that rely on haul out spaces may be forced to gather at increased densities in a smaller number of sites, in turn leading to overcrowding and heightened disease transmission (Burek et al., 2008). Recent surveys suggest that seals, sea lions and otters have been widely exposed to, and infected with, phocine distemper virus in the North Pacific Ocean, due to reductions in

Arctic sea ice, as populations previously separated are now coming into contact across newly navigable areas of the Arctic ocean (VanWormer et al., 2019). The frequency and severity of marine mammal infectious disease-induced mass mortality events are linked to seasonality and global yearly sea surface temperature anomalies, meaning that there may be more negative health consequences for marine mammals with climate change (Sanderson and Alexander, 2020). Many of the zoonotic diseases affecting marine mammals – such as *Brucella*, *Giardia* and influenza A – may also infect humans. As these disease relationships change in the context of a changing climate, collaborations between Indigenous communities, academic researchers and veterinarians in a One Health framework can help us reach a holistic understanding of change in the Arctic (Bradley et al., 2005; Burek et al., 2008).

In the Arctic, Indigenous communities continue to document climate change impacts on their environments, update and apply traditional ecological knowledge, and modify their hunting approaches. For example, Inuvialuit in the Northwest Territories are altering their food preparation techniques as a result of new observations of beluga responses to changing temperatures, extreme weather events and sea-ice reductions (Waugh et al., 2018). Alaskan Native communities, including Yup'ik, Iñupiaq and Cup'ik hunters, have observed that thinner sea ice and more rapid break-up has reduced the time available for hunting and has made walrus (*Odobenus rosmarus*) hunting more difficult (Huntington et al., 2017). However, these changing environmental conditions can also lead to new opportunities, and hunters can adapt if international frameworks allow. For example, while walrus hunting is becoming more challenging, some large whales are shifting their ranges poleward in response to climate and could be used as a protein substitute, but this would need to be considered by the IWC. Given the difficulty of monitoring Arctic marine mammals and the urgent need for data in response to rapid climate change, reciprocally beneficial collaborations between biologists and Indigenous communities remain more vital than ever.

5.8 Stories of Disappointment, Recovery and Hope

5.8.1 Stories of Disappointment

Unfortunately, a second species of cetacean may be about to go extinct, following the path of the baiji (Jaramillo-Legorreta et al., 2019). The vaquita, a small porpoise species endemic to Mexico, is on its last legs, with only about 10–15 individuals left alive, as of this writing (Figure 5.4C). Vaquitas have never been hunted and are instead collateral damage in the extensive and uncontrolled gillnet fishing that occurs in their tiny range in the northern Gulf of California. After the death of an individual in 2017, live capture and potential captive breeding efforts have been abandoned. Still, conservationists hold out a tiny sliver of hope that the species may yet survive. What is required is the removal of gillnets from a very small part of the planet, and if this can be achieved, the species can still make it (Bessesen, 2018).

5.8.2 Stories of Recovery

On a positive note, several marine mammal species have recovered from near extinction. One of the most dramatic examples is the northern elephant seal, which was hunted relentlessly throughout the nineteenth century. By the dawn of the twentieth century, the species was reduced to likely no more than 50–100 individuals. This last colony bred on Guadalupe Island off the coast of Baja California, Mexico. Despite nearly being wiped out through overzealous collection efforts, a handful of seals of this tiny remnant population survived and increased in numbers as hunting ceased (Stewart et al., 1994). Today, there are over 170,000 northern elephant seals alive and they have reoccupied their entire historical range.

Starting in the 1700s, sea otters were hunted mercilessly by fur traders for their luxurious pelts. By the early 1900s, only about 1000 sea otters were thought to have remained, and the California sea otter subspecies was considered to be extinct or nearly so. Protection efforts have been successful, and sea otters have recovered and reoccupied much of their previous range (though currently not the southern part along the Pacific coast of North America). Current estimates of global abundance range between 82,000 and 95,000 otters. However, otters are declining in several parts of their range and even where they are recovering, they can have conflicts with fishermen that result in retaliatory killings over shellfish predation; thus, they are not completely out of danger yet.

Among cetaceans, it is remarkable that whaling activities have not entirely wiped out any species. Whalers in the North Pacific targeted grey whales early on, due to their relatively slow movements and coastal range, which made them easy to hunt from shore. Their breeding lagoons in Baja California, Mexico, famously 'discovered' by Captain Charles M. Scammon, became a 'slaughterhouse' during the winter/spring breeding season. Commercial hunting along the migration route continued up until the early 1970s, but by then the grey whale population had recovered (twice) from drastically reduced numbers. Despite these two 'brushes' with extinction, grey whales in the eastern North Pacific have returned to near historic levels, and currently number about 21,000. A small population in the western Pacific has not fared so well, and is still much reduced, with no more than a few hundred remaining (Clapham and Baker, 2017).

5.8.3 Writing Stories of Hope for the Future

The fates of marine mammals and humans have been connected for millennia. In the Anthropocene, this bond is increasingly strengthened and now forms a complex web as human activities have come to dominate how our planet looks and functions. Of about 137 species of marine mammals, so far only five marine mammal species have been lost through overexploitation and/or our inability or unwillingness to curtail destructive practices. Marine mammals are long-lived and reproduce slowly and are thus much more vulnerable to complete annihilation than most other types of marine wildlife, such as fish and invertebrates. The sad truth is that many more species may 'blink out' during our lifetimes if we do not take action.

As of 2022, recent global political shifts have unfortunately favoured policies that do not protect our oceans and the marine mammals within them. In some cases, governments have actively taken steps in the opposite direction of what is needed to conserve our planet's biodiversity, particularly in the face of global climate change. Such stances are harmful to the health and wellbeing of marine mammals and humans alike.

Tides may be shifting, and it is still not too late for most species and populations. It is certainly debatable whether the vaquita, with a global population of likely less than 15 individuals, can survive. But other species are not in such bad shape, as yet. If we all do our part to support science-based management, there is indeed still hope.

Acknowledgements

We thank an anonymous reviewer for their constructive review of this chapter, and Wang Ding and Maria Cucuzza for permission to showcase their photographs. AMM was supported as a postdoctoral research associate by the University of Oklahoma at the time of this writing.

References

Alter, S.E., Newsome, S.D. and Palumbi, S.R. (2012) Pre-whaling genetic diversity and population ecology in eastern Pacific gray whales: insights from ancient DNA and stable isotopes. *PLoS One* 7: e35039.

Bechshøft, T.Ø., Sonne, C., Rigét, F.F., et al. (2013) Polar bear stress hormone cortisol fluctuates with the North Atlantic Oscillation climate index. *Polar Biol* 36: 1525–1529.

Berta, A., Sumich, J.L. and Kovacs, K.M. (2015) *Marine Mammals: Evolutionary Biology*, Third Edn. New York: Academic Press.

Bessesen, B. (2018) *Vaquita: Science, Politics, and Crime in the Sea of Cortez*. Washington, DC: Island Press.

Bradley, M.J., Kutz, S.J. Jenkin, E. and O'Hara, T.M. (2005). The potential impact of climate change on infectious diseases of Arctic fauna. *Int J Circumpolar Health* 64: 468–477.

Brower, A.A., Clarke, J.T. and Ferguson, M.C. (2018) Increased sightings of subArctic cetaceans in the eastern Chukchi Sea, 2008–2016: population recovery, response to climate change, or increased survey effort? *Polar Biol* 41: 1033–1039.

Brownell, R.L., Jr, Reeves, R.R., Read, A.J., et al. (2019) Bycatch in gillnet fisheries threatens Critically Endangered small cetaceans and other aquatic megafauna. *Endanger Species Res* 40: 285–296.

Burek, K.A., Gulland, F.M. and O'Hara, T.M. (2008) Effects of climate change on Arctic marine mammal health. *Ecol Appl* 18: S126–S134.

Clapham, P.J. and Baker, C.S. (2017) Whaling, Modern. In: Wursig, B. Thewissen J.G.M. and Kovacs, K.M. (Eds.), *Encyclopedia of Marine Mammals*, Third Edn. New York: Academic Press.

Corkeron, P.J. (2017) Captivity. In: Wursig, B. Thewissen J.G.M. and Kovacs, K.M. (Eds.), *Encyclopedia of Marine Mammals*, Third Edn. New York: Academic Press.

de Bruyn, M, Hall, B.L., Chauke, L.F., et al. (2009) Rapid response of a marine mammal species to Holocene climate and habitat change. *PLoS Genet* 5: e1000554.

Doughty, C.E., Roman, J., Faurby, S., et al. (2016) Global nutrient transport in a world of giants. *Proc Natl Acad Sci USA* 113: 868–873.

Estes, J.A., Burdin, A. and Doak, D.F. (2016) Sea otters, kelp forests, and the extinction of Steller's sea cow. *Proc Natl Acad Sci USA* 113: 880–885.

Gregr, E.J., Christensen, V., Nichol, L., et al. (2020) Cascading social-ecological costs and benefits triggered by a recovering keystone predator. *Science* 368: 1243–1247.

Hamilton, C.D., Vacquié-Garcia, J., Kovacs, K.M., et al. (2019) Contrasting changes in space use induced by climate change in two Arctic marine mammal species. *Biol Lett* 15: 20180834.

Hoegh-Guldberg, O., Jacob, D., Taylor, M., et al. (2019) The human imperative of stabilizing global climate change at 1.5 C. *Science* 365: eaaw6974.

Hofman, C.A., Rick, T.C., Erlandson, J.M., et al. (2018) Collagen fingerprinting and the earliest marine mammal hunting in North America. *Sci Rep* 8: 1–6.

Hoyt, E. (2011) *Marine Protected Areas for Whales, Dolphins and Porpoises*, Second Edn. Oxford, UK: Earthscan.

Huntington, H.P., Quakenbush, L.T. and Nelson, M. (2017) Evaluating the effects of climate change on indigenous marine mammal hunting in northern and western Alaska using traditional knowledge. *Front Marine Sci* 4: 319.

Jaramillo-Legorreta, A.M., Cardenas-Hinojosa, G., Nieto-Garcia, E. et al. (2019) Decline towards extinction of Mexico's vaquita porpoise (*Phocoena sinus*). *Royal Soc Open Sci* 6: 190598.

Jefferson, T.A., Webber, M.A. and Pitman, R.L. (2015) *Marine Mammals of the World: A Comprehensive Guide to Their Identification*. New York: Academic Press/Elsevier.

Kraus, S.D. and Rolland, R.M. (2007) *The Urban Whale: North Atlantic Right Whales at the Crossroads*. Boston, MA: Harvard University Press.

Laidre, K.L., Stirling, I., Lowry, L.F., et al. (2008) Quantifying the sensitivity of Arctic marine mammals to climate-induced habitat change. *Ecol Appl* 18: S97–S125.

Lavery, T.J., Roudnew, B., Seymour, J., et al. (2014) Whales sustain fisheries: blue whales stimulate primary production in the Southern Ocean. *Marine Mammal Sci* 30: 888–904.

McCauley, D.J., Pinsky, M.L., Palumbi, S.R., et al. (2015) Marine defaunation: animal loss in the global ocean. *Science* 347: 1255641.

Moore, S.E. and Reeves, R.R. (2018) Tracking arctic marine mammal resilience in an era of rapid ecosystem alteration. *PLoS Biol* 16: e2006708.

Morissette, L., Christensen, V. and Pauly, D. (2012) Marine mammal impacts in exploited ecosystems: would large scale culling benefit fisheries? *PLoS One* 7: e43966.

Nicol, S., Bowie, A., Jarman, S.N., et al. (2010) Southern Ocean iron fertilization by baleen whales and Antarctic krill. *Fish Fish* 11: 203–209.

Nye, J.W., Zangrando, A.F.J., Martinoli, M.P., Vázquez, M.M. and Fogelm, M.L. (2018) Cumulative human impacts on pinnipeds over the last 7,500 years in Southern South America. *SAA Archaeol Rec* 18: 47–52.

Pershing, A.J., Christensen, L.B., Record, N.R., et al. (2010) The impact of whaling on the ocean carbon cycle: why bigger was better. *PloS One* 5: e12444.

Pimiento, C., Leprieur, F., Silvestro, D., et al. (2020) Functional diversity of marine megafauna in the Anthropocene. *Sci Adv* 6: eaay7650.

Popper, A.N. and Hawkins, A. (eds.) (2016) *The Effects of Noise on Aquatic Life II*. New York: Springer.

Prentiss, D.W. (1903) Description of an extinct mink from the shell-heaps of the Maine coast. *Proc US Natl Mus* 26: 887–888.

Reeves, R.R. (2017a) Conservation. In: Wursig, B. Thewissen J.G.M. and Kovacs, K.M. (Eds.), *Encyclopedia of Marine Mammals*, Third Edn. New York: Academic Press.

Reeves, R.R. (2017b) Hunting. In: Wursig, B. Thewissen J.G.M. and Kovacs, K.M. (Eds.), *Encyclopedia of Marine Mammals*, Third Edn. New York: Academic Press.

Reijnders, P.J.H., Borrell, A. Van Franeker, J.A. and Aguilar, A. (2017) Pollution. In: Wursig, B. Thewissen J.G.M. and Kovacs, K.M. (Eds.), *Encyclopedia of Marine Mammals*, Third Edn. New York: Academic Press.

Rodrigues, A.S., Charpentier, A., Bernal-Casasola, D., et al. (2018) Forgotten Mediterranean calving grounds of grey and North Atlantic right whales:

evidence from Roman archaeological records. *Proc Royal Soc B* 285: 20180961.

Roman, J. and McCarthy, J.J. (2010) The whale pump: marine mammals enhance primary productivity in a coastal basin. *PloS One* 5: e13255.

Sanderson, C.E. and Alexander, K.A. (2020) Unchartered waters: climate change likely to intensify infectious disease outbreaks causing mass mortality events in marine mammals. *Glob Change Biol*, 26: 4284–4301.

Schoeman, R.P., Patterson-Abrolat, C. and Plön, S. (2020) A global review of vessel collisions with marine animals. *Front Marine Sci* 7: 292.

Silliman, B.R., Hughes, B.B., Gaskins, L.C., et al. (2018) Are the ghosts of nature's past haunting ecology today? *Curr Biol* 28: R532–R537.

Southall, B.L. 2017. Noise. In: Wursig, B. Thewissen J.G.M. and Kovacs, K.M. (Eds.), *Encyclopedia of Marine Mammals*, Third Edn. New York: Academic Press.

Springer, A.M., Estes, J.A., Van Vliet, G.B., et al. (2008) Mammal-eating killer whales, industrial whaling, and the sequential megafaunal collapse in the North Pacific Ocean: a reply to critics of Springer et al., 2003. *Mar Mamm Sci* 24: 414–442.

Stewart, B.S., Yochem, P. K., Huber, H. R., et al. (1994) History and present status of the northern elephant seal population. In: Boeuf, B.J.L. and Laws, R.M. (Eds.), *Elephant Seals: Population Ecology, Behavior, and Physiology*. Berkeley, CA: University of California Press.

Stoffel, M.A., Humble, E., Paijmans, A.J., et al. (2018) Demographic histories and genetic diversity across pinnipeds are shaped by human exploitation, ecology and life-history. *Nat Commun* 9: 1–12.

Turvey, S. (2008) *Witness to Extinction: How We Failed to Save the Yangtze River Dolphin*. Oxford, UK: Oxford University Press.

VanWormer, E., Mazet, J.A.K., Hall, A., et al. (2019) Viral emergence in marine mammals in the North Pacific may be linked to Arctic sea ice reduction. *Sci Rep* 9: 15569.

Waugh, D., Pearce, T., Ostertag, S.K., et al. (2018) Inuvialuit traditional ecological knowledge of beluga whale (*Delphinapterus leucas*) under changing climatic conditions in Tuktoyaktuk, NT. *Arctic Sci* 4: 242–258.

Wright, A.J., Simmonds, M.P. and Galletti Vernazzani, B. (2016) The International Whaling Commission: beyond whaling. *Front Marine Sci* 3: 158.

SIX

How Birds Reveal the Scale of the Biodiversity Crisis

TRISTRAM ALLINSON

Summary

Over the millennia, and across all cultures, people have developed an intimate bond with birds and, for many, birds are their principal connection to the natural world. With so many eyes trained on the planet's avifauna, birds provide us with a unique insight into the unfolding extinction crisis; the sixth such episode in our planet's 4.5-billion-year history and the first to be driven by the actions of a single species – our own. Avian extinction risk is comprehensively assessed by BirdLife International using the criteria of the IUCN Red List. The situation is alarming – around the world, birds are in steady decline, with approximately one in eight species now at risk of extinction. Each year, more species slip closer to extinction, whilst even once common birds are now disappearing fast. Yet the universal appeal of birds provides cause for hope. Their plight has been a rallying point around which a large and growing conservation movement has coalesced. A century of global bird conservation has demonstrated that when sufficient effort, resources and political will are brought to bear, bird populations can rebound and their habitats can be restored. Although imminent, mass avian extinction is not (yet) inevitable, and may still be averted if we so choose.

Recognised species	11,162	
Extant species	11,003	
Extinct species EX	159	
Extinct in the Wild EW	5	
Critically Endangered CR	225*	globally threatened
Endangered EN	447	
Vulnerable VU	773	
Near Threatened NT	1010	
Least Concern LC	8493	
Data Deficient DD	50	

* 22 Critically Endangered species are listed as Critically Endangered (Possibly Extinct) CR(PE)

6.1 Introduction

There is a great deal that is still unknown about the natural world. Many parts of the planet, such as the deepest reaches of our oceans, remain largely unexplored. We have, for instance, formally described only a tiny fraction of living organisms. The precise number of extant species is a matter of scientific speculation, with estimates ranging from two million to tens of millions. What knowledge we do have is heavily skewed towards vertebrates – the less than 5% of described species possessing a backbone. Of these, it is birds that have ignited our collective curiosity most keenly. From Leonardo da Vinci's captivation with avian flight and the promise it might hold for human imitation, to Charles Darwin's reflections on the finches of the Galápagos, which led him towards his revolutionary theory, birds have been a constant source of inspiration and insight to humankind.

A 'Web of Science' keyword search reveals that since 1990 there have been approximately 160,000 articles in mainstream academic journals with the word 'bird' in the title or abstract – roughly 15 a day, on average. This vast body of academic inquiry is augmented through the findings made by legions of amateur enthusiasts. It is estimated that over 45 million Americans, roughly 14% of the population, spend time observing birds (US Department of the Interior, US Fish and Wildlife Service, and US Census Bureau, 2016), while in the UK, three million people watch birds recreationally and around half a million regularly take part in the country's annual Big Garden Birdwatch event (www.rspb.org.uk). As early as 1916, Julian Huxley was speculating that the 'vast army of bird-lovers and bird-watchers' could begin providing the data scientists needed to address 'the fundamental problems of biology' (Huxley, 1916). Today, the power of the Internet enables scientists to harness the birding 'Crowd' as never before. For instance, *eBird*, an online database for birdwatchers to submit their sightings, receives more than 100 million bird records every year (ebird.org). Through this burgeoning 'citizen science' it is now possible to gather and analyse data on the distribution and abundance of bird species at a scale unthinkable through traditional techniques.

Put simply, birds are far better known than any other comparable group of organisms. For instance, when it comes to stating the number of bird species in the world today, we can do so far more accurately that for other classes of organism. According to BirdLife International, the official Red List Authority on birds for IUCN (see Box 6.1), 11,162 bird species are known to have inhabited the planet since the beginning of the 16th century (1500 being the earliest date after which sufficiently robust records exist). In this time, 159 species have gone extinct, and a further five are now extinct in the wild, but captive populations, and the hope that they can one day be returned to the wild, persist. A further 22 species are likely to be extinct, but, until their demise can be confirmed they remain officially classified as 'Critically Endangered (Possibly Extinct)'. This leaves 10,976 species of bird known to be currently extant on the planet. This figure will be questioned by some, such is the contentious nature of taxonomy. It will also change over time, both through taxonomic revision and genuine new discoveries and rediscoveries, possibly even before this book is published;

Box 6.1
Birds and the IUCN Red List

Much of what we know about how bird species have fared globally over recent decades is down to the IUCN Red List of Threatened Species. The list is produced and maintained by IUCN, together with the Red List Partnership and Species Survival Commission (SSC), a network including more than 140 Specialist Groups, Red List Authorities and Task Forces. One key partner is BirdLife International, the official Red List Authority for birds, responsible for assessing the extinction risk of the world's avifauna. Birds, and BirdLife, have been central to the evolution of the Red List. The task of maintaining the bird records was entrusted to the International Council for Bird Preservation (ICBP; the forerunner to BirdLife) in 1952. In 1964, the first comprehensive lists of threatened mammals and birds were compiled and published as supplements to the IUCN Bulletin (and subsequently republished in 1966 as the 'Red Data Book'). Birds became the first group to be comprehensively assessed when, in 1988, 'Birds to Watch: the ICBP World List of Threatened Birds' by Nigel Collar and Paul Andrew was published. In the 1990s, IUCN established new categories and criteria with clear numeric thresholds relating to five measurable parameters concerning population and range size, and rates of population decline and range contraction. The first application of the new system was carried out by the newly christened BirdLife International in 1994, and published in 'Birds to Watch 2: The World List of Threatened Birds'.

Since this time, BirdLife has updated the Red List annually and undertaken a comprehensive assessment of all avian species every four years (with seven assessments of all species now completed, birds are far better documented than any other taxonomic group, only five others of which have been assessed more than once, and none more than twice). Although the process is coordinated by a team of scientists from BirdLife, it involves collaboration with IUCN bird specialist groups, BirdLife Partners, other NGOs, universities, research institutes and a network of ornithologists, conservationists and bird experts from around the world. Over the years, many thousands of experts have contributed advice, evidence or recommendations; indeed the most recent comprehensive assessment synthesised the collective knowledge of a network of nearly 3000 ornithologists and conservationists. In order to survey the widest possible pool of expertise, and to ensure that decisions are transparent and consultative, all proposed changes to the Red List assessments for birds since 2002 have been posted on online forums for public scrutiny and consultation.

---

however, it is unlikely to change substantially under the taxonomic concepts that are most widely accepted today. Consequently, when it comes to understanding the current state of our global avifauna, we begin from the solid foundations of knowing accurately how many bird species exist.

Birds are so well known and so ubiquitous, being found throughout the world and in virtually all habitats (with the exception of deep caves and the ocean depths), that they serve as a unique barometer of wider ecological health. They are typically mobile and highly responsive to environmental change. The insidious impacts of dichlorodiphenyltri-chloroethane (DDT) pesticides were first noted in birds of prey such as the bald eagle, *Haliaeetus leucocephalus* LC, and peregrine falcon, *Falco peregrinus,* LC, whilst many of the biotic impacts of climate change observed to date have related to changes in the distribu-tion, abundance and phenology of bird species.

6.2 A Historical Perspective: How One Species Came to Dominate All Others

Today, the fate of the world's birds, indeed the fate of all forms of life, rests with one species: our own. Human dominion over the planet is now so total that many suggest we have entered a geological period best characterised as the Anthropocene (Steffen et al., 2007). Indeed, it can be argued that humanity has transformed the biosphere so com-pletely that there is now not a single biological community whose composition and structure is untouched by humankind. To understand how we arrived at this point it is necessary to understand the roots of our growing dominance and the pivotal events that have driven us to ever greater planetary supremacy.

Humans have long been a disproportionate and transformative presence within the biosphere. From the moment humankind expanded out of Africa, roughly 50,000 to 100,000 years ago, our species has had a profound and ever-growing influence on the rest of the natural world. The colonisation of Eurasia, Australasia and the Americas by anatomically modern humans, whilst perhaps not solely responsible for the extinction of the Pleistocene megafauna, certainly hastened its demise. Animals such as Mastodon, Mammoth and Megatherium would have been important keystone species with consider-able influence over ecosystem structure and function. Landscapes denuded of an entire cohort of large herbivores would have been fundamentally changed, thereafter supporting radically different communities of plants and animals, including birds.

The next great change in the relationship between humanity and the rest of the natural world came with the Neolithic Revolution. Around 12,500 years ago, our species transformed from nomadic hunter-gatherers into settled agriculturalists. Humanity was no longer just a superior apex predator, but the planet's pre-eminent ecosystem engineer. Through fire and forest clearance, early farming communities transformed large parts of the Earth's surface. These changes would have disadvantaged species associated with intact forest, but would have favoured those dependent on more open landscapes. Indeed, pre-industrial agrarian societies may have increased species diversity overall by creating a heterogeneous landscape with far greater scope for niche separation. Humanity's whole-scale transformation of the landscape through agriculture not only altered the distribution of species, but even triggered the emergence of new ones. The spread of agriculture from the Near East into Europe enabled the house sparrow *Passer domesticus* LC, a species strongly associated with human settlement, to colonise the continent. When house sparrows reached the Mediterranean they came into contact with Spanish sparrows *Passer hispaniolensis* LC. Hybridisation of the two would eventually result in a genetically distinct population, reproductively isolated from the parental species, and now regarded as a true species in its own right – the Italian sparrow *Passer italiae* VU.

More ominous were advances in maritime technology, which enabled Neolithic communities to spread across the world's seas and oceans, colonising ever-remoter islands. In so doing, they created a wave of ecological disruption and avian extinction described by Jared Diamond as a 'biological holocaust' (Diamond, 1991). Having evolved within more simplistic ecological communities, exposed to only a limited set of competitors and predators, island avifauna proved ill-prepared for exposure to humans and, more crucially, the novel organisms that accompanied them. The spread of the Pacific rat *Rattus exulans* in particular is likely to have been the principal driver of pre-European bird extinction in the Pacific. Indeed, it is suggested that close to 1000 species of non-passerine landbirds alone were extirpated between the initial Polynesian colonisation of the region and the arrival of the first European settlers (Duncan et al., 2013). The comprehensive diminishment of island ecosystems intensified from the end of the fifteenth century as European explorers set out in search of new lands and resources. Whilst European settlers destroyed habitats and directly hunted island birds, the gravest impact came from the exotic animals they brought with them, most significantly stowaway house rats *Rattus rattus* and brown rats *R. norvegicus*. Flightless and fearless, it is widely believed that the dodo *Raphus cucullatus* EX was simply eaten to oblivion by hungry sailors. Yet in reality, it is likely that introduced pigs *Sus domesticus* and crab-eating macaques *Macaca fascicularis* were the principal culprits (Hume, 2017).

BirdLife International and IUCN officially record avian extinctions from 1500 onwards, a cut-off date after which contemporary records are deemed sufficiently comprehensive to provide a reasonably accurate account. Even though most bird species (>80%) live on continents, the overwhelming majority of avian extinctions (89%) have occurred on islands (Szabo et al., 2012). Rates of avian extinction on islands peaked in the 1800s and have subsequently slowed. Doubtless many susceptible species are now already extinct, but also the conservation interventions of the last 50 years have kept others from the abyss. Whilst the elimination of birds on small islands – involving, as it often does, evolutionarily ill-prepared species with only small populations to begin with – has been within humankind's capacity since prehistory, it required the technological advances, and population eruption, unleashed by the Industrial Revolution to make human-driven extinction of continental bird species a reality.

Since 1850, the rate of avian extinction on continents has grown rapidly as humanity's capacity to inflict large-scale destruction on species and habitats has intensified. An early illustration of humankind's unrivalled capacity for industrial-scale killing is provided by the passenger pigeon *Ectopistes migratorius* EX. When Europeans first discovered the Americas, these pigeons may have been the most numerous bird on Earth, totalling 3 billion to 5 billion. Accounts from the middle decades of the nineteenth century describe how the skies would darken as flocks, many millions strong, passed overhead for hours at a time. But relentless persecution, which saw birds shot and trapped on a colossal scale, meant that by the final decade of the nineteenth century there were few pigeons left. The last confirmed wild bird is believed to have been shot in 1901, whilst Martha, the last captive bird, died on 1 September 1914 at Cincinnati Zoo.

The human population has grown rapidly since the Industrial Revolution, from 1 billion in 1800 to 7.9 billion today, more than doubling in the last 50 years. Of the total mammalian biomass on Earth, humans now make up 36% and livestock a further 60%, with wild mammals accounting for just 4%. For avian biomass, 70% is accounted for by domestic chickens and other poultry, while just 30% comprises wild birds (Bar-On et al., 2018). Human dominion over the Earth's systems accelerated sharply in the second half of the twentieth century. So much so, that some authors refer to this latest period of the Anthropocene as the 'Great Acceleration' (McNeill, 2014). Perhaps nowhere epitomises the speed and magnitude of change better than China, with its rapid economic growth and burgeoning urban middle class. Between 2011 and 2013, China used more cement than the USA had used in the entire twentieth century. Since 2000, the country has built, on average, eight new civil airports every year, whilst each year since 2011 the country's road network has grown by a further 10,000 kilometres. The relentless ascendancy of humankind has resulted in a world where 75% of the land and 66% of the oceans are now 'severely altered' by human actions, and where up to 1 million species are likely to be threatened with extinction as a result (IPBES, 2019).

6.3 Birds in the Anthropocene: The Current Status of the World's Avifauna

In December 2021, BirdLife International completed its latest update to the status of the world's birds. It revealed that 1445 species (13% of the 11,003 extant species, roughly one in eight) are threatened with global extinction. These comprise 225 species classified as Critically Endangered (CR 2%), 447 as Endangered (EN 4%) and 773 as Vulnerable (VU 7%). An additional 1010 species are assessed as Near Threatened (NT 9%) – hence a total of 2455 species (nearly a quarter of all the world's birds) are considered to be of significant global conservation concern. Only 50 species (<1% of the total) are deemed too poorly known to be assessed, and so are classified as Data Deficient (DD). This represents a much smaller proportion than in other taxonomic classes, such as mammals (15%), amphibians (21%), corals (19%) and sharks (19%), and is testament to the more complete knowledge that exists about birds.

Threatened species are not evenly distributed among bird groups. For instance, there are particularly high proportions of threatened species among cranes (67%, 10 out of 15), Old World vultures (69%, 11 out of 16), and albatrosses (68%, 15 out of 22). Families and genera with few species have disproportionately high numbers of threatened species (Purvis et al., 2000), as do larger-bodied species and those with low reproductive rates (owing to small clutch sizes and long periods of parental care) (Bennett and Owens, 1997).

The populations of 73% (1058 species) of threatened birds (CR, EN and VU) number fewer than 10,000 mature individuals, and 40% (580 species) have fewer than 2500 mature individuals. Some 69 species have tiny populations that may support no more than 50 mature individuals worldwide. Most threatened bird species have small ranges, and island taxa continue to be disproportionately represented. Forty-six species (3%) have global ranges smaller than 10 km^2, the majority on small islands. For example, the Floreana mockingbird *Mimus trifasciatus* EN is confined to two tiny islets totalling just 0.9 km^2 in the Galapagos archipelago, while two Critically Endangered species, the millerbird *Acrocephalus familiaris* and the Nihoa finch *Telespiza ultima*, are found only on Nihoa, an island of just 0.7 km^2 in the Hawaiian island chain. In total, 108 Critically Endangered or Endangered species are now restricted wholly or overwhelmingly to just one location. For example, a single remnant patch of forest on the Indonesian island of Sangihe supports four Critically Endangered species, the cerulean paradise flycatcher *Eutrichomyias rowleyi*, the Sangihe golden bulbul *Thapsinillas platenae*, the Sangihe whistler *Coracornis sanghirensis* and the Sangihe white-eye *Zosterops nehrkorni*.

Whilst many globally threatened birds are little-known species restricted to remote oceanic islands, mountaintops and forest patches, in recent years there has been a notable, and alarming, rise in the number of once-widespread and familiar species experiencing rapid population declines and now facing extinction. For instance, until recently, the yellow-breasted bunting *Emberiza aureola* was one of Eurasia's most abundant bird species, breeding from Finland to Japan. However, since 1980, its population has declined by 90%, whilst its range has contracted eastwards by 5000 km – a population crash that mirrors almost exactly that undergone by the passenger pigeon *Ectopistes migratorius* EX in the years preceding its infamous demise (Kamp et al., 2015). The species is regarded as a delicacy in parts of China where it is known colloquially as 'the rice bird'. Although banned in the 1990s, trapping continued on a massive scale. In the early 2000s, an estimated one million yellow-breasted buntings were being consumed nationally each year (Chan, 2004). The species is now considered Critically Endangered.

Rampant overexploitation also lies behind the ongoing decline of the grey parrot *Psittacus erithacus* and its recently split sister species, the Timneh parrot *P. timneh*. Once abundant across the forests of equatorial Africa, these intelligent, gregarious birds are now in sharp decline. Their popularity as a pet has fuelled an illegal trade that has seen both species recently listed as globally Endangered. Celebrated in everything from Roman mythology and the Christian Bible to Christmas carols and Shakespeare sonnets, the European turtle dove *Streptopelia turtur* was until recently a familiar summer migrant to Europe, Central Asia and the Middle East from the Sahel zone of Africa. However, in recent decades, agricultural intensification and hunting have taken a heavy toll. Turtle doves have disappeared throughout their range, especially in western Europe, and have recently been uplisted to Vulnerable. The snowy owl *Bubo scandiacus* is surely one of the most widely recognised birds in much of the world, thanks to the popularity of the Harry Potter franchise. It is also widespread, occurring throughout the Arctic tundra of the Northern Hemisphere. Yet, it too is experiencing a rapid decline, most likely connected to climate change, and is now also considered Vulnerable. In the marine realm, the depletion of fish, driven by overfishing and climate change, has caused rapid declines in once-widespread seabirds such as the Atlantic puffin *Fratercula arctica* and the black-legged kittiwake *Rissa tridactyla* – both are now listed as Vulnerable to extinction.

Not so long ago, vultures were a common sight in the skies above much of southern Europe, Asia and Africa. As recently as the 1980s, an estimated 100 million vultures occurred in India alone. Indeed, the white-rumped vulture *Gyps bengalensis* CR was considered the most abundant bird of prey on the planet. These magnificent birds are a vital component of the natural systems in which they occur, performing an essential role in the disposal of carrion. Across their range, their populations are, however, in freefall. The IUCN Red List charts a relentless decline over recent decades. In 1994, 75% of the world's 16 Old World vulture species were classified as Least Concern, meaning that they were not considered at risk of extinction. Only one species – the Cape vulture *Gyps coprotheres* – was thought to be globally threatened and was classified as Vulnerable. Today, just two species remain Least Concern. Of the rest, eight, half of all species, are classified as Critically Endangered and are at risk of imminent extinction, two are almost as imperilled and are classified as Endangered, one is Vulnerable and three are Near Threatened. Populations in South Asia were the first to collapse, with declines of around 95% between 1993 and 2000. These were principally the result of acute poisoning linked to consumption of the carcasses of livestock treated with the veterinary drug diclofenac. However, vultures are now also disappearing across vast swathes of Africa. Over a period of just 30 years, populations of seven African species have fallen by 80–97%. Here, the threats are more varied. Many are killed by carcasses laced with poison, either incidentally, where hyenas and big cats are the intended victims, or intentionally, such as by elephant poachers who kill vultures so that they do not draw attention to their illegal activities. Vultures are also killed for their body parts, which are traded for their supposed mystical properties. Other threats include habitat loss and degradation, decreasing food availability, human disturbance, collisions with wind turbines and power lines, and electrocution on electricity infrastructure. Diclofenac also seems to be affecting vultures in parts of Africa, and its recent licensing for veterinary use in some European countries is also a source of real concern, given its devastating impacts in Asia.

BirdLife has been carrying out comprehensive Red List assessments using a consistent, standardised approach for more than three decades. Consequently, the Red List provides an especially comprehensive measurement of long-term trends in avian extinction risk. Pioneered by BirdLife, the Red List Index (RLI), a metric derived from data on the movement of species between Red List categories resulting from genuine improvement or deterioration in the extinction risk of species, reveals a steady and continuing deterioration in the status of the world's birds since the first comprehensive assessment in 1988 (Figure 6.1a). Although 68 species have improved in status since 1988 (sufficient to be downlisted to a category of lower threat), 389 have deteriorated in status (sufficient to be uplisted to a category of higher threat). One of the species most recently 'uplisted' is the straw-headed bulbul *Pycnonotus zeylanicus*, a species so prized within the Southeast Asian songbird trade it has been systematically trapped out of the region's forests. Regarded as

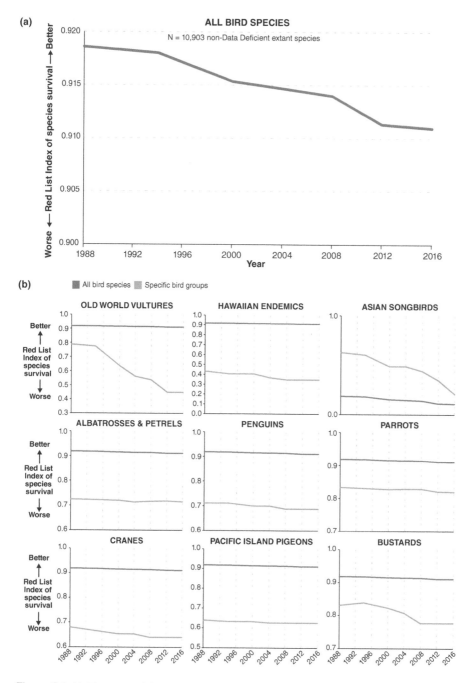

Figure 6.1 (a) The status of the world's birds declined between 1988 and 2016 as shown by the Red List Index (RLI) for birds. The index is based on the number of species in each Red List category and the number that have moved between categories as a result of genuine changes in status (i.e. excluding moves resulting from improved knowledge or taxonomic changes). An RLI value of 1 equates to all species being categorised as Least Concern and hence that none is expected to go extinct in the near future. An RLI value of 0 indicates that all species have gone extinct. (b) The RLI for selected bird groups of particular conservation concern.

Near Threatened in 1988, it has risen sharply through the categories of the Red List, and in 2018 was uplisted from Endangered to Critically Endangered.

The RLI can be disaggregated to show trends for different subsets of species. Birds in terrestrial, freshwater and marine ecosystems (including coastal habitats) have all declined in status over the last 30 years. Pelagic seabirds (those using the open seas) are especially threatened (with the lowest RLI values) and declining faster than other groups, owing to a combination of marine threats (notably from incidental mortality in fisheries) and threats at breeding colonies (particularly the impacts of invasive alien species). Some species groups have been impacted very seriously by human activities and have an exceptionally high proportion of species listed as globally threatened. The RLI can be used to highlight taxonomic groups of concern (Figure 6.1b). For example, Hawaii's endemic avifauna is particularly imperilled, both substantially more threatened than birds in general, and also declining at a faster rate. In contrast, Asian songbirds are less threatened than birds overall, however, they are declining at a much faster rate, suggesting they are an emerging conservation priority.

All countries host one or more globally threatened bird species, with particularly high numbers in the tropical Andes, Atlantic Forests of Brazil, eastern Himalayas, eastern Madagascar and insular Southeast Asia. The highest densities of threatened seabird species are found in international waters in the southern oceans, with a particular concentration around New Zealand. Nineteen countries have more than 50 globally threatened birds, with Indonesia and Brazil top of the list, holding 168 and 165 respectively (Figure 6.2a). In total, 975 threatened birds (67%) have breeding ranges confined to just one country, and 88 countries have one or more such endemic threatened birds. Again, Indonesia and Brazil top the list, with 109 and 89 threatened endemics, respectively, while the proportion of threatened species that are endemic is highest in New Zealand (83% of 66 species), the Philippines (82% of 92 species) and Madagascar (79% of 38 species). Conversely, the ranges of some threatened birds may cross the borders of several countries: the European turtle dove *Streptopelia turtur* VU occurs regularly in 93 countries (and as a vagrant to 20 others) in Europe, Asia and Africa. The avifaunas of some countries are particularly imperilled (Figure 6.2b). These include territories that have highly threatened avifaunas despite relatively low total avian diversity. For example, French Polynesia supports 81 bird species, of which 34 are globally threatened, and the Cook Islands supports 37 species, with 13 globally threatened. Some countries hold far fewer threatened species than expected. For instance, Guyana, Suriname and Congo are all large countries with avifaunas of more than 600 species, yet fortunately few bird species are currently threatened in these countries as they still hold vast tracts of largely pristine forest and host very few restricted-range species.

Even among many of those species that are still relatively widespread and abundant there is cause for concern. Analysis of avifauna, at a range of scales, suggests that between one-third and a half of birds are faring poorly. Three comprehensive assessments of the continental conservation status of all (>500) European bird species have concluded that between 38% and 43% of them are in unfavourable conservation status (Tucker and Heath, 1994; BirdLife International, 2004, 2017), whilst an assessment of all 1154 native

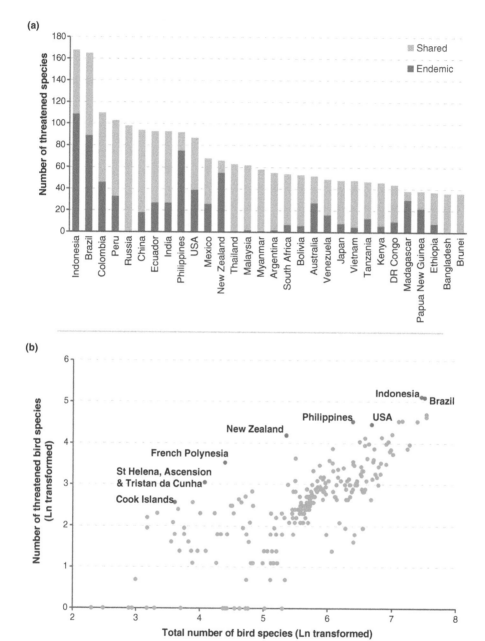

Figure 6.2 (a) Top countries for total number of endemic and shared globally threatened species. (b) Number of threatened species plotted against the total number of bird species per nation using log-transformed data. Some countries have particularly threatened avifauna (marked in red).

bird species that occur in Canada, the continental United States and Mexico reveal that 37% are of significant conservation concern (North American Bird Conservation Initiative, 2016). Indeed, there are estimated to be three billion fewer birds in North America today than there were in 1970 (Rosenberg et al., 2019). BirdLife's data indicates that 52% of bird species worldwide with a known trend have declining populations (5393). In contrast, only 6% are increasing (664), whilst 41% are stable (4240).

6.4 Birds Face a Multitude of Threats

The threats driving avian extinction are many and varied, but they are almost invariably of humanity's making. Most species are impacted by multiple threats and many threats are inter-related. For example, land clearance for agriculture is often preceded by deforestation or wetland drainage. Similarly, many threats act to compound and intensify others: endemic birds in the Hawaiian Islands have already been severely impacted by avian malaria transmitted by introduced mosquitoes, yet climate change is expected to exacerbate the problem still further. At present, mosquitoes are restricted to the lowlands, and the region's globally threatened forest birds, mainly honeycreepers (Drepanididae), have a malaria-free refuge within cooler, high-elevation forests. However, this refuge is under threat. It is predicted that rising temperature will ultimately enable mosquitoes, and the malaria they carry, to spread to much of the remaining montane forest (Benning et al., 2002).

BirdLife systematically evaluates the threats facing globally threatened bird species as part of its work assessing avian extinction risk for the IUCN Red List. This provides a clear insight into the principal drivers of bird declines and extinction. Foremost among them are: agricultural expansion and intensification, which impacts 1120 globally threatened birds (78%), deforestation and logging, affecting 765 species (53%), hunting and trapping, which put 603 (42%) species at risk and invasive alien species, which threaten 578 (40%) species. Climate change, currently affecting 35% of globally threatened species, represents an emerging and increasingly serious threat (Figure 6.3).

6.4.1 Agricultural Expansion and Intensification

The expansion of agriculture, and the resultant habitat destruction, is one of the greatest threats to the world's avifauna. The area of Earth's land surface given over to agriculture has increased more than sixfold over the past 300 years, from less than 6% in 1700 to nearly 40% today. Since 1970 there has been a threefold increase in food production. The conversion of natural habitats to farmland is now occurring most rapidly in tropical regions – driven by cattle-ranching and global demand for commodities such as coffee, cocoa, sugar, palm oil and soya. Between 1980 and 2000, 100 million hectares of land conversion to agriculture took place in the tropics, of which half came at the expense of forest. A recent analysis found that more than 100 bird species are predicted to become extinct based on current farming practices, without conservation interventions (Marques et al., 2019), the vast majority of these are found in Africa, Latin America and Asia, with projected declines driven by cattle farming, forestry and increasing production of seed oils (including palm oil).

At the same time that natural habitats are being lost to agricultural expansion, formerly wildlife-rich farmland is being transformed through agricultural intensification and industrialisation. The diverse mosaic of crops and semi-natural habitats that once characterised Europe's traditionally farmed landscapes has been replaced by vast and highly managed

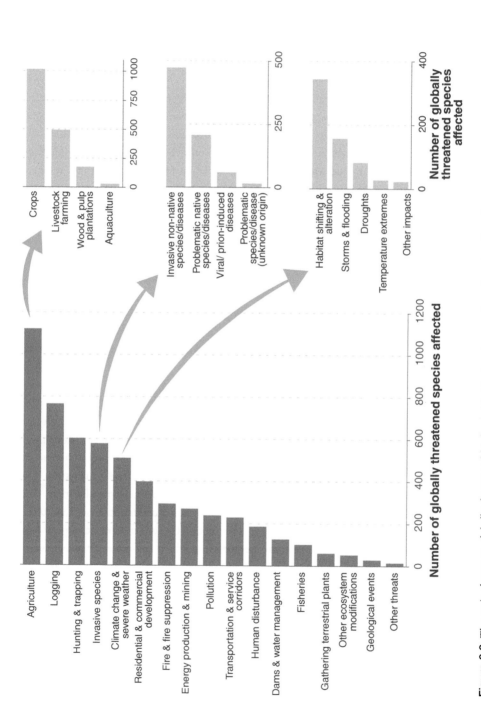

Figure 6.3 The main threats to globally threatened birds worldwide showing number of species affected.

monocultures. It is estimated that between 1980 and 2009, 421 million individual birds of 144 common and widespread species vanished from 25 European countries at a rate close to 1% – about 10 million individuals – each and every year (Inger et al., 2014). These losses have been particularly steep for farmland birds, with an overall decline of 60% between 1980 and 2016 (Gregory et al., 2019). The impact of increasing agrochemical use is particularly apparent. Researchers in Germany report that flying insect biomass has declined by 76% (and up to 82% in midsummer) over the last 30 years (Hallmann et al., 2017), largely as the result of extensive pesticide use. The decimation of insect populations reverberates through the food web. Recent studies in France reveal the impact on those bird species dependent on insects for food. In less than two decades, declines in bird species are equivalent to one-third of birds disappearing from the French countryside. For some species, the declines are particularly catastrophic. The country's grey partridge *Perdix perdix* LC populations have plummeted by 90%, its meadow pipits *Anthus pratensis* LC by 68% and its Eurasian skylarks LC *Alauda arvensis*, whose song is synonymous with summer throughout Europe, by 50% (Suivi Temporel des Oiseaux Communs (STOC), 2019). Even where wildlife-rich agricultural land persists, mechanisation can take a toll. Modern olive-picking techniques involving the use of vacuum-harvesting machinery at night are reported to have inadvertently killed millions of roosting birds in the Mediterranean (da Silva and Mata, 2019). One conservative estimated suggests that some 2.6 million birds may be killed annually in Andalusia, Spain alone (Junta de Andalucia, 2019).

6.4.2 Deforestation and Unsustainable Logging

Nearly two-thirds of bird species globally are found in forests, mainly in the tropics, and many can live nowhere else. Yet more than seven million hectares of forest are destroyed each year, driven by global demand for timber, paper and land for commodity crops and biofuels. Between 1990 and 2015, 290 million hectares of native forest cover was lost due to clearing and wood harvesting (IPBES, 2019). Much of what remains is subject to unsustainable and unlawful forestry practices, with some 10–15% of global timber supplies being provided through illegal forestry. Selective logging degrades standing forests and almost always impoverishes bird communities. Although overall bird species richness can increase following selective logging, due to the influx of habitat generalists, the diversity of forest specialists typically dwindles. Logging activity also facilitates further disturbance, including encroachment and increased hunting pressure, which can have greater and more lasting impacts than the logging itself. For example, forest ecosystems compromised by selective logging are more susceptible than intact forests to devastating fires. Tropical deforestation also affects the world's climate, accounting for 8% of all human-induced greenhouse gas emissions every year (Seymour and Busch, 2016). Indeed, if tropical deforestation were a country, it would rank third in emissions only behind China and the United States.

Deforestation and unsustainable forestry is particularly rampant in South America, South and Southeast Asia, and sub-Saharan Africa. For instance, in parts of Southeast Asia, there is now so little primary forest left that many forests will be logged for the second or third time in the near future. This is especially concerning as these regions support considerable numbers of forest-dependent bird species, including forest specialists that are entirely reliant on intact forest for their survival.

6.4.3 Overexploitation

Hunting for food or sport and trapping for the cage-bird trade has been implicated in the extinction of dozens of bird species and remains a significant and growing threat today. Overexploitation is a particular problem for some bird families, including parrots, pigeons and pheasants, and is most prevalent in Southeast Asia where more than 1000 species are traded for pets, food or traditional medicine. Songbird-keeping is a deeply entrenched pastime in many parts of the region, especially in Indonesia, the largest importer and exporter of wild birds in Asia (Nash, 1993). A recent survey of the bird-keeping habits of households across Java, Indonesia resulted in an estimate that one-third of the Island's 36 million households keep between 66 and 84 million cage birds (Marshall et al., 2019). Despite over half of all birds owned being non-native species, predominantly lovebirds (*Agapornis* spp.) and island canaries *Serinus canaria* (var. *domestica*), there were also huge numbers of some native songbirds, including more than three million white-rumped shamas *Kittacincla malabarica* LC and over two million Oriental magpie-robins *Copsychus saularis* LC. Of all (112) species kept, around 12% are listed as globally threatened or Near Threatened. The bird trade is now recognised as the primary threat to many of the region's species. In 2016, BirdLife uplisted 19 Indonesian songbirds to higher threat categories, including six to Critically Endangered. Some, such as the greater green leafbird *Chloropsis sonnerati* (now EN) were until recently common across the country's forests. Others, such as rufous-fronted laughingthrush *Garrulax rufifrons*, have gone from Near Threatened to Critically Endangered in an alarmingly short time and are now on the brink of extinction. The problem is not confined to songbirds. In 2015, the helmeted hornbill *Rhinoplax vigil* was uplisted from Near Threatened to Critically Endangered. As well as severe loss of its Southeast Asian forest habitat, the species is targeted by hunters for its feathers and for its solid casque, known as 'red ivory', which is illegally traded with China to produce handicrafts.

Illegal hunting remains a major threat to birds across the Mediterranean, Northern and Central Europe, and the Caucasus. Indeed, a staggering 12–38 million individual birds are estimated to be killed or taken illegally every year in the region, many of them on migration (Brochet et al., 2016, 2019). The majority of birds killed are passerines, including 4.7 million house/Italian sparrows *Passer domesticus/italiae* LC, 2.9 million common chaffinches *Fringilla coelebs* LC and 1.9 million Eurasian blackcaps *Sylvia atricapilla* LC. Italy, with 5.6 million birds illegally killed per year, and Egypt, with 5.5 million killed per year, are the countries with the highest death tolls, but, in terms of killing intensity, Malta, with 343 birds killed per km^2 per year, is the most deadly, followed by Cyprus and Lebanon (both with 248 birds killed per km^2 per year; Figure 6.4). For some species, such as the ortolan bunting *Emberiza hortulana* LC, illegal and unregulated hunting is driving local populations to extinction (Jiguet et al., 2019). In addition to those birds killed

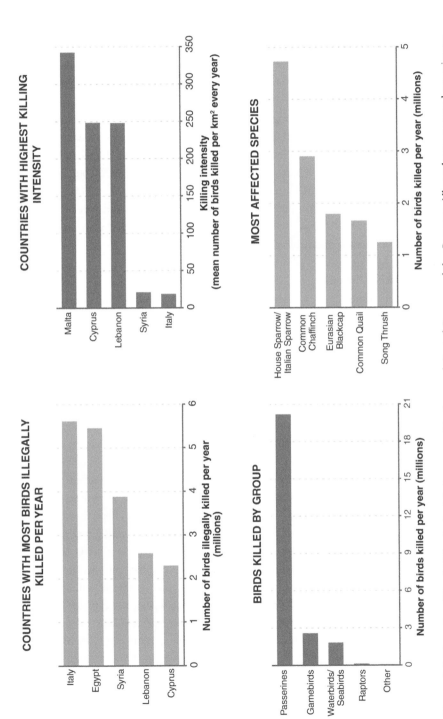

Figure 6.4 The scale of illegal killing in the Mediterranean, Northern and Central Europe and the Caucasus. All numbers are mean best estimates.
Source: Brochet et al. (2016, 2019).

illegally, there is considerable legal hunting. At least 52 million birds are lawfully killed, from 82 permissible quarry species, in the European Union (Hirschfeld et al., 2019). This includes a number of declining and globally threatened species such as the European turtle dove *Streptopelia turtur* VU, the common pochard *Aythya ferina* VU and the velvet scoter *Melanitta fusca* VU.

Large numbers of birds are also killed unintentionally. These include hundreds of thousands of seabirds caught as incidental 'bycatch' in fishing gear. Commercial fisheries have expanded dramatically since the 1960s, both geographically and in their intensity. Gillnet fisheries use a 'curtain' of netting that hangs in the water to catch fish around the gills. They are responsible for over 400,000 seabird deaths each year, mostly of coastal and diving species (Zydelis et al., 2013). Longline fisheries are those that trail lines of baited hooks behind a fishing vessel. Globally, they are thought to cause over 160,000 seabird deaths annually, mostly of albatross and petrel species (Anderson et al., 2011). Trawl fisheries, in which one or two boats pull large nets through the water behind them, cause tens of thousands of seabird deaths each year, typically through collision with the warp cables, or during the setting and hauling of the nets.

6.4.4 Invasive Alien Species

Humans have been transporting animals and plants around the world for thousands of years, sometimes intentionally, as with livestock and companion animals, and sometimes accidentally, as with rats and mice that have stowed away on boats. Typically, introduced species fail to establish themselves in the wild in new locations, but, a proportion thrive and spread. Such 'invasive alien species' can have catastrophic impacts on ecosystems by outcompeting or predating native wildlife, or by modifying their habitat. Over the last 500 years, invasive alien species have been partly or wholly responsible for the extinction of at least 111 bird species, 69% of those known to have gone extinct, making this the most common factor contributing to recent bird extinctions.

As many as 17,000 different organisms have been documented as being established outside their natural geographical ranges as the result of human activity (Seebens et al., 2017). For birds, the greatest risk comes from introduced mammalian predators, which often target chicks and eggs. Rats and cats have had by far the greatest effect, threatening the survival of hundreds of bird species worldwide. Many threatened birds are subject to multiple impacts from a range of non-native species. One such example is the Galápagos petrel *Pterodroma phaeopygia* CR, which has undergone an extremely rapid decline since the early 1980s, owing to a variety of threats, including predation by introduced rats, cats and dogs, and the destruction of breeding habitat by introduced goats and cattle. Birds on remote islands are particularly susceptible to invasive alien species: 70% of globally threatened species on oceanic islands are affected by invasives, compared with 24% on continental islands (islands geologically related to a continental shelf) and just 13% on continental landmasses. A total of 390 islands worldwide support populations of one or more Critically Endangered or Endangered bird species and one or more vertebrate invasive alien species that threatens them.

6.4.5 Climate Change

The climate of our planet is changing as a direct result of human activities, mainly the burning of fossil fuels. In the longer term, this could present the greatest challenge to the future of birds, and indeed all life. Already, many bird species are struggling to adapt to the pace of climatic changes. Rising temperatures are driving species' distributions towards the poles and towards higher ground. Migratory and breeding cycles are changing, leading to disrupted relationships with prey, predators and competitors. In many cases, these effects have driven population declines. One recent analysis suggests that more than a fifth of globally threatened birds may have already been negatively impacted by climate change in at least part of their range (Pacifici et al., 2017). Of those species negatively affected, declines in abundance and range size are the most common impacts. For instance, in Canada, warmer autumns have been linked to reduced breeding success in the grey jay *Perisoreus canadensis* LC, most likely due to increased perishing of hoarded food (Waite and Strickland, 2006).

More damaging than the direct impacts of rising temperatures is the disruption caused to ecological interactions, particularly through phenological mismatches. As European spring temperatures have risen, migratory common cuckoos *Cuculus canorus* LC returning from sub-Saharan Africa have increasingly found their host species already breeding, thus reducing their options for finding suitable nests to parasitise (Møller et al., 2010). Baird's sandpipers *Calidris bairdii* LC, breeding in the high Arctic, time the hatching of their chicks to coincide with the peak emergence of insect prey. However, increasing temperatures have meant that insects now peak in abundance earlier. Sandpiper chicks raised outside the period of peak food availability grow significantly more slowly and are likely to have reduced survival and recruitment (McKinnon et al., 2012).

As warming continues, negative impacts will multiply and intensify. While some species may benefit from rising temperatures, it is likely that more than twice as many species will lose out. Generalist species are typically likely to increase in population and range, while specialist species are expected to decline. Results from studies around the world show that, on average, species are projected to face 10–30% declines in their geographic range sizes, with 30–70% of their current distributions projected to become unsuitable by the end of the century. In North America, modelling shows that 53% of species are projected to lose more than half of their current geographic range by the century's end (Langham et al., 2015). While some may have the potential to colonise new areas, for 40% of these species, loss occurs without associated range expansion. Based on these results, the authors classify one-fifth of North American species as 'climate endangered', and another third as 'climate threatened'.

Species on low-lying islands are particularly vulnerable to sea-level rise. In Oceania, seven species are entirely restricted to islands with a maximum elevation of <10 m, including the Polynesian ground dove *Alopecoenas erythropterus* CR, meaning that coastal flooding could have a devastating impact. Sea-level rise will also impact seabirds. For example, in Midway Atoll, Hawaii, a sea-level rise of 2 m would flood approximately 60% of albatross (Laysan *Phoebastria immutabilis* NT and black-footed *P. nigripes* NT) and 44% of

Bonin petrel *Pterodroma hypoleuca* LC nests, displacing more than 600,000 breeding birds (Reynolds et al., 2015). Extreme weather events are projected to increase in intensity and frequency, which will likely have negative impacts on many species. When Hurricane Matthew swept through the Caribbean in 2016, it devastated the Bahamas' native pine forest, raising concerns as to whether the endemic Bahama nuthatch *Sitta insularis* CR had survived. Exhaustive searches suggest there may be as few as two individuals left. With Hurricane Dorian, the strongest tropical cyclone ever to strike the area, hitting in September 2019, the chances that this species has become the planet's most recent avian extinction are high.

6.5 All is Not Lost: How Conservation Successes Reveal Ways to End the Extinction Crisis

Many dozens of bird species would have been lost were it not for the concerted efforts of dedicated conservation practitioners. Species such as the Lear's macaw *Anodorhynchus leari* EN, the California condor *Gymnogyps californianus* CR and the Asian crested ibis *Nipponia nippon* EN undoubtedly owe their continued existence to the dedication and ingenuity of conservationists. Just this century, 26 species have been brought back from the brink of extinction, in so much as they have been downlisted from Critically Endangered to a lower category due to conservation action (Figure 6.5). In additional, there are many more Critically Endangered species that, although they have not yet recovered sufficiently to warrant downlisting, would have deteriorated further and perhaps even vanished altogether were it not for conservation.

Most of these species have been the beneficiaries of targeted recovery plans. For example, the Azores bullfinch *Pyrrhula murina* or priolo – once Europe's most threatened songbird – has undergone an impressive reversal of fortune thanks to dedicated conservation action led by the Portuguese Society for the Study of Birds (SPEA, BirdLife in Portugal). After decades of decline, which saw the population fall to perhaps as few as 40 pairs, the species is now bouncing back thanks to the restoration of over 300 hectares of native laurel forest through the removal of alien species and the establishment of native plants. As a result, the Azores bullfinch was downlisted from Critically Endangered to Endangered in 2010. Work is now underway to reconnect isolated forest patches to create one large contiguous habitat. The population is now stable at around 1000 individuals. In the 2016 Red List, the species was downlisted for the second time in under a decade – this time to Vulnerable.

In the 1960s, the Seychelles warbler *Acrocephalus sechellensis* was one of the rarest birds on Earth, reduced to a single population on the tiny (0.3 km²) island of Cousin. The island, then a private coconut plantation, was divested of much of its natural vegetation and the prospects for the warbler were bleak. In 1968, with only 26 birds remaining, the ICBP (BirdLife's forerunner) purchased Cousin and so began the species' long road to recovery. Today, through the work of Nature Seychelles (BirdLife in the Seychelles) and others, Cousin Island is once more a functioning natural ecosystem with a population of over 300 Seychelles warblers. In addition, the species has been translocated to four neighbouring

Figure 6.5 Thirty bird species have been downlisted from Critically Endangered since 2000 due to conservation action.

Image credits: First row, left to right: Leonardo Merçon, Dubi Shapiro, Dubi Shapiro, Wang Li Qiang Shutterstock, Dubi Shapiro, Julien Ueda, Dušan Brinkhuizen, Jaime Rojo, Tommy Pedersen. Second row, left to right: Jacques De Spéville, Jonathan Beilby, Richard Jackson, Peter Flood, Trenton Voytko, Mike Danzenbaker, Tone Trebar Shutterstock, Lars Petersson. Third row, left to right: Jon Irvine, Philip Perry, Stanislav Harvančík, Brian Gibbons, Graeme Taylor, Ian Davies, Rémi Bigonneau, Dušan Brinkhuizen. Fourth row, left to right: Bradley Hacker, Dubi Shapiro, Edwar H Guarín, John Cahill, Eric VanderWerf, Alistair Homer. All photos used with permission.

islands where it formerly occurred. The total population is now likely to exceed 2500 birds. In 2015, the species was reclassified as Near Threatened. Similarly impressive recoveries have been achieved for a number of the Seychelles' other endemic birds, including the Seychelles white-eye *Zosterops modestus* VU and the Seychelles magpie-robin *Copsychus sechellarum*. The latter originally occurred on numerous islands in the Seychelles, but by 1965 just 12–15 individuals remained on the island of Frégate and the species seemed destined for extinction. Thankfully, a recovery programme has seen the species translocated to additional islands, and, in 2005, the species was downlisted from Critically Endangered to Endangered. As of 2015, the total population numbered 283 birds across five islands. Although still highly imperilled, the Seychelles magpie-robin would have certainly already been lost were it not for the intervention of conservationists.

On Mauritius, several bird species also owe their existence to the actions of conservationists; indeed no other country has averted more avian extinctions. Much of the credit resides with one man, Carl Jones, a Welsh conservation biologist who started working in Mauritius in 1979. Jones has led five successful recovery programmes, where the starting population has numbered only a handful of individuals: Mauritius kestrel *Falco punctatus* EN, echo parakeet *Psittacula eques* VU, pink pigeon *Nesoenas mayeri* VU, Rodrigues warbler *Acrocephalus rodericanus* NT and Rodrigues fody *Foudia flavicans* NT. The recovery of the Mauritius kestrel is perhaps the most spectacular, having started from just four wild birds (including one breeding pair) in 1974. Persistence, ingenuity and the insight gained through endless hours intimately observing the species enabled Jones to pioneer techniques in captive breeding and release such that by the end of the 1990s several hundred kestrels were living wild across the island.

Many of the birds saved from extinction over recent decades have had small populations and limited ranges, indeed, many are confined to tiny, remote islands. In such circumstances, conservation practitioners are often able to intervene at a population level and manipulate population-limiting factors, such as invasive alien species or habitat quality, within a restricted and relatively closed system. Scaling up conservation interventions to revive the futures of more widely distributed species can prove challenging, but can be achieved. The black-faced spoonbill *Platalea minor* EN is widely but sporadically distributed throughout coastal areas of eastern Asia. The species breeds on offshore islets in the Yellow Sea at sites in China and the Korean peninsula and winters discontinuously from Japan south to the Red River delta in Vietnam, with additional major wintering congregations in Taiwan, Hong Kong, Macau and mainland China. The pressures on coastal habitats in this part of the world are enormous – rapid economic development has driven widespread wetland loss. In addition, agricultural and industrial development creates pollution, and periodic outbreaks of botulism have inflicted a significant toll on the population. Effective conservation therefore requires collaboration, galvanising conservation action across a large area and across national borders. An action plan was published, and there have been a number of workshops involving all major range countries. In 2013, a Black-faced Spoonbill Working Group was set up under the auspices of the East Asia-Australasian Flyway Partnership with the aim to facilitate and promote international collaboration in the species' conservation. Awareness campaigns have helped raise the profile of the species and it is now subject to an annual census of its wintering population. Most significantly, the main breeding and wintering sites have been designated as protected areas. From a low of fewer than 300 individuals in the late 1980s, the species has undergone a steady recovery. The most recent census took place in January 2019. Over 100 wintering sites were surveyed, with a total of 4463 individuals recorded. This is the highest figure yet and a 13% increase on the previous year.

Conservation measures targeted at individual species have resulted in some remarkable successes, and typically delivered wider ecological benefits, such as habitat restoration, yet ultimately the greatest impact is achieved through conservation measures that benefit suites of species and indeed entire habitats and landscapes. The principal mechanism for securing wildlife-rich landscapes is protected area designation. Since Yellowstone National Park became the world's first major protected area in 1872, roughly 215,000 further reserves, parks and sanctuaries have been formally gazetted. The World Commission on Protected Areas (WCPA), part of the International Union for Conservation of Nature (IUCN), recognises a range of protected area types, ranging from strict nature reserves and wilderness areas, in which human intrusion is strictly controlled, through to areas created and maintained through human activity but where nature thrives. Many protected areas have been formally designated for their importance for birds, and the BirdLife Partnership manages over four million hectares of reserves globally. In the European Union, Member States are obliged under the EU Birds Directive to identify Special Protection Areas (SPAs) for the protection of threatened, rare and vulnerable birds, as well as for regularly occurring migratory species. Currently, over 840,000 km^2 of the European Union are protected in this way.

Today, around 15% of the land and 7% of the sea is designated as protected areas globally. Despite this, many areas with rich, endemic or threatened avifaunas remain unprotected. BirdLife has comprehensively identified those sites globally that are significant for the persistence of avian diversity. Using standardised, objective and internationally agreed criteria, it has identified over 13,000 Important Bird and Biodiversity Areas (IBAs) in virtually all of the world's countries and territories, both on land and at sea. Unfortunately, of these sites, 80% are inadequately covered by protected areas and one-third are entirely unprotected. Some IBAs are the only places left on Earth where a highly threatened species can be found. Alarmingly, of the 127 such IBAs, only 26 are completely protected.

Many of the problems facing birds may seem intractable, involving, as they do, often widespread and deep-rooted threats. Yet recent successes in tackling illegal hunting and fisheries bycatch demonstrate huge progress that can be achieved when there is adequate resourcing and political will. For instance, conservationists, in collaboration with the Cypriot authorities and the British military police, have instigated a surveillance programme that is starting to turn the tide on illegal bird trapping on Cyprus. For decades, Cyprus has been an epicentre of illegal bird-trapping. Songbirds, principally Eurasian blackcaps *Sylvia atricapilla* LC, are trapped on an industrial scale to be sold illicitly in restaurants as a local delicacy called 'ambelopoulia', where a dozen birds can sell for 100 Euros. The trapping, using mistnets and limesticks, is indiscriminate, with unwanted species killed and discarded.

Despite being illegal since 1974, the number of birds caught has been on the rise in recent years. Much of the trapping occurs at one of the island's two UK military Sovereign Base Areas: Dhekelia. In autumn 2016, over 880,000 songbirds were trapped on the Dhekelia base. That year, the covert surveillance operation began, and since then more than 20 trappers have been caught and prosecuted, with the Cypriot courts imposing heavy sentences and fines. The latest survey at Dhekelia SBA in autumn 2018 revealed that the number of songbirds trapped had dropped to 121,000 – an 87% reduction in two years.

Notable progress has been made in recent years in reducing the harmful impact of fisheries bycatch on seabirds. In 2005, BirdLife International and the RSPB (BirdLife in the UK) launched the Albatross Task Force, an international team of seabird conservationists tasked with reducing albatross and petrel bycatch in targeted fisheries around the world. Albatross Task Force members embed themselves in regional fisheries, work with government and industry to improve regulations and team up directly with fishermen, providing advice on simple and inexpensive techniques that prevent unintentional seabird deaths. These measures include introducing bird-scaring lines (also known as tori lines) to keep birds away from baited hooks and trawl cables, adding weights to longlines so that the baited hooks sink faster with less opportunity for seabirds to get caught, and encouraging fishing at night when seabirds are less active. One innovative solution has been the 'Hookpod', a device that ensures that the barb of a baited longline hook remains encased in a polycarbonate capsule during line-setting and is only released at a predetermined depth of 10 m, beyond the reach of diving seabirds. The Hookpod has been shown to radically reduce seabird mortality without affecting the catch rate of target fish species (Sullivan et al., 2018). By promoting this range of at-sea mitigation measures, the Albatross Task Force has demonstrated that it is possible to reduce seabird bycatch drastically, typically by as much as 85% and often over 90%. Indeed, in South Africa, albatross bycatch in the hake demersal trawl fleet was reduced by 99% over six years. In Chile, modifying the nets used in the purse-seine fleet reduced bycatch by 98%, and trials in Peru have shown that net lights show promise in reducing seabird bycatch in gillnet fisheries. Following sustained work by the Albatross Task Force, Argentina and Chile have recently announced new seabird bycatch regulations, which are set to save over 10,000 black-browed albatrosses *Thalassarche melanophris* LC in one Argentinean fishery alone.

Examples like those above demonstrate that solutions can be found to the threats facing the world's birds and to nature more widely. However, to end the extinction crisis we must scale up our conservation response. We must implement existing action plans for threatened species swiftly and comprehensively, especially for highly threatened groups such as vultures, and develop and implement new plans as needed. We must introduce measures to restrict the further spread of invasive alien species, and eradicate or control those that are having a detrimental effect on threatened species and important seabird colonies. We must ensure that IBAs are formally protected and effectively managed and go further by restoring and reconnecting wider degraded landscapes, especially in the forested tropics. We must adopt agricultural practices that adequately and equitably feed the world's population, but that are also environmentally sustainable by avoiding farming practices that are resource-

and carbon-intensive, limiting the use of harmful pesticides and reducing food waste. We must eliminate the illegal and unsustainable hunting and trade of birds, especially in Southeast Asia, and ensure that effective seabird bycatch mitigation measures are rolled out across all fisheries. We must tackle climate change by ending our dependency on fossil fuels and switching to clean energy sources, and help bird species to adapt to the climate change to which we are already committed. Ultimately, to achieve this, we must ensure that global investment in conservation is commensurate with the scale of the problem.

Building on data for birds, a study led by BirdLife and the RSPB (BirdLife in the UK) calculated the annual investment needed not just to prevent avian extinctions, but to avoid extinctions of all known threatened species and to protect and manage all sites of importance for nature (McCarthy et al., 2012). The study surveyed 236 experts in bird conservation to ascertain the financial investment needed to improve the conservation status of 211 highly threatened species. The results were modelled to allow extrapolation to all threatened bird species. This provided an estimated annual investment of roughly US$1 billion needed to halt human-driven bird extinction and improve the IUCN Red List status of all threatened bird species. Using data on how the resources needed to conserve birds compare with those required for other taxa, the authors then estimated the annual cost of preventing the extinction of all known globally threatened animals and plants at around US$4 billion. Data on the management costs of safeguarding Important Bird Areas, as well as estimates of land-purchase costs globally, allowed the authors to estimate the cost of adequately protecting and managing all terrestrial sites of global conservation significance at approximately US$76 billion per year.

Put simply, an annual investment of around US$80 billion would safeguard nature and end the extinction crisis. To put this in perspective, this is less than is spent globally each year on pet food and roughly the same as that spent by Americans annually on lottery tickets. When compared with the overall value of the global economy, estimated at $80 trillion, it is a truly trivial figure. Spending just 0.1% of global GDP on wildlife conservation would not only prevent the extinction of an estimated one million life forms, but also safeguard the natural processes on which all life depends and which underpin every aspect of human existence.

Acknowledgements

I am most grateful to Lucy Haskell for assistance on this chapter and to Professor Nigel Collar, Dr Stuart Butchart, Dr Ian Burfield and Kelly Malsch for their helpful comments and suggestions. Much of the information presented is generated by BirdLife International in its role as the IUCN Red List Authority for birds. I would therefore like to acknowledge and thank BirdLife's Founder Patrons, Benjamin Olewine, the Aage V. Jensen Charity Foundation, the A. G. Leventis Foundation, the Tasso Leventis Foundation, the Japan Fund for Science and all BirdLife Species Champions for supporting its Red List assessments and the taxonomic work that underpins them. Thanks also to everyone who contributes information to the Red List assessments, especially via BirdLife's Globally Threatened Bird Forums (https://forums.birdlife.org).

References

Anderson, O.R.J., Small, C.J., Croxall, J.P., et al. (2011) Global seabird bycatch in longline fisheries. *Endanger Species Res* 14: 91–106.

Bar-On, Y.M., Phillips, R. and Milo, R. (2018) The biomass distribution on Earth. *Proc Natl Acad Sci USA* 115: 6506–6511.

Bennett, P.M. and Owens, I.P.F. (1997) Variation in extinction-risk among birds: chance or evolutionary predisposition? *Proc Royal Soc B* 264: 401–408.

Benning, T.L., LaPointe, D., Atkinson, C.T. and Vitousek, P.M. (2002) Interactions of climate change with biological invasions and land use in the Hawaiian Islands: modeling the fate of endemic birds using a geographic information system. *Proc Natl Acad Sci USA* 99: 246–249.

BirdLife International (2004) *Birds in Europe: Population Estimates, Trends and Conservation Status.* Conservation Series No. 12. Cambridge, UK: BirdLife International.

BirdLife International (2017) *European Birds of Conservation Concern: Populations, Trends and National Responsibilities.* Cambridge, UK: BirdLife International.

Brochet, A-L., Van Den Bossche, W., Jbour, S., et al. (2016) Preliminary assessment of the scope and scale of illegal killing and taking of birds in the Mediterranean. *Bird Conserv Int* 26: 1–28.

Brochet, A-L., Van Den Bossche, W., Jones, V. R., et al. (2019) Illegal killing and taking of birds in Europe outside the Mediterranean: assessing the scope and scale of a complex issue. *Bird Conserv Int* 29: 10–40.

Chan, S. (2004) A bird to watch: yellow-breasted bunting *Emberiza aureola. BirdingASIA* 1: 16–17.

da Silva, L.P. and Mata, V.A. (2019) Stop harvesting olives at night: it kills millions of songbirds. *Nature* 569: 192.

Diamond, J. (1991) *The Rise and Fall of the Third Chimpanzee.* London, UK: Vintage.

Duncan, R.P., Boyer, A.G. and Blackburn, T.M. (2013) Magnitude and variation of prehistoric bird extinctions in the Pacific. *Proc Natl Acad Sci USA* 110: 6436–6441.

Gregory, R.D., Skorpilova, J. and Butler, S. (2019) An analysis of trends, uncertainty and species selection shows contrasting trends of widespread forest and farmland birds in Europe. *Ecol Indic* 103: 676–687.

Hallmann, C.A., Sorg, M., Jongejans, E., et al. (2017) More than 75 percent decline over 27 years in total flying insect biomass in protected areas. *PLoS One* 12(10): e0185809.

Hirschfeld, A., Attard, G. and Scott, L. (2019). Bird-hunting in Europe: an analysis of bag figures and the potential impact on the conservation of threatened species. *Br Birds* 112: 153–166.

Hume J.P. (2017) *Extinct Birds,* Second Edn. London, UK: Bloomsbury Natural History.

Huxley, J.S. (1916) Bird-watching and biological science: some observations on the study of courtship in birds. *The Auk* 33: 142–161.

Inger, R., Gregory, R., Duffy, J.P., et al. (2014) Common European birds are declining rapidly while less abundant species' numbers are rising. *Ecol Lett* 18: 28–36.

IPBES; Brondizio, E.S., Settele, J., Díaz, S. and Ngo, H.T. (Eds.) (2019) *Global Assessment Report on Biodiversity and Ecosystem Services of the Intergovernmental Science-Policy Platform on Biodiversity and Ecosystem Services.* Bonn, Germany: IPBES Secretariat.

Jiguet, F., Robert, A., Lorrillière, R., et al. (2019) Unravelling migration connectivity reveals unsustainable hunting of the declining ortolan bunting. *Sci Adv* 5: eaau2642.

Junta de Andalucia. (2019) Informe sobre el impacto generado por la explotacion del olivar en superintensivo sobre las especies protegidas en Andalucia. www.ecologistasenaccion.org/wp-content/uploads/2018/11/informe-sobre-el-impacto-generado-por-la-explotacion-del-olivar-en-superintensivo-sobre-las-especies-protegidas-en-andalucia.pdf (accessed October 2022).

Kamp, J., Oppel, S., Ananin, A.A., et al. (2015) Global population collapse in a superabundant migratory bird and illegal trapping in China. *Conserv Biol* 29: 1684–1694.

Langham, G.M., Schuetz, J.G., Distler, T., Soykan, C.U. and Wilsey, C. (2015) Conservation status of North American birds in the face of future climate change. *PLoS One* 10(9): e0135350.

Marques, A., Martins, I.S., Kastner, T., et al. (2019) Increasing impacts of land use on biodiversity and carbon sequestration driven by population and economic growth. *Nat Ecol Evol.* 3: 628–637.

Marshall, H., Collar, N.J., Lees, A.C., et al. (2019) Spatio-temporal dynamics of consumer demand driving the Asian songbird crisis. *Biol Conserv* 241: 108237.

McCarthy, D.P., Donald, P.F., Scharlemann, J.P.W., et al. (2012) Financial costs of meeting global biodiversity conservation targets: current spending and unmet needs. *Science* 338: 946–949.

McKinnon, L., Picotin, M., Bolduc, E., Juillet, C. and Bêty, J. (2012) Timing of breeding, peak food availability, and effects of mismatch on chick growth in birds nesting in the High Arctic. *Can J Zool*, 90: 961–971.

McNeill, J.R. (2014) *The Great Acceleration: An Environmental History of the Anthropocene since 1945.* Cambridge, MA: Harvard University Press.

Møller, A.P., Saino, N., Adamík, P., et al. (2010) Rapid change in host use of the common cuckoo *Cuculus canorus* linked to climate change. *Proc Royal Soc B* 278: 733–738.

Nash, S.V. (1993) *The Trade in Southeast Asian Non-CITES Birds.* Cambridge, UK: TRAFFIC Southeast Asia.

North American Bird Conservation Initiative (2016) *The State of North America's Birds 2016.* Ottawa, Canada: Environment and Climate Change Canada.

Pacifici, M., Visconti, P., Butchart, S., et al. (2017) Species' traits influenced their response to recent climate change. *Nat Clim Change* 7: 205–208.

Purvis, A., Agapow, P.M., Gittleman, J.L. and Mace, G.M. (2000) Nonrandom extinction and the loss of evolutionary history. *Science* 288: 328–330.

Reynolds, M.H., Courtot, K.N., Berkowitz, P., et al. (2015) Will the effects of sea-level rise create ecological traps for Pacific island seabirds? *PLoS One* 10(9): e0136773.

Rosenberg, K.V., Dokter, A.M., Blancher, P.J., et al. (2019) Decline of the North American avifauna. *Science* 366: 120–124.

Seebens, H., Blackburn, T.M., Dyer, E.E., et al. (2017) No saturation in the accumulation of alien species worldwide. *Nat Commun* 8: 14435.

Seymour, F. and Busch, J. (2016) *Why Forests? Why Now?: The Science, Economics, and Politics of Tropical Forests and Climate Change.* Washington, DC: Brookings Institution Press.

Steffen, W., Crutzen, P.J. and McNeill, J.R. (2007) The Anthropocene: are humans now overwhelming the great forces of nature? *Ambio* 36: 614–621.

Suivi Temporel des Oiseaux Communs (STOC). (2019) Résultats. Paris, France: Muséum National d'Histoire Naturelle, Département Homme et Environnement. Available at: www.vigienature .fr/fr/observatoires/suivi-temporel-oiseaux-communs-stoc/resultats-3413 (accessed October 2022).

Sullivan, B., Kibel, B., Kibel, P et al. (2018) At-sea trialling of the Hookpod: A 'one-stop' mitigation solution for seabird bycatch in pelagic longline fisheries. *Anim Conserv* 21: 159–167.

Szabo, J.K., Khwaja, N., Garnett, S.T. and Butchart, S.H.M. (2012) Global patterns and drivers of avian extinctions at the species and subspecies level. *PLoS One* 7: e47080.

Tucker, G.M. and Heath, M.F. (1994) *Birds in Europe: Their Conservation Status.* Conservation Series No. 3. Cambridge, UK: BirdLife International.

US Department of the Interior, US Fish and Wildlife Service and US Department of Commerce, US Census Bureau. (2016) *National Survey of Fishing, Hunting, and Wildlife-Associated Recreation.* Washington, DC: US Government Printing Office.

Waite, T.A. and Strickland, D. (2006) Climate change and the demographic demise of a hoarding bird living on the edge. *Proc Royal Soc B*, 273: 2809–2813.

Żydelis, R., Small, C. and French, G. (2013) The incidental catch of seabirds in gillnet fisheries: a global review. *Biol Conserv* 162: 76–88.

SEVEN

Reptiles

PHILIP BOWLES

Summary

Reptiles, despite being among the largest and most ecologically important vertebrate groups, have until recently received less research attention than other terrestrial vertebrates and their conservation has been hampered by a lack of both data and interest. Around 20% of reptile species are thought to be at risk of extinction (rising to 50% in turtles), but population trends for most species are not known with certainty and the IUCN Red List does not yet have complete coverage for this group. Reptiles are at particular risk from habitat loss and fragmentation, invasive species and overharvesting. They are thought to be especially sensitive to climate change, the effects of which are probably underestimated due to data limitations. The impacts of a recently identified emergent disease in snakes are unclear but may become a significant driver of future declines. Conservation successes among reptiles are scarce, but notable achievements include population recoveries in most crocodilian species since the 1970s and successful control of invasive species that threatened many island reptiles, particularly in New Zealand. There is a pressing need to better understand the ecology and conservation needs of most reptiles, and to increase their representation in conservation planning.

Table 7.1 gives a summary of the Red List status of each major reptile group as of December 2019. Pre-2004 assessments – outside the focus of this chapter – are included for turtles and crocodilians as a large proportion of each group does not yet have published reassessments, and are included in the figures for Extinct species. Global species numbers are taken from The Reptile Database, updated May 2020.

Table 7.1 *Numbers of species in each category by taxonomic group. Numbers in parentheses – shown only for turtles and crocodilians – include pre-2004 assessments*

	Crocodilians	Lizards	Snakes	Turtles	Tuatara	Amphisbaenians
Global total	**26**	**6827**	**3828**	**359**	**1**	**201**
No. assessed	18 (23)	4760	2661	135 (258)	1	99
LC	8 (12)	2988	1695	33 (44)	1	54
NT	0	291	105	14 (33)	0	2
DD	0	570	546	4 (11)	0	31
VU	3 (4)	325	123	27 (67)	0	3
EN	0	384	125	20 (44)	0	4
CR	7	182	63	35 (50)	0	5
EW	0	2	0	0 (1)	0	0
EX	0	18	4	8	0	0

7.1 Introduction

With more than 11,200 recognised species, reptiles (lizards, amphisbaenians and snakes, crocodilians, turtles and the tuatara) are the most, or after birds the second most, diverse group of terrestrial vertebrates. Reptiles are important predators, in many cases occur in high densities that provide abundant prey resources for other species, and can be important seed dispersers (Böhm et al., 2013). This 'central' role they perform in many ecosystems and their relevance as bioindicators are, however, rarely appreciated (Shine, 2012, Böhm et al., 2013).

In the wake of emerging evidence of widespread decline in amphibian species, the possibility that a corresponding global decline in reptiles may be underway was suggested as early as 2000 by Gibbons et al. (2000). Reptiles remain among the least-studied vertebrates (Todd et al., 2010) and are commonly neglected in conservation plans (Böhm et al., 2013). Although research interest in reptiles has increased over the last 25 years in fields including ecology, taxonomy and physiology, this has for the most part not been accompanied by increased conservation attention. McDiarmid and Foster (2012) reported finding a broad consensus among herpetologists that reptiles had been largely neglected by the conservation community for the 40 years prior to 2002, with the exception of turtles and crocodiles (which together represent less than 4% of reptile diversity), and some lizards and snakes endemic to islands.

These animals have similarly been accorded a low priority in terms of conservation assessments: by 2008 IUCN had completed global Red List assessments for every then-described species of amphibians, mammals and birds, but the corresponding Global Reptile Assessment (GRA) was not completed until 2020, with the final results published in December 2021. This particular initiative has been ongoing for 15 years, but has struggled to secure interest from funding bodies on which IUCN relies to complete assessments.

Reptiles reach their highest diversity in the tropics, where pressures from land use change are greatest, and they are expected to be particularly sensitive to the impacts of climate change. Many species are harvested for food, for use in traditional medicine, for skin products or for the international pet trade. Reptiles are among the most successful vertebrates at colonising and diversifying on islands, resulting in a large number of island endemic species that are now at particular risk from encroachment by humans and invasive species. They generally have narrower distributions than other vertebrates and often narrow ecological niches, both factors likely to increase their sensitivity to threats (Böhm et al., 2013). Turtles, around 50% of which are threatened with extinction, have been recognised as the most threatened group of terrestrial vertebrates.

7.1.1 Summary of Extinction Risk in Reptiles

To date, the only global analysis of extinction risk in reptiles is that of Böhm et al. (2013) who found that, based on Red List assessments for a random sample of 1500 species (a sampled Red List Index or sRLI), 18.9% of reptiles are threatened with extinction, assuming DD species are threatened in the same proportion as the remainder. The

Table 7.2 *Numbers of species in each category in the 2013 sampled Red List Index and the 2019 IUCN Red List*

Red List Category	Böhm et al., 2013		Red List (2004–Dec 2019)	
	Number	%	Number	%
Sample size	1500		7680	
Extinct (EX)	0	0.00%	30	0.4%
Extinct in the Wild (EW)	0	0.00%	2	0.03%
Critically Endangered (CR)	26	1.73%	292	3.8%
Endangered (EN)	92	6.13%	533	6.94%
Vulnerable (VU)	105	7.00%	481	6.26%
Near Threatened (NT)	78	5.20%	412	5.36%
Least Concern (LC)	881	58.73%	4779	62.23%
Data Deficient (DD)	318	21.20%	1151	14.99%
Minimum threatened [CR+EN+VU]	223	14.87%	1306	16.62%
Maximum threatened [CR+EN+VU+DD]	541	36.07%	2457	31.26%
% threatened [(CR+EN+VU)/(N-DD)]		**18.87%**		**20%**

ongoing Global Reptile Assessment has greatly expanded the Red List's coverage of this group to the point where 68% of described reptiles have published assessments, although unlike the sRLI the geographic coverage of this sample is non-random. Comparative results are shown in Table 7.2, excluding species last assessed prior to 2004 (the commencement of the GRA).

Table 7.2 shows that 20% of assessed reptiles are threatened with extinction, suggesting reptiles are at slightly greater risk than previously recognised. The difference between this figure and that of the sRLI reflects the greater level of resolution allowed by the larger sample size, as relatively fewer species are listed as Data Deficient (14.99% vs. 21.2%). Böhm et al. (2013) calculated both a minimum (assuming all DD species would prove to be Least Concern) and maximum (assuming all DD species are threatened) extinction risk for reptiles of 14.87–36.07%. The comparable range from the current stage of the GRA is 16.62–31.26%.

Summary papers based on the reptile assessments for individual regions indicate very high variability in extinction risk for local faunas, ranging from as low as 3.5% in the Arabian Peninsula (Cox et al., 2012) to 39% in Madagascar (Jenkins et al., 2014) (Table 7.3). Both the highest risk of extinction and the highest levels of data deficiency are found in tropical regions (Böhm et al., 2013).

A recent review identified 82 reptile species known to have become extinct in the last 50,000 years, the vast majority from islands, and every recent extinction has been attributed to human impacts (Slavenko et al., 2016). Since then, two additional species have been listed as Extinct on the IUCN Red List: the Christmas Island whiptail skink, following the death of the last known individual in 2014, and Günther's dwarf burrowing

Table 7.3 *Proportions of reptiles in threatened categories (VU, EN or CR) reported for several different regions*

Region	% Threatened	Source
Europe	20	Cox and Temple, 2009
Mediterranean Basin	13	Cox et al., 2006
Arabian Peninsula	3.5	Cox et al., 2012
Madagascar	39	Jenkins et al., 2014
South Africa	5.4	Tolley et al., 2019
Australia	7.1	Tingley et al., 2019
Tanzania	13	Meng et al., 2016

skink, last seen in 1884 and ruled extinct following repeated failures to rediscover it. In April 2019 the only captive female Yangtze giant softshell turtle died. Only two wild individuals of this species are known to survive, of unknown sex, and so this species may well be functionally extinct.

Many DD or Critically Endangered species known only from historical records may now be extinct. Some areas with range-restricted reptiles have 'undoubtedly' suffered extinctions before being visited by scientists (Shine, 2012).

7.1.2 Reptile Taxonomy

The only compiled list of reptile species globally is the Reptile Database. This is widely but not universally followed (Böhm et al., 2013), which can result in disagreements or uncertainty regarding the species concepts associated with individual names. The Reptile Database lists more than 10,970 valid species of reptile, almost a third of which have been recognised since 2000. Undoubtedly, many more species remain to be discovered, and it is believed that current estimates of reptile diversity in the tropics remain 'far too low' (Shine, 2012).

Taxonomic instability in lizards and snakes is extreme and represents a major challenge for accurately evaluating the conservation status of this group. Species previously considered to be widespread have frequently been shown to consist of multiple lineages, each of which is more range-restricted and some of which may have more specialised habitat requirements than previously thought (Fitzgerald et al., 2017). For example, within two years of its Red List assessment, Storr's lerista NT was split into three species, and a new species split from the already Critically Endangered lesser Chinese softshell is on the verge of extinction. Several species long thought to be relatively widespread may in fact be extinct following taxonomic changes that assigned living populations to different species, including two revisions in 2019 alone: an Australian earless dragon and the New Zealand speckled skink. Conversely, animals previously believed to be range-restricted and threatened may belong to more widespread species: *Sphenodon guentheri* was listed on the Red List as Vulnerable but is now treated as a subpopulation of the only recognised tuatara species, *Sphenodon punctatus* LC. Many species assessed on the Red List are recognised as species complexes whose taxonomy is presently unresolved, but which for practical purposes need to be treated as a single conservation unit.

Numerous species (including over 14% of lizards; Meiri et al., 2018) are known from individual specimens or localities, and old descriptions or those based on museum material may lack adequate locality data. This can lead to significant errors: one species described as a new Australian gecko based on museum material proved to be a juvenile African agama, while a purportedly Timorese gecko was recently found to represent a South American species. These cases are comparatively rare and generally do not affect conservation, but are illustrative of the complexity of reptile taxonomy and have the potential to result in non-existent animals receiving Data Deficient assessments or mistargeted survey effort. In a number of cases the only known museum specimen of a named species is poorly preserved or has been lost, and in these it may be impossible to determine whether these names represent valid species (Meiri et al., 2018).

7.1.3 Data Limitations

The ability to identify species and understand their ecological requirements is fundamental to developing conservation strategies (Vitt, 2016), but basic knowledge of species' taxonomy, biology and habitat requirements are lacking for many species and regions, including those where reptiles are at their most diverse.

Reptiles can be difficult to survey or monitor systematically, and studies have rarely had an adequate sampling effort or duration to provide unequivocal support for declines or to elucidate their causes, even in well-known species (Todd et al., 2010). Suitable long-term population studies exist for only 'a handful' of species, and it is unknown for most reptiles whether they experience significant population fluctuations over time (Vitt, 2016) although modelling suggests this is likely for many lizards (Fitzgerald, 1994).

Reptiles include a number of groups that are particularly difficult to monitor, including fossorial species. While most have fast life histories, the class includes long-lived animals for which the appropriate timeframe to identify declines is typically unclear, but may encompass several decades. In tuatara, an analysis of 54 years of survey data found that a long-term declining trend in body condition was only evident with more than 22 years of data (Moore et al., 2007). Similarly, Fitzgerald (1994) found a high degree of sensitivity to year-to-year stochastic events among tegu lizards that is likely to be typical of species with similar life histories. It may consequently require several decades of monitoring to clarify population trends (Fitzgerald, 1994). A subsequent analysis of eight years of harvest data following the implementation of a management programme for the red tegu in Paraguay was only able to conclude that this species was 'probably not declining due to hunting' (Mieres and Fitzgerald, 2006).

This can hamper evaluations of the success of conservation measures in long-lived species; sea turtle populations in Florida are only now responding positively to conservation interventions dating from the 1970s onwards, based on a conclusion with 'relative certainty' that sea turtle nesting activity and hatchling recruitment are increasing significantly (Antworth et al., 2006).

Table 7.4 *Summary of population trends in reptiles on the April 2019 Red List*

Population Status	Number	%
Species	7680	
Decreasing	1064	13.85%
Stable	2779	36.18%
Increasing	42	0.55%
Unknown	3713	48.35%

Almost 50% of Red Listed reptiles are considered to have an unknown population trend (Table 7.4); in most of the remainder a stable trend is inferred from a lack of known threats and declines from surrogate measures such as habitat loss, rather than reflecting true knowledge of a species' population status. Only 42 species are known or suspected to have increasing populations; about a third of these are subject to active conservation management, while the remainder are mainly human commensals whose populations are expanding in response to habitat change.

In some areas, particularly in the tropics, even an understanding of species distributions is 'entirely inadequate' (e.g. in Africa; Tolley et al., 2016). Conversely, some species have been found to have much wider ranges than once believed (Todd et al., 2010), among them the whiptail lizard *Contomastix vittata* VU, which was rediscovered a century after it was last recorded, and the gecko *Matoatoa spannringi* DD, rediscovered at an unexpected locality only a year after it was listed in the Red List as Extinct. This can introduce a high degree of uncertainty into Red List assessments which, in the near-complete absence of adequate population data for most reptiles, have mainly used geographic range in both the sRLI and the GRA.

7.2 Drivers of Decline and Extinction

7.2.1 Habitat Loss and Degradation

Habitat loss and degradation represent the principal causes of reptile declines. Many lizards and snakes are habitat specialists, while crocodilians, most turtles and several snake and lizard lineages are reliant on aquatic – typically freshwater – habitats. Aquatic reptiles other than sea snakes depend on terrestrial habitats for reproduction, and so are exposed to pressures impacting both land and water. Coastal conversion for development threatens sea turtle nesting beaches (Spotila, 2004), and similarly loss of breeding grounds is a major threat to some freshwater turtles. Freshwater habitats are directly destroyed through the excavation or drainage of wetlands (Gibbons et al., 2000) and damming or other flow modification of rivers, as well as general degradation in water quality. These latter have been implicated in, among others, crocodilian declines in the Ganges and Yangtze river systems, declines in North American turtles and the apparent disappearance of the South American water snake *Hydrodynastes melanogigas* following dam construction.

The precise mechanisms by which habitat loss causes declines are in many cases poorly understood, particularly outside forested areas (Gardner et al., 2007). Existing studies exhibit a bias towards the New World, and particularly temperate North America (Gardner et al., 2007), although the majority of reptiles occur in the tropics, and habitat loss has some of its most pronounced impacts on forest-restricted reptiles outside the New World.

Habitat loss is driven principally by agricultural expansion (a threat to over a quarter of all assessed reptiles) but also by timber extraction, urban, commercial and tourist development, fire and mining. More than 70% of African reptiles assessed by the time of a study conducted by Tolley et al. (2016) are at risk from agricultural expansion, 50% from resource extraction (both logging and mining) and 30% from urban development. Unsustainable farming practices in arid and semi-arid lands in the Mediterranean has resulted in desertification, erosion, salinisation and land degradation, and the draining of wetlands on which aquatic reptiles depend (Cox et al., 2006). Reptiles appear to exhibit the greatest diversity and degree of endemism in karst habitats of any animal group in Southeast Asia, and yet limestone mining in this area is extensive and a threat to the survival of numerous species. Small tropical islands are often attractive areas for tourist development, threatening endemic species such as those on Tioman in Malaysia.

Most obviously, land clearance simply removes habitat on which species depend for shelter, breeding sites, shade or food resources. Arboreal species are directly reliant on the presence of trees, while other species are directly susceptible to desiccation in open environments (e.g. the lizard genus *Riama* in northern South America). More indirectly, deforestation can result in declines through longer-term impacts on survival and reproduction, and can expose animals to greater competition from species associated with more open habitats. Replacement of natural forest with monocultures – generally without complex understorey vegetation or deep leaf litter – is typically associated with a reduction in diversity of the reptile fauna. A 50% reduction in leaf litter density has been shown to result in significant declines in lizard encounter rates in Costa Rica (Whitfield et al., 2014).

For highly range-restricted species, removal of key microhabitat features can threaten a species with extinction or contribute to the decline of an already threatened species. The dunes sagebrush lizard VU is a restricted-range species strictly confined to dune blowouts associated with Shinnery oak. This microhabitat is not only highly sensitive to disturbance, but very difficult or impossible to replace through habitat restoration, and population dynamics in the lizard appear to be sensitive to highly localised differences in habitat structure and quality (Ryberg et al., 2015). Even slight disturbance to rocks used by the Australian broad-headed snake VU for shelter can render these refugia unsuitable for the species and may be sufficient to exclude it from extensive areas of otherwise apparently suitable habitat.

Lizards and many snakes typically have limited dispersal abilities and often specialised habitat requirements, and are less able than many vertebrates to disperse between habitat fragments. Although the occurrence of many lizards at high population densities may enable them to maintain viable populations in relatively small patches, fragmentation may have negative long-term implications for genetic diversity within these isolates, and should individual populations become extinct a species is unlikely to recolonise areas from which it has been lost. Metapopulation dynamics in lizards may operate at extremely restricted scales (as little as 100 m in the Grand Skink in New Zealand, for instance), especially for ecological specialists like the dune sagebrush lizard, and so even highly localised impacts can disrupt connectivity between subpopulations and threaten population persistence.

Land clearance is commonly associated with the construction of access roads. While roads themselves are rarely recognised as a major direct threat, they open areas further into the interior for development and expand the area of edge habitat. Additionally, they may be an underappreciated source of direct mortality (Todd et al., 2010): turtles often exhibit sex-biased migratory behaviour in which females are disproportionately likely to cross roads in search of oviposition sites, which may result in elevated female mortality from road kill. Road mortality has been identified as the major current threat to the Milos viper EN, resulting in around 300 deaths every summer in an island endemic species whose annual adult recruitment is estimated to be around 625 individuals (Nilson, 2019).

7.2.2 Invasive Species

Introductions of exotic, typically predatory, species are the primary cause of reptile extinctions and remain the most significant threat to many reptiles, particularly island endemics. Almost exactly 30% of reptiles listed in threatened categories are at risk from non-native species.

Both lizards and turtles decline rapidly on islands following the introduction of invaders that prey on adult animals, eggs or both. Species are frequently lost altogether from small islands. While they usually persist on larger islands or in mainland areas, a notable exception is New Zealand where the tuatara and numerous species of native lizards that were once widespread on the mainland either no longer survive there or have a highly fragmentary remnant distribution. Declines in Galapagos tortoises have been attributed to egg predation by rats and feral pigs (Gibbons et al., 2000).

Böhm et al. (2013) identified that oceanic islands and Australia are at particular risk from invasive species. This has been confirmed for threatened reptiles in full assessments for Australia (Tingley et al., 2019), New Zealand, Oceania and the Caribbean. The invasive Oriental wolf snake has been implicated as the primary cause of extinction for the Christmas Island whiptail skink, and the extinction in the wild of two geckos also endemic to that island, with irruptions of invasive crazy ants likely to have contributed to declines in these species.

Mongooses, several species of rats and cats have represented the major invasive threats to reptiles (Fitzgerald et al., 2017). The most damaging species invasion for reptiles (particularly snakes and ground-dwelling lizards) was the widespread introduction in the nineteenth century of the small Indian mongoose to islands in the Caribbean. Extinctions resulting from this introduction are likely to have been under-recorded, as numerous lizard species have been described from museum material long after they were last seen alive, although it is difficult to prove beyond reasonable doubt that some of these species may not survive on small, unsurveyed islets. During Red List assessments in the Caribbean, many species were consequently listed as Critically Endangered with the 'Possibly Extinct' flag. Many survivors remain in decline as a result of predation pressure from this and other exotic species, and some persist only in areas inhabited by humans from which mongooses are excluded by dogs. The Antiguan racer (CR), at one point described as the world's rarest snake, owes that title to predation by black rats and mongooses, and prior to conservation intervention survived only on a single offshore island from which these mammals were absent.

Crazy ants and Argentine fire ants widely threaten lizards in Oceania, and individual species of invasive reptiles have been implicated in declines and extinctions of island lizards through either predation (as with the Oriental wolf snake on Christmas Island and the brown tree snake on Guam), hybridisation (documented for multiple Caribbean iguana species following invasion by the exotic green iguana) or competition (as with introduced geckos of the genus *Hemidactylus* implicated in declines of island geckos, and invasive *Phelsuma* day geckos on Mauritius). Grazing animals, particularly goats on arid islands, can also threaten the survival of reptiles dependent on vegetation. As a consequence of rat predation and removal of all accessible vegetation on Redonda Island in the Caribbean by goats, three lizards are now extinct and two remaining species are Critically Endangered. Overgrazing by goats and attendant soil erosion are also believed to be responsible for the extinction of the Round Island burrowing boa, which was already rare by the 1940s and has not been seen since 1975.

Although invasive animals are rarely a range-wide threat to mainland reptiles, there is evidence of declines and at least one case of range contraction (the Texas horned lizard LC) as a result of fire ant invasion, and the impacts of this species may be exacerbated by habitat disturbance that facilitates its spread (Todd et al., 2010). Fire ant invasion may also be responsible for declines in the southern hognose snake VU, which has disappeared from much of its former range. Argentine ants, which experiments have found to be inferior prey compared with native ants, which they displace, appear to have contributed to declines in the horned lizard (Todd et al., 2010).

In one notorious case, a toxic prey species, the cane toad, has been responsible for widespread declines in Australian snakes and monitor lizards, as well as individual mortality in crocodiles. The invasion of this species into their ranges has resulted in rapid declines in populations of Mitchell's and Mertens' water monitors over the past three generations, resulting in threatened listings for both species.

Invasive plants can represent a significant threat to reptiles. These are frequently escaped pasture grasses or crop plants, and can become established across wide areas of the mainland. These may increase fire frequency, with negative impacts on species adapted to different fire regimes (such as the gopher tortoise VU) or by vegetation which shades favoured habitats and reduces basking opportunities. Multiple invasive plant species, especially buffelgrass, were identified as threats to lizards in the Australian reptile assessment.

7.2.3 Harvesting

Some reptiles are subject to high levels of commercial and subsistence-level harvesting, for use in food, traditional medicine, skin products and the pet trade. Harvesting is listed as a threat to 708 Red Listed reptiles, including about 20% of threatened species. While sustainable exploitation is an important conservation tool and is largely responsible for the success of crocodile conservation (McDiarmid and Foster, 2012), trade in most reptiles is both unregulated and unmonitored. Exploitation is a secondary threat to most snakes and lizards, but the leading cause of decline in the most threatened reptile group, turtles.

Böhm et al. (2013) reported that 87% of threatened marine and freshwater reptiles – mostly turtles – are at risk from exploitation. Turtles are long-lived, late-maturing and have low reproductive output. Most species are exploited, but it is considered 'nearly impossible' for them to withstand ongoing hunting pressure (Böhm et al., 2013), and Buhlmann et al. (2002) considered levels of exploitation in some freshwater turtles to be at 'crisis levels'. As long ago as 1814, Alexander von Humboldt identified overexploitation as a threat to the communally nesting arrau, a giant freshwater turtle that once exhibited 'enormous' populations in the Orinoco and Amazon rivers. Consumption of eggs and nesting females of this species has not ceased, and while it lacks an up-to-date Red List assessment, the Freshwater Turtle and Tortoise Specialist Group recommended in 2011 that it be considered Critically Endangered.

Human consumption (in the case of sea turtles, in combination with fisheries bycatch) is the primary driver of turtle declines (Buhlmann et al., 2002). Every species of crocodilian has suffered historical declines as a result of the combined impacts of overharvesting and habitat loss (Fitzgerald et al., 2017). Nearly 7 million aquatic snakes are harvested annually for consumption in Cambodia's Tonle Sap, with catches reported to have declined by 74–84% between 2000 and 2005 (Brooks et al., 2007). Jensen (2017) interviewed locals involved in the bushmeat trade in Yaoundé in Cameroon, who universally reported both that snakes had become harder to find in the forest over the preceding five years and that demand for snake meat had increased over the same time period.

In West and Central Africa both the skin trade in pythons and domestic consumption of snake meat, principally of pythons and larger vipers such as the Gaboon viper, are extensive (Jensen, 2017). Southeast Asian species – including the king cobra, as well as some species of ratsnake, cobra and python – are also heavily used in the skin trade.

Most lizards occur at high densities and have fast life histories (Todd et al., 2010), traits that are likely to make them resistant to harvesting pressure. Indeed it has been suggested that the international pet trade in reptiles to supply markets in the USA, Japan and Europe – which is worth millions of dollars annually to local hunters, the commercial trade and wildlife smugglers (Fitzgerald et al., 2017) – could provide incentives for sustainable management of species of commercial interest. Nonetheless, some lizard species that are either highly localised (e.g. the turquoise dwarf gecko and the Union Island gecko (both CR), and a number of chameleon species), that seem to occur in naturally low abundance (including multiple species of Australian leaf-tailed gecko) and/ or have slow life histories, are or may be at risk of extinction at least partially as a result of harvesting for the international pet trade, and in the case of the Union Island gecko the associated destruction of its microhabitat during capture efforts.

Gibbons et al. (2000) reported declines over the preceding 20 years in multiple species of North American turtle which these authors attributed to the pet trade. The angonoka or ploughshare tortoise of Madagascar CR is likely to become extinct in the wild in the near future, and smuggled animals have been seized as recently as March 2016.

Many targeted snakes are slow-growing, low-fecundity species considered sensitive to overharvesting (Todd et al., 2010). This includes vipers, a group disproportionately threated with extinction (Böhm et al., 2013), largely as a consequence of exploitation for food, skins and pets. The pet trade is regarded as a significant threat to insular endemics as well as restricted-range mainland species such as Ashe's pit viper EN and Matilda's horned viper CR in East Africa and the ocellated mountain viper CR in Turkey.

Harvesting for use in traditional medicine − in which snakes are either used in wine or rendered for their fat − is a major threat to a number of Chinese and Southeast Asian snakes. The king cobra VU is subject to a wide range of threats from habitat loss and harvesting, but the primary threat is from traditional medicine. Dried lizards are used medicinally in much of Asia, and a rumour that tokay geckos could be used as a cure for AIDS or cancer resulted in widespread collection of this species in the early 2010s, although this has since declined in at least part of the range. Demand from Asian markets has also resulted in pressure on animals elsewhere in the world, such as the radiated tortoise CR which is exported from Madagascar for its liver as well as for the pet trade.

For most lizards and snakes threatened by collection, overharvesting is a secondary threat to species already at risk from habitat loss. The Indochinese water dragon VU, a popular species in the international pet trade, is associated with lowland forest along large rivers, a habitat particularly accessible for development. All life stages of this animal are exploited, with the eggs and adults being eaten and juveniles captured for export; declines have been reported in areas of surviving habitat in both Vietnam and Cambodia, and are expected to be underway in China. Despite the occurrence of an invasive population in Florida, the Burmese python VU is still harvested for export from its native range − including to the USA − as well as being used for leather products, food and traditional medicine, and this is compounded by threats from loss of its forest habitat.

7.2.4 Climate Change

Lizards and snakes are expected to be more sensitive to climate impacts than other vertebrates, and climate modelling has consistently predicted 'dire outcomes' for lizards, the best-studied reptile group in this regard (Brusch et al., 2016). In a global analysis, 80.5% of 1498 sampled reptiles were considered to be 'highly sensitive' to climate change as a consequence of ectothermy, habitat specialisation and low rates of dispersal (Böhm et al., 2016). This value was higher than for amphibians and birds, but consistent with past studies of climate sensitivity in reptiles from West Africa and Tanzania (Carr et al., 2014; Meng et al., 2016). A widely cited model developed by Sinervo et al. (2010) predicted that lizards may suffer local population extinctions of up to 30% globally, and up to 40% in equatorial regions, by 2080.

Uniquely among terrestrial vertebrates, crocodilians, the tuatara, and many lizards and turtles exhibit temperature-dependent sex determination (TSD). Climate change was highlighted as a risk to these species as early as 1994 by Janzen (1994), who suggested that temperature rises of less than 2 °C during incubation may be sufficient to drastically alter sex ratios, and that changes in the timing and duration of breeding seasons may reduce hatching success. Later breeding seasons linked to climate change have been linked to reduced juvenile success in leatherbacks VU since the 1990s (Saba et al., 2012).

At present, 294 reptile species are listed on the Red List as being threatened by climate change, the lowest figure of any terrestrial vertebrate class. This apparent low risk is likely to reflect both inconsistency in the treatment of climate change on the Red List and the current poor state of knowledge: in a review of climate change studies on reptiles Winter et al. (2016) found only 42 published between 2005 and 2015, 70% of which focused on North America and Europe. The research focus on the northern temperate zone, where climate-linked declines are predicted to be less severe than at the equator, may be inappropriate for predicting broader climate impacts on these animals. Species naturally associated with shaded forest – which make up a higher proportion of tropical than temperate lizards – are especially likely to operate close to their thermal optima, and so may be sensitive to even slight temperature rises (Huey et al., 2009).

Historically, reptiles are likely to have adapted to past climatic changes through dispersal to higher-latitude refugia (Janzen, 1994), but this is no longer possible for many species as a consequence of anthropogenic habitat fragmentation. Wilms et al. (2011) predicted that environmental suitability for a widespread subspecies of the Egyptian mastigure VU may fall by 70–80% by 2080, assuming a 3.5–5 °C increase in temperature, which is likely to result in significant declines. Reptiles are often the most abundant and diverse vertebrates in hot, arid habitats, and this finding is likely to have wider ramifications for dryland reptiles inhabiting environments that are already thermally extreme.

While climate change is often regarded as a future or emerging threat, evidence from some lizard populations suggests that climate-linked declines may have been ongoing since at least the 1970s, the earliest period for which these studies had data. Declines in common species over this period hypothesised to be linked to climate change have been reported in spiny lizards in Mexico (Sinervo et al., 2010) and in anoles in both Costa Rica (Whitfield et al., 2007) and Puerto Rico (Lister and Garcia, 2018). In the latter study, the emerald anole was 10 times less abundant in 2011–2012 than in 1976–1977, while the barred anole could no longer be found in forest within 4 km of the research station. The Retigala day gecko, naturally restricted to mid-to-high elevations within an isolated cloud forest fragment in Sri Lanka's dry zone, could no longer be detected below the top of the mountain following a recent drought, and has not been seen in recent surveys.

Although it is difficult to demonstrate climate change impacts, even on well-studied species, due to confounding factors (Winter et al., 2016), reported declines have been correlated with a reduction over time in the number of dry days (Whitfield et al., 2007; Lister and Garcia, 2018) and thermal modelling found that sites from which the blue spiny lizard LC had been lost were no longer climatically suitable (Sinervo et al., 2010). Four species of *Sphaerodactylus* geckos on Puerto Rico were found to be occupying lowland habitats that were 'stressfully warm' in summer as early as 1991 (Álvarez, 1992).

Many lizards are unlikely to be able to adapt to predicted levels of warming (Sinervo et al., 2010) and are expected to respond to increased ambient temperatures by reducing their activity periods (Brusch et al., 2016). Sinervo et al. (2010) predicted that a loss of less than 4 hours of daily activity could lead to local extinctions; Brusch et al. (2016) found that four presently common and widespread species could experience activity period reductions of as much as 8 hours by 2080 at La Selva in Costa Rica. A 3 °C rise in temperature over the next century has been predicted to exceed the preferred temperature range of the Puerto Rican crested anole, a forest-edge species, at lowland sites at least 68% of the time and almost all the time at midday (Huey et al., 2009).

This phenomenon presents a challenge in accurately assessing extinction risk from climate change in reptiles, given the paucity of population data for this group of animals. In most cases reptile declines are inferred from surrogate measures, principally habitat loss. The impacts of climate change are expected to manifest in reductions in habitat quality or extent driven by extreme weather, increased frequency of fires or sea level rise, or by facilitating invasions of competitors from lower elevations or more open habitats. These studies on lizards suggest, however, that declines may already be underway in seemingly intact habitat (such as Luquillo Experimental Forest, an ecological research site in Puerto Rico, where habitat has been regenerating since the 1950s – Lister and Garcia, 2018) as a direct result of temperature rise, a phenomenon current survey approaches are poorly equipped to detect.

7.2.5 Pollution

Pollution – in two-thirds of cases from agricultural run-off – was highlighted as a potentially major threat to reptiles by Gibbons et al. (2000), is listed as a major threat to 76 threatened reptile species, and was found to threaten 43% of marine and freshwater reptiles by Böhm et al. (2013).

Reptiles remain the least-studied vertebrate group from an ecotoxicological perspective and impacts of contaminants at the scale of populations or species are largely unknown. Almost all reptiles are predominantly or strictly carnivorous, and many can be long-lived, which may result in high concentrations of contaminants in their bodies (Gibbons et al., 2000). Reptiles with environmental sex determination are expected to be sensitive to oestrogen pollution, as has been shown for American alligators (Guillette et al., 1995).

Several die-offs in crocodilians and piscivorous freshwater turtles have been tentatively attributed to the effects of contaminants. Local die-offs in American alligators (1998–2004), gharial (2007–2008) and Nile crocodiles (2008–2009) were characterised by high incidences of disease and poor nutrition, with consumption of contaminated prey fish considered a probable cause, although the true causes of these die-offs remain unexplained. Ross (2018) proposed that the ultimate cause may be blooms of blue-green algae associated with water pollution, with a corresponding increase in abundance of nutrient-poor prey fish.

7.2.6 Disease

Declines linked to upper respiratory tract and shell diseases have been reported in multiple species of North American and European tortoises, the green sea turtle EN and the flatback (Gibbons et al., 2000). Marine habitat degradation has been identified as a potential contributory factor to an increased incidence of Fibropapilloma disease in green sea turtles.

The impacts of disease on these and other reptiles remain poorly understood, but recently concern has emerged over a fungal pathogen in snakes known as snake fungal disease (SFD), caused by the pathogen *Ophidiomyces ophiodiicola*. This was first detected in 2006 in timber rattlesnakes in the USA, although it may have been responsible for declines in a Florida rattlesnake population in the 1990s (Lorch et al., 2016). The 2006 outbreak was associated with a 'precipitous decline' in this population and the fungus has since been reported from other species in the eastern US, from a captive specimen in Canada, and from captive snakes in Europe and Australia (Lorch et al., 2016). It has recently been detected in wild snake populations in Great Britain and the Czech Republic (Franklinos et al., 2017). Lorch et al. (2016) suggested that environmental factors, potentially including climate change, population decline and habitat fragmentation, may be triggering more frequent outbreaks of a long-established pathogen. A very recent study (Agugliaro et al., 2020) reported increases in more than 30% in both resting metabolic rate and evaporative water loss in pygmy rattlesnakes LC infected by *Ophidiomyces ophiodiicola*, and the disease is consequently likely to contribute to significant declines in body condition of animals in infected populations.

Snake fungal disease has the potential to drive populations and possibly species to extinction, but its detection postdates the most recent Red List assessments for most North American and European reptiles and an evaluation of its impacts on wild populations is urgently needed (Sutherland et al., 2015).

7.2.7 Loss of Prey

Reptiles are almost all predatory and may have specialist dietary requirements, putting them at potentially high risk from trophic cascades, a decline following the decline or extinction of their prey species. They often have specialist dietary requirements (Todd et al., 2010), although data to support this hypothesis is so far limited.

The majority of lizards prey on arthropods and other invertebrates, while many aquatic snakes are dependent on amphibian prey. Well-publicised declines in frogs have been linked to declines in formerly common snakes at a site in Panama (Zipkin et al., 2020) and, anecdotally, in the United States (summarised in Todd et al., 2010), while the anole declines recently reported for the Luquilla Forest were correlated with declines in arthropod biomass (Lister and Garcia, 2018). The Panamanian study – based on studies undertaken from 1997 to 2012 – found evidence of declines in both species richness and community heterogeneity following amphibian declines in 2004, as well as of body condition in several species, and this decline was not limited to snakes that relied on amphibian prey, despite the absence of any other apparent changes in habitat quality (Zipkin et al., 2020).

7.2.8 Persecution

In many areas of the world reptiles are persecuted, including most species of snakes and many crocodilians (Fitzgerald et al., 2017). Traditional beliefs have prompted deliberate killing of other reptiles, such as chameleons and geckos.

Although persecution is rarely an extinction-level risk, it can complicate reptile conservation by fostering negative opinions of these animals, particularly of venomous snakes and crocodiles, which are implicated in causing human fatalities, and targeted removal of the largest crocodiles following a death can have negative repercussions for the population as a whole (Fitzgerald et al., 2017).

Historically, viper species were hunted for bounties in many parts of the world, and these have been implicated in drastic population declines and range contractions in the Saint Lucia viper and the Martinique lancehead (both EN).

7.2.9 Enigmatic Declines

There are relatively few reports of enigmatic decline in reptiles. An unexplained decline in a Honduran anole (*Anolis amplisquamosus* CR) was observed in 2005 in Parque Nacional El Cusuco (Townsend et al., 2006). While habitat loss is recognised as a threat to this lizard, the observed decline appears to have taken place in good forest.

Reading et al. (2010) analysed population data (from 1993 or 1997 to 2009) from a variety of snake species in generally well-preserved habitats in Italy, France, the UK and Nigeria, and reported declines in 11 of 17 surveyed species. Most species exhibited a sharp decline in 1998 and showed no evidence of recovery over the following decade, and two-thirds of the study populations collapsed by 2009. This pattern of decline appears to imply a reduction in habitat quality, following which species persisted at reduced density. Reading et al. (2010) were unable to identify the causes of decline, although the similarity of the decline trajectory across different geographic regions, species with different life histories and range sizes, and landscapes subject to differing degrees of land use suggest a common causal agent, possibly linked to climate change or disease.

7.2.10 Synergistic Impacts

More than 80% of species assessed by Böhm et al. (2013) were affected by more than one threatening process, in most cases reflecting varied drivers of habitat loss. A number of species are highly threatened as a result of a combination of habitat loss and harvesting pressure. Among these are sea turtles, to which the principal threat is harvesting, but which are also experiencing the loss of nesting beaches due to coastal development.

Habitat clearance that removes refuge sites can increase animals' exposure to predation, including that from invasive species (as has been documented for the great desert skink VU in Australia following fire) and from targeted harvesting (as has been suggested for the Chinese crocodile lizard EN).

Land use change that fragments species' habitats can increase species' sensitivity to climate change, by preventing animals from migrating to other areas once their existing habitat becomes climatically unsuitable.

Habitat degradation may also increase the sensitivity of reptiles to climate change by removing structural features that naturally preserve cooler, moist microhabitats. While this chapter was in preparation, Red List assessments were completed for the reptiles of the heavily transformed, drought-prone island of Sri Lanka (in which drought conditions are becoming more frequent). Assessors expressed concern for declines and disappearances of species that had previously persisted, and in some cases been common, in tea plantations and secondary forests. Compared with primary forest, these habitats have more open canopies, lack thick leaf litter and may lack moisture-retaining organic soils (humus), all of which may buffer animals against the effects of climate change in natural habitats. Secondary habitats that once represented suitable environments for these species may consequently become uninhabitable as a result of climate change.

Reptiles exposed to human persecution, such as snakes, may be pushed into closer contact with humans in relatively exposed situations by the loss of natural habitat. Even when these animals are ecologically tolerant of habitat loss, their increased exposure to persecution in anthropogenic habitats may exclude them from, or lead to serious decline in, these areas.

Collection and export of live reptiles, most often for the pet trade, has resulted in a number of invasive reptile populations becoming established outside their native range, including the introduction of exotic anoles and of green iguanas to several Caribbean islands where they may outcompete and in some cases prey on native species, and potentially threaten other wildlife. A number of exotic reptiles – including large species such as Burmese pythons and tegus – now have established populations in Florida. In other animal groups, escapes from the pet or food trade are known or suspected to have acted as vectors for disease transmission, and the recent discovery of snake fungal disease in a number of captive species (Lorch et al., 2016) suggests that this may be a risk with this pathogen.

7.3 Positive Developments and Future Directions

Past reviews of the conservation status of reptiles have been heavily skewed towards the north temperate zone by the availability of data, and towards charismatic but low-diversity reptiles like crocodilians, turtles and the tuatara. Knowledge of reptile diversity has been increasing at an 'astounding rate' (Fitzgerald et al., 2017) in recent years, with an expanding network of professional journals devoted to reptile taxonomy, ecology and conservation (McDiarmid and Foster, 2012). Today almost 11,000 reptile species are recognised, over 3200 more than were known as little as 20 years ago (Gibbons et al., 2000), many resulting from new discoveries in previously unsurveyed areas of the tropics.

Reports of genuine reductions in reptiles' risk of extinction are scarce, as the group has received so little attention from conservationists, but the creation by IUCN of the Crocodile Specialist Group (1969) and Sea Turtle Specialist Group (1971) has been credited as a major advance in the conservation of these animals (McDiarmid and Foster, 2012). By the 1970s almost all crocodilians were threatened by overharvesting, but an organised programme of sustainable use combining ranching and farming with management of wild populations – pioneered by the Crocodile Specialist Group – has proven to be effective, and lessons learned from this experience are being applied to other reptile groups targeted for exploitation (McDiarmid and Foster, 2012). Most crocodilian populations have recovered over the 25 years prior to the report by Todd et al. (2010) and are now considered secure, so long as sustainable management continues. In particular, the American alligator LC has been hailed as one of the greatest examples of successful recovery in a vertebrate following conservation intervention.

Increased coverage of reptiles on the Red List, which has accelerated following the establishment of the Snake and Lizard Red List Authority in 2011, and the creation of additional IUCN reptile specialist groups have been important in raising the profile of reptile conservation and provided support for a wider range of threatened species, including tortoises and freshwater turtles, iguanas, chameleons, sea snakes, vipers and skinks.

Over the last 20 years, coordination among non-governmental organisations and improved regulation of wildlife trade has contributed significantly to our knowledge of snake exploitation, particularly in West Africa, and has improved enforcement (Jensen, 2017). Reptile representation in CITES is increasing; for instance, several Sri Lankan dragon lizards received CITES listings in 2019, and the entire Mexican lizard genus *Abronia* was CITES-listed in 2016. Improved national regulation of wildlife trade (for instance, in Chile starting in 1993 and in New Zealand since the 1980s, and management of tegu harvests in Paraguay since 1992) has proven effective and has largely ended the exploitation of endemic lizards in some countries.

The most successful conservation interventions for lizards and snakes have been the eradication of invasive predators and associated management, primarily on islands. A number of species of lizards and snakes in the Caribbean, Mauritius and New Zealand have benefitted from active conservation management and predator exclusion.

Successful captive breeding has been implemented for a number of reptile species, and in some cases has saved species that are now extinct in the wild (e.g. Lister's gecko) or whose remaining wild population may not be viable (as with the angonoka, which has been managed by the Durrell Wildlife Trust since 1986). In 2019 the Galapagos land iguana VU was reintroduced to Santiago, from which it was eradicated in the nineteenth century by invasive mammals. Captive breeding of the Christmas Island blue-tailed skink EW has been highly successful, and in early 2019 Australian news outlets reported plans to reintroduce the animal to the wild at an indeterminate point in the future. The Pinzon giant tortoise VU was reintroduced to the wild a century after its extinction, and survival of new hatchlings was confirmed in 2019.

Despite these limited successes, reptiles' ecological significance remains underappreciated and they are still neglected in conservation, poorly known both taxonomically and ecologically, and there is an extreme scarcity of data on population trends or occurrence. Available natural history data is frequently insufficient to identify key microhabitats of conservation importance. The impacts of climate change, now identified as a major threat to lizards and long-recognised as a risk to turtles and crocodilians with temperature-dependent sex determination, are almost wholly unstudied in snakes, a group whose conservation needs more generally remain poorly understood. Almost nothing is known about most fossorial reptiles, including worm lizards and several groups of lizards and snakes.

Existing IUCN Red List assessments for North America pre-date recent evidence of an emergent disease in snakes and of impacts linked to climate change in Mexican lizards, and the scale of impacts from climate change in particular is only becoming apparent as the Global Reptile Assessment reaches its conclusion. Support for further research into threats to reptiles and into reptile Red Listing that can inform conservation management, and increased attention in conservation planning to this animal group, should be considered a priority.

Acknowledgements

Many thanks especially to Lee Fitzgerald of Texas A&M University for reviewing this manuscript and suggesting revisions. Thanks also to Neil Cox of IUCN and Bruce Young of NatureServe for providing helpful feedback, and to Perran Ross of the University of Florida and the IUCN Crocodile Specialist Group for contributions to the section discussing impacts of pollution on crocodilians.

References

Agugliaro, J., Lind, C.M., Lorch, J.M. and Farrell, T.M. (2020) An emerging fungal pathogen is associated with increased resting metabolic rate and total evaporative water loss rate in a winter-active snake. *Funct Ecol* 34: 486–496.

Álvarez H.J. (1992) *Thermal Characteristics of* Sphaerodactylus *Species in Puerto Rico and Their Implications for the Distribution of Species in Puerto Rico*. San Juan, Puerto Rico:University of Puerto Rico.

Antworth R.L., Pike D.A. and Stiner J.C. (2006) Nesting ecology, current status, and conservation of sea turtles on an uninhabited beach in Florida, USA. *Biol Conserv* 130: 10–15.

Böhm M., Collen B., Baillie J.E.M., et al. (2013) The conservation status of the world's reptiles. *Biol Conserv* 157: 372–385.

Böhm M., Cook D., Ma H., et al. (2016) Hot and bothered: using trait-based approaches to assess climate change vulnerability in reptiles. *Biol Conserv* 204: 32–41.

Brooks, S.E., Reynolds, J.D., Allison, E.H., et al. (2007) The exploitation of homalopsid water snakes at Tonle Sap Lake, Cambodia. In: Murphy, J.C. (Ed.),

Homalopsid Snakes: Evolution in the Mud. Malabar, FL: Krieger Publishing Company.

Brusch G.A., Taylor E.N. and Whitfield S.M. (2016) Turn up the heat: thermal tolerances of lizards at La Selva, Costa Rica. *Oecologia* 180(2): 325–334.

Buhlmann, K.A., Hudson, R. and Rhodin, A.G.J. (2002) *Turtle Conservation Fund: A Global Action Plan for the Conservation of Tortoises and Fresh Water Turtles, Strategy and Funding Prospectus 2002–2007, Washington, DC*. Conservation International and Chelonian Research Foundation. Leominster, MA: MTC Printing.

Carr J.A., Hughes A.F. and Foden W.B. (2014) *A Climate Change Vulnerability Assessment of West African Species*. Cambridge, UK: UNEP-WCMC.

Cox N., Chanson J. and Stuart S. (2006) *The Status and Distribution of Reptiles and Amphibians of the Mediterranean Basin* (No. 2). Gland, Switzerland: IUCN.

Cox N.A., Mallon D., Bowles P., Els J. et al. (compilers). (2012) *The Conservation Status and Distribution of Reptiles of the Arabian Peninsula*. Cambridge, UK and Gland, Switzerland: IUCN, and Sharjah, UAE: Environment and Protected Areas Authority.

Cox, N.A. and Temple, H.J. (2009) *European Red List of Reptiles*. Luxembourg: Office for Official Publications of the European Communities.

Fitzgerald L.A. (1994) The interplay between life history and environmental stochasticity: implications for management of exploited lizard populations. *Am Zool* 34: 371–381.

Fitzgerald, L.A., Walkup, D., Chyn, K., et al. (2017) The future for reptiles: advances and challenges in the Anthropocene. Reference Module in *Earth Systems and Environmental Sciences: Encyclopedia of the Anthropocene* Vol. 3. New York: Elsevier.

Franklinos L.H., Lorch J.M., Bohuski E., et al. (2017) Emerging fungal pathogen *Ophidiomyces ophiodiicola* in wild European snakes. *Sci Rep* 7(1): 3844.

Gardner, T.A., Barlow, J. and Peres, C.A. (2007) Paradox, presumption and pitfalls in conservation biology: the importance of habitat change for amphibians and reptiles. *Biol Conserv* 138(1–2): 166–179.

Gibbons J.W., Scott D.E., Ryan T.J., et al. (2000) The global decline of reptiles, *déjà vu* amphibians: reptile species are declining on a global scale. Six significant threats to reptile populations are habitat loss and degradation, introduced invasive species, environmental pollution, disease, unsustainable use, and global climate change. *BioScience* 50(8): 653–666.

Guillette, L.J., Jr, Crain, D.A., Rooney, A.A. and Pickford, D.B. (1995) Organization versus activation: the role of endocrine-disrupting contaminants (EDCs) during embryonic development in wildlife. *Environ Health Perspect*, 103(suppl 7): 157–164.

Huey R.B., Deutsch C.A., Tewksbury J.J., et al. (2009) Why tropical forest lizards are vulnerable to climate warming. *Proc Royal Soc B* 276(1664): 1939–1948.

Janzen F.J. (1994) Climate change and temperature-dependent sex determination in reptiles *Proc Natl Acad Sci USA* 91(16): 7487–7490.

Jenkins R.K., Tognelli M.F., Bowles P., et al. (2014) Extinction risks and the conservation of Madagascar's reptiles. *PLoS One* 9(8): e100173.

Jensen T.J. (2017) *Snakes of Africa: Exploitation and Conservation*. Masters thesis. Aalborg, Denmark: Aalborg University.

Lister B.C. and Garcia A. (2018) Climate-driven declines in arthropod abundance restructure a rainforest food web. *Proc Natl Acad Sci* 115(44): E10397–E10406.

Lorch J.M., Knowles S., Lankton J.S., et al. (2016) Snake fungal disease: an emerging threat to wild snakes. *Phil Trans Royal Soc B* 371: 20150457.

McDiarmid R.W. and Foster M.S. (2012) Reptile biodiversity: where do we go from here? In: McDiarmid, R.W., Foster, M.S., Guyer, C., Gibbons, J.W. and Chernoff, N. (Eds.), *Reptile Biodiversity: Standard Methods for Inventory and Monitoring*. Berkeley, CA: University of California Press.

Meiri S., Bauer A.M., Allison A., et al. (2018) Extinct, obscure or imaginary: the lizard species with the smallest ranges. *Divers Distrib* 24(2): 262–273.

Meng H., Carr J., Beraducci J., et al. (2016) Tanzania's reptile biodiversity: distribution, threats and climate change vulnerability. *Biol Conserv* 204: 72–82.

Mieres, M.M. and Fitzgerald, L.A. (2006) Monitoring and managing the harvest of tegu lizards in Paraguay. *J Wildl Manag* 70(6): 1723–1734.

Moore, J.A., Hoare, J.M., Daughtery. C.H. and Nelson, N.J. (2007) Waiting reveals waning weight: monitoring over 54 years shows a decline in body condition of a long-lived reptile (tuatara, *Sphenodon punctatus*) *Biol Conserv* 135: 181–188.

Nilson, G. (2019) The ecology and conservation of the Milos viper, *Macrovipera schweizeri*. In: Lillywhite, H.B. and Martins, M. (Eds.), *Islands and Snakes*. New York: Oxford University Press.

Reading C.J., Luiselli L.M., Akani G.C., et al. (2010) Are snake populations in widespread decline? *Biol Lett* 6(6): 777–780.

Ross J.P. (2018) Green ponds, fat fish and dead crocs: a testable hypothesis for crocodylian mass mortality. 26th Crocodile Specialist Group Executive Committee Meeting Universidad Nacional del Litoral, Santa Fe, Argentina, 5 May 2018.

Ryberg, W.A., Hill, M.T., Painter, C.W. et al. (2015) Linking irreplaceable landforms in a self-organizing landscape to sensitivity of population vital rates for an ecological specialist. *Conserv Biol* 29(3): 888–898.

Saba V.S., Stock C.A., Spotila J.R., et al. (2012) Projected response of an endangered marine turtle population to climate change. *Nat Clim Change* 2: 814–820.

Shine, R. (2012) Foreword. In: McDiarmid, R.W., Foster, M.S., Guyer, C., Gibbons, J.W. and Chernoff, N. (Eds.), *Reptile Biodiversity: Standard Methods for Inventory and Monitoring*. Berkeley, CA: University of California Press.

Sinervo B., Mendez-De-La-Cruz F., Miles D.B., et al. (2010) Erosion of lizard diversity by climate change and altered thermal niches. *Science* 328 (5980): 894–899.

Slavenko A., Tallowin O.J., Itescu Y., et al. (2016) Late Quaternary reptile extinctions: size matters, insularity dominates. *Glob Ecol Biogeogr* 25(11): 1308–1320.

Spotila, J.R. (2004) *Sea Turtles: A Complete Guide to Their Biology, Behavior, and Conservation*. Baltimore, MD: Johns Hopkins University Press.

Sutherland W.J., Clout M., Depledge M., et al. (2015) A horizon scan of global conservation issues for 2015. *Trends Ecol Evol* 30(1): 17–24.

Tingley, R., MacDonald, S.L., Mitchell, N.J., et al. (2019) Geographic and taxonomic patterns of extinction risk in Australian squamates. *Biol Conserv* 238: 108203.

Todd, B.D., Willson, J.D. and Gibbons, J.W. (2010) The global status of reptiles and causes of their decline. In: Sparling, D.W., Linder, G., Bishop, C.A. and Krest, S. (Eds.), *Ecotoxicology of Amphibians and Reptiles*, Second Edn. Boca Raton, FL: CRC Press.

Tolley K.A., Alexander G.J., Branch W.R., et al. (2016) Conservation status and threats for African reptiles. *Biol Conserv* 204: 63–71.

Tolley K.A., Weeber J., Maritz B., et al. (2019) No safe haven: protection levels show imperilled South African reptiles not sufficiently safe-guarded despite low average extinction risk. *Biol Conserv* 233: 61–72.

Townsend J.H., Wilson L.D., Talley B.L., et al. (2006) Additions to the herpetofauna of Parque Nacional El Cusuco, Honduras. *Herpetol Bull* 96: 29.

Vitt L.J. (2016) Reptile diversity and life history. In: Dodd, C.K. Jr. (Ed.) *Reptile Ecology and Conservation: A Handbook of Techniques*. Oxford, UK: Oxford University Press.

Whitfield S.M., Bell K.E., Philippi T., et al. (2007) Amphibian and reptile declines over 35 years at La Selva, Costa Rica. *Proc Natl Acad Sci* 104(20): 8352–8356.

Whitfield S. M., Reider K., Greenspan S and Donnelly M.A. (2014) Litter dynamics regulate population densities in a declining terrestrial herpetofauna. *Copeia* 2014(3): 454–461.

Wilms T.M., Wagner P., Shobrak M., et al. (2011) Living on the edge? On the thermobiology and activity pattern of the large herbivorous desert lizard *Uromastyx aegyptia microlepis* Blanford, 1875 at Mahazat as-Sayd Protected Area, Saudi Arabia. *J Arid Environ* 75(7): 636–647.

Winter M., Fiedler W., Hochachka W.M., et al. (2016) Patterns and biases in climate change research on amphibians and reptiles: a systematic review. *Royal Soc Open Sci* 3(9): 160158.

Zipkin, E.F., DiRenzo, G.V., Ray, J.M. et al. (2020) Tropical snake diversity collapses after widespread amphibian loss. *Science* 367(6479): 814–816.

EIGHT

Amphibians

PHILLIP J. BISHOP[†], SALLY WREN, ARIADNE ANGULO
AND RICHARD A. GRIFFITHS

Summary

Amphibians are the most threatened vertebrate class on Earth. They play important roles in ecosystems and are often cited as sentinels of environmental health. Around 84% of the 8208 amphibian species have been assessed by The IUCN Red List of Threatened Species, with 41% categorised as threatened with extinction. As is the case with other species, the main threatening process for many amphibians is habitat destruction, disturbance and fragmentation. However, amphibians are also highly vulnerable to emerging infectious diseases, climate change, invasive species and pollution. These threats often interact, resulting in complex impacts on amphibian populations. Fortunately, there are several initiatives (IUCN SSC Amphibian Specialist Group (ASG), Amphibian Survival Alliance (ASA) and the Amphibian Ark(AArk)) focused on understanding and protecting the many threatened species through global coordination, conservation planning, habitat protection, supporting conservation action, fundraising, emergency rescues and captive breeding for conservation. Diverse amphibian lifestyles, coupled with the complexity of threats, means that different species will respond in different ways and in different places. Consequently there are likely to be 'winners' and 'losers' in a changing world, rather than complete extinction of a class. Amphibian conservation therefore remains one of the greatest challenges of our times.

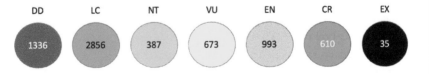

DD	LC	NT	VU	EN	CR	EX
1336	2856	387	673	993	610	35

IUCN assessed amphibian species (2020)

Amphibian Order	DD	LC	NT	VU	EN	CR	EX
Anura	1192	2624	330	565	851	502	32
Caudata	42	167	55	104	133	107	3
Gymnophiona	102	65	2	4	9	1	0

DD = Data Deficient; LC = Least Concern; NT = Near Threatened; VU = Vulnerable;
EN = Endangered;
CR = Critically Endangered; EX = Extinct
Red List Data downloaded July 2020 (6892 species assessed)

8.1 Introduction

Amphibians (Class Amphibia) comprise frogs and toads (Order Anura), newts and salamanders (Order Caudata) and caecilians (Order Gymnophiona). All amphibians are ectothermic vertebrates with a water-permeable skin through which respiration occurs to varying degrees; they inhabit a wide diversity of habitats, and as a group, exhibit a wide variety of life history patterns. They range in size from the giant salamanders of over 1 m in length (*Andrias* spp.) to tiny frogs with an adult size of just 7 mm (*Paedophryne amauensis*). Equally, they can breed in water bodies ranging in size from large lakes to tiny vessels of rainwater captured within the leaves of bromeliads, and even under stones and logs in moist environments.

Amphibians have several life history traits that make them vulnerable to global change. The classic amphibian life cycle involves both terrestrial and aquatic phases, so that many species are open to environmental disruption in both habitat types. Furthermore, different life stages often consume different food, as larvae are normally herbivores while adults are carnivores, exposing individuals to a wider potential for ingesting toxins and exposure to parasites. They are ectotherms, and are therefore sensitive to temperature changes, while their moist, permeable skin leaves many species exposed to pollutants in water and air. Compared to mammals and birds, amphibians have low vagility, so are unable to move too far to escape environmental threats. Amphibian species richness is concentrated in the tropics, where a higher level of environmental change is occurring. Many species, particularly those in tropical regions, have small distributions, so large proportions of a population – or a whole species – can be affected by changes to a relatively small area (Wake and Vredenburg, 2008).

The extent to which amphibians are affected by anthropogenic stressors has led them to be considered as sentinels of ecosystem health, potentially highlighting environmental issues before the impacts are seen more broadly (Whiles et al., 2006; Hopkins, 2007). Ecosystem impacts from declining amphibian populations include increasing invertebrate populations (Teng et al., 2016); increasing algal blooms; and loss of prey for other vertebrate species, reducing trophic transfer in ecosystems (Hocking and Babbitt, 2014; Menéndez-Guerrero et al., 2020; Zipkin et al., 2020). In many forest communities around the world, amphibians constitute the greatest contribution to animal biomass (Semlitsch et al., 2014). Additionally, many aspects of amphibian biology are still unknown, including the scope of the biopharmaceutical properties of their skin secretions, which are known to contain antibacterial, antifungal and antiviral compounds, and are being investigated for their biopharmaceutical properties (Gomes et al., 2007).

Although anecdotal reports of amphibian declines date back to the 1950s, they were first recognised as a global phenomenon following the First World Congress of Herpetology in England in 1989. Shortly thereafter, the Declining Amphibian Populations Task Force (DAPTF) was established by the IUCN Species Survival Commission (SSC) to investigate the causes and severity of the declines. Following the conclusion of the first Global Amphibian Assessment (GAA) in 2004 and a subsequent Amphibian Conservation Summit in 2005, the IUCN SSC's Amphibian Conservation Action Plan (ACAP) was published in 2007 (Gascon et al., 2007). This plan identified key issues that required attention in order to curb this crisis, and provided a framework for interventions. Further actions resulting from the Summit were the merging of the Global Amphibian Specialist Group (GASG), the DAPTF and the Global Amphibian Assessment (GAA) into one entity, committed to implementing a global strategy for amphibian conservation: the IUCN SSC Amphibian Specialist Group (ASG), as well as the formation of the Amphibian Ark to address the *ex situ* component of amphibian conservation.

A third network, the Amphibian Survival Alliance (ASA), was launched in June 2011 and acts as a global organisation-level partnership for amphibian conservation. It is in a pivotal position to support the implementation of ACAP, acting to mobilise a consortium of organisations working together to stem the rapid losses of amphibian populations and species worldwide.

The first GAA assessed 5743 amphibian species – all the known species at the time. A third of these were categorised as Critically Endangered, Endangered or Vulnerable, and therefore threatened with extinction, indicating a global amphibian extinction crisis (Stuart et al., 2004) (Table 8.1).

The rate of new amphibian species descriptions is high, so not all species have been assessed against The IUCN Red List Categories and Criteria (Tapley et al., 2018; IUCN, 2020); however, the second Global Amphibian Assessment (GAA2) is currently working to reassess, or assess for the first time, all amphibian species, and is due to be published in 2023. Of the 6892 amphibian species which have been assessed to date, 33% are listed in a threatened category (IUCN, 2020) (Table 8.1). Although all taxa face grave threats, amphibians are the most threatened vertebrate group that has been comprehensively assessed (Figure 8.1) (Hoffmann et al., 2010).

The percentage of Data Deficient amphibian species adds further complexity – species where so little is known that it is impossible to reliably assess threat status, given associated uncertainties. Currently nearly 20% (1336 species) of amphibians are listed as Data Deficient. If we assume that these species are threatened in the same proportion as those with sufficient data, likely a conservative assumption, we can estimate that approximately 40% of amphibians are currently threatened with extinction (Figure 8.1).

The trend in amphibian threat status is also startling when compared with other major taxonomic groups. The Red List Index (RLI) gives the aggregated change in extinction

Table 8.1 *Percentages and numbers of species in Red List Categories in 2004 and 2020*

Source	DD	LC	NT	CR	EN	VU	EX
2004 (Stuart et al., 2004) 5743 species	22.5% 1294	38.3% 2199	6.3% 359	7.4% 427	13.2% 761	11.6% 668	0.6% 34
2020 (IUCN, 2020) 6892 species	19.4% 1336	**41.4%** 2856	5.6% 387	**8.9%** 610	**14.4%** 993	9.8% 673	0.5% 35

Threatened categories are Critically Endangered (CR), Endangered (EN) and Vulnerable (VU), highlighted in grey; increases in 2020 indicated in bold.

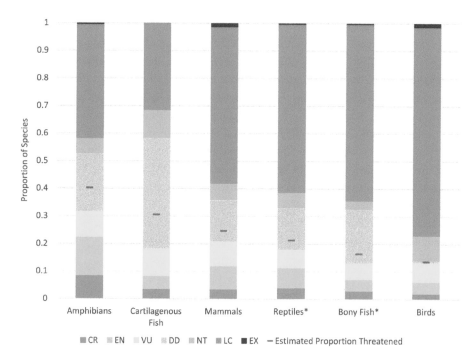

Figure 8.1 Proportion of vertebrate species in different Red List Categories. Horizontal red lines represent the estimated percentage of threatened species, if Data Deficient species are extrapolated to be 'threatened' in the same proportion as data sufficient species. Taxa marked with an asterisk (*) are incompletely assessed. Data from IUCN, 2020.

risk for a group of species over a given period, by examining genuine changes in the Red List category over this period. Within vertebrates, the RLI has been calculated for amphibians, birds and mammals (Hoffmann et al., 2010). While all of these groups show a decline, amphibians exhibit a statistically significantly larger downward trend than the other groups. This equates to 9.9% of amphibian species moving one Red List category closer to extinction during the assessment period of 1980–2004, compared with 2.2% of bird and 2.8% of mammal species being downlisted by one category in their respective RLIs (Stuart et al., 2004; Hoffmann et al., 2010).

Despite concerted efforts by many organisations to halt amphibian population declines, the response to the crisis was insufficient and species continued to decline with 34 amphibian species declared extinct since 1850, likely an underestimate of the true number. Equally the number of Endangered and Critically Endangered species substantially increased between 2004–2020 (Table 8.1).

8.2 Causes of Amphibian Declines

There have been six major factors implicated in amphibian declines: habitat loss and modification, emerging infectious diseases, invasive species, climate change and severe weather events, overexploitation and environmental pollution (Figure 8.2). For some of

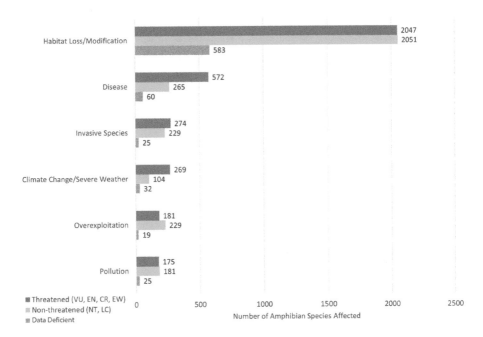

Figure 8.2 Threats to amphibian species. Data from IUCN, 2020.

these threats, there is a solid understanding of the mechanisms that cause declines, but for others research is still needed to clarify the processes and interactions involved (Stuart et al., 2004, 2008; Ford et al., 2020). Since the class Amphibia is such a diverse taxon, the same stressor can affect species in different ways and with differing severity. This adds complexity to assessing the impacts of each threat. Furthermore, most amphibian species are affected by more than one threatening process, and threats may interact synergistically to have an impact that is greater than the sum of their parts (Ford et al., 2020).

8.2.1 Habitat Loss and Fragmentation

The global loss, disturbance and fragmentation of habitats poses the greatest threat to amphibians and biodiversity generally. With fewer places to live, breed and find food, the impacts on species and populations can be stark. Compared to many other vertebrates, amphibians are relatively small-bodied, with a life history that ties them to damp habitats. They often lay large numbers of eggs and tadpoles that naturally suffer high mortality due to competition, predation or water bodies drying out, but in a 'good' year large numbers of young can be recruited to a population. Although life history varies between species, many amphibians have 'boom and bust' periods during population development, with years when reproductive success is very good followed by years when it is very low. These traits have implications for how amphibians respond to habitat change. On the one hand, it means that they can potentially build up populations quickly if the environmental and habitat conditions are favourable. It also means that amphibians can maintain viable populations in habitat that would be too small to support populations of mammals of similar body size. On the other hand, compared to mammals and birds, amphibians have reduced dispersal. Unfavourable habitats or landscape features that present barriers to dispersal pose significant challenges to amphibians. Likewise, their reliance on water means that subtle changes to rainfall patterns, freshwater systems and soil moisture can have dramatic impacts on populations. Such impacts can either be direct, e.g. ponds fail to refill in the spring, or indirect, e.g. habitat change leads to the emergence of a disease or predator that was previously unable to survive or persist.

Whether habitat change involves deforestation, conversion of land to agriculture or construction for commercial development, loss of habitat and fragmentation of habitat go hand-in-hand. These are two related impacts, and the relative importance of the reduction in overall size of habitat available or the fact that what is left is divided up into smaller fragments has been the subject of much debate. Whereas a smaller area of habitat means fewer species and individuals, the effect of dividing up a habitat into smaller patches separated by barriers is more subtle. In nature, many populations exist in patches of suitable habitat situated within a broader matrix of less suitable habitat. Ponds situated within a grassland landscape are a prime example. Providing the grassland between the ponds is not an insurmountable barrier for amphibians to cross, dispersal between the ponds may mean that the species can maintain itself within the landscape, even if the number of animals occupying a single pond may not form a viable population in its own right. This type of system, where the long-term viability of the wider population depends on dispersal between subpopulations, is known as a metapopulation. A good example of this practice is the great crested newt (*Triturus cristatus*) in Kent (Figure 8.3). Great crested newts occupying a group of four ponds located in an agricultural landscape with hedgerows and orchards were studied for 12 years. Over this period, it was clear that breeding success in each of these ponds varied from year to year, and often failed completely when individual ponds dried out or via predation of newt eggs and larvae. In fact, one of the ponds was very deep and never dried out, so even though the newts tried to breed in this pond, there was never recruitment as they were consumed by aquatic predators. This type of pond is known as a population 'sink'. However, another pond in the landscape was more productive and had successful breeding in most years. This 'source' population provided recruits that dispersed to other ponds in the system and kept the wider

Figure 8.3 Pair of great crested newts (*Triturus cristatus*; female above, male below). The viability of great crested newt populations depends on them occupying groups of connected ponds. (Photo: Brett Lewis.)

metapopulation ticking over. A modelling exercise suggested that if that source pond was removed from the landscape, the wider metapopulation would decline because there would no longer be any newts able to disperse and populate other ponds in the system (Griffiths et al., 2010).

The study of amphibian metapopulations has highlighted the importance of good connectivity maintaining dispersal between habitat patches. Metapopulations of amphibians can exist within the landscape at a variety of scales. At one end of the spectrum are some tiny frogs that spend almost their entire lives within specific plants. A small species of frog, Itambé's bromeliad frog (*Crossodactylodes itambe*), is only found living in one species of bromeliad on top of one mountain in Brazil. In this case, the bromeliads form the patches of breeding habitat within the otherwise unhospitable rocky landscape, with the entire global population contained within an area of less than half a square kilometre (Barata et al., 2018). At the other end of the scale, even in large continuous systems such as rainforests, streams and lakes, amphibians are likely to be patchily distributed according to local variations in habitat suitability. At Lake Xochimilco in Mexico, the last remaining axolotls (*Ambystoma mexicanum*) are confined to just a few places within the lake system where water quality and habitat remain suitable for the species (Figure 8.4). Even in this continuous aquatic system, variations in water quality and disturbance may present barriers to dispersal between suitable areas. In such cases, intensive management of the species may be the only way to compensate for the disruption of a functioning metapopulation system. Indeed, the future for the axolotl in the highly disturbed waters of Lake Xochimilco may rely on creating highly managed localised refuges, where water quality can be locally improved and predatory fish excluded (Valiente et al., 2010).

Habitat management for amphibians therefore requires a landscape-level approach, whereby functional metapopulations can be maintained at the appropriate scale. This will need to go hand-in-hand with other aspects of management, such as minimising the risk of habitats suffering from chemical contamination or introduced predators or competitors, and ensuring water levels can be maintained in the face of climate change and reduced water tables. Fires can be something of a mixed blessing for amphibians. In the southeast

Figure 8.4 The axolotl (*Ambystoma mexicanum*). Although widely bred in captivity for research and pets, wild axolotls are now confined to a small number of areas within the Lake Xochimilco system in Mexico. (Photo: Ian Bride.)

USA, occasional fires can increase productivity of ponds by releasing nutrients and improving productivity, while also controlling the encroachment of trees. On the other hand, if fires occur on a regular basis they are likely to negatively impact and prevent establishment of trees that may shade out pond edges. Frequent fires are also likely to negatively impact adult or juvenile amphibians sheltering on land, and rains following fires could lead to siltation of water bodies. Clearly, in the face of climate change, some imaginative conservation actions may be needed to enable amphibian populations to persist.

8.2.2 Disease

Although habitat loss and fragmentation are the biggest threats to amphibians globally, emerging infectious diseases have been implicated in many 'enigmatic' (sensu Stuart et al., 2004) species' declines and extinctions. Frogs have always been model organisms for parasitology and disease research, but it is comparatively recently that the impacts of disease on amphibians at the population level have been appreciated.

Ranavirus is associated with mortality in a wide range of frogs and salamanders, and has also been detected in fish and reptiles. Long-term studies of the effects of ranavirus on amphibians are available for common frogs (*Rana temporaria*) in England and tiger salamanders (*Ambystoma tigrinum*) in North America. In southeast England, ranavirus infections were first reported in the 1990s, and follow-up studies revealed variable impacts on populations. In urban and rural garden ponds, some common frogs disappear following ranavirus outbreaks, in others, populations persist despite some frogs remaining infected, while elsewhere populations recover completely without any further mortality (Teacher et al., 2010). In North American tiger salamanders, disease-driven die-offs have been reported since the 1980s, but it was not until some years later that these were discovered to be caused by a new ranavirus. Although outbreaks of the disease have historically caused die-offs of the salamanders, recent surveys indicate that, while Arizona populations may still be infected, there was little sign of disease or mortality, suggesting that populations may be evolving tolerance to the disease (Greer et al., 2009). Diseases rarely affect all species in the same place in the same way, but in northern Spain, ranavirus infections have been particularly damaging, with mass mortalities in up to six species occurring at the same site (Price et al., 2014).

Of more concern with respect to the speed and scale of mortalities is the fungal disease chytridiomycosis. The significance of this disease for amphibians was linked to the discovery of the fungus *Batrachochytrium dendrobatidis* (or Bd) in 1997 (Berger et al., 1998). Initially discovered in captive poison dart frogs originally from South America, this fungus thrives in cool, damp conditions and is transmitted via a motile zoospore. When it finds a new host the zoospore encysts in the skin and damages the keratin layer. This causes problems with osmoregulation and gaseous exchange across the skin, and the animal can die as a result of organ failure. Bd is thought to be implicated in the declines of over 500 amphibian species worldwide and may have driven over 90 species to extinction (Scheele et al., 2020). However, Bd does not affect all amphibian species in the same way, and it seems to do better in some damp environments than others. The most serious declines and extinctions have occurred in eastern Australia, Central and South America and some upland parts of Europe. Although found in some tropical species, the fungus does not survive for long above 29 °C. Also known from Africa and Asia, Bd does not seem to have affected amphibian populations in these continents in the same way as it has elsewhere. In fact, recent phylogenetic analyses have shown that Bd exists in at least five strains that differ in their pathogenicity, but all seem to have origins in Southeast Asia. The transport of the disease around the world has been linked to the international transport of amphibians for the pet trade and laboratories. In 2013, a new species of chytrid, *Batrachochytrium salamandrivorans* (Bsal), was discovered in the southern Netherlands and Germany as the driver of severe declines in fire salamander populations. Bsal has now been identified in five European countries and, rather worryingly, is causing massive mortality of salamanders (Spitzen-van der Sluijs et al., 2017). North America is a hotspot for salamander species richness, but an extensive survey of wild amphibians confirmed it is currently free of Bsal (Waddle et al., 2020). If Bsal was accidentally transported to North America (likely via international trade) it would likely result in the catastrophic decline and extinction of many susceptible species of salamanders.

The mitigation of disease and its impacts on amphibian populations is a rapidly evolving field of research. Fortunately, amphibians infected with Bd seem to respond well to fungicides such as itraconazole, and for those species that can tolerate higher temperatures, short-term exposure to temperatures above 29 °C. Thus, if disease gets into a captive colony of amphibians, it may be possible to cure the animals of the disease before they succumb. However, the major challenge lies in how the disease can be controlled in the wild. On the island of Mallorca, there has been some success using chemicals to eradicate the disease from the remote rocky gorges inhabited by the island's endemic midwife toad (*Alytes muletensis*) (Figure 8.5). Initially, tadpoles were removed from pools and cleared of Bd in the lab using itraconazole. Unfortunately, after they were returned to the pools they became reinfected, presumably by other toads that were missed in the initial clearance. However, removal and treatment of tadpoles coupled with washing out the pools with the disinfectant Virkon resulted in no cases of infection for at least two years (Bosch et al., 2015).

Despite the success in eliminating Bd from rocky pools in Mallorca, clearing infection would be harder in more complex habitats where the disease may continue to lurk in damp soils or other less vulnerable species. On the island of Montserrat, for example, the endemic mountain chicken frog (*Leptodactylus fallax*) was driven to near extinction by Bd (Figure 8.6). Fortunately, a captive population of frogs was established when the alarm over the declines was first sounded, and these have been shown to respond well to antifungal treatment. However, any frogs that are released back into the wild following treatment are likely to be rapidly reinfected by the abundant robber frogs (*Eleutherodactylus* spp.) that carry the disease without suffering any ill-effects, so provide an ever-present reservoir of Bd (Hudson et al., 2019).

Figure 8.5 A Mallorcan midwife toad (*Alytes muletensis*) breeding pool. The chytrid fungus has been successfully eliminated from such pools by treating tadpoles and the rocky basins with fungicide. (Photo: Richard Griffiths.)

Figure 8.6 Mountain chicken frog (*Leptodactylus fallax*). Although driven to near extinction by disease on the island of Montserrat, frogs have been successfully bred and treated in captivity. (Photo: Richard Griffiths.)

On the positive side, there is evidence that some amphibian populations are starting to recover naturally from Bd-associated declines. A few years after population crashes at certain sites in Panama, some species began to reappear. There was no evidence that Bd had lost any of its historical pathogenicity, so it seems that some species are evolving defences to the disease (Voyles et al., 2018). Globally, although only about 12% of declining species are showing such signs of recovery, ongoing declines continue in 39% of species, and there remains much work to be done in terms of disease mitigation (Scheele et al., 2020).

8.2.3 Invasive Species

Under natural circumstances, most species exist in a state of co-evolution with predators, parasites and competitors. The problem arises when species are introduced into new areas where they have not previously occurred. If the area is unsuitable, then the species may quickly die out. However, if the area is suitable and provides a plentiful supply of prey or parasite hosts that have not evolved the appropriate defences, the introduced species will prosper at the expense of native species.

The impact of invasive species is particularly acute on islands, as these environments have fauna that have evolved in isolation, away from the many different predators, pathogens and competitors that may be widespread on the mainland. Ponds are similar to islands in a terrestrial landscape, and the introduction of fish to such habitats can be just as devastating as the introduction of rats to an oceanic island. Indeed, the release of non-native fish into ponds and lakes is one of the primary reasons for the decline – and sometimes extinction – of amphibians in these habitats. Such declines can come about through direct predation or competition with amphibians, introduction of disease, or sublethal effects that change the behaviour of amphibians in a way that affects growth and reproductive success (Pilliod et al., 2012). That said, some amphibians that inhabit larger water bodies that are frequently occupied by fish have evolved natural defences, such as toxic skins, which allows a degree of co-existence.

The introduction of Asian carp (*Cyprinus carpio*) and tilapia (*Oreochromis nilotica*) to Lake Xochimilco in Mexico has had a profound effect on the whole wetland system, and in particular to the axolotl (*Ambystoma mexicanum*), a salamander that lives and breeds in the lake without ever metamorphosing. Although the axolotl was once the top predator in the system, introduced carp and tilapia collectively comprise 98% of the vertebrate biomass within the lake, and fisherman can harvest 7.5 tons of fish per week. Indeed, netting surveys for the fishes and the axolotl revealed that just 0.5% of catch biomass consisted of axolotls (Zambrano et al., 2010). Now Critically Endangered, the axolotls are only likely to survive in a few small channels where fish have been removed and pollution controlled.

For many amphibians, particularly fully terrestrial ones, the threat may come from introduced invasive mammals such as hedgehogs, cats, rats, mice, stoats, ferrets and mongooses. The native frogs in New Zealand (*Leiopelma* spp.) have evolved in isolation from mammalian predators for over 80 million years and most are fully terrestrial (Figure 8.7). The relatively recent colonisation of New Zealand by humans, with the concomitant introduction of many predatory mammals, has caused the extinction of at least three species of native frogs and severely reduced the ranges of the remaining three species to isolated pockets or predator-free islands (Bishop et al., 2013).

8.2.4 Climate Change

As amphibians are highly dependent on seasonal changes in environmental factors such as temperature and rainfall, climate change would be expected to have far-reaching impacts on their lives. Climate change models predict that different parts of the world will be impacted in different ways. Warming will be generally higher over land than sea, and

Figure 8.7 Hamilton's frog (*Leiopelma hamiltoni*). Once wide-ranging through the South Island of New Zealand, this species became restricted to just two off-shore islands which were never invaded by introduced mammals. (Photo: Phillip J. Bishop.)

higher in the Arctic than the Antarctic. Weather extremes will be more pronounced, with some areas becoming drier and others wetter. Heavy rainfall events are likely at high latitudes and high altitudes in the Northern Hemisphere, and in eastern North America and Eastern Asia. Low-lying coastal areas may become inundated as the sea level rises and the risk of forest fires will increase. The magnitude and timeframe for such changes depends on the rate of global warming, but current temperatures are approximately 1.0 °C above those of pre-industrial levels, and are likely to reach 1.5 °C between 2030 and 2052 at current rates of increase. This will result in significant and long-lasting impacts that may be irreversible (IPCC, 2018).

Where amphibians are concerned, the medium- to long-term impacts can be summarised as shifts in breeding and distributional patterns. Because of the variability in the weather at any one location, determining the impacts of climate change on amphibian breeding phenology requires long-term data spanning two or more decades. A comparative analysis of different taxa showed that amphibians in the Northern Hemisphere are shifting towards earlier reproduction much faster than birds, butterflies and trees (Parmesan, 2007). The populations that are most likely to start breeding earlier are those living towards the northern or southern limits of the species' geographical ranges, as this is where the impacts of climate change will be felt most acutely. Those living in the centre of their natural range may be well within their climatic limits and therefore less affected. Unsurprisingly, other studies have shown variation in the responses of amphibians to climate change, with some species in some areas showing no change (Beebee and Griffiths, 2005).

Shifts in distribution can occur on a latitudinal or altitudinal scale. In both cases the distribution shifts towards cooler areas as the climate warms. Unfortunately, we lack studies that have measured shifts in distribution patterns in relation to climate, so most of our understanding stems from modelling projections under different scenarios. If amphibians were able to disperse in an unlimited way, then most species could accommodate climate change by expanding their ranges. Realistically, however, this is unlikely to be the case and with significant barriers to dispersal most species will lose range. Within Europe, these contractions are more likely to occur in Western Europe, particularly in the

Iberian peninsula, France and northern Scandinavia (Araújo et al., 2006). In contrast to the lack of studies looking at latitudinal shifts in distribution, there has been research on shifts in altitudinal range. In the mountains of northern Madagascar, for example, upslope movements in the distribution of several species of amphibians and reptiles suggests that these animals are already responding to climate change, and that complete habitat loss may occur for some high-altitude species (Raxworthy et al., 2008).

At a global level, a study examining the climate change vulnerability (traits comprising sensitivity, exposure and adaptive capacity) of amphibians, birds and corals found that the amphibians with greatest relative vulnerability to climate change are concentrated in the Amazon basin (Foden et al., 2013). Combining both biological traits and ecologically relevant variables allows for both species- and area-specific interventions and policies.

Shifts in breeding patterns and shifts in distribution result from amphibian populations attempting to track climate change. Before that happens, there may be other more subtle impacts at the local or individual scale. Changes in temperature and rainfall will affect the hydroperiod of breeding ponds and this may have an effect on tadpole growth, development and fitness. Many amphibians display plasticity in development, and are able to speed up development in the face of warming and receding waters. The price that they pay to escape a desiccating pond is a smaller body size at metamorphosis, which may mean they have lower fitness when living on land. However, there is a limit to how fast amphibians can accelerate development, and if ponds dry up too fast and too frequently, then the developing tadpoles will not make it and there will be zero recruitment. If this happens for several years in succession then the population will decline.

One of the classic stories of amphibian declines leading to extinction is that of the golden toad (*Incilius periglenes*) in the Monteverde rainforest of Costa Rica. The golden toad underwent a population crash in 1987 and disappeared completely within two years. Pioneering work by Alan Pounds and his team showed that the decline of the golden toad and other amphibians in this area was associated with reduced frequency of mists, which in turn were related to sea surface temperatures and the El Niño/Southern Oscillation affect. Overall, this led to an extreme dry season that was implicated in the declines and extinction (Pounds et al., 1999). However, there are complex relationships between climate change and disease that are not yet fully understood. Dry conditions can make amphibians more susceptible to disease, and cause them to aggregate together in damp places, thereby increasing disease transmission. Likewise, climate change can shift the temperature profile so that it influences the proliferation of pathogens such as chytrid fungus (Pounds et al., 2006). Further research has suggested that there are complex links between temperature variability, the optimal temperature for chytrid growth and the immune response of the host amphibians (Li et al., 2013).

Although there have been some undoubted conservation success stories in, for example, eradicating invasive species from islands, restoring habitats, and improving water quality, tackling climate change is a much more challenging proposition. We have now gone beyond trying to reduce greenhouse gas emissions to the level they were several decades ago, with current actions aimed at reducing emissions to a rate that prevents widespread ecosystem collapse. Hopefully, this will be sufficiently slow enough to allow some species to adapt and some ecosystem services to remain intact. On a more local scale, there may be opportunities to use innovative methods to offset the impacts of climate change. These may include, for example, use of sprinkler systems and artificial shelters where habitats are drying out, and shading of ponds and manipulation of canopy cover to reduce tempera-ture stress (Shoo et al., 2011). Although collective local actions can make a difference if carried out on a large scale, collective global action is needed if we are to achieve widespread resilience to climate change.

While we know that climate change is having impacts on amphibians, linking popula-tion declines definitively to climate change has proved elusive. With some 40% of amphibians threatened with extinction, some commentators have suggested that we could see the extinction of a whole class of vertebrates under current anthropogenic pressures. However, the ancestors of present-day amphibians have survived previous global extinc-tion events, including the one which wiped out the dinosaurs at the end of the Cretaceous period, so it seems unlikely that the whole class would be eliminated solely by climate change. What is more likely is that there will be 'winners' and 'losers'. There will certainly be more extinctions as climate change progresses, but some species may prosper under the new conditions.

8.2.5 Overexploitation

Amphibians are collected from the wild for the pet and laboratory trade, and to provide food such as frogs' legs. Amphibian trade can be divided into the trade in live animals and the trade in animal products. Globally, wildlife trade has been estimated as being worth over $300 billion, with the illegal trade alone worth $25 billion. Although the trade in amphibians forms only a small component of the total, its impacts can be significant. The conservation issues that arise from the global trade in amphibians concern the transport of disease around the world (as discussed above), overharvesting of populations to the extent that they become vulnerable to extinction, and the deliberate or accidental release of amphibians into the wild that have the ability to compete with, predate upon or spread disease to native species.

The most popular amphibians in the pet trade are those that are colourful, relatively easy to keep and show high levels of daytime activity. Many species of poison dart frogs from South America meet these criteria. Once thought to be quite difficult to breed and difficult to obtain, large numbers of dart frogs have been exported to Europe, North America and the Far East since the 1980s. However, as captive husbandry and breeding success has improved, much of the demand is now met by captive-bred specimens. As a consequence, the proliferation of captive-bred stock may have reduced the price and also the pressure on some wild populations. There is also no doubt that colourful frogs are popular zoo exhibits and may be a useful way to convey important educational messages concerning amphibians and the threats that they face. A counter argument is that the increasing visibility of such species in pet shops and zoos may actually stimulate further trade. Although many of these species are listed on CITES, which means there are regulated quotas of animals that can be collected and exported, illegal collection and trade is very difficult to detect and prevent, and it is not difficult to pass off illegally collected animals as supposedly legal, captive-bred animals (Auliya et al., 2016). In addition, there are also species in trade that are not CITES-listed, in which case they are not regulated and can be legally traded regardless of the status of wild populations.

A wide range of relatively large-bodied amphibian species are utilised for food through-out the world. As human diets vary geographically and culturally, so does the appeal of eating frogs. The consumption of frogs' legs in the EU and USA drives a substantial trade in whole frogs and legs – it was estimated that between 2000 and 2009 approximately 4600 tons of frogs' legs were imported annually by the EU, with up to 84% of these being wild-caught individuals (Auliya et al., 2016). The American bullfrog (*Lithobates catesbeia-nus*) has been spread around the world through frog farms, which has led to its establish-ment in a range of countries. Frog farms can also result in the spread of diseases such as chytridiomycosis, and do not always serve to take the pressure off the exploitation of wild populations. Apart from the invasive species and disease risks, the main impact of the food trade is therefore overharvesting from wild populations. Before the 1990s, around 200 million frogs were exported per year from Asia, which in some countries led to severe population declines. Today, Indonesia and China are the main exporters of frogs' legs, with the majority supplying consumers in western Europe and the USA (Carpenter et al., 2014).

Regulating the trade in amphibians – whether it is live trade or food trade – is fraught with complex problems. CITES is the primary instrument by which the global trade in animals and animal products around the world is regulated. There are 162 (i.e. about 2%) amphibian species listed under CITES appendices, which means that trade is either prohibited or can only be carried out under an import and export permit system. However, only 24 of these species are listed in Appendix I, which means that they are threatened with extinction and trade is prohibited. A further 134 species are listed in Appendix II, where exploitation needs to be regulated to avoid it becoming a significant threat. Currently, 183 countries are parties that have signed up to CITES and are obliged to provide trade statistics on the species that are imported and exported under the permit system. However, there is considerable variation between countries in how CITES has been implemented and delivered. This means that loopholes can often be exploited by unscrupulous traders (e.g. animals collected from the wild can easily be passed off as captive-bred, which may be exempt). Likewise, the level of expertise within border and customs agencies to reliably identify protected species is generally low, and this is confounded by the changing taxonomy of many species. In addition, because many amphibians are small and easily stowed away in small containers, rigorous inspections and checks at borders are very difficult. Furthermore, where frogs are traded packaged as meat, customs officials must rely on the accompanying information to record the species being traded and whether it was farmed or wild-caught. As such, there can be uncertainty in the true origin of frog meat in international trade. DNA barcoding and stable isotope analysis of frog meat imported to Europe has confirmed that mislabelling does indeed occur. As a result, the volume of amphibians in the illegal trade is largely unknown, but suspected to be significant.

A further initiative to try and improve the regulation of the trade is the production of 'black lists' (= negative list) of species that it is not desirable to trade in because of conservation, health or welfare concerns. At the other extreme, 'white lists' (= positive lists) are those species deemed to not be at risk from the trade and/or not likely to pose risks to other taxa. The rationale for both these lists is to reach a voluntary agreement between the various stakeholders along the trade chain, including scientists, conservationists, veterinarians, policy-makers and traders, concerning those species that should – and should not – be traded. The issue here is that it is difficult to reach a consensus between the different stakeholders because there is a lack of hard evidence available to support decisions that are needed either way. A more draconian approach is to produce an outright ban on importing non-native species, or species that might pose a significant risk to biodiversity. This can work in isolated countries with good enforcement infrastructures (e.g. Australia and New Zealand), but is more problematical in countries with porous borders or weak monitoring and enforcement mechanisms. If bans are implemented without the infrastructure to monitor and enforce them, trade may be driven underground, thereby making monitoring and surveillance more problematic.

8.2.6 Pollution

Environmental contaminants comprise a wide range of chemical compounds that are released into the environment either deliberately (e.g. to control agricultural pests or fertilise soils) or as a by-product of other anthropogenic activities (e.g. leakage of inert chemicals from electrical systems). A large proportion of such contaminants are 'pesticides', a term that embraces chemicals to control invertebrate pests, plants, fungi and mammals. By far the most widely used pesticides currently are those used to control plants (herbicides), but historically, wide use of organochlorine pesticides such as DDT have been used to control insects, with far-reaching consequences for other animals and ecological systems. Such organochlorine pesticides have been banned for many years in North America and Europe, but they are still used in other parts of the world. There has been a shift away from using chemicals that can persist in the natural environment towards those that break down quickly after a single application; such short-term exposures can still have long-term impacts on amphibians and other fauna.

Accidental spills of pesticides can have devastating effects. For example, in 1987, a pesticide spill on the island of Jersey wiped out one of the two remaining agile frog (*Rana dalmatina*) populations. It took many years for the site to recover and amphibians to return (Ward et al., 2016). Fortunately, legal regulations and risk assessments make such accidental spillages much less frequent than they used to be, and of more concern are the side-effects of chemicals that are applied to the land as legal pesticides and fertilisers. These may have much more subtle impacts on amphibians and their habitats that can nevertheless produce lasting impacts. It is well-known that chemicals will affect growth, development, morphology and behaviour of amphibians. When pesticides reduce growth rate and development time, it means that tadpoles may be exposed to aquatic predators for longer and metamorphose as smaller, less-fit individuals. Reduced growth may come about as a result of the chemicals reducing activity and feeding behaviour. Alternatively, poor growth may result from pesticides reducing invertebrate prey of salamander larvae, or herbicides reducing algal food resources for frog tadpoles (Boone et al., 2009).

There may also be indirect effects on amphibians via the effects of chemicals on interactions involving predators, competitors and food webs. Low dosages of the pesticide malathion can remove insect predators from a pond and actually increase tadpole survival. However, higher tadpole densities can result in higher levels of competition for food and result in poorer growth and development (Relyea et al., 2005). There may also be complex and sometimes unpredictable effects when different chemicals form complex mixtures (Hayes et al., 2006), and contaminants may also reduce the immune responses of amphibians and make them more vulnerable to disease (Boone et al., 2009). There is less research on the nitrogen compounds that form the basis of most fertilisers than there is on pesticides, although many of the sublethal effects on survival, growth and development appear to be similar to those of pesticides, albeit with considerable variation between species and application scenarios (Baker et al., 2013).

One of the most intriguing and controversial group of chemicals are those that are known as endocrine disruptors. These chemicals disrupt hormonal pathways in animals, causing developmental, reproductive or behavioural changes. One such endocrine disruptor is EE2, an oestrogen-based compound found in human contraceptive pills. Traces of this chemical are excreted and persist through sewage treatments, eventually finding their way into natural systems, albeit at very low concentrations. In laboratory trials, EE2 has been shown to cause feminisation in frogs. Other chemicals, such as polychlorinated biphenyls and the herbicide atrazine, can also act as 'oestrogen mimics' to the same effect. Although such effects have been observed in a range of frog species, the impact varies between species and according to the concentration of the endocrine disruptor. How feminisation relates to sex ratios in the wild, and ultimately, impacts on natural populations remains unclear at present.

Despite considerable research on the impact of contaminants on amphibians in the last two decades (mainly in the global north), most of our knowledge relates to how they affect mortality, growth, interactions with predators and competitors, and food webs. Their impact on population declines has been much more difficult to unravel. Whether or not the use of a pesticide will affect amphibians depends on how, when and where it is applied. The concentration of the chemical, and the method and timing of application will all have an effect on the level of exposure. As discussed above, when different chemicals are being used for different purposes the result may be complex mixtures with complex effects. On top of this, the impact will depend on the environment into which the chemical is being released, and there are significant gaps in knowledge concerning the effects on amphibians in neotropical ecosystems. Rainfall, winds, stream flow, temperature and soil type may affect the dispersion and dilution of the chemical into the environment and its subsequent exposure to fauna and flora. However, there is considerable variation both within and between species in their vulnerability to contaminants (Bridges and Semlitsch, 2001), with some resilient species surviving remarkably well in degraded and quite polluted habitats. Although three areas that are downwind of extensive agricultural areas – the Sierra Nevada of California, Western Australia and mountains of Central America – have all suffered extensive declines (Boone et al., 2009), in Australia and Central America there are also lowland areas close to agriculture that seem to have escaped significant impacts (Lips and Donnelly, 2005). Clearly, then, the impacts of environmental contaminants are highly context dependent.

8.3 Amphibian Conservation Efforts

Although amphibian declines have been reported since the 1950s, it was only at the First World Congress of Herpetology where the global extent of the problem became clear. Since then there has been an increased focus on assessing the extent of the crisis and researching the causes of declines. Despite this increasing focus on amphibian conservation, we are still failing to make significant inroads in reversing, or even mitigating, amphibian declines. An assessment of conservation impact on mammals, birds and amphibians found that conservation efforts had reduced the decline in terms of the Red List Index for both mammals and birds, but that there was little effect of conservation efforts for amphibians (Hoffmann et al., 2010). A revised version of the ACAP is currently being developed which has taken into account feedback from many stakeholders and practitioners and is due for publication in 2023 (S. Wren, unpublished data).

Funding for amphibian conservation is also far behind that available for the 'more charismatic' groups, such as mammals and birds. Further, despite all the efforts to develop a strategic approach, lack of coordination and collaboration is still cited by amphibian experts as a major roadblock for effective conservation. Other factors listed as obstructions include lack of political will and enforcement, amphibians not being prioritised for conservation over other taxa, and no guidance in terms of a formal conservation plan for threatened species (S. Wren, unpublished data). The formation of the North American Bsal Task Force and the completion of a Strategic Plan with a Response Plan highlights how a union of government, academic and NGO scientists and managers in three countries can come together to plan proactive conservation measures (Grant et al., 2016).

With so many threatened species, it is necessary to prioritise where conservation efforts are directed. There are already several tools available to assist with this, including the IUCN Red List, which provides extinction risk assessments that can feed into prioritisation processes; Conservation Needs Assessments (Johnson et al., 2018), which look at conservation priorities by species; as well as Key Biodiversity Areas (www.keybiodiversityareas.org), which identify the most important sites globally to protect and conserve amphibians (and other species) and their habitat in situ. Arguably the most urgent subset of Key Biodiversity Areas to safeguard is the Alliance for Zero Extinction sites, which represent the only location in the world for one or more Critically Endangered or Endangered species; nearly 40% of the 932 AZE sites identified in

2018 were triggered by amphibian species, the largest proportion of any taxonomic group (www.zeroextinction.org).

Once a species, group of species or site has been prioritised, it is necessary to develop appropriate conservation recommendations, normally through a multistakeholder conservation planning process, using the best available conservation evidence and expertise. Conservation evidence is a key research priority to improve the performance of conservation practice (Sutherland et al., 2004). Evidence-based conservation research tests the outcomes of interventions to determine their effectiveness in achieving stated conservation objectives (Sutherland et al., 2004, 2012), thereby increasing our understanding of the consequences of interventions to inform future decision-making. Different interventions can also be tested, using an adaptive management approach for the best conservation outcomes. Publishing research that is useful to conservation practitioners offers potential for valuable societal and environmental impacts, improving the outlook for global conservation interventions. Conservation evidence for amphibians has been reviewed (Sutherland et al., 2019) to improve conservation practice, although continued updates are required to encourage and build on this information and make it available and useful to conservation practitioners. Plans should ideally be holistic, covering all aspects necessary for the conservation of the taxa in question, including in situ and ex situ measures, as well as necessary communication, educational and research components. This so-called 'One Plan Approach' (Byers et al., 2013) integrates all aspects of a plan into a coordinated and collaborative programme. Such plans require significant investment and support from institutions and funders, to be successfully implemented. A flowchart demonstrating the One Plan Approach to amphibian conservation is shown in Figure 8.8.

8.4 Looking to the Future

It has been over 30 years since a wave of publications on amphibian declines followed the First World Congress of Herpetology. One of the many problems faced by amphibian conservationists is that there are a large number of amphibians that have not yet been described or remain in the Data Deficient category, which slows down the Red Listing process. Additionally, when amphibian conservation is successful and results in a genuine downlisting of a species on the Red List, several more species may have been discovered in the interim, and once assessed are in the threatened Red List categories (see Table 8.1). Consequently, any positive achievements are masked by an influx of new species that are also often threatened. Two important publications are due for release in 2023, the updated ACAP and the Global Amphibian Assessment version 2 (GAA2). These publications will highlight the most up-to-date numbers of threatened amphibians (including genuinely downlisted species, e.g. *Agalychnis annae*, Endangered to Vulnerable, *Parvimolge townsendi*, Critically Endangered to Vulnerable) (J. Luedtke, personal communication) and, more importantly, detailed synopses of the current most pressing issues facing amphibians combined with roadmaps of best management practice for amphibian conservation. While the future may seem bleak for amphibians, there are three global amphibian conservation organisations that are working together with a common vision – Amphibians Thriving in

Amphibian conservation flowchart

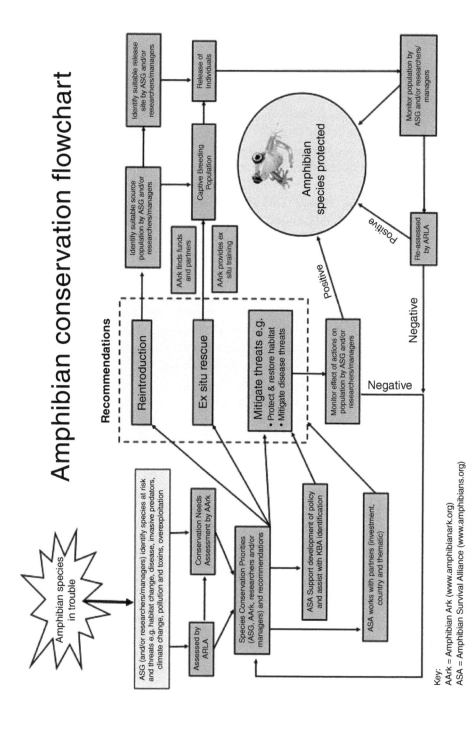

Figure 8.8 Amphibian 'One Plan Approach' conservation flowchart.

Key:
AArk = Amphibian Ark (www.amphibianark.org)
ASA = Amphibian Survival Alliance (www.amphibians.org)
ARLA = IUCN SSC ASG Amphibian Red List Authority (www.iucn-amphibians.org)
ASG = IUCN SSC Amphibian Specialist Group (www.iucn-amphibians.org)
KBA = Key Biodiversity Areas (http://www.keybiodiversityareas.org)

ASA

Conserves amphibians and their habitats through dynamic partnerships worldwide

Leads on coordination, partnerships, outreach (including communication and education), and funding

AMPHIBIANS THRIVING IN NATURE

ASG

Provides the scientific foundation to inform effective global amphibian conservation

Leads on providing the science to guide action

AArk

Ensures the survival and diversity of amphibian species, focusing on those that cannot currently be safeguarded in their natural environment

Leads on ex situ rescue, Conservation Needs Assessments, integrated planning, and capacity-building

Figure 8.9 Diagram illustrating the relationship between the three main amphibian conservation networks. Key: AArk = Amphibian Ark (www.amphibianark.org), ASA = Amphibian Survival Alliance (www.amphibians.org), ASG = IUCN SSC Amphibian Specialist Group (www.iucn-amphibians.org).

Nature – to guide the implementation of global amphibian conservation, driven by expert guidance and best practice (Figure 8.9). These are complemented by a range of other organisations carrying out crucial conservation work at the local, regional or national level. Amphibians as a whole are experiencing 'death by a thousand cuts', but we are starting to understand the threats, and we are making advances in amphibian conservation to halt the decline of many species in the next 30 years.

References

Araújo, M.B., Thuiller, W. and Pearson, R.G. (2006) Climate warming and the decline of amphibians and reptiles in Europe. *J Biogeogr* 33(10): 1712–1728.

Auliya, M., García-Moreno, J., Schmidt, B.R., et al. (2016) The global amphibian trade flows through Europe: the need for enforcing and improving legislation. *Biodivers Conserv* 25: 2581–2595.

Baker, N.J., Bancroft, B.A. and Garcia, T.S. (2013) A meta-analysis of the effects of pesticides and fertilizers on survival and growth of amphibians. *Sci Total Environ* 449: 150–156.

Barata, I.M., Silva, E.P. and Griffiths R.A. (2018) Predictors of abundance of a rare bromeliad-dwelling frog (*Crossodactylodes itambe*) in the Espinhaço Mountain range of Brazil. *J Herpetol* 52: 321–326.

Beebee, T.J.C. and Griffiths, R.A. (2005). The amphibian decline crisis: A watershed for conservation biology? *Biol Conserv* 125(3): 271–285.

Berger, L., Speare, R., Daszak, P., et al. (1998) Chytridiomycosis causes amphibian mortality associated with population declines in the rain forests of Australia and Central America. *Proc Natl Acad Sci USA* 95(15): 9031–9036.

Bishop, P.J., Daglish, L.A., Haigh, A.J.M., et al. (2013) *Native Frog (*Leiopelma *spp.) Recovery Plan, 2013–2018.* Threatened Species Recovery Plan 63. Wellington, New Zealand: Department of Conservation.

Boone, M.D., Davidson, C. and Bridges-Britton, C. (2009) Evaluating the impact of pesticides in amphibian declines. In: Heatwole, H. and Wilkinson, J.W. (Eds.), *Amphibian Decline: Diseases, Parasites, Maladies and Pollution.* Vol. 8 in Amphibian Biology. Baulkham Hills, Australia: Surrey Beatty & Sons.

Bosch, J., Sanchez-Tomé, E., Fernández-Loras, A., et al. (2015) Successful elimination of a lethal wildlife infectious disease in nature. *Biol Lett* 11 (11): 21050874.

Bridges, C.M. and Semlitsch, R.D. (2001) Genetic variation in insecticide tolerance in a population of southern leopard frogs (*Rana sphenocephala*): implications for amphibian conservation. *Copeia* 2001: 7–13.

Byers, O., Lees, C., Wilcken, J. and Schwitzer, C. (2013) The One Plan approach: the philosophy and implementation of CBSG's approach to integrated species conservation planning. *WAZA Magazine*, 14: 2–5.

Carpenter, A.I., Andreone, F., Moore, R.D. and Griffiths, R. A. (2014) A review of the international trade in amphibians: the types, levels and dynamics of trade in CITES-listed species. *Oryx* 48(4): 565–574.

Foden, W.B., Butchart, S.H.M., Stuart, S.N., et al. (2013) Identifying the world's most climate change vulnerable species: a trait-based assessment of birds, amphibians and corals. *PLoS One* 8(6): e65427.

Ford, J., Hunt, D.A.G.A., Haines, G.E., et al. (2020) Adrift on a sea of troubles: can amphibians survive in a human-dominated world? *Herpetologica* 76(2): 251–256.

Gascon, C., Collins, J.P., Moore, R.D., et al. (2007) *Amphibian Conservation Action Plan.* Gland, Switzerland and Cambridge, UK: IUCN SSC Amphibian Specialist Group.

Gomes, A, Giri, B., Saha, A., et al. (2007) Bioactive molecules from amphibian skin: their biological activities with reference to therapeutic potentials for possible drug development. *Indian J Exp Biol* 45: 579–593.

Grant, E.H.C., Muths, E.L., Katz, R.A., et al. (2016) *Salamander Chytrid Fungus (*Batrachochytrium salamandrivorans*) in the United States: Developing Research, Monitoring, And Management Strategies (No. 2015-1233).* Reston, VA: US Geological Survey.

Greer, A.L., Brunner, J.L. and Collins, J.P. (2009) Spatial and temporal patterns of *Ambystoma tigrinum* virus (ATV) prevalence in tiger salamanders *Ambystoma tigrinum nebulosum. Dis Aquat Org* 85: 1–6.

Griffiths, R.A., Sewell, D. and McRea, R. (2010) Dynamics of a declining amphibian metapopulation: survival, dispersal and the impact of climate. *Biol Conserv* 143: 485–491.

Hayes, T.B., Case, P., Chui, D. et al. (2006) Pesticide mixtures, endocrine disruption, and amphibian declines: are we underestimating the impact? *Environ Health Perspect* 114: 40–50.

Hocking, D.J. and Babbitt, K.J. (2014) Amphibian contributions to ecosystem services. *Herpetol Conserv Biol* 9(1): 1–17.

Hoffmann, M., Hilton-Taylor, C., Angulo, A., et al. (2010) The impact of conservation on the status of the world's vertebrates. *Science* 330(6010): 1503–1509.

Hopkins, W.A. (2007) Amphibians as models for studying environmental change. *ILAR J* 48: 270–277.

Hudson, M.A., Griffiths, R.A., Martin, L., et al. (2019) Reservoir frogs: seasonality of *Batrachochytrium dendrobatidis* infection in robber frogs in Dominica and Montserrat. *PeerJ* 7: e7021.

IPCC. (2018) Summary for Policymakers. In: *Global Warming of 1.5 °C*. An IPCC Special Report on the impacts of global warming of 1.5°C above pre-industrial levels and related global greenhouse gas emission pathways, in the context of strengthening the global response to the threat of climate change, sustainable development, and efforts to eradicate poverty. www.ipcc.ch/sr15/chapter/spm (accessed October 2022).

IUCN. (2020) *The IUCN Red List of Threatened Species*. Version 2020–2. www.iucnredlist.org (accessed October 2022).

Johnson, K., Baker, A., Buley, K., et al. (2018) A process for assessing and prioritizing species conservation needs: going beyond the Red List. *Oryx* 54(1): 125–132.

Li, Y., Cohen, J.M. and Rohr, J.R. (2013) Review and synthesis of the effects of climate change on amphibians. *Integr Zool* 8: 145–161.

Lips, R.K. and Donnelly, M.A. (2005) Lessons from the tropics. In: Lanoo, M.J. (Ed.). *Amphibian Declines: the Conservation Status of United States Species*. Berkeley, CA: University of California Press.

Menéndez-Guerrero, P.A., Davies, T.J. and Green, D.M. (2020) Extinctions of threatened frogs may impact ecosystems in a global hotspot of anuran diversity. *Herpetologica* 76: 121–131.

Parmesan, C. (2007) Influences of species, latitudes and methodologies on estimates of phenological response to global warming. *Glob Change Biol* 13: 1860–1872.

Pilliod, D.S., Griffiths, R.A. and Kuzmin, S.K. (2012) Ecological impacts of non-native species. In: Heatwole, H. and Wilkinson, J.W. (Eds.), *Conservation and Decline of Amphibians: Ecological Aspects, Effect of Humans, and Management*. Vol. 10 in Amphibian Biology. Baulkham Hills, Australia: Surrey Beatty & Sons.

Pounds, J.A., Fogden, M.P.L and Campbell, J.H. (1999) Biological response to climate change on a tropical mountain. *Nature* 398: 611–615.

Pounds, J.A., Bustamante, M.R., Coloma, L.A., et al. (2006) Widespread amphibian extinctions from epidemic disease driven by global warming. *Nature* 439: 161–167.

Price, S.J., Garner, T.W.J., Nichols, R.A., et al. (2014) Collapse of amphibian communities due to an introduced ranavirus. *Curr Biol* 24: 2586–2591.

Raxworthy, C.J., Pearson, R.G., Rabibisoa, N., et al. (2008) Extinction vulnerability of tropical montane endemism from warming and upslope displacement: a preliminary appraisal for the highest massif in Madagascar. *Glob Change Biol* 14: 1703–1720.

Relyea, R.A., Schoeppner, N.P. and Hoverman, J.T. (2005) Pesticides and amphibians: the importance of community context. *Ecol Appl* 15: 1125–1134.

Scheele, B.C., Pasmans, F., Skerratt, L.F. et al. (2020) Amphibian fungal panzootic causes catastrophic and ongoing loss of biodiversity. *Science* 363: 1459–1463.

Semlitsch, R.D., O'Donnell, K.M. and Thompson, F.R. (2014) Abundance, biomass production, nutrient content, and the possible role of terrestrial salamanders in Missouri Ozark forest ecosystems. *Can J Zool* 92(12): 997–1004.

Shoo, L.P., Olson, D.H., McMenamin, S.K., et al. (2011) Engineering a future for amphibians under climate change. *J Appl Ecol* 48: 487–492.

Spitzen-van der Sluijs, A., Canessa, S., Martel, A. and Pasmans, F. (2017) Fragile coexistence of a global chytrid pathogen with amphibian populations is mediated by environment and demography. *Proc Royal Soc. B* 284: 20171444.

Stuart, S.N., Chanson, J.S., Cox, N.A., et al. (2004) Status and trends of amphibian declines and extinctions worldwide. *Science* 306(5702): 1783–1786.

Stuart, S.N. Hoffmann, M., Chanson, J.S., et al. (Eds.) (2008) *Threatened Amphibians of the World*. Barcelona, Spain: Lynx Edicions; Gland, Switzerland: IUCN; Arlington, VA: Conservation International.

Sutherland, W.J., Pullin, A.S., Dolman, P.M. and Knight, T.M. (2004) The need for evidence-based conservation. *Trends Ecol Evol* 19: 305–308.

Sutherland, W.J., Mitchell, R. and Prior, S.V. (2012) The role of 'Conservation Evidence' in improving conservation management. *Conserv Evid* 9: 1–2.

Sutherland, W.J., Dicks, L.V., Ockendon, N., Petrovan, S.O. and Smith, R.K. (2019) *What Works in Conservation 2019*. Cambridge, UK: Open Book Publishers.

Tapley, B., Michaels, C.J., Gumbs, R., et al. (2018) The disparity between species description and conservation assessment: a case study in taxa with high rates of species discovery. *Biol Conserv* 220: 209–214.

Teacher, A.G.F., Cunningham, A.A. and Garner, T.W.J. (2010) Assessing the long-term impact of ranavirus infection in wild common frog populations. *Animal Conserv* 13: 514–522.

Teng, Q., Hu, X-F., Luo, F., et al. (2016) Influences of introducing frogs in the paddy fields on soil properties and rice growth. *J Soils Sediments* 16: 51–61.

Valiente, E., Tovar, A., Gonzalez, H., Eslava-Sandoval, D. and Zambrano, L. (2010) Creating refuges for the axolotl (*Ambystoma mexicanum*). *Ecol Restor* 28: 257–259.

Voyles, J., Woodhams, D.C., Saenz,V., et al. (2018) Shifts in disease dynamics in a tropical amphibian assemblage are not due to pathogen attenuation. *Science* 358: 1517–1519.

Waddle, J.H., Grear, D.A., Mosher, B.A., et al. (2020) *Batrachochytrium salamandrivorans* (Bsal) not detected in an intensive survey of wild North American amphibians. *Sci Rep* 10: 13012.

Wake, D.B. and Vredenburg, V.T. (2008) Are we in the midst of the sixth mass extinction? A view from the world of amphibians. *Proc Natl Acad Sci USA* 105(1): 11466–11473.

Ward, R.J., Liddiard, T., Goetz, M. and Griffiths, R.A. (2016) Head-starting, re-introduction and conservation management of the agile frog on Jersey, British Channel Isles. In: Soorae, P.S. (Ed.), *Global Re-introduction Perspectives: 2016. Case-Studies from Around the Globe.* Gland, Switzerland: IUCN/ SSC Re- introduction Specialist Group; Abu Dhabi, UAE: Environment Agency – Abu Dhabi.

Whiles, M.R., Lips, K.R., Pringle, C.M., et al. (2006) The effects of amphibian population declines on the structure and function of Neotropical stream ecosystems. *Front Ecol Environ* 4(1): 27–34.

Zambrano, L., Valiente, E. and Vander Zanden, M.J. (2010) Food web overlap among native axolotl (*Ambystoma mexicanum*) and two exotic fishes: carp (*Cyprinus carpio*) and tilapia (*Oreochromis niloticus*) in Xochimilco, Mexico City. *Biol Invasions* 12: 3061–3069.

Zipkin, E.F., DiRenzo, G.V., Ray, J.M., Rossman, S. and Lips, K.R. (2020) Tropical snake diversity collapses after widespread amphibian loss. *Science* 367: 814–816.

NINE

Freshwater Fishes: Threatened Species and Threatened Waters on a Global Scale

PETER B. MOYLE AND ROBERT A. LEIDY

Summary

Worldwide, freshwater biodiversity is in decline and increasingly threatened. Fishes are the best-documented indicators of this decline. General threats to persistence include: (1) competition for water, (2) habitat alteration, (3) pollution, (4) invasions of alien species, (5) commercial exploitation and (6) global climate change. Regional faunas usually face multiple, simultaneous causes of decline. Threatened species belong to all major evolutionary lineages of fishes, although families with the most imperilled species are those with the most species (e.g. Cyprinidae, Cichlidae). Independent evaluation of California's highly endemic (81%) fish fauna for comparison with IUCN results validates the alarm generated by IUCN evaluations. However, IUCN overall evaluation is conservative, because it does not include many intraspecific taxa for which extinction trends are roughly double those at the species level. Dramatic global loss of freshwater fish species is imminent without immediate and bold actions by multiple countries.

9.1 Introduction

Fishes are appropriate indicators of trends in aquatic biodiversity because their enormous variety reflects a wide range of environmental conditions. Fish also have a major impact on the distribution and abundance of other organisms in waters they inhabit. Examination of the trends of freshwater fish faunas from different parts of the world indicate that most faunas are in serious decline and in need of immediate protection...We conservatively estimate that 20% of the freshwater fish species of the world are already extinct or in serious decline. (Moyle and Leidy, 1992, p. 127)

Tragically, global conditions for freshwater fishes have not stabilised or improved since 1992, but have worsened. Leidy and Moyle (1997), in a status review of the world's marine and freshwater fishes, noted that during the six years since their previous study, freshwater fishes had continued to decline, although this assessment was partly the result of better information. Much of the recorded decline at that time was in regions where the fish fauna had been intensively studied, suggesting that in poorly documented areas most fish declines and extinctions were going unrecorded. This observation has been borne out by Darwell and Freyhof (2015) who found 31% of 7300 freshwater fish species assessed were threatened with extinction (2013 IUCN Red List). Notably, this threatened percentage excluded 1571 species with insufficient data on which to base an assessment as well as 69 species known to be either completely extinct or extinct in the wild. Analysis of the 2022 IUCN database shows that the situation is not improving (Box 9.1).

Box 9.1
IUCN Listed Freshwater Fishes

The IUCN Red List (version 2022-1) database is a useful tool to predict the probable global future of freshwater fishes; it indicates that the future of currently recognised fishes is grim (Table 9.1). The 18,000 species of freshwater fishes represent just over 50% of all known fish species; the IUCN data indicates that about 20–30% of these fishes are threatened with extinction, or nearly so, by the end of the century, with extinction rates varying from region to region. Most of these species are not the subject of conservation plans. IUCN lists 89 freshwater fishes as extinct and another 12 as extinct in the wild. Of 13,276 species of freshwater fishes assessed by IUCN, 728 species are Critically Endangered, 1054 are Endangered and 1156 are Vulnerable. Threatened fishes comprise about 22% (n = 2938) of the total assessed freshwater taxa. Threatened fishes belong to all taxonomic orders, indicating that threatened fishes are globally and taxonomically diverse. Half of all assessed freshwater fishes are considered to be widespread and/or abundant (i.e. Least Concern). Another 2556 taxa have insufficient information to assess extinction risk (i.e. Data Deficient). Decreasing or unknown population trends characterise 14% (n = 1836 spp.) and 67% (n = 8898) of all threatened freshwater fish species, subspecies and subpopulations, respectively. Only 17% of species populations are considered stable and less than 1% are increasing. For Near Threatened Species, 30% have decreasing populations, suggesting that these taxa may soon be threatened.

Table 9.1 *Global status of freshwater fishes by taxonomic order (compiled from IUCN version 2022-1, status abbreviations are defined at bottom of the table)*[a]

CLASS/Order	EX/EW	CR	EN	VU	Subtotal Threatened Species (CR+EN+VU)	NT	DD	LC
CEPHALASPIDOMORPHI								
Petromyzontiformes (lampreys)	1	2	4	2	8	3	3	23
CHONDRICHTHYES								
Carcharhiniformes (groundsharks)	0	2	0	4	6	1	0	0
Myliobatiformes (stingrays)	0	3	6	1	10	1	17	5
Rhinopristiformes (shovelnose rays)	0	5	0	0	5	0	0	0
ACTINOPTERYGII								
Acipenseriformes (sturgeons, paddlefishes)	4	33	15	22	70	0	0	1
Osteoglossiformes (bony tongues)	1	0	6	16	22	5	41	143
Clupeiformes (herrings)	0	4	8	12	23	3	39	112
Anguilliformes (eels)	0	1	3	2	6	4	5	11
Gonorynchiformes (milkfish, hingemouth)	0	0	1	4	5	0	11	17
Cypriniformes (carps, minnows, loaches, suckers, barbs)	44	163	300	339	802	170	676	1443
Siluriformes (catfishes)	2	72	154	156	382	129	664	866
Gymnotiformes (neotropical knifefishes)	0	7	1	14	22	4	30	80
Characiformes (caracins)	0	17	62	70	149	51	203	946
Esociformes (pikes, mudminnows)	0	0	0	1	1	0	0	11
Salmoniformes (salmon, trout, allies)	20	26	33	36	95	8	52	82
Percopsiformes (trout-perches, pirate perches)	0	1	0	0	1	3	0	5
Ophidiiformes (cusk eels)	0	1	4	2	7	2	0	0
Batrachoidiformes (toadfishes)	0	0	0	1	1	0	3	4
Sygnathiformes (pipefishes, seahorses)	0	1	1	1	3	1	17	23

Table 9.1 (*cont.*)

CLASS/Order	EX/EW	CR	EN	VU	Subtotal Threatened Species (CR+EN+VU)	NT	DD	LC
Synbranchiformes (spiny eels)	0	2	6	6	14	4	18	63
Mugiliformes (mullets)	0	0	1	0	1	0	6	32
Beloniformes (needle fishes)	0	7	9	7	23	14	21	54
Atheriniformes (silversides)	1	48	53	44	145	28	31	86
Cyprinodontiformes (rivulines, killifishes, live bearers)	19	108	162	172	497	105	349	1304
Perciformes (perch-likes)	6	156	152	189	596	128	472	1505
Gasterosteiformes (sticklebacks)	1	1	1	2	4	2	1	13
Scorpaeniformes (scorpionfishes and flatheads)	1	3	1	6	10	4	9	87
Tetraodontiformes (puffers, filefishes)	0	0	2	1	3	3	8	35

IUCN Red List Categories: EX/EW = extinct/extinct in the wild; CR = Critically Endangered; EN = Endangered; VU = Vulnerable; NT = Near Threatened; DD = Data Deficient; LC = Least Concern.

[a] Includes species, subspecies and varieties, and subpopulations.

Globally, loss of freshwater biodiversity is a leading crisis in conservation (Darwell et al., 2018; Harrison et al., 2018; Reid et al., 2018; World Wide Fund for Nature, 2020, 2021). Fishes are among the most conspicuous, best-documented indicators of this biotic decline (Dudgeon et al., 2006; Strayer and Dudgeon, 2010; Darwell and Freyhoff, 2015). Ricciardi and Rasmussen (1999) capture this crisis in terms of predicted extinctions in North America of five major groups of freshwater organisms, including fishes, which they estimated will average 4% of the fauna per decade. They comment that '. . .temperate freshwater ecosystems are being depleted of species as rapidly as tropical rainforests' (p. 1220). Given advances in our understanding of this crisis in the last 20 years, the estimates of Ricciardi and Rasmussen (1999) are undoubtedly conservative.

The authors live in a well-defined geographic region of the world, California, USA, with a highly endemic fish fauna (81% of 134 taxa) (Moyle et al., 2011, 2013, 2015). Our most recent analysis indicates that 51% of the total fauna is either extinct or threatened with extinction, with 30% being 'near-threatened' by IUCN standards (Leidy and Moyle, 2021) (Figure 9.1). Only 19% of the fishes can be regarded as secure for the immediate

Figure 9.1 Examples of extinct and threatened California freshwater fishes. (a) The endemic, extinct, thicktail chub, *Gila crassicauda*, was historically one of the most abundant fish in lowland aquatic habitats of Central California. Photo credit: Peter Moyle. (b) Delta smelt, *Hypomesus transpacificus*, a critically endangered member of the Osmeridae. Photo credit: Matt Young, U.S. Geological Survey (c) McCloud River redband trout, *Oncorhynchus mykiss stonei*, an endangered member of the Salmonidae from Trout Creek, California. Photo credit: Michael Carl. (d) The endangered Owens pupfish, *Cyprinodon radiosus*, a small endemic fish that is restricted to isolated springs in arid southeastern California. Photo credit: Joe Ferreira, California Department of Fish and Wildlife. Copyright 2022 by The Regents of the University of California. All Rights Reserved. Used with permission via http://calfish.ucdavis.edu.

future. The situation in California likely reflects the future of freshwater fishes in many other geographic areas of the world. Using the comparatively well-studied fish fauna of California as background, in this chapter we discuss the following topics:[1]

- How many species of freshwater fishes are there?
- What are the general population trends in freshwater fishes?
- Why is the freshwater fish crisis so severe and what are the primary causes of fish declines?
- Are some families of fishes more vulnerable to extinction than others?
- How well does the IUCN Red List represent the status of fish faunas?
- What is the likely future of the world's freshwater fish fauna?

---

[1] For a brief introduction to fish biology and classification, see Chapter 10.

9.2   How Many Species of Freshwater Fishes Are There?

Remarkably, there are now more described freshwater fish species than marine species, a trend that is likely to continue. As of 2022, there are 36,345 recognised species of fishes, of which 18,345 (51%) are freshwater fishes (Fricke et al., 2022). From 2010 through 2020, 4020 new fish species were described, translating to an average of about 365 new fish species per year (Fricke et al., 2022). Three taxonomic orders and one family composed primarily of freshwater fishes account for 65% of the newly described species: Siluriformes, Cypriniformes, Cyprinodontiformes and Cichlidae.

Two factors primarily explain the ongoing discovery of new species of freshwater fishes. First, in part as a response to the freshwater biodiversity crisis, there have been increased efforts by scientists to inventory and describe aquatic faunas in poorly known regions of the world. For example, in 2013, Australian researchers discovered 20 new species of fishes while surveying 17 remote rivers in the Kimberly Region (University of Melbourne, 2016). The discoveries increased the number of described freshwater fishes in Australia by almost 10%. Similarly, the USA's National Science Foundation (NSF) funded multiyear research programmes to understand the global species richness of the two most diverse groups of freshwater fishes, the catfishes (Siluriformes) and the carps and minnows (Cypriniformes) (NSF 2008, 2010). The catfish research project resulted in the astonishing discovery of 430 new species, with another 350–500 new species' descriptions anticipated.

Second, there has been a substantial increase in new freshwater fish species that are part of complexes of cryptic species (Adams et al., 2014). Cryptic species are species that are not recognised because they are hidden under the names of widely distributed, well-recognised species; they often appear morphologically identical to the described species, while they are genetically quite distinct (Bickford et al., 2007). The increasing use and decreasing costs of molecular studies such as DNA barcoding and other genomic techniques continues to reveal new cryptic species and this trend will likely continue. For example, Ramirez et al. (2017), using DNA barcoding, detected potential cryptic diversity within 10 nominal

Figure 9.2 A substantial portion of the increase in new freshwater fish species is from the discovery of cryptic species. For example, a genomic analysis of California roach (*Hesperoleucus* spp.) revealed a complex hierarchy that included two genera, six species, four subspecies, and several distinct population segments. Pictured is a roach *(H. symmetricus navarroensis)* from the Russian River in breeding colours (Baumsteiger and Moyle, 2019). Photo with permission by Don Loarie.

species of the neotropical, species-rich family Anostomidae (Characiformes). Similarly, Adams et al. (2014) used allozyme, mtDNA and morphological techniques on populations of an Australian freshwater fish (*Galaxias olidus*) and found 15 cryptic taxa. Baumsteiger and Moyle (2019) used DNA (RAD) sequencing genomics to clarify and assign taxonomic categories to a comparatively well-studied species complex of two California cyprinids, the California roach (*Hesperoleucus symmetricus*) and hitch (*Lavinia exilicauda*) (Figure 9.2). This genomic analysis revealed a complex hierarchy that included two genera, six species, four subspecies and several distinct population segments. These studies strongly suggest that more analyses are needed to detect cryptic taxa, even within abundant, widely distributed fishes (Adams et al., 2014). In the absence of molecular information on cryptic species, there will be consistent underestimation of numbers of threatened freshwater fish species.

9.3   What Are the Major Trends in Status of Freshwater Fishes?

Understanding population sizes and trends is critical to effective management and conservation of fish species. We used the IUCN Red List (version 2022-1) database as a tool to predict the probable future of freshwater fishes and concluded that the future of currently recognised fishes appears grim (Box 9.1, Table 9.1). There are nine IUCN Red List categories for classifying species global extinction risk (IUCN 2012): (1) an *Extinct* (EX) taxon is one where there is no reasonable doubt that the last individual has died, (2) *Extinct in the Wild* (EW) refers to taxa only known to survive in captivity, or as naturalised populations well outside the native range, (3) taxa are *Critically Endangered* (CE) when considered to be facing extremely high risk of extinction in the wild, (4) taxa are *Endangered* (EN) when facing a very high risk of extinction, (5) *Vulnerable* (VU) refers to taxa facing high risk of extinction, (6) *Near Threatened* (NT) taxa do not meet the criteria for CR, EN or VU, but are close to qualifying for or are likely to qualify for a threatened category in the near future, (7) *Least Concern* (LC) taxa do not meet the criteria of CR, EN, VU or NT, and are widespread and/or abundant, (8) taxa are *Data Deficient* (DD) when there is insufficient information to make a direct, or indirect, assessment of extinction risk based on distribution and/or population status and (9) *Not Evaluated* (NE) means that a taxon has not yet been assessed against the criteria. All taxa listed as Critically Endangered, Endangered, or Vulnerable are considered together as 'threatened'.

Of 13,276 species of freshwater fishes assessed by the IUCN, 5% were Critically Endangered, 8% were Endangered and 9% were Vulnerable. Threatened fishes therefore comprise about 22% (n = 2938) of the total assessed taxa. Population trends for threatened, Near Threatened and Data Deficient freshwater fishes indicate that more species are headed for extinct or threatened status. Decreasing or unknown population trends characterise 14% and 66% of all threatened fish taxa, respectively. Considered stable or increasing are only 18% of known assessed taxa and 9% of threatened and Near Threatened populations, respectively. These statistics indicate that many Near Threatened species will accelerate their slide towards extinction in the future. Unfortunately, another 2418 taxa, or 95% of Data Deficient species, lack information on population trends.

A paucity of information on regional population trends of freshwater fishes exists globally (IUCN, 2022). Regionally, fish species with decreasing populations are most likely to be in

Asia (21% declining populations), especially South and Southeast Asia. Globally, population trends are unknown for 52% and 61% of threatened and Near Threatened fish species, respectively, although it would not be surprising if most are in decline. We have very little information on fish species abundance trends for Sub-Saharan Africa (73% unknown) and South America (86%). Surprisingly, trends are not well known for a significant percentage of the threatened and Near Threatened fishes from some of the better-studied regions of the world, most notably Europe (58%) and North America (45%) (IUCN, 2022).

As of this writing, there are 2236 freshwater fish species or subspecies listed as threatened or near-threatened that need conservation actions based on research, conservation planning, and monitoring (IUCN, 2022). Conservation actions required for these species have been recommended over 4520 times and include land and water protection and management, species management strategies, education and awareness programmes, law and policy changes, and livelihood and economic incentive programmes. Not surprisingly, the most needed conservation actions for freshwater fishes revolve around habitat protection, management and restoration. Research is most urgently needed to resolve population size, distribution and trends, life history and ecology, taxonomy and threats, as well as to develop plans for management, harvest and trade. Most species have multiple conservation issues. Unfortunately, threatened fishes are currently not receiving the conservation, management and research actions that are necessary to reverse continued declines, much less hasten recovery. Alarmingly, 1269 Critically Endangered or Endangered freshwater fishes require multiple conservation actions to prevent imminent extinction. Also, 302 Near Threatened freshwater fishes need conservation actions or research to prevent them from further decline.

Perhaps most troubling, 28% (n = 539) of threatened freshwater fishes need their status assessment updated (IUCN, 2022). It is likely that populations of threatened species that lack current information will continue to decline. The next section shows why this is so likely.

9.4 Why Is the Freshwater Crisis So Severe?

The ultimate cause of the freshwater biodiversity crisis is the ever-increasing human population coupled with increased demand for resources needed for improved standards of living. As more and more of the Earth's water is used to support people, less and less of it is available for other animals and plants. Consequently, a high percentage of rivers, lakes and wetlands of the world are highly altered, overexploited and polluted, putting tremendous stress on aquatic organisms, including fishes. Given that 80% of the world's people live in areas where the poor quality or low availability of water is a threat to their health and wellbeing (Vörösmarty et al., 2010), providing clean and abundant water for fishes could also benefit billions of people directly.

Moyle and Leidy (1992) categorised the more proximate causes of freshwater fish declines into five synergistic, non-exclusive causes of decline, to which we now have added global climate change. Closs et al. (2015) used similar groupings. They include: (1) competition for water, (2) habitat alteration, (3) pollution, (4) invasions of alien species, (5) commercial exploitation and (6) global climate change.

9.4.1 Competition for Water

People require large quantities of freshwater, which is why we build our cities on rivers, lakes and estuaries, create thousands of dams and diversions, and irrigate millions of acres of farmland. According to the United Nations (WWAP, 2019, p. 13):

Water use has been increasing worldwide by about 1% per year since the 1980s... This steady rise has principally been led by surging demand in developing countries and emerging economies (although per capita water use in the majority of these countries remains far below water use in developed countries – they are merely catching up). This growth is driven by a combination of population growth, socio-economic development and evolving consumption patterns... Agriculture (including irrigation, livestock and aquaculture) is by far the largest water consumer, accounting for 69% of annual water withdrawals globally. Industry (including power generation) accounts for 19% and households for 12% ...Global water demand is expected to continue increasing at a similar rate until 2050, accounting for an increase of 20 to 30% above the current level of water use...

Water left in rivers to support fishes and a wide variety of other life is often regarded as water 'wasting to the sea'. The Aral Sea of Kazakhstan is a sad reminder of what can result from competition for water between people and fishes, when people win. Once the fourth largest lake in the world, the Aral Sea has mostly dried up because inflowing rivers are diverted to supply water to grow cotton, with no reductions of water diversion during drought (Figure 9.3). Thirty-two species of native fishes, as well as the fisheries they supported, have been extirpated as a result. At present, a small part of the northern Aral Sea is being restored to a lake-like environment, to conserve remaining endemic fishes and fisheries (Micklin, 2016).

While the Aral Sea disaster is visible from satellites, most habitats of disappearing fishes are small, such as the spring pool systems spread across arid southwestern North America. The endemic pupfishes and similar desert fishes disappear one by one as the water from the aquifers feeding these springs is pumped away for urban and agricultural use. Many of the remaining pools contain aggressive non-native fish species.

9.4.2 Habitat Alteration

Most of the world's major rivers are severely altered from their historical conditions by levees, dams, diversions, roads and other human constructions (Figure 9.4). Our cities and farms typically cover the floodplains and wetlands that have only recently been appreciated for their importance to fish and other components of riverine ecosystems, as well as for flood management (Opperman et al., 2017). Habitat alteration is often continuous from the valley floor lakes and rivers to mountain tributaries, as people attempt to control the movement of water to send it where it is desired, not necessarily where it would flow naturally (Williams et al., 2019). In many areas, intensive use of lands in watersheds for a myriad of purposes, such as timber production, agriculture and urban expansion, results in watersheds with degraded streams and lakes that have lost much of their native fauna.

Increasingly, native fishes are isolated in the least disturbed aquatic habitats or in protected streams because they cannot adapt to new, extreme conditions. This general observation was the basis for the Index of Biotic Integrity (IBI) developed by James Karr in the 1980s, for streams in the Midwestern USA, and widely used as the basis for rapid bioassessment by resource management agencies (Karr, 1991). A fundamental assumption

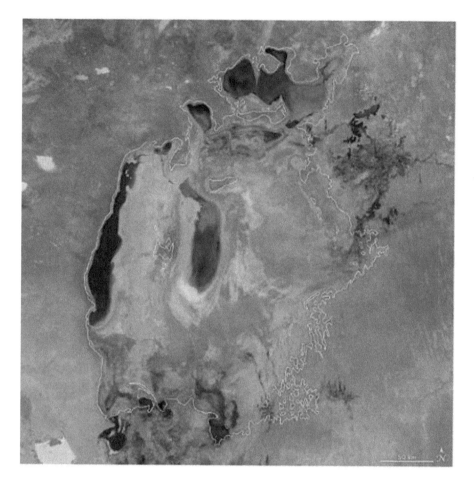

Figure 9.3 The Aral Sea was once the fourth largest freshwater lake in the world. Water diversions for the expansion of agriculture have greatly reduced its size. A 2018 NASA image of the Aral Sea shows the drastic contraction of the sea since 1960 (yellow lines depict 1960 shoreline).
Source: NASA Earth Observatory Explorer 2021.

for IBIs is that the abundance and diversity of native fishes is an excellent indicator of 'healthy' habitat. However, in some highly disturbed waters, native fishes are integrated into fish assemblages that also contain many non-native species, forming novel ecosystems shaped by human presence (Moyle, 2014). Most aquatic habitats of the world today are disturbed to some degree, and thus are increasingly divergent from historical conditions (Figure 9.5). Climate change is accelerating this process, which is leading to increased homogenisation of fish faunas around the world. See Closs et al. (2015) for further discussion of these habitat alteration issues.

9.4.3 Pollution

Streams, lakes, ponds and estuaries are sumps for the waste and other by-products of human activity: all water flows downhill, carrying dissolved materials with it. Pollution,

(a)   (b)

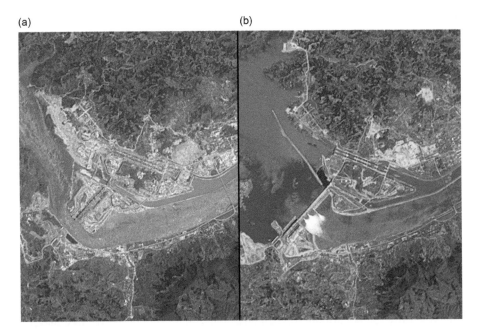

Figure 9.4 The Three Gorges Dam constructed on the Yangtze River is the largest hydroelectric dam in the world. It has severely affected the fish fauna of the river. (a) The 2000 photo depicts river conditions during construction of the dam. (b) The 2006 photo shows the dam following completion. *Source*: NASA Visible Earth 2021.

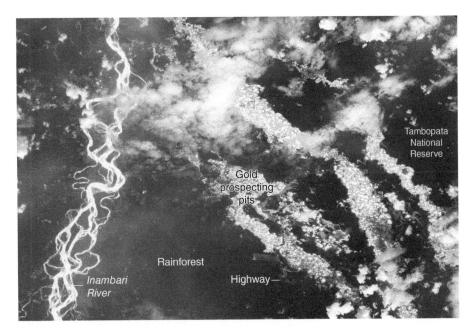

Figure 9.5 Gold mining pits in the Amazon rainforest of eastern Peru result in forest clearing, sedimentation, and the discharge of toxic substances into rivers and wetlands with devastating impacts to freshwater fishes.
Source: NASA Earth Observatory 2021.

from coarse sediment to sewage to 'contaminants of emerging concern' such as residuals of human medications, is ubiquitous. Traces of pesticides and other materials can be found even in the most remote and 'pristine' waters. The vast literature on pollution effects on fishes documents such things as:

- fish kills over broad areas
- reduced survival of eggs and larvae
- reduced growth rates
- altered behaviour, such as reduced ability to migrate
- diminished ecosystem health as the result of the combined effects of multiple pollutants and other elements (Matthaei and Lange, 2016).

9.4.4   Invasions of Non-Native Species

Most waterways around the world support non-native species of fishes. Species with global distributions due to human intervention include brown and rainbow trout (cold waters), common carp, goldfish and mosquitofish (temperate waters), and Mozambique tilapia and guppy (tropical waters). In highly altered habitats (e.g. reservoirs), alien fishes suppress native fish populations through predation, competition or disease. In California, there are over 50 species of alien fishes and about 130 species of native fishes (Moyle and Marchetti, 2006). Generally favoured in altered habitats, non-native species show an increase in abundance as climate change accelerates habitat change and increases competition for water between people and fishes (Moyle et al., 2013). This is a pattern occurring throughout the world. The result will be increased dominance of local fish faunas by a few highly tolerant species, many non-natives (Figure 9.6).

Figure 9.6 Bighead carp (*Hypophthalmichthys nobilis*) are a non-native species established in rivers in the midwestern USA, but have not yet invaded (as of 2021) the Great Lakes. They are plankton-feeding fish that can become extremely abundant, altering food webs and displacing native fishes. *Source*: U.S. Geological Survey 2021.

9.4.5 Commercial Exploitation

Commercial fisheries for wild fish are a significant protein source in much of the world, especially fisheries in tropical rivers (Funge-Smith and Bennett, 2019). In the floodplains of the lower Mekong River, for example, over one million tons of wild fish are harvested each year (Ziv et al., 2012). Not surprisingly, overexploitation of many, if not most, stocks of wild freshwater fishes contributes to the overall decline of freshwater fishes (Allan et al., 2005). Such fisheries are usually not very selective because they employ a wide variety of gear, capturing fishes of all sizes. Allan et al. (2005) noted that 'assemblage overfishing' results in significant, often undesirable, changes in fish faunas in many large waterways, from the Laurentian Great Lakes to major tropical rivers such as the Mekong (Figure 9.7).

9.4.6 Global Climate Change

Rising sea levels, prolonged droughts, massive floods, warmer waters (see Barbarossa et al., 2021) and increasingly distressed human populations are all predictions of global climate change. All of these events will adversely impact freshwater fish abundance and diversity, although a few hardy, widely introduced alien species (e.g. common carp) will no doubt thrive (Moyle et al., 2013) (Figure 9.8). A significant factor affecting native fishes is the predictable human reaction to take actions to fight the changing conditions, which further decreases habitat for fishes. Such actions include construction of additional hardened infrastructure (dams, levees, sea walls, etc.), increased exploitation of remaining fishes, increased diversion of freshwater, invasion of salt water into historically freshwater areas and general degradation of freshwater habitats. Much depends on how and when we let such seemingly inevitable changes take place and how conservation fits into the planning. However, the ever-present desire of most governments for such big projects does not bode well for the fishes.

Figure 9.7 Fishing with a cast net in lower Mekong River basin. Fisheries in the Mekong are an important source of protein for millions of people.
Source: U.S. Geological Survey 2021.

Figure 9.8 Threatened bull trout (*Salvelinus confluentus*) are apex predators in the cold streams and rivers of the western United States. Climate change threatens these fish by decreasing snowpack and stream baseflows, increasing summer water temperatures, and inducing more frequent flooding from rain-on-snow precipitation events.
Source: U.S. Fish and Wildlife Service.

9.5   Are Some Families of Freshwater Fishes More Vulnerable to Extinction than Others?

Every major taxonomic group of freshwater fishes contains at least one threatened species, an indication of the pervasive, detrimental effects of human activities on aquatic ecosystems. For example, according to the IUCN (2022), the number of threatened species within 37 orders containing freshwater fishes ranges from one (i.e. Esociformes, Percopsiformes, Batrachoidiformes, Mugiliformes) to over 802 (Cypriniformes) (Table 9.1). Nine orders comprising 24 freshwater families have greater than 20 threatened species (Table 9.2). The highest numbers of threatened freshwater fish species are within species-rich families such as the Cyprinidae and Cichlidae. However, entire fish families – major evolutionary lineages – are threatened with extinction. For example, within the Galaxiidae (including mudfishes) and Acipenseridae (including sturgeon) 76% and 94%, respectively, of the species are threatened with extinction. Below, we examine the diversity of human threats to five families of freshwater fishes with differing degrees of endemism, distribution, diversity and abundance.

9.5.1   Cyprinidae: Global Distribution, Local Threats

Carps and minnows are one of the most species-rich, abundant and widespread freshwater fish families. Over three thousand species are recognised (Fricke et al., 2022), with the number of taxa being described rapidly increasing. Cyprinids range in size from the giant barb of the Mekong, which reached over 2 m in length with weights of 300 kg (Figure 9.9), to the dwarf minnow (*Paedocypris progenetica*), the world's smallest freshwater vertebrate, from Sumatra, which only reaches 8–12 mm in length. Cyprinid fishes are

Table 9.2 *Freshwater fish families with at least 20 threatened species (compiled from IUCN version 2022-1)[a]*

ORDER/Family	CR	EN	VU	Total threatened species (CR+EN+VU)	Total IUCN assessed freshwater taxa in family (%)
OSTEOGLOSSIFORMES					
Mormyridae (elephantfishes)	0	5	16	21	11
ACIPENSERIFORMES					
Acipenseridae (sturgeons and paddlefish)	32	14	19	65	94
CYPRINIFORMES					
Cyprinidae (carps, minnows and relatives)	67	107	138	312	24
Cobitidae (true loaches)	8	20	14	42	29
PERCIFORMES					
Cichlidae (cichlids)	123	80	113	316	22
Percidae (perches)	10	18	30	58	26
Gobiidae (gobies)	18	27	28	73	15
Eleotridae (sleeper gobies)	19	12	5	36	24
Osphronemidae (gouramies)	16	31	21	68	55
Rivulidae (killifishes)	41	31	48	120	42
Goodeidae (splitfins)	13	14	6	33	83
CYPRINODONTIFORMES					
Nothobranchidae (African rivulines)	11	59	65	135	48
Poeciliidae (poeciliids)	25	23	27	75	24
Cyprinodontidae (pupfishes)	6	15	18	39	56
OSMERIFORMES					
Galaxiidae (galaxiids and mudfish)	25	23	8	56	76
ATHERINIFORMES					
Bedotiidae (Madagascar rainbowfish)	6	9	8	23	82
Melanotaeniidae (rainbowfishes)	20	22	25	67	58
Atherinopsidae (neotropical silversides)	7	9	6	22	40
SALMONIFORMES					
Salmonidae (salmon, trout, chars, whitefish, and graylings)	26	33	36	95	37

Table 9.2 (*cont.*)

ORDER/Family	CR	EN	VU	Total threatened species (CR+EN+VU)	Total IUCN assessed freshwater taxa in family (%)
SILURIFORMES					
Mochokidae (upside-down catfish)	7	15	15	37	18
Loricariidae (armored catfishes)	13	35	24	72	12
Bagridae (naked catfishes)	5	9	10	24	13
Sisoridae (Sisorid catfishes)	3	11	12	26	14
Clariidae (airbreathing catfishes)	6	8	9	23	22

CR = Critically Endangered, EN = Endangered, VU = Vulnerable
[a] Includes species, subspecies and varieties, and subpopulations

Figure 9.9 The giant barb or Siamese carp, *Catlocarpio siamensis*, is the largest carp/barb (Cypriniformes) in the world and is endangered by dams and overfishing. This giant barb was caught on the Mekong River. Photo credit and permission: Zeb Hogan, University of Nevada, Reno.

often the most abundant fishes in river systems and support important fisheries. For example, migratory cyprinids are harvested literally by the billions in the Mekong River and are a principal source of protein and income for residents of the Mekong Basin (Baird et al., 2003).

Cyprinid fishes are native to river systems in tropical and temperate climates of every continent, except Australia and Antarctica. They have adapted to environments from giant floodplain rivers to tiny desert springs and are significant elements of many regional fish faunas, often showing high endemism. Thus, Xing et al. (2016) found that the 654 species of Cyprinidae known in China made up almost half the total fish species (n = 1323) of the country and that 67% were endemic to China. In contrast, some species, such as the common carp and grass carp, have been widely introduced outside their native range, adjusting quickly to new environments, often with harmful effects on native fishes.

It should not be surprising that with such a high diversity of freshwater-dependent species, extinction threatens many cyprinids. Leidy and Moyle (1997) found that 157 species, 8% of the known cyprinids at that time, were threatened. Thirty-five years later, 312 species were listed as threatened by IUCN, which includes 24% of the assessed species (IUCN, 2022). Within China alone, 108 cyprinid species (16.5% of the family) fit the IUCN threatened species criteria (Xing et al., 2016). While such a rapid decline reflects better information, it is also highly likely to be real, led by the loss of species in isolated or highly modified habitats, especially big rivers.

All the factors listed in this chapter as proximate causes of decline affect cyprinids. For example, the Twee River redfin is endemic to a small watershed in South Africa. It is facing extinction through removal of water from the stream by farmers, riparian habitat alteration, pollution from agricultural wastewater and contaminants, and invasions of non-native predators and competitors (Impson et al., 2007), all factors exacerbated by climate change. In the Mekong River, the fisheries, among the most productive in the world, are showing signs of overfishing: they focus more and more on small fishes (usually cyprinids) with wide population fluctuations. Many of the larger species are threatened with extinction, including some of the largest of all freshwater fishes (Hogan et al., 2004; Fengzhi et al., 2019). Even these productive fisheries, however, are threatened by the rapid construction of dozens of large hydropower dams, which change flow timing and volume and capture sediment. New dams proposed for the river, if built as planned, will likely eliminate the vast fish migrations and the fisheries that depend on them (Baran, 2010). They are also likely to decimate the many unexploited endemic fishes that are part of the highly diverse fauna (781 species). Unfortunately, only after dam completions will we find out which cyprinid species have declined or are extinct.

9.5.2 Cichlidae: Food for People, Food for Thought

The Cichlidae are deep-bodied, spiny-rayed fishes adapted for living in lakes, rivers, estuaries and backwaters of tropical Asia, Africa and the Americas. Their complex behaviour, most notably parental behaviour, and adaptability has led to rapid speciation in tropical regions, but especially in the rift lakes of Africa. A handful of tilapia species (Nile, Mozambique and blue tilapias, plus their hybrids) are important aquaculture species throughout the tropics (Figure 9.10). This use has resulted in their becoming widespread in natural environments as well. And, not to be dismissed, the popularity of small brightly coloured cichlids as aquarium fishes has led to the introduction of diverse species into warm waters worldwide. No doubt aquaculture and aquarium species will assure the continued presence of Cichlidae in waters of the world, even if many 'wild' species have disappeared.

The total number of cichlid species is an open question, given that many (if not most) species are undescribed. Fricke et al. (2022) counted 1749 species in the taxonomic

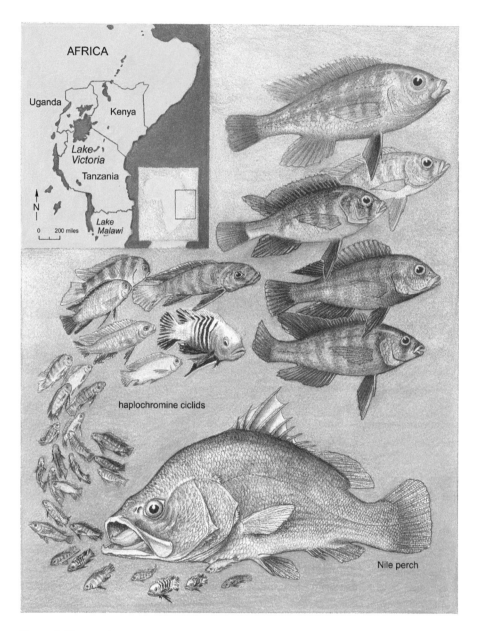

Figure 9.10 Map showing location of African Great Lakes, which support an astonishing diversity of cichlid fishes, with a different group of hundreds of species in each lake. Unfortunately, the predatory Nile perch was introduced into Lake Victoria to establish a fishery. One of its impacts has been to drive many of the lake's cichlid species to extinction through its voracious predation. Pastel drawing created by and copyright held by Chris Mari van Dyck. Used with permission, from Moyle (1993).

literature, but estimates of the number of species in the rift lakes are around 500 for Lake Victoria, 500–1000 for Lake Malawi and 1800 in Lake Tanganyika. Even if these estimates are widely off, they demonstrate three of the most astonishing radiations of fishes on the planet (Hastings et al., 2014) and indicate that conservation efforts need to concentrate on the lakes and their watersheds.

The African rift lake of most concern for cichlid conservation now is Lake Victoria, the world's second largest freshwater lake. The introduction of the Nile perch, a voracious piscivore that grows to 2 m and devours small cichlids of all sorts, threatens the entire endemic cichlid radiation. An additional threat is competition from introduced Nile tilapia, which thrive in the more turbid water. Increased human populations in the watershed have resulted in deforestation and expanded agriculture, which in turn led to more sediment going into the lake and increased pollution and subsequent eutrophication. Fisheries have also grown, while native cichlid populations have crashed in most areas of the lake. Fifty-five percent of the assessed species have been found to be in danger of extinction; many species may already be extinct (Sayer et al., 2018).

In summary, the Cichlidae contains some of the most abundant and widespread (through introductions) freshwater fishes in the world. But it also includes many endemic species threatened with extinction, with numerous taxa not yet described. The future of most cichlid species depends on effective conservation and management of their native waters.

9.5.3   Bedotiidae: Madagascar Endemics

The Indian Ocean island of Madagascar, located off the east coast of Africa, is a freshwater biodiversity hotspot (Ravelomanana et al., 2018). Due to long isolation, Madagascar supports a highly endemic (>50%) freshwater fish fauna of approximately 183 species, with many new endemic species descriptions anticipated (Stiassny and Raminosoa, 1994). Most of these endemic fishes are in decline, as exemplified by the endemic family Bedotiidae, the Madagascar rainbowfishes. The Bedotiidae includes 28 species of small (<10 cm) fishes found in small- to medium-sized rivers and lakes, and in seasonal brackish swamps draining from Madagascar's eastern mountain slopes (IUCN, 2022). Every species is threatened, including six species that are considered Critically Endangered, nine as Endangered and eight as Vulnerable (IUCN, 2022).

Madagascar rainbowfish are declining for multiple reasons. Chronic, widespread clearing of forests for wood and agriculture have decimated aquatic habitats for almost all of Madagascar's native freshwater fishes (Ravelomanana et al., 2018). The IUCN, (2022) identifies deforestation and non-native fishes as the greatest threat to rainbowfish. Deforestation results in loss of fish spawning habitats due to increased sedimentation, increased water temperatures from the reduction of streamside forests, and water quality degradation. The introduction of non-native fish species to support fisheries and aquaculture, including the common carp (Cyprinidae), largemouth bass (Centrarchidae), trout (Salmonidae), several species of tilapia and the Asian snakehead pose severe threats to rainbowfish through direct competition, predation, and disturbance of nesting and spawning sites (Ravelomanana et al., 2018).

Other human activities are also detrimental to rainbowfish (Ravelomanana et al., 2018; IUCN, 2022).They include wetland conversion, subsistence fisheries, farming, grazing and ranching, and mining and forestry operations that exacerbate soil erosion and sedimentation. Increased occurrence of extreme events related to climate change, such as prolonged droughts, and increased flood frequency and intensity also contribute to habitat degradation for these fishes (Ravelomanana et al., 2018).

9.5.4 Sturgeons and Paddlefishes: Big, Valuable River Fishes

The sturgeons (Acipenseridae, 25 species, 2 subspecies, and 42 subpopulations) and paddlefishes (Polyodontidae, two species) are the only living representatives of the ancient order Acipenseriformes (Figure 9.11). They are among the most imperilled lineages of freshwater fishes in the world, in large part because they are the only source of 'true' caviar. Sturgeon and paddlefish are adapted for living in large river systems that include inland seas, large continental rivers and estuaries. All undergo migrations in or to freshwater for spawning. Found in North America and Eurasia, they include the Critically Endangered beluga sturgeon, which is the largest freshwater fish in the world, reaching lengths of 8 m and weights of 1300 kg.

Ninety-four percent of sturgeon species, subspecies or subpopulations listed by the IUCN (2022) are threatened (n = 65) with extinction; 36 have experienced steep decreasing population trends such that they face an extremely high risk of extinction in the wild. The American paddlefish is extirpated from much of its historical range, and remaining populations are in steep decline; the Chinese paddlefish is apparently extinct.

The cumulative effects of all major causes of fish decline discussed in this chapter have severely affected sturgeon and paddlefish populations (Haxton and Cano, 2016). However, global sturgeon populations have suffered most from two factors: illegal

Figure 9.11 The world's largest fishes are some of the most endangered. The American paddlefish (*Polydon spathula*) is native to the Mississippi River drainage, USA, and its conservation status is vulnerable to pollution, overfishing and other factors. Its closest relative, the Chinese paddlefish, recently was declared extinct. Photo credit: Ryan Hagerty, U.S. Fish and Wildlife Service.

overexploitation and the fragmentation of large, free-flowing rivers by dams. Harvest is a problem for these fishes because of the high value of caviar, which only increases in value as wild sturgeon and paddlefish become rare. The caviar fishery for all species focuses on large mature females, which are likely to be 25–100 years old, depending on size and species. Replacement rates are slow, despite high fecundities.

Eurasian sturgeons. Construction of the Volgorad Dam in 1958 on the lower Volga River blocked spawning migrations of beluga, Russian and stellate sturgeons (Ruban et al., 2019). Altered flow regimes below the dam further adversely affected the quality of remaining spawning, juvenile rearing and foraging habitats in the Volga River and the Caspian Sea. Illegal fishing and pollution in the Volga River Delta and the Caspian Sea have also adversely affected reproduction, growth and survival (Ruban et al., 2019). For similar reasons, five of six sturgeon species found in the Danube River and the Black Sea are Critically Endangered (Friedrich, 2018).

Alabama sturgeon. The small (to 0.78 m) Alabama sturgeon is North America's most endangered sturgeon. Dams have reduced its river habitat in the lower reaches of just two rivers in southern Alabama (Kuhajda and Rider, 2016). There are no reliable population estimates for the Alabama sturgeon. Without restored access to historical spawning grounds through the removal of several dams, the Alabama sturgeon has a high likelihood of extinction.

Chinese sturgeon and paddlefish. In the Yangtze River, China, there are several imperilled sturgeon species, as well as the Chinese paddlefish (likely extinct) (Figure 9.12). They suffer from the same human activities that have adversely affected sturgeon elsewhere (Xing et al., 2016), i.e. continued adverse dam operation, new dams and overexploitation.

Because sturgeons and paddlefishes are so valuable, large aquaculture operations exist for some species, mainly to provide caviar. Their value and adaptability to captive conditions create strong incentives to rear species in captivity, despite the high costs of

Figure 9.12 The pallid sturgeon (*Scaphirhynchus albus*) is native to the Mississippi and Missouri River systems, USA, and is considered endangered. Dam construction and dredging have altered its habitat, preventing the sturgeon from reproducing. Photo credit: Ryan Hagerty, U.S. Fish and Wildlife Service.

producing mature fish. However, aquaculture is also a tool to restore sturgeon and paddlefish populations to the wild.

9.5.5 Salmonidae: Hidden Diversity in Cold Water Fishes

The Salmonidae are cold water fishes, adapted for thriving in the dynamic Pleistocene and post-Pleistocene fresh and salt waters of the Northern Hemisphere. Their oily flesh, abundance and high aesthetic qualities have made them the focus of sport and commercial fisheries, as well as aquaculture, worldwide. But their wide distribution and tendency to become easily isolated into small, distinct populations (often recognised as species) means that many species and populations are facing extinction in the modern world.

The most iconic species, the Pacific and Atlantic salmons, are anadromous; they spawn in freshwater but migrate vast distances to forage in northern oceans. Salmonids are masters at adapting to local conditions, so many isolated populations of 'trout' and 'char' are found throughout the family's native range (Kershner et al., 2019), as are species 'flocks' of whitefishes that partition the food resources of the large lakes scattered across the northern landscape. Local adaptation is rapid, so many of these isolated trout, char and whitefishes are now recognised as distinct taxa. Two hundred and fifty-seven known species, subspecies and subpopulations are now recognised by the IUCN (2022), with more being described regularly as new genetic techniques uncover additional taxa. When we wrote about this family in 1997, only 56 species were recognised.

Recognised taxa are only a small part of this family's diversity. Thanks to the enormous interest in the family by the public, fishers and scientists, considerable efforts have been made to understand the evolutionary history and genetic structure of local populations of widespread species. Much of the recent research has been to catalogue diversity so distinctive forms can be protected. To demonstrate the value of this approach, Rand et al. (2012) compiled information on populations of sockeye salmon throughout its range, in spawning streams along the Pacific Rim from eastern Russia to the western USA. They identified 98 'independent populations'. Using IUCN criteria, five of these populations were determined to be extinct, and 27% of the 63 populations evaluated were at risk of extinction. IUCN now includes this information as part of their database on threatened salmonids. In the USA, language of the 1973 Endangered Species Act allows protection of 'distinct population segments' (DPSs) of vertebrate species and today many such DPSs of fishes, especially salmon, are protected under the ESA. For example, in California, three of eight DPSs of Chinook salmon are listed as threatened or endangered species, although all eight segments could qualify (Moyle et al., 2017). This demonstrates the importance of protecting distinct populations of species, both to protect the species as a whole and to make sure each species retains the ability to adapt to changing conditions.

The sockeye salmon discussed above is an excellent example of a widespread species that is likely to persist indefinitely, even with the extirpation of most subpopulations. This persistence will be in part due to its high value in fisheries. Similar species include rainbow trout (steelhead), Chinook salmon and Atlantic salmon. All will persist at some level, perhaps only through hatcheries that produce semi-domesticated juveniles for release into the wild. The North Pacific Ocean now has so many hatchery-origin chum and pink salmon that they are reducing the abundance of other species, even birds (Springer and van Vliet, 2014).

In contrast, many inland species of salmonids are threatened with extinction. The IUCN (2022) lists 95 taxa as being threatened, with about 87% of species needing status updates. The causes are multiple and involve all the factors listed for fishes in general, as described eloquently by Behnke (2002) for salmonids throughout North America and by Kershner et al. (2019) for the world. For many isolated populations of trout, char and whitefish, declines are tied to degradation of watersheds by domestic livestock grazing, logging, mining and other factors, often in combination with invasions of aggressive non-native species such as rainbow trout and brown trout (which now have worldwide distributions in cold water). Restoration or protection of endemic species of salmonids often requires both elimination of non-native species from the watershed and intensive watershed management to restore appropriate ecosystem functions. For example, Eagle Lake rainbow trout in California are now maintained by regular planting of hatchery-reared fish. Long-term restoration of a wild population requires eradication of alien brook trout from their principal spawning stream, as well as protection of the stream and lake from cattle grazing and other disturbances. If present trends continue, the Salmonidae will be represented in the future mainly by a few widely introduced species, remnant or hatchery populations of widespread anadromous species and a few highly managed populations of endemic trout, whitefish and grayling.

The obvious conclusion we reach from this section is that extinction does not respect taxonomic boundaries; no family or lineage is immune to anthropogenic changes. Large families such as the Cyprinidae and Salmonidae are more likely to have representatives in future fish faunas, although species richness will be much lower. Families with few species are candidates for total extinction.

9.6 How Well Does the IUCN Red List Represent the Status of Fish Faunas?

In this chapter, we have relied heavily on data and information from IUCN to make our points about the decline of freshwater fishes worldwide. The task that IUCN has undertaken to track the status of fishes is enormous. New species are being described at a record rate, while entire faunas are in rapid decline, extinctions are occurring and very little information is available on the status of most species and their habitats. Nevertheless, IUCN plans to have all known fishes evaluated by 2022 (W. Darwell, IUCN, personal communication, May 2019).

To understand better how well the IUCN list represents the status of the world's fishes, we compared the status of the fish fauna of California with that of fishes in the IUCN database. California is a geographically defined area, to which most of its fishes are endemic, and suffers from high use and abuse of its limited water supply. We first examined the status of California fishes only at the species level. There are 82 species divided among 13 families with the largest families being Cyprinidae (23 species),

Catostomidae (11) and Cottidae (12); 54 (66%) of the full species are endemic; 42 (51%) of the species have been evaluated by IUCN, which found that 15 (36% of those evaluated) were threatened with extinction (Vulnerable+Endangered+Critically Endangered); 3 of the 42 species were extinct in California but still extant outside the state, and two endemic species were globally extinct (Clear Lake splittail, thicktail chub).

For comparison, we examined the entire list of recognised freshwater fish taxa in California (134 taxa, 81% endemic). This list includes 100 taxa with formal species or subspecies designations, 10 undescribed subspecies and 24 Distinct Population Segments (see Section 9.5.5 for DPS explanation). Eighty-two (61%) of the taxa were either not evaluated by IUCN, were deemed globally extinct, or were Data Deficient. Of the 49 IUCN-assessed taxa (not including three species extinct in California but still extant elsewhere), 13 (27%) were classified by IUCN as Threatened. When we rated the status of all extant species in California using independent measures (Moyle et al., 2015), 63 (49%) were scored in categories reasonably equivalent to the three IUCN categories lumped together as threatened. In short, our evaluation of the status of *all* native fish taxa results in about twice as many taxa being regarded as threatened with extinction than the IUCN evaluations would indicate.

The California example shows that IUCN evaluations of species are reliable, if conservative, for those California fishes fully evaluated. We could independently verify them, although there are many species still to be evaluated. In California, however, much of the diversity that is threatened with extinction is below the species level. This is one reason federal regulatory agencies in the USA use the Distinct Population Segment as a legal basis for protecting many fishes as Threatened or Endangered, such as the Sacramento winter-run Chinook salmon and the southern California steelhead (Moyle et al., 2017). The addition of 98 populations of sockeye salmon to the IUCN list of evaluated species indicates commendable awareness of this issue.

9.7 Conclusions: What Is The Future Of Freshwater Fishes Around The World?

Over 18,000 freshwater fishes have been described so far, representing over half the world's fishes. The discovery of new freshwater fishes continues, especially with the unveiling of cryptic species. But the world seems to be on a path to eliminate species faster than they are discovered. It is likely that several species have become threatened or even extinct during the relatively short time that it has taken us to write this chapter. The decline of freshwater fishes worldwide will continue as long as: (1) the human demand for goods and services keeps growing, (2) climate change continues at its present rapid pace and (3) people fail to realise that healthy aquatic ecosystems are essential to *both* people and fish.

Any prognosis of an improved future for freshwater fishes appears unlikely, as it does for the state of aquatic biodiversity and aquatic ecosystems in general, for which fish are good status indicators (Darwell et al., 2018; Harrison et al., 2018; Tickner et al., 2020). Some

30 years ago, we estimated that 20% of the world's freshwater fish species were already extinct or in severe decline (Moyle and Leidy, 1992). That number has grown substantially. Recent reviews support the conclusion that the current increasing trend in freshwater fish endangerment will not decrease, but will accelerate. Threatened with extinction are about 30% of the 9824 freshwater fish species, subspecies and varieties, and subpopulations assessed by IUCN in 2020; most already have declining populations. This estimate is very conservative, given the information in this chapter. Equally alarming is that we still know very little about the current population status of many freshwater fishes; only about half the known species having been assessed by IUCN so far.

In our view, the information we present here provides a strong indication that without extraordinary measures, at least 40–50% of all freshwater fish species will be extinct in the wild or close to it by the end of the century, if not sooner. Unfortunately, most of these fishes do not have conservation actions in place or planned. It is likely that we will not recognise extinction events until long after they have happened (Baumsteiger and Moyle, 2017). Many persisting species in the future are likely to be found in captivity or small refuges, especially if the fishes cannot survive within new, highly simplified ecosystems. One vision for streams worldwide, especially in urban areas, is to have highly homogenised, if depauperate, fish faunas, part of novel ecosystems dominated by people and non-native species such as the common carp, tilapia, largemouth bass, a catfish or two and mosquitofish. A few hardy native fishes might serve as a distinctive part of each local assemblage.

An urgent question is whether there are conservation strategies that have proven successful in reversing decline of freshwater fishes that might serve as examples for the future. We know what to do to save aquatic biodiversity, but generally lack the will to do it. Several chapters in Closs et al. (2016) thoroughly discuss fish conservation strategies aimed at mitigating the adverse effects of dams, protecting migratory fishes, protecting apex predators, using artificial propagation, managing sustainable fisheries, conserving genetic diversity and using freshwater conservation planning, among other topics. Protecting freshwater aquatic biodiversity will require that multiple strategies and approaches be used depending on the specific circumstances of the challenge (Tickner et al., 2020). However, there is no substitute for protecting and managing a wide variety of rivers, streams, lakes and wetlands in each region of the world to assure that a good fraction of our fish diversity survives into the indefinite future. Whole watersheds need to be managed for their biota, with native fishes as indicators of successful conservation actions. Aquatic refuges cannot just exist as incidental parts of terrestrial reserves, but must be a central focus of a system of aquatic reserves. Successful aquatic reserves will need to be embedded in a broad scheme of river management that integrates the people's needs with those of fishes and their ecosystems. Opperman et al. (2019), for example, present a detailed plan for integrating hydropower development worldwide into conservation strategies for large river systems such as the Mekong River; this river system begins on the Tibetan Plateau and runs through China, Myanmar, Laos, Thailand and Cambodia, emptying into the South China Sea in Vietnam. Without such massive planning and actions by multiple countries, much of the astonishing fish diversity of this large tropical river system will quickly be lost, along with the benefits of their fisheries.

The need for large-scale action to reduce the rapid decline of fish abundance and diversity is widely recognised among aquatic ecologists and biologists (and other professionals) who deal with fish conservation and management. However, the severity of the global situation seems to be underestimated by most. The ever-increasing trend in use and abuse of our freshwaters by people means that the extinction of fish species on a large scale is a near-certainty in the foreseeable future. Given the scope of the problem and conflicts that fish conservation often engenders, large-scale solutions are unlikely to arise. Fish biologists and aquatic scientists should continue to propose solutions to power, such as those discussed above, while engaging in more local actions that might save a species or two. Such professionals have specialised knowledge that gives them special responsibilities to act. Here are examples of the kinds of actions we have in mind:

- Work with local communities and naturalists to protect/enhance/manage the aquatic diversity in a local stream or lake.
- Recognise that captive breeding can 'save' a species, but only if the species can be reintroduced into a restored habitat. This process must happen fast to be effective, with minimal fish domestication. Production fish hatcheries mainly produce domesticated fish, very different from their progenitors.
- Recognise that respect for human diversity should pay dividends in creating more respect for biological diversity.
- Provide input into education at all levels about fish, biodiversity and aquatic conservation. One goal should be to create a new generation of naturalists who can continue fighting to protect fishes and their habitats.
- Work with artists in all media to provide positive views of fishes, streams and lakes.
- Promote the development and expansion of fish collections in museums, so they become more than mausoleums for lost species but major forces for conservation.
- Support or even develop legislation that helps to protect the remaining native species, such as preventing alien species introductions.
- Develop easy-to-use methods for rapid determination of fish status. Ideally, these approaches would link to the more demanding IUCN methods developed for all species (e.g. Moyle et al., 2011, 2013, 2015).

We are sure others can increase and modify this list in many ways. But, regardless, it is important for individuals with a love of aquatic environments to think of themselves as being part of a global conservation effort. Personal success can be measured by the success of small actions at the local level.

We forget that the water cycle and the life cycle are one.

(Jacques Yves Cousteau)

References

Adams, M., Raadik, T.A., Burridge, C.P. and Georges, A. (2014) Global biodiversity assessment and hyper-cryptic species complexes: more than one species of elephant in the room. *Syst Biol* 63: 518–533.

Allan, J.D., Abell, R., Hogan, Z. et al. (2005) Overfishing of inland waters. *BioScience* 55: 1041–1051.

Baird, I.G., Flaherty, M.S. and Phylavanh, B. (2003) Rhythms of the river: lunar phases and migrations of small carps (Cyprinidae) in the Mekong River. *Nat Hist Bull Siam Soc* 5: 5–36.

Baran, E. (2010) *Mekong Fisheries And Mainstream Dams.* Fisheries sections of the Strategic Environmental Assessment of Hydropower on the Mekong Mainstream prepared for the Mekong River Commission by the International Centre for Environmental Management. http://pubs.iclarm.net/resource_centre/WF_2736.pdf (accessed October 2022).

Barbarossa, V., Bosmans, J., Wanders, N., et al. (2021) Threats of global warming to the world's freshwater fishes. *Nat Commun*, 12: 1701.

Baumsteiger, J. and Moyle, P.B. (2017) Assessing extinction. *Bioscience* 67: 357–366.

Baumsteiger, J. and Moyle, P.B. (2019) A reappraisal of the California roach/hitch (Cypriniformes, Cyprinidae, *Hesperoleucus/Lavinia*) species complex. *Zootaxa* 4543(2): 2221–2240.

Behnke, R.J. (2002) *Trout and Salmon of North America.* New York: Chanticleer Press.

Bickford, D., Lohman, D.J., Sodhi, N. S., et al. (2007) Cryptic species as a new window on diversity and conservation. *Trends Ecol Evol* 22: 148–155.

Closs, G.P., Angermeier, P.L., Darwell, W.R.T. and Balcombe, S.T. (2015) Why are freshwater fishes so threatened? In: Closs, G.P., Krkosek, M. and Olden, J.D. (Eds.), *Conservation of Freshwater Fishes.* Cambridge, UK: Cambridge University Press.

Closs, G.P., Krkosek, M. and Olden, J.D. (Eds.) (2016) *Conservation of Freshwater Fishes.* Cambridge, UK: Cambridge University Press.

Darwell, W.R.T. and Freyhof, J. (2015) Lost fishes: who is counting? The extent of the threat to freshwater fish biodiversity. In Closs, G.P., Krkosek, M. and Olden, J.D. (Eds.), *Conservation of Freshwater Fishes.* Cambridge, UK: Cambridge University Press.

Darwell, W.R.T., Bremerich, V., De Weveret, A., et al. (2018) The Alliance for Freshwater Life: a global call to unite efforts for freshwater biodiversity science and conservation. *Aquat Conserv* 2018: 1–8.

Dudgeon, D., Arthington, A.H., Gessner, M.O., et al. (2006) Freshwater biodiversity: importance, threats, status and conservation challenges. *Biol Rev* 81: 163–182.

Fengzhi, H., Zarfl, C., Bremerich, V., et al. (2019) The global decline of freshwater megafauna. *Glob Change Biol* 2019: 1–10.

Fricke, R., Eschmeyer, W.N. and Fong, J.D. (2022) *Eschmeyer's Catalog of Fishes: Species by Family/ Subfamily.* San Francisco, CA: California Academy of Sciences.

Friedrich, T. (2018) Danube sturgeons: past and future. In: Schmutz, S. and Sendzimir, J. (Eds.), *Riverine Ecosystem Management.* Vol 8 in Aquatic Ecology. Cham, Switzerland: Springer.

Funge-Smith, S. and Bennett, A. (2019) A fresh look at inland fisheries and their role in food security and livelihoods. *Fish Fish* 20: 1176–1195.

Harrison, I., Abell, R., Darwall, W., et al. (2018) The freshwater biodiversity crisis. *Science* 362: 1369.

Hastings, P., Walker, H.J. and Galland, G.R. (2014) *Fishes: A Guide to their Diversity.* Oakland, CA: University of California Press.

Haxton, T.J. and Cano, T.M. (2016) A global perspective of fragmentation on a declining taxon: the sturgeon (Acipenseriformes). *Endanger Species Res* 31: 203–210.

Hogan, Z.S., Moyle, P.B., May, B., Vander Zander, M.J. and Baird, I.G. (2004) The imperiled giants of the Mekong. *Am Sci* 92: 228–237.

Impson, N.D., Marriott, M.S., Bills, I.R. and Skelton, P.H. (2007) Conservation biology and management of a critically endangered cyprinid, the Twee River redfin, *Barbus erubescens* (Teleostei: Cyprinidae) of the Cape Floristic Region, South Africa. *Afr J Aquat Sci* 32: 27–33.

IUCN. (2012) *Red List Categories and Criteria: Version 3.1,* Second Edn. Gland, Switzerland and Cambridge, UK: IUCN.

IUCN. (2022) *Red List Version 2022-1*. Gland, Switzerland and Cambridge, UK: IUCN. www .iucnredlist.org (accessed October 2022).

Karr, J.R. (1991) Biological integrity: a long-neglected aspect of water resource management. *Ecol Appl* 1: 66–84.

Kershner, J.L., Williams, J.E., Greswell, R.E. and Lobon-Cervia, J. (Eds.) (2019) *Trout and Char of the World*. Bethesda, MD: American Fisheries Society.

Kuhajda, B.R. and Rider, S.J. (2016) Status of the imperiled Alabama sturgeon (*Scaphirhynchus suttkusi* Williams and Clemmer, 1991). *J Appl Ichthyol* 32(Suppl. 1): 15–29.

Leidy, R.A. and Moyle, P.B. (1997) Conservation status of the world's fish fauna: an overview. In: Fiedler, P.A. and Karieva, P.M. (Eds.), *Conservation Biology for the Coming Decade*. New York: Chapman & Hall.

Leidy, R.A. and Moyle, P.B. (2021) Keeping up with the status of freshwater fishes: a California (USA) perspective. *Conserv Sci Pract* 2021: e474.

Matthaei, C.D. and Lange, K. (2016) Multiple stressor effects on freshwater fish: a review and meta-analysis. In Closs, G.P., Krkosek, M. and Olden, J.D. (Eds.), *Conservation of Freshwater Fishes*. Cambridge, UK: Cambridge University Press.

Micklin, P. (2016) The future Aral Sea: hope and despair. *Environ Earth Sci* 75: 844–859.

Moyle, P.B. (1993) *Fish: An Enthusiast's Guide*. Berkeley, CA: University of California Press.

Moyle, P.B. (2014) Novel aquatic ecosystems: the new reality for streams in California and other Mediterranean climate regions. *River Res Appl* 30: 1335–1344.

Moyle, P.B. and Leidy, R.A. (1992) Loss of biodiversity in aquatic ecosystems: evidence from fish faunas. In Fiedler, P.L. and Jain, S.A. (Eds.), *Conservation Biology: The Theory and Practice of Nature Conservation, Preservation, and Management*. New York: Chapman & Hall.

Moyle, P.B. and Marchetti, M.P. (2006) Predicting invasion success: freshwater fishes in California as a model. *Bioscience* 56: 515–524.

Moyle, P.B., Katz, J.V.E. and Quiñones, R.M. (2011) Rapid decline of California's native inland fishes: a status assessment. *Biol Conserv* 144: 2414–2423.

Moyle, P.B., Kiernan, J.D., Crain, P.K. and Quiñones, R.M. (2013) Climate change vulnerability of native and alien freshwater fishes of California: a systematic assessment approach. *PLoS One* 8(5): e63883.

Moyle, P.B., Lusardi, R., Samuel, P. and Katz, J. (2017) *State of the Salmonids: Status of California's Emblematic Fishes 2017*. San Francisco, CA: Davis Center for Watershed Sciences, University of California and California Trout.

Moyle, P.B., Quiñones, R.M., Katz, J.V.E. and Weaver, J. (2015) *Fish Species of Special Concern in California*, Third Edn. Sacramento, CA: California Department of Fish and Wildlife.

NSF. (2008) All Catfish Species (Siluriformes): Phase I of an Inventory of the Otophysi. Award Abstract #0315963. www.nfs.gov (accessed October 2022).

NSF. (2010) All Cypriniformes Species: Phase II of an Inventory of the Otophysi. Award Abstract #1022720. www.nfs.gov (accessed October 2022).

Opperman, J., Hartmann, J., Carvallo, J.P. (2019) *Connected and Flowing: a Renewable Future for Rivers, Climate and People*. Washington, DC: WWF and The Nature Conservancy,

Opperman, J., Moyle, P.B., Larsen, E.W., Florsheim, J.L. and Manfree, A.D. (2017) *Floodplains: Processes, Ecosystems, and Services in Temperate Regions*. Oakland, CA: University of California Press.

Ramirez, J. L., Birindelli, J.L., Carvalho, D.C., et al. (2017) Revealing hidden diversity of the underestimated neotropical ichthyofauna: DNA barcoding in the recently described genus *Megaleporinus* (Characiformes: Anostomidae). *Front Genet* 8: 1–11.

Rand, P.S., Goslin, M., Gross, M.R., et al. (2012) Global assessment of extinction risk to populations of sockeye salmon, *Oncorhynchus nerka*. *PLoS One* 7(4): e34065.

Ravelomanana, T., Maiz-Tome, L., Darwell, W., et al. (2018) The status and distribution of freshwater fishes. In: Máiz-Tomé, L., Sayer, C. and Darwall, W. (Eds.) *The Status and Distribution of Freshwater Biodiversity in Madagascar and the Indian Ocean Island Hotspot*. Gland, Switzerland: IUCN.

Reid, A.J., Carlson, A.K., Creed, I.F., et al. (2018) Emerging threats and persistent conservation challenges for freshwater biodiversity. *Biol Rev* 94 (3): 849–873.

Ricciardi, A. and Rasmussen, J.B. (1999) Extinction rates of North American freshwater fauna. *Conserv Biol* 13: 1220–1222.

Ruban, G., Khodorevskaya, R. and Shatunovskii, M. (2019) Factors influencing the natural reproduction decline in the beluga (*Huso*, Kinnaeus, 1758), Russian sturgeon (*Acipenser gueldenstaedtii*, Brandt & Ratzeburg, 1833) and stellate sturgeon (*A. stellatus*, Pallas, 1771) of the Volga-Caspian basin: A review. *J Appl Ichthyol* 35: 387–339.

Sayer, C.A., Máiz-Tomé L. and Darwall, W.R.T. (Eds.) (2018) *Freshwater Biodiversity in the Lake Victoria Basin: Guidance for Species Conservation, Site Protection, Climate Resilience and Sustainable Livelihoods*. Gland, Switzerland: IUCN.

Springer, A.M. and van Vliet, G.B. (2014) Climate change, pink salmon, and the nexus between bottom-up and top-down forcing in the subarctic Pacific Ocean and Bering Sea. *Proc Natl Acad Sci USA* 111(18): E1880–E1888.

Stiassny, M.L.J. and Raminosoa, N. (1994) The fishes of the inland waters of Madagascar. In: Teugels, G.G., Guégan, J.F. and Albaret, J.J. (Eds.), *Biological Diversity of Fresh- and Brackish Water Fishes*. Tervuren, Belgium: Musée Royal de L'Afrique Centrale.

Strayer, D.L. and Dudgeon, D. (2010) Freshwater biodiversity conservation: recent progress and future challenges. *J N Am Benthol Soc* 29: 344–358.

Tickner, D. J., Opperman, J.J., Abell, R., et al. (2020) Bending the curve of global freshwater biodiversity loss: an emergency recovery plan. *BioScience*, 70: 330–342.

University of Melbourne. (2016) Twenty new freshwater fish species uncovered in Australia: remote, iconic Kimberley unveiled as biodiversity hub. *Science Daily*, 6 January. www.sciencedaily.com/releases/2016/01/160106110713.htm (accessed October 2022).

Vörösmarty, C.J., McIntyre, B., Gessner, M.O., et al. (2010) Global threats to human water security and river biodiversity. *Nature* 467(731): 555–561.

Williams, J.G., Moyle, P.B., Kondolf, M. and Webb, A. (2019) *Environmental Flow Assessment: Methods and Applications*. Oxford, UK: Wiley.

World Wide Fund for Nature (WWF). (2020) *Living Planet Report 2020. Bending the Curve of Biodiversity Loss: A Deep Dive into Freshwater*. Almond, R.E., Grooten, A. and Petersen, T. (Eds). Gland, Switzerland: WWF.

World Wide Fund for Nature (WWF). (2021) *The World's Forgotten Fishes*. Gland, Switzerland: WWF.

WWAP (UNESCO World Water Assessment Programme). (2019) *The United Nations World Water Development Report 2019: Leaving No One Behind*. Paris, France: UNESCO.

Xing, Y., Zhang, C., Fan, E. and Zhao, Y. (2016) Freshwater fishes of China: species richness, endemism, threatened species and conservation. *Divers Distrib* 22: 358–370.

Ziv, G., Baran, E., Nam, S., Rodríguez-Iturbe, I. and Levin, S.A. (2012) Trading-off fish biodiversity, food security, and hydropower in the Mekong River Basin. *Proc Natl Acad Sci USA* 109(15): 5609–5614.

TEN

The Amazing Yet Threatened World of Marine Fishes

MARK A. HIXON AND BRIAN W. BOWEN

Summary

Fishes are the original and most diverse group of vertebrates, including over 35,000 of the estimated 69,000 species with backbones. Most marine fishes have large geographic ranges that may provide some protection from extinction, but there are very important exceptions:

- *Fishes that move between freshwater and seawater*, including salmon, sturgeon and freshwater eels. The migration from coastal seas to rivers and streams makes these species very vulnerable to capture and habitat degradation.
- *Fishes with very small geographic ranges* can be wiped out by a single catastrophic disturbance or intense fishing. Aquarium fishes with high economic values but small ranges include the resplendent angelfish (*Centropyge resplendens*) that occurs on a single island, and the Banggai cardinalfish (*Pterapogon kauderni*), native to a few islands in eastern Indonesia.
- *Invasive species* can consume naïve native prey or otherwise disrupt ecosystems. The disastrous introduction of the Indo-Pacific lionfish (genus *Pterois*) to the western Atlantic has done both, consuming small-range fishes like the Mardi Gras wrasse (*Halichoeres burekae*) and altering coral reef ecosystems by reducing native fish biomass.
- *Fishes with low reproductive potential* may not be able to recover from overfishing or natural population declines. While many large bony fishes (teleosts) can produce millions of eggs and readily rebound from population depletion, fishes such as the sharks, rays and relatives (chondrichthyans) produce only a few progeny at a time.
- *Overfishing* has brought many species to the brink of extinction. Fishing has historically been the primary cause of declines in marine fishes, both directly in terms of catch and indirectly in terms of bycatch (incidental take of non-targeted species) and fishing gear that destroys seafloor habitat. The introduction of mechanised fishing in the 1880s began a century of severe population reductions, especially via the very destructive practice of bottom trawling.
- *Ocean warming and acidification* are the major threats to the future of marine fishes. These sea changes are expected to result in loss of fish habitat, reduced productivity, behavioural and physiological problems, and disruption of ecological processes that are the basis for healthy fish populations, healthy ocean ecosystems and, by extension, healthy humanity.

10.1 Introduction

Fishes are the ancestors of all vertebrates. They were the wellspring of vertebrate evolution over 500 million years ago (Ma), the progenitors of all biodiversity with a backbone. Because of this high diversity, fishes are known as the insects of the subphylum Vertebrata, with over 35,000 described species (Fricke et al., 2022). Dozens of fish species are still being discovered every year, especially small species of unknown vulnerability. Marine fishes include about half of all known fish species. While freshwater fishes have been devastated by habitat alterations, especially diversion of water for human use (see Chapter 9), the threats to marine fishes are more diverse. Currently at the top of the list is overfishing, followed by seafloor habitat destruction, both possibly soon to be overtaken by the evil twins of ocean warming and acidification.

What is a fish? The most common definitions include vertebrates living in water and typically having gills, scales, jaws and fins. However, none of these traits apply to all fishes. The lungfishes (Subclass Dipnoi) live in stagnant freshwater and breathe air directly, the gills of African and South American species being too atrophied to function for respiration. The moray eels (Family Muraenidae) lack scales, relying instead on a coating of mucus for protection (Figure 10.2A). The ancient hagfishes (Figure 10.2B) and lampreys (Class Myxini) lack both jaws and fins, as well as scales. Faced with the fact that each fishy characteristic is lacking in some fish, we recall the famous words of US Supreme Court Justice Potter Stewart when attempting to define hard-core pornography: 'I shall not today attempt further to define the kinds of material I understand to be embraced within that shorthand description...*but I know it when I see it.*' That definition shall suffice for the purposes of this chapter. For more information about fishes in general and fish conservation in particular, we recommend the books by Facey et al. (2023) and Helfman (2007), respectively.

There are three major groups of living fishes:

'Living fossils' include the jawless hagfishes and lampreys, amazing relicts from a time before the vertebrate jaw evolved, dating back to about 530 Ma. Hagfishes are deepsea scavengers (Figure 10.2B), whereas lampreys mostly persist in specialised freshwater habitats, although the largest are parasites on other fishes and can migrate to the ocean. Another living fossil is the coelacanth, the lobe-finned fish believed to have diverged near the origin of terrestrial vertebrates (tetrapods) (Figure 10.2C). Coelacanths were very abundant in the Jurassic and Cretaceous eras (240–65 Ma), but were believed to have perished with the dinosaurs about 65 Ma. This changed when a fresh specimen was captured in the southwestern Indian Ocean, as chronicled in J.L.B. Smith's classic 1956 adventure book entitled *Old Four Legs: The Story of the Coelacanth.* A second species of coelacanth was recently discovered in Indonesia and the hunt is on for additional species. The extant coelacanths are deepwater fishes that usually occur beyond the reach (and mostly without the knowledge) of local fishermen.

Chondrichthyan fishes are the sharks, rays and their relatives, known from a fossil record dating back to the Devonian (360–420 Ma). They have a cartilaginous skeleton rather than the bony skeleton of most vertebrates. Over 500 species of sharks and over 600 species of rays and ray-like fishes are recognised. Chondrichthyan fishes are overwhelmingly marine, although a few have moved into freshwater, with a stunning radiation of rays in the Amazon River basin. The bull shark (*Carcharhinus leucas*; Figure 10.2D), one of the most dangerous in terms of human attacks, can occur in freshwater, giving some unfortunate swimmers the surprise of a lifetime.

Teleost fishes, the modern bony fishes, are known from the fossil record back to the Triassic (200–250 Ma) and are by far the most abundant and diverse at 96% of living species. This category encompasses among the smallest and largest vertebrates, from the tiny male stout infantfish (*Schindleria brevipinguis*; Figure 10.2E) that measures less than one centimetre as an adult, to the giant ocean sunfish (*Mola mola*; Figure 10.2F) weighing over two tons. Teleosts also include such bizarre creatures as a frogfish that literally fishes for other fish with a fish-like lure (Figure 10.2G) and seahorses that closely resemble seaweeds (Figure 10.2H). Teleosts are *the* evolutionary success story among vertebrates.

Several groups of teleost fishes have shown explosive radiations in recent evolutionary history. The gobies (Family Gobiidae) are the most species-rich group, with over 2000 species. The rockfishes (Family Scorpaenidae) of the temperate eastern Pacific have radiated into over 70 species in a single genus (*Sebastes*). Some regions of the seas are known as wellsprings of species diversity, foremost among them being the Coral Triangle, the corners of which are formed by the Philippines, Indonesia and New Guinea (Allen, 2008). This area hosts over 3000 fish species, including over 50% of the Indo-Pacific fish fauna. By one estimate, 60% of Indo-Pacific reef fishes had ancestors in this region (Cowman and Bellwood, 2013). At the periphery of the Indo-Pacific basin are areas of high endemism (containing species occurring nowhere else) including the Red Sea (13% endemism in fishes) and Hawaiian Archipelago (25% endemism). These areas can also produce and export new species (Bowen et al., 2016). Clearly, regions like the Coral Triangle are conservation priorities to protect the progenitors of future biodiversity.

10.2 Marine Fishes at Risk

Box 10.1 summarises the marine fishes listed as threatened by IUCN. Here we review a half dozen examples in greater detail.

Atlantic halibut (*Hippoglossus hippoglossus*; Figure 10.3A) is among the largest flatfishes, growing to 3 m and exceeding 300 kg. Slow growth and a long time to maturity (over 10 years) make it especially susceptible to overfishing. Whereas European colonists found an abundance of this fish off the North Atlantic coast of America, this species is now rarely encountered. Overfishing has also caused Atlantic halibut to become sexually mature at much smaller sizes. Commercial fishing for this species, now IUCN listed as Endangered, is presently banned in US coastal waters.

Atlantic bluefin tuna (*Thunnus thynnus*; Figure 10.3B) is the largest member of the tuna family (3 m, 678 kg record) and highly prized for sushi and other dishes. It is the

Box 10.1
IUCN Listed Marine Fishes

The International Union for the Conservation of Nature (IUCN) presently lists only six recent extinctions of fishes found in marine waters, all anadromous species (maturing in seawater, spawning in freshwater) that perished due to overfishing and other human activities: the New Zealand grayling (*Prototroctes oxyrhynchus*), the Adriatic Sea stock of the European sturgeon (*Huso huso*) and four populations of Columbia River sockeye salmon (*Oncorhynchus nerka*) (Figure 10.1). However, many marine fishes are threatened, defined by IUCN as having an elevated risk of

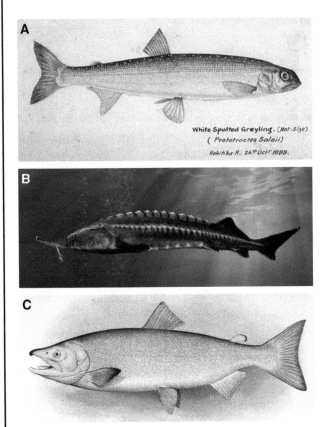

Figure 10.1 Fishes that inhabited seawater (all anadromous species) driven extinct by overfishing and other human activities, as documented by IUCN. (A) New Zealand grayling (*Prototroctes oxyrhynchus*, 22 cm FL) (credit: F.E. Clarke courtesy of the Museum of New Zealand Te Papa Tongarewa). (B) Adriatic Sea stock of the European sturgeon (*Huso huso*, 800 cm TL) (credit: Максим Яковлев). (C) Four populations of Columbia River sockeye salmon (*Oncorhynchus nerka*, 84 cm TL) (credit: B.W. Evermann and E.D. Goldsborough). Maximum fork lengths (FL) and total lengths (TL) from fishbase.org.

extinction, the risk categorised along a gradient from Vulnerable to Endangered to Critically Endangered. Of 988 marine fish species assessed in European waters alone, 15 are Critically Endangered, 22 are Endangered and 22 are Vulnerable, mostly due to overfishing (Nieto et al., 2015). Of 519 Mediterranean species assessed, 15 are Critically Endangered, 13 are Endangered and 15 are Vulnerable, again due to overfishing (Abdul Malak et al., 2011). Most listed species are chondrichthyan fishes (sharks, rays and relatives), of which 36% of over 1000 assessed species are threatened at some level or categorised as Data Deficient (IUCN, 2022). Globally, IUCN currently lists 65 marine fish species as Critically Endangered, 141 as Endangered and 372 as Vulnerable. Importantly, most marine fishes have not been assessed. Beyond IUCN listings, 60% of 825 exploited marine fish species worldwide are projected to experience very high extinction risk from a combination of overfishing and ocean climate disruption if present trends continue (Cheung et al., 2018), especially on coral reefs (McClenachan, 2015).

target of a very lucrative fishery, with individual fish being sold for hundreds of thousands of dollars, and a recent record of 3 million US dollars for a single fish in Tokyo. Management is confounded by the long migrations made by adults, traversing international boundaries and multiple management zones. While other fisheries tend to abate as fish get scarce, the high price of bluefin tuna makes it profitable to hunt them down to the last fish. As a result, the IUCN status for bluefin tuna is Endangered.

Atlantic goliath grouper (*Epinephelus itajara*; Figure 10.3C) exceeds 2 m in length, grows to 300 kg and can live past 40 years. There is a sister (closely related) species in the East Pacific (*Epinephelus quinquefasciatus*). These species are subject to a triple whammy of low reproduction relative to other groupers, overfishing of juveniles before they can reproduce and capture of reproductive adults in spawning aggregations. The Atlantic Goliath Grouper is IUCN listed as Endangered in the Gulf of Mexico, and Vulnerable elsewhere in the West Atlantic. Following a 1990 moratorium on fishing for this species, numbers in US waters are showing impressive signs of recovery.

Orange roughy (*Hoplostethus atlanticus*; Figure 10.3D), originally known as the Slimehead, was rebranded by fisheries to increase appeal to consumers. It is extremely long-lived (up to 149 years) and takes 20–30 years to mature. The damage done by overfishing is amplified by the tendency of this fish to congregate in spawning aggregations, making it easy prey and wiping out reproductive adults. IUCN lists this fish as Vulnerable, likely headed towards Endangered unless overfishing is eliminated.

Smalltooth sawfish (*Pristis pectinata*; Figure 10.3E) is Critically Endangered throughout the Atlantic, with populations reduced by more than 95% over the last century. The primary culprit is mortality in coastal fisheries. While this sawfish is not sought in commercial fisheries, it overlaps extensively with other fishery targets in coastal waters. In these areas, the toothy rostrum ('saw') makes this fish very vulnerable to entanglement

Figure 10.2 Some of the fantastic diversity of marine fishes. (A) Green moray eel (*Gymnothorax funebris*, 250 cm TL) (credit: J. Wilder). (B) Fourteen-gill hagfish (*Eptatretus polytrema*, 93 cm TL) (credit: J.H. Richard). (C) Coelacanth (*Latimeria chalumnae*, 200 cm TL) (credit: R.L. Pyle). (D) Bull shark (*Carcharhinus leucas*) (credit: T. Sinclair-Taylor). (E) One of the smallest vertebrates next to a 1 cm scale, the stout infantfish (*Schindleria brevipinguis*, 0.8 cm SL) of the Great Barrier Reef (credit: Scripps Institution of Oceanography). (F) One of largest fishes, captured at Catalina Island, California, in 1910, the ocean sunfish (*Mola mola*, 333 cm TL) (credit: P.V. Reyes). (G) Warty frogfish (*Antennarius maculatus*, 15 cm TL), showing the modified dorsal spine that resembles a small fish and acts as a fishing lure for this highly cryptic ambush predator (credit: T.W. Pietsch). (H) Leafy sea dragon (*Phycodurus eques*, 35 cm TL), a relative of seahorses that mimics seaweed (credit: J. Rosindell). Maximum total lengths (TL) and standard lengths (SL) from fishbase.org.

Figure 10.3 Some threatened marine fishes. (A) Atlantic halibut (*Hippoglossus hippoglossus*, 470 cm TL) (credit: Wikipedia). (B) Atlantic bluefin tuna (*Thunnus thynnus*, 458 cm TL) (credit: NOAA). (C) Goliath grouper (*Epinephelus itajara*, 250 cm TL) (credit: J.E. Randall). (D) Orange roughy (*Hoplostethus atlanticus*, 75 cm TL) (credit: Pengo). (E) Smalltooth sawfish (*Pristis pectinata*, 760 cm TL) (credit: D.R. Robertson). (F) Winter skate (*Leucoraja ocellata*, 110 cm TL) (credit: NOAA). Maximum total lengths (TL) from fishbase.org.

in fishing nets. A second factor is the desirability of the fins, esteemed in the shark fin trade. The low fecundity of this species, typical of chondrichthyans, limits potential for recovery. In response to these dire population trends, international trade is prohibited under the Convention on International Trade in Endangered Species (CITES), and many nations have imposed total fishing bans, including Brazil, Nicaragua, Mexico and the USA. A decade of intensive management in the USA has paid off in that population trends indicate the beginning of a recovery in US Atlantic waters. However, all sawfish genera (*Pristis* and *Anoxypristis*) are imperilled globally, with two of five species listed by IUCN as Endangered, and the other three listed as Critically Endangered (IUCN, 2022).

Winter skate (*Leucoraja ocellata*; Figure 10.3F) inhabit the northwest Atlantic Ocean and are harvested for fish meal, lobster bait and human consumption. Over the last three decades numbers have dropped by 90%, prompting IUCN to label this species as Critically

Endangered. Due to the low fecundity of skates (like other chondrichthyans), the species will recover slowly if at all, especially because fisheries continue to capture it and remaining numbers are subject to predation from a rebounding population of grey seal (*Haliochoerus grypus*).

10.3 Causes of Extinction Risk

While freshwater fishes have suffered devastating losses from water diversion and habitat disruption (Chapter 9), the fate of marine fishes has not yet been as severe. Documented recent extinctions among marine fishes have been rare so far (Box 10.1). Ignorance about the status of most species may be the primary reason. It may also be that extinction from overfishing is prevented by natural limits on the efficiency of exploitation, with the physical inability or lack of economic incentive to catch the few remaining members of a species (with notable exceptions, such as Atlantic bluefin tuna). Additionally, the paucity of documented extinctions may be due to the enormous expanses of the ocean, where some fish can disperse over entire ocean basins with population sizes in the millions. Coral reef fishes in the vast Indo-Pacific region (which covers over half the planet) have geographic ranges averaging about 9 million km^2, about the size of China (Allen, 2008). Given these possibilities and our lack of knowledge of most species, official tallies presume that marine fish diversity is intact relative to other vertebrates, yet there are clearly important and rapidly multiplying exceptions.

10.3.1 Diadromous Fishes: Marine–Freshwater Double Jeopardy

Diadromous fishes, those that use both marine and freshwater habitats, have been very successful in terms of both abundance and diversity. However, in the age of human exploitation, double benefits can capsize into double jeopardy, as these species are prone to the same hazards as purely marine and purely freshwater fishes. These double-dipping fishes come in two primary varieties.

Anadromous fishes are hatched in freshwater, eat, grow and mature at sea, then return to freshwater and spawn. The most famous example are salmon (Family Salmonidae), a group of very successful fishes that have nourished coastal peoples for thousands of years, becoming cultural icons in the process. Salmon are easy to catch when they return to rivers and hence very vulnerable to overexploitation. While no entire species has yet gone extinct, hundreds of breeding populations have been wiped out by all the various factors that depress freshwater fishes (Chapter 9). The US National Marine Fisheries Service estimates that about one-third of the genetically distinct populations of salmon on the west coast of North America have gone extinct in the last 250 years (Gustafson et al., 2007). Additional anadromous fishes include Striped bass (*Morone saxatilis*), Shad (genus *Alosa*) and Sturgeon (family Acipenseridae), the last being valued for their eggs, known in culinary circles as caviar. Unfortunately for sturgeon, the caviar cannot be extracted without killing the female, and for that reason many species are endangered. Atlantic sturgeon (*Acipenser oxyrhynchus*) longer than 3 m used to be so common that they posed a hazard to river navigation in New England, flipping canoes with the casual swipe of a tail. They are now rarely encountered, and may be effectively extinct in the northern part of their range. As summarised in Box 10.1, all documented extinctions of fishes that inhabit seawater have been anadromous species.

Catadromous fishes do the opposite, living primarily in freshwater but migrating to the ocean where they spawn. The most spectacular examples are the freshwater eels (Family Anguillidae). The European and American freshwater eels inhabit rivers and lakes for most of their lives, then migrate to the Sargasso Sea in the central western Atlantic, where they mass spawn and die. The resulting larva is a bizarre translucent ribbon-like creature known as a leptocephalus (Figure 10.4A) that spends a year or more in oceanic gyres before

Figure 10.4 Some marine fishes of various levels of conservation concern. (A) Leptocephalus eel larva (8 cm TL, credit: U. Kils). (B) Resplendent angelfish (*Centropyge resplendens*, 6 cm TL) (credit: F. Baensch). (C) Threadfin butterflyfish (*Chaetodon auriga*, 23 cm TL) (credit: T. Sinclair-Taylor). (D) Social wrasse (*Halichoeres socialis*, 5 cm TL) (credit: L. Rocha). (E) Banggai cardinalfish (*Pterapogon kauderni*, 9 cm TL) (credit: P. Hound). (F) Orange clownfish (*Amphiprion percula*, 11 cm TL) (credit: T. Sinclair-Taylor). Maximum total lengths (TL) from fishbase.org, except actual length of leptocephalus eel larva photographed.

transforming into a juvenile eel and returning to freshwater. It is this stage, the so-called glass eels, that are subject to intense fishing for subsequent aquaculture or direct consumption. The European eel (*Anguilla anguilla*) has declined by an estimated 80% in the last 50 years. On an evolutionary timescale, switching from marine to freshwater habitats has been a very successful form of exploiting two completely different environments. However, in the age of humans, the confines of a riverine migration expose fish to all the factors that cause declines in freshwater fishes, such as overexploitation, habitat destruction and water quality degradation.

10.3.2 Small-Range Endemics

Restricted geographic range (endemism) is recognised as a primary factor in extinction risk, and some marine fishes have very small ranges that make them more vulnerable to catastrophic decline (Hobbs et al., 2011). The resplendent angelfish (*Centropyge resplendens*; Figure 10.4B) is a living jewel, highly sought after in the aquarium trade, but native only to Ascension Island, a rocky outpost on the Mid-Atlantic Ridge. While it is locally abundant, the restricted range was a primary reason IUCN listed the species as threatened. In contrast, the threadfin butterflyfish (*Chaetodon auriga*) occupies reefs from the Hawaiian Islands to the Red Sea (Figure 10.4C). Such large geographic ranges may be a buffer against extinction, as any catastrophic declines are likely limited to only part of the range. Overall the broad range of most marine species may be their salvation in terms of extinction risk.

10.3.3 Invasive Species

Harmful introduced species are recognised as one of the foremost conservation issues in ecosystems both above and below the waterline. Invasive species seem to be a greater problem for freshwater habitats, perhaps due to the higher population connectivity and fewer barriers in the oceans (Chapter 9). Nonetheless, invasive species also disrupt coastal ecosystems.

For a species introduced by humans to be considered 'invasive,' it must cause declines in the abundance of native species or otherwise be considered a pest. In the 1950s and 1960s, a variety of non-native coral reef fishes were introduced to Hawaii from the South Pacific in an attempt to enhance local fisheries. Unfortunately, the Peacock grouper (*Cephalopholis argus*) has proven to be an unpopular fishery target, due to the accumulation of toxins in its flesh from a dinoflagellate that causes ciguatera (tropical fish poisoning). Another reef fish introduced to Hawaii, the Bluestripe snapper (*Lutjanus kasmira*), brought a nematode parasite that has spread to local fishes.

By far the most devastating invaders among marine fishes have been Indo-Pacific lionfishes (genus *Pterois*), which were likely introduced to the Atlantic sometime in the 1980s, probably the result of multiple aquarium releases. From an initial breeding population in the vicinity of Florida, lionfish have spread across the greater Caribbean region and most recently to Brazil. Lionfishes are very effective predators of small reef fishes, reducing their abundance, in some cases perhaps sufficient to alter coral reef ecosystems (Albins and

Hixon, 2013). Maybe the greatest risk that lionfish pose is to the small-range endemics. The Mardi Gras wrasse (*Halichoeres burekae*), restricted to a few reefs in the Gulf of Mexico, and the Social wrasse (*Halichoeres socialis*; Figure 10.4D) found only on reefs of Belize in Central America, are both regarded as Endangered by IUCN because of restricted ranges and habitat degradation. Predation by lionfish, which target small-bodied fishes, may be sufficient to drive such species to extinction (Rocha et al., 2015). One prominent remedial measure is targeted removals combined with culinary lessons in lionfish as seafood, which seem to be effective in some areas as community events.

10.3.4 Floating Marine Debris

Persistent plastics and other flotsam in the ocean may provide an underappreciated pathway for invasive marine species. The abundance of marine debris in the vast reaches of the North Pacific has allowed a damselfish (*Abudefduf vaigiensis*) to colonise Hawaii. Juveniles of these species inhabit floating ghost nets (abandoned fishing gear) and other marine debris, creating a dispersal mechanism that did not exist previously. The invader is now interbreeding with the Hawaiian Archipelago endemic species (*Abudefduf abdominalis*), which may be genetically swamped out of existence by hybridisation (Coleman et al., 2014). Following the massive 2011 tsunami in Japan, West Pacific fishes such as the striped beakfish (*Oplegnathus fasciatus*) were transported to the other side of the Pacific Ocean with floating debris.

In addition to providing a mechanism for dispersing invasive species, plastic debris has a more insidious negative effect on marine fishes as it breaks down into small particles. These plastic fragments, including microplastics that are often bonded with pollutants, are ingested by marine fishes and their larvae (Worm et al., 2017).

10.3.5 Low Reproductive Potential

Most teleost fishes can produce thousands to millions of eggs, perhaps allowing populations to rebound when adverse conditions are alleviated. In contrast, the sharks, rays and their relatives have a reproductive strategy that is similar to mammals, producing small numbers of well-developed progeny. Overfishing is by far the greatest threat to these fishes, because they cannot quickly rebound from a population crash. The demand for shark fin soup is especially devastating, inducing a barbaric fishery in which sharks are stripped of their fins on the boat deck, and then thrown overboard to die. Similarly, demand for the gill plates of manta and devil rays for traditional Chinese medicine has led to severe overfishing of manta and devil rays. An estimated 36% of sharks and rays are threatened according to IUCN criteria (IUCN, 2022).

Seahorses, pipefish and their relatives (Figure 10.2H) are another group with low reproductive output, in this case coupled with high parental care. Young are born as miniature adults, bypassing the larval stage, and are protected during the first few weeks of life in the father's brood pouch. This strategy has proven successful as seahorses thrive in all tropical oceans. However, this life history becomes a vulnerability under exploitation or habitat loss (Vincent et al., 2011). The Cape seahorse (*Hippocampus capensis*) is the most endangered member of this group. It has a restricted range in a few bays and estuaries in South Africa and is subject to habitat degradation by development and pollution. Millions of seahorses enter the Chinese medicinal trade each year, and hundreds of thousands more are shipped in the aquarium trade. The international trade agreement CITES list them as 'not yet endangered but a species of high concern', with voluntary trade limits observed by the United States and other nations.

The cardinalfishes (Family Apogonidae) are another group with small reproductive potential and unusual breeding habits. They are mouthbrooders, a common strategy in freshwater fishes that protects the young, but rarely seen in marine fishes. The higher survivorship of mouthbrooded young is coupled with a lower reproductive output, as only a few baby fish can fit in dad's mouth. This low reproductive potential, as with the sharks, creates a vulnerability to human disturbances. One extreme example is the Banggai cardinalfish (*Pterapogon kauderni*; Figure 10.4E), native to a few islands in eastern Indonesia. This attractive fish has a small geographic range (5500 km^2, contrasting with the average Indo-Pacific reef fish range of 9 million km^2) and like the seahorses, it lacks a pelagic larval stage. It has been intensively exploited by the aquarium trade, with some collection estimates exceeding 100,000 per month, and numbers are drastically reduced in some parts of the range. As a result of low fecundity, small range and high exploitation, IUCN regards this fish as Endangered. Fortunately, the Banggai cardinalfish can be bred in captivity, which may ultimately provide relief from overexploitation.

10.3.6 Evolutionary Twilight

As noted above, coelacanths were diverse, abundant and widespread in the age of dinosaurs, but are now limited to a few species in deepwater habitats. It is likely that the evolutionary history of coelacanths is almost over. However, natural extinction is a process that may play out over thousands to millions of years, whereas human perturbations occur over periods of decades and centuries. While some of the living fossils may be persisting on borrowed time, we should not hasten their demise by short-term assaults. It is possible that living fossils can break out with new evolutionary innovations (Bowen, 2016), so they have been recognised as Evolutionarily Distinct and Globally Endangered (EDGE) species worthy of conservation in their own right.

10.3.7 Overfishing

To date, the greatest threat to marine fishes has been overfishing: removing more fish from a population faster than the fish can reproduce. Much has been written on this topic, and we refer interested readers to the excellent book by Callum Roberts (2007). Overfishing has occurred since the dawn of civilisation, yet overexploitation skyrocketed with the Industrial Revolution. Large-scale commercial fishing began in the late 1800s with the introduction of steam trawlers in the British Isles. Within a few years, trawlers depleted local flatfish stocks, and began to fish further afield. From that time forward, the major threat to marine fishes has been increasingly efficient industrialised harvest. Reynolds et al. (2005) estimated that commercially exploited marine fishes have declined by 65% in breeding biomass relative to historical levels. Industrial fishing now occurs in >55% of the world ocean and has a spatial extent more than four times that of agriculture on land (Kroodsma et al., 2018). The fishes hardest hit are those with large body size and late maturity, and the net result is depleted continental shelves and a decline in the trophic level of fishery targets, a process known as fishing down the food web (Pauly et al., 1998). As noted above, low fecundity is also a factor, most especially for sharks and rays. The sea yields about 82 million tons of fisheries products per year, compared to about 12 million tons from freshwater.

The overfishing problem is severe. Worm et al. (2009) estimate that 63% of fish stocks are overexploited. Especially troublesome is the practice of targeting the largest fish, which are often the most productive and effective spawners (Hixon et al., 2014). Solutions to overfishing include catch restrictions that are not unduly swayed by political pressures, designating protected areas free from fishing to replenish fished areas and gear modifications to eliminate the most destructive practices. In the last category, bottom trawling can be especially damaging to fish populations as well as seafloor habitats. In addition to clear-cutting the seafloor habitat, trawls tend to produce huge volumes of discarded bycatch (Watling and Norse 1998), unwanted sea life that is mutilated, crushed and usually dead, including the young of many commercially valuable fishes.

10.4 Evil Twins of Ocean Warming and Acidification

Although overfishing has been the greatest threat to marine fishes historically, the twin threats of ocean warming and ocean acidification are rapidly becoming even greater challenges to life in the sea (Gattuso et al., 2015). Because ocean climate disruption is a looming catastrophe unknown to most non-experts, we dedicate much of the chapter to this growing threat. It is as yet uncertain whether these evil twins will merely produce both winners and losers among the fishes in the sea, or only losers.

By way of introduction, recent warming of the ocean as well as the atmosphere is caused by human activities, primarily excessive combustion of fossil fuels (coal, oil, natural gas) and burning of forests. These activities are releasing carbon dioxide and other gases that enhance the heat-trapping greenhouse effect, causing heat waves in the ocean as on land (Oliver et al., 2018). About 93% of the excess heat accumulates in the seas (Cheng et al., 2019), and from 1948 to 1998, the upper layers of the world ocean warmed by over $0.3\ °C$ on average (Levitus et al., 2000). This seemingly small change has already caused intensified storms, altered rainfall patterns, rising sea levels, declining ocean productivity and oxygen levels, bleaching of reef-building corals and melting of polar ice (Gattuso et al., 2015).

Ocean acidification is the other pernicious effect of excess carbon emissions (Doney et al., 2009). About a quarter to a third of the carbon dioxide emitted into the atmosphere by human activities is absorbed directly by the oceans, where it chemically reacts with water and forms carbonic acid. The mean pH (an inverse measure of acidity) of the world ocean has dropped 0.1 units since the industrial era began, and like changes in ocean temperature, this seemingly tiny change has major ramifications for fishes and other sea life. Acidification robs seawater of dissolved carbonate, making it difficult for marine creatures to grow calcium carbonate (limestone) structures. This physiological inhibition has two major effects on marine fishes: direct and indirect. Directly, the inner ear stones or otoliths of fishes are affected, being the only bones of fishes made of calcium carbonate (most of the vertebrate skeleton is made of calcium phosphate). Indirectly, many single-celled planktonic organisms, invertebrates (including corals that build reefs) and even some seaweeds have calcium carbonate skeletons that are inhibited by ocean acidification. These changes are affecting both the food supply and the habitats of marine fishes.

Importantly, the rates at which the oceans are warming and acidifying are accelerating exponentially (Cheng et al., 2019), and these combined threats paint a dire picture for the future oceans (Gattuso et al., 2015). Bryndum-Buchholz et al. (2019) predicted that, if current rates of carbon emissions continue, marine animal biomass will decline by 15–30% in temperate and tropical seas by 2100. Some 60% of 825 exploited marine fish species are projected to experience very high extinction risk from a combination of overfishing and ocean climate disruption (Cheung et al., 2018). Time is short to reverse these dangerous trends (IPCC, 2018), and both grassroots activism and governmental action will be essential to curb carbon emissions and increase carbon sequestration. These are scientific facts which will not go away, even if ignored by corporations and politicians. As Aldous Huxley admonished denialists in his 1927 book *Proper Studies*, 'Facts do not cease to exist because they are ignored.'

10.4.1 Ocean Warming

Accelerating global warming has four major negative ramifications for ocean species and their ecosystems (Gattuso et al., 2015). Like all species, each marine fish has a preferred temperature range to which it is adapted. When the climate warms beyond normal preferences, affected organisms have only three choices: adapt in evolutionary time (centuries to millennia), move in ecological time (years to decades) or suffer physiological stress and increased mortality. With the rapid warming occurring today, the immediate solution is to move, and for marine fishes, this translates to following preferred cooler temperatures by drifting as larvae and/or swimming as juveniles and adults either into higher latitudes or deeper water. The ultimate result of fishes shifting their latitudinal or depth distributions is ecological reorganisation at best, and ecological catastrophe at worst, likely accompanied by lower fishery production (Free et al., 2019). New assemblages of species will eventually form, and there will likely be both winners and losers, with some species or populations going extinct. As reviewed below, those fishes that cannot shift their distributions are already facing physiological costs.

Second, as oceans warm, the timing of reproduction, larval development and other key population processes (i.e. phenology) are disrupted with largely unknown consequences. Species in warming seas have already advanced the timing of important activities, such as spawning, by an average of 4.4 days per decade during the late twentieth century (Poloczanska et al., 2013), with likely negative ramifications for fisheries.

Third, both horizontal and vertical ocean currents are being affected, which can drastically change productivity and thus food sources available to fishes. Typically, as the upper layers of the ocean warm, the ocean stratifies, meaning that a cap of warm water prevents deeper, cooler, nutrient-rich water from reaching the well-lit shallows. Without those upwelled nutrients, many marine plants – mainly the single-celled phytoplankton – cannot grow sufficiently to support complex ocean food webs. As Bakun et al. (2015) concluded bluntly, 'Ecosystem productivity in coastal ocean upwelling systems is threatened by climate change.' Ironically, not only does a warmer ocean provide less food for fishes, but also, because most fishes are 'cold-blooded' (with internal temperature the same as the environment), warmer fish require more food to survive. This situation is a negative double whammy. The resulting increase in respiration by affected sea life, combined with the fact that warmer water necessarily holds less oxygen, has caused the fish-free oxygen minimum zones at 300 m depth and elsewhere in the world ocean to expand.

Fourth, as detailed below, excessively warm seawater causes tropical corals to bleach and die, resulting in loss of coral reefs, which are the rainforests of the sea and the most species-rich assemblages in the ocean.

Distributional Shifts. As the oceans warm, many marine species are moving pole-ward (into higher latitudes) to match preferred water temperatures (Poloczanska et al., 2013). In general, the species that are shifting successfully are both mobile and ecologic-ally generalised – i.e. not requiring special diets or habitats – criteria which fortunately include many fishes. There is also evidence of fishes moving into deeper, cooler waters as the surface layers warm. For example, a variety of North Sea fishes have not only shifted their geographical distributions poleward an average of 100 km over the past several decades (Perry et al., 2005), but also have moved into deeper water at a rate of nearly 4 m per decade (Dulvy et al., 2008). Simultaneous increases in latitude and depth have also been observed in various continental shelf fishes off the northeastern United States, and poleward shifts in the distributions of marine fishes have been documented worldwide.

The anchovies (genus *Engraulis*) that inhabit cold-temperate upwelling zones may be at special risk because they depend on upwelling of nutrient-rich waters. At peak abundance these species yield millions of tons for regional fisheries, the largest fisheries in the world by biomass. Anchovies along continental coastlines may shift into higher latitudes in response to warming. This is feasible along continental coastlines such as Chile and California. However, the anchovies that inhabit the southern tip of Africa have nowhere to go, as a shift into higher latitudes would deprive them of coastal upwelling.

In northern latitudes, boreal (cold-temperate) marine fishes have shifted northward and pushed Arctic fishes out of the Barents Sea, which connects the North Atlantic Ocean to the Arctic Ocean (Fossheim et al., 2015). The good news is that Atlantic cod (*Gadus morhua*) has reached a record high population size in the Barents Sea, despite being severely overfished to the south. Unfortunately, Arctic fishes, including various snailfishes, sculpins and eelpouts, are not coping well with the warming seas. These species are stressed physiologically by warmer temperatures, on top of facing competition and predation by northward-moving boreal fishes. Like the South African anchovy, Arctic species have nowhere to go, and are expected to suffer catastrophic losses. The analogues on land are cool-climate species that eventually become stranded at the tops of mountain peaks, unable to ascend to cooler altitudes as the world warms.

Because there are more species at lower latitudes closer to the equator, as fishes shift their distributions poleward, one would expect the number of species to increase in temperate and polar regions, all else being equal. This pattern has been observed in the North Sea. However, because new mixes of species may cause intensified competition and other negative interactions among species, diversity may also decline. Off southern California, warm-temperate species have displaced cool-water species that originally inhabited this region, resulting in a 15–25% reduction in the number of coastal marine fish species. Exacerbating this decline has been an overall decline in ocean productivity as the ocean warms (Gattuso et al., 2015). On average, with increasing ocean temperatures, marine fish communities become dominated by warmer-water species (Cheung et al., 2013). For example, a 29-year time series of the North Atlantic over 5 degrees of latitude west of Scotland detected a homogenisation of fish assemblages, such that what used to be cooler-water communities are increasingly resembling warmer-water communities (Magurran et al., 2015).

Note that shifts in the geographical ranges of most marine fishes will depend on successful larval dispersal, the drifting and swimming of tiny baby fish in the open ocean that ultimately replenish the adult population. Warming waters are expected to accelerate larval development, thereby reducing larval durations and thus the distance larvae can disperse. Less productive warming oceans may also provide less food for developing larvae (Gattuso et al., 2015). Overall patterns of larval dispersal are likely to shift substantially as the ocean warms (Gerber et al., 2014).

Physiological Effects. Tropical and polar fishes, as well as fish larvae in general, usually are most sensitive to ocean warming because they have narrower temperature tolerances. Over normal environmental ranges, metabolic activity in fish increases by about 10% for every 1°C rise in temperature, and increased metabolism requires additional food. If food is available, then warmer waters result in faster growth of fish. However, given that less food is available in a warming ocean (Gattuso et al., 2015), warmer waters result in decreased activity, decreased growth rates, and increased mortality. Overall, the ability of marine fishes to acclimate to a rapidly warming ocean appears to be limited, and there is evidence that maximum body size of marine fishes may decrease, further negatively affecting fisheries due to altered ecological interactions and reduced fecundity (Cheung et al., 2013).

Habitat Loss. The vast majority of marine fish species inhabit tropical coral reefs (Allen, 2008), which support over 25% of all marine species. Unfortunately, these rainbow gardens of the seas are not only among the rarest of marine habitats – occupying only 0.02% (250,000 km^2) of the surface area of the world ocean – but also the most endangered. Globally, 25–50% of our coral reefs have already been lost due to human activities (Eddy et al., 2021).

One of the main reasons for the death of coral reefs is a phenomenon called 'coral bleaching' (Hoegh-Guldberg, 1999). Reef-building corals provide the structural foundation of coral reefs. These animals are actually partnerships of two organisms: the anemone-like polyp that we see, and special single-celled, plant-like dinoflagellates that live inside the polyp, called zooxanthellae (or simply 'zoox' by coral experts), which give the coral its colour. The association involves mutual feeding: the polyp feeds the zoox nitrogenous wastes that fertilise the microscopic plants, and the zoox in turn provide products of their photosynthesis. (By the way, because the zoox require access to sunlight, corals often assume leaf-like shapes similar to land plants. And corals are often greenish in colour because of the chlorophyll in the zoox.) Healthy corals secrete calcium carbonate (technically, aragonite) skeletons that create the structure of the reef, in turn providing food and shelter for a vast variety of species, especially fishes.

When the surrounding seawater becomes too warm, sometimes as little as 1°C above the normal summer maximum, the marvellous symbiosis between polyp and zoox breaks down and the zoox become more like parasites than mutualists. The coral then expels the zoox, leaving the colourless polyp (hence the term 'bleaching'). If the water does not cool shortly thereafter, the polyp may die. Once the coral dies, the reef begins to erode and crumble, denying fishes and other creatures the shelter and food that the reef once provided. One of us wept in his facemask upon witnessing the complete death and collapse of his favourite coral reef in the Bahamas during the first global coral bleaching event in 1998 (Hixon, 2009).

To date, coral bleaching has been sporadic, yet its frequency and severity is increasing rapidly. It has been projected that tropical coral reefs worldwide will bleach every year by 2040, and that the oceans will be too warm for 46% of the world's coral reefs by 2100. Currently bleached reefs provide a window to the future. One global survey found that 62% of reef fish species declined in abundance within 3 years following 10% (or more) loss of live coral cover (Wilson et al., 2006). Loss of coral due to bleaching can render some fish species more susceptible to predation and intensify competition in other species. Moreover, 10 times as many larval fish settle on healthy corals as on bleached corals. Pratchett et al. (2008) concluded ominously, 'Coral loss has the greatest and most immediate effect on fishes that depend on live corals for food or shelter, and many such fishes may face considerable risk of extinction with increasing frequency and severity of bleaching.' Such losses will directly affect nearby human communities due to declines in fisheries and other reef products.

10.4.2 Ocean Acidification

Ocean acidification is negatively affecting marine fishes directly in terms of developmental and physiological stress, as well as indirectly in terms of food and habitat loss. Because a broad range of marine species are likely to be negatively affected by an acidifying ocean (Doney et al., 2009), the food supply and ecological interactions of marine fishes will certainly shift, mostly in unpredictable ways. As experts Branch et al. (2013) warn, 'Overall effects of ocean acidification on primary productivity and, hence, on food webs will result in hard-to-predict winners and losers.' The ramifications for marine fisheries are even less certain.

Physiological Effects. Efforts to understand the effects of ocean acidification have focused mostly on rearing larval fish in seawater at future low pH values, yet there have also been field studies at locations where natural carbon dioxide vents acidify seawater locally. For most marine fish species studied, ocean acidification causes a variety of physiological and associated sensory and behavioural problems (Heuer and Grosell, 2014). Underlying these problems, acidification negatively affects both protein synthesis and neurotransmitter function. A frequent result is that larval growth and development are stunted.

Declining pH also affects the growth and function of otoliths, the calcium carbonate inner ear stones of fish involved in orientation and hearing. Paradoxically, acidification may result in larger otoliths, yet often disorientation and reduced hearing capabilities. The sense of smell is also inhibited in acidified oceans, negatively affecting both sharks and bony fishes. Some fish even suffer neurological anxiety.

Habitat Loss. Coral reefs are expected to wither tremendously under the combination of coral bleaching caused by ocean warming (discussed above) and ocean acidification, which will likely inhibit the ability of corals to grow their calcium carbonate skeletons (Hoegh-Guldberg, 1999). As corals die, the entire reef ecosystem will shift in unpredictable ways, and may eventually collapse. Indeed, the Great Barrier Reef in Australia has already lost over 50% of the live coral cover. Coral loss in the Indo-Pacific region is increasing at about 2% per year, and it is projected that one-third of reef-building corals face elevated risk of extinction. Given that upwards of 8000 marine fish species are associated with tropical coral reefs (Victor, 2015), and that 8% of assessed reef fish species are already threatened with extinction (McClenachan, 2015), the long-term outlook for coral-reef fishes is dire.

10.5 The Future

We have summarised the life history factors and human assaults that push marine fishes toward extinction, including very small geographic ranges, invasive species, plastic debris, low reproductive rates, overfishing, habitat loss, and the multiple pernicious effects of ocean warming and acidification. However, the extinction crisis that is apparent in terrestrial and freshwater ecosystems has not yet reached the marine fishes. This situation perhaps reflects our ignorance of the trends and status of most species. Large geographic ranges, large population sizes, high fecundity and economic constraints on extreme overfishing may buffer many marine fishes from catastrophic loss. Alternately, these factors may merely slow the process of collapse due to ocean warming and acidification. Many researchers believe that the factors protecting marine fish populations are merely causing a slower march towards extinction. The reduction of many fishes to small populations, due to overfishing and other threats, puts previously abundant species at the same risk as small-range endemics. In other words, there may be an extinction debt that falls due if overfished species are not allowed to recover.

Yet there is also good news. The cases of the Goliath grouper and Smalltooth sawfish reviewed above show that conservation can halt declines and promote recovery in a surprisingly short time. Additionally, marine conservation programmes have increasingly turned from single-species management to ecosystem-based approaches that explicitly include entire ecological systems as well as humans, so-called 'social-ecological systems' (Francis et al., 2007). This holistic perspective now dominates international conservation efforts, as indicated by the United Nations Global Centre for Ecosystem Management and the IUCN Commission on Ecosystem Management. Major tools for ecosystem-based management include marine protected areas (MPAs) where human activities are minimised (Cabral et al., 2020). In keeping with the vast geographic scale of many marine ecosystems and corresponding conservation issues, IUCN has set a goal of permanently protecting 30% of the world's oceans by 2030. It is fortunate that the number of large MPAs is steadily increasing, including the Ross Sea MPA in Antarctica, the Papahānaumokuākea Marine National Monument in the Hawaiian Islands and the Great Barrier Reef Marine Park in Australia. It is unfortunate that meeting the above goals is unlikely, given that, as of 2021, only about 7% of the world ocean is in designated or proposed MPAs, and only 2.7% is in fully implemented, strongly protected areas (Sala et al., 2021).

Fishes are the crowning achievement of vertebrate biodiversity and evolution. As such they have weathered climate changes throughout their 500 million year history, with planetary temperatures and seawater acidity both higher and lower than today. The key understanding for the contemporary climate crisis is not whether the oceans will warm and acidify – which is already happening – it is that ocean temperature and pH are changing extremely rapidly. To some extent the marine fishes will adapt, and they may shift habitats much more easily than their freshwater cousins. However, evolution and adaptation usually work on the scale of millennia, while damage wrought by humanity on our oceans, the cradle of life on Earth, is moving at the timescale of decades.

Many of the threats that beset marine fishes can be addressed by effective ecosystem-based management, yet the issues of ocean warming and acidification are global in scale and require committed governmental efforts to reduce and sequester carbon emissions (Mumby et al., 2017). The fate of marine fishes, and ocean life in general, is contingent on humanity working in common cause. The essential solution is maturation of the human species involving a 'great turning' toward true sustainability and an end to the culture of overconsumption (Korten, 2006).

Acknowledgements

We thank N.K. Dulvy, R.A. Leidy, N. Maclean, P.B. Moyle and J.E. Randall for thoughtful discussion and reviews for this chapter originally completed in 2018, and numerous colleagues for use of their beautiful photos, as credited in the figure captions. We are most grateful to mother ocean for embracing our undersea careers. Long may she thrive. MAH dedicates this work to his grandchildren Nolan and Mila. BWB dedicates this work to RuthEllen, Nichole and Tamaria.

References

Abdul Malak, D., Livingstone, S.R., Pollard, D., et al. (2011) *Overview of the Conservation Status of the Marine Fishes of the Mediterranean Sea*. Gland, Switzerland; Malaga, Spain: IUCN.

Albins, M.A. and Hixon, M.A. (2013) Worst case scenario: potential long-term effects of invasive predatory lionfish (*Pterois volitans*) on Atlantic and Caribbean coral-reef communities. *Environ Biol Fish* 96: 1151–1157.

Allen, G R. (2008) Conservation hotspots of biodiversity and endemism for Indo-Pacific coral reef fishes. *Aquat Conserv* 18: 541–556.

Bakun, A., Black, B.A., Bograd, S.J., et al. (2015) Anticipated effects of climate change on coastal upwelling ecosystems. *Curr Clim Change Rep* 1: 85–93.

Bowen, B.W. (2016) The three domains of conservation genetics: case histories from Hawaiian waters. *J Hered* 107: 309–317.

Bowen, B.W., Gaither, M.R., DiBattista, J.D., et al. (2016) Comparative phylogeography of the ocean planet. *Proc Natl Acad Sci USA* 113: 7962–7969.

Branch, T.A., DeJoseph, B.M. Ray, L.J., et al. (2013) Impacts of ocean acidification on marine seafood. *Trends Ecol Evol* 28: 178–186.

Bryndum-Buchholz, A., Tittensor, D.P., Blanchard, J.L. et al. (2019) Twenty-first-century climate change impacts on marine animal biomass and ecosystem structure across ocean basins. *Glob Change Biol* 25: 459–472.

Cabral, R.B., Bradley, D., Mayorga, J., et al. (2020) A global network of marine protected areas for foods. *Proc Natl Acad Sci* 117: 28134–28139.

Cheng, L., Abraham, J., Hausfather, Z., et al. (2019) How fast are the oceans warming? *Science* 363: 128–129.

Cheung, W.W.L., Watson, R. and Pauly, D. (2013) Signature of ocean warming in global fisheries catch. *Nature* 497: 365–369.

Cheung, W.W.L., Jones, M.C., Reygondeau, G., et al. (2018) Opportunities for climate-risk reduction through effective fisheries management. *Glob Change Biol* 24: 5149–5163.

Coleman, R.R., Gaither, M.R., Kimokeo, B., et al. (2014) Large-scale introduction of the Indo-Pacific damselfish *Abudefduf vaigiensis* into Hawai'i promotes genetic swamping of the endemic congener *A. abdominalis*. *Mol Ecol* 23:5552–5565.

Cowman, P.F. and Bellwood, D.R. (2013) The historical biogeography of coral reef fishes: global patterns of origination and dispersal. *J Biogeogr* 40: 209–224.

Doney, S.C., Fabry, V.J., Feely, R.A., et al. (2009) Ocean acidification: the other CO_2 problem. *Ann Rev Marine Sci* 1: 169–192.

Dulvy, N.K., Rogers, S.I., Jennings, S., et al. (2008) Climate change and deepening of the North Sea fish assemblage: a biotic indicator of warming seas. *J Appl Ecol* 45: 1029–1039.

Eddy, T.D., Lam, V.W.Y., Reygondeau, G., et al. (2021) Global decline in capacity of coral reefs to provide ecosystem services. *One Earth* 4: 1278–1285.

Facey, D.E., Bowen, B.W., Collette, B.B., et al. (2023) *The Diversity of Fishes: Biology, Evolution and Ecology*, Third Edn. Hoboken, NJ: Wiley.

Fossheim, M., Primicerio, R., Johannesen, E., et al. (2015) Recent warming leads to a rapid borealization of fish communities in the Arctic. *Nat Clim Change* 5: 673–677.

Francis, R.C., Hixon, M.A., Clarke, M.E., et al. (2007) Ten commandments for ecosystem-based fisheries scientists. *Fisheries* 32: 217–233.

Free, C.M., Thorson, J.T., Pinsky, M.L. et al. (2019) Impacts of historical warming on marine fisheries production. *Science* 363: 979–983.

Fricke, R., Eschmeyer, W.N. and Van der Laan, R. (Eds.) (2022) *Eschmeyer's Catalog of Fishes: Genera, Species, References*. http://researcharchive.calacademy.org/research/ichthyology/catalog/fishcatmain.asp (accessed October 2022).

Gattuso, J.-P., Magnan, A., Billé, R., et al. (2015) Contrasting futures for ocean and society from different anthropogenic CO_2 emissions scenarios. *Science* 349: aac4722.

Gerber, L.R., Mancha-Cisneros, M.D.M., O'Connor, M.I., et al. (2014) Climate change impacts on connectivity in the ocean: implications for conservation. *Ecosphere* 5: 1–18.

Gustafson, R.G., Waples, R.S., Myers, J.M., et al. (2007) Pacific salmon extinctions: quantifying lost and remaining diversity. *Conserv Biol* 21: 1009–1020.

Helfman, G.S. (2007) *Fish Conservation: A Guide to Understanding and Restoring Global Aquatic*

Biodiversity and Fishery Resources. Washington, DC: Island Press.

Heuer, R.M. and Grosell, M. (2014) Physiological impacts of elevated carbon dioxide and ocean acidification on fish. *Am J Physiol* 307: R1061–R1084.

Hixon, M. 2009. Garden of ghosts. In Hayes, R. (Ed.), *Thoreau's Legacy: American Stories About Global Warming*. Cambridge, MA: Union of Concerned Scientists and Penguin Classics.

Hixon, M.A., Johnson, D.W. and Sogard, S.M. (2014) BOFFFFs: on the importance of conserving old-growth age structure in fishery populations. *ICES J Marine Sci* 71: 2171–2185.

Hobbs, J.-P.A., Jones, G.P. and Munday, P.L. (2011) Extinction risk in endemic marine fishes. *Conserv Biol* 25: 1053–1055.

Hoegh-Guldberg, O. (1999) Climate change, coral bleaching and the future of the world's coral reefs. *Mar Freshw Res* 50: 839–866.

IPCC. (2018) *Global Warming of 1.5 °C: Summary for Policymakers*. Geneva, Switzerland: IPCC.

IUCN. (2022) *The IUCN Red List of Threatened Species*, version 2022-1. www.iucnredlist.org (accessed October 2022).

Korten, D.C. (2006) *The Great Turning: From Empire to Earth Community*. Bloomfield, CT; San Francisco, CA: Kumarian Press and Berrett-Koehler Publishers.

Kroodsma, D.A., Mayorga, J., Hochberg, T., et al. (2018) Tracking the global footprint of fisheries. *Science* 359: 904–908.

Levitus, S., Antonov, J.I., Boyer, T.P. et al. (2000) Warming of the world ocean. *Science* 287: 2225–2229.

Magurran, A.E., Dornelas, M., Moyes, F., et al. (2015) Rapid biotic homogenization of marine fish assemblages. *Nat Commun* 6: 8405.

McClenachan, L. (2015) Extinction risk in reef fishes. In Mora, C. (Ed.), *Ecology of Fishes on Coral Reefs*. Cambridge, UK: Cambridge University Press.

Mumby, P.J., Sanchirico, J.N., Broad, K., et al. (2017) Avoiding a crisis of motivation for ocean management under global environmental change. *Glob Change Biol* 23: 4483–4496.

Nieto, A., Ralph, G.M., Comeros-Raynal, M.T., et al. (2015) *European Red List of Marine Fishes*. Luxembourg: Publications Office of the European Union.

Oliver, E.C.J., Donat, M.G., Burrows, M.T., et al. (2018) Longer and more frequent marine heatwaves over the past century. *Nat Commun* 9: 1324.

Pauly, D., Christensen, V., Dalsgaard, J., et al. (1998) Fishing down marine food webs. *Science* 279: 860–863.

Perry, A.L., Low, P.J., Ellis, J.R. et al. (2005) Climate change and distribution shifts in marine fishes. *Science* 308: 1912–1915.

Poloczanska, E.S., Brown, C.J., Sydeman, W.J., et al. (2013) Global imprint of climate change on marine life. *Nat Clim Change* 3: 919–925.

Pratchett, M.S., Munday, P.L., Wilson, S.K., et al. (2008) Effects of climate-induced coral bleaching on coral-reef fishes: ecological and economic consequences. *Oceanogr Mar Biol* 46: 251–296.

Reynolds, J.D., Dulvy, N.K., Goodwin, N.B., et al. (2005) Biology of extinction risk in marine fishes. *Proc Royal Soc B* 272: 2337–2344.

Roberts, C. (2007) *The Unnatural History of the Sea*. Washington, DC; Island Press.

Rocha, L.A., Rocha, C.R., Baldwin, C.C., et al. (2015) Invasive lionfish preying on critically endangered reef fish. *Coral Reefs* 34: 803–806.

Sala, E., Mayorga, J., Bradley, D., et al. (2021) Protecting the global ocean for biodiversity, food and climate. *Nature* 592: 397–402.

Victor, B.C. (2015) How many coral reef species are there? Cryptic diversity and the new molecular taxonomy. In: Mora, C. (Ed.), *Ecology of Fishes on Coral Reefs*. Cambridge, UK: Cambridge University Press.

Vincent, A.C.J., Foster, S.J. and Koldewey, H.J. (2011) Conservation and management of seahorses and other Syngnathidae. *Fish Biol* 78: 1681–1724.

Watling, L. and Norse, E.A. (1998) Disturbance of the seabed by mobile fishing gear: a comparison to forest clearcutting. *Conserv Biol* 12: 1180–1197.

Wilson, S.K., Graham, N.A.J., Pratchett, M.S., et al. (2006) Multiple disturbances and the global degradation of coral reefs: are reef fishes at risk or resilient? *Glob Change Biol* 12: 2220–2234.

Worm, B., Hilborn, R., Baum, J.K., et al. (2009) Rebuilding global fisheries. *Science* 325: 578–585.

Worm, B., Lotze, H.K., Jubinville, I., et al. (2017) Plastic as a persistent marine pollutant. *Ann Rev Environ Resour* 42: 1–26.

ELEVEN

Insects

MANU E. SAUNDERS, SIMON LEATHER[†],
JENNI A. STOCKAN AND DAVID YEATES

Summary

Insects are the most abundant and diverse group of animals on Earth. They are critical to ecosystem function in terrestrial and aquatic systems, yet they are one of the most understudied groups of organisms. Only a small proportion of the more than five million insect species have been assessed by the IUCN Red List. For most of these species, there is not enough evidence to know what is happening to their populations. In fact, for most insect species globally, there is very little data available on where they live, how they live and what environmental conditions they need to persist in the long term. A number of threats affect insect biology and life cycles generally, including climate change, habitat clearing, invasive species, use of broad-spectrum pesticides, and pollution of soil and waterways. These threats should be addressed immediately to prevent further declines in insect populations. To understand insects better, greater investment in research and documentation of the world's insect diversity is urgently needed.

11.1 Introduction

Insects outnumber all other taxonomic classes of animals, in terms of abundance and number of species. They live in every type of habitat, including arid deserts, ice flows, dense forests, lakes, rivers and oceans. Yet the distribution and lifestyle of most of these insects is a mystery. There are an estimated 5.5 million species of insect, but only about 1 million of these have been given names (Stork, 2018). The global distributions, ecology and life histories for most of these are unknown.

Beetles (Coleoptera) are the most diverse group of described taxa, with more than 320,000 known species. Other highly diverse groups are the moths and butterflies (Lepidoptera) and flies (Diptera), both with over 150,000 known species, and the ants, bees and wasps (Hymenoptera) with over 115,000 known species, and many thousands more to be discovered.

At the global scale, insect diversity is generally higher in warmer tropical regions and lower in cool regions. At smaller scales, insect diversity is intimately linked to the conditions and available resources in different habitats. More than half of all insects depend on living and decaying plants at some stage of their life cycle. Another large fraction of the remaining insects are either predators or parasitoids of the plant-eating insect groups. Therefore, much of the challenge of protecting insect biodiversity depends on also conserving plants and the complex interactions that structure ecosystems.

The sheer diversity and complexity of insect taxa and life cycles makes them difficult, but extremely fascinating, to study. Relative to other animal groups, insects are generally short-lived, produce large numbers of offspring and their populations fluctuate widely in response to environmental conditions. Different life stages of the same species can inhabit vastly different environments and have different resource needs. All of these characteristics mean that it is often difficult to find insects in their natural environment and collect accurate data on their population sizes and distributions. Taxonomic expertise for most insect groups is restricted to a handful of scientists globally, and there are few young scientists entering the field. This is partly due to lack of funding for taxonomic research and the fact that fewer universities are teaching entomology, insect taxonomy and systematics (Cardoso et al., 2011).

The current list of insect species assessed by the IUCN Red List process (Box 11.1) highlights two key facts that are common to insect conservation globally: (1) our tendency to overlook the smallest animals and assume their insignificance has led to huge knowledge gaps and challenges that need to be addressed immediately and (2) based on what we do know, insects have been impacted for many years by the damaging effects human activities are having on ecosystems. The vast knowledge gaps and severe data limitations of current knowledge of global insect diversity make the IUCN Red List a signpost for further research, not an accurate list of current population trends (Cardoso et al., 2012; Fox et al., 2018).

Box 11.1

All Relevant IUCN Red and Green Listed Species

DD	LC	NT	VU	EN	CR	EX
3121	5986	700	893	932	408	59

Insect Order	DD	LC	NT	LR	VU	EN	CR	EX
Bristletails		1			1	1		
Cockroaches	2	10				7	10	1
Beetles	679	592	141		114	184	85	16
Earwigs		1				1	3	1
Flies	45	88	37		36	132	22	4

(*cont.*)

Insect Order	DD	LC	NT	LR	VU	EN	CR	EX
Ice crawlers			1		2	1	1	
Mayflies						1		2
Sucking bugs		6	8		9	20	15	2
Bees, wasps and ants	323	106	27		155	20	12	
Moths and butterflies	98	1121	85		102	92	46	21
Mantids	16	13	3		3	1		1
Lacewings		3						
Dragonflies and damselflies	1730	3389	221		282	298	95	1
Grasshoppers and crickets[a]	205	590	166	3	185	172	111	4
Phasmids	23	62	10		2	1	5	1
Lice							1	
Barklice		2						
Stoneflies		2			2	1	1	1
Caddisflies			1					4
Thrips							1	

[a] One species of cricket (Oahu Deceptor Bush Cricket, *Leptogryllus deceptor*) is currently listed as Extinct in the Wild in the Red List. However, there are no documented captive breeding programmes, so this species has been included in the Extinct category.
DD = Data Deficient; LC = Least Concern; NT = Near Threatened; LR = Lower Risk: Conservation Dependent; VU = Vulnerable; EN = Endangered; CR = Critically Endangered; EX = Extinct.
Data downloaded October 2022 and correct at time of writing

11.2 Summary of IUCN Red Listed Species

Less than 1% of known insect species have been assessed by the Red List process. Most of these species are currently considered to be of Least Concern or Data Deficient. A total of 60 species are listed as Extinct, but for many of these there is scant knowledge of their ecology and life history. Some of these species have since been rediscovered, including moths that feed on American chestnut, a Critically Endangered tree in North America, and the Pecatonica River mayfly (*Acanthametropus pecatonica*) from the United States. Others in the Critically Endangered category may already be extinct, but lack of observation and research effort prevents confirmation of their status.

Population trends are unknown for the majority of living species (Table 11.1). Overall, the population trends for 71% (8675 species) are unknown. Of the remainder, 14% of taxa (1622 species) are identified as having populations in decline, 0.5% (50 species) have populations that are increasing and 11.5% (1134) have stable populations. For many of the

Table 11.1 *Proportion of species in each category showing different population trends*

Category	Declining	Increasing	Stable	Unknown
CR	52.7%	–	1.3%	46%
EN	52%	–	1.7%	46%
VU	40%	–	6%	54%
NT	37.8%	0.5%	7.8%	54%
LC	5.8%	0.8%	20.5%	73%
DD	2.7%	0.03%	0.5%	97%

species identified as 'decreasing', very little data are available on species distribution, life history and ecology; therefore, declines may be localised or extrapolated from limited data.

In the three most threatened categories, 68% of species inhabit terrestrial systems, 6% inhabit freshwater systems, 26% are recorded as using both habitat types (predominantly Odonata) and two species use marine and intertidal habitats. Most (75%) of the Extinct species inhabited terrestrial ecosystems.

There are 27 taxonomic orders of insects, and 20 of these are represented in the Red List. Of the orders that are listed, only a small proportion of the global species diversity for each order has been assessed.

11.2.1 Mayflies (Ephemeroptera)

Mayflies spend most of their life as juveniles in water, emerging onto land for only a few days as adults to reproduce and die. They are critical to ecosystem function in aquatic habitats and are also extremely susceptible to pollution and disturbance of water bodies (Macadam and Stockan, 2015). There are more than 3200 known mayfly species, but only three species have been assessed for conservation status. Of these, the Large Blue Lake mayfly (*Tasmanophlebi lacuscoerulei*) is endemic to New South Wales, Australia. Restricted to just 80 km^2 within the alpine region of Kosciuszko National Park, it is likely to be negatively affected by climate change and as such, its IUCN status was increased to Endangered in 2014.

IUCN lists two mayflies as Extinct, both endemic species to the United States. The Pecatonica River mayfly (*Acanthametropus pecatonica*) was rediscovered in 1987, 60 years after it was considered extinct. Dredging is a likely cause of decline, but population trends are unknown. The robust burrowing mayfly (*Pentagenia robusta*) was endemic to the Ohio River. Likely causes for this species' extinction were water quality (especially sedimentation) and flow.

11.2.2 Caddisflies (Trichoptera)

Caddisflies are another aquatic insect group that depends on clean, healthy waterways to survive. Five caddisfly species have been assessed for the Red List, out of more than 11,500 known species worldwide. Habitat size and quality have been the main factors driving strong population declines of one species, *Limnephilus atlanticus*, which is listed as Near Threatened. Endemic to native forests of the Azores, it is threatened by agricultural pollutants and an invasive plant, *Hedychium gardenerianum* (Kahili ginger), which promotes low habitat heterogeneity. The other four caddisfly species are Extinct; three endemic from the USA and one, Tobias' caddisfly (*Hydropsyche tobiasi*), from Germany. Industrial and military effluent pollution in the Rhine during the twentieth century were blamed for the loss of the latter species.

11.2.3 Stoneflies (Plecoptera)

Stoneflies have similar habitat needs and life cycles to caddisflies and mayflies, and are also threatened by pollution and destruction of freshwater habitats. Over 3600 stonefly species are known, but only seven of these have been assessed. The Critically Endangered Mount Donna Buang wingless stonefly (*Riekoperla darlingtoni*) is decreasing in population size. It is largely confined to the montane region close to the summit of Mount Donna Buang in southern Australia. The flightless adult is restricted to riparian areas along temporary streams, which are the preferred habitat of the immature stages. It is also unusual for a stonefly in having a 3 year life cycle. Mount Donna Buang is a popular tourist area and trampling of the riparian habitat has impacted the species (New, 2008). Other threats are wildfire and plant disease, which reduce the understorey riparian vegetation and affect water quality through sedimentation and turbidity.

Population trends for a further two Vulnerable stonefly species are unknown. Climate change leading to prolonged droughts is the main threat to these species. Loss of riparian habitat through fire or forestry activities are additional threats. The cause of extinction of a fourth stonefly species is unknown.

11.2.4 Dragonflies and Damselflies (Odonata)

Odonates are large, charismatic predatory insects with aquatic larvae and winged adults. Relative to other aquatic insect orders, many dragonflies and damselflies are long-lived and some lineages can fly long distances from their original waterbody. Over 85% of all dragonflies and damselflies worldwide have been assessed; a total of more than 6000 species. The majority of these (92%) have been classified as Least Concern or Data Deficient. In general, the population trends of most odonates are unknown. Species that are increasing, such as the blue dasher (*Pachydiplax longipennis*), tend to be common throughout their range, and are often opportunistic and able to expand their range quickly.

Most of the Critically Endangered and Endangered dragonflies and damselflies are found in Sub-Saharan Africa and South or Southeast Asia. They are at risk from agricultural and forestry activities which destroy habitat and pollute waters (Samways et al., 2011). Climate change is also a major threat to dragonflies and damselflies because it causes loss of habitats or range shifts, which can lead to new overlaps of species distribution and hybridisation. Only the Maui upland damselfly (*Megalagrion jugorum*) from Hawaii is listed as Extinct. It was lost in the 1930s due to overgrazing by feral ungulates.

11.2.5 Beetles (Coleoptera)

The beetles are a highly diverse group of insects, exhibiting a wide range of life histories and functional roles. More than 1800 species of beetle have been assessed for the Red List, which is only a small proportion of global beetle diversity. Most assessed species are terrestrial; just 78 are associated with water bodies. Over half (70%) are identified as Data Deficient or Least Concern, and the population trends for most of these species are believed to be stable or unknown. Population trends for the majority of Critically Endangered and Endangered species are in decline.

Sixteen beetle species are thought to be Extinct, but there is little data to confirm the cause of extinction, or when and where some of these were last seen. The Extinct species are freshwater diving beetles, weevils or ground beetles. Habitat loss is the presumed cause of extinction for the ground beetles and weevils, most of which were restricted to island habitats. As with most animals, the cause is likely to be a result of multiple factors. For example, a weevil (*Rhyncogonus bryani*) endemic to Laysan Island in Hawaii, disappeared as its host plant (*Chenopodium oahuense*) declined due to overgrazing by introduced rabbits. While the host plant is now recovering, the weevil has not been seen since the early 1900s.

Many of the threatened beetle species are associated with woody habitats, especially those rich in decaying wood and organic matter. Nine species of the flightless ironclad beetles (genus *Tarphius*), all endemic to the Azores, and twelve species of fungus weevil endemic to St Helena are under threat from habitat loss. All of these rare species are restricted to small patches of forest where they rely on dead and decaying wood.

11.2.6 Crickets and Grasshoppers (Orthoptera)

Orthopterans are a diverse group of insects, comprising grasshoppers, katydids, crickets and wētās. The group has a long history of association with humans, with many people recognising some grasshoppers and plague locusts as pests. However, most are not pests and they play an important role in ecosystem function, including as nutrient recyclers, soil disturbers, predators and pollinators. They are also important food resources for vertebrates, especially in grassland ecosystems. Only about 7% of the world's orthopterans have been assessed, mostly katydids and grasshoppers, but data on many of these species is limited. Only one species, the Oahu deceptor bush cricket (*Leptogryllus deceptor*) endemic to Hawaii, is Extinct. It is listed as Extinct in the Wild in the IUCN's Red List, but there is no record of captive populations.

Grasshoppers and many katydids depend on open shrubby and grassy habitats and are therefore most threatened by livestock grazing and pasture conversion. Some katydids are also flower feeders and depend on flowering trees and shrubs at different times of the year. Cave crickets and mole crickets live under boulders or leaf litter, in rocky caves and crevices, or dig holes in soil. These species are threatened by agricultural disturbance and intensification, pesticide use, rock quarrying and urban development. Four Vulnerable species of cave cricket from Sardinia and Greece are only known from specific cave locations that are also used for tourism and recreation activities. The effects of tourism on these species persistence is unknown because of lack of available knowledge or research activities.

11.2.7 Moths and Butterflies (Lepidoptera)

Less than 1% of global lepidopterans have been assessed for population trends, and more butterflies (1438 species) are listed than moths (127 species). However, more moths have been listed as Extinct. Most of the extinct moths are noctuids and loopers, families with many species which are sometimes pests in forest systems and agricultural crops. While the main cause of loss is unknown for many of the extinct moths, Hawaii's Poko noctuid moth (*Agrotis crinigera*) declined because of targeted biological control to reduce its effects on local crops. Four butterflies have gone extinct, but the cause is known for only one, the Xerces blue (*Glaucopsyche xerces*) from California. Two endemic species from South Africa, the Mbashe River buff (*Deloneura immaculata*) and the Morant's blue (*Lepidochrysops hypopolia*), are known only from very restricted areas and may have declined naturally.

The majority of listed species are restricted to small geographic areas or specific habitats, increasing their risk of loss as human activities change land uses and habitat quality. Vegetation clearing for agriculture, urban development and mining activities are key drivers affecting lepidopterans, because their larval stages often depend on specific plants for survival. Some Critically Endangered species may already be extinct, as they have not been seen for decades, in spite of targeted searches. For example, a looper moth known from only one specimen collected in 1903 from an Azorean forest, which has since been cleared, has not been found since. Many lepidopterans are classified as Data Deficient, because information on their current range and population trend is too limited to assess their status.

11.2.8 Bees, Wasps and Ants (Hymenoptera)

Hymenoptera are one of the most diverse insect groups, but only a small proportion of the world's species have been assessed. Three-quarters of the 643 Hymenoptera assessed are bees, with the remainder being ants (149 species) and 11 species of wasps. No sawflies have been assessed. There are no known Extinct species. Population trends for more than half of the bees assessed are unknown; the others are either stable or decreasing, with only one species showing an increase in population. For ants, population trends are not known.

Bees depend on flowering plants for survival, so are particularly vulnerable to habitat loss and climate change effects on flowering phenology (Winfree et al., 2010). Invasive pathogens, and residential and commercial development are also detrimental to many bee species. Agriculture has an impact on many bee species through simplification of the landscape, loss of flowering resources and overuse of pesticides. Commercial bumblebee colonies, brought in to provide pollination services for greenhouse and field crops, inadvertently introduce pathogens into native bee populations. This is an additional threat to species such as the Critically Endangered Franklin's bumble bee (*Bombus franklini*).

Threats to ants have not been assessed but for wood ants at least, the main factor is habitat loss.

One of the few wasps assessed is the rare solitary wasp *Tachysphex pechumani* which is listed as Near Threatened. This species is restricted to pine-oak barrens and savannas in parts of the north-eastern USA and south-western Ontario, Canada. Habitat destruction is the main threat, although extreme population fluctuations mean the overall trend for this species is unknown.

11.2.9 Sucking Bugs, Planthoppers (Hemiptera)

Only 60 species from this extremely diverse and widely distributed group have been assessed. There are estimated to be somewhere between 50,000 and 80,000 species worldwide. They comprise four suborders, the Auchenorhyncha (planthoppers, cicadas, etc.), Sternorhyncha (aphids, whiteflies, scale insects etc), Coleorhyncha (moss bugs) and the Heteroptera (stink bugs, waterbugs, harlequin bugs, etc.). They range in size from 1 mm to around 15 cm and are characterised by possession of sucking and piercing mouthparts. They have a wide variety of lifestyles. While the vast majority are plant-eaters, some are predators of other insects and blood suckers of vertebrates. So far only terrestrial species have been assessed and most of these are plant feeders and mainly from two island habitats, the Azores and St Helena. Two mealybug species (*Clavicoccus erinaceus* and *Phyllococcus oahuensis*) are Extinct, both of which were endemic to the island of Oahu in Hawaii. Their loss was likely caused by declines in their host plants, which are threatened by habitat loss. Many of the threatened hemipteran species are specialist herbivores, entirely dependent on one or a few particular plants for survival.

This group suffers from a lack of taxonomic expertise, and taxonomic identification can be difficult. For example, some species of spittle bugs (Ceropidae) are only distinguishable by dissection of the genitalia. Because of the threat to crop production from a minority of species, e.g. aphids, scale insects, psyllids and whiteflies, most research has been directed at control rather than taxonomy and ecology. No long-term data on population trends within this group exist, except for pest species, so it is difficult to assess their status globally.

The most likely factors to threaten the group as a whole are habitat degradation, climate change and loss of endemic host species. Research needs to be directed towards those species living on small isolated islands and those associated with aquatic habitats. Hemipterans living in marine littoral habitats are very poorly known, as are those that live on the open ocean, such as the predatory sea skaters.

11.2.10 Stick Insects (Phasmida)

Phasmids are a fascinating group of herbivorous insects that have a wide range of adaptations to camouflage as parts of the plants they live on. Only about 3% of the world's phasmids have been assessed for the Red List, and nearly all of these are from Australia. Three of the four Critically Endangered species are endemic to Lord Howe Island, off the coast of New South Wales, and are threatened by invasive black rats on the island. All of the Near Threatened species are in decline. They are endemic to rainforest in northern

Queensland and are threatened by invasive ants and loss of habitat. Many of the listed phasmid species have not been seen for decades, highlighting the need for increased research efforts to determine if they are still extant.

11.2.11 Ice Crawlers (Grylloblattodea)

This interesting group of primitive insects, often called ice crawlers or rock crawlers, is only known from caves and glaciers in the far Northern Hemisphere, across Asia and North America. This order was only discovered recently, compared to other insects, in the early 1900s, and only about 34 species are known worldwide. They have adapted to extremely cold temperatures and are highly susceptible when temperatures warm above their narrow tolerance range. This biological feature suggests they are most threatened by the effects of climate change. Only five species are confirmed at risk, four from South Korea and one from the United States. Most are restricted to specific locations, thus they are susceptible to small changes in local environmental conditions.

11.2.12 Praying Mantids (Mantodea)

Mantids are generalist predators of other small animals. They mostly prey on insects, but larger mantids have sometimes been observed catching very small birds and other animals. Globally, only 38 species have been assessed for conservation status, out of approximately 2500 species worldwide, and knowledge of most of these is too limited to know for certain how their populations are faring. One species, the spined dwarf mantis (*Ameles fasciipennis*) from central Italy, was collected once in the 1870s and has not been recorded since. It is listed as Critically Endangered, but may be extinct. A key matter that most threatened and Data Deficient species have in common is that their taxonomy, natural history and distribution are largely unknown.

11.2.13 Flies (Diptera)

Diptera, one of the most diverse insect groups, includes such familiar organisms as houseflies, mosquitoes and gnats. The blood feeding habit of some groups gives the order a reputation as a nuisance, and at worse disease-carrying killers. However, the vast majority of the hundreds of thousands of species of flies are not harmful to humans, and in fact are important pollinators, predators and parasites of other insects, and nutrient recyclers. Three hundred and sixty-four fly species have been assessed, with four found to be Extinct. Two Extinct species were island endemics from Hawaii, another was range restricted in the mountains of California and a fourth had only been found in Essex, England. Other assessed species are endemic to small areas, either in aquatic or terrestrial situations. Two Australian torrent midges (Blephariceridae) are listed, one Endangered and the other Vulnerable. Habitat modification, including the construction of dams that flood white water habitat, is the most significant threat for these species.

The distinctive bone skipper (*Thyreophora cynophila*) with a bright orange head, is an instructive example of how little we know about most of the world's insects. This species is not listed on the IUCN Red List. Only found in northern Europe, it was placed on a list of extinct European species in 2007 because it hadn't been collected for 160 years. A few years later adults were rediscovered in Spain, feeding on the carcasses of large mammals. Further study revealed that this species feeds as an adult on advanced corpses in winter and often after dark, and its larvae feed on bone marrow. This specialised ecology allowed it to elude discovery for almost two centuries (Martin-Vega et al., 2010).

11.2.14 Bristletails (Archaeognatha)

Only three species of this ancient wingless insect group have been assessed, of which two are classed as threatened. Both are endemic to the Azores and are restricted to specific habitats, one in native forests and one in coastal areas, where they feed on algae and lichen. Because of their rarity and endemism, both are predicted to be threatened by habitat decline as climate change and invasive species change environmental conditions on the islands.

11.2.15 Termites and Cockroaches (Blattodea)

Termites and cockroaches used to be considered unrelated, but recent phylogenetic research has discovered they belong to the same lineage, and their classification has been revised to combine them in the same taxonomic order. Four termite species, out of approximately 3000 species worldwide, have been assessed. Two of these, both restricted to small oceanic islands, are Critically Endangered. Very little is known about their population size or trends.

Only 26 species of the world's approximately 4440 species of cockroach have been assessed. The single Extinct species (*Margatteoidea amoena*) and all the threatened species are in the wood cockroach family Blatellidae, and all are endemic to the Seychelles. There is very little known about the populations of most of the species, and some have not been seen for decades, despite surveys. The Extinct species was only known from one small island and has not been recorded for over 100 years. One Endangered species is restricted to grassy coastal areas. All other Endangered and Critically Endangered species live in forests or woodlands, dependent on decaying wood and leaf litter for persistence. Loss of habitat on the islands, from conversion to agriculture, invasive species and urban development, are major threats for these species.

11.2.16 Earwigs (Dermaptera)

Earwigs are predominantly nocturnal animals and hide in crevices and under bark and leaf litter during the day. The common European earwig (*Forficula auricularia*) gets most attention, and has caused a widespread misperception that all earwigs are crop and garden pests. There are about 2000 earwig species worldwide and most rarely interact with humans; only six species have been assessed. The Saint Helena earwig (*Labidura herculeana*) was last recorded on the island in the 1960s and is considered Extinct. It was the world's largest known earwig, living in burrows on rocky plains, in forests and in seabird colonies. Habitat loss and introduced predators are the likely cause of its loss. Four threatened species are endemic to the Seychelles and are restricted to leaf litter in damp forests that are declining from land clearing, climate change and invasive species.

11.2.17 Lice (Phthiraptera)

Some insects depend on specialised interactions with other animals or plants to survive. If one interaction partner declines, so does the other. Only one of the world's approximately 5000 louse species has been assessed for the Red List, the Critically Endangered pygmy hog-sucking louse (*Haematopinus oliveri*) endemic to India. It is an ectoparasite found only on the pygmy hog (*Porcula salvania*), a Critically Endangered mammal that is now restricted to the Assam region of India. More is known about the host than its parasite, suggesting that the louse was only listed because of its interaction with the hog. Knowledge of most of the rest of the world's lice species is limited.

11.2.18 Other Groups

Three other insect orders are represented incidentally in the Red List. Three lacewing (Neuroptera), two barklice (Psocoptera) species and one thrip (Thysanoptera) have been assessed. The lacewings and barklice are currently considered Least Concern with most having stable population trends. The barklice and the Brown lacewing (*Hemerobius azoricus*) are endemic to the Azores, while the other two lacewings are endemic to Saint Helena. The critically endangered thrip (*Chirothrips azoricus*) is also endemic to the Azores, but its population is declining.

Eight orders have not been assessed: silverfish, web-spinners, zorapterans, dobsonflies, fleas, scorpionflies, snakeflies and strepsipterans.

11.3 Causes of Population Changes

Multiple drivers are threatening insect populations around the world (Wagner and Van Driesche 2010; Vanbergen et al., 2013; Sands, 2018). Many of these drivers are related and require complementary efforts from different sectors to address them (Samways, 2007). A key issue with understanding how these drivers affect insect taxa globally is the lack of available evidence. In addition, most drivers affect taxa differently in different systems (e.g. terrestrial, freshwater, marine), yet disciplinary segregation means we still have limited understanding of cross-system effects.

11.3.1 Causes of Extinction

The main cause of extinction is unknown for most Red List species. Extinction can only be confirmed after targeted surveys in known habitats have not found any new individuals over an extended period that is reasonable relative to the individual's life cycle. Because many insects are hard to find and identify, and there are few people with funds and expertise available to conduct searches, this process of confirmation can take many years (Dunn, 2005).

However, where extinction cause is known, habitat loss or human intervention are often to blame. Over half (60%) of the extinct species were endemic to islands, which are

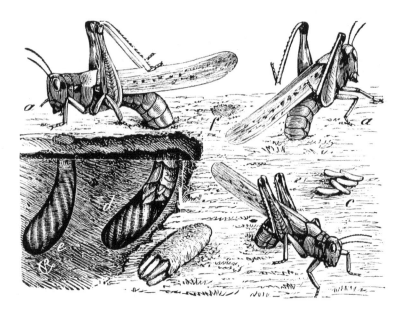

Figure 11.1 The Rocky Mountain locust (*Melanoplus spretus*) depended on damp undisturbed soil in the Great Plains river valleys to reproduce. This illustration from a United States Bureau of Entomology circular in 1904 depicts egg-laying females. The caption noted that 'alfalfa fields throughout the irrigated sections [of its range] constitute an ideal breeding ground' for the locusts, which are thought to have gone extinct because of agricultural development.

far more vulnerable to extinctions than mainland environments. Many of the extinct species were rare or locally restricted, which also increases the risk of extinction. A few species were common across their native region, and even considered pests in large numbers, a factor that in some cases may have contributed to their decline.

The Rocky Mountain locust (*Melanoplus spretus*) was once a devastating plague locust in North America that caused massive damage to homestead crops across large areas in the 1800s. After a particularly damaging plague in 1870s, the expected next wave never came. The species was last recorded in the early 1900s and is considered Extinct, most likely from agricultural modification of the fertile river valleys the grasshoppers relied on to reproduce (Figure 11.1). However, some entomologists have speculated over whether the species may still exist as the solitary phase variant in isolated regions of the Rocky Mountains (Lockwood, 2010).

In Fiji, the Levuana moth (*Levuana irridescens*) was a serious pest of coconut crops in the 1800s, which were an important livelihood for local people. A biological control agent was introduced, a tachinid fly from Malaysia that parasitised the moth, causing a rapid decline in the population. The levuana moth hasn't been seen since the 1920s. A Hawaiian cutworm moth, the Poko noctuid moth (*Agrotis crinigera*), was an indirect victim of another biological control agent. A tachinid fly was introduced to control an introduced cutworm, but targeted the native Poko moth as well. These examples are one of the reasons why biological control programmes are more rigorous today. They are also a timely reminder that pest control strategies of any kind need to be evaluated carefully and the costs and benefits of widespread attempts to eradicate a pest population should be fully investigated before action is taken.

11.3.2 Habitat Loss and Fragmentation

Habitat loss is a key driver of species loss, mostly caused by human activities clearing vegetation or changing land use. Many of the world's threatened species are endemic or restricted to particular habitats or locations, meaning they are highly susceptible to habitat losses or contractions. The Xerces blue butterfly (*Glaucopsyche xerces*) was restricted to coastal sand dunes in parts of the San Francisco peninsula, and was driven extinct by increasing habitat loss and disturbance as urban development expanded. The Antioch Dunes shieldback katydid (*Neduba extincta*) suffered a similar fate. The dunes, which are an ancient remnant of the Mojave Desert in California, have been mostly lost to sand mining, invasive plants and urban development. Only a small fragment of the original dune habitat remains and it has been protected to support a number of endangered plant and insect species. The uniqueness of the shieldback katydid and its dune habitat were unfortunately recognised too late. A specimen was collected sometime before the 1960s and lay in a museum drawer for years before an expert was available to look at it. The specimen was found to be a new species, but subsequent searches in the dune habitat failed to locate any more individuals. Its scientific name, *Neduba extincta*, recognises that it was lost before it was given a scientific name (Rentz, 1977).

Because insects are linked closely with the plants they rely on for food and habitat, the loss of a single plant species can have knock-on effects to the animal species that depend on it. In the United States, five species of moth were collaterally lost when the plant pathogen chestnut blight invaded North America and caused declines in their host plant, the American chestnut. One or two of these species have since been rediscovered, but there is limited data available for any of the five microlepidopteran moths.

11.3.3 Agricultural Intensification

Agricultural development is a leading cause of land use change and associated loss of habitat. A popular myth that is often used to justify expanding agricultural intensification is that we are not producing enough food to feed the world. The reality is very different. Globally, we are producing more than enough food. The problem lies with the type and quality of the food that is being produced and the availability of nutritious food for starving and low-income households. There is a glut of some major commodities, like corn and soy, because the production of these crops far outstrips their demand. This mismatch is largely driven by economic markets. In contrast, nutrient-rich crops that are more valuable to address hunger and poverty, like fruits and vegetables, are limited in supply and often not available to the communities that need them most.

These activities have major impacts on global biodiversity and ecosystems, particularly insects, even beyond the immediate surroundings of individual farms. The increase in

Figure 11.2 (left) Intensive agricultural systems with low plant diversity are inhospitable for most insects. (right) To support insects in agricultural systems, particularly species that contribute ecosystem services to production, farms need to provide high plant diversity across space and time and increase vegetation structure, such as dead wood, leaf litter and mixed herbs, shrubs and trees. Photo credit: Manu Saunders.

intensive production of cash crops, driven by commodity markets and incentives, is causing large-scale vegetation clearing, higher pesticide use, and homogenisation of agricultural landscapes. This has significant, negative consequences for wildlife, which in turn affects agricultural production. Wild insects need multiple types of habitats and diverse resources to live out their full life cycle (Nicholls and Altieri, 2013; Senapathi et al., 2017). While a small proportion of common generalist insect species thrive in the conditions provided by intensive agricultural landscapes, the vast majority of wild insects may suffer decline because there are too many negative impacts and not enough niches for them to survive. Intensive, simplified agricultural landscapes are inherently unstable, in terms of ecosystem function, and support the decline of natural enemies and the prolifer- ation of pest populations, resulting in negative feedback loops affecting production (Jonsson et al., 2012; Landis, 2017). Increasing plant diversity at local and landscape scales is essential to sustain insect diversity and ecosystem services in agricultural landscapes. This can be done, for example, through diversified intercropping systems, retaining flowering ground cover, sowing wildflower strips or meadows, retaining remnant vegetation in paddocks and around crop fields, and using organic management practices (Figure 11.2).

11.3.4 Invasive Species

Predation or competition from invasive species is a key threatening process worldwide, and is one of the main threats identified for many of the Red Listed insect species. Invasive species can directly impact native insects through predation and disease transmission, or cause significant changes to an insect's environment, by destroying a host plant the insect relies on for food or changing habitat structure and resources the insect needs for its life cycle (Wagner and Van Driesche, 2010). The flightless dolichopodid fly (*Campsicnemus mirabilis*) is thought to have been lost from Hawaii after the introduction of invasive *Pheidole* ants. It is not known exactly how the species interacted, but the ants may have

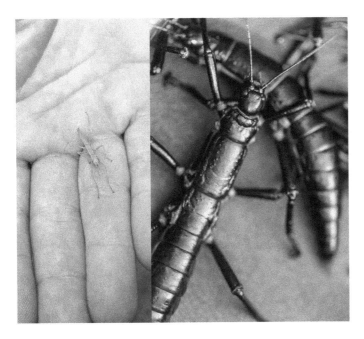

Figure 11.3 One of the rarest insects in the world, the Lord Howe Island phasmid was recently rediscovered and is being bred in captivity to assist the species' recovery. Photos show nymph (left) and adults (right) from captive populations. Photo credits: (left) Bryan Lessard; (right) Corey Hague.

predated directly on the ground-dwelling wingless fly, or they may have competed with the fly for other food and habitat sources.

The Lord Howe Island phasmid (*Dryococelus australis*) (Figure 11.3) was thought to be extinct by the 1920s, largely because of predation by invasive black rats that were released when a foreign steamship ran aground on the island. The phasmid was rediscovered in 2001 by a team of scientists who conducted targeted surveys to verify incidental sightings (Priddel et al., 2003). The insect is now listed as Critically Endangered, with a small wild population known only from Ball's Pyramid, a rocky islet off Lord Howe Island that is difficult to access, and a successful captive breeding programme at the Melbourne Zoo.

11.3.5 Climate Change

Insects are cold-blooded creatures, which means they are highly sensitive to changes in their environmental conditions, particularly temperature and humidity (Deutsch et al., 2008). Many insects are sensitive to extreme cold or heat, and the activity levels of most species are determined by the weather. These biological characteristics mean that insects can be extremely susceptible to population changes driven by climate change. Many species, including common and generalist species, are already showing range contractions or expansions correlated with climate change. Economic pests, like the mountain pine beetle (*Dendroctonus ponderosae*), are rapidly expanding their range and the severity of their impact, in part because of changing climate conditions. Other major agricultural pests are predicted to follow. Other insects, like some bumble bees in North America, are contracting in range or moving upwards in elevation, in response to climatic change. These effects of climate change on insect distribution will also have subsequent effects on plants that rely on these insect species for reproduction and dispersal.

11.3.6 Pollution

Environmental pollution from human activities, particularly around agricultural and urban development, is a major problem for wildlife. In agricultural areas, pesticides and fertilisers pollute soil and waterways and can have long-term damaging effects on insect diversity. In urban environments, there is often less regulation of pesticide use, especially in homes and gardens, and pesticide and nutrient run-off levels can be high (Lowe et al., 2019). Studies testing water quality in urban waterways around the world have shown high levels of pesticides, plastics and heavy metals that have damaging effects on animals that rely on these habitats, especially aquatic insects. One Extinct aquatic insect, Tobias' caddisfly (*Hydropsyche tobiasi*), disappeared from the Rhine River because of industrial pollution during the 1900s. Restoration efforts in these highly impacted urban waterways is extremely important to protect aquatic insect populations (Vaughan and Ormerod, 2012).

Pollution of waterways can also be caused by non-chemical factors. Thermal pollution occurs when industrial manufacturers and energy plants harvest water to cool the operating system and return the water to the waterway at higher temperatures. Such changes in water temperature have damaging effects on aquatic insects and other organisms and can cause long-term changes in the ecology of the waterway (Collier et al., 2016). Sediment pollution, from dredging, erosion or flood mitigation projects, changes the availability and quality of habitat for many aquatic insects. The robust burrowing mayfly (*Pentagenia robusta*), Extinct from the Ohio River, is the only species confirmed to have been lost from increasing sedimentation. However, most aquatic insects are very susceptible to changes in turbidity or sediment quality, because they depend on specific sediment conditions for their larval stages.

11.4 Obstacles to Insect Conservation

The list of insects classified in the Red List is incomplete, covering only a tiny proportion of the millions of insect species on Earth. This is largely because of the limited knowledge available on the distribution and ecology of most insect species, even those that are relatively well-studied. The complex interplay of social, political and scientific systems plays a key role in the availability of this knowledge (Cardoso et al., 2011; Hortal et al., 2015). Three key themes need urgent attention to deliver long-term success for global insect conservation.

11.4.1 Investing in Knowledge

Insects are one of the most understudied groups of organisms, disproportionately relative to their abundance, diversity and importance to ecosystem processes. A number of major knowledge gaps need to be prioritised to achieve successful conservation of global insect diversity.

Museum collections and research in taxonomy and systematics are essential to identifying global insect diversity (Yeates et al., 2016). Yet funding for insect taxonomy research and training has never been commensurate with their diversity, and has declined markedly in recent decades. Many universities have cancelled entomology and taxonomy courses due to low demand, and museums are losing staff and resources as funding sources decline. This means, as current taxonomic experts age and retire, there are fewer scientists training to take their place. The lack of taxonomic expertise and highly specialised available knowledge means that current conservation lists can be biased toward particularly well-studied and charismatic taxonomic groups. This has created a taxonomic impediment to the study of insects, which has major implications for identifying threatened species and understanding how to conserve global insect diversity (Cardoso et al., 2011). Only about 20% of the estimated global insect diversity has been described, and most of these species are the larger and more charismatic fauna, like large beetles, dragonflies and butterflies. Taxonomy is also critical to gain political support for conservation programmes. Establishing species recovery, monitoring or mitigation plans depends on formal identification and clear understanding of their taxonomy, phylogenetic context and distribution. The assessment of many of the Red Listed insect species are based on one or a few specimens that were collected up to 100 years ago and haven't been found since, leaving many questions about their taxonomy and distribution. Some of the listed species are also in need of taxonomic revision to unambiguously assess their conservation status and needs.

Describing species is not enough to save them. There is an urgent need for greater investment in studying the ecology and life cycles of insects, particularly species of conservation concern. A large majority of described species are known only by name; their distribution, habitat needs, host associations, reproductive strategies, life cycle and interactions with other organisms are incompletely known and in some cases largely a mystery. More knowledge is needed of how damaging drivers, like climate change and land clearing, affect different types of insects. Current knowledge of effects is mostly limited to particular species or groups of taxa, but the effects cannot be uncritically translated to other species, even closely related ones.

In addition, current knowledge has been strongly influenced by different scientific disciplines working in isolation. An excellent example is the lack of understanding of insect species that inhabit both aquatic and terrestrial environments throughout their life cycle. Freshwater and terrestrial ecology too often operate as separate disciplines and researchers in each discipline have spent many decades building bodies of knowledge that remain unconnected. Some insect groups, like dragonflies, damselflies and mayflies, are commonly recognised as living in both terrestrial and aquatic habitats. Yet there are many other species that are traditionally thought of as being associated with only one of these habitats, but actually depend on both types of systems. For example some terrestrial flies and beetles have aquatic larvae, or the parasitic adults may depend on aquatic hosts.

Misperceptions about species' life cycles and habitat needs can influence the success of conservation programmes.

Documenting life cycles and habitats needs to be coupled with rigorous research identifying how a species' natural history fits into the complex ecosystem web around it. A particularly important area of research is understanding the interactions that insects depend on throughout their life, and how those interactions structure ecosystems and drive ecosystem processes. Insects are key drivers in pollination, biological control, soil formation, water filtration, decomposition of organic matter and other ecosystem processes, all of which deliver benefits to humans (Yang and Gratton, 2014). To ensure that ecosystem function is maintained to continue supplying ecosystem services to humans, we need to understand more about how insects and their interactions contribute to these benefits. Many of the Red Listed species are dependent on particular plants or animals to live out their life cycle, and some of these hosts are also under threat. Not surprisingly, a recent assessment of cuckoo wasps in Finland found that population trends of the wasps and their hosts were positively correlated (Paukkunen et al., 2018). Many of the saproxylic beetles listed as threatened are dependent on specific trees or wood of a specific age or stage of decay. The Critically Endangered Suckley's cuckoo bumble bee (*Bombus suckleyi*) and the variable cuckoo bumble bee (*Bombus variabilis*), both from North America, have both declined from a variety of reasons, but their declines are associated with declines in their host bee.

All of these important knowledge gaps require greater investment in funding and resources to support researchers and citizen scientists to monitor and study the diverse insect communities around the world. Insects have long suffered from what has been called 'taxonomic chauvinism', a lack of funding relative to the more charismatic fauna, birds and mammals (Clark and May, 2002; Leather, 2009). The challenge for scientists, land managers, educators and policy-makers is to increase public and political support for insects to ensure they receive the attention they deserve.

11.4.2 Law and Policy Issues

Discrepancies in governance and legislative frameworks, especially across different political levels, are a common obstacle in conservation planning and outcomes. For example, in Australia, state-level threatened species lists vary markedly in their comprehensiveness and obligations, and often contain different species to the national-level list, and to the IUCN Red List. These variations can make it difficult to understand and justify the conservation status of insects in different legal or political regions and contexts (New, 2008).

Many countries have limited legal frameworks or national strategies to combat species loss, especially for insect diversity. Much-needed work lies in connecting ecological knowledge of insect diversity and ecology with national policy and legislative frameworks to ensure that insect conservation is embedded in land management and conservation strategies. Guidelines and regulatory reform for industries and systems that have the most damaging effects on insect biodiversity is also urgently needed, particularly agricultural industries and pesticide manufacturing and sales (Lowe et al., 2019).

11.4.3 Public Engagement

Public engagement is critical to insect conservation. Insects are often overlooked or viewed poorly in broader public discussion. With the exception of a few charismatic or useful insect species, like large butterflies and the western honey bee, humans have actively sought to exclude insects from our living spaces for centuries. Insecticides are one of the most commonly used chemicals in urban areas, including inside homes, gardens and public parks. Cultural myths about insects as scary 'creepy crawlies' and damaging pests are ingrained in many people from a young age, and promoted through popular movies, books and television shows. Of course, the stigma is largely undeserved – the vast majority of insects are beneficial and provide critical ecosystem services. Many are among the most beautiful of all invertebrates, and well worthy of our attention. Some insect groups are frequently the object of collectors, watchers, artists and photographers, and some are kept as pets by both children and adults.

Our reliance on agricultural production also promotes the myth that most insects are damaging pests that will destroy crops and cause massive losses to farmers. This misperception fuels the widespread prophylactic use of insecticides in agricultural landscapes. Compounding this, coverage of insects in popular science and news media is often dominated by errors and misinformation. For example, pollinator conservation and crop pollination stories in popular news media are often dominated by the semi-domesticated western honey bee, giving the false impression that this managed species is the only pollinator to be concerned about (Smith and Saunders, 2016). This single bee species, which is not threatened anywhere in the world, has become a mascot for the wild pollinator conservation movement around the world, stealing the spotlight from the huge diversity of insect pollinators globally (Ollerton, 2017). Taking up beekeeping is even promoted as a way to 'save the bees', when in fact it will have very little benefit (and potentially some harm) for wild bee conservation (Colla and MacIvor, 2017). This type of misinformation can be damaging to genuine conservation efforts, detracting funding and attention from the threatened wild insect species that urgently need attention. It is critical for scientists, conservationists and journalists to address this misinformation and find better ways to engage the broader public with the fascinating world of insects.

11.5 The Future

Insects are in urgent need of our attention. As the most abundant and diverse group of animals, even small-scale declines can have massive consequences for ecosystem function. The IUCN Red List is a useful tool to illustrate the importance of conservation efforts, but its value for understanding current insect population trends is limited. Hundreds of thousands of insect species have not been assessed, or have such limited data available on their ecology and distribution that their conservation status is unknown. However, this is no reason to delay action. Our knowledge of the drivers of species decline and the limitations of current data provide enough evidence to prioritise immediate effective actions to support insect conservation in the long term (Box 11.2).

Box 11.2
Priority Actions for Insect Conservation

Policy and regulation:

- reduce levels of deforestation and other forms of habitat modification
- mitigate climate change
- improve the coordination of environmental laws between and across jurisdictions
- greater investment in ecosystem protection and restoration
- reduce environmental pollutants and agrochemicals
- invasive species control
- contain the effects of agricultural, pollution and other anthropogenic disturbances to local systems, thereby limiting their effects in preserves and wildlands.

General research funding priorities:

- greater investment in invertebrate ecology, biology and systematics
- whole-ecosystem research, interactions and ecosystem function
- long-term monitoring and funding
- facilitate collaboration among researchers, land owners, governments, community groups and other stakeholders
- invest in museum collections, natural history and citizen science as valuable knowledge sources.

Education and training (early childhood to adult):

- taxonomy and systematics
- nature study, understanding ecological interactions and food webs
- promote positive insect messaging in classrooms, media and in popular culture.

Acknowledgements

Thank you to David Wagner and Staffan Lindgren for thoughtful comments that improved this chapter.

References

Cardoso, P., Erwin, T.L., Borges, P.A.V and New, T.R. (2011) The seven impediments in invertebrate conservation and how to overcome them. *Biol Conserv* 144: 2647–2655.

Cardoso, P., Borges, P.A.V., Triantis, K.A., Ferrández, M.A., Martín, J.L. (2012) The underrepresentation and misrepresentation of invertebrates in the IUCN Red List. *Biol Conserv* 149: 147–148.

Clark, J.A. and May, R.M. (2002) Taxonomic bias in conservation research. *Science* 297: 191–192.

Colla, S.R. and MacIvor, J.S. (2017) Questioning public perception, conservation policy, and recovery actions for honeybees in North America. *Conserv Biol* 31: 1202–1204.

Collier, K.J., Probert, P.K. and Jeffries, M. (2016) Conservation of aquatic invertebrates: concerns, challenges and conundrums. *Aquat Conserv* 26: 817–837.

Deutsch, C.A., Tewksbury, J.J., Huey, R.B., et al. (2008) Impacts of climate warming on terrestrial ectotherms across latitude. *Proc Natl Acad Sci USA* 105: 6668–6672.

Dunn, R.R. (2005) Modern insect extinctions, the neglected majority. *Conserv Biol* 19: 1030–1036.

Fox, R., Harrower, C.A., Bell, J.R., et al. (2018) Insect population trends and the IUCN Red List process. *J Insect Conserv* 23: 269–278.

Hortal, J., de Bello, F., Diniz-Filho, J.A.F., et al. (2015) Seven shortfalls that beset large-scale knowledge of biodiversity. *Ann Rev Ecol Evol Syst* 46: 523–549.

Jonsson, M., Buckley, H.L., Case, B.S., et al. (2012) Agricultural intensification drives landscape-context effects on host-parasitoid interactions in agroecosystems. *J Appl Ecol* 49: 706–714.

Landis, D.A. (2017) Designing agricultural landscapes for biodiversity-based ecosystem services. *Basic Appl Ecol* 18: 1–12.

Leather, S. (2009) Taxonomic chauvinism threatens the future of entomology. *Biologist* 56: 10–13.

Lockwood, J.A. (2010) The fate of the Rocky Mountain locust, *Melanoplus spretus* Walsh: implications for conservation biology. *Terr Arthropod Rev* 3: 129–160.

Lowe, E.C., Latty, T., Webb, C.E., Whitehouse, M.E.A. and Saunders, M.E. (2019) Engaging urban stakeholders in the sustainable management of arthropod pests. *J Pest Sci* 92: 987–1002.

Macadam, C.R. and Stockan, J.A. (2015) More than just fish food: ecosystem services provided by freshwater insects. *Ecol Entomol* 40(S1): 113–123.

Martin-Vega, D., Baz, A. and Michelsen, V. (2010) Back from the dead: *Thyreophora cynophila* (Panzer, 1798) (Diptera: Piophilidae) 'globally extinct' fugitive in Spain. *Syst Entomol* 35: 607–613.

New, T.R. (2008) Legislative inconsistencies and species conservation status: understanding or confusion? The case of *Riekoperla darlingtoni* (Plecoptera) in Australia. *J Insect Conserv* 12: 1–2.

Nicholls, C.I. and Altieri, M.A. (2013) Plant biodiversity enhances bees and other insect pollinators in agroecosystems: a review. *Agron Sustain Devel* 33: 257–274.

Ollerton, J. (2017) Pollinator diversity: distribution, ecological function and conservation. *Ann Rev Ecol Evol Syst* 48: 353–376.

Paukkunen, J., Pöyry, J. and Kuussaari, M. (2018) Species traits explain long-term population trends of Finnish cuckoo wasps (Hymenoptera: Chrysididae). *Insect Conserv Divers* 11: 58–71.

Priddel, D., Carlile, N., Humphrey, M., Fellenberg, S. and Hiscox, D. (2003) Rediscovery of the 'extinct' Lord Howe Island stick-insect (*Dryococelus australis* (Montrouzier)) (Phasmatodea) and recommendations for its conservation. *Biodivers Conserv* 12: 1391–1403.

Rentz, D.C.F. (1977) A new and apparently extinct katydid from Antioch sand dunes (Orthoptera: Tettigoniidae). *Entomol News* 88: 241–245.

Samways, M.J. (2007) Insect conservation: a synthetic management approach. *Annual Review of Entomology* 52: 465–487.

Samways, M.J., Pryke, J.S. and Simaika, J.P. (2011) Threats to dragonflies on land islands can be as great as those on oceanic islands. *Biol Conserv* 144: 1145–1151.

Sands, D.P.A. (2018) Important issues facing insect conservation in Australia: now and into the future. *Austral Entomol* 57: 150–172.

Senapathi, D., Goddard, M.A., Kunin, W.E. and Baldock, K.C.R. (2017) Landscape impacts on pollinator communities in temperate systems: evidence and knowledge gaps. *Funct Ecol* 21: 26–37.

Smith, T.J. and Saunders, M.E. (2016) Honey bees: the queens of mass media, despite minority rule among insect pollinators. *Insect Conserv Divers* 9: 384–390.

Stork, N.E. (2018) How many species of insects and other terrestrial arthropods are there on Earth? *Ann Rev Entomol* 63: 31–45.

Vanbergen, A.J.; Insect Pollinators Initiative (2013) Threats to an ecosystem service: pressures on pollinators. *Front Ecol Environ* 11: 251–259.

Vaughan, I.P. and Ormerod, S.J. (2012) Large-scale, long-term trends in British macroinvertebrates. *Glob Change Biol* 18: 2184–2194.

Wagner, D.L. and Van Driesche, R.G. (2010) Threats posed to rare or endangered insects by invasions of non-native species. *Ann Rev Entomol* 55: 547–568.

Winfree, R., Bartomeus, I. and Cariveau, D.P. (2010) Native pollinators in anthropogenic habitats. *Ann Rev Ecol Evol Syst* 42: 1–22.

Yang, L.H. and Gratton, C. (2014) Insects as drivers of ecosystem processes. *Curr Opin Insect Sci* 2: 26–32.

Yeates, D.K., Zwick, A. and Mikheyev, A.S. (2016) Museums are biobanks: unlocking the genetic potential of the three billion specimens in the world's biological collections. *Curr Opin Insect Sci* 18: 83–88.

TWELVE

Marine Invertebrates

ALEX DAVID ROGERS, PATRICIA MILOSLAVICH, DAVID OBURA AND OCTAVIO ABURTO-OROPREZA

Summary

Marine invertebrates have the greatest abundance and biomass of animals in the Earth system. As a result, they exert a major influence on the structure and function of marine ecosystems through food-web interactions and as ecosystem engineers. Marine invertebrates are also important in terms of the ecosystem services they provide to humankind. In this chapter we review Red List assessments for marine invertebrates, summarise the levels of extinction threat within this group of animals and examine the drivers of decline in affected species. Our findings suggest that only a small fraction of marine invertebrate species have been assessed for extinction threat and even within 'well'-assessed groups a large proportion of species are categorised as Data Deficient. We find that the proportion of species threatened with extinction can be extremely high (33% in reef-forming corals), with lower levels found for other, less comprehensively assessed groups. The main drivers of extinction risk include habitat loss or degradation through coastal development, pollution or other human activities, overexploitation of species for fisheries, or other purposes, and climate change. Approaches to improve the conservation of marine invertebrates are discussed.

12.1 An Ocean of Invertebrates

It is likely that life originated in the ocean about 3.5 billion years ago, with marine invertebrates appearing in the Neoproterozoic around 650 million years ago (e.g. Cunningham et al., 2016). It has been suggested that because they are so ancient, and seawater provides a relatively benign medium that can support a wide range of body plans, the diversity of higher metazoan taxa in the ocean is much larger than that on land or in freshwater (see Table 12.1; Brusca and Brusca, 1990; May, 1994). Many phyla and subphyla only occur in the ocean (Table 12.1; Brusca and Brusca, 1990), a fact that is

Table 12.1 *Number of accepted extant species in marine and non-marine invertebrates*

Taxon	Marine species	Non-marine species	Lifestyle
Acanthocephala	514	9	Parasitic
Annelida	13,734	1005	Benthic, Commensal, Parasitic, Pelagic
Arthropoda	58,067	29,641	Benthic, Commensal, Parasitic, Pelagic
Brachiopoda	414	0	Benthic
Bryozoa	6451	108	Benthic, Pelagic
Chaetognatha	132	0	Benthic, Pelagic
Cnidaria	11,985	28	Benthic, Parasitic, Pelagic
Ctenophora	205	0	Benthic, Parasitic, Pelagic
Cycliophora	2	0	Commensal
Dicyemida	122	0	Parasitic
Echinodermata	7528	0	Benthic, Pelagic
Entoprocta	198	2	Benthic
Gastrotricha	518	355	Benthic, Pelagic
Gnathostomulida	100	0	Benthic
Hemichordata	132	0	Benthic
Mollusca	50,594	33,930	Benthic, Commensal, Parasitic, Pelagic
Kinorhyncha	335	0	Benthic
Loricifera	31	0	Benthic
Nematoda	6515	6682	Benthic, Parasitic
Nematomorpha	5	0	Parasitic, Pelagic (adults)
Nemertea	1315	13	Benthic, Parasitic, Pelagic
Onychophora*	0	177	Terrestrial
Orthonectida	25	0	Parasitic
Phoronida	13	0	Benthic
Placozoa	3	0	Benthic
Platyhelminthes	13,172	2918	Benthic, Parasitic, Pelagic, Symbiotic
Porifera	9216	232	Benthic
Priapulida	22	0	Benthic
Rotifera	182	118	Benthic, Parasitic, Pelagic, Symbiotic
Tardigrada	217	1019	Benthic, Commensal, Parasitic

Table 12.1 (*cont.*)

Taxon	Marine species	Non-marine species	Lifestyle
Xenacoelomorpha	455	2	Benthic, Pelagic
Chordata	24,299	17,419	

Based on the World Register of Marine Species (https://marinespecies.org/index.php) except * which is based on data from Oliveira et al. (2012). World Register of Marine Species data accessed 2nd December, 2022.

relevant when considering global patterns of biodiversity and occurrence of genetic resources in the natural environment. Estimates of global marine species diversity over the last 10 years vary depending on the methods used, from approximately 300,000 to 2.2 million (Mora et al., 2011; Appeltans et al., 2012; Costello et al., 2012). This is significantly lower than that on land (e.g. May, 1988, 1994; Mora et al., 2011), which is dominated by insects now estimated to number in the region of 5.5 million species (Stork et al., 2015). Looking at global living biomass on Earth gives a very different perspective to the distribution of biodiversity. Marine arthropods are estimated to have the greatest biomass of any group of animals on Earth (~1 Gt) with groups such as copepods and even single species, such as Antarctic krill, *Euphausia superba* (~0.05 Gt), making a significant contribution to global animal biomass (Bar-On et al., 2018). The biomass of terrestrial arthropods, including the insects (0.2 Gt) is estimated to be considerably smaller than that of marine invertebrates (Bar-On et al., 2018) so the past statement 'To a rough approximation...all organisms are insects' (May, 1988) is certainly untrue. The fishes are the second largest group of animals on Earth in terms of biomass (0.7 Gt), being dominated by the mesopelagic fish (those living at 200–1000 m depth in the ocean; Bar-On et al., 2018).

Marine invertebrates are found throughout the ocean, from intertidal and estuarine environments to the deepest ocean trenches (Jamieson, 2015) and from tropical to high-latitude polar oceans. They have evolved to live in the most extreme environments that metazoans can tolerate in terms of temperature, oxygen availability, salinity and the presence of toxic compounds such as hydrothermal vents (e.g. pompei worms, *Alvinella pompejana*; Van Dover, 2000; see Figure 12.1a for examples of vent invertebrates), extreme oxygen minimum zones and hypersaline anoxic basins (e.g. Danavaro et al., 2010). From depths below 8000–9000 m, in the deep hadal zone within ocean trenches, the only animals found are invertebrates (Jamieson, 2015). Marine invertebrates have also adopted a wide range of lifestyles, including fully pelagic (inhabiting the water column; Figures 12.1b and 12.2a,b) planktonic or nektonic forms, sessile and motile epibenthic, endobenthic, epizootic and epiphytic habits, as well as parasitism and commensalism (Table 12.1). Symbiosis is also widespread, including photosynthetic prokaryotic and eukaryotic microbial symbionts such as cyanobacteria and dinoflagellates, mainly in

Figure 12.1 (a) Deep-sea hydrothermal vent from the East Scotia Ridge, Southern Ocean showing yeti crabs (*Kiwa tyleri*), stalked barnacle (*Vulcanolepas scotiaensis*) and snails (*Gigantopelta chessoia*). (b) Squid, possibly *Psychroteuthis glacialis*, photographed in the Kemp Caldera, South Sandwich Islands, Southern Ocean (AD Rogers, NERC CHESSO Project).

Figure 12.2 Pelagic invertebrates: (a) zoea of *Gnathophausia* sp. South West Indian Ridge, Indian Ocean, (b) *Carinaria lamarcki*, a heteropod mollusc, South West Indian Ridge, Indian Ocean (AD Rogers; IUCN / NERC Seamounts Project).

Cnidaria (most notably in reef-forming tropical shallow-water corals) and Porifera but also in Platyhelminthes, Mollusca and Ascidia (Venn et al., 2008). Invertebrates from chemosynthetic habitats, such as deep-sea hydrothermal vents, hydrocarbon seeps and low-oxygen sediments can also host a wide range of chemoautotrophic prokaryotes which oxidise hydrogen sulfide, methane, hydrogen and other reduced compounds which provide energy for carbon fixation, providing energy and materials for biosynthesis (Van Dover, 2000; Figure 12.1a). A wide range of marine invertebrates can produce biolumin-escence, either through a symbiosis with bacteria (e.g. some squid species), by eating light-producing organisms (e.g. Euphausiacea) or by synthesising light-producing compounds (luciferins) themselves (Haddock et al., 2009). This is used for a range of purposes from defensive displays and 'burglar alarm' responses to intraspecies communication, camou-flage and prey capture (Haddock et al., 2009).

12.2 The Importance of Marine Invertebrates

Because of their enormous abundance and biomass, marine invertebrates play a fundamental role in structure and function of marine ecosystems. Their role as grazers in marine food webs provides a critical link between primary producers and predators (e.g. Murphy et al., 2012 for Southern Ocean) as well as a controlling influence on aspects of the carbon (e.g. the biological carbon pump) and other nutrient cycles, particularly in the open ocean, but also in coastal seas (e.g. Beaugrand, 2015). Crustaceans are probably the most important group in this regard, especially the Copepoda and the Euphausiacea (krill), the former of which usually comprise ~70% of the plankton fauna (Raymont, 1983). However, other groups of invertebrates are also important in this regard, such as the Mollusca (e.g. Pteropoda or sea butterflies; Lalli and Gilmer, 1989) and various gelatinous zooplankton groups, including the Ctenophora, Scyphozoa, Siphonophora, Appendicularia (larvaceans) and Tunicata (salps), although these are poorly quantified in terms of abundance, biomass and distribution (Lucas et al., 2014; Lebrato et al., 2019), especially in the deep sea (Robison, 2004). Invertebrates are also important benthic grazers in intertidal and coastal ecosystems, often having an important role in determining the structure and dynamics of macroalgal communities (Little et al., 2009). Invertebrates can also be critical in bentho-pelagic coupling, such as through the role of suspension feeders in capturing planktonic organisms (Gili and Coma, 1998). They can also be important in the transformation of materials to make them available as food or nutrients to other compartments in food webs. Examples include the break-up of marine snow in the mesopelagic zone by zooplankton (e.g. Mayor et al., 2014) and the action of Porifera in conversion of dissolved organic matter to particulate organic matter on coral reefs (e.g. de Goeij et al., 2013; Figure 12.3a). Invertebrates can also represent important mesopredators in marine ecosystems including Cephalopoda (especially squid; Figure 12.1b) in the pelagic realm and decapod Crustacea (e.g. lobsters) in benthic habitats. These can exert significant control on prey populations and often form part of the response of ecosystem cascades resulting from human disturbance to pelagic (e.g. the North Pacific Humboldt

Figure 12.3 (a) Brown tube sponge (*Agelas tubulata*), island of Utila, Honduras, Caribbean. (b) *Holothuria* cf *arguinensis*, rocky shore, Lanzerote, Canary Islands, Northeast Atlantic (AD Rogers).

squid, *Doscidicus gigas*, Zeidberg and Robison, 2007) and benthic ecosystems (e.g. lobsters, shrimp and crab in the NW Atlantic; Worm and Myers, 2003). Invertebrate parasites can also exert important controls on the population dynamics of other species in marine ecosystems (e.g. Marcogliese, 2002).

As well as exerting their effects through food-web interactions, marine invertebrates are also significant ecosystem engineers (Jones et al., 1994). These organisms may influence the physical structure of the marine environment (structural engineers), creating living space for other species, reducing disturbance and altering physical properties such as hydrodynamics, sedimentation and light availability (Berke, 2010). Alternatively, they may influence the properties of ecosystems through their presence or activities, including alterations in light, biogeochemistry, mixing of sediment and turbidity of the water (e.g. bioturbators, light and chemical engineers; Berke, 2010). The most dramatic examples of marine invertebrates as ecosystem engineers are the animal forests they form. These include coral reefs, other coralligenous habitats (e.g. cold-water coral reefs or coral gardens), vermetid reefs, oyster reefs (and other bivalve reefs), serpulid reefs and sponge grounds (Gutiérrez et al., 2003; Paoli et al., 2017). It is estimated that coral reefs are the most species-rich ecosystems in the ocean (e.g. Fisher et al., 2015) and many other animal forests are also characterised by high local diversity (Paoli et al., 2017).

The important functions that invertebrates perform in marine ecosystems means that they are also important in terms of the services they provide to humankind. Ecosystem services are 'the benefits people obtain from ecosystems' (Millennium Ecosystem Assessment, 2005; MA). This is a concept elaborated in the IPBES Global Assessment on Biodiversity and Ecosystem Services (IPBES, 2019) as Nature's Contribution to People (NCP), the positive and negative contributions of living nature to people's lives. Positive benefits (a subset of NCP) include: provisioning services, the production of goods and materials such as food, raw materials and pharmaceuticals, regulatory services, the control of climate, atmosphere and other aspects of the environment that maintain the Earth system, supporting services, those that enable the provision of direct and indirect ecosystem services to humankind, and cultural services, including recreation, tourism, inspiration for art, culture, spiritual experience and cognitive development (De Groot et al., 2012; Costanza et al., 2014; Barbier, 2017).

Marine invertebrates are major contributors to provisioning services, both through capture fisheries and aquaculture. The Humboldt squid (747,010 t), Gazami crab (*Portunus trituberculatus*; 557,728 t) and Akiami paste shrimp (*Acetes japonicus* 531,847 t) are amongst the top 25 species caught in the ocean (FAO, 2018, based on 2016 figures). Many groups of invertebrates with significant fisheries production, including gastropods, crabs, lobsters and shrimps are high value per unit biomass harvested (FAO, 2018). In terms of aquaculture production of marine animals, Crustacea, Mollusca and other invertebrates are currently more than three times as important as finfish (>22 million tonnes versus 6.5 million tonnes; FAO, 2018, based on 2016 figures). Coral reefs perform a range of provisioning (e.g. fisheries), regulatory (atmospheric regulation), supporting (habitat provision) and cultural services (e.g. tourism). They are also important in terms of coastal protection. The economic value of services provided to people by coral reefs globally has been estimated at $9.9 trillion, US (Costanza et al., 2014). There are also many regional to local valuations (e.g. Great Barrier Reef - $56 billion, considering a limited range of ecosystem services, Deloitte Access Economics, 2017), as well as sector-specific valuations (e.g. tourism, >$35 billion globally, Spalding et al., 2017) of ecosystem service provision by coral reefs. Marine invertebrates, especially the Porifera and Cnidaria, but also other groups such as Mollusca, are also the most important sources for marine bioproducts including compounds with anticancer, antibacterial, anti-inflammatory, antifungal, antiviral and analetic properties (Martins et al., 2014; Blasiak et al., 2020).

Therefore, although often not recognised, marine invertebrates are critical in the structure and function of marine ecosystems through their effects on food webs and other interactions with biotic and abiotic components. As such, they exert a significant influence on the Earth system through their impacts on global biogeochemical cycles. They also provide a range of important ecosystem services from which humans benefit, ranging from food provision, coastal protection and tourism to the discovery of new drugs and other useful biocompounds.

12.3 The State of Knowledge of Marine Invertebrates and Implications for Understanding Conservation Status

The numbers of species undescribed has been estimated through a variety of methods from using expert opinion (e.g. Appeltans et al., 2012) to examining patterns of assignment of species to phylum, class, order, family and genus, which can be used to estimate the total number of species in a taxon (e.g. Mora et al., 2011). These studies suggest that somewhere between 10% and a third of marine species have been described (Mora et al., 2011; Appeltans et al., 2012). Examination of the patterns of described species versus estimated global species richness in the ocean reveals that on the whole vertebrate groups are well described, with 77% of taxa described (Pisces including Agnatha) to an estimated 100% (Carnivora and Sirenia; Appeltans et al., 2012; see also Scheffers et al., 2012). Marine invertebrates are much less studied and their diversity can be much higher than vertebrate groups, with as few as 3% of the estimated number of species in the ocean described (e.g. Loricifera and Tantulocarida; Appeltans et al., 2012). Within the invertebrates, taxa with relatively few species (e.g. the crustacean groups Lomisoidea, 1 species or Euphausiacea, 86 species) or those which are relatively large and obvious in the marine environment (e.g. Echinodermata) are relatively well described (Appeltans et al., 2012). Groups with fewer than 20% of species described include a wide range of taxa with a small body size, including the Cycliophora and Loricifera, various groups of peracarid crustaceans and the Nematoda (Appeltans et al., 2012). For these groups, typically hundreds of species remain undescribed, though for some this runs into the tens of thousands or even more than a hundred thousand including the Isopoda (63,150–123,600 species), the Gastropoda (85,000–105,000 species) and Nematoda (50,000 species; Appeltans et al., 2012). Invertebrate groups with relatively few morphological characters, such as the

Hydrozoa and Nemertea are prone to cryptic speciation (species only distinguishable using molecular methods) creating further problems in distinguishing taxa (e.g. Moura et al., 2008; Krämer et al., 2017).

The knowledge deficit of marine invertebrates is relevant as it influences discussions on the current status and trends over time of marine invertebrate species. Analysis of Red List assessments indicates that they have focused on relatively well-described taxa for both marine and terrestrial species (Webb and Mindel, 2015). To date, significant Red List assessments have only been undertaken on shallow-water Cnidaria (mainly stony corals and hydrocorals), Holothuria (sea cucumbers), Mollusca (bivalves, gastropods and cephalopods) and Crustacea (see Table 12.2). For many of these groups, only a small fraction of species has been assessed (e.g. Bivalvia <1%, Gastropoda ~ 2%, Malacostraca <1%; based on numbers of species in the WORMS Register of Marine Species). The only marine groups to have been comprehensively assessed to any degree are the shallow-water Scleractinia (all zooxanthellate stony corals assessed) and the Cephalopoda (octopus, squid, cuttlefish and nautiluses; ~85% of species) with the Holothuria falling to ~20% of species having been assessed (all figures based on numbers of species in the WORMS Register of Marine Species).

12.4 The Current Threat Status of Marine Invertebrates

The summary statistics for Red List assessed marine invertebrate taxa indicate that to date the number of recorded extinctions has been low (four species of Gastropoda; Table 12.2). This is consistent with overall observations of low levels of extinction in marine taxa in general compared to those on land (total marine extinctions including vertebrates and invertebrates = 15 in the last 500 years compared to >500 on land; McCauley et al., 2015). Examining the overall proportion of species within assessed groups that are threatened with extinction (Critically Endangered, Endangered or Vulnerable) gives a range of <1% (Cephalopods) to 26% (Anthozoa, mainly zooxanthellate corals) with other taxa falling between (Holothuroidea 4%, Gastropoda 6%; Table 12.2). However, of these groups, only the Anthozoa and the Cephalopods have been comprehensively assessed and the Holothuroidea have moderate levels of assessment. It is notable that for the Holothuroidea and Cephalopoda there are a high proportion of assessed species categorised as Data Deficient, in other words there are insufficient data for an effective Red List assessment (66% and 55% of species in these groups respectively are rated as Data Deficient). Discarding the Data Deficient species and recalculating the proportion of species threatened with extinction raises the figures to 33% for Anthozoa, 13% for Holothuroidea, 8% for Gastropoda and 1.6% for Cephalopoda. For well-assessed groups of marine and non-marine species, the proportion of threatened species generally lies between 20% and 25% (Webb and Mindel, 2015). The proportion of threatened species of Anthozoa is therefore very high, at a third of all assessed species (see Carpenter et al., 2008). In contrast, the Cephalopoda show a very low level of threat with other, less comprehensively assessed taxa somewhere in between.

Table 12.2 *Summary statistics for marine invertebrate groups which have undergone some level of Red List assessment*

Phylum	Class	Extinct	Critically Endangered	Endangered	Vulnerable	Near Threatened	Least Concern	Data Deficient	Total
Cnidaria	Anthozoa		6	26	202	175	293	166	868
Cnidaria	Hydrozoa		1	2	2	1	8	2	16
Echinodermata	Holothuroidea			7	9		111	244	371
Mollusca	Bivalvia				4		29	20	53
Mollusca	Cephalopoda		1	2	2	1	304	376	686
Mollusca	Gastropoda	4	6	14	30	26	567	184	831
Arthropoda	Malacostraca		2	1	1	2	163	87	256
Total in category		4	16	52	250	205	1475	1079	3081
Total % of species assessed		0.1%	0.5%	1.7%	8%	7%	48%	35%	

Based on data from Rogers et al. (2020).

The paucity of information on marine invertebrate species and lack of comprehensive Red List assessments is a significant barrier to understanding any overall trends in extinction or extinction threat for these animals. Even for the Anthozoa (mainly zooxanthellate, shallow, reef-forming corals), data are based on a single assessment (Carpenter et al., 2008). However, data are consistent with the suggestion that coastal marine species may be more at risk of extinction than oceanic taxa (Webb and Mindel, 2015). It is notable that many Cephalopoda are offshore/oceanic, which may partially explain the low observed extinction risk, but this suggestion is limited by the number of Data Deficient species.

12.5 Drivers of Extinction Risk in Marine Invertebrates

Coral reefs are mainly coastal ecosystems located close to human populations, easily accessible and exposed to multiple direct and indirect anthropogenic stressors (e.g. Carpenter et al., 2008). Whilst there has been a significant focus on the global climate change threats to reef-forming corals, especially the increased occurrence of mass coral bleaching driven by increasing sea surface temperatures (e.g. Hughes et al., 2018) it is apparent from examining the Red List assessment for Anthozoa and Hydrozoa that there are multiple local drivers of extinction threat (Table 12.3, Figures 12.4, 12.5a). Threats range from the effects of coastal development, sedimentation resulting from poor land use and watershed management, sewage discharges, nutrient loading from run-off of agro-chemicals causing eutrophication, coral mining, the collection of corals for the aquarium trade, overfishing of reef-associated biota driving ecological cascades, other forms of human disturbance, outbreaks of disease epidemics, invasion by non-native species and damage from vessels (e.g. Rosenberg et al., 2007; Carpenter et al., 2008; Albins and Hixon, 2013; Raymundo et al., 2018; Bellwood et al., 2019). Many of these stressors, both global and local, interact often additively or synergistically (Pendleton et al., 2016). Because scientific studies have generally focused on a single/small number of species and single drivers of coral stress the prediction of future changes in coral reef distribution, structure and species composition is extremely difficult (Pendleton et al., 2016). Under current projections of future climate change direct, indirect and interactive stresses on reefs from further temperature rise, ocean acidification, sea level rise are set to increase (e.g. van Hooidonk et al., 2016; Perry et al., 2018), leading to projections of a loss of 70–90% of reefs at 1.5 °C of temperature rise to >99% at 2.0 °C of temperature rise (IPCC, 2018). Given that a third of all shallow-water reef-forming corals are already under threat of extinction, this may indicate that this group may be one of the most threatened on Earth. The estimated occurrence of up to a third of all other marine species on coral reefs (Fisher et al., 2015) is therefore a major concern as habitat loss will likely impact many of these, posing a significant extinction risk.

Only a fraction of Gastropoda have been assessed with the genus *Conus* (the cone shells; Figure 12.5b) representing the majority of these, explaining to some extent why they are proportionately the most threatened group observed within the taxon. These animals are threatened by habitat loss arising from coastal development and pollution as well as human disturbance, including the destructive effects of fishing (Table 12.3,

Table 12.3 *Drivers of extinction in threatened species of marine invertebrates (Critically Endangered, Endangered and Vulnerable)*

Taxon (No. of threatened species)	Anthozoa (226)	Hydrozoa (5)	Holothuroidea (16)	Gastropoda (58)	Cephalopoda (5)
Threat					
Residential and commercial development	222	5		20	
Biological resource use	222	5	15	37	5
Pollution	221	5	1	25	
Transport and service corridors	221	5		3	
Invasive species, genes and diseases	221	5	1	4	
Climate change and severe weather	224	5		2	
Human intrusions and disturbance	221	5	1	10	
Agriculture and aquaculture				2	
Energy production and mining				1	
Natural systems modification				5	

Note that a species may have more than one driver of extinction risk so columns do not add up to the total number of threatened species. Based on data from Rogers et al. (2020).

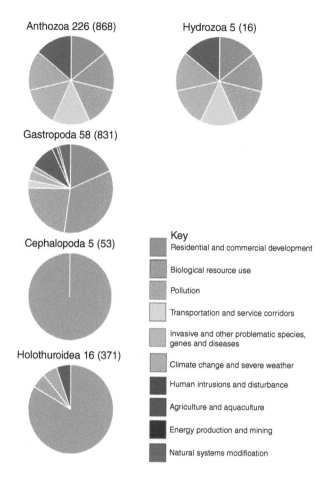

Figure 12.4 Graphic representation of the drivers of extinction risk in marine invertebrate species which are threatened with extinction (Critically Endangered, Endangered, Vulnerable; Rogers et al., 2020).

Figure 12.5 (a) The Endangered scleractinian coral *Orbicella faveolata* from the island of Utila, Honduras, Caribbean. (b) *Conus ventricosus*, Lanzerote, Canary Islands, Northeast Atlantic. The genus includes a high proportion of threatened species (AD Rogers).

Figure 12.4; Peters et al., 2013). This is exacerbated by the extremely small geographic range exhibited by some species (e.g. endemic to single islands in the Cape Verdes; Peters et al., 2013). Cone shells are also intensively exploited for the marine curio trade, shell collecting and for research purposes (Chivian et al., 2003), the latter because conotoxins are a rich source of bioproducts (Martins et al., 2014). All of the Critically Endangered and Endangered species of *Conus* are from Cape Verde and Senegal in West Africa (Peters et al., 2013). The Cape Verde Islands are home to 8.9% of all described *Conus* species, with 53 out of 56 species endemic (Peters et al., 2013). The Cape Verde Islands are undergoing significant economic and social change, with the switch from dependency on fisheries, service industries and developmental aid to coastal tourism (Peters et al., 2013). This switch has been associated with coastal development and road building, and other activites such as illegal sand mining from beaches which impact coastal species like cone shells (Peters et al., 2013).

Other threatened Gastropoda include species of *Haliotis* (abalones) which are highly valued as luxury food items and have been severely overexploited in many parts of the world. There are also a range of marine coastal/supratidal gastropods, also largely threatened as a result of habitat loss. The first deep-sea hydrothermal vent organism, the scaly-foot snail, *Chrysomallon squamiferum*, has also been categorised as threatened because of its extremely small and fragmented population size, based on observations to date and the impending threat of seabed massive sulfide mining at these locations (Sigwart et al., 2019; see also Thomas et al., 2021a, 2021b). Whilst a number of hydrothermal vents have been licensed in the high seas for mining exploration (see: www.isa.org.jm/deep-seabed-minerals-contractors?qt-contractors_tabs_alt=1#qt-contractors_tabs_alt), no commercial mining has taken place to date.

All of the cephalopods at risk of extinction are cirrate octopus which are caught as bycatch in deep-water bottom trawl fisheries (Table 12.3, Figure 12.4). These animals live close to the seabed, they are relatively long-lived, slow growing and exhibit a low fecundity (Collins and Villanueva, 2006), meaning that they have high vulnerability and low level of resilience to bottom trawling.

Holothurians (sea cucumbers; Figure 12.3b) of the families Holothuridae and Stichopodidae have been fished in the Indo-Pacific for more than 1000 years (Bruckner et al., 2003). However, the growing demand for Beche de mer (trepang or Hoi som) prepared from the dried body wall of sea cucumbers primarily as a delicacy or traditional medicine for the Chinese market has driven increased demand over the last 40 years and especially over the last two decades (Purcell et al., 2014; Eriksson and Clarke, 2015; Conand, 2018). This has led to significant overexploitation of populations, first in the southwest Pacific, but following decline of these fisheries, a subsequent expansion across the world including to areas such as the western Indian Ocean, Caribbean, South America (Bruckner et al., 2003; Anderson et al., 2010; Conand, 2018) and even Europe (González-Wangüemert et al., 2018). The large tropical, shallow-water Holothuria are high value, easy to catch and susceptible to overexploitation because they are late to mature, rates of recruitment are low and they exhibit density-dependent reproduction, which renders them vulnerable to the allee effect (Bruckner et al., 2003; Uthicke et al., 2004; Purcell et al., 2014). Initially, many holothurian fisheries were not managed, and many remain unregulated, but even where regulation has been introduced, illegal fishing has been driven by the high prices fetched on the market (Bruckner et al., 2003; Conand, 2018). Therefore, overexploitation is the overwhelming driver of extinction risk in Holothuria (Table 12.3, Figure 12.4), although some species are also affected by climate change impacts and pollution. Efforts to culture sea cucumbers have also led to overcollecting of at least one species for brood stock.

The decline, protection or restrictive management of marine finfish fisheries is thought to have contributed to the increased exploitation of marine invertebrates over past decades with the catch increasing six-fold and number of species exploited doubling since 1950 (Anderson et al., 2011; Eddy et al., 2017). As with the Holothuria, many invertebrate marine fisheries are unregulated or poorly regulated, and there is little idea about the ecological roles or effects of removals of such species on the broader marine ecosystems of which they are part (Anderson et al., 2011; Eddy et al., 2017).

12.6 Mitigation of Extinction Risks to Marine Invertebrates

12.6.1 Lack of Relevant Data

A major barrier to more effective conservation of marine invertebrates is the lack of data on species, their distribution and trends in population status. Put simply, without data on what species of marine invertebrates are present and monitoring of changes in their populations, identifying when species are at risk of extinction is not possible. Both the lack of assessed marine invertebrate groups or species within groups and the number of species within assessed groups categorised as Data Deficient indicate that there is a large knowledge deficit on the threat status for the majority of groups of marine invertebrates (Table 12.2), including those likely to be at risk of extinction (e.g. reef-associated coral and non-coral invertebrates). Coastal States are committed to the monitoring of their bio-diversity through a number of international conventions and agreements, including: the Convention on Wetlands of International Importance especially as Waterfowl Habitat (RAMSAR; 1971), the Convention on International Trade in Endangered Species of Wild Flora and Fauna (CITES; 1973; listed species only) and especially the Convention on Biological Diversity (CBD; 1992). Other international conventions such as the UN Convention on the Law of the Sea (UNCLOS; 1982) and its Implementing Agreements also imply monitoring of commercially exploited species for the purposes of sustainable management, as well as non-target species associated with fisheries so that their reproductive capacity is not significantly affected. Such monitoring should be undertaken by coastal States for their own waters or by fishing States in the case of areas beyond national jurisdiction (ABNJ), where fisheries are subject to management through regional fisheries management organisations (RFMOs). Added to this are regional agreements which may be relevant to biodiversity conservation (e.g. the Oslo Paris Commission aimed at protecting and conserving the North East Atlantic), as well as national legislation.

More focus and more resources are required for assessment of marine invertebrates both in coastal waters and ABNJ. There is a need for the development of adequate inventories of the species present in coastal and oceanic waters to establish baselines from which changes in populations can then be monitored. Such an effort could focus on the already established networks for biodiversity monitoring, including GOOS BioEco (Global Ocean Observing System Biology and Ecosystems Panel; www.goosocean.org/index .php?option=com_content&view=article&id=79&Itemid=273) and the marine component of The Group on Earth Observation Biodiversity Observation Network (GEO BON), MBON (Marine Biodiversity Observation Network; https://marinebon.org/). The latter has already developed a globally coordinated strategy for monitoring biodiversity change using Essential Biodiversity Variables (EBVs) and a system of coordinated Biodiversity Observation Networks (BONs), and data repositories already exist to receive such information (e.g. the Ocean Biogeographic Information System; Navarro et al., 2018). There is also a need to increase data-gathering capacity for catch and bycatch of marine invertebrates in fisheries management organisations/institutions globally. More focus on conservation of biodiversity as a component of ecosystem-based management is required from such organisations, which will in turn need the inclusion of scientific capacity within relevant scientific committees or advisory bodies. A good example of this is the information on biodiversity issues provided by the International Council for the Exploration of the Sea (ICES) through its Expert Groups (e.g. Ecosystem Processes and Dynamics Steering Group and constituent Expert Groups; www.ices.dk/about-ICES/ how-we-work/Pages/default.aspx) to the European Commission and the North East Atlantic Fisheries Commission (NEAFC; www.neafc.org/).

12.6.2 Coral Reefs

Coral reefs are probably the most threatened ecosystem on Earth and reef-forming corals one of the groups of organisms at greatest extinction risk (e.g. *Orbicella faveolata*, Figure 12.5a; Table 12.2). Reducing CO_2 emissions is key to securing the future of coral reefs (Hoegh-Guldberg et al., 2018; IPCC, 2018). Furthermore, the greater the level of climate change the planet experiences, the more limited are the available adaptation measures in terms of management (Gattuso et al., 2015). However, coral reefs are also challenged by a range of regional to local stressors which contribute to extinction risk in the corals themselves (Table 12.3; Figure 12.4). A greater understanding of the full range of stressors on coral reefs, their relative importance, how they interact, the scales over which they operate and how they are changing is required if management actions to address them are to be developed (Wear, 2016; Hughes et al., 2017; Bellwood et al., 2019; Williams et al., 2019). Ultimately, drivers of extinction risk in corals at global to local levels relate to socioeconomic factors, so it is critical that the behaviour of human society is taken into account in terms of stress on reef ecosystems (Hughes et al., 2017; Williams et al., 2019). Many solutions to the coral reef crisis have been discussed and there is insufficient room in the present chapter to enter into a detailed discussion of these. However, several actions are emphasised in the literature, including:

- Building more effective governance to take action across geographic scales to conserve coral reefs. This includes adequately funding international and national efforts to reduce stressors on coral reef ecosystems, as well as strengthening institutions and capacity in science, policy and management for reef conservation (e.g. Hughes et al., 2017; Hoegh-Guldberg et al., 2018; Bellwood et al., 2019).

- Building partnerships between civil society, governments and industry to improve the governance and management of coral reefs at regional to local scales (e.g. Hughes et al., 2017; Bellwood et al., 2019).
- Ecosystem manipulation including active ecosystem interventions. These may include activities such as assisted evolution, assisted migration, coral propagation and replanting on reefs and repair of key ecosystem processes such as herbivory (e.g. Hughes et al., 2017; Hoegh-Guldberg et al., 2018; Bellwood et al., 2019).
- Focus of coral reef conservation activities on a network of localities which have been identified as having a high resilience to projected future climate change impacts (e.g. Hoegh-Guldberg et al., 2018).
- A redefinition of management goals to preserve the ecosystem functions and ecosystem service provision of reef ecosystems (Hughes et al., 2017; Bellwood et al., 2019).

We would point out that the final of these strategies may be associated with a high risk of extinction of 'redundant' species and so poses significant risk for biodiversity. Focusing on a range of resilient coral reefs across a range of geographical areas would appear to have the potential for maximising species conservation. However, should ocean warming continue and coral reef ecosystems progressively decline further, all surviving reef ecosystems will become a priority for conservation.

We would also point out that the vast majority of reef surveys and monitoring programmes currently focus on estimates of coral cover, coral health and reef fish biomass (e.g. Bellwood et al., 2019). Consistent with Section 12.6.1, a greater effort is required to monitor a broad range of reef invertebrates, as many of these may also be subject to extinction risk as a result of the stressors that are affecting coral reefs from global to local levels.

12.6.3 Invertebrate Fisheries

As stated above, there is evidence that fisheries targeting marine invertebrates have undergone a considerable expansion in terms of catch, range of species targeted and geographic areas exploited since 1950 (Anderson et al., 2011). Many of these fisheries are unregulated, with the result that unrecognised overexploitation of populations and/or species has taken place with little or no effective management interventions (Anderson et al., 2011). These fisheries are geographically dispersed, may be located in the waters of developing countries with low capacity for fisheries management and often the distances between where species are captured and where they are processed and marketed are large (Anderson et al., 2010, 2011; Conand, 2018). They are also often small, at a local scale, rendering them uneconomic for conventional science-based fisheries management approaches. Fisheries for marine invertebrates must be better recognised, especially given their potential vulnerability to overfishing (Anderson et al., 2011; Eddy et al., 2017).

New participatory fisheries assessment methods based on indicators such as trends in catch per unit effort, length frequency of caught fish, information on life history attributes etc. (data-poor stock assessment methods; Hilborn and Ovando, 2014) may be more appropriate to such fisheries (Ye and Gutierrez, 2017). Technologies, such as mobile-phone apps may be extremely useful as tools for recording catch in such fisheries. Given that many of these fisheries are small-scale coastal fisheries (especially those affecting groups like the Holothuroidea), community-based fisheries management is likely to be highly effective (e.g. Karr et al., 2017). However, international cooperation is needed both to recognise the scale and nature of such fisheries and to provide capacity and financial assistance for management of such fisheries (Ye and Gutierrez, 2017). This is especially the case where fisheries are taking place in developing countries, but catches are exported to developed countries (Ye and Gutierrez, 2017).

12.7 Concluding Remarks

Marine invertebrates contribute to the structure and function of marine ecosystems underpinning many ecosystem functions and services to humankind. They remain neglected in terms of recognition of their ecological importance and contribution to the Earth's biodiversity. We have surveyed current understanding of extinction threat in marine invertebrates and find that they are inadequately represented in Red List assessments. Even for the few groups of species which have undergone substantive assessments, a large proportion of species remain Data Deficient. The existing assessments indicate that at least one group of marine invertebrates has an exceptionally high proportion of threatened species (reef-forming corals) and there is no evidence that extinction threat overall for marine invertebrates may be any less than for terrestrial species. A dramatically increased effort is required to establish baselines of marine invertebrate populations to enable monitoring of future changes in their status. This is fundamental to addressing the manifestation of the global extinction crisis in the ocean. Marine invertebrates can exhibit biological features that render them highly vulnerable to extinction. It is therefore important to identify the full range of drivers of extinction threat in these animals and to address them through specific management actions coordinated across geographic scales. We have identified coastal development and other forms of habitat destruction, pollution, overexploitation and climate change as the main drivers of extinction risk in marine invertebrates.

References

Albins, M.A. and Hixon, M.A. (2013) Worst case scenario: potential long-term effects of invasive predatory lionfish (*Pterois volitans*) on Atlantic and Caribbean coral-reef communities. *Environ Biol Fish* 96: 1151–1157.

Anderson, S.C., Mills Flemming, J., Watson, R. and Lotze, H.K. (2010) Serial exploitation of global sea cucumber fisheries. *Fish Fish* 12: 317–339.

Anderson, S.C., Mills Flemming, J., Watson, R. and Lotze, H.K. (2011) Rapid global expansion of invertebrate fisheries: trends, drivers, and ecosystem effects. *PLoS One* 6: e14735.

Appeltans, W., Ahjong, S.T., Anderson, G., et al. (2012) The magnitude of global marine species diversity. *Curr Biol* 22: 2189–2202.

Barbier, E.B. (2017) Marine ecosystem services. *Curr Biol* 27: R507–R510.

Bar-On, Y.M., Philips, R. and Milo, R. (2018) The biomass distribution on Earth. *Proc Natl Acad Sci USA* 115: 6506–6511.

Beaugrand, G. (2015) *Marine Biodiversity, Climate Variability and Global Change*. Abingdon, UK: Earthscan from Routledge.

Bellwood, D.R., Pratchett, M.S., Morrison, T.H., et al. (2019) Coral reef conservation in the Anthropocene: Confronting spatial mismatches and prioritizing functions. *Biol Conserv* 236: 604–615.

Berke, S.K. (2010) Functional groups of ecosystem engineers: a proposed classification with comments on current issues. *Integr Comp Biol* 50: 147–157.

Blasiak, R., Wynberg, R., Grorud-Colvert, K. (2020) The ocean genome and future prospects for conservation and equity. *Nat Sustain* 3: 588–596.

Bruckner, A.W., Johnson, K.A. and Field, J.D. (2003) Conservation strategies for sea cucumbers: can a CITES Appendix II listing promote sustainable international trade? *SPC Beche-de-mer Inf Bull* 18: 24–33.

Brusca, R.C. and Brusca, G.J. (1990) *Invertebrates*. Sunderland, MA: Sinauer Associates.

Carpenter, K.E., Abrar, M., Aeby, G., et al. (2008) One-third of reef-building corals face elevated extinction risk from climate change and local impacts. *Science* 321: 560–563.

Chivian, E., Roberts, C.M. and Bernstein, A.S. (2003) The threat to cone snails. *Science* 302: 391.

Collins, M.A. and Villanueva, R. (2006) Taxonomy, ecology and behaviour of the cirrate octopods. *Oceanogr Mar Biol* 44: 277–322.

Conand, C. (2018) Tropical sea cucumber fisheries: changes during the last decade. *Mar Pollut Bull* 133: 590–594.

Costanza, R., de Groot, R., Sutton, P., et al. (2014) Changes in the global value of ecosystem services. *Glob Environ Chang* 26: 152–158.

Costello, M.J., Wilson, S. and Houlding, B. (2012) Predicting total global species richness using rates of species description and estimates of taxonomic effort. *Syst Biol* 61: 871–883.

Cunningham, J.A., Liu, A.G., Bengston, S. and Donoghue, P.C.J. (2016) The origin of animals: can molecular clocks and the fossil record be reconciled? *Bioessays* 39: 1–12.

Danavaro, R., Dell'Anno, A., Pusceddu, A., et al. (2010) The first metazoa living in permanently anoxic conditions. *BMC Biology* 8: 30.

de Goeij, J.M., van Oevelen, D., Vermeij, M.J.A., et al. (2013) Surviving in a marine desert: the sponge loop retains resources within coral reefs. *Science* 342: 108–110.

De Groot, R., Brander, L., van der Ploeg, S., et al. (2012) Global estimates of the value of ecosystems and their services in monetary units. *Ecosyst Serv* 1: 50–61.

Deloitte Access Economics (2017) *At What Price? The Economic, Social and Icon Value of the Great Barrier Reef*. Brisbane, Australia: Deloitte Access Economics.

Eddy, T.D., Lotzke, H.K., Fulton, E.A., et al. (2017) Ecosystem effects of invertebrate fisheries. *Fish Fish* 18: 40–53.

Eriksson, H. and Clarke, S. (2015) Chinese market responses to overexploitation of sharks and sea cucumbers. *Biol Conserv* 184: 163–173.

FAO (2018) *The State of World Fisheries and Aquaculture 2018 - Meeting the Sustainable Development Goals*. Rome, Italy: United Nations Food and Agricultural Programme.

Fisher, R., O'Leary, R.A., Low-Choy, S., et al. (2015) Species richness on coral reefs and the pursuit of convergent global estimates. *Curr Biol* 25: 500–505.

Gattuso, J.-P., Magnan, A., Billé, R., et al. (2015) Risks of warming and acidification for oceans and society. *Science* 349: aac4722.

Gili, J.-M. and Coma, R. (1998) Benthic suspension feeders: their paramount role in littoral marine food webs. *Trends Ecol Evol* 13: 316–321.

González-Wangüemert, M., Domínguez-Godino, J.A. and Cánovas, F. (2018) The fast development of sea cucumber fisheries in the Mediterranean and NE Atlantic waters: from a new marine resource to its over-exploitation. *Ocean Coastal Manag* 151: 165–177.

Gutiérrez, J.L., Jones, C.G., Strayer, D.L. and Iribarne, O.O. (2003) Mollusks as ecosystem engineers: the role of shell production in aquatic habitats. *Oikos* 101:79–90.

Haddock, S.H.D., Moline, M.A. and Case, J.F. (2009) Bioluminescence in the sea. *Ann Rev Mar Sci* 2: 443–493.

Hilborn, R. and Ovando, D. (2014) Reflections on the success of traditional fisheries management. *ICES J Mar Sci* 71: 1040–1046.

Hoegh-Guldberg, O., Kennedy, E.V., Beyer, H.L., McClennan, C. and Possingham, H.P. (2018) Securing a long-term future for coral reefs. *Trends Ecol Evol* 33: 936–944.

Hughes, T.P., Barnes, M.L., Bellwood, D.R., et al. (2017) Coral reefs in the Anthropocene. *Nature* 546: 82–90.

Hughes, T.P., Kerry, J.T., Baird, A.H., et al. (2018) Global warming transforms coral reef assemblages. *Nature* 556: 492–496.

IPBES (2019) *Summary for Policymakers of the IPBES Global Assessment Report on Biodiversity and Ecosystem Services*. Bonn, Germany: Intergovernmental Science-Policy Platform on Biodiversity and Ecosystem Services (IPBES).

IPCC. (2018) *Global Warming of 1.5 °C*. An IPCC Special Report on the impacts of global warming of 1.5°C above pre-industrial levels and related global greenhouse gas emission pathways, in the context of strengthening the global response to the threat of climate change, sustainable development, and efforts to eradicate poverty. Masson-Delmotte, V., Zhai, P., Pörtner, H.-O., et al. (Eds.). Geneva, Switzerland: International Panel on Climate Change.

Jamieson, A. (2015) *The Hadal Zone: Life in the Deepest Oceans*. Cambridge, UK: Cambridge University Press.

Jones, C.G., Lawton, J.H. and Shachak, M. (1994) Organisms as ecosystem engineers. *Oikos* 69: 373–386.

Karr, K.A., Fujita, R., Carcamo, R., et al. (2017) Integrating science-based co-management, partnerships, participatory processes and stewardship incentives to improve the performance of small-scale fisheries. *Front Mar Sci* 4: 345.

Krämer, D., Schmidt, C., Podsiadlowski, L., et al. (2017) Unravelling the *Lineus ruber/viridis* species complex (Nemertea, Heteronemertea). *Zool Scr* 46: 111–126.

Lalli, C.M. and Gilmer, R.W. (1989) *Pelagic Snails: The Biology of Holoplanktonic Gastropod Mollusks*. Stanford, CA: Stanford University Press.

Lebrato, M., Pahlow, M., Frost, J.R. and Küter, M. (2019) Sinking of gelatinous zooplankton biomass increases deep carbon transfer efficiency globally. *Glob Biogeochem Cycles* 33: 1764–1783.

Little, C.W., Williams, G.A. and Trowbridge, C.D. (2009) *The Biology of Rocky Shores*, Second Edn. Oxford, UK: Oxford University Press.

Lucas, C.H., Jones, D.O.B., Hollyhead, C.J., et al. (2014) Gelatinous zooplankton biomass in the global oceans: geographic variation and environmental drivers. *Glob Ecol Biogeogr* 23: 701–714.

Marcogliese, D.J. (2002) Food webs and the transmission of parasites to marine fish. *Parasitology* 124: S83–S99.

Martins, A., Vieira, H., Gaspar, H. and Santos, S. (2014) Marketed marine natural products in the pharmaceutical and cosmeceutical industries: tips for success. *Mar Drugs* 12: 1066–1101.

May, R.M. (1988) How many species are there on Earth? *Science* 241: 1441–1449.

May, R.M. (1994) Biological diversity: differences between land and sea. *Phil Trans Royal Soc B* 343: 105–111.

Mayor, D.J., Sanders, R., Giering, S.L.C. and Anderson, T.R. (2014) Microbial gardening in the ocean's twilight zone: detritivorous metazoans benefit from fragmenting, rather than ingesting, sinking detritus. *Bioessays* 36: 1132–1137.

McCauley, D.J., Pinsky, M.L., Palumbi, S.R., et al. (2015) Marine defaunation: animal loss in the global ocean. *Science* 347: 1255641.

Millennium Ecosystem Assessment. (2005) *Ecosystems and Human Well-Being: Biodiversity Synthesis*. Washington, DC: World Resources Institute.

Mora, C., Tittensor, D.P., Adl, S., Simpson, A.G.B. and Worm, B. (2011) How many species are there on earth and in the ocean? *PLoS Biol* 9: e1001127.

Moura, C.J., Harris, D.J., Cunha, M.R. and Rogers, A.D. (2008) DNA barcoding reveals cryptic diversity in marine hydroids (Cnidaria, Hydrozoa) from coastal and deep-sea environments *Zool Scr* 37: 93–108.

Murphy, E.J., Watkins, J.L., Trathan, P.N., et al. (2012) Spatial and temporal operation of the Scotia Sea ecosystem. In: Rogers, A.D., Johnston, N.M.,

Murphy, E.J., Clarke, A. (Eds.), *Antarctic Ecosystems: An Extreme Environment in a Changing World*. Oxford, UK: Wiley-Blackwell.

Navarro, L.M., Fernández, N., Guerra, C., et al. (2018) Monitoring biodiversity change through effective global coordination. *Curr Opin Environ Sustain* 29: 158–169.

Oliveira, O. de S., Read, V.M. St. J. and Mayer, G. (2012) A world checklist of Onychophora (velvet worms), with notes on nomenclature and status of names. *ZooKeys* 211: 1–70.

Paoli, C., Montefalcone, M., Morri, C., Vassallo, P. and Bianchi, C.N. (2017) Ecosystem functions and services of the marine animal forests. In: Rossi, S., Bramanti, L., Gori, A., Orejas, C. (Eds.), *Marine Animal Forests: The Ecology of Benthic Biodiversity Hotspots*. Cham, Switzerland: Springer International Publishing AG.

Pendleton, L.H., Hoegh-Guldberg, O., Langdon, C. and Comte, A. (2016) Multiple stressors and ecological complexity require a new approach to coral reef research. *Front Mar Sci* 3: 36.

Perry, C.T., Alvarez-Filip, L., Graham, N.A.J., et al. (2018) Loss of coral reef growth capacity to track future increases in sea level. *Nature* 558: 396–400.

Peters, H., O'Leary, B.C., Hawkins, J.P., Carpenter, K.E. and Roberts, C.M. (2013) *Conus*: first comprehensive conservation red list assessment of a marine gastropod mollusc genus. *PLoS One* 8: e83353.

Purcell, S.W., Polidoro, B.A., Hamel, J.-F., Gamboa, R.U. and Mercier, A. (2014) The cost of being valuable: predictors of extinction risk in marine invertebrates exploited as luxury seafood. *Proc Royal Soc B* 281: 20133296.

Raymont, J.E.G. (1983) *Plankton and Productivity in the Oceans*: Vol 2 *Zooplankton*, Second Edn. Oxford, UK: Pergamon Press.

Raymundo, L.J., Licuanan, W.L. and Kerr, A.M. (2018) Adding insult to injury: ship groundings are associated with coral disease in a pristine reef. *PLoS One* 13: e0202939.

Robison, B.H. (2004) Deep pelagic biology. *J Exp Mar Biol Ecol* 300: 253–272.

Rogers, A.D., Appeltans, W., Ballance, L.T., et al. (2020) *Blue Paper 10: Critical Habitats and Biodiversity: Inventory, Thresholds and Governance. Report to the Prime Ministers High Level Panel for a Sustainable Ocean Economy*. Washington DC: World Resources Institute.

Rosenberg, E., Koren, O., Reshef, L., Efrony, R. and Zilber-Rosenberg, I. (2007) The role of microorganisms in coral health, disease and evolution. *Nat Rev Microbiol* 5: 355–362.

Scheffers, B.R., Joppa, L.N., Pimm, S.L. and Laurance, W.F. (2012) What we know and don't know about Earth's missing biodiversity. *Trends Ecol Evol* 27: 501–510.

Sigwart, J.D., Chen, C., Thomas, E.A., et al. (2019) Red Listing can protect deep-sea biodiversity. *Nat Ecol Evol* 3: 1134.

Spalding, M., Burke, L., Wood, S.A., et al. (2017) Mapping the global value and distribution of coral reef tourism. *Mar Policy* 82: 104–113.

Stork, N.E., McBroom, J., Gely, C. and Hamilton, A.J. (2015) New approaches narrow global species estimates for beetles, insects, and terrestrial arthropods. *Proc Natl Acad Sci USA* 112: 7519–7523.

Thomas, E.A., Böhm, M., Pollock, C., et al. (2021a) Assessing the extinction risk of insular, understudied marine species. *Conserv Biol* 36: e13854.

Thomas, E.A., Molloy, A., Hanson, N.B., et al. (2021b) A global red list for hydrothermal vent molluscs. *Front Mar Sci* 8: 713022.

Uthicke, S., Welch, D. and Benzie, J.A.H. (2004) Slow growth and lack of recovery in overfished holothurians on the Great Barrier Reef: evidence from DNA fingerprints and repeated large-scale surveys. *Conserv Biol* 18: 1395–1404.

Van Dover, C.L. (2000) *The Ecology of Hydrothermal Vents*. Princeton, NJ: Princeton University Press.

Van Hooidonk, R., Maynard, J., Tamelander, J., et al. (2016) Local-scale projections of coral reef futures and implications of the Paris Agreement. *Sci Rep* 6: 39666.

Venn, A.A., Loram, J.E. and Douglas, A.E. (2008) Photosynthetic symbioses in animals. *J Exp Bot* 59: 1069–1080.

Wear, S.L. (2016) Missing the boat: critical threats to coral reefs are neglected at global scale. *Mar Pol* 74: 153–157.

Webb, T.J. and Mindel, B.L. (2015) Global patterns of extinction risk in marine and non-marine systems. *Curr Biol* 25: 506–511.

Williams, G.J., Graham, N.A.J., Jouffrey, J.-B., et al. (2019) Coral reef ecology in the Anthropocene. *Funct Ecol* 33: 1014–1022.

Worm, B. and Myers, R.A. (2003) Meta-analysis of cod–shrimp interactions reveals top-down control in oceanic food webs. *Ecology* 84: 162–173.

Ye, Y. and Gutierrez, N.L. (2017) Ending fishery overexploitation by expanding from local successes to globalized solutions. *Nat Ecol Evol* 1: 0179.

Zeidberg, L.D. and Robison, B.H. (2007) Invasive range expansion by the Humboldt squid, *Dosidicus gigas*, in the eastern North Pacific. *Proc Natl Acad Sci USA* 104: 12948–12950.

THIRTEEN

Non-Insect Terrestrial Arthropods

GONZALO GIRIBET

Summary

Numerous non-insect limno/terrestrial arthropods appear in the IUCN Red List of Threatened Species. Nearly all arachnids and myriapods are terrestrial, but within Pancrustacea, many taxa can inhabit marine, limnic and terrestrial environments and it is not possible to easily disentangle the numbers of listed species without sorting them species by species. In some cases, as in Malacostraca, the number provided includes species inhabiting either environment, or even cases of amphidromous species that spend part of their life cycle at sea and part in rivers and streams, as is the case of many shrimp species.

Non-Hexapod Arthropods Red Listed with the Number of Listed Species in Parentheses:

Arachnida (325)
  Araneae (275)
  Opiliones (21)
  Pseudoscorpiones (13)
  Schizomida (6)
  Holothyrida (4)
  Scorpiones (3)
  Amblypygi (2)
  Oribatida (1)
Myriapoda (210)
  Diplopoda (200)
  Chilopoda (10)
Oligostraca (13; marine and limno/terrestrial)
  Ostracoda (13; marine and limno/terrestrial)
Multicrustacea (3126; many are marine)
  Malacostraca (3016; many are marine)
    Decapoda (2892; marine and limno/terrestrial)

Amphipoda (71; marine and limno/terrestrial)

Isopoda (45; marine and limno/terrestrial)

Anaspidacea (4; all limnic)

Copepoda (108; many are marine)

Branchiopoda (42; all limnic)

13.1 Introduction

Arthropods are among the most abundant and diverse terrestrial organisms, but for the most part, as for every other animal phylum, they originated in the sea, where a large fraction of their phylogenetic diversity still resides, especially within the clade Pancrustacea (Giribet and Edgecombe, 2019). Terrestrial invasions have occurred multiple times, and include chelicerates (probably a single invasion with subsequent invasions to freshwater and back to the sea in some mites), myriapods and multiple lineages of pancrustaceans, including the main colonisation of land by hexapods (Lozano-Fernandez et al., 2016; Schwentner et al., 2017). In this chapter I focus on arachnids, myriapods and several lineages of non-insect pancrustaceans. Hexapods are discussed in Chapter 11.

The physiological conditions for colonising limnic and terrestrial environments lead to similar stresses in arthropods and other invertebrates (see Chapter 14), and terrestrial arthropods cannot in general attain the large sizes of many marine species. Nonetheless, the presence of land plants, which seem to have colonised the terrestrial environment earlier than previously thought, around the Cambrian–Early Ordovician (Morris et al., 2018), provided an ideal setting for the early colonisation of land by herbivores (such as modern millipedes) and subsequently for many groups of predators (as is the case for most lineages of arachnids and centipedes).

Extant chelicerates have been traditionally divided into the marine Pycnogonida (sea spiders), the also marine Xiphosura (horseshoe crabs) and the terrestrial Arachnida (spiders, scorpions, harvestmen, ticks, mites, etc.), with a few instances of colonisation of water, mostly by some mite lineages (see a recent review by Giribet, 2018). The diving bell spider (*Argyroneta aquatica*), is the only known spider species that spends almost all its life underwater in freshwater still waters, including to mate, lay eggs and overwinter, only briefly surfacing to replenish its oxygen supply, and occasionally to bring prey to the surface, but as in the case of mites, their aquatic lifestyle is a derived adaptation. Arachnids were thus thought to have colonised the land once (although some authors have considered extant scorpions to have colonised land independently, a hypothesis now discarded). However, recent phylogenomic work has suggested that horseshoe crabs are nested within Arachnida (Ballesteros and Sharma, 2019), and thus must have required a secondary colonisation of water, or arachnids colonised the land multiple times. In contrast, as all known Myriapoda (centipedes, millipedes and their allies) are terrestrial, we can easily postulate a single colonisation of land by the common ancestor of extant myriapods, possibly an euthycarcinoid. Euthycarcinoids are a plausible candidate for the marine myriapod stem-group, a clade that ranges from the late Cambrian to the Middle Triassic (Giribet and Edgecombe, 2019). In Pancrustacea (the traditional 'crustaceans' plus hexapods, including insects), colonisation of limnic and terrestrial environments has occurred multiple times, as entire lineages can be limnic, while others have representatives in the sea, in freshwater and on land (e.g. Isopoda, Amphipoda, Decapoda). Indeed, many insects still have a life cycle with aquatic and terrestrial phases, while others have returned to the aquatic environment altogether, even if requiring air for respiration, using snorkel-inspiring devices. Irrespective of whether oxygen is extracted from water or air, many of these insect larvae or adult insects can be important in the conservation of limnic environments, but they are discussed in Chapter 11.

A related issue for conservation/invasion biology of terrestrial arthropods is the many synanthropic species of insects (not discussed in this chapter) and other arthropods, including the house centipede (*Scutigera coleoptrata*), the common European harvestman (*Phalangium opilio*), the woodlouse spider (*Dysdera crocata*) and many garden spiders (Araneidae), that are found across their originally large native range, but also now in many other areas where Europeans once settled. Their effects on the native species are, however, little understood, as almost no research has been conducted on their impact in their newly invaded territories. Likewise, many parthenogenetic arthropod species have been able to expand their ranges rapidly, in some cases with devastating effects (Gutekunst et al., 2018). Invasion biology of arthropods is full of examples of insects on land and many crustaceans at sea, and prominent examples of more recent freshwater invasions by crayfish are discussed below.

Specialised habitats such as caves and ground waters have emerged as drivers of speciation and places where unique faunas occur, but their limited ranges and low population densities often make these species vulnerable and are important to consider for the conservation of such species. The vulnerability of the stygofauna, when compared to the surface water fauna (De Grave et al., 2015), and the large numbers of short-range endemics of these underground ecosystems (Humphreys, 2008; Guzik et al., 2010) demand that attention be paid to these often neglected environments. Not surprisingly, a large number of extinct and threatened arthropod species are stygobionts or troglobites, some known from a handful of specimens from single caves, as is the case of the pseudoscorpion *Gymnobisium inukshuk*, known only from three specimens from Inukshuk Cave, in Table Mountain National Park, South Africa (Harvey et al., 2016).

Many terrestrial arthropods have small ranges and narrow habitat requirements, often resulting in them being typical short-range endemics (SREs) – a concept that was introduced by Australian arachnologist Mark S. Harvey as of potential utility in conservation biology. SREs were defined as species with naturally small ranges of less than 10,000 km^2 and thus especially vulnerable to anthropogenic change (Harvey, 2002). Many taxa with SREs have similar ecological and life history characteristics, including low vagility and/or confinement to discontinuous habitats (these include ground waters and cave systems, discussed above), such as several groups of arachnids, millipedes and isopod crustaceans. The conservation of such groups is often hampered by poor taxonomic knowledge (Harvey, 2002). These SREs have been the focus of subsequent conservation work, because, by their very nature, these species are most likely to be threatened by habitat loss, habitat degradation and climate change. Thus, and because surveys focusing on all invertebrates are rarely fundable by any governmental agency and are logistically difficult or impossible, it has been argued that by focusing on some of the most vulnerable elements in the landscape – SREs, including troglofauna and stygofauna – we can help to enhance conservation (Harvey et al., 2011).

13.2 Arachnida

Among all arachnids, due to interest in the pet trade, cryptic speciation and territorial behaviour, tarantulas (Mygalomorphae) are a strong focus of conservation (e.g. Hedin and Carlson, 2011; Harvey et al., 2015; Rix et al., 2018). Indeed, among the 53 Critically Endangered arachnids, 45 are spiders, many of which are tarantulas. But of the nine arachnids that are considered Extinct, five are harvestmen, a group that has been used extensively in biogeographic studies because of their extreme low vagility and small ranges (e.g. Clouse and Giribet, 2010; Boyer et al., 2015; Derkarabetian et al., 2016; Richart and Hedin, 2016), yet many species of harvestmen are single locality endemics, but are not listed. This is also the case of Ricinulei, another poorly studied arachnid order inhabiting the tropics of Africa and the Americas (Fernández and Giribet, 2015). Many cave arachnids are considered especially vulnerable, because of their adaptations to these specific habitats and the restricted ranges and low population densities caves are able to support. Yet still, most troglobitic species are not listed (e.g. Figure 13.1.c), despite many having been found only once or only in a single cave system (e.g. Juberthie, 1994; Rambla and Juberthie, 1994). A few species of spiders and harvestmen are synanthropic (e.g. *Phalangium opilio*, *Dysdera crocata*).

13.3 Myriapoda

Millipedes are also common in the pet trade and many are typical examples of SREs, so there is documentation of a good number of species, 3 considered Extinct and 34 Critically Endangered. A large number of the listed millipedes are in three orders, the giant pill-millipedes in the order Sphaerotheriidae (78 listed), endemic to the former Gondwana, and the large cylindrical members of the orders Spirobolida (76 listed) and Spirostreptida (34 listed). Many of these groups have traditionally been poorly studied, and we are just beginning to understand the real numbers of species and their distributions. Conservation work is beginning, especially in places like Madagascar, with great diversity, but rapidly degrading habitats (Wesener and Wägele, 2008; Wesener et al., 2009, 2014), and the Tasmanian fauna is especially well known with many cases of invasions having been documented, especially the large swarms of the black Portuguese millipede (*Ommatoiulus moreletii*). No extinct centipede has been documented, but three Geophilomorpha are listed as Critically Endangered. Centipedes can be SREs, especially in the case of some lithobiomorphs (e.g. Giribet and Edgecombe, 2006), but in general

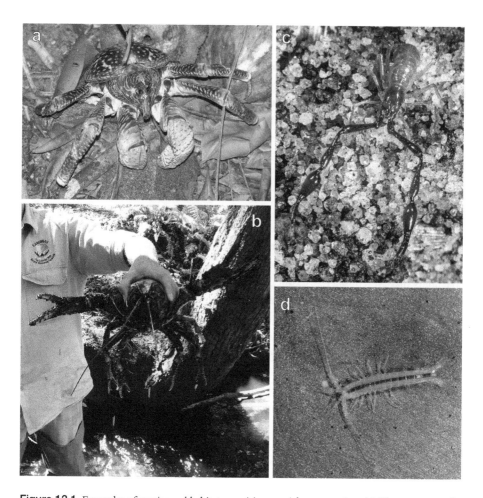

Figure 13.1 Examples of species and habitats requiring special conservation. (a) The coconut crab, *Birgus latro* (Data Deficient), the largest living terrestrial arthropod (photo by Drew Avery; obtained from www.flickr.com/photos/33590535@N06/4091439878). (b) The Tasmanian giant freshwater crayfish or lutaralipina, *Astacopsis gouldi* (Endangered), the largest freshwater invertebrate species in the world (photo by Terry Mulhern). (c) *Gymnobisium inukshuk*, the only troglobitic Gymnobisiidae (Pseudoscorpiones), a species known only from three specimens collected in a single cave in Table Mountain (South Africa), and thus extremely vulnerable, although not Red Listed (photo by the author). (d) The rare spelaeogriphacean *Spelaeogriphus lepidops*, only known from a cave in Table Mountain (South Africa), although not Red Listed (photo by the author).

have broader distributions than millipedes and are therefore less threatened. However, recent genetic analyses have suggested new cryptic species and geographic structure in taxa previously thought to be widespread (Edgecombe et al., 2015), thus questioning the broad distribution of some species with plesiomorphic character states, such as *Newportia stolli*, which constitutes a complex of unrelated species. The blind centipede *Lamyctes coeculus* is a parthenogenetic species that has achieved nearly-cosmopolitan distribution, as has the house centipede (*Scutigera coeloptrata*), although in this case not associated with parthenogenesis.

13.4 Pancrustacea

Crayfish represent one of the most extreme cases of freshwater invasions, probably a result of many species being parthenogenetic (Gutekunst et al., 2018). As an example, in Italy, with 3 natives, 37 species of crayfish have been detected, the native ones being the most vulnerable (Gherardi et al., 2011). One of the most important effects of the invasive species is on the native populations, including those of other species of crayfish. Of the 572 crayfish species that are Red Listed, 4 are considered Extinct and 45 Critically Endangered. The Tasmanian giant freshwater crayfish (*Astacopsis gouldi*) or lutaralipina in Tasmanian Aboriginal language (Figure 13.1.b), the largest freshwater invertebrate species in the world (Mulhern, 2018), is only found in low elevation rivers, below 400 m, in northern Tasmania, and thus it is easily accessible to people. It is listed as Endangered on the IUCN Red List because of overfishing and habitat degradation. Likewise, *Austropotamobius pallipes*, the European crayfish, is listed as Endangered, one of the major reasons for its decline being the introduction of the invasive North American signal crayfish (*Pacifastacus leniusculus*) and red swamp crayfish (*Procambarus clarkii*). In addition to interspecific competition, invasive crayfish native to North America (e.g. *Procambarus clarkii* and *Faxonius limosus*) have acted as vectors of the crayfish plague pathogen (*Aphanomyces astaci*), which has caused dramatic extinctions of European crayfish populations. The literature and reports on invasions and decline of crayfish populations is large.

Freshwater shrimp knowledge has benefitted from a thorough assessment of all known 763 species (De Grave et al., 2015). Among these species, which is probably applicable to other freshwater taxa, the stygofauna is much more threatened than are the surface species. This study listed two species as Extinct with a further 10 being possibly extinct (although not recognised), and almost one-third of species are either threatened or classified as Near Threatened (NT). Threats to freshwater shrimp include agricultural and urban pollution that impact over two-thirds of threatened and Near Threatened species, but invasive species and climate change have the greatest overall impact over freshwater shrimp (De Grave et al., 2015).

Back on land, the coconut crab or robber crab (*Birgus latro*; Figure 13.1.a), the largest living terrestrial arthropod, with a weight of almost 4 kg and up to 1 m in length, has been featured in the news because of its recent population declines. This huge hermit crab is found on islands across the Indo-Pacific region, mirroring the distribution of the coconut palm. Unfortunately, it has been extirpated from most areas with a significant human population, including mainland Australia and Madagascar, and its populations continue to decline, although it is listed as Data Deficient (Drew et al., 2010). Many other species of land crabs are also threatened by land use, invasive species and overexploitation for food. One of these land crabs is the charismatic Christmas Island red crab (*Gecarcoidea natalis*), endemic to Christmas Island and the Cocos Islands in the Indian Ocean, which is well known for its annual mass migration to the sea to lay its eggs in the ocean. Although restricted to a relatively small area, an estimated ca. 44 million adult red crabs once lived on Christmas Island alone, but the accidental introduction of the yellow crazy ant (*Anoplolepis gracilipes*) is believed to have killed about 10–15 million individuals (O'Dowd et al., 2003) and its numbers continue to decline. This invasion by the alien crazy ant has caused a rapid, catastrophic shift in the rainforest ecosystem, as in invaded areas, the ants can extirpate the land crab, the dominant consumer on the forest floor, indirectly slowing litter breakdown.

Many ostracods, especially in Podocopida, are also found in freshwater, but terrestrial species of *Mesocypris* are known from humid forest soils of South Africa, Australia and New Zealand. Some of these limno/terrestrial species are especially vulnerable, but in one case, the Western Cape (South Africa) *Liocypris grandis*, although still listed as Extinct, has now been found in the wild (Martens, 2003). Another southern African limnic ostracod, *Namibcypris costata*, found only in one spring in Namibia, is considered Extinct. Four Tasmanian anaspidaceans, a small group of crustaceans restricted to the surface and ground waters in the former territories of Gondwana, are listed as Vulnerable.

Finally, other groups that should probably be listed are not even considered by IUCN. Among these, Spelaeogriphacea, a group of eyeless, unpigmented peracarid malacostracans represented by very few species from continental subterranean waters, either running or still, in limestone or sandstone caves, or in calcrete aquifers, is especially vulnerable (Jaume, 2008). With only four extant (and two fossil) species known – one from a cave in Mato Grosso (Brazil), another from a cave on Table Mountain (South Africa; Figure 13.1.d), and two from separate Australian aquifers – efforts to protect them should be implemented.

13.5 Conclusions

Arthropods can be some of the most abundant and broadly distributed groups of limnic and terrestrial animals, but many are SREs with restricted habitat requirements, including those inhabiting caves and ground waters, environments especially sensitive to change. While many arthropods are Red Listed, more information for a large number of species is needed before they can be assessed, especially for the many SREs and single-site endemics. Particular threats to many of these species include habitat loss and degradation, as well as competition and/or predation by invasive species, as exemplified by freshwater crayfish and by terrestrial land crabs.

Acknowledgements

I am indebted to Norman Maclean and Rob Cowie for their input and comments.

References

Ballesteros, J.A. and Sharma, P.P. (2019) A critical appraisal of the placement of Xiphosura (Chelicerata) with account of known sources of phylogenetic error. *Syst Biol* 68: 896–917.

Boyer, S.L., Baker, C.M., Popkin-Hall, Z.R., et al. (2015) Phylogeny and biogeography of the mite harvestmen (Arachnida : Opiliones : Cyphophthalmi) of Queensland, Australia, with a description of six new species from the rainforests of the Wet Tropics. *Invertebr Syst* 29: 37–70.

Clouse, R.M. and Giribet, G. (2010) When Thailand was an island: the phylogeny and biogeography of mite harvestmen (Opiliones, Cyphophthalmi, Stylocellidae) in Southeast Asia. *J Biogeogr* 37: 1114–1130.

De Grave, S., Smith, K.G., Adeleret, N.A., et al. (2015) Dead shrimp blues: a global assessment of extinction risk in freshwater shrimps (Crustacea: Decapoda: Caridea). *PLoS One* 10: e0120198.

Derkarabetian, S. Burns, M., Starrett, J. and Hedin, M. (2016) Population genomic evidence for multiple Pliocene refugia in a montane-restricted harvestman (Arachnida, Opiliones, *Sclerobunus robustus*) from the southwestern United States. *Mol Ecol* 25: 4611–4631.

Drew, M.M., Harzsch, S., Stensmyr, M., Erland, S. and Hansson, B.S. (2010) A review of the biology and ecology of the Robber Crab, *Birgus latro* (Linnaeus, 1767) (Anomura: Coenobitidae). *Zool Anz* 249: 45–67.

Edgecombe, G.D., Vahtera, V., Giribet, G. and Kaunisto, P. (2015) Species limits and phylogeography of *Newportia* (Scolopendromorpha) and implications for widespread morphospecies. *ZooKeys* 510: 65–77.

Fernández, R. and Giribet, G. (2015) Unnoticed in the tropics: phylogenomic resolution of the poorly known arachnid order Ricinulei (Arachnida). *Royal Soc Open Sci* 2: 150065.

Gherardi, F., Aquiloni, L., Diéguez-Uribeondo, J. and Tricarico, E. (2011) Managing invasive crayfish: is there a hope? *Aquat Sci* 73: 185–200.

Giribet, G. (2018) Current views on chelicerate phylogeny – a tribute to Peter Weygoldt. *Zool Anz* 273: 7–13.

Giribet, G. and Edgecombe, G.D. (2006) The importance of looking at small-scale patterns when inferring Gondwanan biogeography: a case study of the centipede *Paralamyctes* (Chilopoda, Lithobiomorpha, Henicopidae). *Biol J Linn Soc* 89: 65–78.

Giribet, G. and Edgecombe, G.D. (2019) The phylogeny and evolutionary history of arthropods. *Curr Biol* 29: R592–R602.

Gutekunst, J., Andriantsoa, R., Falckenhayn, C. et al. (2018) Clonal genome evolution and rapid invasive spread of the marbled crayfish. *Nat Ecol Evol* 2: 567–573.

Guzik, M.T., Austin, A.D., Cooper, S.J.B., et al. (2010) Is the Australian subterranean fauna uniquely diverse? *Invertebr Syst* 24: 407–418.

Harvey, M.S. (2002) Short-range endemism among the Australian fauna: some examples from non-marine environments. *Invertebr Syst* 16: 555–570.

Harvey, M.S., Huey, J.A., Hillyer, M.J., McIntyre, E. and Giribet, G. (2016) The first troglobitic species of Gymnobisiidae (Pseudoscorpiones : Neobisioidea), from Table Mountain (Western Cape Province, South Africa) and its phylogenetic position. *Invertebr Syst* 30: 75–85.

Harvey, M.S., Rix, M.G., Framenau, V.W., et al. (2011) Protecting the innocent: studying short-range endemic taxa enhances conservation outcomes. *Invertebr Syst* 25: 1–10.

Harvey, M.S., York Main, B., Rix, M.G., Cooper, S.J.B. (2015) Refugia within refugia: *in situ* speciation and conservation of threatened *Bertmainius* (Araneae : Migidae), a new genus of relictual trapdoor spiders endemic to the mesic zone of south-western Australia. *Invertebr Syst* 29: 511–553.

Hedin, M. and Carlson, D. (2011) A new trapdoor spider species from the southern Coast Ranges of California (Mygalomorphae, Antrodiaetidae, *Aliatypus coylei*, sp. nov,), including consideration of mitochondrial phylogeographic structuring. *Zootaxa* 2963: 55–68.

Humphreys, W.F. (2008) Rising from Down Under: developments in subterranean biodiversity in Australia from a groundwater fauna perspective. *Invertebr Syst* 22: 85–101.

Jaume, D. (2008) Global diversity of spelaeogriphaceans and thermosbaenaceans (Crustacea; Spelaeogriphacea and Thermosbaenacea) in freshwater. *Hydrobiologia* 595: 219–224.

Juberthie, C. (1994) Ricinulei. In: Juberthie, C. Decu, V. (Eds.), *Encyclopaedia Biospeologica*. Moulis-Boucarest: Société de Biospéologie.

Lozano-Fernandez, J., Carton, R., Tanner, A.R., et al. (2016) A molecular palaeobiological exploration of arthropod terrestrialisation. *Phil Trans Royal Soc B* 371: 20150133.

Martens, K. (2003) On a remarkable South African giant ostracod (Crustacea, Ostracoda, Cyprididae) from temporary pools, with additional appendages. *Hydrobiologia* 500: 115–130.

Morris, J.L., Puttick, M.N., Clark, J.W., et al. (2018) The timescale of early land plant evolution. *Proc Natl Acad Sci USA* 115: E2274–E2283.

Mulhern, T.D. (2018) Correcting misconceptions about the names applied to Tasmania's giant freshwater crayfish *Astacopsis gouldi* (Decapoda: Parastacidae). *Pap Proc Royal Soc Tasmania* 152: 1–6.

O'Dowd, D.J., Green, P.T. and Lake, P.S. (2003) Invasional 'meltdown' on an oceanic island. *Ecol Lett* 6: 812–817.

Rambla, M. and Juberthie, C. (1994) Opiliones. In: Juberthie, C. Decu, V. (Eds.), *Encyclopaedia Biospeologica*. Moulis-Boucarest: Société de Biospéologie.

Richart, C.H. and Hedin, M. (2016) Glacial refugia and riverine barriers: biogeography of *Acuclavella* (Opiliones, Ischyropsalidoidea) in Northern Idaho. *Denver Mus Nat Sci Rep* 3: 161.

Rix, M.G., Wilson, J.D., Rix, A.G., et al. (2018) Population demography and biology of a new species of giant spiny trapdoor spider (Araneae: Idiopidae: *Euoplos*) from inland Queensland: developing a 'slow science' study system to address a conservation crisis. *Austral Entomol* 58: 282–297.

Schwentner, M., Combosch, D.J., Nelson, J.P. and Giribet, G. (2017) A phylogenomic solution to the origin of insects by resolving crustacean-hexapod relationships. *Curr Biol* 27: 1818–1824.

Wesener, T. and Wägele, J.-W. (2008) The giant pill-millipedes of Madagascar: revision of the genus *Zoosphaerium* (Myriapoda, Diplopoda, Sphaerotheriida). *Zoosystema* 30: 5–85.

Wesener, T., Enghoff, H. and Sierwald, P. (2009) Review of the Spirobolida on Madagascar, with descriptions of twelve new genera, including three genera of 'fire millipedes' (Diplopoda). *ZooKeys* 19: 1–128.

Wesener, T., Minh-Tu Le, D. and Loria, S.F. (2014) Integrative revision of the giant pill-millipede genus *Sphaeromimus* from Madagascar, with the description of seven new species (Diplopoda, Sphaerotheriida, Arthrosphaeridae). *ZooKeys* 414: 67–107.

FOURTEEN

Terrestrial Invertebrates Other Than Arthropods and Molluscs

GONZALO GIRIBET

Summary

Only four terrestrial invertebrate phyla dealt with in this chapter appear in the IUCN Red List of Threatened Species. Three of these phyla are composed of mostly marine animals, but all the listed species of Nemertea and Platyhelminthes are limnoterrestrial, and of the 224 listed annelids, 222 are limnoterrestrial. Conservation issues related to their marine counterparts are discussed in other chapters of this book.

Non-Mollusc, Non-Marine Invertebrates Red Listed with the Number of Listed Species in Parenthesis:

Annelida (224)

Nemertea (6)

Onychophora (11)

Platyhelminthes (1)

14.1 Conservation of Terrestrial Invertebrates

Of the more than 30 or so accepted animal phyla, only a few are represented in limnic (freshwater) environments, and even fewer in terrestrial environments (Figure 14.1). Arthropods and molluscs, the two largest clades of non-marine invertebrates, are dealt with in separate chapters in this book (Chapters 11, 13 and 15), and most work on conservation and documenting threats and extinctions in terrestrial invertebrates has focused on them. Here I focus on the remaining diversity and on the different problems associated with the members of the phyla Annelida, Nemertea, Onychophora and Platyhelminthes. These issues include extinction and invasiveness, although almost nothing is known about the conservation status of groups such as nematodes, nematomorphs and rotifers, while some literature is available for onychophorans (velvet worms), nemerteans, annelids and flatworms.

Because cells are mostly isotonic with seawater, adaptation to freshwater requires active osmoregulation, while colonisation of land also requires dealing with desiccation and developing structural support. Both constraints are important. For example, echinoderms

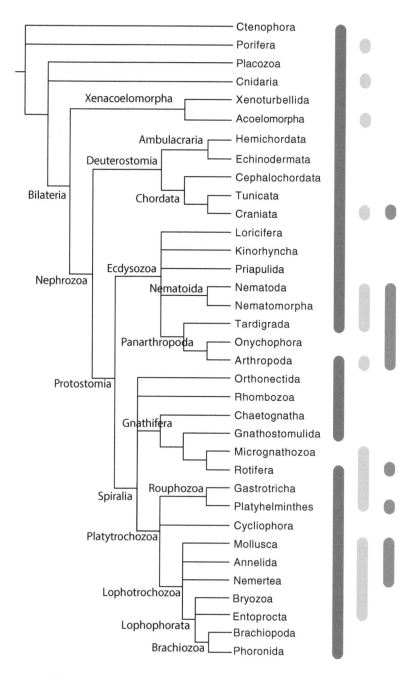

Figure 14.1 Phylogenetic tree of the animal kingdom with phyla as terminals and higher taxa in selected nodes. Dark blue indicates phyla with marine species; light blue indicates phyla with limnic species; brown indicates phyla with terrestrial species. Note that all phyla except Onychophora and Micrognathozoa have marine members. Tree from Giribet and Edgecombe (2020).

have the necessary skeletal support, but their lack of large osmoregulatory/excretory organs has presumably prevented them from colonising freshwater environments, despite being tolerant of exposure to air for long periods in the intertidal. Animal groups with limnic representatives are therefore Porifera, Cnidaria, Craniata, Nematoda, Nematomorpha (only the free-living stages), Tardigrada, Arthropoda, Micrognathozoa, Rotifera, Gastrotricha, Platyhelminthes, Mollusca, Annelida, Nemertea, Bryozoa and Entoprocta. Among these, Micrognathozoa, with a single described species and a couple of other populations reported (Giribet and Edgecombe, 2020; Brusca et al., 2022), is the only phylum without marine representatives. Phyla with terrestrial representatives are even fewer – Craniata, Nematoda, Nematomorpha, Tardigrada, Onychophora, Arthropoda, Rotifera, Platyhelminthes, Mollusca, Annelida and Nemertea – and from these, Onychophora is the only phylum that is entirely terrestrial.

Biotic and abiotic factors are important for explaining species distributions, but despite widespread potentially favourable conditions, many terrestrial small animals have small distributions, and thus are considered short-range endemics (SREs) (see Chapter 13 for a discussion of SREs). SREs are common among, for example, Onychophora, resulting in a large number of cryptic species only recently recognised by the use of molecular techniques (e.g. Trewick, 2000). Extensive work has been done during the last decade or so in recognising large numbers of cryptic onychophoran species with very narrow ranges, in contrast to earlier ideas of widespread species with phenotypic variation (Daniels et al., 2009, 2013, 2016; Daniels and Ruhberg, 2010; McDonald et al., 2012; Ruhberg and Daniels, 2013; Sato et al., 2018), and thus these animals may be useful to understand recent climatic changes (McDonald and Daniels, 2012; Myburgh and Daniels, 2015). Onychophora is not only the only animal phylum that is exclusively terrestrial, but onychophorans have inhabited terrestrial environments at least since the Carboniferous (Garwood et al., 2016), and have evolved and diversified in terrestrial environments since then (Murienne et al., 2014; Giribet et al., 2018). Such an ancient group with SREs is therefore a prime terrestrial taxon for conservation (Hamer et al., 1997; Trewick et al., 2018), and includes one of the few documented cases of continental extinctions of terrestrial invertebrates: *Peripatopsis leonina*, not seen in over a century, although IUCN lists it as Critically Endangered (CR). Eleven Onychophora species are currently Red Listed, including many cavernicolous species, and many more may become Red Listed as most species are presently known from just a few localities. In addition to *P. leonina*, two are listed as Critically Endangered, two as Endangered, four as Vulnerable (including *Peripatopsis alba*, from a cave in Table Mountain, Cape Town; Figure 14.2a) and one as Near Threatened.

Nemerteans are primarily marine. From the nearly 1300 described/accepted species, only a handful inhabit limnic or terrestrial environments (Figure 14.2c). To date, 13 species of fully terrestrial nemerteans have been recognised, although some upper littoral species can also be found in fully terrestrial environments (Gibson et al., 1982; Moore et al., 2001). Most records of terrestrial nemerteans are from islands and many species are widespread (Moore and Gibson, 1985; Gibson and Moore, 1998; Moore et al., 2001), which has led some authors to think that they are dispersed by birds. But terrestrial

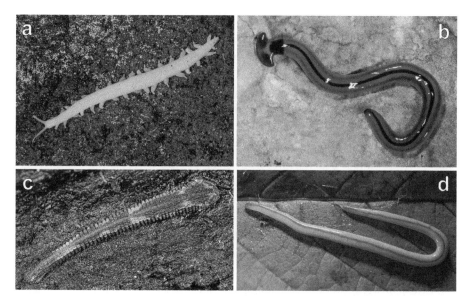

Figure 14.2 Representative members of terrestrial phyla discussed in this chapter. (a) The cavernicolous velvet worm *Peripatopsis alba* (listed as Vulnerable). (b) A species of hammerhead flatworm (Platyhelminthes). (c) The leech *Mesobdella gemmata* (not listed), one of the few terrestrial leeches in South America. (d) The invasive terrestrial nemertean *Geonemertes pelaensis* (not listed). All photos by the author.

nemerteans can also be abundant in pristine continental environments where they are often small and cryptic (Mateos and Giribet, 2008). Many species of terrestrial nemerteans are probably awaiting discovery or adequate description. Others have suffered a decline in abundance. Of the terrestrial species, six are currently Red Listed, one as Extinct (*Geonemertes rodericana*), one as Critically Endangered, one as Endangered and one as Vulnerable. According to Moore et al. (2001), three species could be extinct.

In the case of the 22 freshwater nemertean species, distributional data are extremely deficient (Sundberg and Gibson, 2008) and the validity of the one supposedly extinct species has been questioned (Quigg, 2017). A drastic effect on soil crustaceans has been documented as a result of predation by the non-native terrestrial species *Geonemertes pelaensis* in the Ogasawara Islands, a UNESCO World Heritage site (Shinobe et al., 2017).

Terrestrial invasive predatory species are much better documented for land planarians (Platyhelminthes, Tricladida, Continenticola). For example, the species of hammerhead land planarians in the genus *Bipalium* (see Figure 14.2b) are well-known predators of earthworms (Fiore et al., 2004) and snails (Ducey et al., 2007), and are able to subdue large prey items because of the presence of tetrodotoxin (Stokes et al., 2014), a potent toxin otherwise known only from marine animals. The fact that many planarians are invasive (Justine et al., 2018) is a major concern for soil quality, especially in areas where earthworms are a major player in the soil turnover and have been identified as a cause of snail population declines (Okochi et al., 2004; Ohbayashi et al., 2005).

Among Platyhelminthes, one species is listed as Extinct – the freshwater planarian *Romankenkius pedderensis*, endemic to Tasmanian Lake Pedder prior to its flooding for a hydro-electric power scheme in 1972. However, the species has been reported subsequently (Grant et al., 2006). Long-term studies monitoring the abundances of species through time and possible declines or invasions are rare for some of these terrestrial groups. A 50-year study of land planarians in the Brazilian Atlantic rainforest has revealed the local extinction of some species and the invasion of new ones, including *Endeavouria septemlineata*, an active predator of the alien giant African snail (*Achatina*), but also of native snail species (Carbayo et al., 2008).

Annelida includes a large diversity of limnic and terrestrial species in the clade Clitellata, with ca. 9000 species inhabiting land (e.g. Figure 14.2c), while about 14,000 annelids are marine. This is therefore the most important phylum of terrestrial invertebrates dealt with in this chapter. From the 224 listed annelids in the IUCN Red List, 222 are limnoterrestrial clitellates: 2 are listed as Extinct, 6 as Critically Endangered, 13 as Endangered and 8 are Vulnerable. Many conservation issues are related to overcollecting, as is the case of the European medicinal leech, *Hirudo medicinalis*, now Near Threatened. This has led to the introduction of foreign species to be used for medicinal purposes (Elliott and Kutschera, 2011). However, the great majority of Red Listed annelids are earthworms, including many giant earthworms in the family Megascolecidae (102 listed by IUCN). Many earthworms also have restricted distributions despite their size, and have been excellent models for studying terrestrial biogeography (e.g. Novo et al., 2015). But again, despite the existence of some popular initiatives, little is known about the true distribution of most earthworm species, as their taxonomy is often difficult. Clearly, more research on these key components of the soil is needed from the point of view of conservation.

Although not Red Listed, two other clades of limnoterrestrial invertebrates – Rotifera and Tardigrada – may deserve conservation attention because of their ability to undergo cryptobiosis, mostly anhydrobiosis. Due to these properties, these microscopic animals are a paradigm of the hypothesis that 'everything is everywhere' (the Baas–Becking hypothesis) and thus have potential for long-range dispersal. However, genetic studies have shown that at least some of these purportedly cosmopolitan species, despite having wide distributions, still show geographic structuring (Fontaneto et al., 2008). These two animal phyla have also been the subject of research in two hot topics in biology, the supposed absence of sex in bdelloid rotifers and the extreme extremophile conditions of some tardigrades.

Bdelloids have been referred to as 'sleeping beauties' (Ricci, 2016) and 'evolutionary scandals' (Maynard Smith, 1986), because of their extreme anhydrobiotic capacity and the apparent lack of sex (they are obligate parthenogens) – which paradoxically has made them a model to study the evolution of sex. One of the supposed most extraordinary aspects of bdelloids, a clade known from fossils as far back as the Palaeogene and estimated to be even older based on molecular dating, is this entire absence of sex. Despite much observation of field and laboratory populations and except for one account, neither males, hermaphrodites, mating nor meiosis have ever been reported within the class (Birky, 2010). The fact that bdelloids could have evolved without genetic exchange is, however, hard to accept, and a recent study has suggested a striking pattern of allele sharing consistent with sexual reproduction and meiosis (Signorovitch et al., 2015), even if of an atypical sort. This is, however, not universally accepted and some still consider the question of bdelloid recombination to be open (Nowell et al., 2018).

Tardigrades are well known for being able to push their physiological limits to extremes that most other organisms, including other extremophiles, cannot – these include abiotic factors, such as cold, heat, radiation, vacuum and osmotic stress. Anhydrobiosis, the ability to withstand nearly complete desiccation, sometimes described as an ametabolic state, has evolved in many limnoterrestrial animals, including nematodes and rotifers, but it is best understood in tardigrades. Both tardigrades and rotifers enter the so-called tun, a state that marks the entrance into anhydrobiosis, during which some species undergo 87% reduction of body volume (Halberg et al., 2013). Some species of tardigrades can also enter into a diapause stage by forming a cyst with a cuticular covering that is abandoned once environmental conditions become favourable. Tardigrades can also revive and successfully reproduce after being frozen for more than 30 years (Tsujimoto et al., 2016). Some species are able to survive freezing in their active hydrated state, but this capacity largely depends on the cooling rate (Hengherr and Schill, 2018). Tardigrades are also well known to withstand elevated doses of many stressors, including ionising radiation and UV radiation (Jönsson et al., 2018). At least for the latter, their resistance is conferred both by high capacity for DNA damage repair and DNA protection in the anhydrobiotic state. Tardigrades also have the ability to tolerate high amounts of heavy metals (Hygum et al., 2017). But perhaps the most celebrated experiments related to tardigrade tolerance are those conducted in space, showing potential for survival in space vacuum and radiation, after which, and when returning to Earth, the animals were able to moult and lay eggs (Rebecchi et al., 2009). Clearly, few animals have such remarkable properties.

14.2 Conclusions

Little is known about the conservation status of non-mollusc, non-arthropod, non-marine invertebrates, and in most there is a lack of data necessary to determine conservation priorities. However, because of the SRE status of many species, vulnerability could be the norm, especially with the increasing threat of habitat degradation. Few extinction examples are well documented, but it is clear that additional study is urgently required for many limnic and terrestrial invertebrates. Abundance data through time and genetic data are excellent ways to assess the status of known populations. Further understanding of invasion biology and the effects of invaders on the local invertebrate biota are also sorely needed in many parts of the world and sometimes for entire animal phyla. But extremely small animals with extraordinary capacity for desiccation are also important for a better understanding of the distribution patterns of microscopic organisms, as they all have properties that allow survival in extreme conditions.

Acknowledgements

I am indebted to Norman Maclean and Rob Cowie for their input and comments.

References

Birky, C.W., Jr. (2010) Positively negative evidence for asexuality. *J Hered* 101(Suppl. 1): S42–S45.

Brusca, R.C., Giribet, G. and Moore, W. (2022) *Invertebrates* Fourth Edn. Oxford: Sinauer Associates and Oxford University Press.

Carbayo, F., Pedroni, J. and Froehlich, E.M. (2008) Colonization and extinction of land planarians (Platyhelminthes, Tricladida) in a Brazilian Atlantic Forest regrowth remnant. *Biol Invasions* 10: 1131–1134.

Daniels, S.R., Dambire, C., Klaus, S. and Sharma, P.P. (2016) Unmasking alpha diversity, cladogenesis and biogeographical patterning in an ancient panarthropod lineage (Onychophora: Peripatopsidae: *Opisthopatus cinctipes*) with the description of five novel species. *Cladistics* 32: 506–537.

Daniels, S.R., McDonald, D.E. and Picker, M.D. (2013) Evolutionary insight into the *Peripatopsis balfouri* sensu lato species complex (Onychophora: Peripatopsidae) reveals novel lineages and zoogeographic patterning. *Zool Scr* 42: 656–674.

Daniels, S.R., Picker, M.D., Cowlin, R.M. and Hamer, M.L. (2009) Unravelling evolutionary lineages among South African velvet worms (Onychophora: *Peripatopsis*) provides evidence for widespread cryptic speciation. *Biol J Linn Soc* 97: 200–216.

Daniels, S.R. and Ruhberg, H. (2010) Molecular and morphological variation in a South African velvet worm *Peripatopsis moseleyi* (Onychophora, Peripatopsidae): evidence for cryptic speciation. *J Zool* 282 171–179.

Ducey, P.K., McCormick, M. and Davidson, E. (2007) Natural history observations on *Bipalium* cf. *vagum* Jones and Sterrer (Platyhelminthes: Tricladida), a terrestrial broadhead planarian new to North America. *Southeast Nat* 6: 449–460.

Elliott, J.M. and Kutschera, U. (2011) Medicinal leeches: historical use, ecology, genetics and conservation. *Freshw Rev* 4: 21–41.

Fiore, C., Tull, J.L., Zehner, S. and Ducey, P.K. (2004) Tracking and predation on earthworms by the invasive terrestrial planarian *Bipalium adventitium* (Tricladida, Platyhelminthes). *Behav Proc* 67: 327–334.

Fontaneto, D., Barraclough, T.G., Chen, K., Ricci, C. and Herniou, E.A. (2008) Molecular evidence for broad-scale distributions in bdelloid rotifers: everything is not everywhere but most things are very widespread. *Mol Ecol* 17: 3136–3146.

Garwood, R.J., Edgecombe, G.D., Charbonnie, S., et al. (2016) Carboniferous Onychophora from Montceau-les-Mines, France, and onychophoran terrestrialization. *Invert Biol* 135: 179–190.

Gibson, R. and Moore, J. (1998) Further observations on the genus *Geonemertes* with a description of a new species from the Philippine Islands. *Hydrobiologia* 365: 157–171.

Gibson, R., Moore, J., Randall, F.B.C., et al. (1982) A new semi-terrestrial nemertean from California. *J Zool* 196: 463–474.

Giribet, G., Buckman-Young, R.S., Costa, C.S., et al. (2018) The 'Peripatos' in Eurogondwana? Lack of evidence that south-east Asian onychophorans walked through Europe. *Invertebr Syst* 32: 842–865.

Giribet, G. and Edgecombe, G.D. (2020) *The Invertebrate Tree of Life*. Princeton, NJ: Princeton University Press.

Grant, L.J., Sluys, R. and Blair, D. (2006) Biodiversity of Australian freshwater planarians (Platyhelminthes: Tricladida: Paludicola): new species and localities, and a review of paludicolan distribution in Australia. *Syst Biodivers* 4: 435–471.

Halberg, K.A., Jørgensen, A. and Møbjerg, N. (2013) Desiccation tolerance in the tardigrade *Richtersius coronifer* relies on muscle mediated structural reorganization. *PLoS One* 8: e85091.

Hamer, M.L., Samways, M.J. and Ruhberg, H. (1997) A review of the Onychophora of South Africa, with discussion of their conservation. *Ann Natal Mus* 38: 283–312.

Hengherr, S. and Schill, R.O. (2018) Environmental adaptations: cryobiosis. In: Schill, R.O. (Ed.), *Water Bears: The Biology of Tardigrades*. Switzerland, Cham: Springer Nature.

Hygum, T.L., Fobian, D., Kamilari, M., et al. (2017) Comparative investigation of copper tolerance and identification of putative tolerance related genes in tardigrades. *Front Physiol* 8: 95.

Jönsson, K.I., Levine, E.B., Wojcik, A., Haghdoost, S. and Harms-Ringdahl, M. (2018) Environmental adaptations: radiation tolerance. In: Schill, R.O. (Ed.), *Water Bears: The Biology of Tardigrades*. Switzerland, Cham: Springer Nature.

Justine, J.-L., Winsor, L., Gey, D., Gros, P. and Thévenot, J. (2018) Giant worms *chez moi!* Hammerhead flatworms (Platyhelminthes, Geoplanidae, *Bipalium* spp., *Diversibipalium* spp.) in metropolitan France and overseas French territories. *PeerJ* 6: e4672.

Mateos, E. and Giribet, G. (2008) Exploring the molecular diversity of terrestrial nemerteans (Hoplonemertea, Monostilifera, Acteonemertidae) in a continental landmass. *Zool Scr* 37: 235–243.

Maynard Smith, J. (1986) Evolution: contemplating life without sex. *Nature* 324: 300–301.

McDonald, D.E. and Daniels, S.R. (2012) Phylogeography of the Cape velvet worm (Onychophora: *Peripatopsis capensis*) reveals the impact of Pliocene/Pleistocene climatic oscillations on Afromontane forest in the Western Cape, South Africa. *J Evol Biol* 25: 824–835.

McDonald, D.E., Ruhberg, H. and Daniels, S.R. (2012) Two new *Peripatopsis* species (Onychophora: Peripatopsidae) from the Western Cape province, South Africa. *Zootaxa* 3380: 55–68.

Moore, J. and Gibson, R. (1985) The evolution and comparative physiology of terrestrial and freswater nemerteans. *Biol Rev* 60: 257–312.

Moore, J., Gibson, R. and Jones, H.D. (2001) Terrestrial nemerteans thirty years on. *Hydrobiologia* 456: 1–6.

Murienne, J., Daniels, S.R., Buckley, T.R., Mayer, G. and Giribet, G. (2014) A living fossil tale of Pangaean biogeography. *Proc Royal Soc B* 281: 20132648.

Myburgh, A.M. and Daniels, S.R. (2015) Exploring the impact of habitat size on phylogeographic patterning in the Overberg velvet worm *Peripatopsis overbergiensis* (Onychophora: Peripatopsidae). *J Hered* 106: 296–305.

Novo, M., Fernández, R., Marchán, D.F., et al. (2015) Unearthing the historical biogeography of Mediterranean earthworms (Annelida: Hormogastridae). *J Biogeogr* 42: 751–762.

Nowell, R.W., Almeida, P., Wilson, C.G., et al. (2018) Comparative genomics of bdelloid rotifers: Insights from desiccating and nondesiccating species. *PLoS Biol* 16: e2004830.

Ohbayashi, T. Okochi, I. Sato, H. and Ono, T. (2005) Food habit of *Platydemus manokwari* De Beauchamp, 1962 (Tricladida: Terrricola: Rhynchodemidae), known as a predatory flatworm of land snails in the Ogasawara (Bonin) Islands, Japan. *Appl Entomol Zool* 40: 609–614.

Okochi, I., Sato, H. and Ohbayashi, T. (2004) The cause of mollusk decline on the Ogasawara Islands. *Biodivers Conserv* 13: 1465–1475.

Quigg, S.M. (2017) *Confirming the Status of Lancashire's Endemic Freshwater Nemertean* – Prostoma jenningsi. MSc Thesis. Preston, UK: University of Central Lancashire.

Rebecchi, L., Altiero, T., Guidetti, R., et al. (2009) Tardigrade resistance to space effects: first results of experiments on the LIFE-TARSE mission on FOTON-M3 (September 2007). *Astrobiology* 9: 581–591.

Ricci, C. (2016) Bdelloid rotifers: 'sleeping beauties' and 'evolutionary scandals', but not only. *Hydrobiologia* 796: 277–285.

Ruhberg, H. and Daniels, S.R. (2013) Morphological assessment supports the recognition of four novel species in the widely distributed velvet worm *Peripatopsis moseleyi sensu lato* (Onychophora: Peripatopsidae). *Invertebr Syst* 27: 131–145.

Sato, S., Buckman-Young, R.S., Harvey, M.S. and Giribet, G. (2018) Cryptic speciation in a biodiversity hotspot: multilocus molecular data reveal new velvet worm species from Western Australia (Onychophora: Peripatopsidae: *Kumbadjena*). *Invertebr Syst* 32: 1249–1264.

Shinobe, S., Uchida, S., Mori, H., Okochi, I. and Chiba, S. (2017) Declining soil Crustacea in a World Heritage Site caused by land nemertean. *Sci Rep* 7: 12400.

Signorovitch, A. Hur, J., Gladyshev, E., and Meselson, M. (2015) Allele sharing and evidence for sexuality in a mitochondrial clade of bdelloid rotifers. *Genetics* 200: 581–590.

Stokes, A.N., Ducey, P.K., Neuman-Lee, L., et al. (2014) Confirmation and distribution of tetrodotoxin for the first time in terrestrial invertebrates: two terrestrial flatworm species (*Bipalium adventitium* and *Bipalium kewense*). *PLoS One* 9: e100718.

Sundberg, P. and Gibson, R. (2008) Global diversity of nemerteans (Nemertea) in freshwater. *Hydrobiologia* 595: 61–66.

Trewick, S., Hitchmough, R., Rolfe, J. and Stringer, I. (2018) *Conservation Status of New Zealand Onychophora ('Peripatus' or Velvet Worm), 2018.* NZ Threat Classification Series 26, 1–3.

Trewick, S.A. (2000) Mitochondrial DNA sequences support allozyme evidence for cryptic radiation of New Zealand *Peripatoides* (Onychophora). *Mol Ecol* 9: 269–281.

Tsujimoto, M., Imura, S. and Kanda, H. (2016) Recovery and reproduction of an Antarctic tardigrade retrieved from a moss sample frozen for over 30 years. *Cryobiology* 72: 78–81.

FIFTEEN

Non–Marine Molluscs

ROBERT H. COWIE, BENOÎT FONTAINE
AND PHILIPPE BOUCHET

Summary

Non-marine molluscs stand out as the major animal group under the most severe threat. Among the 8664 mollusc species evaluated for the IUCN Red List (version 2019-1), 300 are considered Extinct out of a total 872 listed Extinct species. However, only ~10% of molluscs have been evaluated and other assessments of the number of extinct species are much higher, 3000 to over 5000, almost exclusively non-marine species. As for most other groups, threats faced by non-marine molluscs are habitat loss, probably the most important, but also impacts of introduced species, exploitation, generally of less concern, and climate change, likely to have serious effects into the future. Oceanic island species, often narrowly endemic, are especially threatened and constitute a high proportion of recorded extinctions. Anthropogenic activities have caused non-marine mollusc extinctions since prehistory, but threats have increased greatly over the last few centuries and will probably continue to increase. Most mollusc species for which a population trend has been evaluated by IUCN are stable or declining; those few that are increasing are primarily introduced and invasive. Most threatened are oceanic island snails, North American and other freshwater bivalves, and the diverse and highly endemic micro-snails of Southeast Asian limestone outcrops.

15.1 Introduction

The IUCN Red List is a rigorous vehicle for assessing the conservation status of plant and animal species. However, although all mammal and bird species and overall almost 70% of all vertebrates recognised by IUCN have been evaluated, only a tiny fraction of invertebrates has been evaluated (IUCN, 2019, Table 1a). As a measure of threat, the Red List is probably quite accurate for birds and mammals, but severely underassesses invertebrates. Non-marine molluscs (Figure 15.1) stand out as the major group under the most severe threat.

Figure 15.1 The diversity of non-marine molluscs: (A) *Ancylastrum cumingianus*, from Tasmania, listed as Critically Endangered by IUCN because of the impoundment of its freshwater habitat and predation by introduced fish (photo: K. Macfarlane), (B) *Iberus gualtieranus*, from southern Spain, listed as Endangered by IUCN as a result of habitat destruction and overexploitation (see text) (photo: Gualtieranus/Wikimedia Commons), (C) *Hamiota altilis*, a North American unionid bivalve, listed as Endangered by IUCN, displaying the lure it uses to attract a host fish (photo: W.R. Haag, US Forest Service), (D) *Carelia turricula*, from Hawaii, went extinct in the mid 20th century, listed as Extinct by IUCN (photo R.H. Cowie), (E) *Zonitarion* sp., an undescribed species, not listed by IUCN, from Gabon rainforest, illustrating the fact that we know nearly nothing about the conservation status of most tropical species from continental areas (photo: B. Fontaine), (F) *Plectostoma crassipupa*, a species from limestone hills in Malaysia, listed as Least Concern by IUCN (photo: Liew Thor-Seng), (G) *Partula hyalina* from the Austral Islands, to which it was introduced

With the development of global taxonomic authority lists, the answers to the question 'How many mollusc species have been described?' are increasingly precise. As of 20 January 2020, MolluscaBase (www.molluscabase.org) had catalogued 74,942 valid described mollusc species, of which 48,704 were marine (estimated >98% complete, i.e. those not in MolluscaBase are described species not yet entered by the editors), 20,521 terrestrial (estimated ~70% complete) and 5884 freshwater (estimated ~80% complete). (The figure of 80,325 (IUCN 2019, table 1a) from MolluscaBase, as accessed by IUCN on 15 March 2019, mistakenly included fossils). The number of Recent described mollusc species is thus around 85,000. However, Recent Mollusca are far from fully inventoried globally, with a yearly increment of about 900 newly described species, with no sign of levelling; the real number of species is well in excess of 100,000, possibly even 150,000–200,000 (Bouchet, unpublished). A not negligible number of these newly described species are recently extinct, described based on specimens from the soil shell bank (e.g. Richling and Bouchet, 2013) or archaeological excavations (e.g. Haag, 2009).

Compared to other invertebrate groups, a relatively high number of mollusc species has been evaluated: 8664 species, just over 10% of the estimated 85,000 described species, with 2231 (26%) considered threatened (Box 15.1). Nonetheless, compared to mammals and birds, that only 10% of molluscan diversity has been evaluated is inevitably because of inadequate funding, not only for molluscs but for all invertebrates. Furthermore, and despite the fact that many of the evaluated mollusc species were chosen because they were judged sufficiently well known, a high proportion (25%) was evaluated as Data Deficient, compared to only 14.5% for all other non-molluscan species evaluated, and in stark contrast to mammals and birds, for which only 5.4% are listed as Data Deficient (Table 15.1). In terms of species listed as Extinct, molluscs stand out, with 300 of the 872 Extinct animal species. Combining this with those listed as Extinct in the Wild (14), Critically Endangered (Possibly Extinct) (141) and Critically Endangered (Possibly Extinct in the Wild) (1), gives a plausible upper estimate of 456 extinct mollusc species in the Red List (IUCN, 2019), i.e. 5.3% of those evaluated.

Of the mollusc species evaluated, only four marine species, all gastropods, are listed as Extinct, and only five cephalopods, four marine bivalves and 45 marine gastropods are listed in the threatened categories (Box 15.1), reflecting the general perception that marine

---

Figure 15.1 (*cont.*) by early Polynesian settlers from its native Tahiti, listed as Vulnerable by IUCN (photo: B. Fontaine), (H) *Pseudosubulina theoripkeni*, described from French Guiana in 2012 and found alive for the first time in 2018, but not listed by IUCN, another species illustrating how little we know about the conservation status of tropical continental species (photo: O. Gargominy), (I) *Vertigo moulinsiana*, from Europe, listed as Vulnerable by IUCN, is more widespread than previously thought (see text) (photo: O. Gargominy), (J) *Australdonta teaae*, from Rurutu, Austral Islands, was already extinct when described but not listed by IUCN, though listed by Cowie et al. (2017) (photo: O. Gargominy), (K) *Helix ceratina*, from Corsica, listed by IUCN (2019) as Critically Endangered but benefitting from habitat restoration (see text) (photo: O. Gargominy). Photos not to the same scale.

Box 15.1

IUCN Listings

Numbers of Mollusca in IUCN *Red List* categories[a] by ecosystem[b] (Red List version 2019-1, via 'advanced search').

Class	EX	EW	CR	EN	VU	NT	LR/CD	DD	LC	Total
Bivalvia										
Marine	0	0	0	0	4	0	4	15	6	29
Freshwater	32	0	72	62	50	55	0	155	312	738
Both	0	0	0	0	0	0	0	5	19	24
Total Bivalvia	32	0	72	62	54	55	4	175	337	791
Gastropoda										
Marine	4	0	5	13	27	29	0	152	488	718
Freshwater	74	3	263	228	416	165	0	922	823	2894
Terrestrial	190	11	317	252	517	431	0	558	1299	3575
Total Gastropoda	268	14	585	493	960	625	0	1632	2610	7187
Cephalopoda										
Marine	0	0	1	2	2	1	0	376	304	686
Total Cephalopoda	0	0	1	2	2	1	0	376	304	686
Total Mollusca	300	14	658	557	1016	681	4	2183	3251	8664

[a] EX – Extinct, EW – Extinct in the Wild, CR – Critically Endangered, EN –Endangered, VU – Vulnerable, NT – Near Threatened, LR/CD – Lower Risk: Conservation Dependent, LC – Least Concern, DD – Data Deficient

[b] A small number of gastropod species are categorised on the Red List as occurring in two and in some cases three ecosystems and are therefore counted more than once in Red List totals. We allocated them reasonably but somewhat arbitrarily to a single ecosystem for the purpose of this analysis.

IUCN has evaluated ~10% of described mollusc species, with the overwhelming majority being gastropods, and of which most are non-marine. Of those listed as Extinct (300) or Extinct in the Wild (14) only 4, all Extinct, are marine. Of those in the threatened categories (Critically Endangered, Endangered, Vulnerable), all but a few are non-marine. However, of all mollusc species evaluated 25% are Data Deficient, with the majority of these being non-marine, reflecting the lack of adequate knowledge for many species.

Table 15.1 *Numbers of Mollusca, of mammals and birds and of all non-mollusc taxa in IUCN Red List categories (Red List version 2019-1)*

	EX	EW	CR	EN	VU	NT	LR/CD	DD	LC	Total
Mollusca	300	14	658	557	1016	681	4	2183	3251	8664
Mammals and birds	237	7	426	960	1329	1363	0	911	11,685	16,918
All non-mollusc taxa	572	55	5256	8618	11,054	5506	204	13,032	45,551	89,848

species are less threatened and have suffered lower extinction rates than non-marine species (e.g. McKinney, 1998). Although this view has been challenged on the grounds that knowledge of marine species is more limited than of non-marine species (e.g. Carlton et al., 1999), we suggest that knowledge of many, especially tropical, land snail species is at least as inadequate as knowledge of many marine mollusc species, and we do not think there is a demonstrated bias in recording marine versus non-marine mollusc extinction.

15.2 Timeframe for Listing Molluscs

The IUCN Red List was initiated in 1964. Molluscs were first included in 1983, when six species, all North American freshwater mussels (Unionida), were listed as Extinct out of 123 mollusc species evaluated (Figure 15.2). Following the realisation that an ill-conceived biological control programme begun in 1977 (Clarke et al., 1984) had caused the extinction of the entire fauna of partulid snails on the island of Moorea in French Polynesia (Murray et al., 1988) and that the extinction of Hawaiian species could be attributed in part to the same cause, initiated in the mid-1950s (Hadfield, 1986), more effort was put into evaluating molluscs for the Red List. In the 1986 Red List 53 species were listed as Extinct (45 Hawaiian land snails, 8 North American freshwater bivalves) out of 323 species evaluated. In 1988, 68 were listed as Extinct (four North American freshwater snails, the same 45 Hawaiian species, 7 *Partula* from Moorea and 12 North American bivalves) of 438 evaluated. The 1990 Red List added just one extinct species, *Parmacella gervaisi* from southern France, out of 513 species now evaluated. Following evaluation of many oceanic

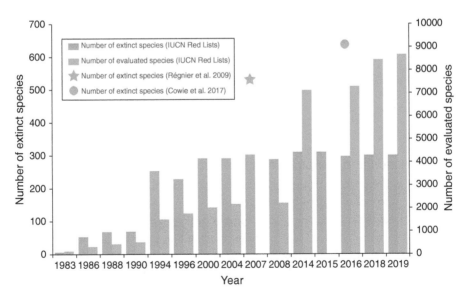

Figure 15.2 Numbers of mollusc species listed as Extinct by IUCN since the initiation of the Red List in 1964 to version 2019–1 (selected versions of the Red List only) with the total numbers of mollusc species evaluated, and estimates of actual known mollusc species extinctions (Régnier et al., 2009; Cowie et al., 2017).

island species, notably from Hawaii and French Polynesia, the 1994 Red List included 253 extinct species out of 1501 evaluated. The 1996 Red List followed a new system of categories, with a number of species previously listed as Extinct recategorised as Not Evaluated, reducing the number listed as Extinct to 228 of 1760 evaluated.

In subsequent lists the number listed as Extinct increased to around 300 and has hovered there for the last two decades, despite the total number of species evaluated having almost quintupled (Figure 15.2). At the time of writing, 300 molluscs were listed as Extinct out of 8664 evaluated (IUCN, 2019).

15.3 Red List Extinctions Underestimate the Real Number

The Red List (IUCN, 2019) lists 872 species (750 animals, 122 plants) as Extinct, including 300 mollusc species. Molluscs, despite the small proportion that has been evaluated, thus represent 34% of all species extinctions and 40% of animal extinctions, as listed by IUCN. Based on bibliographic research and consultation with experts, Régnier et al. (2009) obtained, at that time, a more realistic assessment of the numbers of recorded mollusc extinctions, 533 species, far more than the number on the Red List, leading these authors to comment 'For mollusks [sic] (and all invertebrates) there is a disconnect between extinctions known to experts or published in the scientific literature and extinctions on the IUCN Red List, whereas for birds and mammals, the IUCN Red List is the scientific reference'. Following this approach, Cowie et al. (2017) listed 638 extinct species, 380 possibly extinct and 14 extinct in the wild, a total of 1032 species in these combined categories, and more than twice as many as IUCN listed in these categories. Even so, this approach only considers species with readily available information; it is therefore biased. To overcome this bias, Régnier et al. (2015a) developed an alternative approach using a random global sample of land snails. They found that, based on expert opinion and a probabilistic model, respectively, 10% and 12.5% of land snail species in the random sample should be classified as Extinct. When extrapolated to all non-marine mollusc species, this suggests that 3000–3750 are extinct, or even 5100 species (Cowie et al., 2017), an order of magnitude more, at least, than the IUCN number.

15.4 Causes and Timeframe of Mollusc Extinctions

Although anthropogenic extinctions are best documented in the last two centuries, modern extinctions appear to have begun well before AD 1500, the starting point of the IUCN Red List. The following paragraphs outline some examples of non-marine mollusc extinctions and their causes over the course of time up to the present. Habitat loss is probably the most important threat, although interactions among the various causes may be complex.

15.4.1 Non-Anthropogenic Causes

There is a rich molluscan fossil record, the vast majority of species having gone extinct long before the advent of *Homo sapiens*. For others, in some cases known as 'subfossils' (e.g. Régnier et al, 2015b), the relative roles of climate, habitat change and anthropogenic impact are unknown. However, there are few Recent documented land snail extinctions for which anthropogenic impact is excluded, e.g. the land snail *Zonites santoriniensis*, endemic to Santorini in the Aegean Sea, which probably did not survive the cataclysmic eruption of the island in around 1500 BC (Riedel and Norris, 1987).

15.4.2 Habitat Loss

Loss of habitat is probably the main cause of extinction and continues to be a major threat, because of deforestation, cultivation, mineral extraction and urbanisation.

On Porto Santo, in the Madeiran archipelago, at least nine geomitrid land snail species are known only from empty shells. They are presumed to have gone extinct before the nineteenth century scientific exploration of the island (De Mattia et al., 2018), no doubt a result of massive deforestation that also impacted the land snails of Madeira itself (Goodfriend et al., 1994).

The freshwater mussel *Reginaia apalachicola* is known only from pre-Columbian archaeological sites dating from 650 to 1500 years BP in the Apalachicola basin of the southeastern USA. Its demise has been related to the clearing and settlement of the Apalachicola basin, but it is possible that although it became extinct before it was described, it may have persisted into the late nineteenth century and no other mussel extinctions were documented in North America until 1924 (Haag, 2009).

Oceanic islands, particularly Pacific islands, have seen more mollusc extinctions than any other geographical region (Chiba and Cowie, 2016). In the Hawaiian Islands, which supported a documented fauna of >750 land snail species, it has been estimated that 65–90% of the fauna has gone extinct (Lydeard et al., 2004). Some of these extinctions may have occurred before human discovery and settlement of the islands 1200–800 years ago, but most happened subsequently (Régnier et al, 2015b).

Elsewhere in the Pacific, similar scenarios have affected many land snail groups, and while some extinctions through habitat destruction took place following early colonisation of the islands, the rate of habitat loss and consequent land snail extinction increased markedly following European arrival (e.g. Neubert et al., 2009; Sartori et al., 2014). For example, in the Gambier Islands, deforestation began with the first arrival of Polynesian people around 1000 years ago and peaked in the seventeenth and eighteenth centuries, with total destruction of the native flora (Conte and Kirch, 2008). A few of the 46 known land snail species were yet extant in the 1840s–1860s, but no living specimens of any but the three still extant in 1997 have been collected since the nineteeth century; the remainder were described from shells collected from the shell bank of the soil (Richling and Bouchet, 2013). Habitat destruction and species loss will probably continue, especially on islands not yet so severely affected (e.g. Rundell, 2010).

Although the Pacific islands stand out, snails of other oceanic islands have suffered similarly. In the Atlantic, soon after St. Helena was discovered in 1502, habitat destruction began and continued through to the mid-twentieth century, when a goat eradication programme (ultimately unsuccessful; Campbell and Donlan, 2005) was undertaken and the need for wood fuel had declined. But by then the natural vegetation had disappeared from most of the island, and of the 20 endemic snail species, only one or perhaps two remained; predation by rats, introduced at least by the end of the sixteenth century, may also have played a part in their extinction (Ashmole and Ashmole, 2000).

Much the same train of events led to the demise of many of the land snails of Mauritius. First colonised in the seventeenth century, gradual expansion of deforestation resulted in ~80% loss of native vegetation by the end of the nineteenth century, with less than 2% remaining at the end of the twentieth century; of the 81 endemic land snail species only 36 remain (Griffiths and Florens, 2006). Predation, notably by introduced rats but possibly also toads, in remnant snail populations may have been the death knell for these species.

Even once habitat loss has been arrested, which in most parts of the world it has not, there may still be an extinction debt to pay; we have not seen the last of land snail extinctions caused by past habitat destruction (Otto et al., 2017).

While anthropogenic extinction of non-marine molluscs has taken place over centuries, many species are still threatened by recent and ongoing habitat loss. For example, the freshwater snail *Melanopsis parreyssii* was listed as Critically Endangered on the Red List in 2013. It was extremely narrowly endemic in Romania but had been introduced to Hungary and Bulgaria. However, by 2010 these introduced populations had vanished (Sîrbu et al., 2013). The Romanian locality was part of a system sustained by a geothermal aquifer that was a nature reserve and a Natura 2000 Site of Community Importance. Yet despite the ostensible protection, rapidly increasing development of the geothermal waters, especially for tourism, led to shrinking of the thermal lakes to the point at which only one tiny lake remained. By 2011 the spring serving it ceased activity (Sîrbu et al., 2013) and by 2015 it had become little more than a puddle supporting no molluscs except an invasive bivalve; *M. parreyssii* was therefore deemed extinct in the wild (Sîrbu and Benedek, 2016), although it remains Critically Endangered on the Red List (IUCN, 2019).

A species of *Powelliphanta* is another example of a species on the brink of extinction from loss of its entire habitat. First collected in 1996 on Mount Augustus, a peak in New Zealand's South Island and the site of a large open cast coal mine, it was not recognised as a possible new species until 2003, by which time much of its habitat had been destroyed, with the entire remaining 8.5 ha of ridge-top habitat under severe threat (Walker et al., 2008). The species was described as *Powelliphanta augusta* in 2008 (Walker et al., 2008). Following legal action (see Walker et al., 2008), all snails and eggs that could be found were brought into captivity, beginning in 2006. Soon thereafter, all but a tiny piece of snail habitat was destroyed (Walker et al., 2008). Many of the snails were transferred back to the wild at three sites with supposedly similar habitat, but they were invaded by weeds and the mortality rate in these populations meant they were unlikely to survive (Morris, 2010). The captive snails exhibit slower growth and higher hatchling mortality than in the original wild population, and tragically, a large proportion died following an electrical malfunction in their temperature-controlled facility (James et al., 2013).

Limestone outcrops in Southeast Asia support extremely narrow endemic land snails, in some cases endemic to a single outcrop, with many undescribed. But they are under severe threat from mining of their habitat for cement production and for marble and road-surfacing materials (Schilthuizen et al., 2005). One species from Peninsular Malaysia was even named *Charopa lafargei* after the Lafarge cement company that was threatening its habitat, despite the company's stated positive biodiversity goals (Vermeulen and Marzuki, 2014). At the time of writing it remains extant (J.J. Vermeulen, personal communication).

Ancient oligotrophic lakes are another kind of 'island' that host highly endemic freshwater gastropod faunas that may vanish even before being documented. They are threatened by eutrophication and landfilling. For example, *Tchangmargarya ziyi* is a large (45 mm) recently described viviparid from Lake Babuhai in Yunnan, China, most of which has been filled for golf course construction, with the population probably now extinct (Zhang, 2017). Ancient lakes in the Balkans face severe reduction of habitat quality because of eutrophication and excessive water abstraction for agriculture. For example, 37% of the malacofauna of Lakes Prespa and Mriki Prespa is endemic to the lakes. Surveys conducted during 2003–2010 demonstrated a decline and potential loss of mollusc diversity, with all endemic species being of conservation concern (Albrecht et al., 2012); five are classified as Critically Endangered, although one of these (*Vinodolia lacustris*) was not found during the survey and could well be evaluated as Extinct.

Many reaches of large rivers, especially rapids, riffles and shoals that are key habitats for numerous freshwater molluscs are threatened everywhere by the construction of dams and by blasting to remove obstacles to navigation. Examples of extinct, probably extinct or extinct in the wild species from such habitats include *Helicostoa sinensis*, from the Yangtze (Wilke, 2019), *Melanoides agglutinans*, from the Congo (IUCN, 2019), and species of *Aylacostoma*, from the Paraná (Vogler et al., 2016; Cowie et al., 2017). *Helicostoa sinensis* (not listed by IUCN, 2019) and *Melanoides agglutinans* (Critically Endangered; IUCN, 2019) became Extinct without any conservation action. *Aylacostoma guaraniticum* and *A. stigmaticum* are Extinct (listed Extinct in the Wild; IUCN, 2019) and *A. chloroticum* and *A. brunneum* are Extinct in the Wild (the former so listed, the latter not listed; IUCN, 2019) and held in a captive breeding programme. Habitat loss from impoundment and channelisation of streams and rivers has been considered the main cause of the extinction of many species of North American mussels, although the ongoing decline may also be due to other, enigmatic causes (Haag, 2009, 2019). With so many such construction projects worldwide, this is a serious conservation issue.

Many more examples of decline and extinction of non-marine molluscs resulting from habitat loss could be provided, and as vast tracts of the Earth continue to be altered, often irreversibly, it is difficult to imagine that such trends will slow. Many species will no doubt not be described or even discovered prior to their demise.

15.4.3 Impacts of Introduced Species

It is generally difficult to demonstrate definitively that an invasive species has caused the extinction of another species. For example, following the zebra mussel (*Dreissena polymorpha*) invasion of North America beginning around 1985, many native freshwater mussels (Unionida) were considered doomed (Ricciardi et al., 1998). At localities with high zebra mussel densities, native mussel populations were being extirpated and some species were in steep decline or becoming regionally extinct. Over 60 species were thought to be in danger of global extinction from the combined effects of zebra mussels and habitat degradation (Ricciardi et al., 1998). However, a decade later, Strayer and Malcom (2007), focusing on four species, showed that although they had declined steeply following zebra mussel invasion, by 2000–2004 their populations had stabilised at 4–22% of their pre-invasion densities, offering hope that they could co-exist with the invaders, albeit at much lower densities. Another species of *Dreissena*, the Quagga mussel (*D. bugensis*), had been introduced at around the same time. It also became widespread in North America, but less is known about it and its distribution seems not to have expanded as comprehensively as that of *D. polymorpha*; it seems less likely to affect native unionids (Karatayev et al., 2015). Another mussel, *Limnoperna fortunei*, is having similar impacts in South America (Darrigran et al., 2012), but no extinctions have been attributed to it.

In contrast, the prime example of an invasive species causing extinction of mollusc species is the introduction of the predatory snail *Euglandina rosea* (in fact a species complex; Meyer et al., 2017) to the islands of the Pacific, notably to the Hawaiian Islands and the Society Islands of French Polynesia, but also elsewhere (e.g. Cowie and Cook, 2001), in poorly considered efforts to control the invasive giant African snail, *Achatina fulica* (Hadfield, 1986; Murray et al., 1988). The clearest evidence of direct impact was that as *E. rosea* spread across the island of Moorea, the endemic *Partula* tree snail species vanished in its wake (though a few remnant populations were subsequently discovered and represent most of the major genetic lineages; Haponski et al., 2019); it did not control *A. fulica* (Murray et al., 1988; Chiba and Cowie, 2016). On the other islands of the Society group the same story played out, with the exception of a few remnant populations surviving on Tahiti in addition to those on Moorea (Coote and Loève, 2003; Gerlach, 2016). As currently recognised (Gerlach, 2016), of 18 Moorean and Tahitian species, 6 are Extinct, 5 are Extinct in the Wild, 4 are represented by remnant wild individuals and 3 by both captive and remnant wild individuals (Haponski et al., 2019). Taxonomic revision of these partulid species is sorely needed to resolve the discord between the traditional morphological taxonomy (Gerlach, 2016) and molecular (including phylogenomic) data (Haponski et al., 2019).

In Hawaii, the combination of *E. rosea* and invasive rats, following on from habitat destruction, caused the decline of endemic achatinelline tree snails (Hadfield, 1986). Another introduced predatory snail, *Oxychilus alliarius*, may yet impact endemic Hawaiian species, notably the single species in the monotypic helicarionid genus *Kaala* (Curry et al., 2016), and potentially other oceanic island species (Curry et al., 2019). Rats have been widely implicated in land snail extinction in the Pacific (Chiba and Cowie, 2016). The invasive predatory flatworm *Platydemus manokwari* has caused the extinction of endemic Pacific island snails, notably in the Ogasawara Islands (Chiba and Cowie, 2016). Competition between invasive and native snails may also be important, but few definitive instances have been documented (e.g. Riley and Dybdahl, 2015).

The impacts of invasive species are often inextricably linked to those of habitat loss, as invasive species such as ungulates (especially goats) and rats, may drastically alter habitat, rendering it unsuitable for native animal species, and habitat alteration may facilitate the spread of additional invasive species. As such, invasive species can be at least the partial cause of extinction, acting in concert or consecutively with habitat alteration. But, with some clear exceptions, it is difficult to say that invasive species, per se, have been the cause of specific mollusc extinctions.

15.4.4 Exploitation and Collecting

Numerous non-marine mollusc species are exploited for human consumption. In Europe, and especially in Mediterranean countries, various larger species of land snails are eaten, most notably *Helix pomatia*, *Helix lucorum* and *Cornu aspersum*, which used to be collected in the wild but are now increasingly farmed. Despite local declines in *Helix pomatia* abundance, whether this is a conservation issue is unknown. Various other species are eaten around the Mediterranean (Yildirim et al., 2004) but few seem to have attracted concern, for instance *Iberus gualtieranus* (Figure 15.1b), a species from southern Spain, which is listed as Endangered in part because of to indiscriminate and uncontrolled collecting, as it has great gastronomic appeal. In New Caledonia, the endemic 'bulimes' (genus *Placostylus*) have regressed everywhere because of habitat loss (Neubert et al., 2009), but they remain common on the Isle of Pines, where they are harvested for the gourmet trade, necessitating regulations that prohibit export from the island. In Asia, various species of Ampullariidae, Viviparidae and Pachychilidae are eaten, as are a number of clams and mussels (e.g. Köhler et al., 2012), and Achatinidae are eaten in West Africa (e.g. Nyoagbe et al., 2016); but none of these species has attracted great concern.

A few land snails are used for medicinal and religious purposes (Cowie and Robinson, 2003; Neto et al., 2012) but there is no evidence that these usages have led to their decline and certainly not extinction.

In the nineteenth century, freshwater mussels (Unionida) were commercially harvested for their pearls, notably in the USA and Europe; overharvesting led to their decline and the fishery was largely abandoned (Anthony and Downing, 2001). However, soon thereafter, the demand for freshwater mussel shells for making buttons burgeoned, causing further declines and adding to the already serious and increasing threats from habitat degradation; but this industry essentially died out with the advent of plastics (Anthony and Downing, 2001), although it persists in other parts of the world (Beasley, 2001). However, the discovery in Japan that mussel shell material could act as nuclei for cultured pearl production, resulted in a further phase of exploitation in the USA for export, although as mussel stocks declined, so the industry began to wane (Anthony and Downing, 2001). Although overexploitation caused severe declines of some species, habitat degradation has been considered the primary cause of mussel extinction (Haag, 2009, 2019).

The shell-collecting hobby and associated trade focuses more on marine than non-marine species. However, among non-marine species there are a few notable instances in which shell collecting and ornamental use may have been at least partially responsible for the decline and perhaps extinction of certain species. For example, collecting of snails by late nineteenth- and early twentieth-century shell collectors quite possibly had an important impact on some of the larger and more colourful Hawaiian species (Hadfield, 1986). Partulids, achatinellines and other species have been used in the Pacific islands to make necklaces and other ornaments. For example, *Cyclomorpha flava* was heavily collected for this purpose on the island of Anaa (Tuamotu archipelago), possibly impacting its populations (Fontaine, personal observations). The collection of ~10,000 shells of the partulid *Eua zebrina* that were used to make the chandeliers in the lobby of American Samoa's then main hotel (Cowie and Cook, 2001) must have significantly reduced some of its populations. While collection and trade of shells of non-marine species is much more limited than of marine species, it nonetheless may lead to endangerment. However, the Convention on International Trade in Endangered Species (CITES) lists only three non-marine gastropod taxa: the genus *Achatinella*, with 39 species listed as either Extinct (15) or Critically Endangered (24) by IUCN (2019), the genus *Polymita*, with no species evaluated, and *Papustyla pulcherrima*, listed as Near Threatened.

Overall, therefore, exploitation and collecting have not been major causes of non-marine mollusc extinction.

15.4.5 Climate Change

Land snails may be especially susceptible to the ramifications of anthropogenic climate change (Nicolai and Ansart, 2017), but there is as yet no instance of extinction of a mollusc species that can be definitely attributed to such change. However, continued warming will probably have more serious effects in the future.

Rhachistia aldabrae, an endemic cerastid from Aldabra Atoll, was widespread and abundant in the 1970s, but was thought to have gone extinct by the late 1990s as a result of declining rainfall, and was therefore placed on the Red List as Extinct. This is the only instance of a mollusc reported as having gone extinct because of climate change. However, although in 2014 an adult and a few juveniles were located, it seems likely that with ongoing climate change it may yet succumb. It is now listed as Critically Endangered (IUCN, 2019).

Pearce and Paustian (2013) undertook extensive elevational surveys in Pennsylvania, USA, to assess whether, with climate warming, species forced ever upward would eventually be unable to retreat further. Of the 69 species recorded, 5 appeared especially susceptible. Such susceptibility is of particular concern on oceanic islands. On many Pacific islands, habitat destruction and establishment of invasive species at lower elevations has resulted in most of the remaining endemic land snails being confined to higher elevations (e.g. Régnier et al., 2015b), either because their lower elevation populations were extirpated or because they are evolutionarily adapted to the lower temperatures at these higher elevations and historically only ever occurred there (e.g. *Nesoropupa* spp. on Tahiti; Gargominy, 2008). A similar situation obtains in the Azores (Cameron et al., 2012). As such, with limited opportunity to move to higher elevations as the climate warms, these species face extinction.

There have also been several studies on the negative impact of climate change on freshwater mussels (e.g. Hastie et al., 2003).

Climate change has many complex and inter-related ramifications and while it may directly lead to extinction of non-marine molluscs as the climate exceeds their physiological tolerances, habitat change and the facilitation of invasive species resulting from climate change may also do so to the extent that the proximate cause of extinction may be the result of broader environmental change.

15.5 IUCN Species Trajectories

While the statistics regarding extinction of molluscs are depressing, the explicit goal of the Red List is not to assess extinction but to assess relative extinction risk, thereby focusing attention on conservation needs. Thus for each species, IUCN now evaluates (if there are adequate data) whether it is declining, stable or increasing, based on the IUCN Red List Categories and Criteria (IUCN, 2012), which generally means that trends are determined over 10 years or three generations, whichever is longer, up to 100 years.

Of the 7678 non-extinct gastropods in the Red List (Box 15.1), trajectories have been evaluated for 6578 (Table 15.2). However, among these, the trajectories of a high proportion of both gastropods (72%) and bivalves (65%) were evaluated as 'unknown'. Among the remainder, bivalves appeared to be declining more than gastropods; only 37% of these bivalves were stable, while 75% of the gastropods were stable. Very few were evaluated as increasing: 6 of 238 bivalves (2.5%) and 35 of 1,647 gastropods (2.1%).

Reliance on the '10-year rule' (Fox et al., 2019) to assess trends of invertebrates has, however, received criticism, with 10 years considered too short to detect a real trend. Few mollusc species are monitored with sufficient frequency, which is a factor in the high proportion with 'unknown' trends. The number for which a trend could be evaluated may be highly biased.

Notwithstanding this criticism, among all 41 increasing species, the range of 27 at least has expanded because of anthropogenic introductions (Table 15.3). All but two of these

Table 15.2 *Population trends of those bivalve and gastropod species evaluated, by ecosystem[a], based on Red List evaluations (Red List version 2019–1)*

	Unknown	Stable	Decreasing	Increasing	Total
Bivalvia					
Marine	18	1	0	0	19
Freshwater	417	86	145	6	654
Total Bivalvia	**435**	**87**	**145**	**6**	**673**
Gastropoda					
Marine	532	45	15	0	592
Freshwater	2254	195	168	17	2634
Terrestrial	1472	999	190	18	2679
Total Gastropoda	**4258**	**1239**	**373**	**35**	**5905**
Total	**4695**	**1326**	**519**	**41**	**6578**

[a] A small number of gastropod species are categorised on the Red List as occurring in two and in some cases three ecosystems and are therefore counted more than once in Red List totals. We have allocated them reasonably but somewhat arbitrarily to a single ecosystem only for the purpose of this analysis.

Table 15.3 *Species of bivalves and gastropods evaluated as increasing, and whether introduced or invasive as reported in their Red List (IUCN, 2019) species accounts*

Species	Category	Habitat	Introduced/invasive
Bivalvia			
Dreissena polymorpha	LC	Freshwater	'Invasive'
Elliptio complanata	LC	Freshwater	Not known as introduced, 'stable'
Dreissena bugensis	LC	Freshwater	'Invasive'
Corbicula fluminea	LC	Freshwater	'One of the worst invaders of aquatic ecosystems'
Corbicula fluminalis	LC	Freshwater	'Introduced'
Limnoperna fortunei	LC	Freshwater	'Introduced'
Gastropoda			
Monacha fruticola	LC	Terrestrial	'Introduced'
Tandonia serbica	LC	Terrestrial	'Probably introduced'
Xerocrassa molinae	NT	Terrestrial	Not known as introduced
Pachnodus silhouettanus	NT	Terrestrial	Not known as introduced
Gyraulus chinensis	LC	Freshwater	'Introduced'
Brephulopsis cylindrica	LC	Terrestrial	'Widespread alien species'
Haitia acuta	LC	Freshwater	'Widely introduced'
Deroceras sturanyi	LC	Freshwater	'Very widely spread through introduction'
Cipangopaludina chinensis	LC	Freshwater	'Introduced widely in North America'
Oxychilus cellarius	LC	Terrestrial	'Introduced to many parts of the world'
Oxychilus draparnaudi	LC	Terrestrial	'Introduced to many parts of the world'
Xerocrassa meda	LC	Terrestrial	'Introduced'
Pomacea canaliculata	LC	Terrestrial	'One of the worst invaders'
Pseudosuccinea columella	LC	Freshwater	'Highly invasive'
Trochulus clandestinus	LC	Terrestrial	Not known as introduced
Ferrissia dohrnianus	LC	Freshwater	Not known as introduced
Chilostoma sphaeriostoma	LC	Terrestrial	'Expanded its range…possibly due to…human activities'
Discus macclintocki	LC	Terrestrial	Not known as introduced 'stable'
Biomphalaria choanomphala	LC	Freshwater	Not known as introduced
Biomphalaria pfeifferi	LC	Freshwater	'An invasive species'
Oxychilus alliarius	LC	Terrestrial	'Introduced…often invasive'
Tandonia kusceri	LC	Terrestrial	'Introduced'
Arion hortensis	LC	Terrestrial	'Outside Europe all records are likely to be introductions'

Table 15.3 (*cont.*)

Species	Category	Habitat	Introduced/invasive
Gyraulus convexiusculus	LC	Freshwater	'Introduced'
Viviparus acerosus	LC	Freshwater	Not known as introduced
Trochoidea caroni	LC	Terrestrial	Not known as introduced
Gyraulus rossmaessleri	LC	Freshwater	Not known as introduced
Biomphalaria alexandrina	LC	Freshwater	Not known as introduced but 'a pest'
Charpentieria itala	LC	Terrestrial	'Introduced'
Deroceras invadens	LC	Terrestrial	'Invasive'
Bulinus liratus	LC	Freshwater	Not known as introduced
Tarebia granifera	LC	Freshwater	'Very widely introduced'
Ferrissia fragilis	LC	Freshwater	'Wide introduced distribution'
Bellamya constricta	LC	Freshwater	Not known as introduced
Melanoides tuberculata	LC	Freshwater	'Introduced'

increasing species are evaluated as Least Concern. The two others, *Xerocrassa molinae* and *Pachnodus silhouettanus*, are listed as Not Threatened, the former exhibiting a slight increase perhaps because the islands on which it lives are protected, and the latter increasing by actively colonising abandoned coconut plantations. The majority of these increasing species are introduced, often invasive, species. Also, two species, the bivalve *Elliptio complanata* and the gastropod *Discus macclintocki*, are indicated in the assessment text as stable but categorised as increasing. Thus only 15 (or perhaps 13) species are increasing naturally or in one case because of conservation action, a tiny fraction of the total of 1885 species for which a trajectory could be determined. But at least if species that were evaluated as stable really are stable over the long term then their conservation status is good.

15.6 Global Status

Although this chapter focuses heavily on mollusc extinction, noting that this is particularly severe on oceanic islands, it is becoming clear that much greater numbers of non-marine molluscs, though not yet extinct, are under considerable threat. For example, the European Red List of terrestrial molluscs (Neubert et al., 2019) considers 2469 species as native in Europe, but only five of these as Extinct, apparently in marked contrast to the picture painted above. However, 19.5% of the species are Critically Endangered, Endangered or Vulnerable. Adding the Near Threatened species, increases those at risk to 33.5%, and hypothesising that the Data Deficient species may also be threatened, gives a maximum of 43.6%, almost half the terrestrial malacofauna of Europe. Extrapolating to the rest of the world, suggests that over 9000 terrestrial mollusc species are at risk. The situation for freshwater species is probably worse. For example, in 2011, of 624 African species, although only 14 were considered Extinct, 57% were evaluated as being in one of the threatened categories or as Data Deficient (Seddon et al., 2011).

Arguably then, although the likely number of recent mollusc extinctions is great, especially on oceanic islands, the overall global picture is even worse because close to half of all extant mollusc species are probably under some level of threat. Given the enormous and ongoing habitat loss in tropical continental regions, this scenario may not be exaggerated.

15.7 Notable Conservation Efforts

Despite all the threats faced and extinctions suffered by non-marine molluscs, committed people have undertaken diverse projects to protect and save many threatened species. These projects include efforts to breed threatened species in captivity for introduction to the wild once, optimistically, threats are ameliorated, habitat protection to support populations of endangered species, inventory surveys to locate populations of threatened species and to identify hotspots of threatened diversity, and surveys to locate as yet undescribed species before they vanish.

Numerous projects have been undertaken by or under the aegis of the IUCN Mollusc Specialist Group. Particularly notable is the captive breeding and currently ongoing release programme for Society Island partulids (Coote et al., 2019). Other captive breeding programmes include those in Hawaii for achatinelline tree snails (e.g. Sischo et al., 2016), in Bermuda for *Poecilozonites* spp. (Outerbridge et al., 2019) and in the Ogasawara Islands of Japan primarily for *Mandarina* spp. (Mori et al., 2020), as well as for endangered bivalves in both North America (e.g. Neves, 2004) and Europe (e.g. Kyle et al., 2017).

Major efforts have continued to be made by IUCN to evaluate additional mollusc species in key regions including eastern Mediterranean freshwater species, European terrestrial molluscs and Pacific island land snails, among others referenced by Cowie et al. (2017), as well as the freshwater molluscs of Madagascar (Van Damme et al., 2018). Other concerted surveys have been undertaken over large regions, e.g. eastern and southern Africa (Seddon et al., 2005), and more narrowly focused but intensive surveys of highly endangered and locally endemic groups that have already suffered catastrophic extinction, e.g. Hawaiian Amastridae (Régnier et al., 2015b), have also been undertaken, in some cases rediscovering species previously considered extinct.

One of the few mollusc-specific conservation success stories is that of the endemic Corsican land snail *Helix ceratina* (Figure 15.1k). When rediscovered in 1994, it had not been seen since the 1910s and was confined to less than 7 ha of habitat in the suburbs of Ajaccio, squeezed between the airport, a large car park and beach access paths (Bouchet et al., 1997). It became the object of the first-ever 'Arrêté préfectoral de Biotope' project undertaken in France specifically for an invertebrate. Habitat was restored, including closure and restoration of the 2 ha car park to its natural state. This was accompanied by outreach promoting the value of *H. ceratina*, not so much for its scientific or ecological importance, but more for the heritage and cultural value of this narrow-range endemic.

Because many of the threats faced by non-marine molluscs (and many other species) are related to habitat degradation and loss, significant international efforts have been made to preserve and restore key habitats. For example, the European Union's 'Habitats Directive' aims to preserve habitats in order to conserve a large number of species listed in its Annexes, particularly Annex II, which lists 29 gastropod and 4 bivalve species. Among these are four species of wetland land snails in the genus *Vertigo*. As a result, there was a burgeoning of research on *Vertigo* spp. within the framework of the Habitats Directive. In England, when a population of *V. moulinsiana* was discovered in the path of a major road development, an entire segment of habitat, with snails, was moved to a location away from the road's path and additional habitat was created (Stebbings and Killeen, 1998). The project failed, but at least prompted additional surveys that revealed that the species was more widespread than previously thought (Williams, 2006). The Habitats Directive has, however, been criticised because of its highly vertebrate bias and because it is not adequately focused on rare and threatened species (Fontaine et al., 2007a).

Freshwater molluscs suffer from pollution and other impacts on water quality (e.g. Pérez-Quintero, 2011). Improving water quality may therefore improve the conservation status of threatened species. The problem of water quality has spawned national and regional policies and efforts that have reduced pollution, for example in Europe (e.g. bij de Vaate et al., 2006) and North America (Bogan, 2006). However, there seems to have been little effort to assess any direct effect of such improvement on threatened molluscs, and, indeed, repopulation (to the extent recorded) of improved habitat may involve primarily non-native species, thereby negatively affecting remnant native species (e.g. bij de Vaate et al., 2006) or species that are not threatened (Locy et al., 2002). In North America, filter/suspension feeding bivalves have been promoted for their ability to improve water quality, which in turn could focus attention on conservation and enhancement of those species chosen to implement such efforts (Kreeger et al., 2018), although these efforts are unlikely to focus on seriously threatened species.

Finally, the incorporation of molecular genetics in conservation has advanced more sophisticated efforts to, for instance, identify cryptic molluscan species via integrated taxonomic approaches (e.g. Collado et al., 2019), delineate evolutionary significant units or lineages within molluscan species (e.g. Buckley et al., 2014) and assess and avoid inbreeding in captive breeding programmes for molluscs (Price & Hadfield, 2014).

15.8 Conclusion

In 1983, 123 mollusc species were evaluated for the IUCN Red List, 6 of them deemed Extinct. By 2019, 300 of 8664 species evaluated were deemed Extinct (IUCN, 2019), although more realistic estimates of the number of extinctions are much higher (Régnier et al., 2009, 2015a, b; Cowie et al., 2017). Molluscs face diverse threats but because most are not 'charismatic', efforts to stem the rate of extinction and ameliorate the threats face an uphill battle. Nonetheless, small groups of dedicated people are doing everything they can to aid this effort, as attested to by the many articles from all over the world published in *Tentacle*, the IUCN Mollusc Specialist Group newsletter (www.hawaii.edu/cowielab/Tentacle.htm).

Often, when considering the daunting task of invertebrate conservation, vertebrate specialists will invoke the 'umbrella species' concept, suggesting that if we conserve the charismatic megafauna, then the invertebrates in the same habitats will also be conserved, almost by default. But conservation strategies for often narrowly endemic invertebrates, notably many of the threatened mollusc species discussed here, cannot be the same as those for wide-ranging vertebrates (Fontaine et al., 2007b), especially as many species are facing highly specific threats, e.g. predation by an introduced snail predator or elimination of a specific limestone outcrop.

There are more recorded extinctions among non-marine molluscs than in any other animal group; those that remain face a diversity of ongoing threats. Efforts to save some of the most threatened species continue, but their long-term chances of success may be slim. We are in a race against time. We need to continue to describe species before they vanish and place them on the conservation radar screen before they go extinct. We need to augment single-species approaches with broader conservation initiatives, identifying key habitats, regions, ecosystems and hotspots. Conservation-related research should be promoted in neglected regions of the world and should include generation of more basic knowledge of life history, habitat preferences, etc. Finally, if mollusc conservation is to surmount the huge barriers it faces, we must advocate, advocate, advocate.

Acknowledgements

We thank Eike Neubert and Gonzalo Giribet for reviews of drafts of the manuscript and Reuben Clements, Olivier Gargominy, Wendell Haag, Kevin Macfarlane and Liew Thor-Seng for providing photos in Figure 15.1. Publication number 11584 of the University of Hawaii School of Ocean and Earth Science and Technology.

References

Albrecht, C., Hauffe, T., Schreiber, K. and Wilke T. (2012) Mollusc biodiversity in a European ancient lake system: lakes Prespa and Mikri Prespa in the Balkans. *Hydrobiologia* 682: 47–59.

Anthony, J.L. and Downing, J.A. (2001) Exploitation trajectory of a declining fauna: a century of freshwater mussel fisheries in North America. *Can J Fish Aquat Sci* 58: 2071–2090.

Ashmole, P. and Ashmole, A. (2000) *St Helena and Ascension Island: A Natural History*. Oswestry, UK: Anthony Nelson.

Beasley, C.R. (2001) The impact of exploitation on freshwater mussels (Bivalvia: Hyriidae) in the Tocantins River, Brazil. *Stud Neotrop* 36: 159–165.

bij de Vaate, A. Breukel, R. and van der Velde, G. (2006) Long-term developments in ecological rehabilitation of the main distributaries in the Rhine delta: fish and macroinvertebrates. *Hydrobiologia* 565: 229–242.

Bogan, A.E. (2006) Conservation and extinction of the freshwater molluscan fauna of North America, In: Sturm, C.F., Pearce, T.A., Valdés, A. (Eds.), *The Mollusks: A Guide to Their Study, Collection, and Preservation*. Pittsburgh, PA: American Malacological Society.

Bouchet, P., Ripken, T. and Recorbet, B. (1997) Redécouverte de l'escargot de Corse *Helix ceratina* au bord de l'extinction. *Rev Écol* 52: 97–111.

Buckley, T.R., White, D.J., Howitt, R., et al., (2014) Nuclear and mitochondrial DNA variation within threatened species and subspecies of the giant New Zealand land snail genus *Powelliphanta*: implications for classification and conservation. *J Molluscan Stud* 80: 291–302.

Cameron, R.A.D., Pokryszko, B.M. and Frias Martins, A.M. (2012) Land snail faunas on Santa Maria (Azores): local diversity in an old, isolated and disturbed island. *J Molluscan Stud* 78: 268–274.

Campbell K. and Donlan J.C. (2005) Feral goat eradications on islands. *Conserv Biol* 19: 1362–1374.

Carlton, J.T., Geller, J.B., Reaka-Kudla, M.L. and Norse, E.A. (1999) Historical extinctions in the sea. *Ann Rev Ecol Syst* 30: 515–538.

Chiba, S. and Cowie, R.H. (2016) Evolution and extinction of land snails on oceanic islands. *Ann Rev Ecol Evol Syst* 47: 123–141.

Clarke, B., Murray, J. and Johnson, M.S. (1984) The extinction of endemic species by a program of biological control. *Pacific Sci* 38: 97–104.

Collado, G.A., Vidal, M.A., Aguayo, K.P., et al. (2019) Morphological and molecular analysis of cryptic native and invasive freshwater snails in Chile. *Sci Rep* 9: 7846.

Conte, E. and Kirch, P.V. (2008) One thousand years of human environmental transformation in the Gambier Islands (French Polynesia). In: Clark, G., Leach, F. and O'Connor, S. (Eds.), *Colonization, Seafaring and the Archaeology of Maritime Landscapes*. Islands of Inquiry (Terra Australis 29). Acton, Australia: Australian National University Press.

Coote, T. and Loève, É. (2003) From 61 species to five: endemic tree snails of the Society Islands fall prey to an ill-judged biological control programme. *Oryx* 37: 91–96.

Coote, T., Garcia, G. and Clarke, D. (2019) Fourth year of *Partula* species reintroductions into natural habitat on Tahiti and Moorea. *Tentacle* 27: 35–38.

Cowie, R.H., and Cook, R.P. (2001) Extinction or survival: partulid tree snails in American Samoa. *Biodivers Conserv* 10: 143–159.

Cowie, R.H. and Robinson, D.G. (2003) Pathways of introduction of nonindigenous land and freshwater snails and slugs. In: Ruiz, G. and Carlton, J.T. (Eds.), *Invasive Species: Vectors and Management Strategies*. Washington, DC: Island Press.

Cowie, R.H., Régnier, C., Fontaine and B., Bouchet, P. (2017) Measuring the Sixth Extinction: what do mollusks tell us? *Nautilus* 131(1): 3–41.

Curry, P.A., Yeung, N.W., Hayes, K.A., et al. (2016) Rapid range expansion of an invasive predatory snail, *Oxychilus alliarius* (Miller 1822), and its impact on endemic Hawaiian land snails. *Biol Invasions* 18: 1769–1780.

Curry, P.A., Yeung, N.W., Hayes, K.A. and Cowie, R.H. (2019) The potential tropical island distribution of a temperate invasive snail, *Oxychilus alliarius*, modeled on its distribution in Hawaii. *Biol Invasions* 22: 307–327.

Darrigran, G., Damborenea, C., Drago, E.C., et al. (2012) Invasion process of *Limnoperna fortunei* (Bivalvia: Mytilidae): the case of Uruguay River and emissaries of the Esteros del Iberá Wetland, Argentina. *Zoologia* 29: 531–539.

De Mattia, W., Neiber, M.T. and Groh, K. (2018) Revision of the genus-group *Hystricella* R.T. Lowe, 1855 from Porto Santo (Madeira Archipelago), with descriptions of new recent and fossil taxa (Gastropoda, Helicoidea, Geomitridae). *ZooKeys*. 732: 1–125.

Fontaine, B., Bouchet, P., Van Achterberg, K., et al. (2007a) The European Union's 2010 target: putting rare species in focus. *Biol Conserv* 139: 167–185.

Fontaine, B., Gargominy, O. and Neubert, E. (2007b) Priority sites for conservation of land snails in Gabon: testing the umbrella species concept. *Divers Distrib* 13: 725–734.

Fox, R., Harrower, C.A., Bell, J.R., et al. (2019) Insect population trends and the IUCN Red List process. *J Insect Conserv* 23: 269–278.

Gargominy, O. (2008) Beyond the alien invasion: a recently discovered radiation of Nesopupinae (Gastropoda: Pulmonata: Vertiginidae) from the summits of Tahiti (Society Islands, French Polynesia). *J Conchol* 39: 517–536.

Gerlach, J. (2016) *Icons of Evolution: Pacific Island Tree-Snails of the Family Partulidae*. Cambridge, UK: Phelsuma Press.

Goodfriend, G.A., Cameron, R.A.D. and Cook, L.M. (1994) Fossil evidence of recent human impact on the land snail fauna of Madeira. *J Biogeogr* 21: 309–320.

Griffiths, O.L. and Florens, V.F.B. (2006) *A Field Guide to the Non-Marine Molluscs of the Mascarene Islands*. Mauritius: Bioculture Press.

Haag, W.R. (2009) Past and future patterns of freshwater mussel extinctions in North America during the Holocene. In: Turvey, S. (Ed.), *Holocene Extinctions*. Oxford, UK: Oxford University Press.

Haag, W.R. (2019) Reassessing enigmatic mussel declines in the United States. *Freshw Mollusk Biol Conserv* 22: 43–60.

Hadfield, M.G. (1986) Extinction in Hawaiian achatinelline snails. *Malacologia* 27: 67–81.

Haponski, A.E., Lee, T. and Ó Foighil, D. (2019) Deconstructing an infamous extinction crisis: survival of *Partula* species on Moorea and Tahiti. *Evol Appl* 12: 1017–1033.

Hastie, L.C., Cosgrove, P.J., Ellis, N. and Gaywood, M.J. (2003) The threat of climate change to freshwater pearl mussel populations. *AMBIO* 32: 40–47.

IUCN. (2012) *IUCN Red List Categories and Criteria.* Version 3.1. Second Edn. Gland, Switzerland; Cambridge, UK: IUCN.

IUCN. (2019) *The IUCN Red List of Threatened Species.* Version 2019-1. Gland, Switzerland; Cambridge, UK: IUCN.

James, A.F., Brown, R., Weston, K.A. and Walker, K. (2013) Modelling the growth and population dynamics of the exiled Stockton coal plateau landsnail, *Powelliphanta augusta. NZ J Zool* 40: 175–185.

Karatayev, A.Y., Burlakova, L.E. and Padilla, D.K. (2015) Zebra versus quagga mussels: a review of their spread, population dynamics, and ecosystem impacts *Hydrobiologia* 746: 97–112.

Köhler, F., Seddon, M., Bogan, A. and Do, T.V. (2012) The status and distribution of freshwater molluscs of the Indo-Burma region. In: Allen, D.G., Smith, K.G., Darwall, W.R.T. (Eds.), *The Status and Distribution of Freshwater Biodiversity in Indo-Burma.* Gland, Switzerland; Cambridge, UK: IUCN.

Kreeger, D.A., Gatenby, C.M. and Bergstrom, P.W. (2018) Restoration potential of several native species of bivalve molluscs for water quality improvement in mid-Atlantic watersheds. *J Shellfish Res* 37: 1121–1157.

Kyle, R., Reid, N., O'Connor, N. and Roberts, D. (2017) Development of release methods for captive-bred freshwater pearl mussels (*Margaritifera margaritifera*). *Aquat Conserv* 27: 492–501.

Locy, D., Proch, R. and Bogan, A. (2002) *Anodonta suborbiculata* (Say, 1831) added to the freshwater bivalve fauna of Pennsylvania. *Ellipsaria* 4(3): 10.

Lydeard, C., Cowie, R.H., Ponder, W.F., et al. (2004) The global decline of nonmarine mollusks. *BioScience* 54: 321–330.

McKinney, M.L. (1998) Is marine biodiversity at less risk? Evidence and implications. *Divers Distrib* 4: 3–8.

Meyer, W.M., III, Yeung, N.W., Slapcinsky, J. and Hayes, K.A. (2017) Two for one: inadvertent introduction of *Euglandina* species during failed bio-control efforts in Hawaii. *Biol Invasions* 19: 1399–1405.

Mori, H., Inada, M. and Chiba, S. (2020) Conservation programmes for endemic land snails on the Ogasawara Islands: captive breeding and control of invasive species. *Tentacle* 28: 23–27.

Morris, R. (2010) An unfortunate experiment. *Forest Bird* 337: 14–18.

Murray, J., Murray, E., Johnson, M.S. and Clarke, B. (1988) The extinction of *Partula* on Moorea. *Pacific Sci* 42: 150–153.

Neto, N.A.L., Voeks, R.A., Dias, T.L.P. and Alves, R.R.N. (2012) Mollusks of Candomblé: symbolic and ritualistic importance. *J Ethnobiol Ethnomed* 8: 10.

Neubert, E., Chérel-Mora, C. and Bouchet, P. (2009) Polytypy, clines, and fragmentation: the bulimes of New Caledonia revisited (Pulmonata, Orthalicoidea, Placostylidae). *Mém Mus Natl Hist Nat* 198: 37–131.

Neubert, E., Seddon, M.B., Allen, D.J., et al. (2019) *European Red List of Terrestrial Molluscs.* Cambridge, UK; Brussels, Belgium: IUCN.

Neves, R.J. (2004) Propagation of endangered freshwater mussels in North America. *J Conchol Spec Publ* 3: 69–80.

Nicolai, A. and Ansart, A. (2017) Conservation at a slow pace: terrestrial gastropods facing fast-changing climate. *Conserv Physiol* 5(1): cox007.

Nyoagbe, L.A., Appiah, V., Nketsia-Tabiri, J., Larbi, D. and Adjei, I. (2016) Evaluation of African giant snails (*Achatina* and *Archachatina*) obtained from markets (wild) and breeding farms. *Afr J Food Sci* 10: 94–104.

Otto, R., Garzón-Machado, V., del Arcoet, M., et al. (2017) Unpaid extinction debts for endemic plants and invertebrates as a legacy of habitat loss on oceanic islands. *Divers Distrib* 23: 1031–1041.

Outerbridge, M.E., Ovaska, K. and Garcia, G. (2019) Back from the brink: recovery efforts for endemic land snails of Bermuda. *Tentacle* 27: 16–18.

Pearce, T.A. and Paustian, M.E. (2013) Are temperate land snails susceptible to climate change through reduced altitudinal ranges? A Pennsylvania example. *Am Malacol Bull* 31(2): 213–224.

Pérez-Quintero, J.C. (2011) Freshwater mollusc biodiversity and conservation in two stressed Mediterranean basins. *Limnologica* 41: 201–212.

Price, M.R. and Hadfield, M.G. (2014) Population genetics and the effects of a severe bottleneck in an ex situ population of critically endangered Hawaiian tree snails. *PLoS One* 9(12): e114377.

Régnier, C., Fontaine, B. and Bouchet, P. (2009) Not knowing, not recording, not listing: numerous unnoticed mollusk extinctions. *Conserv Biol* 23: 1214–1221.

Régnier, C., Achaz, G., Lambert, A., et al. (2015a) Mass extinction in poorly known taxa. *Proc Natl Acad Sci USA* 112(25): 7761–7766.

Régnier, C., Bouchet, P., Hayes, K.A., et al. (2015b) Extinction in a hyperdiverse endemic Hawaiian land snail family and implications for the underestimation of invertebrate extinction. *Conserv Biol* 29: 1715–1723.

Ricciardi, A., Neves, R.J. and Rasmussen, J.B. (1998) Impending extinction of North American freshwater mussels (Unionoida) following zebra mussel (*Dreissena polymorpha*) invasion. *J Animal Ecol* 67: 613–619.

Richling, I. and Bouchet, P. (2013) Extinct even before scientific recognition: a remarkable radiation of helicinid snails (Helicinidae) on the Gambier Islands, French Polynesia. *Biodivers Conserv* 22: 2433–2468.

Riedel, A. and Norris, A. (1987) An undescribed species of *Zonites* from the island of Santorini, Greece. *J Conchol* 32: 377–378.

Riley, L.A. and Dybdahl, M.F. (2015) The roles of resource availability and competition in mediating growth rates of invasive and native freshwater snails. *Freshw Biol* 60: 1308–1315.

Rundell, R.J. (2010) Diversity and conservation of the land snail fauna of the western Pacific islands of Belau (Republic of Palau, Oceania). *Am Malacol Bull* 28: 1–90.

Sartori, A.F., Gargominy, O. and Fontaine, B. (2014) Radiation and decline of endodontid land snails in Makatea, French Polynesia. *Zootaxa* 3772: 1–68.

Schilthuizen, M., Liew, T.-S., Bin Elahan, B. and Lackman-Ancrenaz, I. (2005) Effects of karst forest degradation on pulmonate and prosobranch land snail communities in Sabah, Malaysian Borneo. *Conserv Biol* 19: 949–954.

Seddon, M.B., Tattersfield, P., Herbert, D.G., et al. (2005) Diversity of African forest mollusc faunas: what we have learned since Solem (1984). *Rec West Aust Mus Suppl* 68: 103–113.

Seddon, M.[B.], Appleton, C., Van Damme, D. and Graf, D. 2011. Freshwater molluscs of Africa: diversity, distribution, and conservation. In: Darwall, W.R.T., Smith, K., Allen, D., et al. (Eds.), *The Diversity of Life in African Freshwaters: Under Water, Under Threat. An Analysis of the Status and Distribution of Freshwater Species Throughout Mainland Africa.* Gland, Switzerland; Cambridge, UK: IUCN.

Sîrbu, I. and Benedek, A.M. (2016) Requiem for *Melanopsis parreyssii* or the anatomy of a new extinction in Romania. *Tentacle* 24: 26–28.

Sîrbu, I., Gagiu, A. and Benedek, A.M. (2013) On the brink of extinction: fate of the Peţea thermal lake (Romania) and its endemic species. *Tentacle* 21: 35–37.

Sischo, D.R., Price, M.R., Pascua, M.-A. and Hadfield, M.G. (2016) Genetic and demographic insights into the decline of a captive population of the endangered Hawaiian tree snail *Achatinella fuscobasis* (Achatinellinae). *Pacific Sci* 70: 133–141.

Stebbings, R.E. and Killeen, I.J. (1998) Translocation of habitat for the snail *Vertigo moulinsiana* in England. *J Conchol Spec Publ* 2: 191–204.

Strayer, D.L. and Malcom, H.M. (2007) Effects of zebra mussels (*Dreissena polymorpha*) on native bivalves: the beginning of the end or the end of the beginning? *J N Am Benthol Soc* 26: 111–112.

Van Damme, D., Köehler [sic], F., Andriamaro, L., Darwall, W. and Máiz-Tomé, L. (2018) The status and distribution of freshwater molluscs. In: Máiz-Tomé, L., Sayer, C. and Darwall, W. (Eds.), *The Status and Distribution of Freshwater Biodiversity in Madagascar and the Indian Ocean Islands Hotspot.* Gland, Switzerland: IUCN.

Vermeulen, J.J. and Marzuki, M.E. (2014) '*Charopa*' *lafargei* (Gastropoda, Pulmonata, Charopidae), a new, presumed narrowly endemic species from Peninsular Malaysia. *Basteria* 78: 31–34.

Vogler, R.E., Beltramino, A.A., Strong, E.E., Rumi, A. and Peso, J.G. (2016) Insights into the evolutionary history of an extinct South American freshwater snail based on historical DNA. *PLoS One* 11(12): e0169191.

Walker, K.J., Trewick, S.A. and Barker, G.M. (2008) *Powelliphanta augusta*, a new species of land snail, with a description of its former habitat, Stockton coal plateau, New Zealand. *J Royal Soc NZ* 38: 163–186.

Wilke, T. (2019) Helicostoidae Pruvot-Fol 1937. In: Lydeard, C. and Cummings, K. (Eds.), *Freshwater Mollusks of the World: A Distribution Atlas*. Baltimore, MD: Johns Hopkins University Press.

Williams, N. (2006) Road to oblivion. *Curr Biol* 16: R617–R618.

Yildirim, M.Z., Kebapçi, Ü. and Gümüş, B.A. (2004) Edible snails (terrestrial) of Turkey. *Turk J Zool* 28: 329–335.

Zhang L.-J. (2017) A new species of freshwater snail *Tchangmargarya* (Gastropoda: Viviparidae) endemic to a vanished small lake in Yunnan, China. *Molluscan Res* 37: 252–257.

SIXTEEN

An Account of the Diversity and Conservation of Fungi and Their Close Relatives

GREGORY M. MUELLER AND JESSICA L. ALLEN

Summary

Neither animals nor plants, the organisms traditionally treated as fungi are distributed across three kingdoms: Fungi, Chromista and Protista. These organisms are critical for society both through direct impacts on human health and the economy and through their intimate involvement in most essential environmental processes. Yet, less than 5% of the estimated 2–4 million species of true fungi have been described, data on species abundances and distributions are fragmentary at best, even for lichens, mushrooms and other macrofungi, and information on their life history and ecology remains woefully incomplete. Fungi are not immune to the stressors that threaten animals and plants, these include habitat loss, overharvesting and climate change. However, the paucity of data on the diversity, distribution and population status of most fungal species has severely limited efforts to assess the extinction risk of fungi. This dearth of data, coupled with perceptions by the conservation community that fungi are not amenable to conservation assessments due to their biology has hindered the development of fungal conservation. This perception is changing, and progress in assessing the conservation status of fungi has been made over the past 5 years, but much work remains. The July 2022 update of the IUCN Red List of Threatened Species includes only 597 of the nearly 150,000 described species of fungi, and these are restricted to only two of the 12 phyla of fungi, Ascomycota and Basidiomycota.

16.1 Introduction

This chapter provides a brief discussion on the current knowledge of the diversity, conservation status and threats to organisms traditionally studied by mycologists, as well as some recommendations for taking the topic forward.

Fungi and fungal-like organisms occur throughout the world in virtually every habitat from deep oceans to mountain tops, and from deserts to geothermal soils and hot springs to tropical rainforests, as well as all human-dominated systems. They are decomposers of organic material, endoparasites of animals, pathogens of plants and animals, and disease agents, but they also are important food resources, indispensable industrial agents, sources of some of our most used pharmaceutical products, essential mutualists of bacteria, plants and animals, and more. The trophic diversity of fungi (i.e. where they acquire their primary nutrients) is astounding, especially when compared to plants, which are almost all photosynthetic. In short, life as we know it would not exist without fungi, and the vast and varied niches they fill in all global ecosystems.

Centuries of mycological research have culminated in a wealth of knowledge about fungal diversity, distributions and ecology. One of the recent important advances in mycology has been the substantial data refuting the paradigm of unlimited dispersal in fungi. Species-level taxonomy has consistently shown that fungi that were once thought to have multicontinental distributions are actually species complexes comprised of some-times startling diversity. More recent advances in genomics has shown that fungi can have highly geographically structured populations, and that they are adapted to local environ-mental conditions. These findings, taken together, suggest that fungi are even more diverse than we once thought, and we can expect threats like habitat fragmentation to effect fungi similarly to plants and animals. Perhaps even more importantly, coupling current technologies and analytics with traditional morphological and field data provides mycologists with a wealth of resources that bring answers to outstanding research ques-tions within our reach.

Despite continued advances in mycological research, and the recognition that fungi are essential for life, our knowledge of the diversity, distribution, biology and conservation status of fungi and fungal-like organisms is still very incomplete. While much of the estimated species diversity of oomycetes and slime moulds has been described, only a fraction, less than 150,000, of the estimated 2–4 million species of true fungi are described and named (Catalogue of Life: 2020-06-04 Beta version, Hawksworth and Lücking, 2017). The actual distribution of many of the described species remains uncertain, as they are known from few collections and/or environmental DNA samples. Information on their population status is even less well known, limiting efforts to assess the conservation status of described fungi. Currently only 597 species have been included on the global IUCN Red List (Version 2022-1, Figure 16.1), see Table 16.1 and Mueller et al., (2022).

Advancements in knowledge of fungal biodiversity and distribution has accelerated with the advent of multiple citizen science platforms. Contributions by citizen scientists through informal observations (e.g. iNaturalist) and participating in formal initiatives (e.g. Fungal Diversity Survey or FunDiS, FungiMap, etc.) are significantly adding to our knowledge of the distribution of macrofungi. Environmental sampling using metabarcod-ing is generating huge amounts of diversity and distribution data (e.g. Yahr et al., 2016; Ritter et al., 2020), with the caveat that these data have limitations (Hofstetter et al., 2019). Together, these new data sources and enhanced public engagement coincide with

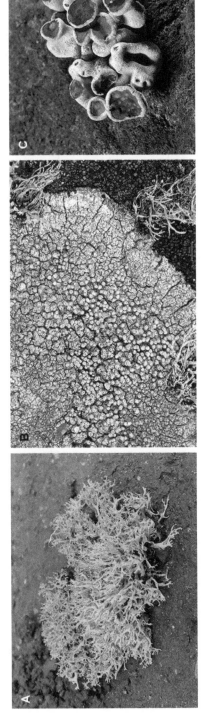

Figure 16.1 Threatened fungal species on the IUCN Red List. (A) Arctic orange-bush lichen (*Seirophora aurantiaca*) occurs only along the coastline of the Inuvialuit Settlement Region in the Canadian Western Arctic, where it can be found growing on the tundra. As an Arctic and coastal species, climate change impacts pose serious threats, including coastal erosion, saline wash from storm surges, and permafrost melting. Thus, it is assessed as Endangered. (Photo: Troy McMullin.) (B) Gladys' mountain spikes (*Lepra andersoniae*) is a rock-dwelling lichen endemic to the Appalachian Mountains of eastern North America. Its name honours Gladys P. Anderson (1888–?) who collected the type specimen in the early twentieth century. Shifts in habitat quality due to logging, invasive species and climate change, along with recreation, are threats to this species currently assessed as Endangered. (Photo: Jason Hollinger.) (C) Coastal popcorn lichen (*Mobergia calculiformis*) can be found in the fog desert along the Pacific coast of the Baja California peninsula, in Mexico where it grows on small stones, boulders and cliffs. It has historically been documented from habitats along the Pacific coast, from northwestern Mexico all the way into California, but the species has now been extirpated from the US. Few viable populations remain in Mexico, most of which are threatened by expanding agriculture and urbanization. The species is assessed as Endangered. (Photo: Frank Bungartz.)

Table 16.1 *Numbers of published globally listed fungal species arranged by class and threat category (IUCN Red List, July 2022)*

Fungal Order/Class	CR	EN	VU	NT	LC	DD
Basidiomycota (447)	14	58	114	50	171	40
Agaricomycetes (444)	14	58	112	50	170	40
Ustilagomycetes (3)	0	0	2	0	1	0
Ascomycota (125)	18	37	23	6	30	11
Lecanoromycetes (85)	14	32	15	1	23	0
Pezizomycetes (11)	1	1	3	3	1	2
Sordariomycetes (8)	2	0	1	0	1	4
Leotiomycetes (8)	0	1	1	1	5	1
Geoglossomycetes (2)	0	0	2	1	0	1
Eurotiomycetes (5)	0	0	1	0	1	3
Arthoniomycetes (3)	0	3	0	0	0	0
Dothidiomycetes (2)	1	0	1	0	0	0
Not Assigned (1)	0	0	1	0	0	0

DD = Data Deficient; LC = Least Concern; NT = Near Threatened; VU = Vulnerable; EN = Endangered; CR = Critically Endangered

an increased interest in, and support for, fungal conservation within the mycological and broader conservation community (Mueller et al., 2014; Ainsworth et al., 2018; May et al., 2019).

16.2 Fungi vs. fungi

Fungi in the broad sense were classified as plants until the middle of the twentieth century. Kingdom Fungi then included organisms now known to be unrelated (oomycetes, slime moulds) and lacked some groups now recognised as true fungi (e.g. *Microsporidia*). These disparate groups were originally treated together because they look similar, produce spores and acquire their nutrients through external digestion and absorption. While we now know that they are evolutionarily distantly related, they continue to be treated by mycologists and included in courses on fungi. Colloquially this traditional broad group of fungi and former fungi have been referred to as fungi (lower case 'f') in contrast to true Fungi (upper case 'F'). The classification of fungi and fungal-like organisms has undergone major changes over the past 30+ years, and continues to evolve (James et al., 2020). While most major lineages (phyla and classes) are now resolved and stable, some key questions remain, most notably the placement of Chromista among protists, branching patterns at the base of the fungal tree (Tedersoo et al., 2018; Wijayawardene et al., 2018; Li et al., 2021) and the placement of several enigmatic taxa within the fungal tree of life (Hibbett et al., 2018; James et al., 2020). This chapter covers the range of organisms treated as fungi, but with a focus on those groups that have been included in conservation initiatives.

16.3 Myxomycetes, Dictyostellids and Protostellids: Amoebozoa

(See further discussion of these groups in Chapter 17.)

Slime moulds are members of the *Amoebazoa*, a group of protists which forms a monophyletic sister clade to the clade comprised of fungi and animals (Schilde and Schaap, 2013; Maclean, Chapter 17). Slime moulds are divided into three groups, Dictyostellids, Protostellids and Myxomycetes. The latter two are considered plasmodial slime moulds because they exist as a plasmodial mass full of many nucleii, which can be thought of as essentially one large cell, during the vegetative stages of their life cycles.

Dictyostellids are cellular slime moulds that have a fascinating life cycle. The majority of their life cycle is spent in a unicellular, haploid state. When food is scarce, the individual cells aggregate, forming a multicellular 'slug'-like structure that can move to a suitable place to establish a spore-forming body. Thus, they are both unicellular and multicellular organisms, and are sometimes called social amoeba. One species in particular, *Dictyostelium discoideum*, is an important model organism for studying development and cell biology.

Protostellids are unicellular or plasmodial, and feed on bacteria, yeast and fungal spores in soil and freshwater systems.

Myxomycetes are plasmodial slime moulds of which there are approximately 1000 species. They commonly occur in moist, decaying wood and in soil. One species of mycomycete, *Physarum polycehpalum*, is frequently used in experimental cell biology as a model organism. Compared to other groups of fungal-like organisms, myxomycetes are a relatively well-known group, but the conservation status of most species has not been assessed. The IUCN SSC Chytrid, Zygomycete, Downy Mildew and Slime Mould Specialist Group is focused on raising awareness of slime moulds and the need to consider them in conservation discussions.

16.4 Oomycota: Chromista

Oomycota encompass ~1000 species that are now placed in the Kingdom Chromista and the sub-Kingdom group Heterokonta (Lévesque, 2011). Members of Heterokonta are characterised by the presence of two flagella in at least part of their life cycle, one smooth flagellum and one hairy flagellum. Some members of Heterokonta are photosynthetic, including diatoms and brown algae, while others, like the Oomycetes, are not. Oomycetes are largely filamentous, and their asexual spores have the two flagella typical of Heterokonta. Most species exist as saprotrophs in aquatic, both freshwater and marine, and terrestrial ecosystems. However, species that parasitise plants and animals have gained the most notoriety. The most well-known oomycete is *Phytophthora infestans*, the causative agent of late blight in potatoes, which led to the Irish potato famine. Most species of *Pythium* are plant pathogens, often causal agents of damping off disease of seedlings while *Pythium insidiosum* is an animal pathogen. Species of *Saprolegnia* can be fatal pathogens of fish, both free-living and in aquaria.

16.5 Fungi

Fungi has been recognised as a distinct Kingdom more closely related to animals than plants since the middle of the twentieth century. The composition of the Kingdom and phylogenetic relationships within the Kingdom have been revised many times since then as new data became available. A coordinated effort to understand phylogenetic relationships of Fungi based on multigene data was published in a special issue of Mycologia referred to as Deep Hypha (Blackwell et al., 2006). A classification to the level of class by Hibbett et al. (2007) has been published. Advances since then have focused on higher-level relationships based on genomic data (e.g. Hibbett et al., 2018; James et al., 2020).

16.5.1 Chytridiomycota, Mucormycotina and Glomeromycota

Early diverging lineages of fungi have undergone drastic taxonomic revision in recent decades, leading to the relatively recent recognition of numerous phyla (Hibbett et al., 2007; Tedersoo et al., 2018; Wijayawardene et al., 2018; Li et al., 2021). Here we treat three groups that include well-known species with important conservation implications. The Chytrid species *Batrachochytrium dendrobatidis* has gained global infamy as the causative agent in widespread and drastic loss of amphibians. Current estimates suggest that a total of 501 species' populations have declined due to chytridiomycosis, and 90 of those have become extinct (Scheele et al., 2019). However, the vast majority of Chytridiomycota are not parasites or pathogens of animals, fungi and plants, and are instead saprotrophs living in soil, and fresh- and saltwater. Species can be unicellular or filamentous, and they form motile spores with a single flagellum. Mucormycotina include filamentous species that are saprotrophs, plant, animal and fungal pathogens, ectomycorrhizal and essential gut microbiota of arthropods. The group is not speciose, it includes ~1000 species, but there are a few species that are familiar to many people. Two species, *Rhizopus oligosporus* and *Actinomucor elegans*, are used to ferment soy beans and produce tempeh and tofu, respectively. *Rhizopus stolonifer*, a species of common bread mould, is also widespread and familiar to many people.

Glomeromycota are commonly referred to as arbuscular mycorrhizal fungi (AMF) or endomycorrhizal fungi (Smith and Read, 2010). They form symbiotic relationships with land plants and develop highly branched structures inside root cells, called arbuscules, which resemble the branching of a tree. There are currently 220 described species of AMF (Stürmer et al., 2018). They are biologically anomalous as they have not been observed reproducing sexually, a phenomenon some have called the 'ancient asexual scandal'. However, genomic data suggest that they undergo some process of recombination (Yildirir et al., 2020). More than 80% of the plants on the planet have AMF living in their roots, including numerous foundational food crops (Smith and Read, 2010). AMF effectively drastically expand the surface area of the root system, allowing plants to access exponentially more water and nutrients than the plant would be able to with their organs alone. Symbioses with AMF are hypothesised to be a key innovation that allowed plants to colonise land (Smith and Read, 2010). In experiments where plants with and without AMF are grown in the same conditions and compared, plants with AMF reliably produce higher above-ground biomass than plants without AMF. Indeed, AMF have been shown to reduce stress effects in plants, including frost and low soil moisture content. Thus, plant function and consequently terrestrial ecosystem health planet-wide depends on AMF communities.

A review of Glomeromycota conservation outlined multiple threats to biodiversity in the group, and discusses the role of protected areas in their conservation (Turrini and Giovannetti, 2012). These authors found that AMF diversity is negatively impacted by habitat loss and disturbance, and that these impacts vary by taxa. Approximately 43% of species in Glomeromycota have cosmopolitan distributions, while the remaining 57% show some degree of endemism, supporting the 'moderate endemicity model' in the group (Stürmer et al., 2018). Communities are shaped by abiotic and biotic variables at multiple spatial scales, with soil, climate and habitat heterogeneity being some of the strongest drivers (Chaudhary et al., 2018). Plant communities fundamentally rely on AMF and they can be instrumental in supporting conservation of rare plant species.

16.5.2 Ascomycota

Overview

Encompassing more species than any other group of fungi on the planet, the Ascomycota are ubiquitous and trophically diverse (Hibbett et al., 2018). They are united by two characteristics: (1) sexual spores produced in sacs called asci, and (2) a set of small proteins called Woronin bodies that are located at openings between cells and clog the opening if cells are damaged. Most species in this group are filamentous, but some are unicellular yeasts. Some species display beautiful and elaborate spore-forming bodies, while others produce only microscopic structures throughout their life cycle. Famous fungi in Ascomycota include morels (*Morchella* spp.), fungi that produce the antibiotic penicillin (*Penicillium* spp.) and most lichens, which are fungi that form obligate symbioses with algae and/or cyanobacteria. Some infamous plant pathogens are also in the Ascomycota, including chestnut blight, *Cryphonectria parasitica* and ergot, *Claviceps purpurea*.

Ecological Importance

Many Ascomycota share ecological roles with fungi in other phyla (e.g. saprotrophs, endophytes, mycorrhizas and pathogens), but the ecological contribution of lichenised fungi is unique to Ascomycota (Figure 16.1). There are a few lichenised lineages of fungi in Basidiomycota (Lawrey et al., 2009), but the vast majority are Ascomycetes. Lichens are hubs of interspecies interactions, and live at the fulcrum of the macroscopic and microscopic worlds. They occur in every terrestrial ecosystem on the planet, where they fix nitrogen and carbon, stabilise soils and interact with diverse animals (Brodo et al., 2001). Caribou and reindeer (*Rangifer* spp.) are arguably some of the highest profile animals reliant on lichens. Lichens comprise the majority of their diet in winter, and a substantial portion of their summer diet in some regions. Caribou are able to differentiate among lichen species, and tend to favour certain species in the genera *Alectoria*, *Bryoria*, *Cladonia* and *Stereocaulon*. Declines in woodland caribou populations are tightly linked to timber extraction-driven habitat loss. The reduction in ground-dwelling lichen cover in the Arctic is also concerning for tundra caribou populations. Other large mammals (e.g. moose, deer, bighorn sheep, etc.) use lichens as a winter forage. Birds, especially hummingbirds, use lichens as nesting material, small mammals eat lichens, and some, like the northern flying squirrel, also use them for nesting material. Insects and spiders are exquisitely adapted to use lichens as camouflage, with some of the most incredible examples including lacewing larvae and spiny leaf insects. While there are numerous examples of macroscopic biodiversity interacting with, and relying on, lichens, the quantity of microscopic biodiversity integrated with lichens is even more astounding. Microinvertebrates, including nematodes, collembola and water bears abound in and on lichens. Additionally, they harbour unique fungal communities that live in and among the scaffold of the thallus as commensalites and parasites, many of which are unique to lichens. Lichens harbour more than just one main photosynthetic partner, they contain whole communities of Eukaryotic algae and cyanobacteria (Moya et al., 2017). Finally, their bacterial microbiome is more diverse than any other microscopic component, and, indeed, the quantity of bacterial cells associated with lichens is much more than all other components combined (Grimm et al., 2021). In short, conserving lichen biodiversity translates to safeguarding shelter and food for myriad other organisms.

Human Uses

Ascomycete fungi fundamentally shape some of the most important elements of human cuisine and culture. Furthermore, major advancements in human health and environmental monitoring rely on members of the Ascomycota. *Saccharomyces cerevisiae*, the primary fermenting agent in bread and alcohol production, supports the most widespread uses of fermentation in foods and beverages worldwide and its evolution closely tracks the history of human civilisation (Legras et al., 2007). Other species, like morels (*Morchella esculenta*) and truffles (*Tuber melanosporum*), are highly sought after as a culinary delicacy. The discovery and development of the first antibiotic, penicillin, in the early twentieth century has saved untold human lives, and is a compound produced by the species *Penicillium notatum*. Penicillin remains one of the most widely used antibiotics (Karwehl and Stadler, 2016). Some Fungi provide detailed information about environmental health. Lichens are used globally to monitor air quality. By studying which species are present in an area and how abundant they are, it is possible to quantify the type and severity of air pollution in that area. Furthermore, they sequester elements from the atmosphere, and can be used to monitor deposition rates, including heavy metals and nitrogen. Here we have presented just a few key examples of human uses of Ascomycota.

Conservation Highlights

Conservation assessments and actions improve the outlook for species in Ascomycota. Here we highlight three species from three different continents as case studies: *Ophiocordyceps sinensis*, *Sarcosoma globosum* and *Cetradonia linearis*. The caterpillar fungus (*Ophiocordyceps sinensis*) parasitises moth larvae and grows only in the Himalayas and the Tibetan Plateau (Yang, 2020). It is harvested from the wild and used as an aphrodisiac and to treat kidney and lung diseases. Overharvesting and habitat degradation, among other threats, has resulted in the species being assessed as globally Vulnerable according to the IUCN Red List (Yang, 2020). Some countries and regions have taken steps to control harvesting rates of the species, while in other regions it remains unregulated. The Convention on International Trade in Endangered Species of Wild Fauna and Flora (CITES) does not regulate the international trade of at-risk fungi, thus this species is afforded no international protection. While there are clear actions that can be taken to improve the conservation status of the Chinese caterpillar fungus, and some have been taken, there are still key regulatory frameworks missing to ensure its long-term viability.

Witches cauldron, *Sarcosoma globosum*, is a soil-dwelling species that occurs in Europe and eastern North America. It relies on old-growth forests, and logging throughout its range has led to population declines and, in some eastern European countries, even extirpation (Dahlberg, 2015). The declines throughout its range have led to the species being listed as Near Threatened on the IUCN Red List, and its inclusion on numerous country-level Red Lists. The species cannot survive clear-cutting, thus forests managed for timber production where the species occurs should instead be selectively thinned.

The rock gnome lichen (*Cetradonia linearis*) is narrowly endemic to the southern Appalachian Mountains of southeastern North America where it grows on rocks at high elevations and in streams, especially near waterfalls. It was assessed as Endangered and is protected at the national level by the Endangered Species Act (Allen et al., 2022). Its populations are diverse and highly structured, thus each population harbours unique genetic diversity. The most serious threat to the rock gnome lichen is habitat loss and degradation, and its continued protection is essential.

16.5.3 Basidiomycota

Overview

Basidiomycota is the second largest Phylum of fungi, with nearly 50,000 described species (Catalogue of Life: 2020-06-04 Beta version). They are characterised by having their meiospores formed externally on specialised club-shaped cells termed basida. While there are a few yeast-like Basidiomycota, the vast majority are multicellular and form extensive mycelia. Most species display an extended dikayotic mycelial phase due to a delay in nuclear fusion (karyogamy) following successful mating. Karyogamy, followed by meiosis, occurs in the basidia. The phylum consists of three monophyletic Subphyla (Hibbett et al., 2007): Pucciniomycotina, Ustilaginomycotina and Agaricomycotina.

Pucciniomycotina includes over 8000 species that form a monophletic clade at the base of the Basidiomycota (Aime et al., 2014). It is best known as the clade that encompasses the rust fungi, but it also includes rhizoplane fungi and some orchid mycorrhizal species. Rust fungi are often characterised by having complex life cycles, and some require two different hosts to complete their life cycle. Cereal rust, *Puccinia graminis* and cedar-apple rust, *Gymnosporangium juniperi-virginianae*, are two of the best known and economically import-ant rust species. Species in the Atractiellomycetes have been shown to form mycorrhizas with terrestrial and epiphytic tropical orchids (Kottke et al., 2010).

Ustilaginomycotina includes the smut fungi and forms a monophyletic clade of less than 2000 species (Begerow et al., 2014). All species are obligate biotrophs. Most are phytopathogens, often strongly host specific, but a few are pathogens of other organisms, including the mammal-pathogenic genus *Malassezia*. Corn smut, *Ustilago maydis* is the best known species of the group. Corn smut disease can be managed and it is not a serious pathogen in parts of its range. The infected corn kernels are a delicacy in Mexico, and *huitlacoche* can be found being sold fresh in markets as well as canned for export. *Ustilago maydis* is a model organism used to study plant disease and plant genetics. *Tilletia horrida*, rice kernel smut, is an important pathogen of rice.

Agaricomycotina encompasses nearly 40,000 described species distributed in three classes, Tremellomycetes, Dacrymycetes and Agaricomycetes (Hibbett et al., 2007). Tremellomycetes and Dacrymycetes, the 'jelly fungi,' are characterised by having septate or 'tuning fork' basidia. Species of Agaricomycete have unseptate 'holobasidia' and make up the majority of species in the subphylum.

All species of *Tremella* are parasitic on other fungi, and most are dimorphic, growing in a 'yeast' or filamentous phase, depending on conditions. Two species of *Tremella*, *T. fuciformis* and *T. aurantialba*, are cultivated for food. *Tremella mesenterica* is a common jelly fungus, 'witches butter,' frequently found on dead but attached recently fallen branches. It is a parasite of wood decay fungi in the genus *Peniophora*.

Darcrymyces is the only genus in the Dacrymycetes with around 40 described species. Most species in the genus form small, orange, gelatinous sporocarps growing on sticks and branches. While species of *Dacrymyces* can look similar to some species of *Tremella*, they differ by having 'tuning fork' non-septate basidia, vs. cruciately septate basidia in *Tremella*, and by being wood decomposers rather than fungal pathogens.

Agaricomycetes is by far the largest and most diverse class in the subphylum encompassing 35,000 of the 40,000 species (Matheny et al., 2006). Morphologically, the group ranges from forming thin, waxy crusts to truffle-like hypogeous sporocarps, to coral fungi, mushrooms and brackets over 1 m in diameter. Ecologically, the group includes pathogens, decomposers and species forming mycorrhizal associations with a diversity of plants, including orchids. Chanterelles, *porcini* and the common store mushroom are examples of the many edible fungi, while some species of *Amanita* and *Galerina* can cause death if eaten. The psychedelic substance psilocybin found in some species of the mushroom genus *Psilocybe* is increasingly being investigated as treatment for a variety of psychiatric and behavioural disorders (e.g. www.hopkinsmedicine.org/psychiatry/research/psychedelics-research.html).

16.5.4 Threats

While too few assessments have been completed to make a rigorous analyses of threats to fungal species, patterns are emerging (Mueller et al., 2022). Habitat loss/transformation is the most reported threat to species of both plants and fungi, with land development and agriculture being the two primary drivers of loss. Logging and wood harvesting are together the third most frequently listed threat, followed by climate change and severe weather, fire and fire supression. Threats differ between lichenised and non-lichenised fungi. The top three threats in order from most frequent to least frequent for lichenised fungi are climate change and severe weather, land development and disturbance, and for non-lichenised fungi they are land development, agriculture and logging.

16.6 Conserving Fungal Diversity

A focus on fungal conservation is relatively new. The previously held paradigm that most species of fungi had very broad, oftentimes multicontinental, distributions and low ecological conservatism minimised concern about species loss. Added to this, the cryptic nature of fungi due to their growth within substrata, coupled with the paucity of data on the taxonomy, ecology and population trends of most species, led many mycologists to believe that assessing the conservation status of fungi using IUCN Red List or other systems was somewhat intractable (Dahlberg and Mueller, 2011).

Pioneering work by members of the European Council for the Conservation of Fungi in the mid 1980s began to change this perception (Dahlberg et al., 2010; Heilmann-Clausen et al., 2015). An edited volume, *Fungal Conservation: Issues and Solutions* (Moore et al., 2001) summarised the state of fungal conservation and suggested a course for future work, and similar publications and meetings were organized focused on specific groups of fungi, like lichens (Nimis et al. 2002), in that same period. By 2010, a number of European countries, plus Japan and New Zealand, included at least some fungi in their National Red Lists (Dahlberg and Mueller, 2011). But global assessments were nearly totally lacking until recently, e.g. the 2013 update of the IUCN Global Red List included only one mushroom and two lichens. Five IUCN SSC fungal specialist groups were established in 2009 as part of efforts to address the need to raise the profile of fungal conservation and build capacity for assessing the extinction risk of fungal species: *Chytrid, Zygomycete, Downy Mildew and Slime Mould; Cup-Fungus, Truffle, and Aly; Lichen; Rust and Smut Fungi;* and *Mushroom, Bracket, and Puffball.* The Global Fungal Red List Initiative initiated in 2013 (Mueller et al., 2014), focused on capacity building and engagement by the mycological community resulting in a relatively rapid increase in the number of listed fungal species (IUCN Red List version 2022).

2012 saw the passage of a motion during the World Conservation Congress in Jeju, Korea that focused on increasing the attention given to the conservation of fungi (WCC-2012-Res-033). The motion called on 'all of the component parts of IUCN, including Members, Commissions and the Secretariat, and the conservation movement more generally, to place much greater emphasis and priority on the conservation of fungi...' and '...all governments to give greater priority to mycology...' Recognition of the importance of fungi and the need to conserve them has continued to build, and 2021 saw the IUCN SSC, Re:wild and other conservation organisations make public statements calling for the explicit recognition of fungi on a par with plants and animals (www.iucn.org/news/species-survival-commission/202108/rewild-and-iucn-ssc-become-first-global-organizations-call-recognition-fungi-one-three-kingdoms-life-critical-protecting-and-restoring-earth). This recognition of the importance of fungi is reflected in recent initiatives by the global conservation community to document and conserve soil biodiversity, e.g. FAO's Global Soil Partnership launched the International Network on Soil Biodiversity (NETSOB) in December 2021 (www.fao.org/global-soil-partnership/resources/highlights/detail/en/c/1457777/) and the Society for the Protection of Underground Networks (SPUN) (https://spun.earth/) was announced that same week.

16.7 Challenges to Conservation Efforts and Opportunites for Overcoming Them

Although there is growing support for fungal conservation from the conservation community, progress in assessing fungi and developing conservation action plans lags behind efforts on plants and most animal groups (Hochkirch et al., 2020; Lughadha et al., 2020).

16.7.1 Challenges

Fungi are a megadiverse group at multiple scales. As discussed above, Kingdom Fungi encompases up to 12 phyla (James et al., 2020) with taxa ranging from single-celled endoparasites to clonal individuals visible from aeroplanes. A wide variance in the estimated number of fungal species have been published over the last 30 years, ranging from a minimum of nearly 1 million to 2 million (e.g. Hawksworth, 1991; Schmit and Mueller, 2007) to more than 5 million (Blackwell, 2011), with the current most accepted estimate at 2.2–3.8 million (Hawksworth and Lücking, 2017). All of these estimates place fungi as the second most species diverse group of eukaryotes following insects, and the least known, with less than 5% of the estimated species described. But taxonomic richness is not the only challenge. Several hundred fungal species can be recovered from a few grams of soil with a different community documented from nearby samples (Peay et al., 2016). This high alpha and beta diversity, coupled with their cryptic nature, can make documenting diversity, and estimating their abundance at local and regional scales difficult. It is not surprising, given these challenges, coupled with gaps in geographic sampling and the paucity of professionally employed field mycologists compared to most animal and plant groups, that most fungi have not had their conservation status assessed. However, progress is being made.

16.7.2 Opportunities

Basic data needed to assess the conservation status of any organism include information on their distribution, population size and changes in population size over time. Ongoing fieldwork targeting undersampled regions have made significant advances in documenting global fungal diversity based on a combination of traditional field studies and environmental sampling of soil, roots and leaves (e.g. Geml et al., 2014; Tedersoo et al., 2014; Ritter et al., 2020). While next-generation metagenomic sequencing of environmental samples has proven highly valuable for documenting diversity, challenges in data quality and interpretation remain (e.g. Yahr et al., 2016; Hofstetter et al., 2019). Specimens and their associated data housed in natural history collections are important but underutilised resources for documenting fungal diversity and distributions (Andrew et al., 2018). The development of data portals such as the Global Biodiversity Information Facility (www .gbif.org) and national and regional sites (e.g. Miller and Bates, 2017) have greatly facilitated access to these important resources.

Even with these advances by the mycological community, much work remains to document fungal diversity and distribution. There remains great opportunity for discovery. This provides the opportunity and need for engaging citizen scientists to document what species are occurring where and when, and how these patterns are changing (Heilmann-Clausen et al., 2015). Websites like iNaturalist (www.inaturalist.org/) provide the public with the opportunity to document fungal diversity and distributions. By December 2021, iNaturalist had over 5 million fungal observations posted by nearly 500,000 individuals! While the quality of observations varies (McMullin and Allen, 2022), and there is taxon bias toward macrofungi and lichens, with care, the data are useful for making conservation assessments. Several citizen science inititives have documented the high value of engaging citizen scientists in focused projects to generate many high-quality data points useful for conservation efforts, e.g. Australia's FungiMap (https:// fungimap.org.au/), the UK's The Lost and Found Project (www.kew.org/read-and-watch/lost-and-found-fungi) and the US West Coast Rare Challenge coordinated by The Fungal Diversity Survey (https://fundis.org/protect/take-action).

Population size and changes in population size over time are the other essential data needed to assess a species conservation status. A species with a stable or increasing population is likely not currently threatened. While a species undergoing population loss, depending on its population size and rate of loss, may need attention/intervention to mitigate the loss. Progress is being made in fungal population biology (e.g. Vincenot and Selosse, 2017; Branco 2019), but our knowledge of the size of individuals and their population structure lags behind the documentation and understanding of fungal diversity and distribution patterns. Addressing these questions are needed to better assess the conservation state of fungal species.

16.8 Moving Forward

Fungi are essential to life – both ecologically and economically. They are taxonomically, ecologically and morphologically diverse. They also face the same threats as animals and plants. Since human and financial resources are limited, determining which species are thriving and which are rare or declining is crucial for targeting conservation action towards species in greatest need. Yet the conservation status of the vast majority of fungal species has not been assessed regionally or globally. This has greatly hindered the inclusion of fungi in conservation discussions, access to funding programmes, policy decisions and conservation action. Progress is being made, but concerted efforts are needed to advance fungal conservation at the rate needed. For this reason May and colleagues (May et al., 2019) called for the creation of the discipline of conservation mycology to identify gaps in our knowledge and address issues unique to fungi (Box 16.1).

Box 16.1

Benefits of establishing the explicit discipline of conservation mycology

- Facilitates framing research questions
- Focuses on associations of fungi with other biota in addition to 'single species' approach to conservation
- Recognises that practices developed for other organisms in ecosystem management may not be optimal for fungi
- Fosters two-way communication between conservation mycology researchers and practitioners
- Encourages the creation of designated conservation mycologists in universities and management agencies.

Adapted from May et al., 2019.

References

Aime, M.C., Toome, M. and McLaughlin, D. (2014) The Pucciniomycotina. In: McLaughlin, D. and Spatafora, J.W. (Eds.), *The Mycota VII Part A: Systematics and Evolution*, Second Edn. Berlin, Germany: Springer-Verlag.

Ainsworth, A.M., Canteiro, C., Dahlberg, A., et al. (2018) Conservation of fungi. In: K. J. Willis (Ed.), *State of the World's Fungi*. Kew, UK: Royal Botanic Gardens.

Allen, J., Lendemer, J. and McMullin, T. (2022) *Cetradonia linearis*. In: *The IUCN Red List of Threatened Species 2015*: e.T70386009A70386019. https://dx.doi.org/10.2305/IUCN.UK.2015-4.RLTS.T70386009A70386019.en (accessed October 2022).

Andrew, C., Diez, J., James, T. Y. and Kauserud, H. (2018) Fungarium specimens: a largely untapped source in global change biology and beyond. *Phil Trans Royal Soc B* 374: 1–11.

Begerow D., Schäfer, A.M., Kellner, R., et al. (2014) 11 Ustilaginomycotina. In: McLaughlin D. and Spatafora J. (Eds.), *Systematics and Evolution: The Mycota (A Comprehensive Treatise on Fungi as Experimental Systems for Basic and Applied Research)*. Vol. 7A. Berlin, Heidelberg, Germany: Springer.

Blackwell, M. (2011). The fungi: 1, 2, 3. . . 5.1 million species? *Am J Bot* 98(3): 426–438.

Blackwell, M., Hibbett, D.S., Taylor, J.W. and Spatafora, J.W. (2006) Research Coordination Networks: a phylogeny for kingdom Fungi (Deep Hypha), *Mycologia*, 98(6): 829–837.

Branco, S. (2019) Fungal diversity from communities to genes. *Fungal Biol Rev* 33(3–4): 225–237.

Brodo, I.M., Sharnoff, S.D. and Sharnoff, S. (2001) *Lichens of North America*. New Haven, CT: Yale University Press.

Chaudhary, V.B., Cuenca, G. and Johnson, N.C. (2018) Tropical-temperate comparison of landscape-scale arbuscular mycorrhizal fungal species distributions. *Divers Distrib* 24(1): 116–128.

Dahlberg, A. (2015) *Sarcosoma globosum*. *The IUCN Red List of Threatened Species 2015*: e.T58515314A58515381. https://dx.doi.org/10.2305/IUCN.UK.2015-4.RLTS.T58515314A58515381.en (accessed October 2022).

Dahlberg, A. Genney, D.R. and Heilmann-Clausen, J. (2010) Developing a comprehensive strategy for fungal conservation in Europe: current status and future needs. *Fungal Ecol* 3: 50–64.

Dahlberg A. and Mueller, G.M. (2011) Applying IUCN Red Listing Criteria for assessing and reporting on the conservation status of fungal species. *Fungal Ecol* 4: 147–162.

Geml, J., Gravendeel, B., van der Gaag, K.J., et al. (2014) The contribution of DNA metabarcoding to fungal conservation: diversity assessment, habitat partitioning and mapping Red-Listed fungi in protected coastal *Salix repens* communities in the Netherlands. *PLoS One* 9(6): e99852.

Grimm, M., Grube, M., Schiefelbein, U., et al. (2021) The lichens microbiota, still a mystery?, *Front Microbiol* 12: 623839.

Hawksworth, D.L. (1991) The fungal dimension of biodiversity: magnitude, significance, and conservation. *Mycol Res* 95: 641–655.

Hawksworth, D.L. and Lücking, R. (2017) Fungal diversity revisited: 2.2 to 3.8 million species. *Microbiol Spectr.* doi: 10.1128/microbiolspec. FUNK-0052-2016.

Heilmann-Clausen, J., Barron, E.S., Boddy, L., et al. (2015) A fungal perspective on conservation biology. *Conserv Biol* 29(1): 61–68.

Hibbett, D.S., Binder, M., Bischoff, J.F., et al. (2007) A higher-level phylogenetic classification of the Fungi. *Mycol Res* 111: 509–547.

Hibbett, D.S., Blackwell, M., James, T.Y., et al. (2018) Phylogenetic taxon definitions for Fungi, Dikarya, Ascomycota and Basidiomycota. *IMA Fungus* 9(2): 291–298.

Hochkirch, A., Samways, M.J., Gerlach, J., et al. (2020) A strategy for the next decade to address data deficiency in neglected biodiversity. *Conserv Biol* 35(2): 502–509.

Hofstetter, V., Buyck, B., Eyssartier, G., et al. (2019) The unbearable lightness of sequenced-based identification. *Fungal Divers* 96: 243–284.

IUCN. (2022) *The IUCN Red List of Threatened Species.* Version 2021-1. Gland, Switzerland; Cambridge, UK: IUCN.

James, T.Y., Stajich, J.E., Hittinger, C.T. and Rokas, A. (2020) Toward a fully resolved fungal tree of life. *Ann Rev Microbiol* 20(74): 291–313.

Karwehl, S. and Stadler, M. (2016) Exploitation of fungal biodiversity for discovery of novel antibiotics. *Curr Top Microbiol Immunol* 398: 303–338.

Kottke, I., Suárez, J.P., Herrera, P., et al. (2010) Atractiellomycetes belonging to the 'rust' lineage (Pucciniomycotina) form mycorrhizae with terrestrial and epiphytic neotropical orchids. *Proc Royal Soc B* 277: 1289–1298.

Lawrey, J. D., Lücking, R., Sipman, H.J.M., et al. (2009) High concentration of basidiolichens in a single family of agaricoid mushrooms (Basidiomycota: Agaricales: Hygrophoraceae). *Mycol Res* 113(10): 1154–1171.

Legras, J.-L., Merdinoglu, D., Cornuet, J.-M. and Karst, F. (2007) Bread, beer and wine: *Saccharomyces cerevisiae* diversity reflects human history. *Mol Ecol* 16(10): 2091–2102.

Lévesque, C.A. (2011) Fifty years of oomycetes - from consolidation to evolutionary and genomic exploration. *Fungal Divers* 50: 35–46.

Li, Y., Steenwyk, J.L., Chang, Y., et al. (2021) A genome-scale phylogeny of the kingdom Fungi. *Curr Biol* 31(8): 1653–1665.

Lughadha, E.N., Bachman, S.P., Leão, T., et al. (2020) Extinction risk and threats to plants and fungi. *Plants People Planet* 2: 389–408.

Matheny, P. B., Curtis, J.M., Hofstetter, V., et al. (2006) Major clades of Agaricales: a multilocus phylogenetic overview. *Mycologia* 98: 982–995.

May, T., Cooper, J., Dahlberg, A., et al. (2019) Recognition of the discipline of conservation Mycology. *Conserv Biol* 33(3): 733–736.

McMullin, R.T. and Allen, J.L. (2022) An assessment of data accuracy and best practice recommendations for observations of lichens and other difficult to identify taxa on iNaturalist. *Botany* 100: 491–497.

Miller, A.N. and Bates, S.T. (2017) The mycology collections portal (MyCoPortal). *IMA Fungus* 8(2): 65–66.

Moore, D., Nauta, M.M., Evans, S.E. and Rotheroe, M. (2001) Fungal conservation issues: recognizing the problem, finding solutions. In: Moore, D., Nauta, M.M., Evans, S.E. and Rotheroe, M. (Eds.), *Fungal Conservation: Issues and Solutions.* Cambridge, UK: Cambridge University Press.

Moya, P., Molins, A., Martínez-Alberola, F., Muggia, L. and Barreno, E. (2017) Unexpected associated microalgal diversity in the lichen *Ramalina farinacea* is uncovered by pyrosequencing analyses. *PloS One* 12(4): e0175091.

Mueller, G.M., Dahlberg, A. and Krikorev, M. (2014) Bringing fungi into the conservation conversation: the Global Fungal Red List Initiative. *Fungal Conserv* 4: 12–16.

Mueller, G.M., Cunha, K.M., May, T.W., et al. (2022) What do the first 597 global fungal Red List assessments tell us about the threat status of fungi? *Diversity* 14(9): 736.

Nimis, P.L., Scheidegger, C. and Wolseley, P.A. (2002) *Monitoring with Lichens: Monitoring Lichens.* Dordrecht, the Netherlands: Springer.

Peay, K.G., Kennedy, P.G. and Talbot, J.M. (2016) Dimensions of biodiversity in the Earth mycobiome. *Nat Rev Microbiol* 14(7): 434-447.

Ritter, C.D., Dunthorn, M., Anslan, S., et al. (2020) Advancing biodiversity assessments with environmental DNA: long-read technologies help reveal the drivers of Amazonian fungal diversity. *Ecol Evol* 10(14): 7509–7524.

Scheele, B.C., Pasmans, F., Skerratt, L.F., et al. (2019) Amphibian fungal panzootic causes catastrophic and ongoing loss of biodiversity. *Science* 363(6434): 1459–1463.

Schilde, C. and Schaap, P. (2013) The Amoebozoa. *Meth Mol Biol* 983: 1–15.

Schmit, J.P. and Mueller, G.M. (2007) An estimate of the lower limit of global fungal diversity. *Biodivers Conserv* 16: 99–111.

Smith, S.E. and Read, D.J. (2010) *Mycorrhizal Symbiosis.* New York: Academic Press.

Stürmer, S.L., Bever, J.D. and Morton, J.B. (2018) Biogeography of arbuscular mycorrhizal fungi (Glomeromycota): a phylogenetic perspective on species distribution patterns. *Mycorrhiza* 28(7): 587–603.

Tedersoo. L., Bahram, M., Põlme, S., et al. (2014) Global diversity and geography of soil fungi. *Science* 346(6213): 1256688.

Tedersoo, L., Sánchez-Ramírez, S., Kõljalg, U., et al. (2018) High-level classification of the Fungi and a tool for evolutionary ecological analyses. *Fungal Divers* 90(1): 135–159.

Turrini, A. and Giovannetti, M. (2012) Arbuscular mycorrhizal fungi in national parks, nature reserves and protected areas worldwide: a strategic perspective for their in situ conservation. *Mycorrhiza* 22(2): 81–97.

Vincenot, L. and Selosse, M.-A. (2017) Population biology and ecology of ectomycorrhizal fungi. *Ecol Stud* 230: 39–59.

Wijayawardene, N.N., Pawłowska, J., Letcher, P.M. et al. (2018) Notes for genera: basal clades of Fungi (including Aphelidiomycota, Basidiobolomycota, Blastocladiomycota, Calcarisporiellomycota, Caulochytriomycota, Chytridiomycota, Entomophthoromycota, Glomeromycota, Kickxellomycota, Monoblepharomycota, Mortierellomycota, Mucoromycota, Neocallimastigomycota, Olpidiomycota, Rozellomycota and Zoopagomycota). *Fungal Diver* 92: 43–129.

Yahr R, Schoch, C.L. and Dentinger, B.T.M. (2016) Scaling up discovery of hidden diversity in fungi: impacts of barcoding approaches. *Phil Trans Royal Soc B* 371: 20150336.

Yang, Z.-L. (2020) *Ophiocordyceps sinensis* (amended version of 2020 assessment*). The IUCN Red List of Threatened Species 2020*: e.T58514773A179197748. https://dx.doi.org/10.2305/IUCN.UK.2020-3.RLTS.T58514773A179197748.en (accessed October 2022).

Yildirir, G., Malar, C.M. Kokkoris, V. and Corradi, N. (2020) Parasexual and sexual reproduction in arbuscular mycorrhizal fungi: room for both. *Trends Microbiol* 28(7): 517–519.

SEVENTEEN

Simple Life Forms

NORMAN MACLEAN

In Chapter 1 it was emphasised that the first cellular life forms to evolve were bacteria, and that photosynthetic bacteria called cyanobacteria released oxygen through photosynthesis and thus set in train the conditions which allowed the many forms of aerobic life to evolve.

In this chapter I will discuss the separation of bacteria into eubacteria and archaea, and the eventual evolution of other simple forms of life such as protozoa, slime moulds, *Mycoplasma* and Oomycota. None of these life forms is under threat on the planet to the best of my knowledge, but they are included in this chapter for the sake of completeness to ensure that all forms of life on our Planet Earth are considered.

Providing an account of these simple life forms is not without its difficulties. The first problem arises with the Archaea grouping. These organisms were originally called Archaebacteria but are now known, on the basis of gene sequencing of some of the intracellular RNA molecules, to be quite distinct from normal bacteria. The eukaryotic cell is now believed to have evolved from a fusion of a bacterial cell and an archaeal cell, although where the nucleus originated remains obscure.

The second difficulty arises with the single-celled protozoan grouping. These were once thought to be a distinct phylum, but it is now clear that they have originated from more than one phylum, and are a conglomerate of organisms that have arisen from different sources. Protozoa are hugely varied and internally complex, including amoeboid, ciliate and flagellate forms, and species such as *Trichonympha*, an internal symbiont of the termite gut, which has a very complex structure.

This chapter should also discuss some other somewhat mysterious organisms such as the slime moulds *Dictyostelium* and *Physarum*. The cellular slime mould *Dictyostelium* is now included in the Rhyzopoda and the plasmodial slime moulds are now classed as Myxomycota.

A third issue arises about where to place the Oomycota group, which includes organisms such as potato blight (*Phytophthora infestans*). In the nineteenth century these organisms destroyed the entire potato harvest in Ireland and Germany, resulting in widespread famine. It is now clear that many other cultivated crops have their own specialist blight organisms, quite distinct from bacteria or fungi.

I will not discuss viruses here, important though they are. Viruses have evolved from cellular components and depend on cells for their replication. Nor will I discuss prions which are misfolded proteins from eukaryotic cells. Prokaryotic cells have their own viruses known as bacteriophage.

17.1 Bacteria

Let us start with bacteria, which are believed to represent the first forms of life to evolve on Planet Earth. Many bacteria are pathogenic, causing diseases and sepsis in animals and disease in plants, but most are not. Bacteria are anucleate cells with cell walls and in favourable conditions can replicate very rapidly. In mammals, bacterial infection triggers an immune response, which may prevent any resulting disease or reduce its effects. Cyanobacteria can photosynthesise and produced the first oxygen on Planet Earth.

One group of bacteria were once recognised as archaebacteria, but these are now called the archaea and are seen as quite distinct from true bacteria. I will discuss them after the true bacteria. In the evolution of life on Earth, early eukaryotic cells are believed to have formed by the fusion of bacteria and archaeal cells. Both bacteria and archaea are prokaryotes, meaning that they do not possess nuclei. Most life on Earth is prokaryotic and a single gram of soil may contain 100 million individual prokaryotic cells. Leguminous plants and some other plants have root nodules containing bacteria which fix nitrogen.

Bacteria may be spherical, spiral or rod-shaped, and some are motile through the possession of flagellae. Some bacteria, like *Chlamydia*, reproduce entirely within cells. Some pathogenic bacteria release toxins which kill or injure the cells of the host, and these include some of the most toxic substances known, such as tetanus and diphtheria toxins, and pseudomonas exotoxin.

In size, most bacteria range from 2 to 500 microns in length, and most are about 0.5 to 1 microns in diameter. They are bounded by a rigid cell wall, within which is a cell membrane. There is a central DNA chromosome which is usually circular and may contain from a few hundred to several thousand genes.

Some bacteria are filamentous, some occur in long chains, and others spiral like spirochaetes. The flagellum, if present, is driven by a 'motor' in the cell membrane. Round bacteria are often referred to as cocci.

Bacteria are everywhere, in water, soil, in our guts and on many surfaces. Many are killed by copper, and so copper surfaces in a kitchen are usually sterile. Most are killed by exposure to temperature above 60 °C but some, such as the extremophile bacteria in hot springs can tolerate 100 °C. The polymerase chain reaction (PCR) is based on enzymes derived from such bacteria, namely *Taq* polymerase from *Thermus aquaticus*. So not all extremophile organisms are archaea.

Many bacteria can produce endospores, which enables the organism to withstand harsh conditions for long periods of time.

17.2 Archaea

As already emphasised, these prokaryotic organisms are quite distinctive from bacteria, and exist in many environments. Unlike true bacteria, none are pathogenic, but many are so-called extremophiles, able to survive high temperatures in ocean hydrothermal vents and hot springs, and some are tolerant of high radiation levels. They are structurally fairly similar to true bacteria, but have some genes and metabolic pathways that resemble those of eukaryotes rather than those of bacteria. No archaea are flagellated. Some are methanogens, which are used in sewage treatment.

17.3 Protozoa

These organisms, although single-celled for the most part, are much more complex in structure than bacteria and archaea. They are also very varied and those with chloroplasts are actually plants. All are nucleated and some, like some ciliates, have a macronucleus and one or more micronuclei. In size, protozoan cells range from a few microns to a few millimetres. Many, such as the malaria parasite *Plasmodium falciparum* and the *Trypanosoma* which causes sleeping sickness, are serious pathogens. Most, but not all, protozoa are motile, either through possession of cilia or flagellae, or, as in *Amoeba*, moving by amoeboid movement. Structurally they are usually bounded by a stiff pellicle.

Many protozoa reproduce asexually by binary or multiple fission, but some exchange genetic material with other cells of the same species in sexual reproduction (typically involving conjugation). Meiotic sex is known in various protozoa including *Giardia*, *Plasmodium*, *Toxoplasma* and *Trichomonas*.

Some protozoa can form resting cysts to survive harsh conditions, much as some bacteria can form endospores.

The life cycles of some protozoa such as *Plasmodium* can be complex, while the internal structure of many is also complex, as in *Trichonympha* mentioned above (see Figure 17.1).

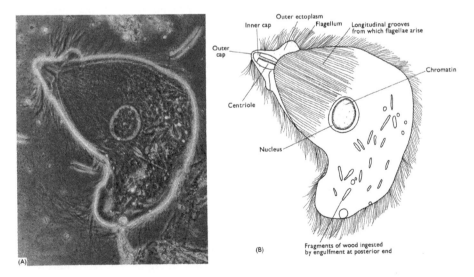

Figure 17.1 (A) Phase contrast photograph of *Trichonympha campanulata*, from the gut of a termite. ×500 approx. (B) Diagram of the photograph shown in (A). (Reproduced with permission from Maclean, 1977.)

Simple multicellular organisms include the slime moulds, *Physarum* and *Dictyostelium*, and also the organisms which cause potato blight and other blight diseases, and are now classed as Oomycota. I do not propose to discuss the many other simple multicellular eukaryotes, but the books in the references to this chapter by Margulis and Schwartz (1998) and Tudge (2000) will provide more information on such organisms.

As indicated earlier, I have chosen to discuss only two of the numerous groups of simple invertebrate, namely the slime moulds *Physarum* and *Dictyostelium*, and the blight organisms characterised by potato blight, *Phytophthora infestans*, classified as belonging to the Oomycota.

17.4 *Physarum*

This is classified as belonging to the Myxomycota, the plasmodial slime moulds. They exist as wet scum on fallen logs and other surfaces, especially in tropical rainforest. The separate amoebae combine to form a multinucleate plasmodium of the Myxamoebae. The plasmodium produces a sporophore fruiting body from which separate amoebae bud off. These are often binucleate, and may or may not possess flagellae. They combine to form a zygote from which new multinucleate plasmodium grows.

17.5 *Dictyostelium*

These organisms, the cellular slime moulds, belong to the Rhizopoda, which also contains amastigote amoeba. The best known example of *Dictyostelium* is *D. discoideum*, widely cultured in laboratories (see Figure 17.2). The separate amoebae on the forest floor are the dispersed feeding stage, and these may aggregate to form a cellular pseudoplasmodium or slug. This is migratory, and eventually produces a stalked sporophore with a cap or sorus, from which individual spores produce the individual feeding amoebae. These eventually aggregate to form the migratory slug referred to above. The life history of this organism is often quoted as an example of simple cellular differentiation. The separate amoeba can produce a pheromone called acrasin (which is actually cyclic adenosine monophosphate) which attracts the separate amoebae to aggregate to form the pseudoplasmodium. In some species the stalk cells of the sporophore are different from the spore cells, and this is the simple form of cell differentiation referred to above.

17.6 Oomycota or Blight Organisms

These organisms are sometimes called water moulds, downy mildews or white rusts, and are best characterised by potato blight (*Phytophthora infestans*). This organism occurs on the leaves and stems of crop potato plants in warm damp conditions, and can totally destroy a crop. At present, potato farmers spray their potato crops with fungicide a few times prior to the development of what are known as blight conditions. This organism produces fungus-like threads or hyphae which release digestive enzymes and thus absorb nutrients from the host.

The pseudomycelium also has a reproductive cycle, producing zoospores. These germinate to produce a new oomycote thallus. In the sexual phase, the tips of the growing hyphae produce specialised male and female structures called antheridia and oogonia. The

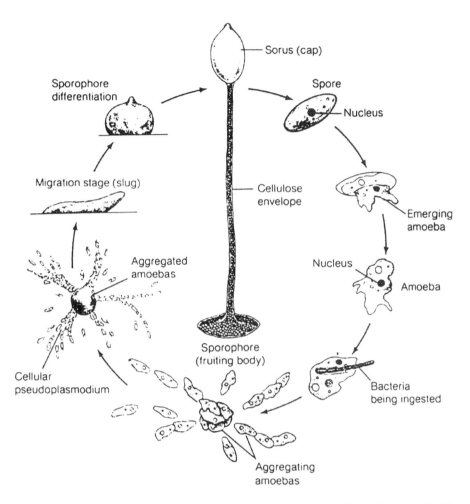

Figure 17.2 The life cycle of the cellular slime mould *Dictyostelium discoideum*. Reproduced with permission from Maclean and Hall (1987) and also Margulis and Schwartz (1985).

male nucleus migrates through a fertilisation tube which penetrates the oogonial tissue and allows fusion. Fertilisation takes place inside the walled oogonium, within which oospores produce zygote cells called oospores.

Essentially, every crop plant can develop its own specialised blight, and hundreds of species are on record.

17.7 Algae

The group of plants called Algae are not monophyletic, meaning that they do not share a common ancestor and are not all related to one another. Algae range from single-celled creatures like diatoms and desmids in freshwater to the huge range of green, brown and red seaweeds in the world's oceans. Single-celled algae also live commensally with corals in coral reefs, allowing the corals to utilise the products of photosynthesis for food. They also co-exist in some sponges.

In freshwater, single-celled algae are sometimes lumped together with other single-celled organisms like amoebae, ciliates and flagellates in the Protozoa, while marine unicellular algae are part of the Phytoplankton, and contribute to the food of manta rays, whale sharks, and some baleen whales.

Further information on algae can be found in a substantial article in Wikipedia under this name (https://en.wikipedia.org/wiki/Algae). The photosynthetic abilities of Algae are based on plastids derived from cyanobacteria. Fossilised filamentous algae have been found in the Vindhya basin, which dates back to 1.7 billion years ago (Bengston et al. 2009). The origin of the algal chloroplasts from cyanobacteria has occurred on separate occasions in different algal lineages, emphasising their separate origins.

A term that has come to be used for aggregations of algae in both fresh and marine water environments is 'algal turf'. Some marine algal turf aggregates provide part of the diet for mammalian dugongs and manatees.

The first land plants are thought to have evolved from Algae like chara some 500 million years ago.

Some marine algae are consumed as food, others are gathered to be used as green manures (and were used in the Scottish Hebrides for the cultivation of potatoes in so-called 'lazy beds').

Seaweed farming occurs in countries such as Indonesia and Malaysia, while there is a modern take on this by the use of algal bioreactors in which algae are cultivated for biomass production in so-called reactors. Algal bioreactors are used not only to produce animal feed but also to produce biodiesel and bioethanol. Agar, a gelatinous substance derived from red algae, is widely used as a laboratory medium on which to grow bacteria and fungi, since these organisms cannot digest agar.

Also some algal products are used as pigment alternatives to synthetic compounds in dyes used in clothing and carpet manufacture.

Acknowledgement

I am much indebted to Professor Nigel Brown, Emeritus Professor of Microbiology at Edinburgh University, for numerous corrections and improvements to this chapter.

References

Bengston, S., Belivanova, V., Rasmussen, B. and Whitehouse, M. (2009) Three-dimensional preservation of cellular and subcellular structures 1.6 billion-year-old crowd-group red algae. *Proc Natl Acad Sci USA* 106(19): 7729–7734.

Maclean, N. (1977) *Differentiation of Cells: Genetics – Principles and Perspectives*. London, UK: Hodder & Stoughton Educational.

Maclean, N. and Hall, B.K. (1987) *Cell Commitment and Differentiation*. Cambridge, UK: Cambridge University Press.

Margulis, L. and Schwartz, K.V. (1985) *Five Kingdoms: Illustrated Guide to the Phyla of Life on Earth*. New York: W.H. Freeman.

Margulis, L. and Schwartz, K.V. (1998) *Five Kingdoms*. New York: W.H. Freeman & Co.

Tudge, C.(2000) *The Variety of Life*. Oxford, UK: Oxford University Press.

EIGHTEEN

Assessing Species Conservation Status: The IUCN Red List and Green Status of Species

MOLLY GRACE

Summary

The conservation status of the taxa in this book is measured using the criteria of the Red List of Threatened Species™. The Red List is overseen by the International Union for Conservation of Nature (IUCN), and categorises species according to extinction risk. This chapter summarises the history of the Red List and explains the criteria used to assess species' extinction risk, as well as the quality control procedures in place today. This chapter also introduces a new part of the Red List, formalised in 2021: The Green Status of Species, a set of metrics which assess species' progress towards functional recovery across its range and the impact of conservation actions.

18.1 What is the International Union for Conservation of Nature?

The International Union for Conservation of Nature (IUCN)[1] was established in 1948 and is widely acknowledged as the 'global authority on the status of the natural world and the measures needed to safeguard it' (www.iucn.org/about). In October 2022, the Union had over 1400 members, including scientific and conservation-focused institutions, governments, educational institutions and non-governmental organisations. IUCN advises on conservation policies regionally and globally, helping craft international agreements such as the Convention on Illegal Trade in Endangered Species of Wild Fauna and Flora (CITES) and the Convention on Biological Diversity; IUCN also has United Nations observer status. In addition to these roles, IUCN is perhaps best-known as the custodian of The IUCN Red List of Threatened Species™ (hereafter 'Red List'): the most widely used measure of species conservation status worldwide (Rodrigues et al., 2006).

---

[1] Until 1956, IUCN was known as the International Union for the Protection of Nature (IUPN); it was also referred to for a time (1990 to 2008) as the World Conservation Union, but this name is no longer commonly used and its use is actively discouraged.

18.2 What Does it Mean if a Species Has a Red List Assessment?

To assess a species for the Red List is to evaluate its probability of extinction. Because all species are 'doomed to extinction' on a geological time scale (Mace and Lande, 1991), Red List methods are designed to flag extinctions likely to happen in the near future (i.e. within the next 100 years). It is important to note that a species does not have to be facing any significant current risk of extinction to be evaluated using the Red List Criteria; in fact, for about half of species listed using the criteria in 2022, the probability of extinction is considered negligible (www.iucnredlist.org/search/stats). However, many people consider the term 'Red Listed' to be synonymous with 'threatened'. This is not surprising, considering how the Red List has evolved over the decades.

Since its beginnings in the 1950s, the system has undergone major changes in both format and scope (for a full history of the Red List see Hilton-Taylor, 2014). The Red List as we know it today has its origins in the work of the IUCN Species Survival Commission (SSC). The SSC was established in 1949[2] to gather and disseminate information on 'all species of fauna and flora that appear to be threatened with extinction' (Scott et al., 1987) with a goal 'to prevent the extinction of species, and to preserve viable wild populations in their native habitats' (Thornback and Jenkins, 1982). To begin this process, information about presumably threatened mammal and bird species was catalogued in a card index, which by 1960 included a few dozen species (Scott et al., 1987; Burton, 2003; Hilton-Taylor, 2014). In 1964, two supplements to the IUCN Bulletin were published – a 'List of Rare Birds' and a 'Preliminary List of Rare Mammals' (see Hilton-Taylor, 2014). Available in English and French, 10,000 copies were sent to IUCN Members, making the information widely available. Hence, 1964 is considered the official start date of the IUCN Red List.

During the 1960s and 1970s, the pace of data collection increased, allowing the SSC to release looseleaf 'Red Data Books', updated every 6 months, for selected species of mammals (Simon, 1966–1971), birds (Vincent, 1966–1971), reptiles and amphibians (Honegger, 1968–1979), freshwater fishes (Miller, 1968–1977) and angiosperms (Melville, 1970–1971). Species in these volumes were assigned to a status such as 'Endangered', 'Vulnerable' and 'Rare', based on expert opinion (Table 18.1). Complete copies of these early editions are difficult to find today, especially because they were 'living documents': when updates were issued, owners were instructed to destroy the old looseleaf pages and replace them with new ones (Burton, 2003). These original Red Data Books were considered 'specialist editions' and were not intended for public use (Scott et al., 1987), though a popular version which primarily focused on mammals and birds was also published (Fisher et al., 1969).

The 1980s saw the trickle of information turn into a flood, with Red Data Books introduced for new groups of species (e.g. invertebrates; Wells et al., 1983) and previous versions expanded; for example, the Red Data Book for mammals had swelled to

---

[2] Then called the IUCN Survival Service Commission.

Table 18.1 *Changes to the Red List Categories over time*

Dates of use	1966–1998	1994–2000 (IUCN, 1994)[a]	2001–present (IUCN, 2001)
	Extinct (Ex)	Extinct (EX)	Extinct (EX)
	Endangered (E)	Extinct in the Wild (EW)	Extinct in the Wild (EW)
	Extinct/Endangered (Ex/E)[b]	Critically Endangered (CR)	Critically Endangered (CR)
	Vulnerable (V)	Endangered (EN)	Endangered (EN)
	Rare (R)	Lower Risk/conservation dependent (LR/cd)	Vulnerable (VU)
	Indeterminate (I)	Lower Risk/near threatened (LR/nt)	Near Threatened (NT)
	Out of Danger (O)	Lower Risk/least concern (LR/lc)	Least Concern (LC)
Categories	Threatened (T)[c]	Data Deficient (DD)	Data Deficient (DD)
	Commercially Threatened (CT)[c]	Not Evaluated (NE)	Not Evaluated (NE)
	Threatened Community (TC)[c]		
	Threatened Phenomenon (TP)[d]		
	Not threatened (nt)		
	No Information (?)[e]		
	Insufficiently Known (K)		
Evidence used	Expert opinion	Quantitative thresholds	Quantitative thresholds

[a] The old system was still being used for plants during this time period.
[b] Used for plants.
[c] Used for animals.
[d] Used for listing monarch butterfly migration sites in the Americas.
[e] Used for invertebrates.

encompass over 320 species (Thornback and Jenkins, 1982). The accelerating pace of data collection, as well as the need to keep track of changes and updates to species status, was the impetus for the establishment of the IUCN Conservation Monitoring Centre in Cambridge, which created databases to store the rapidly growing number of species accounts. In 1999, the Red List Unit was set up and all data were moved to a single database.

Other big changes were happening around this time as well. In 1984, the IUCN General Assembly held a workshop to improve definitions for the Red List categories of extinction risk, which were inconsistently applied and relied on subjective expert opinion (Fitter and Fitter, 1987; Rodrigues et al., 2006). In 1991, a proposal was made to introduce quantitative thresholds based on principles of population biology – the Red List Categories and Criteria – to the Red List process, to provide a more objective measure of extinction risk (Mace and Lande, 1991; Mace et al., 1992). There were also proposed changes to the categories to which taxa could be assigned. Over the next few years, the proposed Red List Categories and Criteria were developed through consultation and testing until the new version was formally adopted (IUCN, 1994; version 2.3). As this revision was implemented on a large scale, certain desirable changes were identified, particularly to improve its applicability to taxa such as plants, trees and marine fishes[3] (Mace et al., 2008). In 2001, a third version of the Red List Categories and Criteria was approved (IUCN, 2001; version 3.1). It is this third version that is in use today. The applications of the Red List Categories and Criteria are supported by a detailed set of guidelines (IUCN SPC, 2022) that are updated regularly, providing information on how to incorporate new types of data (such as remote sensing), methods of analysis (e.g. for inferring extinctions and for modelling habitat), and emerging threats (such as climate change) into Red List assessments. Today, print versions are no longer published; all Red List species accounts are available online (https://www.iucnredlist.org/).

18.3 The Red List Categories and Criteria (Version 3.1)

Since 2001, Red List assessments have followed Version 3.1 of the Red List Categories and Criteria (IUCN, 2001). These criteria can be applied at the taxonomic level of species or below (e.g. subspecies, variety, subpopulation) but are most often applied to species. When considering a taxon for classification, there are nine categories into which it may be placed (Figure 18.1). Most of these potential categories reflect the probability that extinction has occurred or will occur. A taxon is placed in the *Extinct (EX)* category when there is 'no reasonable doubt' that the last individual has died, which is demonstrated when exhaustive surveys throughout the species' known or expected range, under conditions appropriate to the species' life history (e.g. activity patterns, life cycle), fail to uncover any

[3] Resolution WCC1996-RES-1.5 requested the IUCN to review the IUCN Red List Categories and Criteria to ensure the criteria are effective indicators of extinction risk across the broadest possible range of taxonomic categories, especially in relation to marine species, particularly fish, taking into account the dynamic nature of marine ecosystems, species under management programmes and the time periods over which declines are measured.

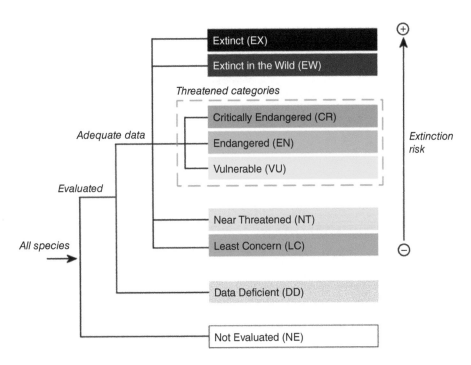

Figure 18.1 IUCN Red List Categories. Reproduced with permission from IUCN (2001).

individuals (IUCN, 2001). The Christmas Island pipistrelle bat was assessed as Extinct in 2016 after ultrasonic detectors had not recorded the species anywhere on the island since 2009, following years of documented decline (Lumsden et al., 2017). A taxon is considered *Extinct in the Wild (EW)* when the conditions for the Extinct category are fulfilled, save for any individuals surviving in captivity/cultivation or in naturalised populations well outside its native range; for example, the scimitar-horned oryx, native to the African Sahel, is considered Extinct in the Wild despite there being as many as 11,000 free-living individuals on ranches in the United States (IUCN SSC Antelope Specialist Group, 2022). Considering the relative costs of wrongly declaring an extant species to be EX or EW, and of failing to list an extinct species as EX, IUCN is developing new guidance based on recent developments in inferring extinctions (Akçakaya et al., 2017; Keith et al., 2017; Thompson et al., 2017).

The next three potential categories are considered the *threatened* categories, and taxa must meet quantitative criteria to be placed in one. The threatened categories reflect descending order of extinction risk: extremely high risk, *Critically Endangered (CR)*, very high risk, *Endangered (EN)* and high risk, *Vulnerable (VU)*. The magnitude of extinction risk is a combination of the probability of extinction and the timescale over which that probability is spread, with Critically Endangered species facing a higher probability of extinction over a shorter period of time than Endangered species, and likewise Endangered vs. Vulnerable species.

Table 18.2 *Summary of the five criteria used to determine if a taxon belongs in one of the three threatened categories (Version 3.1)*

A. Population size reduction. Population reduction (measured over the longer of 10 years or 3 generations) based on any of A1 to A4			
	Critically Endangered	**Endangered**	**Vulnerable**
A1	≥ 90%	≥ 70%	≥ 50%
A2, A3 & A4	≥ 80%	≥ 50%	≥ 30%

A1 Population reduction observed, estimated, inferred, or suspected in the past where the causes of the reduction are clearly reversible AND understood AND have ceased.	(a) direct observation *[except A3]*
	(b) an index of abundance appropriate to the taxon
A2 Population reduction observed, estimated, inferred, or suspected in the past where the causes of reduction may not have ceased OR may not be understood OR may not be reversible.	(c) a decline in area of occupancy (AOO), extent of occurrence (EOO) and/or habitat quality
A3 Population reduction projected, inferred or suspected to be met in the future (up to a maximum of 100 years) *[(a) cannot be used for A3]*.	*based on any of the following:* (d) actual or potential levels of exploitation
A4 An observed, estimated, inferred, projected or suspected population reduction where the time period must include both the past and the future (up to a max. of 100 years in future), and where the causes of reduction may not have ceased OR may not be understood OR may not be reversible.	(e) effects of introduced taxa, hybridization, pathogens, pollutants, competitors or parasites.

B. Geographic range in the form of either B1 (extent of occurrence) AND/OR B2 (area of occupancy)			
	Critically Endangered	**Endangered**	**Vulnerable**
B1. Extent of occurrence (EOO)	< 100 km²	< 5,000 km²	< 20,000 km²
B2. Area of occupancy (AOO)	< 10 km²	< 500 km²	< 2,000 km²
AND at least 2 of the following 3 conditions:			
(a) Severely fragmented OR Number of locations	= 1	≤ 5	≤ 10
(b) Continuing decline observed, estimated, inferred or projected in any of: (i) extent of occurrence; (ii) area of occupancy; (iii) area, extent and/or quality of habitat; (iv) number of locations or subpopulations; (v) number of mature individuals			
(c) Extreme fluctuations in any of: (i) extent of occurrence; (ii) area of occupancy; (iii) number of locations or subpopulations; (iv) number of mature individuals			

C. Small population size and decline			
	Critically Endangered	**Endangered**	**Vulnerable**
Number of mature individuals	< 250	< 2,500	< 10,000
AND at least one of C1 or C2			
C1. An observed, estimated or projected continuing decline of at least (up to a max. of 100 years in future):	25% in 3 years or 1 generation (whichever is longer)	20% in 5 years or 2 generations (whichever is longer)	10% in 10 years or 3 generations (whichever is longer)
C2. An observed, estimated, projected or inferred continuing decline AND at least 1 of the following 3 conditions:			
(a) (i) Number of mature individuals in each subpopulation	≤ 50	≤ 250	≤ 1,000
(ii) % of mature individuals in one subpopulation =	90–100%	95–100%	100%
(b) Extreme fluctuations in the number of mature individuals			

D. Very small or restricted population			
	Critically Endangered	**Endangered**	**Vulnerable**
D. Number of mature individuals	< 50	< 250	D1. < 1,000
D2. *Only applies to the VU category* Restricted area of occupancy or number of locations with a plausible future threat that could drive the taxon to CR or EX in a very short time.	-	-	D2. typically: AOO < 20 km² or number of locations ≤ 5

E. Quantitative Analysis			
	Critically Endangered	**Endangered**	**Vulnerable**
Indicating the probability of extinction in the wild to be:	≥ 50% in 10 years or 3 generations, whichever is longer (100 years max.)	≥ 20% in 20 years or 5 generations, whichever is longer (100 years max.)	≥ 10% in 100 years

Reproduced from the IUCN website (https://www.iucnredlist.org/resources/summary-sheet).

Species are placed into one of the three threatened categories if they meet the category thresholds for at least one of the five criteria A–E (Table 18.2). Thus, taxa are assessed against all five criteria, which forces assessors to consider the full suite of extinction risk indicators decided upon by IUCN consultation. A species may qualify for different categories based on the criterion under consideration; for example, a species may qualify as VU under criterion A and EN under criterion B. In this case, the higher risk category (EN) is assigned.

The fact that extinction risk can be detected using any one of five distinct criteria means that the Red List framework is sensitive to the different sources of evidence which are likely to be available for different taxa. The large kidney fern is listed as Critically Endangered under criterion B because it occupies an area of less than 10 km^2, is declining and has a severely fragmented population (Lambdon and Ellick, 2016). However, it would be difficult to assess this species for the Red List if extinction risk could only be indicated by the number of mature individuals (required for criteria C and D), as this information is often not known for plant species.

In most cases, data available for the species are incomplete and uncertain. The assessment process allows and encourages incorporating these uncertainties. All data entered into an assessment can be expressed as an interval (minimum and maximum plausible values) in addition to a best estimate. These data uncertainties are then propagated through the criteria based on fuzzy arithmetic methods (Akçakaya et al., 2000). Additional flexibility in applying the criteria is provided by allowing estimated, inferred, projected or suspected values of some of the parameters. A species' category is reassigned if new data become available; see Section 18.7, Re-evaluation of Red List Status.

If a taxon is assessed against the five criteria and is not found to meet any of the thresholds, there are two categories to which it could potentially be assigned. If it does not currently meet any of the criteria, but is close to meeting them such that it is likely to do so in the near future, the taxon is classified as *Near Threatened (NT)*. The witches cauldron fungus (*Sarcosoma globosum*, also known as the charred pancake-cup) is experiencing an ongoing reduction in habitat estimated to be just under 30% over 50 years (Dahlberg, 2015), which means that it very nearly qualifies for threatened status (VU) under criterion A (Table 18.2) and is therefore considered NT. Finally, if the species is not close to meeting any of the thresholds, it is classified as *Least Concern (LC)*. The puma (also known by the names mountain lion, cougar and panther) is one of the few large-bodied felids in this category.

In some cases, not enough is known about the taxon to generate a meaningful estimate of extinction risk, resulting in a *Data Deficient (DD)* classification. For example, the Algerian oak (*Quercus canariensis*) is known to have a wide distribution spanning North Africa and the Iberian Peninsula, so it would not qualify for one of the threatened categories under criterion B (Table 18.2), but data on population size and trends are lacking, so it cannot be assessed against the other criteria (Gorener et al., 2017). However, a species must be assigned to this category only if there is such doubt that the species could potentially rank anywhere from Critically Endangered to Least Concern. If this is not the case, and expert opinion indicates that any other category may be appropriate, the precautionary principle should be followed.

Finally, if a species has not yet been assessed using Red List Criteria, it is considered *Not Evaluated (NE)*. It is a goal of IUCN to reduce the number of species in this category.

18.4 Regional Applications of Red List Categories and Criteria

Whilst these categories and criteria are usually applied to the global population of a taxon, there are also guidelines for applying them at subglobal spatial scales (IUCN, 2012). This can be useful for guiding regional and/or national conservation efforts, especially when a region contains a significant proportion of the global population. Regional assessments began to appear in the 1970s (Scott et al., 1987).

18.5 Who Performs Red List Assessments?

In theory, anyone with sufficient knowledge of a species can perform a Red List assessment, which will be passed through the appropriate quality control channels before publication (see Section 18.6, Quality Control). In practice, however, the majority of Red List assessments are coordinated by a taxon-specific Red List Authority (Figure 18.2). The Red List Authority can be an IUCN partner organisation (e.g. BirdLife International), but in most cases the Red List Authority is a dedicated Specialist Group under the auspices of the IUCN Species Survival Commission. There are over 140 Specialist Groups, each with its own taxonomic focus. Some groups have a narrower scope than others; the Pangolin Specialist Group covers only eight species, whereas there are more than 15,000 species which could be assessed by the Freshwater Fish Specialist Group. New groups are still being formed to help share the load and begin assessments for neglected taxa; in 2018 for example, the Mayfly, Stonefly and Caddisfly; Ladybird; Firefly; Hoverfly; and Skink Specialist Groups came into existence.

18.6 Quality Control

The introduction of quantitative thresholds in 1991 made it much easier to identify the reasoning behind assignment of a taxon to a particular category and greatly reduced the ambiguity of Red List assessments. Despite this, because assessments are often made using the precautionary principle and rely on estimation or inference, it is critical that all assumptions and sources of information which have been used to determine the species' category are documented. Therefore, each species assessment on the Red List website (www.iucnredlist.org/) contains, in addition to a brief summary of the information on the species, a full detailed report with additional information where relevant (as a Supplemental Information PDF linked to from the species' assessment webpage). Each assessment is also available as a downloadable PDF. It is also important to note that submitted Red List assessments go through several rounds of quality control checks, including independent review by named reviewers and checks by a dedicated Red List Unit, prior to publication, to ensure that they reflect accurate information (Figure 18.2).

18.7 Re-evaluation of Red List Status

Because the Red List is a measure of extinction risk, it is crucial to re-evaluate species status regularly (usually every five to ten years) to determine if a new status is appropriate or if new conservation actions are needed. The process of moving a species from one category of extinction risk to another varies depending on the circumstances calling for the

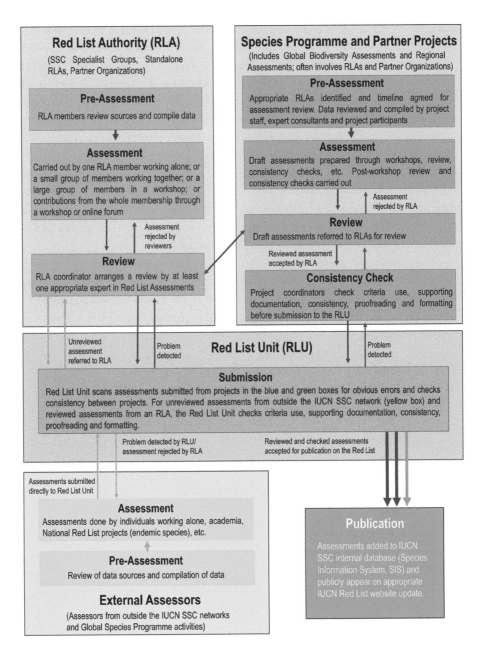

Figure 18.2 Process of submission and quality control for Red List assessments. Adapted from the IUCN website (www.iucnredlist.org/assessment/process).

move. If there is compelling evidence for *uplisting* (moving from a lower risk category to a higher one, e.g. Vulnerable → Endangered), the change in status takes effect immediately. Likewise, if a *downlisting* is called for because a previous assessment was based on incomplete information which indicated a higher risk of extinction than the species was actually facing, the change in status is also immediate. The exception to this rule is a downlisting based on a *genuine change* in species status. Under the precautionary principle, a species must meet the criteria for the lower risk category for at least 5 years before the change can take effect. For example, if the number of mature individuals of a species increases enough so that it would no longer be considered Endangered under criterion D, it must maintain that increase for five years before it can be reclassified as Vulnerable.

Tracking genuine changes in species' Red List status over time allows us to create a *Red List Index*, a powerful tool to assess improvement or deterioration of a group of species over time. Genuine improvements in species status increase the group's index, while genuine deteriorations decrease it. To date, the RLI has been calculated for mammals, birds, amphibians, cycads and corals, groups for which all species have been assessed twice or more. Unfortunately, but perhaps not unsurprisingly, the RLI of all five groups deteriorated from the first assessment to the most recent.

IUCN has set a goal of assessing 160,000 species from across all taxonomic groups. Such a representative sample would provide an indication of the relative extinction risk of the world's major species groups, a kind of *Barometer of Life* (www.iucnredlist.org/about/barometer-of-life). The progress of these groups will be tracked over time as a measure of planetary change.

18.8 Is Assessing Extinction Risk Enough?

The IUCN Red List has become the global standard for assessing the risk of extinction each species on Earth faces. This large-scale adoption has led to harmonised national and international polices, allowed the impact of multiple forms of development on species to be evaluated, and has resulted in more efficient allocation of conservation actions and resources. Recently, however, there has been international interest in developing new metrics of conservation success to work in parallel with the Red List.

This call for new metrics is not a criticism of the Red List. For one thing, the call comes from within IUCN, the keeper of and primary advocate for the Red List. The Red List does what it is designed to do – assess the likelihood of imminent extinction – well. Instead, the request for new metrics reflects a conceptual shift in conservation which advocates that avoiding extinction, while truly the first and foremost priority in species conservation programmes, should not be the end goal. Rather, the end goal should be the *recovery* of species and their associated ecosystem functions. To truly understand the conservation status of a species, we must understand not only its risk of extinction, but also where it is on the road to recovery.

Focusing solely on extinction risk can provide an incomplete picture of a species' conservation status. Take the example of the puma. This felid is considered Least Concern on the Red List, as it has a huge, continent-spanning range, and the large population is not undergoing steep global reductions in size. Least Concern is a completely accurate description of the Puma's imminent extinction risk. However, when we consider factors besides extinction risk, our picture of the species' conservation status becomes less clear. For one thing, the species has experienced a severe range contraction over the past centuries; due to extreme hunting pressure it was extirpated from at least a third of its range (Nowell and Jackson, 1996). It is well-documented that pumas exert considerable top-down influence on the ecosystems they inhabit, with their removal causing negative shifts in the relationship between large herbivores and woody vegetation (Ripple and Beschta 2006, 2008). Should we be concerned about the absence of this top predator, and its associated ecosystem functions, from so many areas?

18.9 The IUCN Green Status of Species: Measuring Species Recovery and Conservation Impact

The field of species conservation has, in the Red List, an excellent way to measure the likelihood of what we want to avoid – species extinction – but there has not historically been a consistently applied method to measure progress toward what we want to achieve – species recovery. An optimistic vision of species conservation that presents a road map on how to achieve recovery, once the threat of extinction has been averted, is also needed. Recognising this, IUCN decided to expand the Red List assessment process to include metrics of species recovery.

The idea of such an expansion to the Red List, termed the 'Green Status of Species' (IUCN, 2021), was endorsed by the IUCN membership at the World Conservation Congress in 2012. The Resolution requested that the Species Survival Commission 'develop objective, transparent and repeatable criteria… that systematically assess successful conservation of species'.[4] The idea is that the Red List (extinction risk measure) and Green Status (recovery measures) will work together to tell a more complete story of a species. Since this resolution was adopted, IUCN has convened ten consultations to develop a framework for a Green Status of Species: March 2014, Cuernavaca, Mexico, where an inaugural meeting on conservation success metrics was convened between the SSC, WCPA and CEM; September 2014, Tallinn, Estonia, among members of the IUCN SSC Steering Committee; September 2015, Abu Dhabi, United Arab Emirates, among the wider leadership of the SSC and close partners; April 2016, Cambridge, UK, which brought together 22 participants from around the world to advance the framework methods; September 2016, Hawai'i, USA, among participants to the 6th IUCN World Conservation Congress; and four scientific development meetings between 2017 and 2019 in Oxford and Cambridge, UK. A final online consultation open to all IUCN members was carried out in 2020.

---

[4] The Resolution (WCC2012-RES-41) called for the creation of three Green Lists: The Green List of Protected Areas, the Green List of Species and the Green List of Ecosystems. The Green List of Protected Areas, the first of these to be completed, is a certification scheme that identifies well-managed protected areas (IUCN, 2016). The species metric, however, was not designed to identify only 'recovered' species, and due to this conceptual difference, the name was changed from 'Green List of Species' to Green Status of Species'. The Green List of Ecosystems followed suit, and the Green Status of Ecosystems will be developed according to the principles of the Green Status of Species (just as the Red List of Ecosystems mirrors the Red List of Threatened Species).

In November 2016, an IUCN Task Force on Assessing Conservation Success was formed, convened under the joint auspices of the IUCN Red List Committee and Species Survival Commission.[5] This Task Force published a draft Green Status of Species framework (Akçakaya et al., 2018), which was further developed to produce the Green Status Standard (IUCN, 2021) with accompanying Background and Guidelines (IUCN SCSTF, 2020). The Green Status defines a 'fully recovered' species as one that is viable and ecologically functional across its indigenous (pre-impact and future) range. In practice, progress toward this goal is measured by dividing the range into subsections (*spatial units*) and assessing the population within each spatial unit as *Absent, Present, Viable* or *Functional*. This is then converted into a *Green Score (G)*, or percentage of full recovery, using the formula

$$G = \frac{\sum_s W_S}{W_F \times N} \times 100$$

where W_S equals the weight given to the status in each spatial unit,[6] W_F equals the weight given to the Functional status (the maximum value possible for a spatial unit), and N equals the total number of spatial units. If a species were Absent in all spatial units, it would receive a Green Score of 0% (e.g. it is Extinct in the Wild). If a species were Functional in all spatial units, it would receive a Green Score of 100% (Fully Recovered).

Defining recovery in this way has several advantages. For one, it explicitly incorporates variation in status across the species' range. Often status does vary considerably across the range, but because the Red List is primarily used to assess extinction risk globally, the status of the largest or best-off population can obscure this variation. The Green Status definition of recovery is also designed to account for temporal variation in species status. In the Green Status of Species framework, range is defined by the historical, pre-impact distribution of the species.[7] This avoids the trap of shifting baselines (Papworth et al., 2009) and makes recovery targets more ambitious (Akçakaya et al., 2018). Finally, the Green Status definition of recovery includes functionality, recognising that species are embedded in ecosystems and that we are aspiring to maintain populations that contribute to ecological processes.

Applying the Green Score formula to assess the current state of species recovery provides new information, complementary to the Red List, and progress can be measured by reassessing the species every few years to see if the species is moving forward or

---

[5] In the Species Survival Commission (SSC), the Task Force is called the Species Conservation Success Task Force.

[6] In the default method, Absent = 0, Present = 3, Viable = 6, Functional = 9; there are also fine-scale weightings for use in certain circumstances. For more information, see the Green Status Standard (IUCN, 2021) and the Background and Guidelines document (IUCN SCSTF, 2020).

[7] This 'indigenous range' represents the distribution of the species at a temporal baseline. The baseline varies from species to species, because it is meant to represent a time before humans became a major factor limiting the species' distribution. For many species, 1750 CE (the start of the Industrial Revolution) may be an appropriate baseline and so is recommended as the default in cases where information about species-specific human impacts is unknown (IUCN 2021).

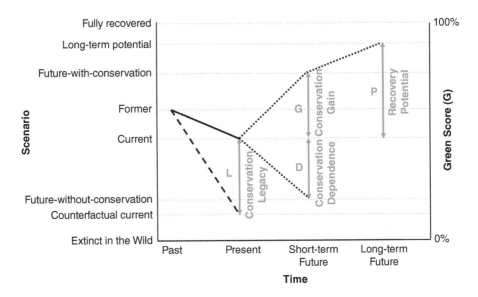

Figure 18.3 Derivation of the four Green Status metrics, where the solid black line represents observed change in the state of the species since 1950, the long-dashed black line represents the past change expected in the absence of past conservation efforts, the dashed black lines represent future scenarios of change expected with and without current and future conservation efforts, the dotted black line represents long-term potential change expected with future conservation innovation and efforts. Modified with permission from IUCN (2021).

backward along the road to recovery. However, there are four additional metrics produced by the Green Status assessment which will enhance species conservation efforts (IUCN, 2021): by calculating a species' *Conservation Legacy*, *Conservation Gain*, *Conservation Dependence*, and *Recovery Potential* (Figure 18.3).

18.10 Measuring Conservation Success: Four Metrics

Conservation efforts can sometimes seem futile, if years of effort and expenditure of resources do not result in a change in Red List status. The Javan rhinoceros, for example, has been listed as Critically Endangered since 1996, despite concerted conservation efforts (van Strien et al., 2008; Ellis and Talukdar, 2020). However, Akçakaya et al. (2018) suggest that preventing declines in status should also be celebrated as a conservation victory. Therefore, the Green Status of Species can also be used to calculate the *Conservation Legacy* of a species – the difference between the current Green Score and the estimated score if no conservation actions had been taken. By asking assessors to estimate[8] how conservation to date has impacted the species, the Green Status of Species

---

[8] Standardized methods for robustly estimating species status under different scenarios can be found in IUCN SCSTF (2020).

framework can be used to show that conservation has indeed had a legacy – even if this has not caused the Red List category to change.

A similar exercise can be used to assess the species' *Conservation Dependence*, the expected deterioration in Green Score if all conservation efforts were to cease. While this may seem like a far-fetched scenario, often conservation funding is linked to Red List Categories, with priority given to species in more threatened categories. This makes sense from a prioritisation viewpoint, but it can also create perverse incentives to under-report conservation success; if conservation has had a positive impact on a species, celebrating that fact could result in a loss of funding, sending the species back into threatened status within a few years (see Mallon and Jackson, 2017). By assessing Conservation Dependence, the Green Status of Species can provide a justification for continued conservation funding if necessary.

The final two conservation metrics which can be generated by the Green Status of Species consider future species recovery. *Conservation Gain* considers the planned conservation actions for a species and calculates a Green Score based on their estimated impact. *Recovery Potential*, on the other hand, is an estimate of the recovery that is possible in the long term, an upper limit to ambitions for the species. It calculates the maximum possible recovery that could be achieved, e.g. if we had unlimited funds, where would it be feasible to restore this species and where would it be highly improbable/impossible to do so? This optimistic but realistic measure allows expectations to be managed appropriately; for one species, it may only be possible to achieve 30% recovery, while for another, full recovery is possible.

18.11 The Future of Species Conservation: Red + Green

The Green Status of Species recovery framework has been tested for scientific robustness on a range of species and taxonomic groups in partnership with IUCN SSC Specialist Groups and independent species experts (Grace et al., 2021a). This feedback has produced an objective measure of recovery for species which all present different types of conservation challenges, including terrestrial, marine and freshwater species, plants, fungi, invertebrates and vertebrates, long- and short-lived species, species with very different geographic range sizes, and species with different amounts and quality of data. Input has also been sought from various stakeholders representing governmental agencies, non-governmental organisations, intergovernmental organisations, and zoos, aquaria and botanic gardens (Dudley and Timmins, 2021; Grace et al., 2021b).

Now that the Green Status of Species protocol has been finalised and made available (IUCN, 2021), conservationists have two equally important ways to frame the status of their species: The Red List of Threatened Species, which acts an alarm bell signalling imminent danger to the persistence of the species, and the Green Status of Species, which allows us to consider the longer process of species recovery. With these two complementary systems working in tandem, we will soon have a much fuller understanding about the conservation status of the diverse species of our planet.

Acknowledgements

I sincerely thank Craig Hilton-Taylor and Resit Akçakaya for editing this chapter and for sharing their deep knowledge of the history of IUCN and the development of the Red List. I am also grateful to NERC for their support of my work on the Green Status of Species via a Knowledge Exchange Fellowship.

References

Akçakaya, H.R., Keith, D.A., Burgman, M., et al. (2017) Inferring extinctions III: a cost-benefit framework for listing extinct species. *Biol Conserv* 214: 336–342.

Akçakaya, H.R., Bennett, E.L., Brooks, T.M., et al. (2018) Quantifying species recovery and conservation success to develop an IUCN Green List of Species. *Conserv Biol* 32: 1128–1138.

Akçakaya, H.R., Ferson, S., Burgman, M.A., et al. (2000) Making consistent IUCN classifications under uncertainty. *Conserv Biol* 14(4): 1001–1013.

Burton, J.A. (2003) The context of Red Data Books, with a complete bibliography of the IUCN publications. In: H.H. de Iongh, O.S. Bánki, W. Bergmans and M.J. van der Werff ten Bosch (Eds.), *The Harmonization of Red Lists for Threatened Species in Europe, Proceedings of an International Seminar 27 and 28 November 2002.* Mededelingen No. 38. Leiden, the Netherlands: The Netherlands Commission for International Protection.

Dahlberg, A. (2015) Sarcosoma globosum. *The IUCN Red List of Threatened Species 2015*: e. T58515314A58515381. www.iucnredlist.org/species/58515314/58515381 (accessed October 2022).

Dudley, N. and Timmins, H.L. (Eds.) (2021) *A Survey of User Attitudes Towards the Proposed IUCN Green Status of Species.* Gland, Switzerland: IUCN.

Ellis, S. and Talukdar, B. (2020) Rhinoceros sondaicus. *The IUCN Red List of Threatened Species 2020*: e. T19495A18493900. https://www.iucnredlist .org/species/19495/18493900 (accessed October 2022).

Fisher, J., Simon, N. and Vincent, J. (1969). *The Red Book: Wildlife in Danger.* New York: HarperCollins.

Fitter, R. and Fitter, M. (Eds). (1987). *The Road to Extinction*, pp. 1-5. Gland, Switzerland: IUCN.

Gorener, V., Harvey-Brown, Y. and Barstow, M. (2017) Quercus canariensis. *The IUCN Red List of Threatened Species 2017*: e.T78809256A78809271. www.iucnredlist.org/species/78809256/ 78809271 (accessed October 2022).

Grace, M., Akçakaya, H.R., Bennett, E.L., et al. (202 coauthors). (2021a) Testing a global standard for quantifying species recovery and assessing conservation impact. *Conserv Biol* 35(6): 1833–1849.

Grace, M., Timmins, H., Long, B., et al. (2021b) Engaging end-users to maximise uptake and effectiveness of a new species recovery assessment. *Conserv Soc* 19(3): 150–160.

Hilton-Taylor, C. (2014) A history of the IUCN Red List. In: Smart, J.S., Hilton-Taylor, C. and Mittermeier, R.A. (Eds.), *The IUCN Red List: 50 Years of Conservation.* Washington, DC: Cemex and Earth in Focus, Inc.

Honegger, R. (1968–1979) *IUCN Red Data Book*, Vol. 3. Reptilia-Amphibia. Morges: IUCN.

IUCN. (1994) *IUCN Red List Categories. Version 2.3.* IUCN Species Survival Commission. Gland, Switzerland; Cambridge, UK: IUCN.

IUCN. (2001) *IUCN Red List Categories and Criteria: Version 3.1.* IUCN Species Survival Commission. Gland, Switzerland; Cambridge, UK: IUCN.

IUCN. (2012) *Guidelines for Application of IUCN Red List Criteria at Regional and National Levels: Version 4.0.* Gland, Switzerland; Cambridge, UK: IUCN.

IUCN. (2016) *IUCN Green List of Protected and Conserved Areas: Standard, Version 1.1.* Gland, Switzerland: IUCN.

IUCN. (2021) *IUCN Green Status of Species: A Global Standard for Measuring Species Recovery and Assessing Conservation Impact. Version 2.0.* Gland, Switzerland: IUCN.

IUCN Species Conservation Success Task Force (IUCN SCSTF). (2020) *Background and Guidelines* for the *IUCN Green Status of Species. Version 1.0.* Prepared by the IUCN Species Conservation Success Task Force. www.iucnredlist.org/resources/green-status-assessment-materials (accessed October 2022).

IUCN Standards and Petitions Committee (IUCN SPC). (2022). *Guidelines for Using the IUCN Red List Categories and Criteria. Version 14.* https://www.iucnredlist.org/resources/redlistguidelines (accessed October 2022).

IUCN SSC Antelope Specialist Group. (2022) Oryx dammah. *The IUCN Red List of Threatened Species 2016*: e.T15568A50191470. http://dx.doi.org/10.2305/IUCN.UK.2016-2.RLTS.T15568A50191470.en (accessed October 2022).

Keith, D.A., Butchart, S.H., Regan, H.M., et al. (2017). Inferring extinctions I: a structured method using information on threats. *Biol Conserv* 214: 320–327.

Lambdon, P.W. and Ellick, S. (2016) Dryopteris cognata. *The IUCN Red List of Threatened Species 2016*: e.T67373923A67373935. www.iucnredlist.org/species/67373923/67373935 (accessed October 2022).

Lumsden, L., Racey, P.A. and Hutson, A.M. (2017) Pipistrellus murrayi. *The IUCN Red List of Threatened Species 2017*: e.T136769A518894. https://www.iucnredlist.org/species/136769/209549918 (accessed October 2022).

Mace, G. M. and Lande, R. (1991) Assessing extinction threats: toward a reevaluation of IUCN threatened species categories. *Conserv Biol* 5(2): 148–157.

Mace, G.M., Collar, N., Cooke, J., et al. (1992) The development of new criteria for listing species on the IUCN Red List. *Species* 19: 16–22.

Mace, G.M., Collar, N.J., Gaston, K.J., et al. (2008) Quantification of extinction risk: IUCN's system for classifying threatened species. *Conserv Biol* 22: 1424–1442.

Mallon, D.P. and Jackson, R.M. (2017) A downlist is not a demotion: Red List status and reality. *Oryx* 51(4): 605–609.

Melville, R. (1970–1971). *IUCN Red Data Book*, Vol. 5. Angiospermae. Morges, Switzerland: IUCN.

Miller, R.R. (1968-1977). *IUCN Red Data Book*, Vol. 4. Pisces. Morges, Switzerland: IUCN.

Nowell, K. and Jackson, P. (1996). *Wild Cats. Status Survey and Conservation Action Plan.* Gland, Switzerland; Cambridge, UK: IUCN/SSC Cat Specialist Group.

Papworth, S.K., Rist, J., Coad, L. and Milner-Gulland, E.J. (2009) Evidence for shifting baseline syndrome in conservation. *Conserv Lett* 2: 93–100.

Ripple, W.J. and Beschta, R.L. (2006) Linking a cougar decline, trophic cascade, and catastrophic regime shift in Zion National Park. *Biol Conserv* 133(4): 397–408.

Ripple, W.J. and Beschta, R.L. (2008) Trophic cascades involving cougar, mule deer, and black oaks in Yosemite National Park. *Biol Conserv* 141(5): 1249–1256.

Rodrigues, A.S., Pilgrim, J.D., Lamoreux, J.F., Hoffmann, M. and Brooks, T.M. (2006) The value of the IUCN Red List for conservation. *Trends Ecol Evol* 21(2): 71–76.

Scott, P., Burton, J.A. and Fitter, R. (1987) Red Data Books: the historical background. In: Fitter, R. and Fitter, M. (Eds.), *The Road to Extinction.* Gland, Switzerland: IUCN.

Simon, N. (1966–1971). *IUCN Red Data Book*, Vol. 1. Mammalia. Morges, Switzerland: IUCN.

Thompson, C.J., Koshkina, V., Burgman, M.A., Butchart, S.H. and Stone, L. (2017) Inferring extinctions II: A practical, iterative model based on records and surveys. *Biol Conserv* 214: 328–335.

Thornback, J. and Jenkins, M. (1982) *The IUCN Mammal Red Data Book, Part 1.* Gland, Switzerland; Cambridge, UK: IUCN.

van Strien, N.J., Steinmetz, R., Manullang, B., et al. (2008) Rhinoceros sondaicus. *The IUCN Red List of Threatened Species 2008*: e.T19495A8925965. www.iucnredlist.org/species/19495/18493900 (accessed October 2022).

Vincent, J. (1966–1971). *IUCN/ICBP Red Data Book*, Vol. 2. Aves. Morges, Switzerland: IUCN.

Wells, S., Pyle, R.M. and Collins, N.M. (1983) *IUCN Invertebrate Red Data Book.* Gland, Switzerland; Cambridge, UK: IUCN.

NINETEEN

Problems with the World's Ecosystems: The Future and Attempts to Mitigate Decline

MATT W. HAYWARD

Summary

One species – humans – is ultimately responsible for devastating much of the only planet in the cosmos that is known to support life – Earth. Our population has expanded exponentially since the Industrial Revolution and this, along with the resources required to sustain us, is ultimately driving the decline in the condition of the world's ecosystems. Examples of species threatened by development (residential/commercial), agriculture, energy production and mining, transportation, biological resource use, natural system modification, invasive species, pollution and climate change are provided. Yet there are solutions to these problems and many species and ecosystems have bounced back from the brink of extinction. Provided the general public and politicians have the will to invest sufficiently in conservation, it can be highly successful. This chapter ends by exploring the variety of ways that humanity can use to improve the status of the world's ecosystems.

19.1 Introduction

The Earth is the only planet in the universe where life is known to exist. Beyond the Earth's atmosphere, conditions are inhospitable to almost all forms of life. Notwithstanding the Sun's energy, the diversity of life that has evolved on Earth over the past 4.28 billion years is almost completely reliant upon the resources available here. Diversion of those resources by one species (humans) away from others, reduces the number of species that can be sustained. Since the 1980s, the exponential population increase and resource use of our species has consumed more than the global regenerative capacity of the biosphere (Wackernagel et al., 2002). Humans – the most widespread mammal on the planet – are using more resources each year than can be renewed. Of all the threats to the world's ecosystems, human activities are the most pervasive and have the greatest impact.

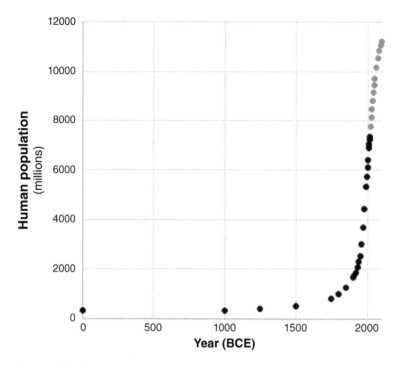

Figure 19.1 Human population growth over time (data from United Nations Department of Economic and Social Affairs Population Division). Historical data are shown in dark grey, and future projections to the year 2100 in light grey.

Following the evolution of our species (*Homo sapiens*), the human population on Earth remained low for hundreds of thousands of years, before beginning a more rapid increase with the advent of farming (Figure 19.1; Shennan and Edinborough, 2007). From the Neolithic period, human population growth accelerated until an exponential rate of increase began during the Industrial Revolution that shows little sign of abating today (Figure 19.1). Future population projections suggest this rate of increase will slow, but the human population will continue to increase for the foreseeable future (Figure 19.1). Humans have gone from a species utterly reliant upon the resources available in local environments and thereby constrained in abundance by the carrying capacity of the land, to one capable of living in the most inhospitable areas on the planet, and even in outer space, at densities far beyond those prevalent in human evolution prior to the Agricultural Revolution.

19.2 Factors Threatening Ecosystems

The direct impact on the world's ecosystems of this enormous human population is habitat loss and degradation associated with producing raw materials for housing and feeding us, producing energy and transporting this around the globe (Figure 19.2). However, humanity's resource overexploitation is not the only problem we have wrought on the

Figure 19.2 Factors threatening ecosystems: (a) Housing development in Ontario, Canada, (b) land clearing for agriculture in the Amazon, (c) phosphate mine in Togo, (d) wind farm developments in the Solway Firth, Scotland, (e) transportation corridor through forests in Europe, (f) oil pollution fire from BP's Deepwater Horizon rig, (g) invasive zebra mussels and (h) shrinking areas of ice through climate change affecting polar bears.

world's ecosystems. The indirect impact of humanity includes pollution, the spread of invasive species and diseases, and climate change (Figure 19.2).

19.2.1 Measuring Problems with the World's Ecosystems

The International Union for the Conservation of Nature and Natural Places (IUCN) was established in 1948 and is now the pre-eminent global non-government organisation devoted to the conservation of biodiversity in all its forms. IUCN was created through an intergovernmental agreement to conduct conservation assessments and actions on behalf of its 161 member states. There are currently 217 states and governmental agencies listed as members of IUCN, plus an additional 1066 NGOs.

The IUCN Red List is the most comprehensive and robust assessment of the conservation status of biodiversity in the world. The Red List uses more than 16,000 experts to assess the state of the world's species and ecosystems. To date, the IUCN Red List has assessed over 85,000 species, but this represents less than 5% of the total number of species described (www.iucnredlist.org/about/summary-statistics). For some well-studied taxa, however, the assessments are more comprehensive, notably for birds, mammals, reptiles and amphibians. As the taxon-specific chapters earlier in this book illustrate, the evidence from the IUCN Red List is that the world's ecosystems are in poor shape and this is likely to continue to decline in the foreseeable future without concerted conservation efforts.

The IUCN Red List defines 12 threatening processes that are negatively affecting the world's ecosystems: residential and commercial development, agriculture and aquaculture, energy production and mining, transportation and service corridors, biological resource use, human intrusions and disturbances, natural system modification, invasive and other problem species/genes/diseases, pollution, geological events, climate change and severe weather, and 'other'. Below are some examples of species threatened by each of these factors (Figure 19.3). These species were selected at random from the Red List to illustrate the ecological and biogeographical diversity of species threatened by each factor. Each major threatening process is listed along with the subsections used by IUCN in the Red List.

19.2.1.1 Residential and Commercial Development

Development as a threatening process is divided into three subcategories: housing development, commercial development and tourism development. The entire known population of the Bolivian chinchilla rat (*Abrocoma boliviensis*) occurs within an area of less than 100 km^2 between 1800 and 2270 m above sea level in the Bolivian cloud forest. This range is divided by a road along which housing development is occurring, and so this species is listed as Critically Endangered (IUCN, 2022). *Banara caymanensis* is a woody shrub within the family Flacourtiaceae with only 30 mature individuals known to exist and these are severely threatened by residential and tourism development with one locality on Cayman Brac within 250 m of such a development site (IUCN, 2022). Selective logging in the forests of Pará and Maranhão in the Brazilian Amazon for housing and commercial development in an area within the region with the highest human population

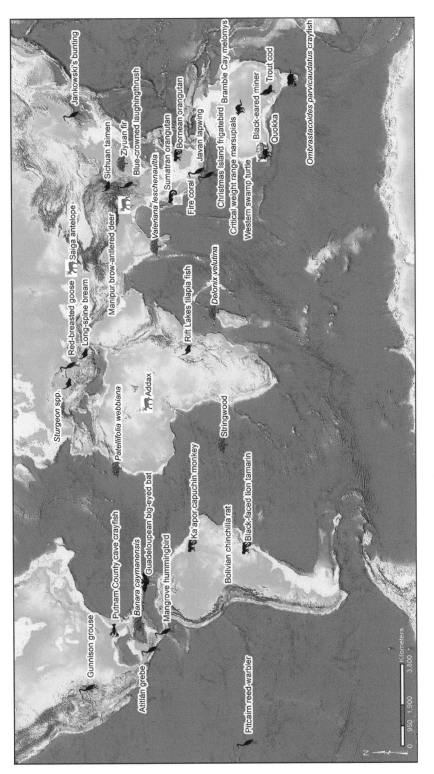

Figure 19.3 Map showing the location of species mentioned in the text.

density has severely impacted the Ka'apor capuchin monkey (*Cebus kaapori*) such that it is now listed as Critically Endangered (IUCN, 2022). The Critically Endangered western swamp turtle (*Pseudemydura umbrina*) is restricted to two freshwater lakes surrounded by residential land on Perth, Western Australia's, coastal plain (Webb et al., 2014) such that the lack of opportunity for the population to grow has led to assisted colonisation projects to save it (Dade et al., 2014).

19.2.1.2 Agriculture and Aquaculture

The agriculture and aquaculture threat category is separated into crops, plantations, pastoralism and aquaculture on the Red List. Shifting cropping on a 3 year rotation removed the original woodland habitat of the Manipur brow-antlered deer (*Rucervus eldii eldii*), and this woodland was then replaced by unpalatable bamboo rather than grasses upon which the deer feeds (IUCN, 1980), such that it is now listed as Endangered (IUCN, 2022). Smallholder agriculture is seen as one of the most pressing global threats to cacti, affecting 55% of all species (Goettsch et al., 2015). *Delonix velutina* is a Malagasy tree that grows to 15 m in dry forest on limestone-derived soils that is being cleared for shifting, slash-and-burn (swidden/tavy) agriculture to the extent that the species is listed as Endangered (IUCN, 2022), and this may lead to a chain of extinction and also endanger the sunbirds (Philepittidae) that feed on it (Du Puy et al., 2002).

The widespread and rapid increase in oil palm plantations in Southeast Asia places many species at risk of extinction. The Sumatran and Bornean orangutans (*Pongo abelli* and *P. pygmaeus*) are both listed as Critically Endangered with over 3000 km^2 of natural habitat in Borneo alone cleared annually, largely for oil palm plantations (IUCN, 2022). Oil palm plantations are not just a threat to Asia's wildlife, as oil palm plantation expansion plans in Africa suggest numerous primate species there will also be threatened (Wich et al., 2014). However, ceasing the use of palm oil will not solve this problem because oil palms yield more oil per hectare than any other crop species, so moving from palm oil to other vegetable-based oils will cause an increase in habitat loss.

Pastoralism directly affects ecosystems via the conversion of native vegetation to improved, but species-poor, grazing lands, but goes further to include competition for food between livestock and wildlife, along with human–wildlife conflict, the transmission of disease and a diversion of resources (e.g. nutrients and water) away from native species. Disease and human persecution (conflict) are listed on the Red List as unique threats, but clearly they are associated with the expansion of humanity into the ranges of wildlife. The main threat to the 500 or so Jankowski's bunting (*Emberiza jankowskii*) remaining in China, Russia and North Korea is the conversion of its grassland habitat for pastoralism and the species is now listed as Endangered (IUCN, 2022).

Aquaculture threatens biodiversity through habitat loss, where it occurs along the coast, and also pollution and disease transmission. Habitat loss associated with the construction of shrimp aquaculture ponds are destroying mangroves required by the mangrove humming-bird (*Amazilia boucardi*) throughout its distribution on Costa Rica's Pacific coast, wherever the threatened mangrove *Pelliciera rhizophorae* occurs (IUCN, 2022). Entire mangrove ecosystems are threatened by some forms of aquaculture (Gunawardena and Rowan, 2005). The Atlantic salmon (*Salmo salar*) aquaculture fishery in 1997 required 1.8 million tons of wild fish for feed, but only produced 644,000 tons of salmon – an enormous net loss of protein (Naylor et al., 1998). The Nordic salmon farming industry discharges nitrogen and phosphorous in amounts equivalent to the untreated sewage of over 1.7 million people (Naylor et al., 1998). The escape of farmed aquatic fauna threatens other species by way of genetic introgression of genes for domestication into wild stock or competition with wild species (Diana, 2009).

19.2.1.3 Energy Production and Mining

In comparison to many other threatening processes, mines and energy production sites tend to be largely point source disturbances around the actual site of activities, and so these only generally impact range-restricted species; however, they can have broader impacts. For example, although hunting caused the initial decline of the Critically Endangered addax (*Addax nasomaculatus*; IUCN 2022) – the most arid-adapted, desert-dwelling antelope – the only (almost) viable population in Termit Tin Toumma National Nature Reserve in Niger has been subject to disturbance by oil exploration and production, and shooting by their military escorts (Duncan et al., 2014).

The Christmas Island frigatebird (*Fregata andrewsi*) is a largely black, fork-tailed seabird with a bright red gular pouch in males that is endemic to Australia's Christmas Island, but which is now Critically Endangered – predominantly through the clearing of a quarter of its breeding area for a phosphate mine before 1946, and thereafter phosphate dust further damaging breeding habitat (IUCN, 2022). The construction of the Crotty hydroelectric dam on Tasmania's King River seems likely to send the Critically Endangered *Ombrastacoides parvicaudatus* crayfish extinct in the near future (Hansen and Richardson, 2007). The thousands of wind turbines proposed for the Dobrudhza area of Bulgaria and Romania are considered a major recent threat to the vulnerable red-breasted goose *Branta ruficollis*, unless mitigation measures are implemented (IUCN, 2022).

19.2.1.4 Transportation and Service Corridors

Transportation and service corridors tend to be long, continuous linear features that destroy habitat locally, but also serve to fragment habitat, often into isolated remnants where issues of loss of genetic diversity become problematic (Figure 19.2). Roads also provide access into areas humans previously rarely occurred and thereby introduce a range of other threatening processes (Kleinschroth et al., 2017). Species threatened by these man-made features include the blue-crowned laughingthrush *Garrulax courtoisi*, which has had several breeding sites destroyed by road development in Jiangxi Province, China (Figure 19.3) leading to very severe declines (IUCN, 2022). In the USA, the fragmentation arising from roads and powerlines in the sagebrush habitat of the Gunnison grouse *Centrocercus minimus* are fundamental to its Endangered status (IUCN, 2022).

19.2.1.5 Biological Resource Use

Biological resource use can take the form of hunting, plant collection, logging and wood harvesting, and fishing and harvesting aquatic resources. The Critically Endangered saiga antelope *Saiga tatarica* is endemic to the Eurasian steppe and once occurred in the millions; however, uncontrolled hunting for horns, which are used as traditional Chinese medicine, and meat, since the break-up of the former USSR, has led to a catastrophic decline to around 50,000 from 1.25 million in the 1970s and these have continued more recently due to disease (Milner-Gulland, 2015). *Valeriana leschenaultia* is a Critically Endangered herb found only in the Nilgiri Hills of India's Western Ghats, where it is threatened by collection for local medicinal use as the roots and rhizomes are used to treat eye diseases, hysteria, hypochondriasis and stress (IUCN, 2022). The Sumatran orangutan is also threatened by logging activities. The Sichuan taimen *Hucho bleekeri* is a salmonid fish that is Critically Endangered because of illegal fishing of adults during the spawning season in the headwaters of the Yangtze River in China (IUCN, 2022).

19.2.1.6 Human Intrusions and Disturbances

Human intrusions and disturbances can take the form of recreation, war or civil unrest, or work activities. Disturbance by tourists in Brazil's Superagüi National Park is the most serious threat to the Critically Endangered black-faced lion tamarin *Leontopithecus caissara* (IUCN, 2022). The last surviving population of the Critically Endangered beet *Patellifolia webbiana* is threatened by military training activities on Gran Canaria (IUCN, 2022). Although much of the decline of the Critically Endangered Javan lapwing *Vanellus macropterus* has been attributed to 'merciless hunting and trapping', it seems more likely that high levels of human disturbance associated with nearby aquaculture and agricultural activities were responsible (IUCN, 2022).

19.2.1.7 Natural System Modification

There are a myriad of ways natural ecosystems have been modified, from changes in fire regimes to water management and other similar perturbations. The quokka *Setonix brachyurus* is a small, vulnerable marsupial wallaby that was decimated by the introduction of European red foxes *Vulpes vulpes*, but changes from high-frequency Aboriginal burning regimes to less frequent, but higher intensity, wildfires make them far more susceptible to predators, as the swamp habitats become more open and lose their ability to provide refuge from predators (Hayward et al., 2005). The trout cod *Maccullochella macquariensis* of Australia's Murray–Darling river system is Endangered by river regulation following the construction of numerous locks and weirs to aid river travel that have altered the flow patterns from winter–spring floods to higher flows in summer today.

19.2.1.8 Invasive and Other Problem Species/Genes/Diseases

In 1999, the Invasive Species Specialist Group of IUCN identified a list of 100 high-profile invasive species to boost global awareness of their impacts and this highlighted the diversity of taxa that impact biodiversity worldwide from microorganisms to plants and animals (Lowe et al., 2004). These cause huge economic costs to our society. For example, it is estimated that over 50,000 invasive non-native species have been introduced to the USA alone since 1900 and these cost almost US$120 billion per year in environmental and agricultural damage (Pimentel et al., 2005). However, the ecological costs are also vast, with hundreds of native species threatened by invasive alien species (Butchart et al., 2010). For example, the arrival of yellow crazy ants *Anoplolepis gracilipes* on islands has decimated biodiversity (Lowe et al., 2004). Their arrival on Christmas Island has led to a 98% decline in native forest skink *Emoia nativitatis* such that it is now considered Critically Endangered (IUCN, 2022). The intentional introduction of Nile perch *Lates niloticus* to Africa's Rift Lakes led to the extinction of more than 200 other fish species. Introduced predators (red foxes and feral cats) have been responsible for the extinction of at least 23 critical-weight-range mammals in Australia since European colonisation in 1788 (i.e. those weighing between 0.035 and 5.5 kg; Burbidge and McKenzie, 1989). The brown tree snake was introduced to Guam after World War II and reached peak densities of 100 per hectare, which led to the extinction of 12 native species and huge social and economic impacts (Lowe et al., 2004). *Caulerpa taxifolia* seaweed is native to the Indian Ocean, but has invaded the Mediterranean Sea and the coastal waterways around Australia, leading to complete dominance of the benthos, such that other species are competed to extinction (Lowe et al., 2004). Even humans invading new areas have been implicated as the cause of numerous extinctions (Barnosky et al., 2004; Faurby and Svenning 2015).

But it is not just invasive species that threaten biodiversity. Introduced genetic material and diseases can also be problematic. The black-eared miner *Manorina melanotis* is Australia's rarest bird and it is threatened by hybridisation by another native – the yellow-throated miner *M. flavigula* – that has expanded into more arid regions via the construction of artificial water points and thereby come into contact with its rarer relative (Clarke et al., 2001).

Newly spread diseases are also a threat to biodiversity. For example, rinderpest decimated bovids in Africa (Plowright, 1982) and avian malaria similarly affected Hawaiian birds (Lowe et al., 2004). Chytridiomycosis is an invasive disease caused by the fungi *Batrachochytrium dendrobatidis* (that affects frogs) and *B. salamandivorus* (that affects salamanders), which has decimated amphibian populations worldwide, including causing the extinction of amazing species such as the southern gastric-brooding frog from *Rheobatrachus silus* (Kilpatrick et al., 2010). Devil facial tumour disease is a cancer spread by direct contact that is currently largely responsible for causing the Tasmanian devil *Sarcophilus harrisii* population in Tasmania to plummet from over 100,000 in 1996 to less than 30,000 today (McCallum et al., 2007).

19.2.1.9 Pollution

Pollution as a threatening process can arise from domestic/urban sources, industrial/military effluent, agriculture/forestry, garbage/solid waste, airborne pollution or excess energy. The pollution of Lake Gölbasi arising from urban wastewater (sewage) is threatening the Critically Endangered long-spine bream *Acanthobrama centisquama* in

Turkey (IUCN, 2022). Sturgeon species throughout Europe have declined through pollution arising from industrial and agricultural run-off (Lenhardt et al., 2006). The Putnam County cave crayfish *Procambarus morrisi* is Critically Endangered, largely through a Volkswagen motor vehicle being dumped into the Devil's Sink Cave, Florida – the only place this species is known to exist (Hobbs and Franz, 1991).

Other forms of pollution are also damaging to biodiversity. Light pollution from human activities has led to a suite of problems, such as disorienting migrating birds and turtles, and changing the distribution patterns of bats (Irwin, 2017). The synthetic oestrogens used in the contraceptive pill are excreted by humans into sewerage systems and eventually reach natural waterways. The chronic exposure of these has feminised fat-headed minnows *Pimephales promelas* in Lake Ontario such that males virtually disappeared and the population crashed (Kidd et al., 2007). Noise pollution is also a threat and has been shown to alter bird communities and their interactions (Francis et al., 2009).

19.2.1.10 Geological Events
Geological threats can take the form of volcanoes, earthquakes/tsunamis and avalanches. Volcanic activity on Montserrat may have destroyed the remaining habitat in the five known locations where the Endangered Guadeloupean big-eyed bat *Chiroderma improvisum* has been recorded (Larsen et al., 2007). The Atitlán grebe *Podilymbus gigas* was driven extinct when an earthquake in 1976 that killed 23,000 people in Guatemala reduced the water level in Atitlán Lake by 4.5 m, reducing the amount of vegetation available for roosting and nesting, and reducing nursery areas for key food items (fish, crabs, invertebrates) (LaBastille, 1983). The Ziyuan fir *Abies ziyuanensis* is a rare tree that only occurs on five of the highest mountains in Guangxi, China, where it is Endangered, largely through the repeated landslides that destroy individuals (IUCN, 2022).

19.2.1.11 Climate Change and Severe Weather
Climate change is threatening fauna worldwide through shifting habitats, increasing droughts, storms and flooding, and changing temperatures (Parmesan, 2006). Coral reefs are experiencing unprecedented levels of bleaching (dying). Some species threatened by this include the Critically Endangered (possibly extinct) fire coral (*Millepora boschmai*) from the eastern Indian and Pacific Oceans (IUCN, 2022). Sea level rise associated with climate change has driven the Bramble Cay melomys *Melomys rubicola* extinct on Australia's Torres Strait islands (Gynther et al., 2016). There are also concerns that range-restricted species inhabiting small isolated habitat patches, such as the Endangered Pitcairn reed-warbler *Acrocephalus vaughani*, may be unable to cope with the changes in habitat associated with climate change (IUCN, 2022).

19.2.1.12 'Other' Threatening Processes
Where threats to a species cannot be placed into one of the other threat categories, they are lumped into the 'Other' category of the IUCN Red List. The stringwood *Acalypha rubrinervis* was last recorded on St. Helena in 1875 and, although habitat loss undoubtedly

affected the species persistence, there are still fragments of cloud forest present on the island that support a rich endemic flora, so the ultimate cause of its extinction is unknown (IUCN, 2022).

19.3 Summary of Threats

More than 77,300 species have been assessed on the IUCN Red List and the results illustrate a key problem for today's ecosystems in that we are losing individual species and, perhaps as importantly, the ecological functions they perform. Today, 63% of cycads, 41% of amphibians, 33% of corals, 34% of conifers, 25% of mammals and 13% of birds are threatened with extinction (IUCN, 2022). Losing this number of species would mean the loss of ecosystem services such as fire suppression (Hayward et al., 2016), disease reduction (Ogada et al., 2012), improved fisheries productivity (Worm et al., 2006), carbon storage, regulation of climate and water flow, provision of clean water and the maintenance of soil fertility (Benayas et al., 2009). The processes threatening the world's ecosystems are predominately driven by humanity, with agriculture/aquaculture the most significant factor (Figure 19.4).

While species and subspecies are the current focus of IUCN, it is also worth pointing out that IUCN is currently in the process of devising a Red List of Ecosystems and their

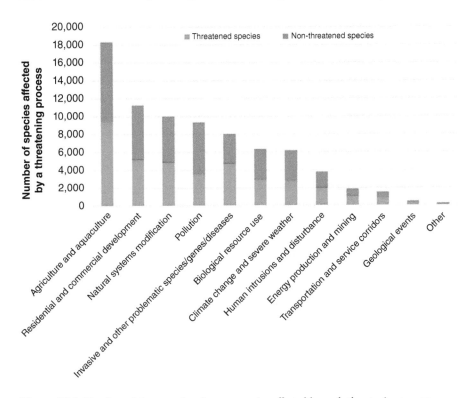

Figure 19.4 Number of threatened and secure species affected by each threatening process (IUCN, 2015).

functioning (https://iucnrle.org/). The Red List of Ecosystems will provide standardised categories and criteria as a technical basis for the systematic assessment of global risk of collapse of all freshwater, marine, terrestrial and subterranean ecosystems (Rodríguez et al., 2015). This will provide an additional, perhaps more holistic, measure of the problems with the world's ecosystems, in association with the Red List of Threatened Species. Although the process is new, to date there have been 12 global Red List of Ecosystems assessments for ecosystems and 21 regional assessments from 15 countries (https://iucnrle.org/) that show the Aral Sea ecosystem in Uzbekistan and Kazakhstan has entirely collapsed, the Coorong and Murray River mouth estuary and Lord Howe Island cloud forest in Australia, and the Gonakier forests of the Senegal River floodplain in Senegal and Mauritania are Critically Endangered, and the Coolibah-Black Box woodlands of Australia, giant kelp forests of Alaska, Tapia forest of Madagascar and the Yellow Sea tidal flats of China and Korea are all Endangered. Reedbeds in Europe are considered Vulnerable, while the Antarctic's shallow invertebrate-dominated ecosystems are considered Near Threatened, and Venezuela's Tepui shrubland ecosystems are secure.

The extinction of these species and ecosystems has far-reaching consequences for current generations. For example, bee extinctions would threaten the pollination of numerous crops, megafaunal extinctions would threaten the viability of the tourist industries in many African countries, the decimation of the Great Barrier Reef would damage Australia's tourist industry and degraded dam catchments would threaten the water quality of many of the world's cities. But the loss of these species and ecosystems also has potentially greater implications for intergenerational equity, whereby future generations will miss out on seeing the majesty of these lost ecosystems and species, and on the invaluable ecosystem services they currently offer and could offer in the future. A big challenge we currently face is the uncertainty in predictions of the impacts that these altered ecosystems will have, which means we are unable to plan, prioritise or implement mitigation measures to ameliorate them.

19.4 Solutions

Clearly there are major problems facing today's ecosystems and the species that comprise them. Yet there is good evidence that conservation action is successful in protecting the Earth's ecosystems (Hoffmann et al., 2010), and conservation actions are considered to have averted the extinction of 20% of birds that would otherwise have occurred over the past century (Brooks et al., 2009). Similarly, despite a population size of only ~150 adults, the Iberian lynx *Lynx pardinus* has been downlisted from Critically Endangered to Endangered due to the increase in population size following reintroduction programmes, habitat reconstruction and rabbit restocking (Simón et al., 2012). The Seychelles warbler *Acrocephalus sechellensis* has been downlisted to Near Threatened, having been on the verge of extinction, with only 26 birds alive on Cousin Island in 1968 after successful reintroductions to other islands have increased the population to over 3000 adults (www.iucnredlist.org/species/22714882/178746590). New Zealand's brown teal *Anas chlorotis* has seen similar successful conservation management via reducing predation by introduced mammals, improving habitat modified by drought, and minimising road mortalities such that it has also been downlisted to Near Threatened. Rigorous protection from poaching has seen the Tibetan antelope *Pantholops hodgsonii* improve in status from Endangered to Near Threatened (www.iucnredlist.org/species/15967/50192544).

Clearly, conservation management can, and often does, work. For example, rinderpest (cattle plague) is a *Morbillivirus* that decimated 90% of cattle and huge numbers of antelopes in Africa upon its introduction in 1896, but was considered globally eradicated in 2011. Tiger *Panthera tigris* numbers have increased at 6% per annum in India since 2010 due to antipoaching activities saving tigers and improving the density of their prey, and village relocations to areas outside of protected areas (https://theconversation.com/some-good-conservation-news-indias-tiger-numbers-are-going-up-121055). Yet successes such as these require financial, political and community support, and to date there has been insufficient levels of this to successfully achieve broad-scale conservation successes (Waldron et al., 2013), despite notable exceptions, like New Zealand's plan to eradicate all invasive pest species by 2050 (Owens, 2017). Until our society values biodiversity or recognises its value sufficiently to alter the views of politicians, this is unlikely to change (Ehrlich and Ehrlich, 2013).

The managed development of less developed countries with assistance from wealthy nations is crucial to the protection of the Earth's ecosystems. The world's rich have benefitted enormously from the natural resources of their own countries and often also of the resources of less developed countries, but now need to use the wealth and technological advancements this has yielded to assist the less developed world in a more sustainable development path. Expectations of continued economic growth will lead to catastrophic biodiversity loss.

This managed development also ties in to intergenerational equity. The wealth many people experience today has arisen through the use of non-renewable or slowly renewable resources that will not be available to future generations. Therefore, we owe future generations some form of compensation (either financial or technological) that will ensure current generations are not restricting the wealth of future generations. As things currently stand with increasing human-derived carbon dioxide emissions likely to cause substantial climate change, non-renewable resources approaching their reserves and an ailing, ageing population that has not budgeted sufficiently for a long retirement, intergenerational inequity looks increasingly likely (Santoyo-Castelazo and Azapagic, 2014; Stebbing and Spies-Butcher, 2016; Hayward et al., 2022).

Given that food production is the major process threatening biodiversity (Figure 19.4), we urgently need to develop ways in which humanity can be adequately fed in a globally sustainable manner. Currently, 30–40% of food in both the developed and developing worlds is wasted along the food chain (Godfray et al., 2010). Intensification of practices may produce more food, but as the IUCN Red List illustrates, this will have a cost, and reducing food waste is a clear opportunity of benefit to humanity and biodiversity. Particularly in the developed world, farmers tend to be large landowners with disproportionate political influence, yet they also exhibit vastly different views on biodiversity than the broader public (e.g. Table 3 in Nilsen et al., 2007). Currently, farming in many areas is uneconomical without government subsidies (Piccinini and Loseby, 2001), and if free market economic practices were implemented, then alternative land uses that may favour natural ecosystems could become competitive (e.g. Rewilding Europe, 2012).

Agricultural practices could also evolve to more environmentally friendly practices. Changing our dietary practices may also improve the state of the world's ecosystems, largely through a reduction in humanity's consumption of meat (Machovina et al., 2015). While agricultural intensification is viewed as a method to improve our ability to feed the expanding human population, sustainability is often tagged alongside this, with little real consideration of biodiversity. Land sparing (via segregating land for production and nature) and land sharing (via integrating biodiversity within agricultural landscapes in wildlife-friendly farming) are two paradigms of sustainable intensification of agriculture, but neither have satisfactorily protected natural ecosystems during agricultural intensification to date (Tscharntke et al., 2012).

The increasing urbanisation of our society offers opportunities and costs. The movement of rural farming communities to urban areas in Eastern Europe has led to a natural rewilding of the landscape and an expansion of large predators (Chapron et al., 2014). The trend for increasing urbanisation is predicted to occur globally over the coming decades, which, when coupled with the slowing human population growth rate, provides some hope that we may be at the peak of pressure on the Earth's ecosystems. Conversely, urban dwellers are becoming increasingly disconnected from biodiversity and natural ecosystems (Miller, 2005), such that they may be less inclined to support or engage with ecosystem conservation programmes. This disconnect may have led to the evolution of concepts such as 'novel ecosystems' (Aronson et al., 2014) and 'compassionate conservation' (Ramp et al., 2013) that both threaten to homogenise global biodiversity (Hayward et al., 2019). Irrespectively, conservation needs to ensure that local communities obtain benefits from both the presence of biodiversity, which itself is often costly and this cost burden tends to be focused on the developing world (Lindsey et al., 2017), and the presence of conservationists (Gillingham and Lee, 1999). Studies to date indicate that there are indeed benefits to living alongside biodiversity, at least in urban areas of developed countries with evidence of experiences of nature leading to improved physical and mental health outcomes (Shanahan et al., 2016).

Methods to ameliorate other threats are also available. There is some evidence to suggest that active support for on-ground conservation action by way of ranger patrols is effective in reducing poaching (Moore et al., 2017); however, other empirical studies have found that armed rangers do not have an effect (Barichievy et al., 2017). Non-governmental conservation organisations that invest heavily in on-ground conservation management by having staff living on site and implementing intensive conservation actions, such as African Parks (www.african-parks.org/) and the Australian Wildlife Conservancy (www.australianwildlife.org/), illustrate what can be achieved with sufficient effort (Innes et al., 2015). Government conservation agencies have also achieved substantial successes, such as the conservation of European bison *Bison bonasus* in Poland (Kerley et al., 2012) or the southern white rhinoceros *Ceratotherium simum* in South Africa (Hayward et al., 2018).

Some threatening processes are well suited to specific conservation management actions (Hayward, 2011). For example, conservation fencing has the potential to separate biodiversity from a range of direct threats, including introduced species and persecution from humans (Hayward and Kerley, 2009); however, fencing developed for purposes other than conservation can have devastating impacts on biodiversity (Linnell et al., 2016). Conservation fencing is often viewed as highly invasive to natural ecosystems by stopping movements and gene flow of other native species not protected within the fences; however, there are ways to mitigate this (Crisp and Moseby, 2010). The expense of conservation fencing is also often invoked as problematic; however, it seems more justified when longer perspectives that go beyond the political cycle given the long-term nature of large-scale pest animal poisoning programmes (Armstrong, 2004) compared to fence maintenance and 25 yearly replacement costs.

Other threatening processes are less specifically addressed by mitigation measures (Hayward, 2011). Climate change requires a global effort just to keep temperatures within 2 °C of those today. 'Wicked' problems involving so many stakeholders are inherently more challenging than those involving few stakeholders. In light of this, protected area networks are fundamental and there is evidence that systematically planned, representative conservation networks have had great success in protecting the Earth's ecosystems (Brooks et al., 2006). Yet for mammals, occurrence within protected areas is insufficient to improve conservation status, and more active conservation management is often required, including translocation, invasive species control and captive breeding (Hayward, 2011).

19.5 Conclusion

Despite developing a better understanding of the threats to the world's ecosystems and methods to ameliorate them, conservation is still losing ground (Butchart et al., 2010). The conservation sector has long been seeking a silver bullet to ensure today's ecosystems are conserved into the future. The traditional view of conservation is that the environment and biodiversity should be conserved for their inherent intrinsic values and our ethical responsibility; however, recently a 'new' conservation agenda has been promoted by linking biodiversity to the benefits it provides humans (Kareiva and Marvier, 2012). The selling of conservation to corporate interests has raised numerous concerns (Noss et al., 2013; Soulé 2013; Spash 2015) as another example of failed neoliberal philosophies (Kopnina et al., 2018), and it seems likely that humanity will need to make major concessions in economic and population growth for the world's ecosystems to be successfully conserved. Thus, we will be left with the hard graft of sacrificing land that could be developed for housing or agriculture to biodiversity protection, but following that with intensive on-ground actions to ensure connectivity in the long term.

For wildlife conservation to be successful, the broader society needs to acknowledge the value of the world's ecosystems and desire their conservation. If this occurs, the world's political class may support actions to protect our global natural heritage, and invest sufficiently to achieve this. We need to understand the threats to the world's ecosystems to enable us to successfully conserve them so that we leave a planet for our children in as good or better ecological condition that we received it.

Acknowledgements

This chapter has been improved by the reviews of Norman MacLean, Gina Hayward and Andrew Knight.

References

Armstrong, R. (2004) Baiting operations: Western Shield review – February 2003. *Conserv Sci W Aust* 5: 31–50.

Aronson, J., Murcia, C., Kattan, G.H., et al. (2014) The road to confusion is paved with novel ecosystem labels: a reply to Hobbs et al. *Trends Ecol Evol* 29: 645–646.

Barichievy, C., Munro, L., Clinning, G., et al. (2017) Do armed field-rangers deter rhino poachers? An empirical analysis. *Biol Conserv* 209: 554–560.

Barnosky, A.D., Koch, P.L., Feranec, R.S., et al. (2004) Assessing the causes of late Pleistocene extinctions on the continents. *Science* 306: 70–75.

Benayas, J.M.R., Newton, A. C., Diaz, A., et al. (2009) Enhancement of biodiversity and ecosystem services by ecological restoration: a meta-analysis. *Science* 325: 1121–1124.

Brooks, T.M., Mittermeier, R.A., da Fonseca, G.A.B., et al. (2006) Global biodiversity conservation priorities. *Science* 313: 58–61.

Brooks, T.M., Wright, S.J. and Sheil, D. (2009) Evaluating the success of conservation actions in safeguarding tropical forest biodiversity. *Conserv Biol* 23: 1448–1457.

Burbidge, A.A. and McKenzie, N.L. (1989) Patterns in the modern decline of Western Australia's vertebrate fauna: causes and conservation implications. *Biol Conserv* 50: 143–198.

Butchart, S.H.M., Walpole, M.J., Collen, B., et al. (2010) Global biodiversity: indicators of recent declines. *Science* 328: 1164–1168.

Chapron, G., Kaczensky, P., Linnell, J.D., et al. (2014) Recovery of large carnivores in Europe's modern human-dominated landscapes. *Science* 346: 1517–1519.

Clarke, R.H., Gordon, I.R. and Clarke, M.F. (2001) Intraspecific phenotypic variability in the black-eared miner (*Manorina melanotis*); human-facilitated introgression and the consequences for an endangered taxon. *Biol Conserv* 99: 145–155.

Crisp, H. and Moseby, K.E. (2010) One-way gates: initial trial of a potential tool for preventing overpopulation within fenced reserves. *Ecol Manag Restor* 11: 139–141.

Dade, M., Pauli, N. and Mitchell, N. (2014) Mapping a new future: using spatial multiple criteria analysis to identify novel habitats for assisted colonization of endangered species. *Animal Conserv* 17: 4–17.

Diana, J.S. (2009) Aquaculture production and biodiversity conservation. *BioScience* 59: 27–38.

Du Puy, D.J., Labat, J.-N., Rabevohitra, R. et al. (2002) *The Leguminosae of Madagascar*. Kew, UK: Royal Botanic Gardens.

Duncan, C., Kretz, D., Wegmann, M., et al. (2014) Oil in the Sahara: mapping anthropogenic threats to Saharan biodiversity from space. *Phil Trans Royal Soc B* 369: 20130191.

Ehrlich, P.R. and Ehrlich, A.H. (2013) Can a collapse of global civilization be avoided? *Proc Royal Soc London B* 280: 1–9.

Faurby, S. and Svenning, J. C. (2015) Historic and prehistoric human-driven extinctions have reshaped global mammal diversity patterns. *Divers Distrib* 21(10): 1155–1166.

Francis, C.D., Ortega, C.P. and Cruz, A. (2009) Noise pollution changes avian communities and species interactions. *Curr Biol* 19: 1415–1419.

Gillingham, S. and Lee P.C. (1999) The impact of wildlife-related benefits on the conservation attitudes of local people around the Selous Game Reserve, Tanzania. *Environ Conserv* 26: 218–228.

Godfray, H.C.J., Beddington, J.R. Crute, I.R., et al. (2010) Food security: the challenge of feeding 9 billion people. *Science* 327: 812–818.

Goettsch, B., Hilton-Taylor, C., Cruz-Piñón, G. et al. (2015) High proportion of cactus species threatened with extinction. *Nat Plants* 1: 15142.

Gunawardena, M. and Rowan, J. (2005) Economic valuation of a mangrove ecosystem threatened by shrimp aquaculture in Sri Lanka. *Environ Manag* 36: 535–550.

Gynther, I., Waller, N. and Leung, L. (2016) Confirmation of the extinction of the Bramble Cay melomys *Melomys rubicola* on Bramble Cay, Torres Strait: results and conclusions from a comprehensive survey in August–September 2014. Unpublished report to the Department of Environment and Heritage Protection. Brisbane, Australia: Queensland Government.

Hansen, B. and Richardson A.M. (2007) A revision of the Tasmanian endemic freshwater crayfish genus Parastacoides (Crustacea: Decapoda: Parastacidae). *Invert Syst* 20: 713–769.

Hayward, M. W. (2011) Using the IUCN Red List to determine effective conservation strategies. *Biodivers Conserv* 20: 2563–2573.

Hayward, M.W. and Kerley, G.I.H. (2009) Fencing for conservation: restriction of evolutionary potential or a riposte to threatening processes? *Biol Conserv* 142: 1–13.

Hayward, M.W., Callen, A., Allen, B.L., et al. (2019) Deconstructing compassionate conservation. *Conserv Biol* 33: 760–768.

Hayward, M.W., de Tores, P.J. and Banks, P.B. (2005) Habitat use of the quokka *Setonix brachyurus* (Macropodidae: Marsupialia) in the northern jarrah forest of Australia. *J Mammal* 86: 683–688.

Hayward, M.W., Meyer, N.F.V., Balkenhol, N. et al. (2022) Intergenerational inequity: stealing the joy and benefits of nature from our children. *Front Ecol Evol* 10. doi:10.3389/fevo.2022.830830.

Hayward, M.W., Ripple, W.J., Kerley, G.I.H., et al. (2018) Neocolonial conservation: Is moving rhinos to Australia conservation or intellectual property loss. *Conserv Lett* 11: e12354.

Hayward, M.W., Ward-Fear, G., L'Hotellier, F., et al. (2016) Could biodiversity loss have increased Australia's bushfire threat? *Animal Conserv* 19: 490–497.

Hobbs, H.H. and Franz, R. (1991) A new troglobitic crayfish, *Procambarus (Lonnbergius) morrisi*, (Decapoda: Cambaridae) from Florida. *Proc Biol Soc Washington* 104: 55–63.

Hoffmann, M., Hilton-Taylor, C., Angulo, A., et al. (2010) The impact of conservation on the status of the world's vertebrates. *Science* 330: 1503–1509.

Innes, J., Burns, B., Sanders, A., et al. (2015) The impact of private sanctuary networks on reintroduction programmes in Australia and New Zealand. In: Armstrong, D.P., Hayward, M.W., Moro, D. and Seddon, P.J. (Eds.), *Reintroduction Biology in Australia and New Zealand*. Melbourne, Australia: CSIRO Publishing.

Irwin, A. (2017) The dark side of light: how artificial lighting is harming the natural world. *Nature* 553: 7688.

IUCN. (1980) *Threatened Deer: Proceedings of a Working Meeting of the Deer Specialist Group*. Morges, Switzerland: IUCN Deer Specialist Group, 46.

IUCN. (2015) *IUCN Red List of Threatened Species*. Version 2014.3. Gland, Switzerland: IUCN.

IUCN. (2022) *2022 Red List of Threatened Species*. www.redlist.org (accessed October 2022).

Kareiva, P. and Marvier, M. (2012) What is conservation science? *BioScience* 62: 962–969.

Kerley, G.I.H., Kowalczyk, R. and Cromsigt. J.P.G.M. (2012) Conservation implications of the refugee species concept and the European bison: king of the forest or refugee in a marginal habitat? *Ecography* 35: 519–529.

Kidd, K.A., Blanchfield, P.J., Mills, K.H., et al. (2007) Collapse of a fish population after exposure to a synthetic estrogen. *Proc Natl Acad Sci USA* 104: 8897–8901.

Kilpatrick, A.M., Briggs, C.J. and Daszak, P. (2010) The ecology and impact of chytridiomycosis: an emerging disease of amphibians. *Trends Ecol Evol* 25: 109–118.

Kleinschroth, F., Healey, J.R., Gourlet-Fleury, S., et al. (2017) Effects of logging on roadless space in intact forest landscapes of the Congo Basin. *Conserv Biol* 31: 469–480.

Kopnina, H., Washington, H., Gray, J., et al. (2018) The 'future of conservation' debate: Defending ecocentrism and the Nature Needs Half movement. *Biol Conserv* 217: 140–148.

LaBastille, A. (1983) Drastic decline in Guatemala's giant pied-billed grebe population. *Environ Conserv* 10: 346–348.

Larsen, R.J., Boegler, K.A., Genoways, H.H., et al. (2007) Mist netting bias, species accumulation curves, and the rediscovery of two bats on Montserrat (Lesser Antilles). *Acta Chiropterol* 9: 423–435.

Lenhardt, M., Jaric, I., Kalauzi, A. et al. (2006) Assessment of extinction risk and reasons for decline in sturgeon. *Biodivers Conserv* 15: 1967–1976.

Lindsey, P.A., Chapron, G., Petracca, L.S., et al. (2017) Relative efforts of countries to conserve the World's megafauna. *Glob Ecol Conserv* 10: 243–252.

Linnell, J.D.C., Trouwborst, A., Boitani, L., et al. (2016) Border security fencing and wildlife: the end of the transboundary paradigm in Eurasia? *PLoS Biol* 14: e1002483.

Lowe, S., Browne, M., Boudjelas, S., et al. (2004) *100 of the World's Worst Invasive Alien Species: A Selection from the Global Invasive Species Database.* Gland, Switzerland: Invasive Species Specialist Group of the World Conservation Union (IUCN).

Machovina, B., Feeley, K.J. and Ripple, W.J. (2015) Biodiversity conservation: the key is reducing meat consumption. *Sci Total Environ* 536: 419–431.

McCallum, H., Tompkins, D.M., Jones, M., et al. (2007) Distribution and impacts of Tasmanian devil facial tumor disease. *EcoHealth* 4: 318.

Miller, J.R. (2005) Biodiversity conservation and the extinction of experience. *Trends Ecol Evol* 20: 430–434.

Milner-Gulland, E.J. (2015) Catastrophe and hope for the saiga. *Oryx* 49: 577.

Moore, J.F., Mulindahabi, F., Masozera, M.K., et al. (2017) Are ranger patrols effective in reducing poaching-related threats in protected areas? *J Appl Ecol* 55: 99–107.

Naylor, R.L., Goldburg, R.J., Mooney, H., et al. (1998) Nature's subsidies to shrimp and salmon farming. *Science* 282: 883–884.

Nilsen, E.B., Milner-Gulland, E.J., Schofield, L., et al. (2007) Wolf reintroduction to Scotland: public attitudes and consequences for red deer management. *Proc Royal Soc London B* 274: 995–1002.

Noss, R., Nash, R., Paquet, P., et al. (2013) Humanity's domination of nature is part of the problem: a response to Kareiva and Marvier. *BioScience* 63: 241–242.

Ogada, D.L., Torchin, M.E., Kinnaird, M.F., et al. (2012) Effects of vulture declines on facultative scavengers and potential implications for mammalian disease transmission. *Conserv Biol* 26: 453–460.

Owens, B. (2017) Behind New Zealand's wild plan to purge all pests. *Nature* 541: 148.

Parmesan, C. (2006) Ecological and evolutionary responses to recent climate change. *Ann Rev Ecol Evol Syst* 37: 637–669.

Piccinini, A. and Loseby, M. (2001) *Agricultural Policies in Europe and the USA: Farmers Between Subsidies and the Market.* New York: Springer.

Pimentel, D., Zuniga, R. and Morrison, D. (2005) Update on the environmental and economic costs associated with alien-invasive species in the United States. *Ecol Econ* 52: 273–288.

Plowright, W. (1982) The effects of rinderpest and rinderpest control on wildlife in Africa. In: *Symposia of the Zoological Society of London.* New York: Academic Press.

Ramp, D., Ben-Ami, D., Boom, K., et al. (2013) *Compassionate Conservation: A Paradigm Shift for Wildlife Management in Australasia. Ignoring Nature No More: The Case for Compassionate Conservation.* Chicago, IL: University of Chicago Press.

Rewilding Europe. (2012) *Rewilding Europe.* Niljmegen, the Netherlands: ARK, Conservation Capital, WWF, Wild Wonders of Europe. https://rewildingeurope.com/wp-content/uploads/2013/11/Rewilding-Europe-Brochure-2012.pdf (accessed October 2022).

Rodríguez, J.P., Keith, D.A., Rodríguez-Clark, K.M., et al. (2015) A practical guide to the application of the IUCN Red List of Ecosystems criteria. *Phil Trans Royal Soc B* 370: 20140003.

Santoyo-Castelazo, E. and Azapagic, A. (2014) Sustainability assessment of energy systems: integrating environmental, economic and social aspects. *J Cleaner Prod* 80: 119–138.

Shanahan, D.F., Bush, R., Gaston, K.J., et al. (2016) Health benefits from nature experiences depend on dose. *Sci Rep* 6: 28551.

Shennan, S. and Edinborough, K. (2007) Prehistoric population history: from the Late Glacial to the Late Neolithic in Central and Northern Europe. *J Archaeol Sci* 34: 1339–1345.

Simón, M.A., Gil-Sánchez, J.M., Ruiz, G., et al. (2012) Reverse of the decline of the endangered Iberian lynx. *Conserv Biol* 26: 731–736.

Soulé, M.E. (2013) The 'New Conservation'. *Conserv Biol* 27: 895–897.

Spash, C.L. (2015) Bulldozing biodiversity: the economics of offsets and trading-in Nature. *Biol Conserv* 192: 541–551.

Stebbing, A. and Spies-Butcher, B. (2016) The decline of a homeowning society? Asset-based welfare, retirement and intergenerational equity in Australia. *Housing Stud* 31: 190–207.

Tscharntke, T., Clough, Y., Wanger, T.C., et al. (2012) Global food security, biodiversity conservation and the future of agricultural intensification. *Biol Conserv* 151: 53–59.

Wackernagel, M., Schulz, N.B., Deumling, D., et al. (2002) Tracking the ecological overshoot of the human economy. *Proc Natl Acad Sci USA* 99: 9266–9271.

Waldron, A., Mooers, A.O., Miller, D.C., et al. (2013) Targeting global conservation funding to limit immediate biodiversity declines. *Proc Natl Acad Sci USA* 110:12144–12148.

Webb, J.K., Harlow, P.S. and Pike, D.A. (2014) Australian reptiles and their conservation. In: Stow, A., Maclean, N. and Holwell, G.I. (Eds.), *Austral Ark: The State of Wildlife in Australia and New Zealand*. Cambridge, UK: Cambridge University Press.

Wich, S.A., Garcia-Ulloa, J., Kühl, H.S., et al. (2014) Will oil palm's homecoming spell doom for Africa's great apes? *Curr Biol* 24: 1659–1663.

Worm, B., Barbier, E.B., Beaumont, N., et al. (2006) Impacts of biodiversity loss on ocean ecosystem services. *Science* 314: 787–790.

TWENTY

Conservation Methods and Successes

NORMAN MACLEAN

Summary

This chapter will provide details and discussion about methods and actions currently employed in the conservation of animals and plants, together with a list and discussion of species which have benefitted most from these conservation methods.

I would like at the outset to suggest that Costa Rica provides an exemplary case of how a country can be managed to the benefit of its wildlife. Many years ago the Costa Rican Government decided to abandon the development of armaments and an Army, and instead to spend the money thus saved to help conserve its wildlife and to promote ecotourism. This policy has proved to be an outstanding success. It is a few years since I last visited this country, but when I did I was astonished by the rich wildlife diversity. On my own and without a guide, in a period of a week I notched up over 300 bird species, including such flagship species as the resplendent quetzal, blue-crowned motmot, boat-billed heron, sun bittern, scissor-tailed flycatcher, and a host of colourful tanager species. Amongst mammals I saw both two-toed and three-toed sloths.

20.1 Establishing Protected Areas

The first and still the most important aspect of conservation is the creation of national parks and smaller reserves. Initially people were excluded from some of these in order to favour the wildlife and protect it from disturbance, but increasingly visitors are welcomed and viewing opportunities such as hides and blinds are provided to help visitors to see the wildlife. This is partly because the revenue from visitors both directly and indirectly helps to fund the protected areas.

It has been calculated that 15% of the planet's land and 10% of its territorial waters are covered by some form of protected area (see Wikipedia 'Marine protected area'; https://en.wikipedia.org/wiki/Marine_protected_area). In many countries plans are afoot to increase this protection and in Wilson's book *Half Earth*, the author argues for half of the planet's land surface to be protected for wildlife (Wilson, 2016).

While most national parks are designed primarily to conserve wildlife, some, such as Monument Valley National Park in the State of Utah in the USA, are designed partly to protect the remarkable scenery and partly in this case to ensure survival of the Navaho tribal Americans who live within the Park.

Arguably, Yellowstone and Yosemite Parks are the American examples best known for their wildlife, and the reintroduction of the grey wolf (*Canis lupus*) to the former has proved highly successful and has helped return the ecology of the park back to its earlier state. The park contains geothermal hot springs which help ensure the winter survival of bison and other mammals found in the park.

Other important parks outside the USA include the Serengeti and Kruger Parks in Africa, the Rainforest and Barrier Reef reserves of Queensland, Australia, the Galapagos, Madagascar and Antarctica, the Manu Reserve in Peru, Coto Donana in Spain, Torres del Paine Park in Southern Chile, Corcovado Park in Costa Rica and the Bialowieza Forest Park in Poland. Some of these parks are huge at over 6000 square miles. Some like the Serengeti Reserve in Tanzania are mainly visited and viewed by tourist groups taken out by rangers in adapted Jeeps and Land Rovers, while others, like Kruger in South Africa can be visited by tourists in their own cars. Despite the presence of armed wardens in these African Parks, illegal trade in ivory and rhino horn still leads to the killing of animals by poachers.

Increasingly there are also marine reserves in which restrictions are placed on fishing and tourist activity. Less than 1% of the world oceans had been set aside for reserves in 2007 but it is probably much more now. Particular problems in the marine environment include the shark fin industry, whale watching, which sometimes involves disturbance of the whales, and overfishing of marine fish stocks of tuna and cod. Also the survival of marine turtles and the conservation of the beaches in which they ovulate.

Although the Sea of Cortez in Southern California is not at present a reserve, it should be (see Steinbeck's book *The Log from the Sea of Cortez*; Steinbeck, 1951). It is the breeding area of the American grey whale and the remarkable tameness of these animals during migration to the Arctic has encouraged a large tourist industry organised from small boats, in which the whales come alongside and seem to welcome being stroked by the visitors on the boats. In the UK the government has designated 103 marine sites for special protection. These marine areas are mainly managed by Wildlife Trusts, which are discussed below.

20.1.1 Smaller Protected Areas

In the UK, most counties have Wildlife Trusts with local membership and these manage a number of small enclosed nature reserves, most charging a fee for entry, but some being free. Often there are guided tours provided and in some, food such as grain is provided for wintering wildfowl. These small reserves have proved to the very successful, especially for birds such as the avocet (*Recurvirostra avosetta*), bittern (*Botaurus stellaris*), common crane (*Grus grus*), Whooper and Bewick's swans (*Cygnus cygnus* and *C. columbianus*) and many duck species such as the mandarin duck (*Aix galericulata*) and winter visiting pochard (*Aythya ferina*), wigeon (*Anas penelope*) and gadwall (*Anas strepera*), and in the Scottish Highlands birds such as the osprey (*Pandion haliaetus*) and goldeneye ducks (*Bucephala clangula*).

20.2 The Role of Zoos, Botanical Gardens and Aquaria for Breeding and Display Of Endangered Species

In recent years there have been some notable successes in the breeding of endangered birds and mammals and subsequent reintroduction. These include the successful breeding of the Hawaiian goose or nene (*Branta sandvicensis*) and its reintroduction to Hawaii, from Severn Wildfowl Trust Reserve at Slimbridge, England. There is a current programme there for the breeding and subsequent release of the endangered spoon-billed sandpiper (*Calidris pygmaea*), which breeds in Northern Russia and overwinters in Southeast Asia. A somewhat similar programme was followed prior to the reintroduction of the California condor (*Gymnogyps californianus*) in that American state, and there is a promising programme of captive breeding of the New Zealand Parrot, the kakapo (*Strigops habroptilus*) prior to subsequent release. The clearing of the New Zealand island of Tiritiri Matangi of invasive alien species and the introduction of threatened native birds such as the kokako (*Callaeas cinereus*) and takahe (*Porphyrio mantelli*) has been very successful. There is also a population of little spotted kiwi (*Kiwi pakupuka*) on this island.

The continued survival of healthy Tasmanian devils (*Sarcophilus harrisii*) on Maria Island, New Zealand and also in captivity, promises to allow release of healthy examples after a facial tumour disease has led to its extinction in most of Tasmania, as is expected to be the outcome of the present situation.

20.3 2020 as a Year of Special Conservation Effort

Following up on the Extinction Rebellion movement and with international concern about increasing extinction rates, 2020 was supposed to be a year of special conservation effort. Unfortunately because of the Covid-19 pandemic these advances have not been realised. As a result of the pandemic, tourism and the policing of some African reserves have declined, and 2020 has seen a return to elephant and rhino poaching. It is too early to tell what the main effects of the pandemic will be on wildlife around the world. Many wildlife areas have been quieter because of reduced car and aeroplane noise, and there has been less human intrusion because of international lockdown.

20.4 Problems with Invasive Alien Species and Attempts to Remove Them From Sensitive Areas

Throughout the world, invasive alien species have proved problematic. Thus New Zealand conservationists now regret the introduction of some marsupial mammals from Australia, and Australia regrets the introduction of the cane toad (*Rhinella marina*), the camel (*Camelus dromedarius*) and the rabbit (*Oryctolagus cuniculus*).

The native honeycreeper birds of Hawaii have suffered from avian malaria, spread by local mosquitoes from infected introduced exotic species; this has already led to some extinctions, and others may follow.

The introduction, intentional or accidental, of species such as pigs, mongooses, goats, rats and mice to places such as the Galapagos and Hawaii, and some remote islands such as Gough Island, as well as botanical floral species such as Japanese knotweed (*Fallopia japonica*), Himalayan balsam (*Impatiens glandulifera*), water hyacinth (*Eichhornia crassipes*), gorse (*Ulex europaeus*) and lantana (*Lantana camara* and other species) has posed serious problems in many countries. Expensive but successful eradication procedures for rats (*Rattus rattus* and *R. norvegicus*) and mice of a few species on islands such as Gough Island and the Scottish Shiant Isles has led to dramatic recoveries of threatened seabird hole-nesting species like puffins, auks and petrels.

20.5 International Co-ordination and Collaboration and the Legislation Which Supports It

Growing concern over the crisis in biodiversity has led to some important legislation. This include the following:

(1) The Convention on International Trade in Endangered Species of Wild Fauna and Flora (CITES) was enacted in 1973. It currently affords protection for almost 6000 animals and 30,000 plant species. There are currently 183 signatory countries.
(2) The Convention on Biological Diversity (CBD) adopted at the 1992 Rio-de-Janeiro Earth Summit. There are 196 signatory countries.
(3) The Bonn Convention on the Conservation of Migratory Species of Wild Animals (CMS); 130 states have signed up and there is an Appendix 1 to the Convention which lists the threatened species included.
(4) The Ramsar Convention on Wetlands. This was adopted in 1971 and there are 170 member states signed up. There are more than 2300 Ramsar Sites listed.

I should not conclude this section without commenting on the now International 'Extinction Rebellion Movement' which urges governments to be more active in the battle to counter climate change.

20.6 Species Which Have Benefitted From Conservation Methods by Recovery and in Some Cases, Reclassification in the IUCN Listing of Threatened Species

Note that some of these species, such as the southern right whale and humpback whale, are essentially international, while others, such as the Australian saltwater crocodile (*Crocodylus porosus*) and Wallace's giant bee (*Megachile pluto*) in Indonesia, are very localised. Two UK stories are remarkable and deserve special mention. They are the recovery of the large blue butterfly (*Maculinea arion*) and the red kite (*Milvus milvus*). Through the dedicated work of a few individuals, the ecology of these two species has come to be understood, leading to appropriate local management and successful reintroduction, leading to recoveries from single figures 20 years ago to many thousands now. The successful reintroduction of the white-tailed sea eagle (*Haliaeetus albicilla*) to the UK is not far behind. Other UK species which have dramatically recovered include the water vole (*Arvicola amphibius*), in which the southern population was decimated by escaped American mink (*Neovison vison*), and also the great bustard (*Otis tarda*), a bird which now has a small breeding population on Salisbury plain, following its reintroduction using eggs from a population in Eastern Europe.

20.7 A Problem with Vultures

There was a tragic decline in the numbers of various vulture species in the 1980s and 1990s, originally in India and neighbouring parts of Southern Asia, but also later in Spain. The vulture species involved in India were the Himalayan griffon vulture (*Gyps himalayensis*), the cinereous vulture (*Aegypius monachus*), the red-headed vulture (*Sarcogyps calvus*), the white-rumped vulture (*Gyps bengalensis*) and the long-billed vulture (*Gyps indicus*). The Eurasian griffon vulture (*Gyps fulvus*) was affected both in India and Spain.

The cause of the declines has been established to be a veterinary drug, diclofenac, which is given to cattle by intramuscular injection for its anti-inflammatory and painkilling effects. The drug persists in dead animal carcasses and poisons vultures that feed on them resulting in kidney disease. The drug is still widely used by humans under the name of Voltarol. It was widely used by farmers in India from 2000 to 2008, although it was officially banned for such use in 2006. It is still used illegally in both India and Spain, and vulture deaths continue, but at a low level. The population of the white-rumped vulture declined in India during this period by more than 99%. The topic is discussed on a website 'Save Vultures' (https://save-vultures.org/). Since 2009 the vulture populations in India and Spain have substantially recovered, although, as mentioned above, the problem persists at a much lower level. But in the main the conservation news is positive for vulture populations in both India and Spain since 2009, which is why it is mentioned here.

20.8 The Dramatic Recovery of the Peregrine Falcon (*Falco peregrinus*)

This charismatic bird has an almost worldwide distribution, apart from tropical rainforest, and to the best of my knowledge, New Zealand. Its taxonomy is complex and it is currently divided into almost 20 subspecies, which may or may not include the bird known as the Barbary falcon (*Falco perginoides*).

Due to a number of factors, the bird came close to extinction in Britain and North America in the 1970s. This decline was partly a result of the early craze for egg collecting, the persecution of the bird during the Second World War because it was perceived as a major predator of pigeons, some of which were birds returning from Europe following release by aircraft pilots whose planes had been downed by gunfire. Most of all, the era of DDT use in agriculture led to dramatic egg-shell thinning in peregrine clutches during the 1960s and early 1970s, until Rachel Carson's message in *Silent Spring* led to a ban on the use of DDT in the early 1970s. In the UK, the Royal Society for the Protection of Birds believes that there are now at least 2000 nesting pairs in the UK and a similar recovery has occurred in the USA. If only John Baker could have lived to see this day. He foretold its ultimate demise in his amazing book *The Peregrine* (Baker, 1967).

The peregrine has always attracted human attention, partly because of its popularity with falconers (which has both a downside and an upside, the former being the stealing of nestlings for rearing in captivity for future falconry training, and the latter being the contribution of escaped falconer's birds to the breeding population in the wild), and partly because it is by far the fastest bird in the skies, since when stooping on a prey bird it has registered speeds of over 270 mph.

Perhaps the most remarkable aspect of the recovery of the peregrine is its present liking for nesting on town buildings and predating town populations of pigeons. The placement of cameras on some of these building ledges has allowed many people with no previous interest in wild birds to become engaged with watching the fortunes of these nesting peregrines. It has also had another unexpected result, namely the realisation that these falcons often hunt at night, and cameras have recorded the night capture of migrating black-necked grebes, virginia rails and common quails.

20.9 Species Which Have Prospered as a Result of Conservation Activity

20.9.1 Plants

Erica verticillata – South Africa

Hibiscus liliiflorus – Reunion Island

Ramosmania rodriguesi – Rodrigues Island

Melocactus matanzanus – Cuba

Biscutella neustriaca – France

In addition to the above, many plants are now very rare in the wild but fairly common in gardens and greenhouses. These include:

Gingko biloba – China

Araucaria araucana – Chile and Argentina

Tecophilaea cyanocrocus – Chile

Wollemia nobilis – Australia

Brighamia insignis – Hawaii

20.9.2 Arthropods

Lord Howe Island stick insect (*Dryococelus australis*) – Lord Howe Island (see Mikheyev et al., 2017)

River clubtail dragonfly (*Gomphus flavipes*) – Europe

Golden presta dragonfly (*Syncordulia legato*) – South Africa

Green gomphid dragonfly (*Ophiogomphus cecilia*) – Austria

Fisher's estuarine moth (*Gortyna lunata*) – UK

Large blue butterfly (*Maculinea arion*) – England (see Thomas et al., 2019)

Violet copper butterfly (*Lycaena helle*) – Luxemburg

Wallace's giant bee (*Megachile pluto*) – Indonesia (see Main, 2019)

White-clawed crayfish (*Austropotamobius pallipes*) – Spain
Ladybird spider (*Eresus sandeliatus* – England

20.9.3 Mollusca
Freshwater pearl mussel (*Margaritifera margaritifera*) – Belgium

20.9.4 Fishes
Twaite shad (*Alosa fallax*) – UK
Mediterranean killifish (*Aphanius fasciatus*) – Slovenia
North Sea houting - (*Coregonus oxyrinchus*) – North Sea
Devils Hole pupfish (*Cyprinodon diabolis*) – Nevada, USA

20.9.5 Amphibians
Spadefoot toad (*Pelobates fuscus*) – Estonia
Kihansi spray toad (*Nectophrynoides asperginis*) – Tanzania
Mallorcan midwife toad (*Alytes muletensis*) – Mallorca
European tree frog (*Hyla arborea*) – Belgium
Variable harlequin frog (*Atelopus various*) – Costa Rica
Bornean rainbow toad (*Ansonia latidisca*) – Borneo
Hula painted frog (*Latonia nigriventer*) – Israel

20.9.6 Reptiles
European pond turtle (*Emys orbicularis*) – Lithuania
Saint Croix ground lizard (*Pholidoscelis polops*) – Saint Croix
Hungarian meadow viper (*Vipera ursinii*) – Hungary
Loggerhead turtle (*Caretta caretta*) – Cyprus
Green turtle (*Chelonia mydas*) – Cyprus
Kemp's ridley sea turtle (*Lepidochelys kempii*) – Tortuga
Philippine crocodile (*Crocodylus mindorensis*) – Philippines
Australian saltwater crocodile (*Crocodylus porosus*) (see Whitaker and Whitaker, 2008)
Jamaican iguana (*Cyclura collei*) – Jamaica
Bolson tortoise (*Gopherus flavomarginatus*) – Mexico
Espanola giant tortoise (*Chelonoidis hoodensis*) – Galapagos
Island night lizard (*Xantusia riversiana*) – California, USA
Antiguan racer snake (*Alsophis antiguae*) – Antigua
Pinzon giant tortoise (*Chelonoidis duncanensis*) – Pinzon
American alligator (*Alligator mississippiensis*) – Mississipi, USA
Aldabra giant tortoise (*Aldabrachelys gigantea*) – Aldabra
Western swamp turtle (*Pseudemydura umbrina*) – Australia

20.9.7 Birds
Corncrake (*Crex crex*) – Latvia and UK
Yelkouan shearwater (*Puffinus yelkouan*) – Malta

Mediterranean storm petrel (*Hydrobates pelagian*) – Malta

Little tern (*Sternula albifrons*) – Netherlands

Great bustard (*Otis tarda*) – Portugal and UK

Saker falcon (*Falco cherrug*) – Hungary

Eastern imperial eagle (*Aquila heliaca*) – Slovenia

Spanish imperial eagle (*Aquila adalberti*) – Spain

Dalmatian pelican (*Pelecanus crispus*) – Europe

Lesser kestrel (*Falco naumanni*) – Spain

Mauritius kestrel (*Falco punctatus*) – Mauritius

Eurasian bittern (*Botaurus stellaris*) – UK

Eurasian stone curlew (*Burhinus oedicnemus*) – UK

Pygmy cormorant (*Phalacrocorax pygmaeus*) – Bulgaria

Ferruginous duck (*Aythya nyroca*)– Bulgaria

Egyptian vulture (*Neophron percnopterus*) – France

Black vulture (*Aegypius monachus*) – France

Griffon vulture (*Gyps fulvus*) – France

Bearded vulture (*Gypaetus barbatus*) – France

Eurasian spoonbill (*Platalea leucorodia*) – France and UK

Black stork (*Ciconia nigra*) – Hungary

Kakapo (*Strigops habroptila*) – New Zealand

Lear's macaw (*Anodorhynchus leari*) – Brazil

Madagascar pochard (*Aythya innotata*) – Madagascar

California condor (*Gymnogyps californianus*) – California, USA

Short-tailed albatross (*Phoebastria albatrus*) – Torishima Island

Mauritius fody (*Foudia rubra*) – Mauritius

Puerto Rican Amazon parrot (*Amazona vittata*) – Puerto Rico

Red-vented cockatoo (*Cacatua haematuropygia*) – Philippines

Saint Helena plover (*Charadrius sanctaehelenae*) – Saint Helena

Seychelles magpie-robin (*Copsychus sechellarum*) – Seychelles

Snowy egret (*Egretta thula*) – North America

Spoon-billed sandpiper (*Calidris pygmaea*) – Russia

Whooping crane (*Grus americana*) – North America

Yellow-eared parrot (*Ognorhynchus icterotis*) – Columbia

Pale-headed brush-finch (*Atlapetes pallidiceps*) – Ecuador

Northern bald ibis (*Geronticus eremita*) – Morocco

North Island kokako (*Callaeas wilsoni*) – New Zealand

Millerbird (*Acrocephalus familiaris kingi*) – Hawaii

Little spotted kiwi (*Apteryx owenii*) – New Zealand

Kirtland's warbler (*Setophaga kirtlandii*) – Michigan, USA

Crested ibis (*Nipponia nippon*) – China

Hawaiian goose (*Branta sandvicensis*) – Hawaii (see Black and Ellis-Joseph, 1994)

Black robin (*Petroica traversi*) – New Zealand

Campbell teal (*Anas nesiotis*) – New Zealand

Bald eagle (*Haliaeetus leucocephalus*) – USA

Bermuda petrel (*Pterodroma cahow*) –Bermuda

Pink pigeon (*Nesoenas mayeri*) – Mauritius

Echo parakeet (*Psittacula eques*) – Mauritius

Azores bullfinch (*Pyrrhula murina*) – Azores

Cirl bunting (*Emberiza cirlus*) – England

Red kite (*Milvus milvus*) – UK

White-tailed eagle (*Haliaeetus albicilla*) – UK (see https://en.wikipedia.org/wiki/White-tailed_eagle)

Osprey (*Pandion halioetus*) – UK

Peregrine falcon (*Falco peregrinus*) – UK

Common crane (*Grus grus*) – England

White-rumped vulture (*Gyps bengalensis*) – India

Trumpeter swan (*Cygnus buccinator*) – North America

20.9.8 Mammals

Brown bear – Italy

Eurasian otter – Netherlands and UK

Northern chamois – Slovakia

Greater horseshoe bat – UK

American bison – USA

Southern white rhino – Africa

Golden lion tamarin – S. America

Grey wolf – Europe and America

Guanaco – Argentina

Eurasian beaver – UK

Tasmanian devil – Tasmania

European mink – Eastern Europe

Iberian lynx – Spain

Grey whale – USA

Greater one-horned rhino – Nepal

Giant panda – China

Hartmann's zebra – Africa

Bridled nail-tail wallaby – Australia

Sperm whale[1]

Santa Cruz Island fox – Santa Cruz

Saiga antelope – Asia

Black-footed ferret – USA

Vicuna – Andes

---

[1] As most whales are circumpolar, no locations are given.

Vancouver Island marmot – Canada

Scimitar-horned oryx – North Africa

Southern right whale

Przewalski's horse – Mongolia

Northern elephant seal – North America

Northern chamois – Asian Mountains

Mountain gorilla – Uganda

Mexican pronghorn – Mexico

Iberian ibex – Spain

Indian blackbuck – India

Humpback whale

Hawaiian monk seal – Hawaii

Greater bamboo lemur – Madagascar

Golden-crowned sifaka – Madagascar

Golden-headed lion tamarin – Brazil

European bison – Poland

Cantabrian chamois – Spain

Cotton-top tamarin – Columbia

Bontebok – South Africa

Arabian oryx – Arabia

Alpine ibex – Italy

Northern muriqui monkey – Brazil

Southern muriqui monkey – Brazil

Water vole – UK

Bengal tiger – India

Acknowledgement

I wish to acknowledge the help received from Dr Tris Allinson, who gave this chapter a critical review and suggested ways in which it could be improved.

References

Baker, J.A. (1967) *The Peregrine*. New York: HarperCollins.

Black, G.A. and Ellis-Joseph, S. (1994) Survival and breeding of Hawaiian Goose (*Branta sandvicensis*). *J Wildfowl Manag* 61: 1161–1173.

Main, D. (2019) World's largest bee, once presumed extinct, filmed alive in the wild. *Nat Geo*. www.nationalgeographic.com/animals/article/worlds-largest-bee-rediscovered-not-extinct (accessed October 2022).

Mikheyev, A.S., Zwick, A, Magrath, M.J.L, Grau, M.L., et al. (2017) Museum genomics confirms that the Lord Howe Island stick insect survived extinction. *Curr Biol* 27: 3157–3161.

Steinbeck, J. (1951) *The Log from the Sea of Cortez*. New York: The Viking Press.

Thomas, J., Meridith, S. and Simcox, D. (2019) Re-establishing the large blue butterfly in Britain. *Br Wildlife* 31: 7–14.

Whitaker, R. and Whitaker, N. (2008) Conservation of Australian saltwater crocodile (*Crocodylus porosus*). *IUCN Crocodile Specialist Group* 27: 26–30

Wilson, E.O. (2016) *Half Earth*. New York: Liveright.

Further Reading

Kolbert, E. (2014) *The Sixth Extinction*. London: Bloomsbury.

Maclean, N. (2010) *Silent Summer: The State of the Wildlife in Britain and Ireland*. Cambridge, UK: Cambridge University Press.

Mittermeier, R.A. (2017) *Back from the Brink*. New York: Global Wildlife Conservation.

Mountford, G. and Hosking, E. (1958) *Wild Paradise: The Story of the Coto Donana Expeditions*. Boston, MA: Houghton Mifflin Company.

Wernham, C., Siriwardena, G.M., Toms, M., et al. (Eds.) (2002) *The Migration Atlas: Movements of Birds of Britain and Ireland*. Lake Dallas, TX: Helm.

TWENTY ONE

What Does the Future Hold for Our Planet and its Wildlife?

NORMAN MACLEAN

Summary

This chapter will attempt to predict what the future will hold for life on Planet Earth. It reviews the changes which have come about and which will continue as a result of factors such as climate change. The chapter also discusses the emergence of the Extinction Rebellion movement, the likely future declines in insects and other species, as discussed in the 2019 State of Nature report, and the factors that are likely to continue to impact survival of wild species on Planet Earth. In closing, the chapter outlines some likely future increases in species adapting to life in large cities.

Gazing into a crystal ball to find out what is in store is rarely satisfactory, and never more so than in predicting the future of the wildlife on our planet. For a start, it is frankly impossible to be very optimistic, although I will list some positives below (and see the list of recovering species in Chapter 20). So much damage has already been inflicted on our world that it is impossible to completely put the clock back. We are stuck with something of a mess.

21.1 Climate Change in the Future

Despite the valiant efforts of the Extinction Rebellion movement (https://en.wikipedia .org/wiki/Extinction_Rebellion and https://rebellion.global), the governments of the world, especially China, USA and Russia, still seem intent on ignoring what has to be done to reverse the present climate changes. Perhaps the worst present effects are to be found at the poles, where increased ice melting threatens the livelihood of species such as the polar bear, walrus, some seals, the arctic fox and some polar bird species. It seems likely that in future many of these species will become extinct and be replaced by the movement of subpolar species into these areas. Already red foxes are moving into the Arctic and co-existing with arctic foxes, although whether they will be able to adapt the amazing hunting strategies of the latter species remains to be seen. Changes are also likely with some penguin species in the Antarctic and with some of the wildlife in the Tasmanian islands, especially McQuarrie Island. The melting of the polar ice is also resulting in rising sea levels, which currently threaten many areas, such as the Indonesian islands, and this seems likely to continue.

In addition to rising temperatures in the Arctic, the hottest and driest countries, such as Australia and Namibia, will have more bush fires and less water, so the local people and wildlife will have further problems. Some plants can cope with fire very effectively, but others will be unable to survive.

The years 2019 and 2020 have seen unprecedented bush fires in Australia, destroying a lot of habitat and killing much wildlife. No doubt global warming has increased Australia's long-standing tendency to have bush fires. It is now calculated that more than 3 billion animals were killed in these fires, and 72,000 square miles of land were scorched. Amongst the worst affected species were the following 10 notable animals: koala, Kangaroo island dunnart, Hastings river mouse, bush-tailed rock wallaby, greater glider, glossy black cockatoo, northeastern bristlebird, regent honeyeater, western ground parrot and corroboree frog (see Richards et al., 2020 and links therein)

Climate change may also have an impact on the Galapagos, where El Niño years bring warmer ocean temperatures, which may become more frequent and impact on future populations of seals, sea lions, sharks and marine iguanas for which the islands are famous.

The CO_2 output and resulting ocean acidification may decline in future, although there are stories of widespread coral bleaching in the Great Barrier Reef. In this connection there are reports of being able to rescue the reef by the introduction of cultured pieces of coral and the growth of such pieces in aquaria from the collection of living coral eggs and sperm recovered from wild reefs during coral reproduction.

Even as I finish this chapter, an international climate summit in Glasgow called COP26, has just concluded. Its finishing statements are very disappointing. At the last moment the determination to 'phase out' the use of coal was watered down to 'phase down' at the insistence of China and India. It is clear that the end point of reducing climate change to an increase of only 1.5 °C in global warming will not be met, but instead the increase is likely to be 2.4 °C over the next few years. The compensation proposed to be paid by rich nations to poor nations to help them adapt to climate change was agreed in the Paris meeting of COP21 to be 100 billion dollars, but to date less than half of this amount has been raised. The aim to reduce carbon emission to 'net zero' by 2030 will clearly not be met. So taken together, the projections from COP26 must be regarded as 'too little' and 'too late'. Not a good outcome for the planet or its wildlife.

On the positive side Poland, Vietnam and Chile have agreed to greatly reduce their dependence on coal, and Indonesia, one of the signatories, has stated that it is 'unfair' to expect the poorer countries to reach targets which the rich nations will not, in fact a problem mainly caused by the past and present use of coal, oil and gas by the richer nations.

21.2 The Extinction Rebellion Movement

The Extinction Rebellion Movement highlights the following:

- Donald Trump's (former President) negative views on climate change
- Economic development of China

- Rise in human population of Earth
- Replacement of rainforest with oil palm in Indonesia
- Destruction of Amazon rainforest
- Increase in vegetarianism and veganism
- Problems of cars, roads and atmospheric pollution, and also gradual increase in electric and hybrid cars
- Indoor production of livestock
- Depletion of ponds and pools on farmland
- Use of pesticides and herbicides
- Tourism, air and sea travel
- Worldwide drive for human equality, and bridging the gap between rich and poor
- Low value placed on wildlife by most people living in cities
- Plastic and elastic bands/seabirds etc.
- Seahorses and oil extraction
- Coral bleaching as a result of ocean acidification following high CO_2 levels, with consequent threats to many coral reef resident species.

21.3 Insect Declines

As emphasised in Chapter 11, insect decline is already worldwide, and since insects are at the bottom of so many food chains, the knock-on effects of insect decline are felt throughout other invertebrates and vertebrate species, especially birds and mammals. A review of insect decline authored by Sanchez-Bayo and Wyckhuys (2019) indicates that the present rates of insect decline are twice those reported for mammals, and that one-third of all insect species are threatened with extinction in the countries under study. Also, the rates for aquatic insects are higher than those for terrestrial species and pollution-tolerant species will represent most of the survivors. The rate of insect decline in the UK is 60% higher than it was 40 years ago; for Europe it is 44% and for the world 41%. This study is not trivial, since it was based on scrutiny of 10 different insect orders (there are over 20 in toto). Insect biomass is reported to be declining by 2.7% annually in the rainforest canopy of Costa Rica, and in Germany a study recently recorded an annual decrease of 2.8% (Hallmann et al., 2017; Lister and Garcia, 2018). The major factor causing these declines seems to be continuation of pesticide spraying on farm crops, and no big change in this scenario can be predicted for the future. So the effects of insect decline in future will be widespread because of their functions as flower pollinators and, in some cases, their ability to keep populations of other pest insects in check.

There is increasing concern about the continued use of pesticides containing neonicotinoids and their effect on bees and other insects (see Goulson, 2020).

21.3.1 Insects on Car Windscreens

Those of us who are over 80 years of age, of whom I am one, can remember that some 50 years ago, in Europe, and maybe elsewhere, those of us who owned a motor car bought special plastic devices which we attached to the central front of the car bonnet.

These were insect deflectors, to help reduce the spattering of our car windscreens with insects. Even with these devices fitted, many insects splattered our windscreens, and when we drove into petrol stations, an attendant would come out to clean them.

The need for these devices and the attentions of the attendants has long since gone, a startling piece of evidence of European insect decline.

21.3.2 An Important New Book on Insect Decline

In recent months, a new book has been published. It is *Silent Earth* by Dave Goulson (2021).

This book details lots of evidence from the last 50 years of the dramatic reduction in insect numbers. There is a figure on page 50 which graphs the startling decline in insect biomass in German nature reserves between 1989 and 2014. The total weight in grams per trap per day declined by 76% over these 26 years.

Goulson then shows figures on page 60 which illustrate the geographic ranges of wild bees and hoverflies in the UK between 1980 and 2012. The graphs show how much space, on 1 km grid cells, was occupied by these insects. In both cases the insect numbers show a drop of over 30% in grid occupancy. He also states on the same page that 23 follower-visiting bee and wasp species have become extinct in the UK between 1850 and the present.

Nor are these insect declines confined to Europe. Goulson also cites a 97% drop in the numbers of Western Monarch butterflies in North America (counted in their hibernating sites in California). The Eastern population of this insect is a little better, with an 80% decline in their Mexican overwintering population.

21.4 Other Reported Declines

Even as I write this chapter, the 2019 'State of Nature' report (https://nbn.org.uk/wp-content/uploads/2019/09/State-of-Nature-2019-UK-full-report.pdf) has appeared online, the result of over 80 organisations such as WWF, RSPB, Plantlife, Butterfly Conservation, the Woodland Trust and many others. The report attempts to outline where we currently stand. The results are broadly in line with the other projections mentioned, namely that over the short term, between 2011 and 2016, 46% of the species studied showed strong or moderate decreases, and 35% dramatic decreases. In the November 2019 issue of *British Birds*, it was reported that the total population of North American birds has declined by 25%, a loss of three billion birds. The report details losses of more than 860 million birds of 'sparrow' species (of which there are some 38 species in North America), 440 million blackbirds (of which there are some 10 species in North America) and more than 600 million New World warblers (which along with sparrows make up the Family Emberizidae). There are about 48 North American warbler species.

21.5 Trade in Pangolins

The pangolin is arguably the most threatened of all mammals. In Asia, as reported by IUCN, all four wild species are affected. The animals are traded for bushmeat and also for the supposed medical benefits of eating pangolin scales. The skin is also turned into a type of leather. In 2017, China seized the equivalent of 20,000 pangolins. The main countries importing pangolins illegally are Vietnam and China. There is also a demand for pangolin leather in the USA. So clearly a big international effort is needed to stop this catastrophic trade in pangolins.

21.6 Future Genome Sequencing

The Welcome Trust-funded Sanger Centre in London, UK, which has worked for some years on sequencing the genomes of human individuals, is proposing in future to turn its attention to sequencing the genomes of other vertebrate species (see www.sanger.ac.uk/science/data/#). This is aimed to provide better understanding of relationships between species, although, looking at the development move sceptically, it provides future work for an already highly developed technology.

21.7 Wilding and Rewilding

In recent years this terminology has appeared and it refers to permitting and assisting farmland to return to the pristine state of heath, copse or forest. An important book has appeared which describes the wilding of a farm estate in Sussex known as the Knepp estate (Tree, 2018).

This describes a remarkable return to nature, and several endangered species such as purple emperor butterflies and white stork birds have bred well, with dramatic increases in number. If this model could be applied elsewhere it could indeed put the clock back and allow recovery of many threatened wildlife species.

21.8 Other Future Losses and Decreases to be Expected

We may well expect in the future further decreases in species such as seahorses and sand eels, reduction in alpine and cold-tolerant plants and animals as a result of global warming, and increases in bush fires and desertification. Some pest species which have learned to live in cities alongside humans, such as brown rats, cockroaches, some corvids and some invasive plants such as water hyacinth and Japanese knotweed will continue to increase. Roof-nesting gull species such as herring gulls and lesser black-backed gulls will surely persist in the UK, especially with their marked preference for feeding at nearby rubbish dumps.

Ignorance of the natural world may well increase as children are urbanised and cut off from countryside experiences. It is hard to see long-term reduction in atmospheric and soil pollution, even if we begin to win the battle against plastic waste and can become less dependent on pesticides and herbicides.

Fortuitously 600 conservation experts signed a letter initiated by the wildlife charity WWF, in which they drew attention to the precarious balance faced by the Earth's wildlife. In addition to the points listed above, this letter draws attention to the plight faced by pangolins, which are caught and sold in illegal wildlife trade, and to that of river dolphins in freshwater rivers such as the Amazon and a number of rivers in Asia.

In this letter the following aspects are highlighted as most in need of urgent action:

1. Overfishing and plastic pollution of the high seas, including birds and mammals being caught up in the remains of discarded nets (see 7. below).
2. Deforestation of rainforest in the Amazon, Borneo and elsewhere.
3. The continuing illegal wildlife trade in species such as pangolin, tortoises and parrots.
4. Land degradation. The letter states that three-quarters of the world's land surface has been seriously degraded, with no hope of reversal. Mining of tar sands in Florida and Vancouver are highlighted.
5. Melting of polar ice in the Arctic and Antarctic with threats to survival of walrus, polar bears and many penguin species in Antarctica.
6. Threats to many freshwater species, ranging from insects to mammals. Freshwater species are believed to have declined by 83%. Freshwater dolphins are all in steep decline.
7. It was reported in the press in 2020 that plastic waste in the ocean could triple by 2040 unless something radical is done to prevent the increase. The predicted increase could be from 11 million tons per year to 29 million tons per year by 2040. The total amount in 2040 could be 600 million tons. This was reported in a paper in the *Science* journal by the Pew Charitable Trust, together with the company Systemiq.
8. The loss of wildlife corridors, especially between patches of rainforest, since such corridors help to reduce inbreeding of isolated populations and ensure that species such as birds and mammals have enough space to allow them to survive and spread.

The factors which continue to threaten wildlife and are likely to do so in the future are:

1. Agricultural intensification involving the use of pesticides, herbicides and synthetic fertilisers.
2. Deforestation
3. Overfishing at sea
4. Climate change
5. Pollution of air, water and soil by pesticides with long lives
6. Desertification due to lack of water
7. Plastic garbage on land and sea
8. Increased salination and acidification of seawater and problems for coral reefs
9. Spread of invasive alien species
10. Increases in human population with urban and industrial sprawl and more demand for resources
11. Increasing air travel resulting in more atmospheric pollution
12. Increasing number of children and young people with no knowledge or understanding of the natural world.

However, some of these factors could be partly counterbalanced in future if climate change can be partially reversed by activities such as those of Extinction Rebellion, farmers putting out grain to feed birds in place of earlier stubble feeding, reversal of oil palm plantation spread in Indonesia and reduction in new prawn farms.

To try to end on an optimistic note, I see no reason why much of the huge fauna on the African plains will not persist, especially if the bans on ivory and rhino horn become more effective. The grasses and acacia species which provide their food are well adapted to the drought and seasonal rains which characterise the area. So too with the ban on whaling, many species of great whales should survive into the future, especially the humpback and American grey whale. However commercial whaling on a limited scale continues by Japan, Norway and Greenland. I have listed in Chapter 20 many species which have recently responded to conservation and are on the increase, and Tris Allinson in Chapter 6 lists and illustrates some bird species which are currently doing well. So the future will not be devoid of species. The crocodilians have proved to be the great dinosaur survivors, they too look likely to persist in many of the tropical countries. The desert specialists such as the red kangaroo in Australia will surely survive, alongside many Australian birds which continue to prosper.

There has been very encouraging news about the numbers of tigers in the wild. Conservation bodies devised a scheme to help tiger numbers. This was called Tx2. When the scheme was launched in 2006 it was estimated that only 3200 animals remained in the 13 countries in which the species survives, chiefly Bhutan, China, India, Nepal and Russia. This figure has now more than doubled and the population in India alone has increased by 33% in 4 years (the actual figure is 741 more tigers; see Jhala et al., 2019).

There is more recent good news about the endangered one-horned rhino in Nepal. The population there has increased from 645 in 2015 to 752 in 2021. This population exists in four national parks in the Southern plains of Nepal.

Another likely future advance is that many current invasive pest species around the world will be reduced or eliminated by intensive conservation actions, especially on islands. Some of the worst offending species currently are brown and black rats, rabbits, many species of mice, feral cats, feral goats, brushtailed possum in New Zealand, and Indian mongooses; also cane toads, bullfrogs, Nile perch, mosquitofish and brown tree snakes in Guam, and the Burmese python in the Florida Everglades. Some pest insects that could be eradicated include the harlequin ladybird, tawny crazy ant and Africanised honey bee.

Invasive plant species that might be eradicated are lantana (*Lantana camara* and other species), kudzu vine (*Pueraria lobata*), water hyacinth (*Eichornia crassipes*), and many others.

We discussed in Chapter 20 the importance of national parks and conservation areas. In the future these areas will be even more important. There was no mention in Chapter 20 of town gardens and parks, but now through people feeding birds from artificial feeders, and ceasing to use garden insecticides, these areas will be life lines to many wildlife species and efforts are underway to ensure that there are wildlife corridors linking neighbouring parks and gardens to prevent inbreeding and social isolation. Some European birds such as herring gulls, peregrine falcons and red kites are breeding on town buildings or in neighbouring parks, while in the United States both common nighthawks and killdeer plovers now commonly nest on flat-roofed buildings in towns. Bird species which are now commonly using bird feeders in British gardens include goldfinches, greenfinches, siskins, great spotted woodpeckers, nuthatches and reed buntings, which is all good news. The provision of nest boxes in gardens and nature reserves has also greatly boosted numbers of many species, none more so than the North American purple martin, with a current population of around 7 million, which now nests almost exclusively in communal nest boxes provided in many towns and gardens. The feeding of parrots and parakeets is also a common practice in gardens and reserves on the east coast of Australia.

These species which are benefitting from the use of garden feeders and nest boxes represent only one aspect of the many animal species which are prospering from urbanisation.

There are some dramatic stories emerging about how some animal species are adapting to urban life. The peregrine falcon is now a frequent bird in British cities, nesting on the ledges of buildings as if they were ledges on sea cliffs. And it is not only in the UK, since New York City in the USA has an amazingly high population of these falcons, and, as in the UK, feral pigeons provide an attractive food source. Racoons are also common nocturnal visitors to houses in the USA, feeding on local scraps and garbage, and often remaining to rear their young in sheltered corners and chimneys of household dwellings. The last example which deserves mention here is the Indian leopard. In a number of Indian cities, and in particular Mumbai, leopards are regular nocturnal visitors. People are now sometimes attacked by these prowling cats, but their main prey are the young piglets in litters of pigs kept in the backyards of houses in these cities.

Urbanised species now also include the racoon, North American black bear, spotted hyena, red fox, feral pigeon, rose-ringed parakeet, common magpie and, amongst insects, species such as honey and bumble bees, which now commonly breed in cities, and many dragonfly species which breed in garden ponds.

In addition to the above, other future changes likely to persist include the architectural use of green walls on city buildings, in which numerous plant species can thrive by being planted in the plastic pockets of these walls, as well as the construction of flat-roof gardens of dwarf plants such as mosses and sedums, and the successful use of artificial trees, as currently employed in Singapore in which trees and other plants self seed and a variety of bird species come to nest.

The unpredictable nature of the future is underlined by the fact that the world's human population is only now recovering from a prolonged lockdown following the widespread pandemic of the virus Covid 19. The infection is thought to have originated in the large animal market in Wuhan, China. Fortunately, a number of excellent vaccines have been prepared to provide immunity against this virus, and these include those from Astra Zeneca and Pfizer. Most older people in the UK have now had three injections of one of these vaccines and this provides strong immunity. A campaign to vaccinate the rest of the world's human population is underway.

To add to the problem posed by the Covid 19 virus, a wave of avian influenza has now arrived in late 2022 in Europe, and many seabirds and migratory ducks, geese and swans are now dying as a result of this infection.

The effects of these viral infections on the world's wildlife have yet to be determined. As a result of the Covid 19 pandemic, there is less tourism, and the rural environment is comparatively quiet. Whether the poaching of elephant ivory and rhino horn will increase or decrease as a result is as yet unclear. Such pandemics in the human population are not a new phenomenon, since there was a serious human influenza epidemic in 1918–1919, and more soldiers died from this epidemic than died in the trenches. My own father caught the infection but recovered.

Another recent and important development is the signing in Montreal in December 2022 of what is called the COP15 agreement. Most countries in the world have signed up to this and it commits the world to set aside 30% of the Earth's landmass for wildlife by the end of 2030. The official name for this agreement is the Kunming-Montreal pact. The rights of many indigenous people who occupy much of the rural environment of the Earth have also been emphasised and protected.

Another recent development is that Sir David Attenborough has revealed that he has put together a television programme (Frozen Planet II) to be used to inform the nations of the world and their governments how one species, ourselves, has exploited and changed Planet Earth to benefit ourselves, but at the expense of the other wildlife species with which we share the planet. The programme shows that this is now the eleventh hour, in which we can mend our ways and strive to conserve what is left of the planet's ecosystems and their wildlife.

At the initial interview in which Sir David outlined this ambitious project, he also emphasised the importance of reducing the human culture of waste of such things as power, food and plastic. 'Don't waste. This is a precious world. Celebrate and cherish'. He also highlighted Costa Rica as an outstanding example of a country which had decided to dispense with its army and armaments and instead spend its financial resources on wildlife conservation and ecotourism. This last is especially relevant to this book (see the discussion about Costa Rica at the beginning of Chapter 20).

A Life on Our Planet, David Attenborough's book (Attenborough, 2021), alluded to at the end of Chapter 1 of this book, also needs a mention for the future, since this present book on the state of the world's wildlife complements the future predictions of David Attenborough, providing the essential detail on which his case depends.

Acknowledgement

I wish to acknowledge the help received from Dr Tris Allinson, who gave this chapter a critical review and suggested ways in which it could be improved.

References

Attenborough, D. (2021) *A Life on Our Planet: My Witness Statement and a Vision for the Future*. London: Witness Books/Penguin Random House.

Goulson, D. (2020) Neonics in salmon farming. *Br Wildlife* 31(6): 391–392.

Goulson, D.(2021) *Silent Earth: Averting the Insect Apocalypse*. London, UK: Jonathan Cape.

Hallmann,C.A., Sorg, M., Jongejans, E., et al. (2017) More than 75 percent decline over 27 years in total flying insect biomass in protected areas. *PLoS One* 12(10): e0185809.

Jhala, Y.V., Qureshi, Q. and Nayak, A.K. (Eds.) (2019) *Status of Tigers, Co-predators and Prey in India 2018. Summary Report*. New Delhi, India: National Tiger Conservation Authority, Government of India; Dehradun, India: Wildlife Institute of India. TR No./2019/05.

Lister, B.C. and Garcia, A. (2018) Climate-driven declines in arthropod abundance restructure a rainforest food web. *Proc Natl Acad Sci USA* 115 (44): E10397–E10406.

Richards, L., Brew, N. and Smith, L. (2020) 2019–20 Australian bushfires - frequently asked questions: a quick guide. Research Papers 2019–20, Parliament of Australia. www.aph.gov.au/About_Parliament/Parliamentary_Departments/Parliamentary_Library/pubs/rp/rp1920/Quick_Guides/AustralianBushfires (accessed October 2022).

Sanchez-Bayo, F. and Wyckhuys, K.A.G. (2019) Worldwide decline of the entomofauna: a review of its drivers. *Biol Conserv* 232: 8–27.

Tree, I. (2018) *Wilding: The Return of Nature to a British Farm*. Southampton, UK: Picador.

Species Index

Page numbers in *italic* refer to figures; those in **bold** to tables; Common names are also indexed where available

Subject Index

Page numbers in *italic* refer to figures; those in **bold** to tables

For named plant/animal examples *see* species index